The Gambia & Senegal

Katharina Lobeck Kane

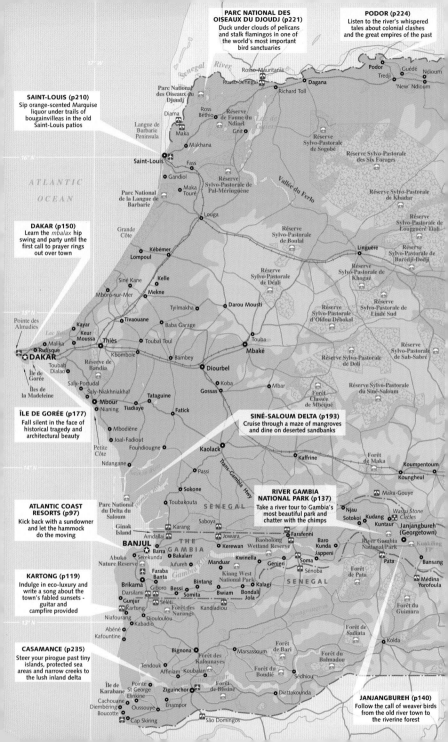

PARC NATIONAL DES OISEAUX DU DJOUDJ (p221)
Duck under clouds of pelicans and stalk flamingos in one of the world's most important bird sanctuaries

PODOR (p224)
Listen to the river's whispered tales about colonial clashes and the great empires of the past

SAINT-LOUIS (p210)
Sip orange-scented Marquise liquor under trails of bougainvilleas in the old Saint-Louis patios

DAKAR (p150)
Learn the *mbalax* hip swing and party until the first call to prayer rings out over town

ÎLE DE GORÉE (p177)
Fall silent in the face of historical tragedy and architectural beauty

SINÉ-SALOUM DELTA (p193)
Cruise through a maze of mangroves and dine on deserted sandbanks

RIVER GAMBIA NATIONAL PARK (p137)
Take a river tour to Gambia's most beautiful park and chatter with the chimps

ATLANTIC COAST RESORTS (p97)
Kick back with a sundowner and let the hammock do the moving

KARTONG (p119)
Indulge in eco-luxury and write a song about the town's fabled sunsets - guitar and campfire provided

CASAMANCE (p235)
Steer your pirogue past tiny islands, protected sea areas and narrow creeks to the lush inland delta

JANJANGBUREH (p140)
Follow the call of weaver birds from the old river town to the riverine forest

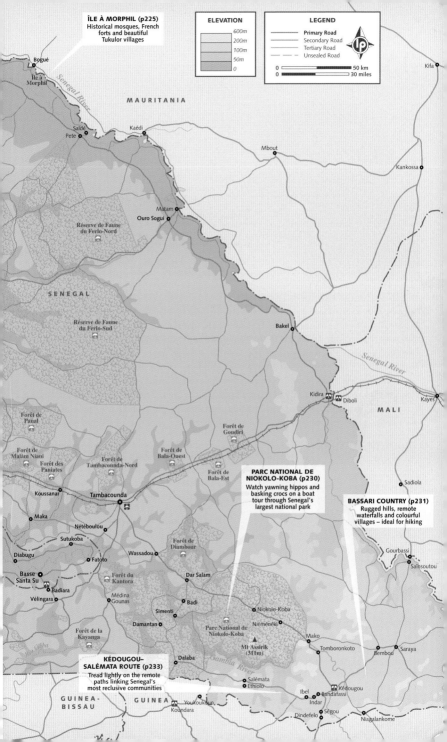

ÎLE À MORPHIL (p225)
Historical mosques, French forts and beautiful Tukulor villages

ELEVATION

600m
200m
100m
50m
0

LEGEND

Primary Road
Secondary Road
Tertiary Road
Unsealed Road

0 —————— 50 km
0 —————— 30 miles

Bogué
Île à Morphil

MAURITANIA

Kifa

Saldé
Pete
Kaédi

Mbout

Kankossa

Matam
Ouro Sogui

Réserve de Faune du Ferlo-Nord

SENEGAL

Réserve de Faune du Ferlo-Sud

Bakel

Senegal River

Kidira
Diboli

MALI

Kayes

Forêt de Paoul

Forêt de Goudiri

Forêt de Malâm Niani
Forêt des Panjates
Forêt de Tambacounda-Nord
Forêt de Bala-Ouest

Forêt de Bala-Est

Sadiola

Koussanar
Tambacounda

PARC NATIONAL DE NIOKOLO-KOBA (p230)
Watch yawning hippos and basking crocs on a boat tour through Senegal's largest national park

BASSARI COUNTRY (p231)
Rugged hills, remote waterfalls and colourful villages – ideal for hiking

Maka
Nétéboulou
Sutukoba
Diabugu
Fatoto
Basse Santa Su
Badiara
Vélingara

Wassadou

Forêt de Diambour

Gourbassi
Sainsoutou

Forêt du Kantora
Médina Gounas
Simenti
Damantan

Dar Salam
Badi

Niokolo-Koba
Niéménéki

Mako
Tomboronkoto
Bembou
Saraya

Forêt de la Kayanga

Parc National de Niokolo-Koba

Mt Assirik (311m)

Dalaba

KÉDOUGOU–SALÉMATA ROUTE (p233)
Tread lightly on the remote paths linking Senegal's most reclusive communities

Salémata
Ethiolo

Ibel
Indar
Kédougou
Bandafassi
Ségou

GUINEA-BISSAU

GUINEA

Youkounkoun
Koundara

Dindefelo
Niagalankome

On the Road

KATHARINA LOBECK KANE Author

Keeping family life in Dakar (p150) above chaos level can take so much time and energy that the country's biggest rewards – the beaches, mangroves and deserted river spots – don't get to see as much of me as I'd like. Researching this book was a great way of seeking out even the most distant corners of Senegal and Gambia: steering boats through meandering deltas, being awed by the village wrestling matches in honour of the king of Oussouye (p243) and helping to plant a million mangroves together with village kids in the Casamance (p235). And how great to know that Dakar was always there, waiting for my return with its rough embrace, pushing me gently back into an ever-changing restaurant, fashion and party scene, and having me road-test the city's offerings for children under my daughter's critical guidance.

ABOUT THE AUTHOR

Ever since the seductive tremor of a Fula flute first lured Katharina to West Africa in 1997, she hasn't been able to spend more than a few months without a stint in Africa. A year of PhD research in Guinea was followed by work visits to dozens of countries on the continent, usually clutching a camera and a voice recorder, to dig up gems from local music scenes. When London threw her out in 2005, she moved to Senegal. Katharina currently works as a writer, radio producer and presenter, and projects manager. Unless Berlin or Cologne have embraced her, you'll find her in Dakar.

MY FAVOURITE TRIP

Travelling for me has always been about music. Dakar, with its dazzling live-music scene (p172), is hard to leave if you love music. In May Saint-Louis holds its spectacular jazz festival (p60). Podor (p224) is the place to hear Fula music, perhaps during Baaba Maal's Festival du Fleuve. For the really rootsy stuff, Salémata (p233), with its vibrant Bassari culture, and Kartong (p119), site of a bustling festival, are my destinations of choice. Ziguinchor in Casamance is best visited during its carnival (p240), and Abéné (p253) during its reggae-fuelled New Year's festival. Brikama is the place to indulge in some masterful kora playing (p125).

The Gambia & Senegal Highlights

On these pages, travellers and Lonely Planet authors share their top experiences in The Gambia and Senegal. Do you agree with their choices, or have we missed your favourites? Go to lonelyplanet.com/thorntree and tell us your highlights.

NIC BOTHMA / CORBIS

1 **DUNES OF LOMPOUL**

The wind sweeps through dunes in the Désert de Lompoul (p203), so mighty you feel lost. An endless, starlit sky provides shelter.

Karoline Lobeck, Traveller, Berlin

ANDREW BURKE

DAKAR'S URBAN BEAT

The streets of Dakar (p150) kept calling us out of our recording studio and we set up our gear everywhere – in booming basements, among *ataaya* tea sippers and clouds of bats on a bare Médina terrace, in sandy backstreets vibrating to drumbeats. The city imposed its own rhythm. We tore up our careful plans and allowed ourselves to be swept away. And, strangely, the musical currents took us right back to our native South America, in one straight line. So confusing, so deep, so hard to leave.

Ivan Duràn, Record Producer

ARIADNE VAN ZANDBERG

2

ATLANTIC COAST & SEREKUNDA

Dust, heat and fumes just seem to pearl off those rustling robes people wear on Friday, the day of prayer. We were never able to match that incredible elegance, not even when draped in our newly sewn outfits, hand-picked on our walks through the frantic urban village of Serekunda (p97).

Sarah Legrand, Traveller, France

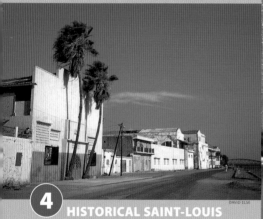

DAVID ELSÉ

4

HISTORICAL SAINT-LOUIS

Everything in Saint-Louis (p210) changes once night has fallen. The waves lapping against the wooden pontoon of Hôtel Sindoné (p216) murmur soft secrets and I'm sure I can hear the old buildings behind hum quiet tunes as the glow of the candles touches them.

Stephanie Masure, Senegal

MANGROVES OF THE SINÉ-SALOUM

I took my ultralight aircraft from France to the Siné-Saloum (p193) and, when I flew over Palmarin, I just kept circling, unable to take my eyes off those meandering creeks, white sandbanks and the bright pink dots of the salt basins. Then I spotted M'boss Dor (p193), seemingly suspended between sky and mangrove, and I knew this was where I was going to live.

Frédéric Vezia, Senegal

DAVID ELSE

PODOR, TRANQUIL RIVER TOWN

There are no cars and few people in Podor (p224). The water flows and time has no meaning. For once I switch off my phone – one conversation is enough and the river has plenty to say. I think of my grandfather and that I should visit his grave. Perhaps he used to sit right here, between the silent walls of Podor's old warehouses and the wide band of the river, thinking of *his* ancestors. This is where I come from, this region that I barely know that still whispers 'home' whenever I pass.

Souleymane Kane, Senegal

ANDREW BURKE

SECRETIVE BASSARI COUNTRY

Our motorbike jumped over earth mounds and through deep troughs, past green hills and over red laterite. Dust settled everywhere, like a second skin. We washed it off in the rock pool of the waterfall at Dindefelo (p233), then set out on a hike to their source. After months in Senegal, there were finally hills.

Ines Gontek, Senegal

7

ARIADNE VAN ZANDBERGEN

8

ARIADNE VAN ZANDBERG

RIVER GAMBIA NATIONAL PARK

The first flicker of sunlight sparks a symphony of baboon barks, bird calls and the morning shrieks of the chimps on the island in River Gambia National Park (p137). The cool water of the outdoor shower trickles down my spine and, as I walk across the wooden platform for my morning coffee, I'm convinced that those cheeky red colobus monkeys are debating about the curious creature that has come to join their treetop haven.

Katharina Lobeck Kane, Lonely Planet Author

ANDREW BUR

9

BEACHES OF N'GOR

You have to wake up early – very early – to catch the waves at N'Gor (p161). At 6am I'm on the beach, shivering, scanning the sea. Then I'm in there, playing the ocean's game. When I ride on a wave into the day, I forget that I haven't slept, perhaps for days, working to protect those waters.

PJ, Environmental Worker

Contents

Regional Map Contents

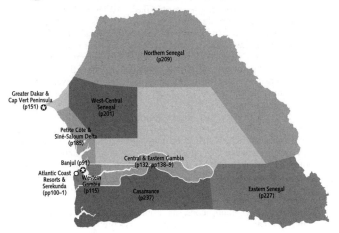

Northern Senegal (p209)

Greater Dakar & Cap Vert Peninsula (p151)

West-Central Senegal (p201)

Petite Côte & Siné-Saloum Delta (p185)

Banjul (p91)

Atlantic Coast Resorts & Serekunda (pp100–1)

Western Gambia (p115)

Central & Eastern Gambia (p132, pp138–9)

Casamance (p237)

Eastern Senegal (p227)

Destination
The Gambia & Senegal

Among all the random border constructs that trouble the African continent, the country-within-a-country set-up of Senegal and Gambia is perhaps the most puzzling. A fleeting glance at the West African map forces the question of why those two nations are just that – an anglophone sliver wedged into a vast, francophone side of land. There's a lot that links the two countries (a lot more than citizens of either usually like to admit). Wolof is the main tongue in both and the sandy beaches that embrace the Atlantic with smile-shaped bays merely shrug at the idea of human-made borders.

While national identities are clearly defined and often fiercely opposed, other, more ancient civilisations have washed over territories of both nations and tie their people closely together. On either side of the Senegal–Gambia border, *griots* (West African praise singers) will treat you to their epic narrations of the exploits of 13th-century hero Soundiata Keïta and the historical battles of the Kaabu Empire, accompanying their poetry with hypnotic patterns trickling from a *kora* (lute-harp). In both Dakar and Banjul, glittering nightclub crowds gyrate seductive hips to the toe-tripping beats of *mbalax*, while the chants of devout Muslims ring eerily through the night. Sound contradictory? Not in Senegal and Gambia. Culture here is shaped from a patchwork of enticing paradoxes, logic slips through your fingers like fine sand and reality stubbornly defies rational reasoning. As people move through the cities, they seem to at once perform journeys through time and space. A hard-nosed businessman may calmly swap his designer suit for a billowing *boubou* and kneel down in the middle of the street for his Friday prayer. You'll find feminist fighters wedged in polygamous marriages, where they've carved out niches of astonishing freedom. And even the staunchest defenders of cold logic might secretly wear protective charms, like backups for the possible power failures of reason.

> 'Move away from the main tourist centres and, along with the persistent grains of Sahel sand, you'll take memories of thought-provoking encounters home with you.'

But the sharpest contrasts are, sadly, the economic ones, and even the shortest trip through Dakar impresses those on you. While a small percentage of the nation is driving skyward in flashy 4WDs, most people are left to cough up the clouds of dust in their wake. The polished cocktail bars, top-brand boutiques and luxury hotels all have their local clientele, but those who weigh up the luxury of bread for breakfast versus a bus ticket to town remain far more numerous. And yet it's hard to escape the sense of endless possibility as you walk Dakar's hustler-ridden streets – the sense that, one day, the creative energy currently invested in designing clever con jobs and pushy souvenir-selling strategies may be applied to shaping the foundations of a few new businesses.

In Senegal, in particular, the environment seems fertile, as the country is not only stable, but is also one of Africa's few nations where real political debate seems possible. In 2008 the nation proved the maturity of its democracy once again when the opposition's alliance won major cities in local elections and the government accepted that 'slap on the wrist' thoughtfully. All across Dakar those dramatic results were noisily debated alongside football scores, marital issues and celebrity gossip in tiny *tanganas* (roadside cafes) and over strongly brewed *ataaya* tea in the sand-strewn backstreets of the capital's lively neighbourhoods. In Gambia, where the idea that a government might grant an inch to oppositional voices is a pretty alien one, people held their breath after Senegal's unexpected results. Where Senegal's rulers have been eager to portray themselves as democracy-favouring, France-friendly, intellectually gifted rulers, Gambia's leader, Yahya Jammeh, has modelled himself on his idea of a legendary West African hero. Since his coup d'état in 1994, he has ruled the nation like a one-man show, clamping down on critics, boosting the secret service and trying to impress the nation with his big gowns, kingly cane, ebony prayer beads and claims of magic powers. As a result, people are more wary of expressing political opinions and you might not be able to engage people in Gambia in keen political and religious sparring matches as quickly as in Senegal.

Still, in both countries, your travels are likely to be safe ones and, though you'll certainly cross paths with a few tricksters and indefatigable touts, real hospitality will prove a more enduring companion. Move away from the main tourist centres and, along with the persistent grains of Sahel sand, you'll take memories of thought-provoking encounters home with you.

Getting Started

Whether it's a lazy beach holiday you're after or a solitary tour around remote villages, myriad mangrove swamps and savannah plains, you'll be well served in Gambia and Senegal.

For a brief stay in the built-up tourist zones – such as the Atlantic resorts in The Gambia, and Saly and Cap Skiring in Senegal – you won't need much advance preparation, especially if you travel with an organised tour.

Independent travellers and those intending to venture far off the beaten track should spend a good amount of time crouched over maps and travel guidebooks – if you know where you're hoping to stay, many of the isolated lodgings upcountry can help you with transport if you contact them in advance. The Senegalese Casamance is a particularly exciting area for tours around tiny islands and white beaches, and a visit here is easily combined with a Gambia holiday – just don't let the language difference scare you.

The budget you need to plan for depends largely on where in the region you're headed. Prepare for European prices on a city holiday to Dakar. Upcountry, accommodation and food are much cheaper, but transport costs may increase, particularly if you plan to travel by boat. Despite the price tag, weaving your way through creeks and river paths may well be the most amazing thing you'll do on your trip.

WHEN TO GO

By far the most popular tourist season in Gambia and Senegal is the period from November to February, when conditions are dry and relatively cool. This is also the best time to watch wildlife and birds (including many European migratory species) in the countries' many national parks, and the season you're guaranteed best access to all regions, as the absence of rain makes even the remotest dirt road reasonably accessible. And if you want to party, the urban centre of Dakar is a great place to spend Christmas and New Year.

Several of Senegal's famous dance and music festivals, however, tend to take place between April and June, when temperatures are higher and the climate is still dry.

The wet season (late June to late September) is the time keen hobby fishers come here to participate in deep-sea outings offered by specialist providers.

DON'T LEAVE HOME WITHOUT...

- your vaccination certificate with a yellow-fever stamp – you never know when you might have to show it
- making copies of all official documents – it will make getting any necessary replacements much easier
- a torch (flashlight) – many remote places don't have electricity, and power cuts are frequent even in the urban zones
- binoculars – even those with no ornithological inclination whatsoever are likely to be converted in this region
- a set of smart clothes – don't be outshone by the impeccably dressed locals
- a warm jersey – January nights in Dakar can get wool-sweater chilly
- an unlocked mobile phone in which you can insert a local SIM card – the easiest way of being reached while abroad

---

VISITS DURING RAMADAN

Ramadan, the holy month of the Islamic calendar, is a time of religious contemplation dedicated to prayer and the study of the Koran. Most importantly, it's the fasting month – Muslims are not allowed to eat, drink, smoke or have sex from dawn until dusk.

The Ramadan fast completely changes the rhythm of life in the Muslim world. Many people wake around 5am for an early breakfast before sunrise, and some businesses cancel the usual lunch break and finish around 4.30pm.

For travelling, this isn't the ideal time. Many restaurants, bars and nightclubs close for the 30 days and there won't be many live concerts, as music and other worldly pleasures are frowned upon for its duration. The combination of heat and collective hunger also means rising tempers, especially towards the late afternoon. A Ramadan traffic jam before dusk is always a scene of loud arguments and occasional fist fights.

As a non-Muslim you won't be expected to fast, and most people won't take offence if you eat in their presence. Just bear in mind that most others around you are running on empty stomachs, and be considerate of their needs. If you use the services of a driver, allow for prayer stops and try to get back before the break of the fast. If that's impossible, make sure you put in a stop when the prayer is called after dusk, allowing him to take in a hot drink and a bite to eat. The fast is usually broken with a handful of dates, so you can offer the driver some if you're running late and want to show your appreciation. Generally, be patient with the occasional show of grumpiness. If you want to know what it's like, try to live the Ramadan rhythm for a while. You'll understand what most of the locals are experiencing.

Most other tourists avoid it. The rains wash away some of the roads, rendering certain journeys upcountry impossible. Malaria is widespread, the humidity can become stifling and many national parks (and a few hotels) shut down. But there's a positive side to this, too. Everything is greener, you get to experience some awesome tropical storms, and independent travellers will enjoy the absence of large tourist groups as well as price reductions of up to 50%.

See Climate Charts (p261) for more information.

October and November are again fairly dry, though very hot. If you can take the temperatures, this is a great time to come. You can still enjoy the sight of lush greens, swelling rivers and large waterfalls while staying dry yourself. The beaches aren't packed yet and you're bound to find a hotel room.

Since you're travelling to a predominantly Muslim region, it's worth checking the lunar calendar, particularly for the dates of the fasting month of Ramadan (see the boxed text, above). Though it's perfectly possible to visit during Ramadan, and the month's special ambience is an experience in itself, many restaurants close and the entertainment scene goes into hibernation.

COSTS & MONEY

Gambia and Senegal are expensive destinations compared with other African countries. Shoestringers can get by on a budget of around US$40 per day, but that means battered minibuses, cheap hostels, street food and leaving Dakar on the earliest bush taxi you find. Spending US$40 to US$100 allows for some creature comforts. With US$100 you'll be at ease, though it takes around US$400 for almost unlimited access to the luxuries available.

Locally produced items (including food and beer) are much cheaper than in Europe or America, but as soon as you head for the supermarket for some French yoghurt or a box of cornflakes, you pay at least twice the amount you would at home.

All around the region, you can get a generous platter of rice and sauce in a local-style restaurant for US$4 or even less, but a three-course meal for two at the smart restaurants of Dakar or the coastal resorts of Gambia will set you back US$40 or more. In between, you get the whole range of quality and cost.

Hotel prices vary enormously between the urban centres and upcountry villages. In Dakar even staying in a bug-infested hostel might set you back US$30, while the same amount will get you a spacious double room in a *campement* (hostel accommodation in bungalows) in rural Senegal or Gambia.

On average allow US$40 to US$100 for midrange hotels; top-notch establishments go for anything from US$150 to far, far above. Couples can save on accommodation costs, as double rooms often cost only 25% more than singles and might even go for the same price. In most hotels, children sharing with their parents stay free of charge up to the age of two and are charged around 50% of the full price between two and 10.

It's in transport that differences in costs are most notable. Bush taxis (minibuses or *sept-places*) are fairly cheap (around US$4 per 100km) but rough, slow and unsafe. For more comfort, you have to hire your own transport – around US$60 to US$100 per day for a private taxi, and US$120 or more per day for a 4WD with driver.

TRAVELLING RESPONSIBLY

There's plenty on offer in Senegal and Gambia for anyone wishing to travel in an ecofriendly, community-supportive way. Gambia has a particularly impressive infrastructure for eco-travel, patiently grown via organisations such as ASSET (see the boxed text, p104) and a couple of private investors. It boasts some of the most luxurious and fully developed eco-lodges in the whole of West Africa, excellent birdwatching opportunities, and a number of fascinating community projects that open their doors to visitors. In Senegal, the best options for travelling responsibly are found in the Casamance and Siné-Saloum regions, where you can stay in pretty community *campements* tucked away on river edges or hide from the world in remote eco-lodges. For more information on planning a holiday that's not only enjoyable but also leaves a positive impact, see Responsible Travel, p68, and check our GreenDex (p319), which indicates recommended destinations.

TRAVEL LITERATURE

Very few travel books have been published about the region, but you can still read your way into the countries' culture through a whole range of related topics.

The most famous work relating to The Gambia is probably *Roots,* by Alex Haley, which was written in 1976. A mix of fiction and historical fact, this hugely influential book describes the African-American author's search for his African origins.

For historical insights into the region, give Mungo Park's *Travels in the Interior of Africa* a try. The classic tome details the author's expeditions through Gambia and Senegal to the Niger River in the late 18th and early 19th centuries. His descriptions of the musical performances by *griots* (West African praise singers) could still apply to their timeless art today.

Finally translated, Fatou Diome's *The Belly of the Atlantic* (2008) is a beautiful novel that grants an intimate insight into complex issues surrounding emigration.

The stunning art book *Senegal Behind Glass* (1994), by Anne-Marie Bouttianaux-Ndiaye, contains reproductions of beautiful *sous-verre* paintings (see p53), from historical to contemporary examples, giving artistic insights into the country's religion, culture and arts scene.

A Saint in the City (2003), by Allen and Mary Roberts, takes a similar approach, discussing aspects of Senegalese culture through the images of Senegal's great Sufi leader Cheikh Amadou Bamba (see p205) that you'll find painted on houses, walls and taxis.

TOP PICKS

SENEGAL

Dakar

Banjul

Mali

TOP FESTIVALS

It's hard to come to Senegal and not find a festival in full swing. The country has a fantastically vibrant arts and music scene, as well as a population that loves a good party. Gambia is barely keeping up, though it also has a couple of events that mustn't be missed.

- Kartong Festival (p266), Kartong, March/April
- Dak'Art Biennale (p163), Dakar, every two years in May
- Saint-Louis International Jazz Festival (p213), Saint-Louis, May
- Kaay Fecc (p164), Dakar, June
- International Roots Festival (p266), throughout Gambia, every two years in June
- Les Blues du Fleuve (p265), Podor, dates vary
- Regards sur Courts (p178), Gorée, May

TOP RIVER SPOTS

Between them, Senegal and Gambia have three major waterways, each with tucked-away river camps and old trading towns.

- Tranquil Podor (p224)
- Classic Saint-Louis (p210)
- Lush River Gambia National Park (p137)
- Island-set Janjangbureh (Georgetown; p140)
- Vast Parc National de Niokolo-Koba (p230)
- Stunning Pointe St George (p244)
- Mangrove-lined Niomoune (p245)

TOP BIRDWATCHING SITES

Senegal and Gambia are among the world's major birdwatching destinations, and you never have to venture far to get some shiny feathers in front of your binoculars. See also p70.

- Abuko Nature Reserve (p122)
- Baobolong Wetland Reserve (p134)
- La Langue de Barbarie (p219)
- Pointe St George (p244)
- Marakissa (p126)
- Parc National des Oiseaux du Djoudj (p221)
- Réserve de Popenguine (p186)
- Tanji River Bird Reserve (p116)
- Toubakouta (p198)

Most works on Senegal are written in French. If you're familiar with the language, *Sénégal* (2005), Christian Saglio's musings on the country, is a great choice. The former head of Dakar's Institut Français has spent the greater part of his life in Senegal, where, among other things, he helped conceive the fabulous network of *campements villageois* (traditional-style village lodgings; see p243) in Casamance in the 1970s.

For an easy-to-read and entertaining account of travels around West Africa's music scene, try Mark Hudson's *Our Grandmother's Drum*. The amusing *Music in My Head*, by the same author, describes the power, influence and everyday realities of modern African music, and is set in a mythical city that is instantly recognisable as Dakar.

Overland travellers to the region must read *Sahara Overland – A Route & Planning Guide*, by Chris Scott, which covers every tiny detail you might

The website www .wootico.com is a brilliant resource on cultural events and top destinations in Senegal.

need to know. First published by Trailblazer in 1999, it can be 'upgraded' at Scott's website (www.sahara-overland.com).

INTERNET RESOURCES

Access Gambia (www.accessgambia.com) Seemingly bigger than the country itself, this comprehensive site contains pretty much everything, from information on hotels to music clips, maps and telephone listings.

ASSET (www.asset-gambia.com) The home page of the Gambian Association of Small Scale Enterprises in Tourism lists plenty of interesting small businesses, from juice pressers and hotels to fashion designers and taxi drivers. The perfect guide for responsible travel off the beaten track.

Au-Senegal (www.au-senegal.com) Information overload – no detail of practical information, cultural/historical background or news has been left out. You can book hotels online, get the latest updates on the political situation and much, much more.

Lonely Planet (www.lonelyplanet.com) Up-to-date information on travelling to the region and links to other good travel resources.

Senegalaisement (www.senegalaisement.com) Quite disorganised and very opinionated, this French site contains very detailed historical, cultural and practical information on even the smallest destination in Senegal.

Wow (www.wow.gm) The place to read and comment on news from Gambia.

Itineraries
CLASSIC ROUTES

GAMBIA – COASTAL COMFORTS
TO RURAL REMOTENESS
One to Two Weeks

The Gambia's compact size makes it an ideal destination for a one- or two-week visit. From Banjul airport, head for the **Atlantic coast** (p97), where you'll find the biggest choice of places to stay. Spend a couple of days at the beaches, and take the occasional day trip to the surrounding areas once the glamour of sea and sun alone has worn off. The busy market of **Serekunda** (p97) is close by, arts lovers will enjoy the proximity of **Tunbung Arts Village** (p118) and **Tanji Village Museum** (p117), while anyone interested in 'green options' will find plenty of choice in **Gunjur** (p119) and **Kartong** (p119). Spend the night in one of the fabulous eco-lodges there, then visit the bustling junction town of **Brikama** (p124) and the bee farm in **Sifoe** (p127). Carry on to **Makasutu** (p123), visit the Culture Forest and then head back to the coast.

Abuko Nature Reserve (p122), Gambia's smallest stretch of protected nature, is only a short drive away from the coast. A trip here can be combined with a meal at **Lamin Lodge** (p122), a creaking wooden restaurant that nestles in the mangroves.

The small and dusty capital of **Banjul** (p89) sits roughly 20km from the coastal resorts, and tempts with a lively market and colonial architecture. Take the ferry to the north bank for a visit to **Jufureh** (p129), then spend the night on beautiful **Ginak Island** (p128).

If you have two weeks, take a journey upcountry. A river trip to **Janjangbureh** (p140) is an absolute treat. Take the road to **Bintang Bolong** (p132), then combine driving and boat trips to Janjangbureh, taking in **Wassu** (p137) and the **River Gambia National Park** (p137) on the way. Put in a day trip to **Basse Santa Su** (p144) before the long journey home.

This itinerary travels the entire country, taking you to all the major sites, from the beaches and fishing villages of the Atlantic coast to the most important national parks – Ginak Island in the west and River Gambia National Park in the east. Approximate return distance is 1000km.

THE MANY FACES OF SENEGAL'S COAST   Two to Three Weeks

Travel north from Dakar to Saint-Louis' nearby national parks for birdwatching, then south past the dunes of Lompoul and along the Petite Côte, ending up in the Siné-Saloum Delta. Starting and ending in Dakar, this tour is around 1050km.

Most flights go to **Dakar** (p150), where you're plunged straight into the city's exciting nightlife, arts and restaurant scenes, and maze of markets. Prepare your escape with day trips to peaceful **Île de Gorée** (p177) and **Îles de la Madeleine** (p179).

Next, head north to historical **Saint-Louis** (p210) and from here day-trip to **Parc National des Oiseaux du Djoudj** (p221) and **Parc National de la Langue de Barbarie** (p220).

Return south, taking in the **Désert de Lompoul** (p203) on your way to the Petite Côte. Stop at the chilled-out fishing village of **Toubab Dialao** (p184), before following the shoreline south to **Mbour** (p190). Be awed by the sounds and smells of the town's giant fish market, then discover the quieter side of the resort zone of Saly by booking a room in **Saly-Niakhniakhal** (p190). Past the seashell town of **Joal-Fadiout** (p192), take the laterite route to **Palmarin** (p193), the stunning entry port to the Siné-Saloum Delta region. Spend a romantic night on nearby **Île M'boss Dor** (p193) or **Dionewar** (p194). Back on the mainland, follow the dirt road via Sambadia to **Ndangane** (p195), where you can cross via pirogue to the tranquil, bird-rich island of **Mar Lodj** (p195). A star-studded stay at **Fimela** (p196) crowns the journey.

ROADS LESS TRAVELLED

THE SENEGAL RIVER ROUTE   Two to Three Weeks

This historical itinerary follows the Senegal River, the country's national border with Mauritania, tracing the route of French colonial incursion. Start in **Saint-Louis** (p210), the ancient capital of French West Africa, where you can learn about the town's unique history and culture on guided city tours and through independent exploration. From here you can either take the classic *Bou El Mogdad* upriver to Podor, or mirror the ship's journey on a trip by road. Past the industrial monument of **Makhana** (p222), the town of **Richard Toll** (p223) is the place to taste delicious dairy products and visit the sugar factory. Stay for a while in **Podor** (p224), visit the ancient fort, the old photographer and the newly renovated quay, then head off on an off-road journey around the **Île à Morphil** (p225), where classic Omarian mosques, stunning savannah countryside and Tukulor villages line the bumpy dirt roads. Further along you'll reach **Matam** (p225), a place to meet the local community, and **Bakel** (p225), framed by gentle hills and a windswept shoreline. A short hop south and you reach **Kidira** (p234) at the Malian border. You can return to Dakar via **Tambacounda** (p227), but if you've still got a few days, first head to **Wassadou** (p229), where you can arrange your tour to the **Parc National de Niokolo-Koba** (p230). Once you've reached **Kédougou** (p231) and **Bassari country** (p231), you may feel like never going home, especially as you've got a 700km journey to **Dakar** ahead of you.

This takes you along the rarely travelled road following the Senegal River, past the ancient forts of Podor, Matam and Bakel. You'll visit Senegal's largest national park and hike through the hills of Bassari country. Starting in Saint-Louis and finishing in Dakar, this tour is about 1800km.

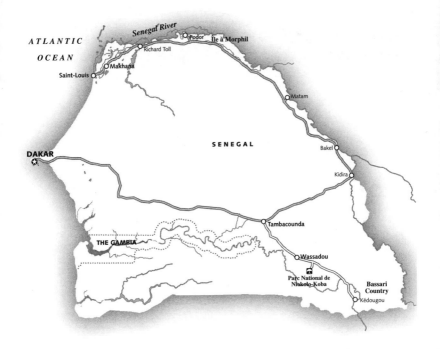

STRADDLING BORDERS
Two to Three Weeks

This is a perfect holiday – a tour around Gambia's developed coastline, combined with either a circuit of Senegal's stunning Siné-Saloum Delta or the diverse scenery of the beautiful Casamance. Starting and finishing at the Atlantic coast, it's around 1500km, depending on which route you take.

Combining trips to Gambia with excursions to the Senegalese regions across the border is becoming increasingly popular – an easy way of experiencing the best of two worlds. You'll arrive at Banjul, and spend your first days at the **Atlantic coast resorts** (p97). Take your pick from day excursions (see the Gambia itinerary, p19), and prepare your bags for the trip via the Karang border crossing to **Toubakouta** (p198) and the beautifully secluded eco-camp of **Bamboung** (p198). **Missirah** (p199) and the adjacent **Forêt de Fathala** (p194) are a short hop to the south. North of Toubakouta, the community of **Sokone** (p197) opens its doors to visitors. Circumvent the Delta to rejoin it on the western side, where **Fimela** (p196) has the most stunning lodge of all, and **Simal** (p196) in the mangroves has rootsy, traditional huts for intrepid visitors.

Even less travelled, and still more attractive, is the Gambia–Casamance route. Start as above, but instead of heading north to Toubakouta, go to **Brikama** (p124), from where you'll find transport to **Kafountine** (p251) and **Abéné** (p253). Before reaching those chilled-out villages, put in a detour to secluded **Niafourang** (p254), temptingly close to **Kartong** (p119) in Gambia (ensure you've all the legal stamps to cross). Take the road southwards to **Ziguinchor** (p238), the capital of the Casamance, possibly taking in the community stays of **Koubalan** and **Dioubour** (p249) on the way. Take the straight route to **Oussouye** (p243), put in a day of kayaking and cycling, then speed down to **Cap Skiring** (p246) and stay still for a bit, spread-eagled on the widest, whitest beaches of the region.

TAILORED TRIPS

AS THE CROW FLIES

Senegal and Gambia are among the best destinations for birdwatching in West Africa.

In Gambia the chirping of hundreds of species greets you before you've even left your hotel, in the backyards of the Senegambia Beach Hotel in **Kololi** (p107) or the Corinthia Atlantic Hotel in **Banjul** (p94). The **Abuko Nature Reserve** (p122) and the **Tanbi Wetland Complex** (p94) are more 'regular' birdwatching sites, complete with guides and hides.

On the south coast, the **Tanji River Bird Reserve** (p116) is a great place to spot a variety of waders. Inland, **Marakissa** (p126) attracts a huge diversity of species, being set between river and forest. **Baobolong Wetland Reserve** (p134) is a playground for herons, egrets and owls, and **Kiang West National Park** (p135) attracts huge numbers but is hard to explore. In **Janjangbureh** (p140) try a stay at Bird Safari Camp, great for variety with its forest-river location, and take a trip towards **River Gambia National Park** (p137), where you can cruise past weavers and herons perched on small islands.

In Senegal, the *bolongs* (creeks) of the **Siné-Saloum Delta** (p193) and the **Casamance** (p235) are bird-watchers' dream destinations, with hundreds of sea birds and waders nesting on river islets and circling above mangrove forests. Other highlights are the **Parc National des Oiseaux du Djoudj** (p221), the world's third-largest bird sanctuary, and the stunning peninsula of **Parc National de la Langue de Barbarie** (p220).

ARCHITECTURAL GEMS

Trace the history of colonisation by following the architectural 'monuments' of Gambia and Senegal. If it's local culture you're after, check out the different building styles of the countries' various regions.

For colonial impact, **Île de Gorée** (p177) and **Saint-Louis** (p210), with their partly preserved French buildings, are must-sees. **Rufisque** (p182) and **Banjul** (p89) have similar colonial houses, though in a less well-kept state.

Along the Senegal River, the Folie de Baron Roger in **Richard Toll** (p223) is a monument to the grand aspirations of colonialism, as are the Faidherbian forts of **Podor** (p224) and **Bakel** (p225). On **Île à Morphil** (p225), the Sudanese architecture of the Omarian mosques is a reminder of local resistance to colonisation.

In Gambia, the British **Fort James** (p130) is partly preserved, and **Janjangbureh** (p140) has a couple of crumbling colonial warehouses. In Casamance, you can sleep in the old governor's house and mission on **Île de Karabane** (p245), visit the old fort and administrative buildings of the former colonial capital **Sédhiou** (p254), and admire the *cases à étages* (two-storey mud buildings) in **M'Lomp** (p244) and the *cases à impluvium* (round mud houses) in **Enampor** (p243) and **Affiniam** (p250).

THE BEST RIVER SPOTS

There's something special about a tranquil journey up a major waterway. Cut through by three large rivers, the region offers plenty of choice.

Great spots on the Gambia River include the rickety mangrove cabins of **Bintang Bolong** (p132) and, further north, **Tendaba Camp** (p133), perfectly located near the **Baobolong Wetland Reserve** (p134) and **Kiang West National Park** (p135), which teem with birds. Further east, where the lush vegetation starts, **River Gambia National Park** (p137) is a dream spot, great for hippo, chimpanzee, and baboon spotting. A little further eastwards, you reach the pretty island town of **Janjangbureh** (p140), and the market centre of **Basse Santa Su** (p144), where you can cross the stream in a metal tub.

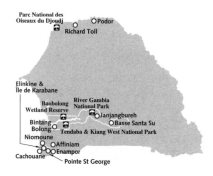

A tour along the Casamance River takes you to numerous secluded community *campements* (hostels). Pirogues leave from Ziguinchor, and can take you to **Enampor** (p243) and **Affiniam** (p250). **Elinkine** (p245) is a centre for pirogue tours, from where you can easily connect to the stunningly beautiful **Pointe St George** (p244), historical **Île de Karabane** (p245), mangrove-framed **Niomoune** (p245) on the north bank and **Cachouane** (p249) near the river mouth.

In the far north of Senegal, the best river trip is done aboard the historic boat *Bou El Mogdad* (see p215), which stops at **Parc National des Oiseaux du Djoudj** (p221), **Richard Toll** (p223) and **Podor** (p224).

TRAVELLING GREEN

In Gambia you'll find some of the most fully developed and luxurious options for sustainable travel. Sandele Eco-Retreat in **Kartong** (p121) and Footsteps Eco Lodge in **Gunjur** (p119) combine eco-awareness and comfort in an amazing package. At the **Makasutu Culture Forest** and **Ballabu Conservation Project** (p123) you'll find Gambia's most exclusive eco-lodge, and an inspiring example of community-based conservation. For outings, visit the beekeepers' association in **Sifoe** (p127) and the **Gambia Is Good Farmyard** (p126).

In Senegal, the Océanium uses village-run *campements* to finance the Marine Protected Area of **Bamboung** (p198) and **Pointe St George** (p244). Along the lush banks of the Casamance River, numerous tucked-away *campements villageois* (traditional-style village lodgings) enable basic community stays, notably in **Koubalan** (p249) and **Affiniam** (p250). The **Campement Villageois d'Elinkine** (p245), the cute guest houses at **Cachouane** (p249) and **Niomoune** (p245), and the *campement* at **Dioubour** (p249) are privately managed, but invest in the community they're based in. The setting of Tilibo Horizons in **Niafourang** (p254) is particularly stunning and the owners also offer tours with a sustainable edge, as does the managing association of Fadidi Niombato at **Sokone** (p197). We were completely besotted by the children's project of the Village d'Outouka in **Kafountine** (p253). Right up north, the Maison Guillaume Foy contributes to responsible tourism development in **Podor** (p224), and the village of **Makhana** (p222) raises community income by organising visits to the historical pumping station.

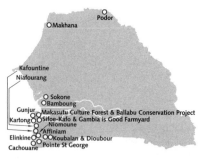

History

Senegal and Gambia are young nations, formed in the wake of the independence movements that swept through Africa in the 1950s and 1960s. Yet those few decades are a mere blip in a past that spans centuries, during which illustrious African emperors charged on horseback through the lands of the Sahel, marking territories and fighting over souls. People moved and settled, united and dispersed with the currents of time, adopting new faiths or defiantly strengthening old ones. Their unwritten stories shaped the shifting cultural grounds that still determine life today.

EARLY RESIDENTS

In a large circle spanning today's Gambia, parts of Senegal's east and the mangrove-dotted western coast, a scattering of ancient sites tease researchers and provoke speculation about this area's earliest citizens. Near the banks of the Gambia River, large rings of smoothly hewn laterite stones guard the secrets of the sophisticated early civilisation that built them, probably around AD 750. It is almost certain that these enigmatic monuments indicate burial sites, just like the fascinating seashell tumuli found in Senegal's Siné-Saloum region (see the boxed text, p26).

More is known about the gradual development of trade routes in the 1st millennium AD, linking West Africa to the north of the Sahara. The desert had long been too big an obstacle to brave, until someone had the simple but brilliant idea of using camels to transport gold and salt across these hostile lands. The caravans traced early economic arteries, along which settlements were founded that grew first into wealthy trading stations, then powerful federations.

AGE OF THE EMPIRES

The first state to grow rich from the lucrative trade routes was the Empire of Ghana. At its height between the 8th and 11th centuries, it spanned large parts of eastern Senegal and western Mali, and probably would have continued to expand happily, had the trade routes that built it not also opened the path for the forces that destroyed it. Around 1075, the legendary Almoravid dynasty rode in from the north, eager to spread Islam and, naturally, extend its territories

---

THE GAMBIA

The Gambia's official name always includes 'The', but this is often omitted in everyday situations. In this book we have usually omitted 'The' for reasons of clarity and to ensure smooth-flowing text.

TIMELINE

AD 750	1030s	1324
Stone circles, such as those of Wassu and Kerr Batch, and seashell burial mounds, such as Diorom Boumag near Toubakouta, indicate that sophisticated civilisations inhabited this region in a time that we still know very little about.	The Halpulaar (Tukulor) leaders of the Tekrur Empire in northern Senegal convert to Islam. Their religious and economic rivalry with the Ghana Empire makes them natural allies of the Almoravids in their war against Ghana.	Mansa Kankan Musa, the 10th emperor of the mighty Mali Empire, causes the first global financial crisis when he carries so much gold with him on his pilgrimage to Mecca that he crashes the global markets.

BURIED IN OYSTERS

Giant baobabs cling with mighty roots to the tiny island of Diorom Boumag near Toubakouta. Baobabs love calcium-rich soils, and that's why they flourish on this unusual island. Diorom Boumag is in fact a human-made mound, shaped entirely from the shells of oysters and mussels, thrown here on a massive pile many centuries ago. There are more than 200 such sites across the Siné-Saloum region in Senegal, and around 20 stand out for another reason. Excavations have uncovered human bones among the shells, dating back to around AD 730–1370 and suggesting that the shell dumps were also used as burial sites. Little is known about the people who shaped these fascinating islands, but they provide fascinating proof of early habitation of this part of West Africa.

---

southwards. Ghana put up a fight, but eventually succumbed to the combined forces of the Almoravids and the northern Senegalese Tekrur Empire.

From the 11th century onwards, West African history brims with stories of horseback warriors, passionate preachers and insatiable emperors. Most famous of all is Soundiata Keïta, whose praise songs are still today on the lips of every Manding *griot* (West African praise singer). This hero of epic proportions led wars, conquered peoples, defeated the sorcerer king Soumaoro Kanté and built the greatest West African kingdom of all – the Mali Empire. By the 14th century this mighty realm stretched from the Atlantic coast across to present-day Nigeria, spreading its wealth, hierarchical social make-up and Manding culture across the region.

In a far-flung corner of the kingdom (the territories of present-day Gambia and Guinea-Bissau), one of Soundiata's generals, Timakhan Traoré, set up an outpost of the empire, the small state of Kaabu, where he could reign and gain fame. Today, the founder-general has largely been forgotten, eclipsed by the awe-inspiring persona of Janke Waali, the dreadlocked animist king who fought Kaabu's last battle in 1867 against Muslim Fula pushing in from the south.

The Empire of Mali itself saw numerous rulers come and go. Few are remembered today. What remains, though, is the story of a realm that rose to dazzling greatness before stretching too far, breaking in the process. By the mid-15th century Mali had begun to wane, and a new contender for greatness, the Songhaï Empire, rose in its place.

In the far west, Mali's decline turned its former vassal state, the Jolof Empire, into a self-governing realm. For Jolof, however, the waning of central control came at a difficult time. An influx of Portuguese trading wealth had reinforced divisions between the empire's individual member states that proved impossible to resolve. Thus weakened, Jolof was no match for the rebellious spirit of Koli Tenguella, who waged war against its northern states and snatched them to his newly formed Fouta Toro Empire on the Senegal River. Jolof crumbled and by 1600 had to be content with the status of a microstate that co-existed with its former components.

1360	1443	1537
The Wolof people establish the Jolof Empire, uniting the small coastal kingdoms Siné and Saloum and the northern Waalo, Kayor and Baol in a visionary federal state whose cultural legacy remains strong to this day.	Portuguese ships reach the mouth of the Senegal River, and a year later they land on the coast of Senegal at a peninsula they name Cabo Verde, meaning Green Cape. (It is now called Cap Vert, and is the site of Dakar.)	As the Mali Empire declines, the former outpost of Kaabu becomes a kingdom in its own right. It eventually falls in a series of fierce battles between the animist Mandinka rulers and Muslim Fula forces.

EUROPEAN AMBITIONS

The shattering of the Jolof Empire was an indication of major changes. By the 15th century, new forces had joined the battle over territories, riches and beliefs in West Africa – those of the European empires. Dazzled by the West African gold that had made it to their courts, they started vying for the lands that harboured such extraordinary riches.

Travelling across the desert wasn't an option for the Europeans – the Sahara trade routes were controlled by Arab states. The empire that therefore gained an advantage over its rivals was Portugal, which possessed a superior fleet of ships and was eager to send it out. The 15th-century Prince Henry of Portugal, fittingly nicknamed Henry the Navigator, encouraged explorers to sail down the coast of West Africa. In 1443 Portuguese ships reached the mouth of the Senegal River, and a year later they landed on the coast of Senegal at the peninsula that houses present-day Dakar. No matter that they'd reached an inhabited area with its own cultures and traditions; steeped in the spirit of 'discovery', they swiftly bestowed their own name on the area, calling it Cabo Verde (Green Cape; today called Cap Vert). A few negotiations with local chiefs followed, and the Portuguese established a trading station on Île de Gorée, a short distance off the coast. Unbeatable sea travellers at the time, the Portuguese were able to sail around large parts of the West African coast, and dotted its shores and islands with commercial centres from where slaves and commodities were shipped back to Europe.

THE TRAGIC TRADE

Over the following centuries, West Africa's fate depended on developments in an entirely different part of the globe – the so-called New World, which included South America, the Caribbean and the south of what became the USA. Portugal had established settlements in Brazil by 1530, which grew into large commercial sugar estates between 1575 and 1600. Their expansion led to a demand for labourers, which the Portuguese met by importing slaves from West Africa – a development that was to have huge and serious repercussions throughout the continent.

Although local slavery had existed in West Africa for many centuries, the Portuguese developed the trade on a massive scale. By the 16th century, other European powers had joined in and rivalled Portugal in its commercial ambitions. The French had been defying the Portuguese monopoly for some time, and between 1500 and 1530 captured hundreds of Portuguese vessels with their human cargo. By the 1650s Portugal had largely been ousted from the coasts it had opened to European exploitation, while other powers engaged in fierce and ugly struggles over the region's territories and people. The Netherlands entered the scene, taking over the settlement on Île de Gorée in 1617. The British and French directed their attention to the two main waterways that cut through the region. While Britain gained control over

African Civilization Revisited: From Antiquity to Modern Times (1990) is only one of many accessible works on African history by the influential writer Basil Davidson.

1617	**1633**	**1659**
The Dutch turn the trading station on Île de Gorée into a major slave port. The French eventually take Gorée from the Dutch in 1677.	The French establish La Compagnie du Cap Vert et du Sénégal, the main trading company operating in France's African colonies.	French traders put down roots on the barely inhabited island of N'Dar at the mouth of the Senegal River. They rename the place Saint-Louis, after the French emperor, and build an important urban centre.

the Gambia River, France focused on the Senegal River in the north. Both controlled trade through forts and trading stations (*comptoirs* in French) that they established on strategically placed islands near the river deltas.

Key colonial settlements, such as James Island, Île de Gorée and France's *comptoir* of Saint-Louis, founded in 1659 on the barely inhabited island of N'Dar, were fiercely embattled and changed hands several times between the British and French. For the French, the port of Saint-Louis was the most treasured site of all, and the one they lavished most attention on. The town became far more than a mere shipping port. Here the Franco-African *métis* (mixed race) merchant class that already characterised Île de Gorée developed into a unique, urban culture. The most amazing symbol of this was the *signares,* mixed-race women who married French traders (for the duration of their stay in Saint-Louis) and gained status, wealth and even political influence through this connection. Their style and festivities, such as the famous *fanals* (lantern processions) still inspire nostalgia today. *Métis* residents attained important posts within the colonial administration – on a walk through modern-day Saint-Louis, you'll find streets and buildings named after them, and probably talk to many of their descendants.

The growth of such a unique culture through intermarriage was perhaps the most positive way in which life in West Africa was affected by European expansion. Far more sinister was the fact that the steadily increasing demand for slaves encouraged the more powerful local communities, particularly those who had built their own kingdoms through servant culture and slavery, to invade neighbouring peoples and take captives that they'd sell to the European merchants.

Between the 16th and 19th centuries, up to 20 million Africans were captured as slaves. More than a quarter, and possibly half, of all captives died on the journey to the New World, due to the inhumane conditions on the boats and the duration of travel. Of the approximately 10 million slaves who reached the Americas, around 50% died within a few years as a result of malnourishment and ruthless treatment. Historical sites, such as La Maison des Esclaves (p180) on Île de Gorée in Senegal and James Island (p130) in Gambia, are stern reminders of this catastrophic trade, whose economic and above all human legacies changed the world forever.

The comprehensive website http://webworld .unesco.org/goree covers the history of Senegal's Île de Gorée, and includes a virtual tour of its infamous Maison des Esclaves.

MAKING PEANUTS

The British imposed a ban on slavery in 1807, and while Napoleon officially abolished the trade in 1815, it wasn't until 1848 that it finally stopped. This was also the time of the Napoleonic Wars (1799–1815) and tensions between Britain and France were high. The slavery ban gave Britain a good excuse to attack the old enemy – French ships off the coasts of Gambia and Senegal were frequently chased and captured by the British navy, and slaves were freed and resettled.

1664	1677	1756
Britain wins the battle over the fort on James Island, established initially by Baltic Germans and later held by the Dutch. It changes hands several times more between the French, the British and even pirates.	The French gain control over the trading station of Île de Gorée, founded in 1455 by the Portuguese, then fought over by the Dutch, British and French. Gorée's architecture shows the legacies of all its occupants.	Britain and France are opposed in fierce territorial battles lasting seven years. Britain briefly gains control of all of France's possessions in the Senegal area, though soon has to return them.

In 1816 Britain bought an island called Banjul (meaning bamboo) on the south side of the mouth of the Gambia River from a local chief. Popular legend has it that a few iron bars sufficed to gain the land. They renamed the place Bathurst, and declared the Gambia River and its surrounding lands a British protectorate in 1820. The Gambia was administered from the British colony of Sierra Leone, further along the West African coast, which had been established as a haven for freed slaves in 1787. Several forts were built along the river, such as Fort Bullen in 1826 and Georgetown (now called Janjangbureh) in 1828.

The protectorate enabled Britain to focus its attention on the development of plantations and the trade in agricultural products, now that the slave trade had ceased to provide revenue. In the French areas, a similar change in focus was pursued in an aggressive way. Strongly urged by powerful trading companies such as Maurel & Prom, whose warehouses you can still see in Saint-Louis and Podor, the French government laid out a plan whereby a series of forts along the Senegal River would serve to gain control over the acacia gum trade in those areas. This new focus suited the expansionist zeal of Louis Faidherbe, governor since 1854. Under his rule, forts were established in Dagana, Podor, Matam and Bakel, as well as in present-day Mali. Of these fortifications, those of Dagana and Podor have today been restored.

Not only the gum trade, but also large groundnut (peanut) cultivations were brought under French control, and strongly expanded in subsequent years. First introduced by the Portuguese, the humble peanut was easily cultivated, and increasingly sought after, as Europe's economies found greater use for its precious oil.

The developments inland gave renewed impetus to Saint-Louis, at once the gateway to the Senegal River and the port from which products were shipped. Proud capital of the vast French-governed terrain of Afrique Occidentale Française (AOF; French West Africa), the town evolved at an ever-increasing rate and its vibrant urban culture developed to cosmopolitan heights.

French expansionist efforts weren't looked upon kindly in the region and were eventually fiercely opposed. One of the biggest challengers of the French was Islamic leader El Hajj Omar Tall, who frequently clashed with the French in fights motivated by economic, religious and territorial competition.

Ethnic Groups of the Senegambia, by Patience Sonko-Godwin, tells the stories of the main peoples of Gambia and Senegal, tracing their histories back to the era of the great West African empires or earlier. It's available locally.

BROTHERHOOD OR FRATRICIDE?

To some people, he's West Africa's greatest resistance fighter, an anti-European, Africa-building unifier; to others, a bloody invader. The name of El Hajj Omar Tall doesn't leave anyone from Senegal to Mali indifferent. Born in humble circumstances in Alwar, a small town near Podor in 1797, this son of a weaver rose to great ambitions when an Islamic marabout introduced him to the teachings of the Sufi brotherhood Tijaniya. Following trips to far-flung corners of West and North Africa to deepen his understanding of Islam (including, naturally, a pilgrimage to Mecca in 1828), El Hajj Omar

1783	**1794**	**1807**
The Treaty of Versailles delineates the spheres of anglophone and francophone influence that dominate the region to this day. Gambia is given to the British, and Gorée returned to the French. Later attempts at unifying the territory fail.	The slave trade is abolished by France, only to be reinstated by Napoleon eight years later. It is finally abolished once and for all in 1815.	Britain imposes a ban on slave trading, although existing slaves are still legally held until the Slavery Abolition Act is passed in 1833.

Tall set out to found the largest Muslim theocracy and last great empire of the region through a series of battles, starting in 1850. From his adopted home in Dinguiraye (Guinea-Conakry), he formed an army of disciples and launched a jihad (holy war) that he hoped would unify most of West Africa under the banner of the Tijaniya brotherhood. At its height, his empire stretched from northern Senegal as far as Timbuktu (Mali).

Muslim faith had been introduced to West Africa as early as the 10th century, yet had for a long time remained the religion of the wealthy and the rulers, who tolerated the practice of traditional faiths among their subjects. Although El Hajj Omar Tall wished to put an end to the animist practices still prevalent in Segou (Mali) and other areas in his path, the Islamic practice he helped spread contained elements that had been absorbed from traditional religions, rendering it uniquely African.

Islam in West Africa takes the form of Sufism, a belief system that emphasises mystical and spiritual attributes. It allows for the influence of holy men called marabouts, many of whom are credited with having divine powers and the ability to communicate with Allah. El Hajj Omar Tall was a marabout and, like many others, he became an influential figure and counterforce to European powers, for whom the universal spread of Islam, and its related territorial expansion, was the ultimate red cloth.

Donald Cruise O'Brien's book *The Mourides of Senegal* is a comprehensive discussion of the origins of the powerful Senegalese brotherhoods. Published in the 1980s, it's largely still relevant to an understanding of religion in Senegal today.

El Hajj Omar Tall clashed frequently with French forces, and even celebrated victories, but ultimately couldn't compete with the military strength of the colonisers. Unable to drive out the French, he focused his attention on the eastern areas of Mali, where he fought the Bambara Empire of Segou and the Fula kingdom of Macina (1862). His unrelenting fight for occupation of the Muslim Fula theocracy of Macina is the clearest exposure of his expansionism, rather than religious zeal, as his forces opposed another Islamic community of the same ethnic group in long, bloody battles, claiming the lives of over 70,000 people. Ultimately, it was the combined force of the Bambara, Fula, Tuareg and other ethnic groups that put an end to his life in 1864 (he died in a gunpowder explosion), and ultimately to his leaderless empire.

El Hajj Omar Tall's missionary zeal and opposition to the French inspired clashes for more than three decades after his death. While in large areas of present-day Gambia, the Soninke-Marabout wars pitted Muslim clerics against Mandinka rulers in enduring battles over faith and influence, in Senegal's Siné-Saloum region further north, Islam became the unifying factor in the struggle against French expansion. Here, in the kingdom of Cayor, the legendary leader Lat Dior converted to Islam in 1861, hoping that powerful Muslim alliances, strong enough to protect even non-Muslim states, would provide sufficient force against the French. Recognising the strategic advantage the Dakar–Saint-Louis railway would grant the colonial force, he put up fierce resistance against its construction, though he was ultimately defeated in 1886, and the railway completed.

1820	1827	1848
Gambia is declared a British proctectorate and, after failed attempts by Britain to exchange it for other colonial territories, it becomes a full colony in 1886.	A 30-year-old El Hajj Omar Tall undertakes life-changing journeys to Niger, Sokoto (today's Nigeria), Cairo, Mecca and beyond in order to increase his understanding of Islam and forge new relations.	The key colonial centres of Rufisque, Dakar, Gorée and Saint-Louis become self-governing communes, where citizens enjoy the same rights as those of France.

The final thorn in the French colonials' side was another marabout called Cheikh Amadou Bamba. By 1887 this pacifist leader and founder of the Mouride brotherhood had gained a large following, proposing a religious practice that provided a strong social and cultural identity to communities under colonial domination. Fearing his force, the French exiled him first to Gabon (1895–1902), then to Mauritania (1903–07), which only increased his huge popularity. (See p205 for more details.) Today the Mouride brotherhood is the most influential in Senegal and Gambia (see p46), and Cheikh Amadou Bamba and his disciple Cheikh Ibra Fall are revered by large parts of the population – just check out the number of wall paintings and shops bearing their names across the region.

THE SCRAMBLE FOR AFRICA

Africa's modern boundaries were defined far from the continent's soil. In 1884–85 the European powers met in a boardroom at the Berlin Conference, drawing lines, swapping annexed territories, bartering and fighting over an entire continent and its inhabitants. The conference was called to put an end to the Scramble for Africa, which saw the big European nations (notably France, Belgium, Britain and Germany) engage in an undignified land grab in the late 1870s and early 1880s.

The scramble had been triggered in 1879 when King Leopold of Belgium claimed the Congo (now the Democratic Republic of the Congo). France responded by establishing a territory in the neighbouring area, which became known as the French Congo (now the Republic of the Congo) and Gabon. Meanwhile, the British were increasing their influence in East Africa, as part of a strategy to control the headwaters of the Nile. Germany's leader, Otto von Bismarck, also wanted 'a place in the sun' and claimed various parts of Africa, including territories that later became Togo and Cameroon. In 1883 Britain staked a claim to much of East Africa and to territories in West Africa, such as Gambia, Sierra Leone, the Gold Coast (modern-day Ghana) and Nigeria.

The attribution of territories to different European forces rang in a feverish period of colonial activity, as each nation ran to strike deals with local chiefs in order to gain official possession of the lands. Over the following years, African forms of governance were abolished and replaced by colonial administrations. The consequences on the ground in Africa were terrible. Coherent ethnic groups were suddenly divided by frontiers. New colonial identities were placed upon old community ties, and people with different languages and cultures were forced into one national bond. The seeds were sown for cycles of conflict that plague the continent to this day.

'Africa's modern boundaries were defined far from the continent's soil.'

CARVING OUT THE GAMBIA

Nowhere is the implausibility of the colonial constructs more obvious than in the case of Gambia, a tiny sliver of land that almost splits Senegal in two.

1857	**1864**	**1881**
France opens a military post at the Lebou village of Ndakaru. This act is considered by many as the official founding of Dakar, even though the town had been a flourishing Lebou community since the 17th century.	Omar Tall's forces are finally defeated by the French, but his missionary zeal inspires followers to keep fighting jihads, the so-called Marabout Wars, for another three decades.	The legendary leader Lat Dior starts a brave struggle against the construction of the railway linking Saint-Louis and Dakar, and thereby crossing the Kayor territories he rules over.

CANNONBALL RUN

The boundaries of Gambia largely follow the course of the Gambia River. From about 50km upstream, every bend of the river is echoed by a precise twist or turn in the borders, which run parallel to the river, less than 20km to the north and south. Local legend tells that the border was established by a British gunship sailing up the river and firing cannonballs as far as possible onto each bank. The points where the balls fell were then joined up to become the border. While this may not be strictly true, Gambia was initially established as a protectorate, and in the 19th century protection could be most easily administered by gunship.

Although Gambia was a British protectorate from 1820 and became a full British colony in 1886, the decision-makers in London didn't really want this strip of riverbank, inconveniently surrounded by French territory. Attempts were made to exchange Gambia for land elsewhere – a common practice among the colonial powers of the time – but no matter how much the British talked up the qualities of the territory, no one was interested. Thus Britain was lumbered with Gambia, and the little colony was almost forgotten as events in other parts of Africa and India dominated British colonial policy in the first half of the 20th century. Little wealth came out of Gambia and as a result very little development was attempted – administration was limited to a few British district commissioners and the local chiefs they appointed.

In the 1950s Gambia's groundnut plantations were improved as a way to increase export earnings, and some other agricultural schemes were set up. There was little in the way of services, and by the early 1960s Gambia had fewer than 50 primary schools and only a handful of doctors. While the rest of West Africa was gaining independence, this seemed unlikely for Gambia; there was hardly any local political infrastructure and Britain was against the move. A federation with Senegal, which had just gained independence from France, was considered but came to nothing.

Around this time David Jawara, a Mandinka from the upcountry provinces, founded the People's Progressive Party (PPP). It was the first party to attract mass support from rural Mandinkas, the overwhelming majority of Gambia's population. To prepare for at least partial self-government, a Gambian parliament – the House of Representatives – was instituted and elections were held in 1962, with prompt victory by Jawara's PPP.

AFRICA – THE FRENCH WAY

One can only imagine what Blaise Diagne might have felt when addressing the French parliament for the first time in 1914 – the first black African to obtain such a position. Only two years later, he pushed through a law granting full citizenship to the residents of the communes of Dakar, Gorée, Rufisque and Saint-Louis. Dashing, young and incredibly bright, the Gorée-born politician

1884–85	1887	1895
Colonial powers gather around a conference table in Berlin 'carving up' the African continent in line with their territorial interests. In over 90% of African territories, all forms of autonomous reign are brought to an end.	Eight years before he will be sent into exile by the French, Cheikh Amadou Bamba, leader of the Mouride brotherhood, founds the town of Touba. His religious and political legacy remains hugely important in Senegal and Gambia to this day.	Saint-Louis in Senegal becomes the capital of the vast, French-owned area of Afrique Occidentale Française (AOF; French West Africa), stretching from Senegal in the west to present-day Sudan in the east.

represented Senegal's young generation of thinkers, who were consciously African yet very close to France. He was vocal in his fight for equal rights for anyone, regardless of their skin colour, though he never opposed French rule. Quite the opposite: the French cultural values that included equality and freedom were aspects that fuelled his thinking. In that vein, it was not a contradiction for him to encourage young Senegalese soldiers (the so-called *tirailleurs*) to join the French army during WWI – after all, the 'motherland' needed support.

Diagne's persona exemplified the French colonisation style, called assimilation, which aimed to turn residents of the colonies into 'African French' through education and culture, and stood in stark contrast with British imperial policy. Another 'product' of assimilation was a young tutor by the name of Léopold Sédar Senghor. His command of the French language baffled even France's most gifted intellectuals. And language became his most powerful weapon – as a poet and thinker, and as a gifted speaker. But despite his very French education and style, Senghor's focus was firmly on Africa. One of the co-founders of the Négritude movement, he actively promoted African culture, which was what got him noticed at a time when Senegal's fledgling political class was gaining in strength.

Senghor's first great political break came after WWII, when France granted each of its colonial territories the right to its own assembly. He became the elected candidate for Senegal-Mauritania, and quickly drew attention to himself through his support for the population (as during a rail strike where he sided with the workers rather than the colonial administration) and his political skill. Though a Catholic, he was able to gain the backing and respect of Senegal's powerful marabouts when he allowed them partial autonomy and control of the lucrative groundnut economy – an act that certainly helped swing rural areas in his favour.

> During WWI 13,339 Senegalese *tirailleurs* (soldiers) were recruited to fight in the French army against Germany. Usually sent right to the battle frontline, most perished for their supposed 'motherland'.

THE GENERAL'S CHOICE

In the 1950s independence movements gained in strength across Africa. For the French colonies, which formed a pretty coherent territory in West Africa, the question was not 'whether to be free or not to be free', but 'how to be free'. Considering the geographical make-up, the idea of a federal union of all French territories represented a real alternative to the separate autonomy of each colony. Senghor was strongly in favour of a federation, fearing the weakening and division that might follow independence otherwise. His main rival was Côte d'Ivoire's leader, Felix Houphouët-Boigny, whose preference for a neat split stemmed mainly from the fact that he headed a rich nation and didn't necessarily want to have to support poorer states. Just as Senghor gained support from French Sudan (present-day Mali), Upper Volta (present-day Burkina Faso) and Dahomey (present-day Benin) to form a single union (the Mali Federation), the French General Charles de Gaulle

1889	1901	1906
After the demarcation of colonial territories at the Berlin Conference, it takes France and Britain another five years to agree on the current borders between Senegal and Gambia.	British colonial forces, helped by the French, kill the infamous Muslim leader Foday Kabbah, effectively putting an end to the Soninke-Marabout wars, and paving the way for indirect British rule of Gambian territories.	Léopold Sédar Senghor is born in a small fishing village in the Siné-Saloum region. A sharp intellectual, he follows simultaneous careers in politics and poetry, and becomes the first president of independent Senegal.

Ousmane Sembène's moving film *Camp de Thiaroye* (1987) tells of an uprising of returned Senegalese *tirailleurs*, whose request of due payment was violently quashed by the French. The movie was long banned in France.

interrupted the debate with a sudden, extreme choice. On his historic 1958 tour of West Africa, the general proudly presented two options: complete independence and a total break from France, or limited self-government and the renouncing of independence within a French-controlled union. De Gaulle was certain that total autonomy would not be the route the colonies would choose, and he was almost right. Apart from brave, rebellious Guinea-Conakry, the French territories opted to stay in France's favour. The ambitious Mali Federation crumbled, and on 20 August Senegal was born in its current boundaries.

Senghor, the charismatic thinker and poet, became the country's first president and managed to consolidate his position throughout the 1970s, despite initial conflicts with students and labour unions. In 1980, after 20 years as president, he stepped down voluntarily (a move previously unheard of in Africa), making room for his successor, former prime minister Abdou Diouf.

THROWING OFF THE BRITISH YOKE

Against all the gloomy predictions, Gambia braved the step into independence in 1965, with David Jawara as prime minister and Britain's Queen Elizabeth II as titular head of state. Initially, the world's economic climate conspired to give the tiny nation a flying start. For a decade after independence, the world price for groundnuts increased significantly, raising Gambia's GNP almost threefold. A second event had an even more resounding effect: European travellers discovered the beauty of the country's beaches. In 1966 the number of tourists visiting Gambia was recorded as 300. By the end of the 1960s this figure had risen to several thousand, with numbers increasing at a dramatic, and reassuring, rate.

Economic growth translated into political confidence: Gambia shed the last hold Britain had over the country by becoming a fully independent republic, and now-president Jawara made tentative moves towards building a democracy by allowing opposition parties and encouraging a free press.

Still, the PPP was viewed as conservative and Jawara's opponents accused his government of benign neglect and financial corruption. The troubles of the nation surfaced starkly in the early 1980s, when two attempted coups threatened to put an end to Dawda Jawara's reign and possibly his life. Controversial military support by the Senegalese army ignited talks of closer collaboration, which culminated in the creation of the Senegambia Confederation in 1982. Despite deep cultural and ethnic ties, and the fact that the countries are shaped like one big bear hug, the attempt at approaching the topic of uniting the two nations did not bear any fruit. National identities and individual political interests had become too strong, and the Senegambia Confederation crumbled only seven years later, at a time when Senegal-Gambia relations were at an all-time low.

1914–18	1960	1965
France drafts over 200,000 Senegalese men, the so-called *tirailleurs*, to fight for the French army during WWI. The same recruitment process is repeated during the second world war. Veteran *tirailleurs* had to fight for their pensions until 2006	On 4 April Senegal and Mali are granted independence as a joint federation – an idea strongly supported by Senghor. But the alliance only lasts four months before the two countries are split.	The Gambia becomes an independent country, with David Jawara as prime minister and Queen Elizabeth II as titular head of state.

THE DIOUF ERA

For Senegal, a union with Gambia would probably have been particularly useful. The fact that Gambia separates Senegal's northern regions from the southern Casamance has certainly contributed to strong separatist feelings in the south. There had been periodic calls for independence in Casamance for many years, but they came to a head in 1990, when rebels from the Mouvement des Forces Démocratiques de la Casamance (MFDC) started attacking government installations (see p236).

The 1980s were also testing times for Senegalese president Abdou Diouf, as he struggled to maintain democratic dialogue in the face of challenges. While his Parti Socialiste (PS) won the 1983 elections easily, the Parti Démocratique Sénégalais (PDS), under charismatic leader Abdoulaye Wade, enjoyed increasing popularity. He represented a new leadership at a time when the current government was perceived as slow, stale and unable to propose solutions to economic and social troubles. Wade channelled anti-Diouf feelings and united a number of opposition groups under the slogan *sopi* (change), catchy enough to work as a song title and T-shirt print and be shouted by large groups. And those turned out in swelling numbers when the leader was arrested alongside others for allegedly posing a threat to state security, and when he was freed a short time later. He chose voluntary exile in France for a while before returning home. As calls for change attained a deafening volume, the government clamped down more severely in an effort to protect its place. Yet by the late 1990s, increasing electoral gains by Wade made it clear that it was only a matter of time until change – *sopi* – would come.

The name Senegal is thought to be derived from the Wolof term *sunu gal,* meaning 'boat'.

JAMMEH TAKES CHARGE

If the Western world remembers the 1980s largely as an era of poodle perms and the first stirrings of bling culture, the era was anything but a disco dance for most African nations. Economies across the continent went into free fall, and painful restructuring programs by the International Monetary Fund (IMF) enforced cuts in public spending. Gambia was particularly hard hit by a drop in groundnut prices that took a direct toll on its fragile economy. Though the voices of discontent grew louder, Jawara and the PPP were re-elected for a sixth term in April 1992. Only two years later, an army protest over late salaries turned into a coup d'état. The coup leader was Lieutenant Yahya Jammeh, who found himself suddenly swept to the most powerful position in the country at only 29 years of age. He hastily assembled a government, headed by the Armed Forces Provisional Ruling Council (AFPRC). The AFPRC and Jammeh had solemnly promised to return to the barracks once they'd put the country back in balance, but Jammeh found it hard to let go of the presidential seat and simply announced that he'd stay – for years, and perhaps a bit longer.

1970	1980	1981
Gambia becomes a full republic. David Jawara's role changes from prime minister to president, and he promptly Africanises his name from David to Dawda.	Senegal proves its democratic maturity when president Senghor steps down after losing the elections and makes room for former prime minister Abdou Diouf. Diouf will repeat the same, smooth transition when voted out of power in 2000.	Newly elected Senegalese president Abdou Diouf leads his first military intervention – in neighbouring Gambia. Though his army's support helps thwart a coup, 500 people are killed in the events, causing hostilities between the two nations.

Pressure from international governments couldn't change his mind, but the gradual decline in tourist numbers, largely caused by Britain's refusal to continue to recommend the destination, proved more effective. In 1995 he announced that elections would be held the following year, a simple phrase that did the trick. The FCO (Foreign and Commonwealth Office) lifted the travel warning and tourists returned to the beaches; an economic crisis had been averted.

Victorious at the promised 1996 elections, and a couple of later ones too, Jammeh and the APRC (now neatly renamed the Alliance for Patriotic Reorientation and Construction) remained in control and have been there ever since. Despite claims of vote rigging, Jammeh appeared genuinely popular with many Gambians, especially in the early days, when ambitious schemes to rebuild the country's infrastructure and economy, and the opening of clinics and schools brought hope. Then again, each election was fiercely contested by opponents, and incidents of muzzling the press occurred frequently.

CHANGE COMES TO SENEGAL

In Dakar public mood and popular concerns can often be read from house walls and bridges, where youngsters put up their hopes and grievances via a simple spray can. In 2000 only one word was scribbled there: *sopi*. In the run-up to the elections, there was no doubt where people had placed their hopes for new economic growth, a return to the liberal climate the country used to enjoy, and the resolution of the ongoing Casamance conflict. People wanted change; they wanted Abdoulaye Wade and the PDS, who had built their entire campaign on promising just that. An unprecedented number of people, especially young people, turned out to vote and their voices brought about the historic victory they'd longed for. President Diouf ceded his place without any contestation and Senegal made history as a rare African country that had enjoyed two peaceful transitions of power.

In the early years of Wade's rule, things improved rapidly and visibly, with promising economic measures, strengthening of public services and a supportive climate of hope. But then stagnation set in. Wade's government seemed lost in internal power struggles. Ministers were nominated and dismissed, and parliaments dissolved and reformed so quickly it was hard to keep track of who occupied which post at any point in time. Despite growing discontent, a now 81-year-old Wade was re-elected in 2007. He no longer enjoyed the heroic status of the previous polls, but lacking any strong alternatives, people preferred the 'devil they knew' to the risk of change.

HEALING POWERS & A DREAM ABOUT OIL

Though Gambia has been a stable country under Jammeh's rule, his leadership style is increasingly marked by intimidation, such as the detention of opposition voices and critical journalists by forces of the government and the National Intelligence Agency, as reported by Amnesty International

Every year, young men leave Senegal's shores aboard tiny, wooden boats, hoping to reach Europe. Many perish on the eight-day journey; those arriving are immediately repatriated. It has become the most tragic symbol of the hardships felt by many.

1990s	1994	2000
Throughout this difficult decade, the separatist movement in Senegal's Casamance clashes frequently with government forces, claiming the lives of hundreds of people and damaging the tourist industry that flourished in the region.	After a military coup in Gambia, Yahya Jammeh, leader of the Armed Forces Provisional Ruling Council, becomes the new president.	Abdoulaye Wade, leader of the Parti Démocratique Sénégalais, becomes president of Senegal in democratic elections, running a campaign with the slogan *sopi* (change).

THE JOOLA FERRY – A SENEGALESE TRAGEDY

When you take the ferry from Dakar to Ziguinchor, you'll be impressed by the boat's impeccable quality, timing and rigorous application of safety measures. But there's a tragic background to all this comfort and care. In 2002 the MV *Le Joola* ferry that had travelled this route for years capsized in the worst tragedy Senegal has ever experienced. Almost 2000 people perished in the disaster; only 68 escaped with their lives. The high death toll points directly to one fact of this tragedy: the boat was dangerously overloaded. This, combined with serious technical problems, is likely to have caused the disaster, although investigations into the exact events are still going on. All along the coast, from Ziguinchor to Gambia, victims of the disaster lie buried in small cemeteries. Memorial spaces in Dakar and Ziguinchor serve as lasting reminders of the tragedy and meditative sites for the families of the victims.

and Reporters without Borders. Perhaps most worrying is Jammeh's recent retreat into the 'world of magic'. As reported by local media and international watchdogs, around 1000 people were detained in 2008 under accusations of witchcraft; several died from herbal potions they were forced to drink. Jammeh himself likes to play the role of a healer, administering homemade cures for asthma and AIDS to sufferers before the rolling cameras of the national TV station. International bodies and AIDS organisations have reacted with outrage to such displays in a country marked by thriving sex tourism. In country, few voices openly dispute the president's self-proclaimed powers.

After four decades of independence, Gambia remains today not only one of Africa's smallest countries but also one of its poorest, despite what the flourishing coastal zone may suggest. Considering the difficult global climate, things don't seem set to improve soon – though Jammeh seems overly keen to spread hope here as well, setting imaginations alight in 2003 with the pronunciation of the charmed words 'offshore oil'. The jury's still out on whether there's any substance to his claims; drilling certainly hasn't started yet.

CHEWING ON CONCRETE

Senegal today presents the paradoxical picture of a nation reaching for the skies at the risk of toppling off its shaky foundations. The capital Dakar radiates new prosperity as well as deepening poverty and despair. Brand-new roads, bridges, tunnels, street lighting, skyscrapers and a scattering of luxury hotels on the city's coastline speak of rapid progress. A new airport is planned, a multilane motorway is under construction and even the battered old taxis are gradually being replaced by shiny new Iranian and Indian cars (put together at Senegal-based assembly plants). But for every new 4WD that plies the modern streets, there's also a horse-cart driver who finds it harder to feed his family every day. Power cuts, still almost unknown in the early 2000s, now last for hours every day of the rainy season. Gas shortages

2002	2003	2004
Nearly 2000 people are killed when the ferry MS *Joola* capsizes between Dakar and Ziguinchor, a catastrophe provoked at least partly by dangerous overcrowding. Senegal's biggest disaster leaves the country in shock.	President Jammeh's claims that major oil resources have been found off the Gambian coast provoke scepticism on one side, hope on the other. There were no signs of exploitation at the time of writing.	Prominent Gambian journalist and government critic Deyda Hydara is assassinated while under surveillance by secret service agents. The still-unsolved murder brings the issue of press freedom in Gambia into sharp focus.

have become more frequent and frustration among the nation's poor so prominent that Dakar's image as a safe city is being shaken by gradually increasing street crime.

In 2008 the worldwide spiralling cost of petrol painfully hurt the country's small businesses, while rapidly increasing food prices left parts of the population desperately hungry. This situation slammed the issue of national self-sufficiency back onto the governmental table. Senegal imports over 80% of its basic foods, rendering the country particularly vulnerable to price shifts in the global markets. In response, Wade announced a wildly ambitious program (GOANA) to increase local food production over the next few years. Farmers only smiled at the plan, colourfully promoted on giant posters, dismissing the proposed scale as fantastic and pointing to the fact that Senegal simply doesn't have the natural make-up to become an agricultural nation.

The overwhelming feeling, actively expressed in Senegal's relatively free press, is that politicians are lost for ideas that could provide real solutions, and hide behind finger-pointing and political infighting. In local elections in 2009, Senegal's population demonstrated their dissatisfaction by voting opposition leaders into key local councils *(mairies)*. The fact that this was possible and quietly accepted by the current government was a reassuring sign that Senegal's democracy is a fairly stable and mature one.

2004	2006	2008
Many peace agreements have been signed between the Senegalese government and the MFDC rebel leaders in the Casamance. This one, however, seems to hold, and the situation has largely remained quiet ever since.	Following an alleged coup attempt in Gambia (claimed to be the sixth in 12 years), over 60 people are arrested without warrants and unlawfully detained. Eventually, 21 are charged with treason.	After huge increases in the cost of imported food, Wade announces a wildly ambitious program (GOANA) to increase local food production.

The Culture

THE NATIONAL PSYCHE

Skimming any holiday brochure about Senegal, you'll sooner or later stumble across the term *teranga,* meaning 'hospitality'. Senegal takes great pride in being the 'Land of Teranga': the national football team is called 'Lions of Teranga' and many hotels and restaurants have likewise adopted the name. As with Gambia's claim of being 'The Smiling Coast', much of this is promotional hype, but don't lose faith just because you've spent a day shaking off overeager souvenir sellers or trying to cut through the stone-faced look of a hotel receptionist. To understand what people mean, leave the big tourist centres or see what happens if you have a car breakdown far out in the sticks. You'll find a village ready to help you, offering you a bed for the night, food and plenty of helping hands.

In Senegal and Gambia, conversation is the key to local culture, and the key to conversation is a great sense of humour and a quick-witted tongue. People love talking, teasing, and testing you out, and the better you slide into the conversational game, the easier you'll get around. Someone mocks your habits? Don't tense up, retaliate with a clever remark. You've gathered the courage to try your first feeble *mbalax* dance steps and earn nothing but noisy amusement? Don't blush and hide in the corner – join in the hilarity and keep copying the gyrating hips around you. People don't mean any harm and the ability to laugh at yourself is just as important an item to bring with you as your malaria pills and T-shirts.

Having mastered the art of conversation, there's only one other crucial ground rule: don't hurry. If you're on holiday, you're likely to be positively inclined towards the idea of a turtle's pace; if you're on business, the slow speed of society can be frustrating – if you keep fighting it. Senegal and Gambia are governed by a great paradox of time – the more you relax, the quicker you'll get things done. Fit into the local rhythm and you won't have quite such a rocky ride.

DAILY LIFE
The Extended Family

Visitors to Africa are often struck by the staggering size of most families and the importance of parental ties in a person's life. As in most African cultures, individuals are closely tied to their extended family, including uncles, aunts and distant cousins.

MASLA

Among the many cultural codes that govern conversation and interaction in Senegal, *masla* is perhaps the hardest to grasp. Unlock it and you'll suddenly fly past the traps and conflicts that used to frustrate you. There's no direct translation for this Wolof term, but it can loosely be defined as 'the art of the elegant compromise'. *Masla* means that you'll do anything to avoid hurting others through harmful words or comments. From here develops the fine art of couching criticism in carefully chosen phrases and of unpicking a compliment to unravel the small disapproval it might actually contain. When someone says he'll call you, definitely, when he's next in town, it may well be a *masla* way of saying goodbye. When everyone seems to approve of your idea, then offers confusingly contradictory thoughts, it's the *masla* kind of gentle disagreement. It's tricky, but try to listen with the awareness that not every spade here really is a spade and you'll soon get the hang of elaborate politeness.

Unmarried children stay at their parents' home until they wed, at which time men found their own household and women join that of their husband. Marrying is an expensive business and many men don't have the necessary means at their disposal to take this step until they are in their mid-20s. It's therefore not unusual (nor discreditable) for adults of this age to still occupy a room in their parents' house. It's also common for a man who enjoys greater financial success than his parents to invite them to move into his home, thus bringing the whole big family back together.

In the case of divorce, women usually rejoin their families, bringing their children with them. Single-woman or single-mother households are virtually unheard of in Gambia and Senegal.

Relationships between family members are clearly defined and govern a person's responsibilities towards a given relative and the respect one owes a next of kin. Generally, elder relatives are to be treated with the greatest deference and aunts and uncles are to be respected like one's own mother and father. Children are expected to help in the house and will interrupt recreation to run some errands for a family member.

Having to fulfil the expectations of a large group of relatives is an enormous responsibility – just ask any emigrant from Senegal or Gambia who lives abroad. Most families in the region have at least one family member, usually a young man, who has emigrated to Europe or America. In some rural communities, this has led to an eerie absence of male citizens, but has brought in an extra influx of cash – money sent to Senegal and Gambia by emigrated nationals today constitutes one of the largest 'economic branches' of the nations. The meagre earnings of an expatriate in the West never belong to him or her alone, but are to be shared with those who have stayed at home. This puts enormous strains on the émigré, and many are reluctant to return home as they feel they can't fulfil financial expectations.

On the other hand, family solidarity means that elderly people will always be looked after by kin and children are raised in a family environment even if both parents work. There's no alienation between generations, as the young and old are in permanent contact with one another.

Education

Providing basic education for all is still a challenge in both Senegal and Gambia. Although gross primary enrolment figures are encouraging, with 74% of children enrolled in Gambia and 80% in Senegal, completion rates stand at only 50% to 60% in both countries. In theory, state primary education is available to all children, though poverty still bars many children from attending school – even if fees are paid, there may not be enough money for books, and some low-income families need their children's helping hands to supplement family income.

The lack of government funds for education compounds the problem. Classes are often large, sometimes holding up to 100 pupils in spaces intended for half that number; teachers are underpaid; and resources are limited.

Boys generally continue their education to higher levels than girls. While numbers are fairly equal during the early years of primary school, few girls complete their primary exams and even fewer carry on to secondary or university level, either because scant resources for education are focussed on sons rather than daughters or due to early marriage.

However, in both Gambia and Senegal, several government initiatives are trying to redress the balance. In Gambia, efforts have been made to increase the number of schools, and there are proposals to offer free schooling to girls. In Senegal, there has been an additional focus on the preschool age, with a countrywide program of state-funded nurseries.

If you're fair skinned, when you walk through Senegal and Gambia your passage will spark screams of *'toubab'* from little children. *Toubab* means 'white person' and, though the shouts get very annoying, they don't indicate hostility and aren't pejorative.

Despite recent initiatives, literacy rates in Gambia and Senegal remain low. The UNDP Human Development Index ranks the countries 153rd and 160th respectively out of 179 nations, with adult literacy rates of around 40%. For girls, rates are usually 15% to 20% lower than for boys.

Weddings

Take a weekend stroll around the streets of Dakar and you are bound to pass groups of elegant women, decked out in their finest *boubous* (dresses; see the boxed text, p43) and most delicate heels. They'll have blocked the road with rows of plastic chairs and they sit there, looking magnificent and listening to distorted praise songs by the family *griots* (West African praise singers) carried through the neighbourhood via battered amplifiers. There's always a wedding on somewhere and the celebrations are mainly women's business. They meet and chat, dance and laugh, cook, serve food from huge pots, and eat, while the men go about the more serious business of 'tying the marriage' at the mosque. In the Muslim cultures of Senegal and Gambia, weddings are at least as much about the families as about the couple itself. The male relatives of the groom will offer cola nuts to the parents of the bride, asking for her hand in marriage. If the offer is accepted, they will convene at the mosque at around 5pm, while the bride and groom stay at home. It's even possible for parents to marry off their sons and daughters while they are abroad – a phone call will tell them about their new status.

Among the Tukulor, it's common for cousins to be married to one another, although incidences of this tradition are beginning to decline, particularly in urban settings, where children increasingly demand a choice in the arrangement of their marriage.

Gifts are important, not only to equip the couple with household items, but also as a means of financial redistribution. If you receive large presents on your big day, you're supposed to double the expense when it's the donor's turn to celebrate. Women often form 'party circles', attending each other's weddings and keeping close track of the value of gifts.

Especially in urban settings, traditional weddings are usually followed by evening receptions, where the bride will change from her *boubou* into rustling folds of white satin and cut the obligatory three-tier cake.

POPULATION

When travelling around Gambia and Senegal, you'll quickly notice how closely the two nations are linked culturally, but also how diverse each nation is in terms of social make-up and traditions. Before colonisation, the territory of Senegal and Gambia was home to several indigenous empires. To this day, the cultural and social practices that emerged in their wake, together with the ethnic groups associated with those empires, determine life in the region.

Ethnic Groups of The Gambia & Senegal
WOLOF

The Wolof, for the most part Muslim, are the largest ethnic group in the region, accounting for 43% of the population in Senegal and 16% in Gambia. Their language (see p308) has become the lingua franca in both countries. Wolof culture was largely defined during the days of the 14th-century Jolof Empire, which later split into several smaller kingdoms, including those of Walo and Cayor. Today, the Wolof are particularly concentrated in the regions of those ancient empires, notably in the central area to the north and east of Dakar and along the coast. Traditionally farmers and traders, the Wolof today control a great deal of commerce, especially in Senegal. Smaller

CODES OF INTERACTION

Greetings

Extended greetings are an important part of social interaction and many doors will open for you if you are capable of exchanging simple greeting phrases in the local language. (Some basic words and phrases are provided in the Language chapter, p303.)

Upon entering someone's home, announce your arrival with a confident *'Salaam aleikum'* (peace be with you), and your presence will be acknowledged with *'Aleikum salaam'* (and peace be with you).

This is followed by enquiries about your health and that of your family, the state of your affairs and your children. You're never expected to give an honest answer at this point. In Gambia things are always fine; in Senegal the response is always *'Ça va'*. Never mind the real troubles that might be plaguing you – these can be mentioned later in the conversation.

Although it's not necessary for foreigners to go through the whole routine, it's important to use greetings whenever possible. Even if you're just changing money or asking directions, precede your request with a simple, 'Hello, how are you? Can you help me please?', rather than plunging right in.

Shaking Hands

You'll shake a lot of hands during your stay. Particularly for men it's important to shake hands with other men when entering and leaving a gathering. In social settings you are expected to go around the room and greet everyone with a handshake. Veiled women won't shake hands with men and some Muslim elders won't greet women with a handshake. They'll indicate this politely – don't take offence if your outstretched arm is left unanswered.

Deference

In traditional societies, older people and those of superior social status are treated with deference. On your travels that includes immigration officers, police and village chiefs. Officials are normally courteous, but manners, patience and a friendly smile are essential to ensure a pleasant exchange. Undermining an official's authority or insulting their ego will only tie you up in red tape. When visiting small villages, it's polite to go and see the chief to announce yourself and ask for permission before setting up camp or wandering through the village.

Eye contact is often avoided: if a local doesn't look you in the eye during a conversation, they're being polite, not cold.

Giving Money & Presents

Charity and giving to the poor are part of Islamic culture. Especially on Fridays you'll see many affluent Senegalese and Gambians donate small sums to beggars on street junctions and outside mosques. As a *toubab* (foreigner) in Senegal and Gambia, you're rich compared to most people and it's hard not to want to give if you're faced with the sight of poverty. However, giving, receiving, demanding and donating are regulated by cultural mechanisms and crossing those means upsetting vital social structures.

In the tourist zones, you'll often find yourself followed by children asking for gifts, pens, money and sweets. Don't answer their demands. If you want to make a contribution, support the head of a family or a village, or donate money to a charity working with children. Giving to individual children in the street upsets the rules of social interaction – children aren't supposed to ask older people for money – and encourages the shouts of *'toubab'* that you'll soon find an unwelcome companion.

Don't respond to random requests from strangers, as some can be outright scams. But do be generous, especially if eliciting services. If you've been offered food or a bed for the night, you should repay the kindness by handing the host some money when it's time for goodbyes. Just consider what you'd have paid for a similar meal or hotel room, and judge the amount you give from there.

Giving money is usually done discreetly and sometimes without discussing amounts or even demanding payment up front. If people help you out, they will usually expect to be paid something at the end. Consider whether someone has had to pay for their own transport to meet you – you should give them that amount before they go back home.

ethnic groups may sometimes complain about an increasing 'Wolofisation' of their culture, especially via music and language, yet few are those not glad for a unifying local tongue and the feverish *mbalax*, a Wolof rhythm.

MANDINKA & MALINKÉ

The Mandinka live mainly in Gambia, where they constitute 42% of the population, and in the Casamance in Senegal. The Mandinka form part of the Mande cultural groups, which also include the Malinké and Bambara in Mali. All Mande people once belonged to the vast 13th-century Mali Empire that spanned West Africa. Today, Mande surnames still tell of the social standing each family held in the days of their great ruler, Soundiata Keïta. The Mande dialect of Gambia's Mandinka people differs strongly from the Mande dialect spoken by the Malinké in Mali. The Mandinka migrated to the Gambia region between the 13th and early 16th centuries and the popular Mande instrument, the *kora* (harp-lute), came with them.

FULA

The Fula (also known as Peul, Fulbe or Fulani) are one of West Africa's largest, most diverse and widespread ethnic groups. You find Fula groups from Senegal to Sudan and Mauritania to Nigeria. In Gambia around 18% of the population is Fula; in Senegal, 24%. Their language (see p307) is the strongest unifying factor of the different Fula groups.

Traditionally, the Fula were nomadic cattle herders and the constant search for grazing land partly explains their wide dispersal across the region. The early adoption of Islam by some Fula branches also contributed to their spread, as converts introduced the religion throughout West Africa and created several Muslim theocracies in northern Nigeria and Guinea. While most Fula groups settled centuries ago, the majority maintain a strong attachment to cattle and the presence of a large herd of cattle is usually a sign of a Fula residence.

In Senegal, Fula groups are mainly found around the Haute Casamance and Kédougou, as well as in Fouta Toro (around the Senegal River) in the north, where the Tukulor, a sub-branch of the Fula, is the dominant community.

Tukulor (Halpulaar)

The Tukulor, constituting around 10% of the population in Senegal, are a culturally distinct branch of the Fula. They refer to themselves as Halpulaar (Fula-speakers).

DRESS

Especially on Friday, the most important day of the week in Muslim countries, and on public holidays, you'll find the streets filled with people in shimmering, embroidered garments, often of stunning elegance. These billowing robes are called *boubous*. A *grand boubou* for men consists of a flowing robe that reaches to the ground. It's worn with baggy trousers and a shirt underneath. A woman's *boubou* is similar, though often more colourful, and worn with a wraparound skirt and matching headscarf. *Boubous* can be as simple or elaborate as the occasion requires: one worn for a celebration such as a wedding should dazzle in the sunlight and rustle when you walk.

In general, people in Gambia and Senegal place immense importance on appearance and try to dress in the best clothes they can. Unless combined with a matching, tailored top, a wraparound skirt or sarong, so favoured by Western women travelling to Africa, is usually only worn around the house by local women. Travellers turning up in tatty clothes, shorts and simple T-shirts are frowned upon, especially in rural areas.

Their cultural roots date back to the Tekrur Empire, a 9th-century kingdom spread across a wide area in the Senegal River zone (the Fouta Toro region). This is still where most Tukulor live. They embraced Islam early, in the 10th or 11th century, when the religion was first carried south across the Sahara from Morocco, and played a major role in spreading their faith to other ethnic groups. The most famous Tukulor leader, El Hajj Omar Tall, built a vast Islamic empire in the mid-19th century, which reached as far as Segou in Mali.

Bitter irony: the valley of the Senegal River, where the French colonialists were strongly opposed by the armies of El Hajj Omar Tall, is today a region where the entire male populations of certain villages have emigrated to France.

SERER

The Serer, representing around 14% of Senegal's population, are concentrated in the Siné-Saloum region of Senegal, in central Senegal, and just across the border in northwest Gambia. They are thought to have migrated from southern Senegal in the 16th century. The Serer resisted Islamisation for a long time; their 11th-century refusal to succumb to North African Almoravids led them to migrate to the regions of Baol, Siné and Saloum, where they established important kingdoms. Today, most Serer have adopted either Christian or Muslim faith, and their region is renowned for the peaceful cohabitation of both religious communities.

DIOLA

In Senegal, the Diola (also spelt Jola) live in the Casamance and in the southwest, from where they spread as far as Guinea-Bissau. In Gambia, around 10% of the population are Diola, compared with 5% in Senegal. They preserve a strong spirit of independence, partly inspired by their very distinctive culture. They are one of the few ethnic groups in the region whose society is not hierarchical, but segmented and flexible, and they have largely rejected Islam, preferring either their own traditional beliefs or conversion to Christianity.

The Ceddo, Senegal's ancient warriors, have a solid place in popular mythology. Their images are used in paintings, the classic *griot* song 'Ceddo' tells their story and Ousmane Sembène treated the subject in the eponymous film.

As oral history is not preserved and passed down by *griots,* as among the more hierarchically organised groups, their origins are slightly obscure. It is thought that they probably lived in the area for many centuries. Their territory presumably used to reach as far as the Gambia River, from where they were probably pushed southwards with the 13th- to 16th-century Mandinka migrations.

SERAHULI

The Serahuli live in the eastern part of Senegal and far eastern Gambia. Almost exclusively Muslim, they are also known as Soninke and spread as far as Mali and Burkina Faso. Soninke is also the Mandinka word for 'king' and the battles of the late 19th century between traditional Serahuli rulers and Islamic leaders were often called the Soninke-Marabout Wars. The origins of the Serahuli are unclear: they may have migrated to this area after the breakup of the ancient Songhaï Empire in present-day Mali at the end of the 15th century; another theory has it that they have been in the region for longer and are the descendants of the original Ghana Empire.

Anyone who has ever travelled by battered bush taxi and been entertained by the lively conversations of the local passengers will love Moussa Touré's hilarious movie *TGV Express,* which is set in one such clapped-out vehicle.

OTHER GROUPS

Other small groups in Senegal include the Bassari and the Bédik, largely animist or Christian, who live in the remote southeastern part of Senegal and have maintained a very strong, individual culture known for its impressive masked dances and initiation ceremonies.

The Lebou, Senegal's famous fishermen, are another distinct group, living almost exclusively around Yoff outside Dakar and along the coast. In Gambia, the Aku people (see the boxed text, opposite) are similar to the Krio found in other parts of West Africa.

THE AKU

In Gambia the Aku are a small but significant ethnic group, mostly descendants of freed slaves brought to the country in the early 19th century when the British established a protectorate here. Some came from plantations in the Americas, while others were released from slave ships leaving West Africa. Many also came from Sierra Leone, where a similar group of freed slaves settled (usually referred to as Krio people). The Aku language – a mix of 18th-century English and various indigenous tongues – is similar to the Krio and pidgin spoken in other former British colonies in West Africa.

Today there are still strong links between the Aku and Krio (the terms are sometimes used interchangeably), with many families having members in both Gambia and Sierra Leone.

The Aku are mostly Christian and generally have names of British origin, such as Johnson or Thompson. Traditional Aku houses have steep tin roofs, gabled windows and weatherboard walls, a design thought to have originated in the southern states of the USA. They can still be seen in the old part of Banjul.

In colonial times, the administration often chose their civil servants among the Aku. The distinction between the former civil servants and other locals can render social interaction uneasy to this day.

Both Senegal and Gambia have significant Mauritanian and Lebanese communities, which are often involved in trade.

Social Structures

Most of the ancient West African empires were based on a clearly defined hierarchical system. Senegal's main cultural group, the Wolof, and the Tukulor and Mandinka groups are organised in such a way. These traditional 'pyramid structures' continue to define social interaction to a large extent, alongside other factors, such as economic success or education. Family surnames still largely reflect a person's place in society.

At the top of the pecking order sit the 'freeborn', ancient families of nobles and warriors who formed the traditional ruling elite. Slightly lower, though still freeborn, are farmers and traders. Lower down the scale are the artisans – blacksmiths, leather workers, woodcarvers and *griots* – occupational groups whose status is defined by their traditional profession. Though a child bearing a blacksmith's surname may never work metal, he is still a blacksmith by birth and in theory has the 'right' to exercise his parent's métier.

At the bottom of the hierarchy were the captives, originally taken in wars or bought from traders, but kept in this position for many generations. Although this status no longer officially exists, aspects of 'servant culture' continue to survive to this day. Especially in rural regions, you may even find that the descendants of former captives still work as tenant farmers for the families of their former masters.

In reality, this social system is, of course, much more complex and fluid than this brief outline suggests. Social status only explains a small part of a person's place in society, and 'inferior' groups often play alternative roles, which allow them to exercise great influence despite their relatively low rank. *Griots* (*gewel* in Wolof, *gawlo* in Fula and *jali* in Mande), for instance, may be considered unsuitable 'marriage material' by a higher ranking member of society, and yet they command great respect as they are the ones who can glorify a person's name and even enshrine it in history. See also p55.

RELIGION

Senegal and Gambia are often cited as examples of religious harmony. The vast Muslim majority (90% of the population) lives in peaceful respect next to the countries' Christian and animist minorities. Christian faith is most

COMMUNITY BANKING

In countries where financial institutions cater for less than half the total population, informal banking systems thrive. Senegal and Gambia are crossed by an elaborate web of financial support structures, usually called *tontin*. Tightly managed by women, the *tontin* unites a small group of relatives, colleagues or friends in joint saving. Each month, every participant pays in an agreed figure and every month the total amount is given to the person who needs it most. When you've received the spoils, you need to wait for your next turn – until everyone has cashed in once. Sometimes additional payments are made that can be released if a member faces a particularly tight spot or needs extra cash to prepare for a wedding, baptism or funeral. It's fascinating to imagine how much money circulates in this way. And, unlike a bank, the *tontin* fulfils a social function, tying families or friends together and uniting communities in overcoming poverty together.

widespread among the Diola, Serer and Bassari and traditional religious forms are most commonly practised in the predominantly Christian areas. Both Islam and Christianity in Senegal and Gambia are interwoven with elements of traditional religious practice.

Islam

Muslims across the world are united in their faith in God (Allah) and Muhammad, his Prophet. While some elements of religious practice, such as submission to the Five Pillars of Islam and study of the Holy Koran, are observed across the Islamic world, others differ from one culture to the next, depending on regional context. Islam reached Gambia and Senegal when the Almoravids (Berber warriors) conquered parts of today's northern Senegal in the 11th century. Regional practice evolved over the following centuries, and was refined in the 19th century with the spread of the Muslim Sufi brotherhoods *(confréries)*. These brotherhoods follow the teachings of spiritual leaders called marabouts, who are deeply revered by the people, hold great political and economic power and define many aspects of national culture.

MARABOUTS & BROTHERHOODS

Take a tour around Dakar and you are bound to notice the images of two veiled men – one dressed in white, the other in black – painted on numerous walls, cars and shop signs. They are the portraits of Cheikh Amadou Bamba, the 19th-century founder of the Mouride brotherhood, and Cheikh Ibra Fall, his illustrious follower and spiritual leader of the Baye Fall, a branch of Mouridism. Garages and tailor's workshops are named after them and minibuses are painted with their words in a bid to voice religious belonging and bestow spiritual protection on the named site. On the national charts, Senegal's stars sing their praises to hip hop, *mbalax* and pop beats.

While orthodox Islam holds that every believer is directly in touch with Allah, Muslim faith in Senegal and Gambia is more commonly channelled via saintly intermediaries (marabouts), who are ascribed divine powers and provide a link between God and the common populace. The concept of the marabout-led brotherhood was brought to Senegal from Morocco, where a spiritual leader is known as a *cheikh* or *caliph,* terms that are also used in Senegal. The earliest brotherhood established south of the Sahara was Qadariyyah in the 16th century, which encouraged charity and humility and attracted followers throughout the northern Sahel. In Senegal and Gambia, Qadariyyah teachings remain particularly popular among the Mandinka.

The Morocco-based Tijaniya brotherhood was introduced to Senegal by El Hajj Omar Tall in the mid-19th century and remains powerful today, with important mosques in the towns of Tivaouane and Kaolack. Later in the 19th century, a smaller brotherhood called the Layen broke away from the Tijaniya under a marabout called Saidi Limamou Laye. Most Layen are Lebou people, and the famous Layen Mausoleum is found in the Lebou village of Yoff outside Dakar.

With more than two million followers, the Mouridiya, established by Cheikh Amadou Bamba, is by far the most important brotherhood (see the boxed text, p205) and its power has consistently grown since the mid-19th century. The initial rise of Mouridism is closely connected to colonial expansion and popular resistance to the measures imposed by the French. The colonial administration weakened or completely disabled traditional structures of governance, rendering chiefs powerless and leaving their subjects without respectable leaders. The evolving structures of the brotherhoods mirrored the demolished societal organisation, thereby providing a kind of socio-cultural refuge for a population that sought to preserve its autonomy and oppose the colonial power.

For many years Cheikh Amadou Bamba was merely a humble marabout, no more renowned than any other religious leader of his time. Part of his remarkable rise to fame is due to the total adherence of his most famous *talibe* (disciple), Cheikh Ibra Fall, who demonstrated his profound commitment less through religious study than through hard physical labour. 'Lamp' Fall (meaning 'Fall, the light'), as he is often called, publicly renounced Koranic study and refused the Ramadan fast, stating that, in order to serve God, he required all his time and bodily force to work hard. He soon gathered his own group of followers, the Baye Fall. Baye Fall adepts are traditionally recognisable by their long dreadlocks, heavy leather amulets containing pictures of their marabout, and patchwork clothing (though not all follow the dress code), and to this day the Baye Fall tend to be the hardest workers in the region of Touba, building mosques and preparing fields for cultivation.

As the Mourides and Baye Fall gained popularity, the French began to fear their impact and forced Bamba into exile on an island in Gabon. His

---

ISLAMIC HOLIDAYS

Below are the most important Islamic holidays, when commercial life in Gambia and Senegal comes to a stop:

Eid al-Moulid (Mawlid) Birthday of the Prophet Muhammad.

Grand Magal Celebrated in the Senegalese town of Touba on the anniversary of the return from exile of Cheikh Amadou Bamba, founder of the Mouride Islamic Brotherhood.

Korité (Id al-Fitr) Celebrates the end of Ramadan, the month of the Muslim holy fast.

Tabaski (Id al-Adha) The most important Muslim holiday. Commemorates Abraham's willingness to sacrifice his son on God's command. God rewarded Abraham by replacing the child with a ram and Muslims across the world remember this by sacrificing a sheep.

Tamkharit (Ashura) Tenth day of the lunar year, celebrating the Prophet's arrival at Medina as well as commemorating the death of his grandson.

Since the Islamic calendar is based on 12 lunar cycles, Islamic holidays fall roughly 11 days earlier than in the previous year. The exact dates depend on what hour the moon is seen by the astronomers of Mecca, therefore the dates below might vary by a day or two:

Event	2009	2010	2011
Eid al-Moulid	9 Mar	26 Feb	16 Feb
Ramadan begins	20 Aug	10 Aug	31 Jul
Korité	19 Sep	8 Sep	29 Aug
Tabaski	26 Nov	15 Nov	5 Nov
Tamkharit	26 Dec	15 Dec	4 Dec

THE TALIBE

You'll see them all around Dakar and the urban resorts of Gambia: young boys in torn clothes begging on the roadside with rusty tomato tins. They're called *talibe*, an Arabic term meaning 'disciple', and many are indeed students of Islamic marabouts. Learning humility by singing for food and living ascetically has long been part of the rigorous education that takes place at Koranic schools. In the urban centres of Senegal and Gambia, this tradition has often become distorted into a serious social problem.

Children are sometimes sent away from their families for reasons of poverty, often from neighbouring countries – it's estimated that most of the boys on the streets of Dakar today come from Guinea-Bissau.

While some of those boys genuinely do get educated by their Islamic teachers, others are being exploited, and others again are street children who no longer belong to any social network. According to Unicef estimates, there are more than 100,000 child beggars in Senegal alone and the problem is growing.

For a traveller to the region, it's impossible to know which kids will be asked to leave their small gains with a marabout at the end of their begging day and which are simply hungry. If you don't want to contribute to upholding an exploitative system but don't want to ignore the children either, you can always give food, which will benefit them directly.

return from there in 1907 is still celebrated by the annual Magal pilgrimage to Touba.

Today the Mourides, together with the ensemble of other brotherhoods, hold considerable power in politics and economics as they largely control groundnut (peanut) cultivation and trade and have the ear of the population: about a quarter of the population follow the words of the leading Mouride *caliph* (a position passed down among the descendents of Bamba). His words can thus impact on the outcome of an election, something that Senegal's politicians are keenly aware of.

Christianity & Traditional Religions

Missionary zeal in Africa, the close companion of colonial expansionism, reached its high point in the mid-19th century, when the French and British established Christian missions across their annexed territories. However, their impact wasn't as strong as desired, as Islam had already been successfully introduced to the region.

The roughly 10% of Christians in Gambia and Senegal belong mainly to the Roman Catholic Church; Pentecostal and Protestant churches also have minor followings and the influence of evangelist preachers has grown as economic conditions decline.

The Diola in Senegal's Casamance constitute the largest Christian community. Along with the Bassari and Bédik of the Kédougou region, they are also the main group that still follows traditional religions, often combined with the practice of Christianity.

There are hundreds of traditional religions in West Africa and, while there are no written scriptures, beliefs and traditions have long been handed down by oral transmission. Their practice usually involves a high degree of secrecy. The following is only a broad, very simplified overview.

Almost all traditional religions are animist: based on the attribution of life or consciousness to natural objects or phenomena. A certain tree, mountain, river or stone may be sacred because it represents a spirit or is home to a spirit. Instead of 'spirit', some authorities use the terms 'deity' or 'god'. The number of deities each religion accepts can vary, as can the phenomena that represent them.

Several traditional religions accept the existence of a supreme being or creator, a factor that largely facilitated the combination of Christianity, Islam and animist practices. In many African religions ancestors play a particularly strong role. Their principal function is to protect the community or family and they may, on occasion, show their pleasure or displeasure at the acts of their successors. Droughts, bad harvests or epidemic diseases can thus be interpreted as adversarial acts of ancestral spirits. Communication with ancestors or deities may take the form of prayer, offerings or sacrifice, possibly with the assistance of a holy man (or, occasionally, a holy woman).

'Fetishes' are an important feature of traditional religions. These are sacred objects (or charms) that can take many forms. The most common charms found throughout West Africa are small leather amulets worn around the neck, arm or waist. These are called *grigri* and are used to ward off evil or to bring good luck. *Grigri* are also worn by West African Muslims, whose leather object encloses a written verse from the Koran. This is only one example of the myriad connections between traditional religions and Islam or Christianity.

WOMEN IN GAMBIA & SENEGAL

The societies of Senegal and Gambia are predominantly Muslim and patriarchal, which impacts on the role of women. Women rarely live on their own – a woman usually only leaves her parental home to live with her husband. Harshly put, this means that submission to her parents is immediately replaced by submission to her husband, who, if Muslim, may take up to four wives.

Though women are taught a whole repertoire of methods for pleasing their men, running a household, looking after kids and being seductive (and available) after every long day of working at home or the office, you'll search in vain for the stereotypical 'oppressed wife'. Women are very much part of public life; they're assertive and strong. Few women are veiled and the ones that are probably made that choice for themselves. Many have found ways of social and economic assertion, for instance via women's cooperatives *(groupements de femmes)* that can play important roles in combating female circumcision – a practice that still occurs despite being banned in both Senegal and Gambia – or under-age marriage, which remains particularly common in the north.

The majority of married women look after the house and children, yet many do work and some achieve high ranks in the political, economic or artistic arenas (in Senegal, 42% of the work force and 19% of the members of parliament are women). Even those who remain at home often engage in some form of commerce – perhaps a small street stall or importing and selling jewellery – to boost their financial means.

Senegalese women, in particular, dress with incredible elegance, donning matching outfits, shoes and handbags for even the tiniest occasion, like a walk to the shops. Hours are spent putting on make-up and perfecting a style – all in a bid to please guys, outdo female rivals and, most of all, assert self-confidence and pride in one's beauty. Dakar dance floors are usually packed with stunningly (and daringly) clothed *disquettes* (stylish young girls), while the presence of successful, cosmopolitan businesswomen (often referred to as *dirianké*) is amplified by billowing *boubous* and jingling gold jewellery. And breathtaking looks go hand in hand with a whole universe of uniquely female knowledge – the art of seduction. From tinkling, scented waist beads and arousing mixes of perfume, incense and soaps to culinary secrets, women here have an expansive and creative repertoire of methods to prevent a husband from straying.

MARRIAGE & DIVORCE *Katharina Lobeck Kane*

Aissatou is an impressive woman in every single way. With her size, her height, the weight of her gold earrings and the folds of her rich *boubou*, she cuts an imposing figure and looks at ease in the most conservative sectors of Senegalese society. And yet, as a single mother, four times divorced, living alone and running her own successful business, she breaks about every cultural rule of appropriate female behaviour. As I've always admired her for her skilful negotiation of that fine balance between tradition and modernity, submission and freedom, the news that she'd become someone's fourth wife came as quite a shock. From the steering wheel of her 4WD, she sends me a broad smile. 'Don't look so upset', she says, 'let me explain. I like this man and I like spending time with him. What am I to do? Taking a lover would mean social ostracism. Becoming someone's full-time wife means waiting on a husband hand and foot – and with a business to run, I really don't have time for that. Until society allows me to just be, without being married, this looks like a pretty good solution'.

Admittedly, it did, apart from the risk of sexually transmitted diseases at least. But rare are the women who choose polygamy as an act of defying tradition (can there be a greater paradox?) – most co-spouses have little choice in the matter.

The Holy Koran, which guides the lives of the vast Muslim majority of Gambia and Senegal, allows men to take up to four wives, normally on the condition that they can provide equally for and love all of them. And that's really the crux of the issue – can one equally love four women? Most women would say no, pointing an accusatory finger at the many men who bring a beautiful young wife into the family home once they've 'tired' of their first, ageing spouse. Though many of Senegal and Gambia's women are resigned to this reality, few welcome it with joy, secretly praying that their partner will proudly spell the word 'monogamy' when asked about his choice at the civil wedding.

To Western men who might dream of having such rights, a word of warning: managing a polygamous household is very hard work. Wives are commonly jealous of one another and such resentment is often spread from the mothers to their children. All of this means a family home where tensions brew easily and it's the head of the household who is expected to calm escalating situations.

MEDIA
The Gambia

The watchdog association Reporters Without Borders classifies Gambia as a country in a 'difficult situation' with regard to freedom of the press. Following the still-unpunished murder of outspoken journalist Deyda Hydara, editor of independent newspaper the *Point* and correspondent of Agence France-Presse, journalists fear repression if publishing controversial articles. His suspicious death under secret service surveillance and subsequent warnings to members of the press have for now put an end to hopes that a truly free press might find its place in a state veering towards the authoritarian.

Senegal

Senegal had long been considered one of the best climates for free press in Africa. The nation's dailies debate government action very critically – far more so than TV or radio – but occasional incidents of stifling free expression give cause for concern. Throughout 2008 the topic of free press under Wade's reign became a subject of national debate when two journalists were beaten by police following a football match and the government failed to condemn the incident, and the offices of two antigovernmental voices (*24 Heures Chrono* and *L'As*) were damaged. On the other hand, the fact that those issues became the focus of a heated public debate in itself shows that relative openness still dominates the press and public expression.

SPORT
Football
There's no better opportunity to find a break in Dakar's eternally gridlocked streets than when the national football (soccer) team is playing a televised match. The entire country will be grouped around TV sets and businesses come to a virtual standstill. Be home before the game is over, though: if the national team loses, youngsters are likely to run riot and commit random acts of violence – after Senegal's 2008 draw with Gambia and subsequent disqualification from the 2010 World Cup and Africa Cup of Nations, angry fans left a trail of burnt-out cars and stolen goods. Gambia partied and declared a national holiday, even though the draw didn't lead them to qualification either.

Like most of Africa, these two nations are football crazy. Being a professional kicker is every boy's dream – just check out the number of improvised football grounds on busy streets and beaches.

Any larger town has an official football stadium. The main one in Senegal is the Léopold Sédar Senghor Stadium on the northern side of Dakar. In Gambia, it's the Independence Stadium in Bakau near Banjul.

Wrestling
Traditional wrestling (*la lutte* in French) is a hugely popular spectator sport in both Senegal and Gambia. In Senegal, it's mostly practised by the Serer and Diola. From September to November, following harvest season, the Siné-Saloum and Casamance regions buzz with wrestling matches. You'll find entire villages united around dust-filled terrains lit by kerosene lamps. The repetitive wail of *griots,* wildly distorted by clattering amplifiers, tears the air. The wrestlers enter the arena clad in nothing but loincloths and leather *grigri* strapped to their arms, back and chest. Girls cheer them on and sprinkle their heroes' bare chests with white powder, spurring them on to perform dance steps worthy of warriors. An evening consists of a string of matches, culminating in the encounter of the most renowned fighters. Wrestlers will circle one another cautiously, carefully preparing their next rapid move. The winner is the one who manages to pin his opponent to the ground, shoulder blades touching the floor. Diola wrestling is more exciting for technique and craft – unlike the Serer and Wolof fights, it doesn't allow punches or kicks.

Senegal's most famous annual wrestling encounter takes place on 1 January in the national stadium.

ARTS
Music
The music of Senegal and Gambia alone is worth the price of the plane ticket. Senegal is home to some of Africa's most famous musicians, including singers such as Youssou N'Dour, Baaba Maal and Ismaël Lô. Gambia's star has slightly faded internationally, but it still has a fantastic reggae scene. See p55 for a detailed discussion.

Painting, Sculpture & Photography
From traditional sculpture to contemporary photography, there's a lot on offer here outside the spray-painted canvases proffered on roadside souvenir stalls.

The tradition of sculpture in Senegal and Gambia is rooted in the creation of wooden statues and masks, originally produced for ritual purposes and today for sale en masse in tourist markets and boutiques. Some of these figures can be fascinating (Dakar's IFAN museum and Banjul's national museum show some good examples), but the countries have also produced

If you can't make it to a wrestling match yourself, check out the photographs by Mamadou Gomis and Pape Seydi, two young Senegalese photo reporters who have documented the sport in a stunning black and white series.

The Dakar-based in-line skating association Accro Roller, set up by skater Babacar Ndiaye, today has over 100 members and offers affordable classes to dozens of children. Check www .accro-roller.com for the most fun to be had in Dakar.

some amazing contemporary sculptors. The Senegalese sculptor Ousmane Sow remains the reference in this field. He is famous for his gigantic stone figures with eerily lifelike eyes. Other artists include Gabriel Kemzo, who has a workshop on Île de Gorée; Séni Camara, whose mythical clay sculptures are for sale at the local market in Bignona, Casamance; and Ndary Lô.

Iba Ndiaye, one of the most important painters of African modernism, passed away in 2008. He was one of the great leaders of the École de Dakar, Senegal's influential 1960s visual arts movement, which influences painters to this day. Contemporary painters of renown in Senegal include Souleymane Keïta, Soly Cissé, Cheikhou Bâ, Amadou Kane Sy and Mohamadou 'Douts' Ndoye among many others. Besides canvas painting, Senegal is particularly renowned for its unique tradition of glass painting (*sous-verre;* opposite). There's also an important photography scene. Key names include Boubacar Touré Mandémory, Mamadou Gomis, Pape Seydi, Jacky Ly and Podor's doyen Omar Ly (see p223).

Famous painters in Gambia include Baboucarr Etu Ndow and Njogu Touray, both of whom run creative centres that are open to visitors (see p118 and p102 respectively). They have shaped a school of art distinctive through its imaginative use of natural media, including sand and cowry shells, as well as through the vibrant colours of their works.

Textile & Fashion Design

Classic textile design techniques in Senegal and Gambia include wax printing, tie-dyeing and *bazin* (dyed fabrics that are beaten to a shine with wooden clubs). You'll be able to admire *bazins* on any Friday in town, when people head to the mosque in their finest *boubous*. Watching traditional weavers at work is fascinating: they produce slim strips of roughly woven cloth on long, narrow looms, which are erected on footpaths in the artisans' quarters. The strips are then sown together to make a *pagne* (a length of colourful cloth worn as a skirt).

Dakar is all style, cheek and nonchalant saunter. The young designers Ndiaga Diaw and Cheikha create outfits that match the Dakar spirit perfectly. See the boxed text, p174, for details.

Contemporary artists and fashion designers are taking these traditional crafts in new directions. Senegalese artists Rackie Diankha and Aïssa Dione have exhibited and sold their fabulous woven oeuvres, and Baboucar Fall and Toimbo Laurens are advancing contemporary batik printing in Gambia.

Fashion-conscious Senegal is also home to some of Africa's most renowned designers. Best known internationally are Oumou Sy and Collé Ardo Sow, whose stunning Afrocentric creations have been exhibited in many international fashion shows. Dakar's annual fashion fair, Sira Vision, unites some of the most promising creators on one catwalk. Upcoming designers include Angélique Dhiedhiou, whose label Toolah proposes a contemporary elegance rooted in African styles; and Cheikha's label Sigil and Ndiaga Diaw's Fitt, which take Afro-fashion to a cool street level.

Literature

For information on cultural events in Gambia, including everything from the latest reggae release to the origins of the Kankurang masquerade, go to www.onegambia .com. In Senegal, www .ausenegal.com contains a complete cultural calendar, special articles and portraits.

THE GAMBIA

Along with many countries of the Sahel, Gambia's literary tradition is partly based upon the family histories and epic poems told over the centuries by the *griots* (see p55).

In more recent times, especially since independence, a number of contemporary writers have emerged, although compared with many other West African countries, Gambia does not have a major literary output.

Gambia's best-known novelist is William Conton. His 1960s classic *The African* is a semiautobiographical tale of an African student in Britain. A story about the trials and tribulations of a young man seeking his identity in a newly born nation, it was an influential bestseller in postindependence Africa.

SOUS-VERRE – THE SENEGALESE ART OF GLASS PAINTING

Enter Moussa Sakho's charmingly chaotic atelier at the Institut Français in Dakar (p159) and you're greeted by a group of smiling faces looking out from a surface of colourfully painted glass. Moussa Sakho is one of the leading contemporary artists of *sous-verre*, Senegal's distinctive art of reverse glass painting. In this special technique, images are drawn onto the back of a glass surface, which lends them radiance and protection.

The origins of this tradition aren't entirely clear, but the practice reached an early high point in the late 19th century. Islamic imagery was initially the most prominent theme of the *sous-verres*, something that didn't please the French administration. Colonial governor William Ponty famously forbade their creation, fearing that their wide distribution would aid the expansion of Islam. But his decree didn't have the intended result. Quite the contrary – fearing for the few religious works they possessed, painters started copying the works and the art of *sous-verre* entered its most prolific phase; it was now considered a countercolonial force.

The most popular *sous-verres* today portray contemporary styles, fashions, and the minutiae of daily life in Senegal. To find good-quality *sous-verre*, you have to look past the tourist stalls. Moussa Sakho's workshop is a good place to start. Other artists of renown include Babacar Lô, Andy Dolly, Séa Diallo, Mbida and Gora Mbengue.

Whereas Conton has his roots in the colonial era, author Ebou Dibba is seen as part of the new generation of Gambian writers, even though his first and best-known novel, *Chaff on the Wind* (1986), is set in the preindependence period. This book follows the fortunes of two rural boys – one keen and studious, the other looking only for a good time – who come to work in the capital city, both eventually suffering at the hands of fate despite their attempts to control their own destinies.

Another new-generation writer is Tijan Salleh. Primarily known as a poet – his main collection is *Kora Land*, published in 1989 – he has also written essays and short stories.

SENEGAL

Senegal is one of the West African countries with the most prolific literary output; however, most works are only published in French.

Film-maker Ousmane Sembène was initially a writer and is still among the country's best-known authors. His classic *God's Bits of Wood* (1970) tells of the struggles of strikers on the Dakar–Bamako train line in the late 1940s and describes the emergence of a grassroots political consciousness in preindependence Africa.

Senegal's most influential writer is probably Léopold Sédar Senghor, the country's first president. Studying in France during the 1930s, he coined the term 'Négritude', which emphasised black African ideas and culture, countering the colonial policy of assimilation.

The most famous female author is Mariama Bâ, whose short but incisive novel *So Long a Letter* was first published in 1980 and won the Noma Award for publishing in Africa. It's one of the most sensitive, intimate and beautiful contemplations of female lives in a polygamous society.

Aminata Sow Fall came to fame with her 1986 novel *The Beggars' Strike*. An ironic story highlighting the differences between rich and poor, it questions the power of the political elite – two recurring themes in modern Senegalese literature.

The novel *An Ambiguous Adventure* by Cheikh Hamidou Kane is a true Senegalese classic. It's a deeply philosophical discussion of issues relating to colonialism, religion and the social transformations of early-20th-century Senegal.

Gifted photographer Mama Casset has created a series of memorable portraits depicting early-20th-century Senegalese styles. The booklet *Mama Casset*, published by Revue Noire, is in French, but the collection of images speaks for itself.

Young author Fatou Diome shot to fame in 2004 with her debut, *The Belly of the Atlantic*. A brilliant treatment of the topic of emigration, it was a best seller in France and has recently been translated into German and English.

Cinema

Senegal is one of the leading nations in African cinema and, while the scene was in its prime in the years following independence, today there's a resurgence of young film-makers emerging against all financial odds. The doyen of Senegalese cinema was Ousmane Sembène, who passed away in 2007. He studied film in Russia after hustling his way through '50s France as a seaman, dock worker and builder. He used cinema to shed a critical eye on Senegalese society, history and culture, from his first 1962 directed work *Borom Saret* – a moving black-and-white tale about an inner-city horse-cart driver – through to the 2006 release *Moolaadé,* which broaches the sensitive subject of female circumcision.

The illustrious Djibril Diop Mambéty surprised the movie world with daring, experimental works such as his 1973 'Senegalese road movie' *Touki Bouki,* a surreal story of a young Dakar couple, and the 1992 *Hyenas.*

Contemporary talents include Moussa Sene Absa *(Teranga Blues)* and Joseph Gaï Ramaka, whose controversial 2001 work *Karmen Geï* sets the classic story of *Carmen* in a Senegalese context and breaks boundaries by touching on sensuality and lesbian love in a daring way. Dakar's annual Festival International du Film de Quartier (p164) is a good place to spot future big names.

Architecture

The story of West Africa's ancient empires isn't easily traced through architectural remains, as the powerful rulers didn't enshrine their memory in monumental building work as did their counterparts elsewhere. What survives to this day are the contrasting architectural styles of ordinary housings, which differ greatly from one region to the next. In the north, the *banco* (mudbrick) constructions of Tukulor houses have much in common with Sudanese architecture. In the same region there are late-19th-century mosques, organic shapes built from mudbricks by the followers of El Hajj Omar Tall. The Kédougou region is home to the round stone huts typical of the Bassari, while in the area of Siné-Saloum huts are made from thatch and mud.

Besides African building work, Senegal has many examples of European architecture, some dating back to the Portuguese era. The islands of Gorée and Saint-Louis and the Senegal River settlements of Richard Toll, Podor, Matam and Bakel are virtual time capsules of 18th- and 19th-century French and Portuguese architecture. Many of the old houses on Île de Gorée (p178) have now been beautifully restored, as has the ancient fort in Podor (see p224).

The impact of Breton settlers on Île de Carabane at the remote mouth of the Casamance River is still plain to see in its large church and mission (now a hotel). In Gambia, Banjul is home to wide avenues of grand homes once occupied by the colonial elite, while nearby stand small, unpretentious Aku-style homes. Fortifications were also important to the British colonists and not far from Banjul you can see the remains of Fort James (James Island) and Fort Bullen (Barra), while Janjangbureh (Georgetown) and Basse both have examples of colonial warehouses.

For contemporary architecture, visit Arch 22 (p92) and Banjul Airport, both designed by Senegalese star architect Pierre Goudiaby Atepa.

Music

You don't have to look hard to find music in Senegal and Gambia – just step into a taxi and commence your search. The driver of your clapped-out Peugeot is likely to have his stereo fully turned up, sweetening his endless tours around Dakar's sand-blown tarmac with the latest Youssou N'Dour or some homemade hip hop. On a weekend, he'll probably pass several aching sound systems that carry the distorted voice of a *griot* (West African praise singer) or some local reggae through the bustling boroughs, entertaining radiant wedding parties or enticing tea-sipping youngsters to dance. If you're in Dakar, ask the driver to steer his cab straight into the impossibly crammed streets of Marché Sandaga, where scratchy stereos compete for attention, and where impatient car horns, clicking heels, rustling *boubous* (robes), shouts of bartering, and calls to prayer from the mosque mingle into a unique hymn to urban Dakar. This heaving downtown market is also home to several tiny stalls stacked sky-high with CDs that deliver the latest local music releases to an eagerly waiting public – works the stallholders have probably just copied in the backrooms of their boutiques.

When it comes to music, no one teaches West Africans anything. You'll be the one keen to learn the seductive hip swing of *mbalax* or the sensual sway of the latest zouk (a style of dance music, originally from Guadeloupe, that mixes African and Latin-American rhythms).

A POTTED HISTORY OF GAMBIAN & SENEGALESE MUSIC

Even the most contemporary Senegalese and Gambian music trends evoke ancient roots, with their proud poise and soaring voices. The history of modern music in the region begins several centuries ago, in the days of the 13th-century Mali Empire of the Malinké, the 15th-century Jolof Empire established by the Wolof, and other influential kingdoms of precolonial Africa. The epic of Soundiata Keïta, illustrious founder of the Mali Empire, famously recounts the important role of his *griot* Bala Fasseke, and explains the establishment of a social hierarchy in which musicians had a clearly defined place. Along with blacksmiths, woodcarvers and other artisans, *griots* occupied the place in society of professional groups, ranked lower than the 'freeborn' families of rulers and traders, and above the slaves. 'Griot' is a French word – local terms for this social group are *jali* in Mande, *gewel* in Wolof and *gawlo* in Fula.

Griots are born musicians; they're born with the right to sing the praises of their rulers, act as political advisers, recite genealogies and, importantly, memorise and spread the region's oral history and pass it on to future generations. This is how the stories of Africa's ancient kingdoms have survived the centuries. It's also how the *griots'* classic repertoire has been transmitted from one generation to the next. Any accomplished *griot* today can still transport his listeners into past times, instilling pride in their family legacy – a gift that an appreciative audience rewards with generous offers of money or cloth.

One of the Mande *griots'* most famous instruments is the *kora* (harp-lute), an icon of African music throughout the world. The history of this stringed instrument started in Gambia. This tiny country became a centre of *kora* playing when one of Soundiata Keïta's generals led a group of Malinké people here and established an outpost of the mighty Mali Empire. Gambia boasts a wide variety of *kora* styles, notably the dry patterns of the eastern regions around Bansang and Basse, and a softer style more common in the west of the country.

The stories of West Africa's great empires are kept alive in the songs of the *griots*. 'Kelefa' tells the story of the ancient empire of Kaabu, while 'Tara' praises the heroism of El Hajj Omar Tall.

Take a time-machine ride from the precolonial era to the 1960s and you land directly on a swinging Cuban dance floor – right in the heart of Dakar. Cuban music was incredibly influential in the '60s and was first played in cosmopolitan dance clubs, such as the Miami, to the affluent French and Senegalese elite. Brought over from France's fashionable dance floors, it quickly struck a chord with the Senegalese population. After all, Cuban rhythms were a 'New World' adaptation of musical styles originally brought to the Americas from Africa. Having now returned to their source, they once again became infused with African flavours.

Sunjata: Gambian Versions of the Mande Epic, by Bamba Suso and Banna Kanute, tells the story of the 13th-century ruler of the Mali Empire in the words of two renowned Gambian *griots.*

Independence brought a whole new national consciousness, which left its traces in the music of the region. Inspired young musicians, notably Ibra Kasse and his Star Band, started to transform the imported Cuban beats by infusing them with a uniquely Senegalese twist. Salsa sections were increasingly broken up with bursts of frenetic drumming, drawn from traditional ceremonies. Dancers went crazy on the floor, rotating hips, thrusting groins and spinning legs, spurring the drummers on to even faster playing. There was no going back. In this polyrhythmic marriage Senegal had found its own beat – the *mbalax.*

The birth of *mbalax* is mainly associated with one name, Youssou N'Dour, who proudly dons the epithet 'king of *mbalax*'. In the late '70s, he was a young kid singing with the Étoile de Dakar, an offshoot of the Star Band. It was this group that took the novel Senegalese-Cuban sounds to a whole new level, by introducing the street sound of live *sabar* drums into the nightclubs. The sound proved irresistible and launched N'Dour into a superstardom that still seems to grow. Today, *mbalax* continues to evolve through the combination of new sounds. The music is getting even faster, yet its core sound, the rolling drumbeat called by the *sabar* and *tama* drums, hasn't changed.

If you enter any Gambian music shop today, you'll find about the same selection of music as in Senegal. After all, Wolof texts and rhythms are understood beyond the artificial border, and Dakar has the bigger musical kitchen. Leading local artists include Jalibah Kouyateh and Tata Dindin Jobarteh. Both mix *mbalax* with Gambian Mandinka sounds.

If Senegalese music is a dominant force in Gambia today, it has to recognise that its initial inspiration came from the shores of the Gambia River. In the late '60s the Afro-funky Super Eagles ruled the stages of Banjul and opened the doors for a fantastically flourishing music scene in Gambia. That music made a huge impact in Senegal at the time, and provided the inspiration that led to the creation of *mbalax*. And even though Senegal likes to think of itself as the one and only source of the busy beat, the spark might never have been lit without a mighty musical push from the small neighbouring nation.

Senegalese star Youssou N'Dour created the music for the French children's film Kirikou et la Sorcière, and a member of the rap group PBS Radical provided Kirikou's voice. The clever and cheeky Kirikou has become a cartoon hero for West African children.

Gambia's young generation has chosen an entirely different route – that of reggae. The lazy beat blasts from improvised sound systems around the country, each echoing pulse proving that the nation's nickname 'Little Jamaica' is entirely deserved.

In Senegal, reggae is competing for youth attention with a vibrant local hip hop scene. Senegalese hip hop has been made famous worldwide by groups such as Positive Black Soul and Daara J, who sneer at the permanently overdressed, glittering *mbalax* crowd. Unperturbed, *mbalax* audiences gathered in style at concerts by the likes of the R&B-influenced Viviane N'Dour, the streetwise Omar Pene and a host of excellent young singers. In the 30th year of his career, Youssou N'Dour is still unrivalled in popularity – neither the soft-voiced Thione Seck, Youssou's eternal challenger in Senegal, nor the nasal-voiced Baaba Maal, the better-known name abroad, have ever been able to topple him from his throne.

TRADITIONAL MUSIC

The boundaries between traditional and modern music styles are fluid. During the day an artist (probably a *griot*) can recite the story of Soundiata and his warriors with a soaring voice in a way that brings their tales of heroism truly to life. Yet in the evening, you might easily encounter the same artist backed by a full electric ensemble, experimenting with a *kora*-funk crossover. The difference between traditional and modern is perhaps best defined by context, rather than style. Music that's played for social occasions, such as weddings or naming ceremonies, is usually considered traditional, while a nightclub setting demands modernity and the scream of an amplified *kora* riff.

Established families often have their own *griots,* who perform praise songs and recite genealogies at celebrations, and are usually showered with crumpled CFA franc or dalasi notes in return. But there's more to the traditional music of the region than the refined songs of the *griots* alone. Every ethnic group has its own rhythms, dances and instruments, and a tour around Gambia and Senegal will reveal the spectacular array of styles – ranging from the flute and fiddle troupes of the Fula herders to stunning polyphonic Serer songs and the sky-high leaps that accompany Wolof *sabar* drumming. If you're serious about experiencing the region's variety of traditional music, head for the tiny villages. The best chance to see such music is at a family celebration, and if you approach the local wedding party respectfully, your presence is unlikely to offend.

Particularly spectacular are the masked dances and songs of the Bassari and Diola. These are mainly performed for initiation ceremonies, and the stunningly decorated dancers usually represent supernatural spirits that either protect or try to harm the newly circumcised boys. Masked shows have survived only in the non-Islamic regions of the country. Their deep connection to traditional religion, the spiritual associations of the drum and the representation of non-Islamic spirits via masks makes them largely incompatible with Muslim faith. There are some exceptions to this rule, though: the dance of the Kankurang of the Malinké – where a spirit is represented by a rustling, grass-covered mask – has found its way into the region's Islamic culture, just as the protective amulets worn by followers of traditional religions are now worn by most Muslims.

Traditional Instruments

DRUMS

The *tama* drum of the Wolof has gained much attention through its use in *mbalax*. The tiny size of this double-headed tension drum belies the frenzy it can cause among dancers. Watch out for the *tamakat* – the player of the drum – at any Youssou N'Dour gig. Once he gets up and starts pounding the stretched drum skin with a stick, women leap up from their chairs and dance until their shiny *pagnes* (skirts) and headscarves unravel.

Another Wolof drum is the *sabar*. This tall, thin drum is played in an ensemble and forms the clanging basis of the *mbalax* beat.

The ubiquitous *djembe* is probably the most popular of all African drums, and its appeal has reached beyond Africa and deep into Europe. The *djembe*-like *bougarabou* stems from the Casamance region.

Kafountine and Abéné in the Casamance are Senegal's favourite destinations for aspiring *djembe* players, with plenty of informal drumming courses. In Dakar, try the **Centre Culturel Blaise Senghor** (Map p158; Rue 10, Dakar).

Famous Senegalese drummers:

Assane Thiam Youssou N'Dour's famous *tama* player.

Doudou N'Diaye Rose Most renowned *bougarabou* player, who has fathered a diaspora of equally gifted sons.

Mbaye Dieye Faye Youssou N'Dour's equally famous *sabar* player.

STRINGED INSTRUMENTS

The variety of stringed instruments ranges from the Mandinka single-string *moolo* (plucked lute) and the *riti* (bowed fiddle) to the 21-string *kora* (harp-lute).

The harp-lute *kora* is the classic instrument of the *griots,* and is arguably one of the most sophisticated instruments in sub-Saharan Africa. With its delicate tumble of shimmering notes, it has captured the souls of many listeners abroad, and has been incorporated into a wide array of crossover works, ranging from jazz to Western classical music and even hip hop.

Another important instrument of the *griots* is the *xalam* (a Wolof word, pronounced kha-lam). It is known by a variety of names, including *konting* in Mandinka and *hoddu* in Fula, and has from three to five strings that are plucked to produce a dry, guitarlike sound. It's believed that the banjo evolved from the *xalam*.

The best place to learn to play the *kora* is Brikama (see the boxed text, p125), a dusty town in Gambia where the famous *griot* families of Dembo Konté and Malamini Jobarteh reside.

Famous *kora* players:

Amadou Bansang Jobarteh The doyen of Gambia's dry, eastern style.

Dembo Konté One of the Brikama masters; has gained fame for his *kora* duets with the Casamance-born Kausu Kuyateh.

Jali Nyama Suso Outstanding Gambian *kora* player who wrote his country's national anthem.

Edou Manga A young *kora* player from the Casamance who experiments with new styles as a member of Ekankan and Carlou D's ensemble.

Malamini Jobarteh Another member of a famous Brikama clan; his sons Pa and Tata Dindin Jobarteh are among Gambia's most popular musicians today.

WIND INSTRUMENTS

The Fula flute, with its husky call, is West Africa's most famous wind instrument. Flute musicians combine singing with playing sharp trills and tumbling descending patterns. The Fula flute stems from the Fouta Jallon in Guinea, but many flute players *(nyamakala)* have moved to Gambia and southern Senegal, where they often perform their hilarious, acrobatic shows for the entertainment of hotel guests. To learn the instrument properly, you should really go to Guinea. Otherwise, try Brikama (the Konté family can point you in the right direction; see p125) or the Théâtre Daniel Sorano (p174) in Dakar.

Famous Fula flautists:

Ali Wague Based in Paris; plays on dozens of West African albums.
Issa Diao The flautist of Dakar's Théâtre National du Sénégal.

XYLOPHONES

The wooden *balafon,* whose dry tone is accompanied by the gentle buzz of vibrating gourds attached to each slab, is another typical *griot* instrument. It's most widespread in Guinea, but Malinké *griots* play it all across Gambia and Senegal. To arrange xylophone courses in a calm environment, Brikama and the Théâtre Daniel Sorano are once again the addresses to remember.

El Hajj Sory Kouyate is a famous Guinean *balafon* player. His double CD *Guinée: Anthologie du Balafon Mandingue* is a great way to experience *balafon* music.

CONTEMPORARY MUSIC

Senegal's pop scene is thriving – find yourself in the epicentre of an exploding *mbalax* dance floor and you'll see how passionately people feel about their music. Dakar's contemporary music scene is fantastically varied. Anything from hip hop to reggae, salsa, folk, jazz and pop is available – all homemade and spiced with potent local flavours. The glitzy Senegalese scene compares to that of The Gambia in the same way the two capitals do: the former is a vibrant party queen, the latter smoothly rippled by the bass drop of a reggae beat.

Dance Orchestras

In the 1970s the pop-music scene in Senegal was dominated by large bands, complete with multipart horn sections, bass and rhythm guitar, and several singers and dancers. These mighty beasts are usually referred to as 'dance orchestras', an apt name considering their football-team size. The most famous of these, Orchestra Baobab, was the undisputed leader of the Senegalese scene throughout the '70s, before a younger generation snatched its audiences away with cheek and a healthy dose of rebellious innovation. Right now the grand Baobab is living its second spring. It reformed in 2001 and now tours regularly, luring audiences worldwide onto the dance floor, thanks to the members' inimitable grandfatherly charm.

The father of the Senegalese dance orchestra style, however, was an artist who is lesser known today. Ibra Kasse was a reputed tyrant when it came to working with talented musicians, and was the leader of a fantastically gifted group called the Star Band de Dakar. In the line-up were Pape Seck and the illustrious Gambian-born lead singer Labah Sosseh. When the Star Band divided into glittering pieces Étoile de Dakar emerged, providing the rocket launcher for Senegalese uberstar Youssou N'Dour.

Songlines (www .songlines.co.uk) is a quarterly music magazine with a large reviews section and a good variety of features.

Salsa

In the 1960s the dance floors of newly independent Senegal and Gambia swayed to catchy rhythms from Cuba. Based on African beats in the first place, the fashionable Cuban sounds quickly caught on all across Africa,

---

SAINT-LOUIS JAZZ

Saint-Louis shares its name with St Louis, Missouri, and it seems that the great blues city of the USA may have shared its musical secrets with northern Senegal's capital too. Jazz is a big thing here, and the tradition goes back to the 1940s, when jazz ensembles from Saint-Louis undertook their first tours to Paris and other European cities. After independence, the blue notes tinted the Afro-Cuban big-band sounds of the great Saint-Louis orchestras. And in the 1990s the tradition was honoured with the creation of the Saint-Louis Jazz Festival. Since then, international and local jazz and blues outfits have graced the stages of the city's small, smoky clubs and open-air platforms for a week every May. Now managed by a new, young team, the famous festival is being infused with new flavours from across Africa and the diaspora.

For more background, have a look at *St-Louis Jazz,* a book by Hervé Lenormond, which outlines the history of jazz in Senegal and has some wonderful photos of musicians from Africa, America and Europe performing in Saint-Louis. Festival programs and dates can be checked on www.saintlouisjazz.com (in French), or with the Syndicat d'Initiative (p212).

---

and hit the local airwaves in their original Cuban form, as well as draped in colourful African guises from Guinea and the Congo.

Senegalese bands interpreted Spanish lyrics and Cuban rhythms so perfectly that they almost passed for the original. Bands like Orchestra Baobab, Pape Fall & African Salsa, and Africando still draw huge audiences – mainly among the middle-aged, who'll saunter onto the dance floor and start swinging to the sounds that coloured their first date rose.

Mbalax

Mbalax is the heart and soul of Senegalese music – and the legs, thighs, hips and backsides, too. Several Gambian artists of the '60s created the fiery sound from a mixture of Cuban beats and traditional *sabar* drumming. *Mbalax* was made famous by Youssou N'Dour, who is still the unrivalled leader of the scene. He is also one of the biggest names in world music, a shrewd businessman, a cultural icon – and then some.

Since its inception, *mbalax* has evolved by adapting to changing fashions, without ever losing its essence. One example of the genre's versatility is the *mbalax* by impeccably suited-and-tied Thione Seck, who has married the beat with Indian-style vocals. In 1974 Senegal's 'street kid' Omar Pene and his band Super Diamono were the first to replace the congas of a standard *mbalax* outfit with a drum kit – a move that has been copied by every artist since.

Youssou N'Dour's sister-in-law Viviane N'Dour is one of Senegal's major style icons, mixing sexy *mbalax* beats with breathy, R&B-inspired vocals. Other *mbalax* artists causing havoc on the region's dance floors include Abdou Guité Seck, Ablaye Mbaye, Aliou Mbaye N'Der, Titi and Jali Ba Kuyateh.

Afro-Jazz, Rock, Folk & Fusion

Senegal has a long tradition of jazz. The northern city of Saint-Louis, which was the first important cosmopolitan city in Senegal, has harboured brilliant jazz combos since the 1940s and is still home to West Africa's most renowned jazz festival (see the boxed text, above). Within Senegal jazz-related forms are often referred to as *Afro.*

In the 1980s the group Xalam, which proposed a unique African-flavoured rock, attained such great heights internationally that they played support for the Rolling Stones. In Senegal itself, they never achieved nearly as much fame, though they reunited in 2008 to have another go at that. Also in the '80s, the band of brothers known as Touré Kunda set out from its Casamance home to conquer the world – with some success. The new sound, brewed from

The monthly music magazine *fRoots* (www.frootsmag.com) is a good source for reviews and articles and looks beneath the surface of the music scene.

traditional Casamance styles, reggae, folk and rock, was embraced first by France, where the band went all the way to the national charts.

In recent years, Afro-folk has become immensely popular here, largely due to the sexy success of a young performer named Carlou D. He left a hip hop background to shape a unique blend of folk, rap, reggae, country and plenty more, and fills stadiums in Senegal and Gambia. His success has even brought the old masters of Afro-folk, the Frères Guisse, to a second season of glory, and inspired youngsters, such as Yoro and Biba, to try to mirror his success.

Although Baaba Maal's acoustic works are sometimes classed as folk, it's hard to categorise his music. He has produced a spectacularly varied catalogue, toying with hip hop and dance beats among plenty of other styles. And Cheikh Lô, another well-known name in the West, stormed onto the scene with a moving blend of Latin rhythms, subtle hints of *mbalax* and praise lyrics to Cheikh Amadou Bamba, spiritual leader of the Baye Fall (see p46).

Hip Hop & Reggae

Senegal has maintained a vibrant hip hop scene since the mid-'80s, when the brash young trio PBS (Positive Black Soul) stormed the international scene. Dakar's kids have coupled the American beats with local rhymes and sounds, turning the music into a powerful tool for voicing discontent. The scene enjoyed a revival in 2004, when Daara J sold unexpected numbers of records, shifting the global spotlight right onto the urban youth culture of Senegal. Other leading hip hop artists in Senegal include the Xuman, Nixx, Biss Bi Clan, Matador, Gaston and many others.

Gambia is more Kingston than New York, a country where reggae artists such as Egalitarian, Rebellion the Recaller and Dancehall Masters do an amazing job of transferring Jamaican swagger into a Gambian context. Many have performed with some of the greatest names in reggae, and even the president enjoys public mingling with Jamaican stars like Morgan Heritage and Sizzlah.

Find out all about Gambia's vibrant reggae scene at www.onegambia .com, where you can put together your own mix of Gambian reggae.

The most comprehensive website discussing releases of African urban music is www .africanhiphop.com.

Environment

From Sahel plains in the north to the abundant greenery in the south, and specked with mangrove-lined river deltas and white beaches in the west, Gambia and Senegal offer rich natural surroundings. Naturally, the diversity of scenery attracts a large variety of wildlife – not the 'big five' of East Africa, but hundreds of bird species that will have you wield binoculars in no time. As elsewhere in the world, natural surroundings are threatened by an almost overwhelming array of environmental issues. A large number of sustainable tourism options allow you to find out about the issues at stake, while ensuring that your own impact on these fragile surroundings is minimised.

THE LAND

Gambia and Senegal belong to the Sahel zone, the savannah belt that stretches from the Sahara desert in the north to the tropical forests of the south. For the most part, the land is so flat that even minor elevations like the volcanic Mamelles in Dakar or the cute escarpment that delineates the Gambia River in Kiang West National Park are indicated to visitors like major attractions.

Towards the far southeastern corner of Senegal, however, the terrain does get mountainous enough to strap on hiking boots. The highest peak, Mt Asserik, still stands at only 311m, but it forms part of a beautifully varied landscape with steep climbs, tucked-away waterfalls and lush greens lining narrow mountain paths.

Check out the work of nature and environmental photographers Hellio and Van Ingen on www.hellio-vaningen .fr, both to marvel at the land's beauty and catch a vivid glimpse of ongoing protection work.

The Gambia River snakes its way through Bassari country and the Parc National de Niokolo-Koba before forming the centre of the country Gambia, whose narrow shape is defined by the wide stream. In the northeast, from Basse to the River Gambia National Park, the lush riverine vegetation looks almost Amazonian. Inland, tropical landscapes and gallery forest have largely been diminished by deforestation. As you travel westwards, saltwater is carried in from the shore, and palm trees give way to thick mangrove swamps that line the Gambia River from the labyrinthine Baobolong wetlands to the Atlantic coast.

Creeks, islets, lagoons and mangroves also define the elaborate Senegalese deltas of the Saloum River to the north (partly protected as a national park) and the Casamance River in the south. The latter is the waterway that irrigates Senegal's most fertile region – the Casamance. The abundance of green here almost makes up for the total absence of it in other parts of Senegal and Gambia. It's an area where you'll be awed by the magnificent size of tropical trees, and where September storms soak you in a second and wash away the path you travelled on a minute ago. This is one of Senegal's main agricultural zones, where rice, millet, sorghum and many varieties of fruit are cultivated.

The second most important farming zone is found right in the north, along the shores of the Senegal River, which marks the border between Mauritania and Senegal. The landscape here is very different, with barely a

---

HIDDEN GAMBIA

'The river is Gambia's most prominent feature, and you get to see a completely different side of the country if you travel the water way', says Mark Thompson, successfully persuading us to take a boat downstream. He was so struck by the beauty of the Gambia River and its shores that he founded Hidden Gambia (see p288), a company offering tours upriver.

HARMATTAN HAZE

The harmattan is a dry wind that blows from the north, usually from December to March. During this period the skies of most West African countries are grey from Sahara sand carried by the wind, and even when the wind stops blowing, skies remain hazy until the first rains fall. The effects are more noticeable away from the coast, and generally travel isn't too badly affected. Photographers can expect hazy results, while people with contact lenses should be prepared for problems.

---

spot of green to break up the sand and red dust blown in from the Sahara further north. Only the irrigation zones closest to the river provide enough water to cultivate grains. Senegal's vast northeastern region, barely inhabited and even less visited, is marked by those dry, flat lands.

Senegal is the country that lies furthest to the west of the African land mass – only the Cape Verde islands point further westwards. From the westernmost Pointe des Almadies near Dakar, the gentle slope of the Grande Côte stretches northwards with wide beaches beaten by wind and waves.

South of Dakar, the Petite Côte is more protected from the forces of nature and stretches as one long beach paradise to the mangroves of the Siné-Saloum. Past the Siné-Saloum Delta, the Gambia greets the ocean with 80km of coast that continues in the Casamance to the south all the way to the wide sand strands of Cap Skiring.

ANIMALS

Senegal and Gambia aren't the kinds of countries that tempt tourists with huge safari parks. There is some wildlife to be seen, but it's much more humble than the herds of zebras and giraffes you can observe in other parts of Africa.

Although the region can't show off with mighty elephants or rhinos, it beats most other destinations when it comes to birds. The Parc National des Oiseaux du Djoudj in Senegal, for instance, is the world's third-largest bird sanctuary, while tiny Gambia attracts large numbers of birdwatchers with hundreds of species and a well-organised system of birdwatching tours (see p70 for more information).

Popular and easily recognised mammals in forested areas include baboons, and vervet, patas and the stunning red colobus monkeys. Abuko Nature Reserve in Gambia is one of the best places to see these monkey species. Chimpanzee populations occur naturally in Senegal's Parc National de Niokolo-Koba and near Ethiolo, though the best place to spot them is in the River Gambia National Park, home to the fabulous chimpanzee rehabilitation project initiated by Stella Brewer (see the boxed text, p141).

Oribi and duikers (small members of the antelope family) are common in some of the forest zones, including the Reserve de Guembeul, which also works on the reintegration of dama gazelles and oryxes. Some areas of dry grassland are inhabited by kobs, roan antelopes, waterbucks and Derby elands.

Wild boars are very common throughout Gambia and Senegal. In Niokolo-Koba, they are one of the few types of animals you're guaranteed to come across. And as Pumbaa in *The Lion King* was modelled on a wild boar, your kids may even forgive you if they don't get to see the leopards and lions they were promised (the giant cats inhabit the park but are very rarely seen).

The Réserve de Bandia (southeast of Dakar) has a whole range of large mammals, including rhinos, buffalos and giraffes, though some are not indigenous to Senegal and have been brought here as a tourist attraction.

Hyenas are common in parts of the Siné-Saloum Delta and in the northeast of Gambia. They're shy animals and, though you might not see them,

---

MANGROVES

The mangrove, a tropical evergreen plant, is typically found in the tidal mud flats and inlets of areas such as the Siné-Saloum Delta and the mouth of the Casamance – zones where large rivers spill into the ocean. The mangrove plays a vital role for both the local population and wildlife and has a fascinating reproductive system, perfectly adapted to its watery environment. It is one of very few plants that thrive in salt water, and this allows rapid growth in areas where no other plant would have a chance.

Two types of mangrove – red and white – can be seen in Gambia and Senegal and are easily identified. The red is the most common and has leathery leaves and a dense tangle of stiltlike buttress roots. The white mangrove is mainly found on ground that is covered by water only when there are particularly high tides. It does not have stilt roots; you can recognise it by its breathing roots, which have circular pores and grow out of the mud from the base of the tree.

Oysters cling to the mangrove's roots as the tide comes in and are easily collected during low waters. Mangrove trees catch silt, vegetation and other floating debris in their root systems, including their own falling leaves. As this mire becomes waterlogged and consolidated, it forms an ideal breeding ground for young mangroves. In this way, the mangrove creates new land. As the stands expand on the seaward side, the older growth on the landward side gradually gets further from the water. Eventually the trees die, leaving behind a rich soil.

---

you'll probably hear their distinctive cries at night and see their tracks in the morning.

Hippos are regularly seen along the Gambia River. Good viewing sites include River Gambia National Park, Niokolo-Koba, Wassadou and Mako. If you're out hippo spotting by boat, be careful not to get too close: this peaceful-looking creature can be very aggressive (see the boxed text, p140).

A trip to the cute Sakura arts studio (p102) of Gambian painter Njogu Touray is a great introduction to his original ways of marrying environmental dedication to creative talent.

Wherever large rivers enter the sea, you have a vague chance of catching a glimpse of dolphins. They're common at the mouth of the Casamance River and may sometimes follow your ferry on its way to Île de Gorée. Thanks to the tireless efforts of Senegal's Océanium (see p161), the manatee (sea cow) populations near Pointe St George are now protected by a sanctuary. Visit during low tide, and you're bound to see them. They're also found in the River Gambia National Park and in the Senegal River near Matam, but sightings are less common there, as the ancient, shell-covered creatures tend to remain hidden by the muddy water. Another river inhabitant in Senegal and Gambia is the crocodile, both the more common Nile species and the very rare dwarf crocodile.

Other reptiles to watch out for (but that shouldn't inspire bush paranoia) are snakes. Gambia and Senegal have venomous and harmless snakes (including pythons, cobras and mambas), but most fear humans and you'll be lucky to even see one. Other reptiles include lizards (including large monitor lizards), geckos and tortoises.

The website www .chimprehab.com gives excellent background information on the chimpanzee rehabilitation project in River Gambia National Park (see the boxed text, p141). You can even adopt your own chimp.

PLANTS

If you trace Senegal's main east–west artery from Dakar to Tambacounda, you'll get a 400km introduction to the dry and dusty sparseness of Sahel vegetation. From Dakar to Kaolack, huge baobab trees stand scattered across the red earth like solitary giants. Further eastwards low shrub and the flat tops of thorny acacia trees dot the arid lands. While parts of northern and western Senegal come close to being desert, there's more to vegetation in this Sahel country than the dust-sprayed branches of leafless baobabs.

Lush tropical forest exists only in the Basse Casamance, but pockets across Senegal and Gambia are dotted with thick gallery forest, a type of vegetation that is similar to rainforest, though not as thick and dense. As it's fed primarily through ground water, many of the vines and epiphytes that characterise a picture-book jungle are absent. You'll find beautiful stretches of gallery forest in northern Senegal (Reserve de Guembeul), along wide areas of Niokolo-Koba in the east, and in various, often protected, corners of Gambia, such as Kartong, Kunkiling and zones surrounding Janjangbureh (Georgetown).

Apart from the baobab, Senegalese symbol of strength, endurance and patience (see the boxed text, below), a typical tree of the region is the kapok, also known as the silk-cotton tree. It's instantly recognisable by its huge, exposed roots, which form a maze around the base of the trunk. In Senegal this tree is called the *fromager* (from *fromage,* the French word for cheese) because the wood of the trunk is soft and light. Many villages are built around an ancient kapok tree because they are believed to have special significance, harbouring spirits who protect the inhabitants from bad luck. The men of the village use the tree as a *bantaba* (meeting place) and the exposed roots often make comfortable benches.

Common palm trees include the rhun palm (also called ron and, in French, *ronier*), easily identified by its bulging trunk and fan-shaped leaves. With hard wood that is naturally termite proof, it is a highly desired building material, which means its numbers are in decline in many regions. The coconut palm, reaching up to 35m, and the Senegal date palm, which grows to 8m and produces small red berries, are also widespread.

NATIONAL PARKS

Senegal and Gambia have an impressive number of protected areas, ranging from tiny community reserves to vast World Heritage–listed parks. Not all of the protected areas are equally well maintained: while some are impressively well managed, others suffer from understaffing, lack of funding or governmental support, or merely from the absence of one dedicated soul to make a real difference. In Gambia, the Department of Parks & Wildlife Management is responsible for looking after the country's six national parks, which cover a total of 3.7% of Gambian lands. In Senegal, the Direction des Parcs Nationaux manages six parks, including Parc National de Niokolo-Koba, the region's largest protected area.

GENTLE GIANTS

The mighty baobab *(Adansonia digitata)* is probably Africa's most characteristic tree. With its thick, sturdy trunk and stunted rootlike branches, it's an instantly recognisable symbol of the continent. Baobabs grow in most parts of Gambia and Senegal; the flat savannah lands between Dakar and Kaolack in particular are richly covered with baobabs of all sizes and ages.

Legend has it, in a number of local cultures, that a displeased deity plucked a tree in anger and thrust it back into the ground upside down, creating the baobab – hence the thick, sprawling branches. Despite this mythical beginning, the baobab is held in high regard by local people. Its wizened appearance, combined with an ability to survive great droughts and live for many hundreds of years, means the baobab is often deemed to be sacred and is believed to have magical powers. Very old trees develop cavities and, in ancient times, these were sometimes used as burial places for *griots,* the praise singers and oral historians common to many West African societies.

The baobab has many practical uses too. The hollow trunk can hold rainwater, which may have percolated in from cracks higher up in the tree, forming a useful reservoir in times of drought. The tree's large pods (sometimes called 'monkey bread') contain seeds encased in a sherbetlike substance that can be eaten or made into a drink. The leaves can be chopped, boiled and made into a sauce; dried and ground they produce a paste used as a poultice for skin infections and sore joints.

NATIONAL PARKS OF THE GAMBIA & SENEGAL

Park	Features (Biomes; Animals)	Activities
Abuko Nature Reserve (p122)	gallery forest; bushbucks, monkeys, crocodiles, turacos	walks, birdwatching trail with hides
Marine Protected Area of Bamboung (p198)	mangrove swamps, savannah woodland; sea birds, waders, warthogs, hyenas	walks through mangroves, pirogue tours
Baobolong Wetland Reserve (p134)	wetland, marshes; herons, egrets, sunbirds, manatees	pirogue tours
Bijilo Forest Park (p99)	woodland; monkeys, birds	guided walks
Kiang West National Park (p135)	mangrove creeks, woodland; bushbucks, birds of prey, warthogs	pirogue tours, guided walks
Parc National des Îles de la Madeleine (p179)	islets, rock pools; black kites, cormorants, dolphins, turtles	pirogue tours, swimming
Parc National de la Langue de Barbarie (p220)	sandbanks, river; sea birds, waders	pirogue & kayak tours, walks, swimming
Parc National de Niokolo-Koba* (p230)	savannah woodland & gallery forest; porcupines, lions, hyenas, monkeys, elephants	guided 4WD tours, hides at waterholes
Parc National des Oiseaux du Djoudj* (p221)	woodland, creeks, mud flats; sea birds, waders, crocodiles	pirogue tours
Réserve de Popenguine (p186)	gallery forest; sea birds, sunbirds, rollers, birds of prey	guided walks through forest & lagoon
River Gambia National Park (p137)	islands, woodland; chimpanzees, hippos, birds	pirogue tours
Tanji River Bird Reserve (p116)	woodland, islands; Caspian terns, turtles	walks, pirogue tours
Réserve de Guembeul* (p218)	woodland, wetlands; oryx, dama gazelles	walks, pirogue tours
Marine Protected Areas Kassa & Pointe St George (p244)	mangroves, river, woodland; manatees	guided walks, pirogue tours

* denotes a World Heritage Site

In addition to those grand national zones, both countries have numerous smaller gazetted areas, including community forests, Marine Protected Areas and community-managed lagoons. A couple of the most important ones have been listed along with the national parks in the table, below.

For detailed information on each protected area, see individual chapters. To find out how to volunteer or arrange visits to certain areas, contact **Makasutu Wildlife Trust** (☎ 7782633, 4473349; m.wildlifetrust@yahoo.co.uk; Abuko Nature Reserve) in Gambia, or **Océanium** (☎ 33 822 2441; www.oceanium.org; Route de la Corniche-Est, Dakar) in Senegal, which looks after the management of most Marine Protected Areas of the country.

For comprehensive information on Gambia's nature reserves or on volunteering at the Abuko Nature Reserve near Banjul, check out the fantastic work of the Makasutu Wildlife Trust at www.darwingambia.gm.

ENVIRONMENTAL ISSUES
Coastal Erosion

The human activity of sand mining (see the boxed text, p161) compounds the coastal erosion that occurs naturally on the Atlantic shores. In Gambia, the disastrous combination of the two had already threatened to destroy the one thing that fuels the nation's tourist industry – its wide, white sand beaches. Ironically, it was the increased demand for sand to build tourist complexes, roads and resorts near the beaches that sped up their decline. A huge, American-funded program, using Dutch technology to trap the sand and thus rebuild the beaches inch by inch, is showing impressive results. In areas such as Kololi, the erosion process has today largely been reversed and beaches stretch once again temptingly into the sea. One can only hope that swimmers alone – not construction companies – will be allowed to give in to the sand's lure.

Overfishing

Fishing is one of Senegal's economic lifelines, a sector that today employs around 600,000 people but is facing severe problems. Still a sustainable industry until the mid-20th century, rapidly increasing demand for fish, both from within the country and for export, have caused the industry to grow and the balance to tip. Fish stocks have dwindled dramatically and the Senegalese Department of Maritime Fishing estimates that catch volumes have fallen by more than 50% between 1994 and 2005.

In light of emotional debates over trade agreements and illegal emigration (see the boxed text, below), this serious situation is often painted as an unfair fight between the EU trawlers and the small fishing pirogues of the Senegalese fishermen. Yes, there are a number of efficient industrial vessels that come here from the EU, as well as often undeclared Asian boats, but today, with EU trawlers in decline, more than 75% of the total amount of fish caught in a year (some estimates go much higher) is brought in by the humble, colourful pirogues of Senegal's so-called 'artisanal fishermen'. Their boats are small and their methods labour intensive, but a large number of minor operators can do a great deal of damage too, especially in the absence of regulations or their enforcement. Growing demand for fish both in Senegal and abroad have caused the number of fishermen to rise dramatically. Today around 15,000 pirogues are estimated to work along Senegal's 700km of coast.

The economic perils of this problem are huge and are widely debated among the Senegalese government, the UN, the EU and a string of NGOs. Entire communities around Dakar and Saint-Louis live off the sector and are struggling to sustain themselves as their local economies collapse. And the problem is not confined to Senegal – neighbouring countries fear civil unrest caused by the migration of Senegalese fishermen and the subsequent overexploitation of fishing stocks in coastal areas outside Senegal. In the context of those debates, the environmental dimension is almost treated as an afterthought. But the chain reaction caused by the disappearance of entire species (particularly precious bottom feeders) will eventually affect every aspect of life along the Senegalese coast.

Though a viable solution to this complex problem is not in sight, the Marine Protected Area in Bamboung (see the boxed text, p198) on the

Ever since Dakar's industrial zone discovered an easy way of dumping sewage – directly into the waters near the U-shaped Plage de Hann – the palm-fringed sands have turned into one of Senegal's big environmental catastrophes.

For a diving holiday with an eco-mission, contact Océanium (www .oceanium.org), based in Senegal, which knows fabulous diving spots in Senegal and does amazing work to protect them.

THE HUMAN FACE OF OVERFISHING

Amadou Ba sits in the tiny house he owns in the busy fishing village of Kayar; next to him his young wife feeds a tiny baby. 'When I tried to leave Senegal, my wife was pregnant', he says calmly, 'I didn't know how I'd feed a family. So I thought I'd try my luck abroad'. Amadou is one of hundreds of young men who have attempted to reach the Canary Islands by wooden pirogue from the Senegalese coast – a perilous journey of several days in a tiny boat beaten by the waves. Unlike others, Amadou made it there, barely alive, only to be repatriated on the next plane to Senegal.

It's a reckless undertaking of men without hope, ready to risk their lives to leave a desperate situation. Not all of the men attempting the crossing are fishermen or Senegalese, but many of the desperate emigrants have come from the fishing villages along the Senegalese coast. They face a particularly precarious economic situation, and, as they don't fear the ocean, many may find the idea of a long sea journey easier to conceive of than the thought of working in a sector other than fishing in Senegal.

RESPONSIBLE TRAVEL

As the world becomes more conscious of the huge environmental challenges we're all facing, responsible, eco- and sustainable tourism have grown increasingly fashionable. Fantastic – except that the soul-soothing terms occur today as buzz words in the most unlikely settings, confronting anyone keen to travel green with hard choices.

Does your village stay really support the local community or does it disrupt local structures? Is your eco-camp with views over the mangroves really there to sustain them or does their waste water spill directly into the river? Some travel companies may claim to be practising 'eco-tourism' just because they do things outdoors or talk about community support, when all they really offer is an 'exotic' tour to far-flung, traditional places.

It's tough to accept, but activities such as desert driving, and hiking, camping and boating trips to remote and fragile areas can be more environmentally or culturally harmful than a conventional holiday in a developed resort.

The GreenDex (see p319) can give you some guidance for putting together a low-impact, high-pleasure holiday. Below is an overview of a few things you can do (or refrain from doing) to render your vacation a little greener. Many of the small steps that make a difference don't even depend on your chosen hotel or way of travel – even if you stay in the biggest sun and sea resort in the area, you can work responsible thinking into your planning.

- Don't book an all-inclusive holiday. Instead check out locally owned restaurants, tour operators, shops and bars. You'll spread your dollar beyond the walls of your possibly foreign-owned hotel and contribute to the diversity of the local tourist industry.

- Don't give money, pens or sweets to kids in the street. Yes, they need pens for school, but children aren't supposed to ask elders or strangers for things. Your well-intentioned act contributes to forming a generation of 'beggars'. There's a simple question you can ask yourself: would I be happy if a stranger offered my child money in the street? Probably not. The same goes for the communities you're visiting. If you want to help, donate to a school or educational NGO.

- Spend money! Yes! Many people tend to think of eco-tourism as cheap travel with a backpack strapped to your shoulders. It doesn't have to be. A luxury three-course meal in a good restaurant can arguably do more for the local economy than a bush taxi trip with family stays.

Siné-Saloum Delta has achieved remarkable success in stock regeneration. As important as the environmental successes are the economic ones: at least some of the hard-up fishermen have found lucrative employment in alternative sectors, either as marine patrollers or in the sustainable tourism initiative built to finance the protected zone.

If you're considering purchasing a djembe *drum, think twice. The* dimb *tree used to manufacture this much-loved percussion instrument has almost become extinct in the region, due to the staggering increase in European demand for* djembes.

Deforestation

Away from the coast, deforestation is another major environmental issue faced by both Gambia and Senegal. Woodland is partly cleared to match a growing demand for farmland, but trees are also felled to make firewood and charcoal, much of which is used to smoke fish. On a larger scale, wooded areas are often diminished by bushfires to make room for cash crops, notably groundnuts (peanuts), to promote new growth for livestock, to control pests such as the tsetse fly, and to flush out wild animals for hunting.

The clearing of natural woodland has many disastrous effects. Besides leading to soil erosion and with it the reduction of cultivable areas, it means reduced water catchment and a decrease in the availability of traditional building materials, foodstuffs and medicines. Perhaps most visibly, forest destruction causes the disappearance of rare plants and the loss of vital habitats for many of the region's bird and animal species.

In Gambia, attempts at redressing this situation have been made by creating community forests. Rather than fencing off the forest and keeping the

■ Stay in community-run hotels or places that invest back in the village. These include the *campements villageois* in the Casamance and several privately owned camps that make an effort to train and invest locally. Our GreenDex includes some options.

■ Avoid eating young *thiof* (grouper), which frequently features on menus in Senegal and Gambia – you'll be contributing to the gradual extinction of the species if you eat little fishes that haven't had the chance to reproduce yet.

■ Try to pick an environmentally friendly hotel – the GreenDex gives you some examples.

■ Ask permission before photographing people. If they refuse, respect their wishes.

■ Respect religious and cultural habits. That also means dressing a little more conservatively (long skirts and trousers) in Muslim regions.

■ Don't participate in hunting activities organised by big hotels – despite their claims, many of them don't only go shooting in the legal zones.

■ Be economical in your use of water and electricity – although you won't necessarily feel the cuts in these resources if you're staying in a tourist zone, the local population will.

■ Don't buy a *djembe* drum as this will contribute to deforestation.

The following organisations can advise you on responsible travel:

Association of Small Scale Enterprises in Tourism (ASSET; www.asset-gambia.com; Timbooktoo Bookshop, Fajara) It's been awarded several Responsible Tourism Awards for its impressive work in support of local Gambian businesses.

Océanium (www.oceanium.org; Route de la Corniche-Est, Dakar) Does amazing work in furthering environmentally friendly tourism, including the establishment of Marine Protected Areas and the organisation of eco-diving courses.

Makasutu Wildlife Trust (☎ 7782633, 4473349; m.wildlifetrust@yahoo.co.uk; Abuko Nature Reserve, Gambia) Based at Abuko Reserve and close to Makasutu Culture Forest, it can inform you of its fantastic range of projects, including conservation work in collaboration with the Eden Project, UK, and the establishment of a community-run reserve.

locals out, the resident community reaps the benefits from helping to sustain the woodland. For example, dead wood can be used for timber and other products of the forest can also be utilised for cooking or the production of items. Villagers get employed as guides, taking visitors along eco-trails and on birdwatching trips, gaining an income from eco-tourism initiatives.

In Senegal, Océanium is running similar projects to restore the mangroves (see the boxed text, p250).

Birds

Gambia and Senegal are home to a hugely diverse range of birds, including many migrants that spend the European winter months here. The region is at an ecological crossroads between the rich fauna of equatorial Africa, the arid vastness of the Sahara, the bulk of continental Africa and the Atlantic coast. This important transition zone, especially vital for migratory birds, supports a mosaic of habitats in which some 660 species of birds have been recorded.

The bird diversity of Gambia reaches a concentration that seems out of all proportion to the tiny size of the country itself. More than 560 species have been recorded – just 80 fewer than in Senegal, which is almost 20 times larger – and the country's unique shape makes many good birdwatching sites easily accessible.

Thanks to a well-organised network of birdwatching tours and guides, Gambia in particular attracts large number of birdwatchers, particularly between November and February.

BIRD HABITATS

Many birds are found across wide areas, but the majority have feeding, breeding or other biological requirements that restrict them to one group of habitats. Following is a brief rundown of bird habitats in Gambia and Senegal.

Cities, Towns & Villages

Before you even leave your urban lodging for remote regions, you'll be able to see plenty of birds, even in the most built-up areas. The grey-headed sparrow is the main representative of this cosmopolitan group; the red-billed firefinch frequents grain stores and village compounds; and swifts, swallows and martins nest under the eaves of buildings. Many travellers have their first introduction to the region's birds on a hotel estate – the Senegambia Beach Hotel in Kololi (p107) has a well-deserved reputation for sheltering dozens of birds in its vast tropical garden. Look out for the gorgeous little cordon-bleu flitting among the vegetation, and for starlings and the brilliant yellow-crowned gonolek feeding on lawns; weavers make their presence felt in noisy colonies. The piapiac, a long-tailed member of the crow family, can also be seen around towns, and on any Dakar evening you'll see large numbers of kites crossing the skies in wide circles.

While there have as yet been no cases of avian flu in Gambia or Senegal, it has been much discussed, particularly as the region attracts huge numbers of migratory birds. Regular checks are now being conducted in some areas, most notably the Parc National des Oiseaux du Djoudj.

Ocean Shore & Estuaries

The coastlines of the region are rich habitats for creatures such as crustaceans and molluscs, attracting humans and animals alike to feast on them. Birds likely to be seen feeding in these habitats include waders such as oystercatchers and plovers, and the reef egret, which stalks fish and crabs.

The Gambia and Casamance Rivers both have extensive mangrove-lined estuaries. Historically they have been dismissed as 'swamps', but mangroves are now recognised as an important ecological resource. At low tide the fine mud floor is exposed and makes a rich feeding ground for migratory waders such as curlews, sandpipers, stints, godwits and plovers. Small birds such as sunbirds feed in the mangrove canopy, while larger water birds, such as ibises, herons, egrets and spoonbills, roost and nest among the larger stands.

Waterways

The major river systems of Gambia and Senegal – and the associated fringing forests, grasslands and swamps – support an astonishing variety of birds. Some hunt along the shoreline or probe the soft mud at the water's edge, whereas long-legged species stride into deeper water to seek prey. Some kingfishers dive from overhanging branches into the water, while warblers and flycatchers hunt insects in riverside vegetation. For the beginner and expert birdwatcher alike, freshwater habitats provide some of the best viewing opportunities.

Low-lying areas may flood after the rains to create extensive ephemeral swamps, which are often superb for birdwatching. Egrets, herons and other wading birds stalk the shallows; dainty African jacanas walk across floating vegetation on their bizarre long, splayed toes; and rails skulk in reed beds.

Savannah & Woodland

Large swaths of central and southeastern Senegal, plus adjoining parts of Gambia, are characterised by savannah vegetation dominated by a mixture of small trees. There can be rich pickings for birdwatchers in this habitat, from the perplexing cisticolas to huge birds of prey, plus weavers, finches, starlings, rollers and many more.

The southern part of the region once supported extensive woodland, and though most of this has now been cleared or modified by human activities, patches of it still remain near Pointe St George and in the Abuko Nature Reserve. A number of rare birds, such as the African pied hornbill, the grey-headed bristlebill and the little greenbul, are found only in these protected areas.

Arid Areas

The northern part of Senegal is sub-Saharan semidesert, a sparsely vegetated landscape that has been shaped by the low rainfall inherent in this area. This habitat is seldom visited by birdwatchers but supports a few interesting species, including wheatears, desert finches and migratory birds stopping on their way to or from the northern hemisphere.

THE BIRDS

The Senegal parrot is the most famous bird of the nation it is named after. It's known in French as *youyou* and scientifically as *Poicephalus senegalus*.

The following is a group-by-group description of some of the diverse birds visitors may see during a trip to Gambia or Senegal. This is not a comprehensive list – refer to one of the guides (p76) for further information. Many birds have been left out: for example, a peculiarly African group known as flufftails are so hard to spot as to be virtually invisible.

To look up the names of birds, with translations in several European languages, check http://avibase.bsc-eoc.org, a seemingly unlimited resource.

Barbets & Tinkerbirds

Barbets are closely related to woodpeckers but, rather than drilling into bark after grubs, they have strong, broad bills adapted to eating fruit and a variety of insect prey. Most of the region's seven species are found in Senegal. Barbets are often brightly coloured and perch in conspicuous locations. Tinkerbirds are a noisy but tiny variety of barbet, and are sometimes difficult to see.

Bee-Eaters & Rollers

One of the pleasures of birdwatching in Africa is that beautiful and spectacular species aren't always rare. The various bee-eaters are often brilliant and always watchable; eight members of this colourful family are found in the region. Bee-eaters are commonly seen perched on fences and branches – sometimes in mixed flocks – from which they pursue flying insects, particularly, as their name suggests, bees and wasps. They may congregate in the thousands – you won't quickly forget seeing a flock of stunning carmine bee-eaters.

MY BIRD BAPTISM *Katharina Lobeck Kane*

It takes us over one hot hour, and the help of four strong farmers, to free our 4WD from the muddy clutches of a rice field near Senegal's Pointe St George. Jean Goepp, coordinator at the environmental association Océanium, is itching to get going. 'I made an appointment that I want to keep', he says, and checks his watch. Around us, a fascinating landscape stretches into the distance. Tall bush grass and rice plants cover the ground, specked with rare *Parinari macrophylla* trees and spooky *Acacia albida*, whose bare branches look as though they're covered in ice. With whom did he set up a meeting, in this uninhabited land?

Jean races along an overgrown path, and suddenly slams on the brakes. 'Look to your left. Your nine o'clock appointment, ma'am.' A small northern red bishop proudly shows off its crimson plumage against the bright green of the bush. 'He's always here. Every time I drive here in the morning, he sits there.'

The startlingly red bird doesn't only look like a royal guard; he turns out to be the gatekeeper to a fascinating world that has me wildly wielding binoculars, excited with each new discovery. Abyssinian rollers, Western grey plantain eaters and African goshawks accompany our journey, and a rare sandgrouse flutters up as we approach.

A few metres on, the landscape changes suddenly, as we approach the Forêt de Kanoufa, a band of woodland whose shade houses entirely different species. The lamenting call of a wattle-eye greets us as we climb a tall viewing platform that grants magnificent views across the forest and surrounding lands. Jean laughs at my futile efforts at searching for the little bird with the mighty voice. 'Give up,' he says, 'this one is a teaser. He's an amazing singer, but unremarkable to look at. You'll never find him'. I don't. But I'm determined. And as long as I haven't caught a glimpse of the songbird, I've always got a reason to come back to this magical corner, tucked away between the Casamance River and the bush.

Rollers are closely related to bee-eaters but are not as gaudy, decked out usually in blues and mauves. The Abyssinian roller sports two long tail feathers. Most of the five species are common to the region.

Birds of Prey

Hawks, eagles, vultures and falcons number more than 50 species in the region. Their presence is almost ubiquitous and travellers will soon notice a few types, from soaring flocks of scavenging vultures to the stately bateleur eagle watching for prey. Several have specialised prey or habitat requirements. The osprey and striking African fish-eagle, for instance, feed almost exclusively on fish.

Cisticolas

These drab little warblers are common and widespread but sometimes difficult to see and even harder to identify. Many are so similar that they are most easily separated by their calls, a characteristic that has led to common names such as singing, croaking, siffling and zitting cisticolas. Many of the region's 12 species are typically found in long grass and riverside vegetation.

Cranes

These graceful birds resemble storks and herons but are typically grassland dwellers. The one species found in the region – the black-crowned crane – is eccentrically adorned with a colourful crest.

Finches, Weavers & Widows

This large group includes many small but colourful examples. They are readily seen in flocks along Gambian and Senegalese roads and wherever long grass is found in the region. All are seed eaters, and while some, such as the various sparrows, are not spectacular, others develop showy courtship plumage and tail plumes of extraordinary size. A finch typical of the region is the crimson-coloured red-billed firefinch.

Weavers are usually yellow with varying amounts of black in their plumage. A weaver-inhabited tree, full of tiny nests that tremble with the permanent flitting in and out of the noisy birds, is a spectacular sight. The village weaver often forms big nesting colonies right in the centre of towns.

Widows, like sparrows, typically come in shades of brown and grey when not breeding, but males moult to reveal black plumage with red or yellow highlights when courting. The whydah, a type of weaver, develops striking tail plumes during courtship; the enormous tail of the exclamatory paradise whydah can be more than twice the bird's body length.

Honeyguides

Displaying some of the most remarkable behaviours of any bird, honeyguides seek out the help of mammals such as the ratel (aka honey badger), or even humans, in order to 'guide' them to a beehive. Once it has attracted the attention of a 'helper', a honeyguide flies a short way ahead then waits to see if it is being followed. In this way it leads the helper to the hive (and its next meal), which the obliging creature breaks open and robs, while the honeyguide feeds on wax and bees' larvae and eggs.

Hornbills

Found in forests and woodland, hornbills are medium-sized birds that sport massive, down-curved bills. The African grey and red-billed hornbills are reasonably common. The rarer black Abyssinian ground hornbill is an extraordinary bird that stands about 1m high. It rarely flies, instead moving about in small groups along the ground.

Kingfishers

Colourful and active, the nine species of kingfishers found in Gambia and Senegal can be divided into two groups: those that typically dive into water after fish and tadpoles (and as a consequence are found along waterways), and those less dependent on water because they generally prey on lizards and large insects.

Among those that dive into water, the giant kingfisher reaches 46cm in size, while the jewel-like malachite kingfisher is a mere 14cm. Forest-dwelling kingfishers are generally less colourful than their water-diving relatives. The blue-breasted kingfisher, however, is a boldly patterned example.

Mention should also be made here of the hoopoe (related to the kingfisher), a black-and-white bird with a salmon-pink head and neck and a prominent crest.

Nightjars

These small birds are a nocturnal group, unrelated to owls. Their plumage is soft and their flight silent. Nightjars roost on the ground by day, their subtle colouration making a perfect camouflage among the leaves and twigs. At dusk they take flight and catch insects. Although they are not uncommon, you may be oblivious to their presence until one takes off near your feet. The identification of several species is difficult and often relies on their call, but when spotted during the day nightjars typically perch on a nearby branch, allowing a closer look. The standard-winged nightjar is the region's most spectacular example; with two feathers unadorned except at the ends, the bird seems to be flying flags to herald its flight.

Few nature films have images of birds in flight as stunning as Jaques Perrin's acclaimed *Winged Migration* (2001). It features a long extract about pelicans and other migratory birds, filmed in Senegal's Parc National des Oiseaux du Djoudj.

Owls

These nocturnal birds of prey have soft feathers (which make their flight inaudible) and exceptional hearing, and can turn their heads in a 180-degree arc to locate their prey. Owls have inspired fear and superstition in many cultures, but their elusiveness makes them eagerly sought after by birdwatchers. There are 12 species in the region, ranging from the diminutive scops owl to the massive eagle owl, which measures up to 65cm in length. Their prey varies according to the species, with insects, mice and lizards eaten by the smaller species, and roosting birds and small mammals favoured by others. Pel's fishing owl hunts along rivers and feeds exclusively on fish.

Pigeons & Doves

Familiar to city and country dwellers alike, members of this family have managed to adapt to virtually every habitat. For example, the various turtledoves and the tiny Namaqua dove feed on the ground, while the African green pigeon leads a nomadic life following the seasonal fruiting of trees. Two of the dove species, the cosmopolitan rock dove and the laughing dove, are common inhabitants of gardens and human settlements.

'Gambia and Senegal are home to a hugely diverse range of birds, including many migrants that spend the European winter months here.'

Sea Birds

Into this broad category can be grouped a number of bird families that hunt over the open sea. They include the various petrels and shearwaters, which usually live far out to sea and return to land only to breed; beautiful gannets, which plunge into the sea from a great height to feed on fish; and fish-eating cormorants (shags), which also live in brackish and freshwater habitats.

Starlings

Africa is the stronghold of these gregarious and intelligent birds, and there are 11 species found in Gambia and Senegal. Several species of the so-called glossy starlings, including purple, long-tailed and blue-eared varieties, may be seen in fast-flying, noisy flocks around the region. All are magnificent birds in iridescent blues and purples, although they may prove an identification challenge when they occur in mixed flocks. The yellow-billed oxpecker is another member of this family and can be seen clinging to livestock, from which it prises parasitic ticks and insects.

Sunbirds

Sunbirds are small, delicate nectar feeders with sharp down-curved bills. The males of most species are brilliantly iridescent, while the females are more drab. Spectacular species include the pygmy sunbird, whose slender tail plumes are almost double its 9cm length, the copper sunbird and the violet-backed sunbird.

Swifts & Swallows

Although unrelated, these two groups are superficially similar and can be seen chasing flying insects just about anywhere. Both groups have long wings and streamlined bodies adapted to life in the air; both fly with grace and agility after insects; and both are usually dark in colouration. Swallows, however, differ in one major aspect: they can perch on twigs, fences or even the ground, while swifts have weak legs and rarely land except at the nest. In fact, swifts are so adapted to life in the air that some are even known to roost on the wing. There are many examples of the swallow family in Gambia and Senegal; two often seen around towns and villages are the red-rumped and mosque swallows.

Turacos

These often beautifully coloured, medium-sized forest birds can be difficult to see because they tend to remain hidden in the canopy, but three species (the violet turaco, green turaco and western grey plantain-eater) are common in the region. The violet turaco is a stunning bird, although you may only be lucky enough to catch a tantalising view when it flies across a clearing, showing its deep-violet wing patches.

Waders

Resident waders include the odd dikkop and the boldly marked lapwings – lanky, nocturnal species with grey spotted wings and weird wailing cries.

LONG-LEGGED WADERS

Virtually any waterway will have its complement of herons, egrets, storks, spoonbills and ibises. All have long legs and necks, and bills adapted to specific feeding strategies: herons and egrets have daggerlike bills for spearing fish and frogs; spoonbills have peculiar, flattened bills that they swish from side to side in the water to gather small creatures; ibises have long bills, curved down to probe in soft earth and seize insects; and storks have large, powerful beaks to snap up small animals and fish. Members of this group range from the tiny, secretive bittern to the enormous goliath heron, which stands 1.4m tall, and the ugly marabou stork, which feeds, along with vultures, on carrion. An unusual member of this group is the little hamerkop (aka hammerhead), which makes an enormous nest of twigs and grass.

'The Senegal parrot is the most famous bird of the nation it is named after.'

MIGRATORY WADERS

Every year migrating shore birds leave their breeding grounds in the northern hemisphere and fly to their wintering spots south of the Sahara. Generally nondescript in their winter plumage, these migratory waders provide an identification challenge for the keen birdwatcher. They're usually found near waterways, feeding along the shore on small creatures or probing intertidal mud for worms. The migrants include the long-distance champions, sandpipers and plovers.

Waterfowl

As their collective name suggests, this large group is found almost exclusively around waterways, and includes the familiar ducks and geese. Waterfowl are strong flyers and can travel vast distances in response to rainfall. The increased availability of food after the rains means they may be more easily seen at this time. In particular, the large, black-and-white spur-winged goose is often abundant at such times. Despite the significance of water as a habitat in Senegal and Gambia, there are comparatively few species of ducks and geese in the region.

WHERE TO LOOK

You will encounter birds virtually everywhere on your travels, although weather and temperature can affect bird activity. Both Gambia and Senegal have a number of reserves set up for the protection of wildlife and habitat, and these are good places to concentrate your birdwatching efforts, although some nonprotected areas can also be rewarding. Following is a brief rundown of popular sites; for more details see the relevant destinations in this book.

In Gambia, Abuko Nature Reserve (p122) is closest to Banjul and hosts a surprising diversity within its 105 hectares. Many forest species are easier to see here than in other parts of the country and conveniently located observation hides have been set up. Tanji River Bird Reserve (p116), on the coast, protects a patchwork of habitat on the flyway for migrating birds. More than 300 species have been recorded in the park's 612 hectares. Kiang West National Park (p135) is one of the country's largest protected areas and a good spot to see a variety of wildlife, including birds. The adjacent Baobolong Wetland Reserve (p134) is also very rewarding. Other recommended areas include Niumi National Park (p128), an extension of the Parc National du Delta du Saloum in neighbouring Senegal, and Bijilo Forest Park (p99), which is easy to reach from the Atlantic coast resorts.

Senegal has six national parks, as well as several other areas set aside as reserves to protect wildlife. Near the mouth of the Senegal River in the north of the country are the Parc National de la Langue de Barbarie (p220) and Parc National des Oiseaux du Djoudj (p221) – both superb sites famous for flocks of pelicans and flamingos. Djoudj is also a Unesco World Heritage Site, where some 350 bird species have been recorded. In the southeast, the vast Parc National de Niokolo-Koba (p230) protects more than 9000 sq km of savannah and associated habitats; about 350 bird species have been recorded here. Near Dakar, the Îles de la Madeleine (p179) are tiny volcanic islands inhabited by red-billed tropic birds, great cormorants, bridled terns and other varieties, while the small reserves of Popenguine (p186) and La Somone (p187) are home to many woodland and water-dwelling species. Absolutely worth exploring are the beautiful Siné-Saloum Delta (p193), an accessible area of coastal lagoons, mangroves, sandy islands and dry woodland, and the delta of the Casamance River, which boasts the Sanctuaire Ornithologique de la Pointe de Kalissaye and the highly rated Sanctuaire Ornithologique de Kassel (see the boxed text, p254). Both deltas are easily reached from Gambia.

> Hotels offer some of the best bird sightings in Gambia. The Senegambia Beach Hotel in Kololi, the Footsteps Eco Lodge in Gunjur and the Marakissa River Camp in Marakissa are just three lodgings where large varieties of species are regularly spotted.

RESOURCES
Books
Gambia's popularity as a birdwatching destination has inspired a number of illustrated books and other publications. *A Field Guide to the Birds of The Gambia & Senegal,* by leading ornithologists Clive Barlow and Tim Wacher, with illustrations by award-winning artist Tony Disley, is undeniably the best. It lists more than 660 species (illustrating 570), with colour plates, detailed descriptions and in-depth background information. This 400-page hardback is no featherweight, but it's as essential as a pair of binoculars for any serious birdwatcher. It is usually also available from Timbooktoo bookstore (p98) in Fajara, Gambia.

More portable is *Birds of The Gambia,* by M Gore, an annotated checklist with extra information on habitat, distribution and vegetation, illustrated with photographs. It can be hard to find, though.

Another useful guide is *A Birdwatchers' Guide to The Gambia,* by Rod Ward, a finely researched book concentrating on birdwatching sites and likely sightings, rather than detailed species descriptions. It includes 28 maps.

A Field Guide to the Birds of West Africa, by W Serle and GJ Morel, is part of the long-running Collins field-guide series, though with a broader ambit than is usual for this series.

For more detailed information – plus excellent illustrations – on all African birds, refer to the six-volume *The Birds of Africa,* by EK Urban, CH Fry and S Keith, or try *Birds of Western Africa,* by Nik Borrow and Ron Demey, a 784-page monster that was released in 2002.

Websites
The internet is a rich resource of information on birds, with databases of birds and their geographic distribution, tour-booking sites, trip reports and forums.

BIRDWATCHING TIPS

A pair of binoculars will reveal subtleties of form and plumage not usually detected by the naked eye, allowing you to nut out the subtle differences between species. Be warned, though – once you've seen the shimmering iridescence of a glossy starling or the brash hues of a bee-eater through binoculars you may get hooked!

Basic binoculars can be purchased quite cheaply from duty-free outlets. If you like to keep baggage weight down, look for a light and compact model – some of them are very good. If you're serious about your birds, though, consider investing in better-quality optics; expensive brands such as Leica, Zeiss and Swarovski should last a lifetime and offer unrivalled quality.

A spotting scope gives stunning views with a magnification at least twice that of binoculars. They're huge, though, and usually need to be mounted on a tripod. Some models can be attached to a camera and double as a telephoto lens.

To help you get the most out of birdwatching, bear the following in mind:

- Try to get an early start, as most birds are generally active during the cooler hours of the day. This is particularly so in arid regions and during hot weather.

- Many species are quite approachable and will allow observation and photography if you approach slowly and avoid sudden movements or loud noises.

- If you're on foot, try to dress in drab clothing so as not to stand out. Birds are not usually too concerned about people in a vehicle or boat, and stunning views can often be obtained from the roadside. Cruises on rivers and through mangroves are rewarding and great fun.

- Water birds and waders respond to tidal movements. As the tide goes out, more food is available and larger flocks are attracted, but the birds are spread out; as the tide comes in the birds may be 'pushed' closer to your observation position.

- Do not disturb birds unnecessarily and never handle eggs or young birds in a nest. Adults will readily desert a nest that has been visited, leaving their young to perish.

- Remember that weather and wind can adversely affect viewing conditions and you should not expect to see everything at your first attempt.

African Bird Club (www.africanbirdclub.org) Set up by a charity aimed at the conservation of bird habitats, this site has features on both Gambia and Senegal, and regular bulletins and updates.
Birdlife International (www.birdlife.org) This site of a global collective of conservation societies has detailed pages listing species you're likely to see in particular habitats of Senegal and Gambia.
Birds of the Gambia (www.birdsofthegambia.com) Home page of ornithologist Clive Barlow, with a virtual birdwatching tour; you can also book trips to Gambia.
West African Ornithological Society (http://malimbus.free.fr) Not for the hobby ornithologist, this site contains specialised articles and reference materials on birds in West Africa.

Birdwatching Guides

Gambia has a well-developed network of professional birdwatching guides, as well as tour operators that specialise in birdwatching excursions. Use this fabulous resource. Trained local guides know the region well, and know how to find exciting spots even for knowledgeable ornithologists.

Unfortunately, there is no equivalent set-up in Senegal, where even the rangers in some of the main national parks aren't always very knowledgeable about birds. The Siné-Saloum and Casamance regions of Senegal are in close proximity to Gambia, and easily visited on a tour from there in the company of your Gambian guide. Many offer combined trips to those areas as well as in Gambia. Gambia Experience (p288), via its Senegalese branch Senegal Experience, also organises trips to the Siné-Saloum area, particularly to Toubakouta and Palmarin.

To contact good birdwatching guides in Gambia, try the following.

African Bird Club (www.africanbirdclub.org) This excellent online resource contains an almost exhaustive list of guides, including recommendations from travellers who have worked with some of them.

Bird Safari Camp (☎ 5676108; www.bsc.gm; Janjangbureh) This camp in Janjangbureh is one of many good birdwatching sites, sitting between a forest and the river. It also organises trips upriver through Hidden Gambia (www.hiddengambia.com), which allow you to explore habitats including wetlands and forest. Guides usually come through Habitat.

Habitat (☎ Solomon Jallow 9921551, 9907694, 4472208; habitatafrica@hotmail.com) Solomon Jallow is the name any search for good bird tours and guides leads to. His highly recommended network of guides can put together itineraries and organise transport and accommodation.

West African Bird Study Association (Wabsa; Abuko Nature Reserve; Lamin Jobarteh ☎ 7776821; laminjobarteh2002@yahoo.co.uk; Solomon Jallow ☎ 9921551, 9907694, 4472208; habitatafrica@hotmail.com) Gambia's main birdwatching association works towards the advancement of bird study and environmental protection and counts many good guides among its members.

Food & Drink

Two words summarise the basis of Senegalese and Gambian cuisine: rice and sauce. Sound boring? Spend a week tasting the myriad flavours that can inspire a rich, stomach-filling rice dish and you're bound to change your mind. Those with a taste for delicacies should put up camp near the mangrove-adorned embouchures of the Gambia, Saloum or Casamance Rivers, where an ordinary day can quickly turn into a luxurious affair with a breakfast of freshly shucked oysters.

STAPLES & SPECIALITIES

Breakfast local style is a steaming cup of milky instant coffee accompanied by French bread and butter. If you're from a part of the world where breakfast is a big deal or good coffee is essential to staying alive, this may not bode well. But worry not: the French legacy has left the Senegalese with a taste for croissants and pastries, easily satisfied at any of Dakar's refined patisseries.

Lunch usually consists of generous rice dishes, and dinner sometimes too, though urban households often prepare lighter meals, such as salads or sandwiches for dinner. The queen of all local dishes is *thiéboudienne* (spelt in myriad different ways and pronounced chey-bou-jen), in Gambia called *benachin*. *Thiéboudienne* literally means fish and rice but is so much more than that. A platter of this delicious meal is quite a sight – chunks of fish stuffed with a parsley-garlic paste, carrots, cassava and other vegetables are served carefully arranged on a bed of red rice, which owes its colour to the tomato sauce it's cooked in. The festive version of this national dish is *thiébouyape* (also called *riz yollof*), where fish is replaced by meat.

Another favourite is *yassa poulet* – grilled chicken marinated in a thick onion-and-lemon sauce – which features on many a restaurant menu. Occasionally chicken is replaced by fish or meat, in which case it's called *yassa poisson* (fish) or *yassa bœuf* (beef).

In either country, if you're in the mood for something rich, ask for some *mafé* or *domodah* – you'll be served a platter of rice covered with a thick, smooth groundnut (peanut) sauce with fried meat and vegetables.

At the house of a Fula or Tukulor family, chances are you'll be presented with a delicious plate of steamed millet couscous, either prepared with a vegetable sauce *(haako)* or meat. Couscous served cold with sour or fresh milk *(lacciri e kosan)* is the archetypal food of the Fula – and a delicacy at that.

The creators of the food and travel blog www.culinaryanthropologist.org have done an amazing amount of tasting and savouring. Check their recommendations (and warnings).

TRAVEL YOUR TASTEBUDS

You've been in the region for a while? A simple *thiéboudienne* (fish and rice dish) must be far too ordinary by now. Put your taste buds to the test with a plate of *soupoukandia* – a slippery stew of okra and vegetables – that's definitely not for the faint hearted. If the flavour is too strong, you can always drown it in homemade chilli sauce, an obligatory addition to every Senegalese meal.

Or try a scoop of the creamy Jamaican sorrel (roselle hibiscus) sauce *bissap* (not to be confused with the juice of the same name), a delicacy dotted over a festive plate of *thiéboudienne*. This humble accompaniment tastes sweet, sour, spicy and fresh all at the same time and, once you've learnt the secret of its preparation, your home cooking will never taste the same again.

If dairy products are your thing, you'll love *chakri* (a sugary millet mix covered with rich, sweet yoghurt) and *lait caillé* (sweetened sour milk). For really fresh flavours, visit the Fula regions, where cattle-herding families prepare the creamiest milk products of all.

CONSUMING LOCALLY

Even though the vast majority of people in Senegal and Gambia work in agriculture, most basic foods are imported, including 80% of all rice, the base of most local dishes. Even local-style dairy products are mainly made from imported powdered milk – with one major exception: those of the Senegalese Laiterie de Berger. Created by Baba Bathily in 2005, this small enterprise works with over 600 cattle herders in the region of Richard Toll (p223), where the dairy is based. Every day trucks travel to distant villages to collect milk under European standards of hygiene – a huge undertaking considering that local cows only tend to produce 1L per animal per day. The milk is then checked, filtered, pasteurised and packed, with some used to produce yoghurts and other dairy products, before being distributed to all corners of Senegal on bumpy roads and tracks. The profit margins for the *laiterie* are tiny – the benefits for rural economies and consumers' health, however, are enormous. When Baba bravely set up his company, many dismissed his efforts as idealistic. But today, as the price hikes of imported produce cause economic instability and civil unrest and scares of poisonous milk powder rock the media, his small efforts to strengthen local economies and improve local consumption suddenly shine like the work of a visionary.

You can purchase the fresh products of the Laiterie de Berger in any of Senegal's supermarkets.

Main ingredients for a good, spicy sauce vary from one region to the next. Along the coast, fish tends to be the preferred base, while meat is more common inland (for those who can afford it). Every housewife's favourite fish is the *thiof*, a type of grouper. Also common are barracuda, monkfish *(lotte)*, sole, Nile perch and swordfish *(espadon)*. Prawns, crabs, oysters, lobster and other seafood are also found in local markets. They're rarely cooked in family homes but are staple ingredients in dishes in most of the better restaurants. Lamb and beef are the most commonly prepared meats. As most people are Muslim, pork isn't widely consumed, though in the Casamance, where a large percentage of Christians live, you'll find the occasional place selling pork skewers or steaks.

DRINKS
Nonalcoholic Drinks

Even the tiniest, most remote, barely inhabited hamlet has a red-and-white-painted stall selling Coca Cola. But if you want a taste of something else, try some of the rich and creamy local juices – they may not be any less sugary, but they have a few vitamins and surprise with great flavours.

The most ubiquitous drink is the deep-purple *bissap*, made from hibiscus, sugar and water. Zingy ginger juice (*gingembre* in French) is often strong enough to make you wince and is perfect for any time of day: it's considered a wake-up boost worthy of a couple of press-ups, as well as an aphrodisiac (particularly if enhanced with extra spices). Then there's *bouyi*, a thick, sugary drink made from the fruit of the baobab tree, and the creamy soursop juice *corosol*, both particularly good for making ice cream. *Ditakh,* finally, is a smooth, bright green mix that looks very healthy, tastes divine and is fibrous enough to replace a small sandwich.

In the hot-drinks department, instant coffee (usually Nescafé) rules the game – just check out the number of two-wheeled Nescafé trolleys that mingle with local traffic. Better restaurants also serve real (ie espresso) coffee. Worth trying is the Senegalese *café touba*, a spicy brew served in small cups at roadside stalls and by wandering sellers.

Local teas include the sweetly flavoured *kinkiliba*, brewed from the leaves of the eponymous shrub *(Combretum micranthum)* and said to have medicinal and detoxifying properties. For a real caffeine punch, try a glass of *ataaya* (see p84), usually served with the free offer of an afternoon's socialising.

There's no end to the commercial ventures of Senegal's superstar musician Youssou N'Dour. In 2004 he coauthored the cookery book *La Cuisine de ma Mère,* containing recipes for some of Senegal's most popular dishes.

As the quality of tap water varies, it's best to rely on mineral water. This also means avoiding ice cubes in drinks – one of the most frequent sources of tummy bugs. Definitely steer clear of the tap in Senegal's Siné-Saloum region. The water here has a dangerously high fluoride content that discolours teeth and causes health complications.

Alcoholic Drinks

Though Gambia and Senegal are Muslim regions, beer is widely available and is consumed in bars and restaurants. The main Senegalese brands are the watery Gazelle and the stronger Flag. In Gambia, JulBrew is the local label. Good wine is available from supermarkets (especially in Senegal), but is expensive.

As for liqueurs, flashy city bars boast anything from a potent G&T to sophisticated cocktails and in every village you'll find a small drinking hole serving whisky or gin behind stained plastic curtains. Drinking is mainly a bar activity: few people drink at home, no one takes a secret sip in the street and open displays of drunkenness are very much frowned upon. Remember, you're in a predominantly Muslim region and, though many Muslims do drink, they tend to do it in a discreet fashion – just check the speed with which the beer bottles vanish as soon as the club photographer makes the rounds. Drinking yourself into a stupor is not a way to gain 'cool' points in this part of the world.

Palm wine (see below) is popular in the villages of Gambia and Casamance. If you're not used to it, it might give you a runny tummy, but it's pretty safe to savour, unlike its potent cousin *kana* or the cashew-liqueur *soumsoum* – both are high-percentage, unpredictable brews and are not always produced under clean, controlled conditions.

> Ever tried sweet passionfruit liqueur or a dose of high-percentage coconut and lime? Kim Kombo (p102) in Gambia and Liqueur de Warang (p191) in Senegal produce top-quality, locally distilled liqueurs – and have tasting sessions!

CELEBRATIONS

As elsewhere in the world, food is the real centre of many celebrations (and possibly the most persuasive reason for attending). Weddings, naming ceremonies and other family events are always as opulent here as the bank manager will allow. This is when the whole extended family unites and there'll be enough food to feed a couple of neighbouring streets. At a medium-size wedding, the food budget can easily reach US$2000 – a lot considering basic foodstuffs aren't all that expensive in these countries. The meals served are

---

COLLECTING PALM WINE

As you travel along the back roads of Gambia and southern Senegal, you'll almost certainly see men perched precariously on palm trees, collecting the plant's precious sap. Frothy, white palm wine is a much-loved drink that gets sold by the canister. The strong, yeasty flavour takes some getting used to, but once you've learnt to appreciate it, it's a sure gateway to a few hilarious village moments.

It's impressive to watch the liquid being collected. Men skilfully climb up tall palms with the help of a simple loop of handmade rope (called a *kandab* in Diola) that fits around them and the tree, holding them close to the trunk. Just below the point where the palm fronds sprout from the tree, the collector punches a hole through the soft bark until he reaches the sap. The liquid drips slowly through a funnel into a bottle or – the traditional-style – a natural gourd. At the end of the day, the collector comes back to pick up the container, now filled with thick, white sap. Almost free of alcohol when freshly tapped, the wine gets stronger by the day as it ferments.

To savour the brew, ask around in the villages of Gambia or Casamance and you might get taken to the local seller, who often presides over a shack filled with canisters of wine in various stages of fermentation. A bottle won't cost you more than a few dalasi or CFA.

more refined versions of the usual staples, with the addition of extra meat, a more expensive sauce or any other way to make a difference.

During naming ceremonies in Senegal, *lakh* or *ngalakh,* a delicious millet porridge served with sweet yoghurt or baobab cream, is typically served in large bowls – taste it and you'll understand why people don't miss these parties.

Small fried doughnuts, usually given to guests in small plastic bags, are also obligatory at naming ceremonies and weddings.

For most celebrations, some animal has to give up its life – a sheep in most cases or a cow if the family is really big or immensely wealthy. At Tabaski (see p47) sheep are slaughtered in the homes of all Muslim families. Days before the feast rams as big as calves line all major roads, only an eerie quiet and a few sheep droppings remain after the big day.

Gambia Is Good supports over 1000 local farmers, 90% of whom are women, in selling their produce to restaurants, hotels and shops. Visit its farmyard and check out the goods (see p126). For more information see www.concern-universal .org.

WHERE TO EAT & DRINK

Dakar and the urban zones along Gambia's Atlantic coast are blessed with an excellent restaurant scene. You'll find sophisticated local and international cuisine, beach restaurants with sunbeds and luxury venues with spectacular food, and sometimes even excellent service.

If you're on a budget, hunt out the tiny local eateries, called 'chop shops' in Gambia and *gargottes* in Senegal. Many are nameless but easily spotted: look out for vinyl-cloth-covered tables on the roadside, surrounded by rickety benches. That's your place. There's no menu – it's rice with a daily changing sauce. *Tanganas* (literally meaning 'hot stuff') look the same and usually serve deep-fried omelettes squeezed into French bread that you'll wash down with instant coffee, sweetened with large doses of condensed milk. A *dibiterie* in Senegal or *afra* in Gambia is a grilled-meat stall (open from evening until early morning); it's the place people head to before a night out on the town or when returning home after dancing the night away. And if you've partied Dakar-style, you'll only be ready to leave the nightclub at breakfast time, in which case you do what the locals do and head straight for one of the patisseries.

The *thiof* (grouper), Senegal's best-loved fish, is so appreciated that Senegalese women refer to a good-looking (or tasty?) young man as *thiof* (or *super thiof,* but only if they're being served top quality…).

Quick Eats

For food on the go, the trusted hamburger will be a good travel companion, though the more popular alternative is the Lebanese *shwarma,* a kebab-style sandwich made from thin, grilled slices of lamb or chicken wrapped in thin bread. They are sold at busy fast-food stops. Sandwiches tend to be intimidating affairs, with fries, meat, mayonnaise and forlorn salad leaves all squeezed into a stick of French bread.

EATERIES

Here are some useful words to know when you're hungry. Terms marked 'G' or 'S' are used only in Gambia or Senegal respectively.

Afra (G) Grilled-meat stall; grilled meat.

Boulangerie A bakery that only sells bread (usually French bread).

Chop (G) Meal, usually local style.

Chop shop (G) Basic local-style eating house or restaurant.

Dibiterie (S) Grilled-meat stall.

Patisserie A bakery selling bread, croissants and cakes.

Salon de thé (S) Tea shop.

Tangana A roadside cafe serving hot drinks and snacks.

Terminus A popular place to eat and mingle after a night out, usually a *dibiterie* or a *patisserie.*

LE MENU

In Senegal's smarter restaurants, the *menu du jour* (often shortened to *le menu*) is the meal of the day – usually comprising a starter, a main course and a dessert – at a set price. If you want to see the menu (ie the list of dishes available), ask for *la carte* instead. This may include the *plat du jour* (dish of the day), usually at a special price too. It is often a good idea to go for *le menu* or *plat du jour* – any other choice may take much longer to prepare and be more expensive.

Selling food on the street is a way for many local women to add to the household income, hence the number of informal stalls near bus stops and markets. They usually sell roast peanuts or *brochettes* (skewered meat or fish), grilled fish, fried plantain – even plates of rice and sauce – and get busy over lunchtime and in the evenings. Leave any nightclub and there'll be a street stall outside, tempting you with something hot and grilled.

If you want to consume your street food sitting down, try a *tangana* or *gargotte*, and join the traders, drivers and other working folk on their break.

These roadside places charge only a handful of dalasi or CFA francs and, while eating there can save money, it's also the quickest way of catching a stomach bug. The interior of a place can tell you a lot about its attitude to hygiene – ramshackle doesn't mean bad quality, but leftovers that haven't been cleaned up, dirty tablecloths and, well, stray cockroaches definitely do.

The unique culture of Saint-Louis' glamorous *signare* ladies includes the brewing of their own liqueur (Marquise). It's made from a white-wine base, gently spiced with orange. Try it at Saint-Louis' hotel La Résidence.

VEGETARIANS & VEGANS

For vegetarians, this region will be a challenge. If you eat fish and seafood, you'll be fine, but prepare for hard times if you follow a strict vegetarian or vegan diet. Few restaurants serve vegie food, let alone a choice of dishes, and there's little understanding as to why someone who can afford meat won't eat it – vegetables are for the poor. When you order a dish without meat, you might therefore find that you still get the meat sauce poured over your rice, just without the chunks.

The easiest way to get your message across is to say you have an allergy or that your beliefs don't allow you to touch meat. Still, prepare for a rather limited variety of food choices during your stay.

Vegie fabulous are the spicy cooked beans served on street corners (especially in Gambia). They're called *niebe* and are made from a blend of soft black beans, tomatoes, onion and spices. The whole lot is wrapped in a large chunk of French bread and sprinkled with hot sauce.

Throughout the book, restaurants that offer a good selection of vegetarian foods, or are happy to prepare you a delicious nonmeat meal on request, have been labelled with a big, proud Ⓥ.

For an exhaustive report on Senegalese cuisine, complete with recipes and links to Dakar's restaurants, go to www .au-senegal.com (English version), click on 'Noon and Evening' and then on 'Cooking'.

HABITS & CUSTOMS

If you get invited to share a meal with a local family, there are a few customs to observe. Traditionally, meals are served on huge platters placed on mats on the floor. You'll be pointed to your place (in some families men, women and children eat apart), expected to take off your shoes (even if nothing is said) and probably be given a spoon. Whether you use a spoon or try the hand, make sure you use the right and only the right hand – the left is strictly reserved for personal hygiene.

Eating with your fingers means learning the skill of forming small balls of rice and sauce, then placing them elegantly in your mouth. It also means washing your hands before you dig in – there's usually a plastic bowl and kettle available for that.

Are you the sweet or spicy type? Find your personal chilli flavour at the Pimenterie de Saint-Louis. It blends locally grown chillies with imaginative ingredients, including sweet *bissap* juice. More info can be found at www.pimentissimo.com.

TEA TIME

From midafternoon to midnight, you see them everywhere in Senegal – groups of boys and men, sometimes joined by women, grouped around a tiny, chipped enamel kettle, a steaming stove and a tray holding a few tiny glasses. They're brewing *ataaya*, West Africa's classic pick-me-up. This is a punchy, bittersweet brew made from fistfuls of green tea leaves and a generous amount of sugar. While its high caffeine content does help you to stay awake in the suffocating midday heat, brewing *ataaya* is really about whiling away a hot afternoon people watching, about meeting old friends and making new ones, and about gossip, stories, jokes and football matches.

Brewing *ataaya* is a social ritual that follows a precise set of tiny, immutable laws that are repeated precisely all across the Sahel region. The main rule: making tea shall never be rushed. The leaves are left to infuse with a little water and plenty of sugar for hours. The tea maker in charge has to watch the kettle and take it off the heat when the lid starts rattling; the first infusion is usually ready after an hour or so. He blends the concoction by pouring it into the glasses from an impressive height to create the perfect froth, then back into the kettle and finally back into the glasses, which are now heated and covered in sweet froth.

The first infusion is a pungent wake-up call, usually offered to the men who dare; the second one is strong, sugary perfection; the third is 'sweet as love' (as the locals would have it). You down your hot tea as fast as your throat permits; the tea maker will be waiting to collect the glass so it can be rinsed, refilled and passed to the next in line.

As an honoured guest you might be passed chunks of meat by the head of the household. It's polite to finish eating while there's still food in the bowl. The shocked comments of 'You haven't eaten anything; dig in' are more an acceptance of your finishing, rather than an invitation to eat more. The same goes for invitations to eat whenever you pass someone about to take a meal – it's polite to invite, but you're not always expected to take it up.

EAT YOUR WORDS

For English speakers, dining in Gambia is no problem. However, a few words and phrases in French will come in handy in Senegal.

For tips on pronunciation, see p303.

Useful Phrases

Do you know a good restaurant?
Connaissez-vous un bon restaurant?   ko·nay·say·voo un bon res·to·ron

What time does this restaurant open/close?
À quelle heure ouvre/ferme le restaurant?   a kel er oo·vrer/fairm ler res·to·ron

I've just eaten.
Je viens juste de manger.   zher vyen zhoost der mon·zhay

Can I have the menu please?
Est-ce que je peux avoir la carte?   es ker zher per a·vwar la kart

Do you have a menu in English?
Est-ce que vous avez une carte en anglais?   es ker voo zavay ewn kart on ong·glay

How much is the meal of the day?
Combien coûte le plat du jour?   kom·byun koot ler pla dew zhoor

I'm a vegetarian.
Je suis végétarien/végétarienne.   zher swee vay·zhay·ta·ryun/ryen

I don't eat meat.
Je ne mange pas de viande.   zher ner monzh pa der vyond

I'm allergic to (meat/seafood).
Je suis allergique   zher swee za·lair·zheek
(à la viande/aux fruits de mer).   (a la vyond/o frwee der mair)

Can I have this dish without meat?
Est-ce que je peux avoir ce plat sans viande?   es ker zher per a·vwar ser pla son vyond
Do you have any Senegalese dishes?
Est-ce que vous avez des plats sénégalais?   es ker voo za·vay day pla say·nay·ga·lay
What's your speciality?
Quelle est votre spécialité?   kel ay vo·trer spay·sya·lee·tay
Is this dish very spicy?
Est-ce que ce plat est très épicé?   es ker ser pla ay tray ay·pee·say
Do you have any dishes for children?
Est-ce que vous avez des plats pour les enfants?   es ker voo za·vay day pla poor lay zon·fon
A juice without ice cubes, please.
Un jus sans glaçons, s'il vous plaît.   un zhew son gla·son seel voo play
Thank you, I'm full.
Merci, j'ai assez mangé.   mair·see zhay a·say mon·zhay
Excuse me, I ordered quite some time ago.
Excusez-moi, j'ai commandé il   ek·skew·zay·mwa zhay ko·mon·day eel
y a assez de temps.   ee a a·say der tom
Can I have the bill please?
L'addition, s'il vous plaît?   la·dee·syon seel voo play

Food Glossary

DAIRY

le beurre	ler ber	butter
le fromage	ler fro·mazh	cheese
le lait	ler lay	milk
le lait caillé	ler lay kay·yay	sour milk
le yaourt	ler ya·oort	yoghurt

FISH & SEAFOOD

le calmar	ler kal·mar	squid
les crevettes	lay krer·vet	prawns
les fruits de mer	lay frwee der mair	seafood
la langouste	ler long·goost	lobster
le poisson	ler pwa·son	fish

FRUIT

l'ananas	la·na·nas	pineapple
la banane	la ba·nan	banana
la mangue	la mong·ger	mango
la noix de coco	la nwa der ko·ko	coconut
la papaye	la pa·pa·yer	papaya

VEGETABLES, NUTS & GRAINS

les arachides	lay za·ra·sheed	groundnuts/peanuts
les légumes	lay lay·gewm	vegetables

TOP FIVE RESTAURANTS

Butcher's Shop (p108; Fajara, Gambia) Has the best steak and local fruit juices in the region.
Green Mamba (p110; Kololi, Gambia) Excellent Oriental wok in a calm garden setting.
Le Cozy (p168; Dakar, Senegal) Imaginative global cuisine in ice-cool surroundings.
Hôtel Sindoné (p216; Saint-Louis, Senegal) Tasty seafood served on a wooden river terrace.
Chez Boum (p199; Toubakouta, Senegal) Tiny straw shack that serves unexpected delicacies and the best *mousse au chocolat* in the country.

les pommes de terre	lay pom der tair	potatoes
le riz (*thieb* in Wolof)	ler ree	rice

OTHER FOOD

les frîtes	lay freet	fries
le pain	ler pun	bread (usually French bread)
le piment	ler pee·mon	small red pepper
le sel	ler sel	salt
le sucre	ler sew·krer	sugar

DRINKS

bissap	bee·sap	a purple drink made of water, sugar and hibiscus leaves
bouyi	boo·yee	sweet, thick juice made from the fruits of the baobab tree
(un) café au lait	(un) ka·fay o lay	(a) coffee with milk
(un) café touba	(un) ka·fay too·ba	(a) spiced black coffee
corossol	ko·ro·sol	thick, white juice made from the fruits of the soursop tree
jus de pomme	zhew der pom	apple juice
jus d'orange	zhew do·ronzh	orange juice
kinkiliba	keen·kee·lee·ba	local herbal tea
l'eau minérale	lo mee·nay·ral	mineral water
(un) petit café	(un) pe·tee ka·fay	(an) espresso
bière pression	bee·yair pray·syon	draught beer
(un) thé	(un) tay	(a) tea (usually black)
vin du palme	vun dew pal·mer	palm wine

The Gambia

VERONICA GARBUTT

THE GAMBIA

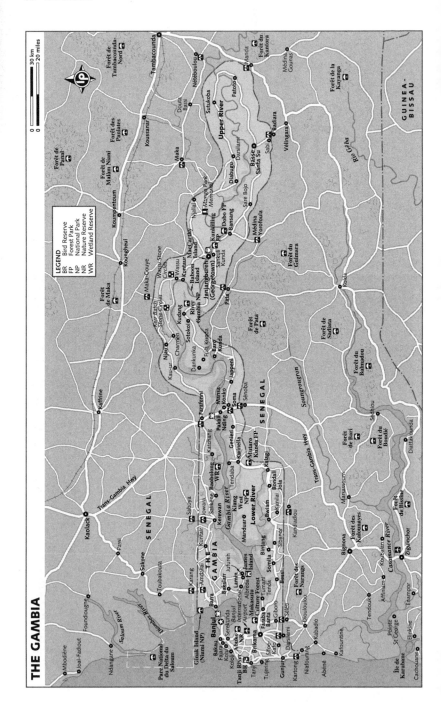

Banjul

It's hard to imagine a more unlikely, more consistently ignored capital city than the sleepy seaport of Banjul. Just 30 minutes from the thriving tourist zones of the Atlantic coast, the city sits on its island like a sulking little sister who's stopped vying for attention. But despite the shadow of abandonment that haunts its sand-blown streets, Banjul is a fascinating destination.

Lively Albert Market, at the heart of the city, is one of Gambia's best places to snap up a souvenir bargain and soak up the atmosphere of eager buying, selling and bartering that makes the narrow alleyways and ramshackle stalls hum with excitement. Down the road from the market, Banjul's hectic harbour is another vibrant slice of inner-city Africa. This is where Gambia's main ferry chugs back and forth, heaving huge trucks, traders bearing wares, hustlers and travellers across the mouth of the Gambia River. The constant comings and goings and the bustle that accompanies the urban ritual are worth taking in, especially from one of the makeshift roadside cafes.

Banjul's 'old town', a mile of fading colonial structures, is imbued with a sense of history that the plush seaside resorts are lacking, and the National Museum, a charming institution with dusty exhibits, reinforces this atmosphere of a precious, though slightly neglected, past.

Perhaps the most curious and enticing aspect of the capital is that its urban developments are walking distance from the wildlife-boasting wilderness of the Tanbi Wetland Complex. It's a neat countryside escape, and you don't even have to leave town to take it in.

HIGHLIGHTS

- Stir your pirogue through the thick **Tanbi Wetland Complex** (p94), Banjul's magical front yard

- Imagine family histories as you wander the streets of the **old town** (p93)

- Smell the spices and drown in colour among the rickety stalls of **Albert Market** (p93)

- Travel back in time on a visit to the **National Museum** (p92)

- Climb the giant structure of **Arch 22** (p92) to get a view over The Gambia's forgotten capital

HISTORY

Flat, swampy and plagued by malarial mosquitoes, Banjul (the Mandinka word for bamboo) was an unremarkable little island. Few people chose to live there, but for Captain Alexander Grant, mission leader for the British Crown, the spot was a dream location. In 1816 he was on the lookout for a strategic spot from which the British could enforce the observance of the Slavery Abolition Act (1807) by other European powers, as well as strengthen their advantage over the interior of the country. He arranged payment of a few iron bars to the local King of Kombo and put up a new nameplate, calling his newly acquired bit of flood zone Bathurst, after Henry Bathurst, the secretary of the British Colonial Office. Many soldiers lost their lives through tropical disease and overly strenuous work during the construction of army barracks, the building of Albert Market and the laying down of MacCarthy Sq (today's July 22 Sq) with its government buildings. The colonial outpost kept growing in strength: it soon stretched over a handful of distinctive neighbourhoods and the number of inhabitants multiplied rapidly. The population swelled particularly in the 1830s, when freed slaves from Sierra Leone were settled here. The crumbling remains of the houses they built, reminiscent of the Victorian architecture adaptations typical of Freetown, Sierra Leone, indicate where they first settled.

When Gambia achieved independence in 1965, Bathurst was granted city status and became the capital of the young nation. Eight years later it shed its colonial name, and reinvented itself once again as Banjul – the bamboo island.

With the growth of Gambia's coastal towns into major tourist areas, Banjul experienced a strong decline, reflected in a shrinking population and the move of major businesses towards the coast. Today it's mainly an administrative centre, while a capital-worthy lifestyle is found in the resort zones.

ORIENTATION

Banjul is small, and certainly not expanding. You can explore the city in an easy walk. The centre is July 22 Sq, a small public park from which several main streets run south, including Russell St, which leads past the bustling Albert Market into Liberation St. South of the October 17 roundabout is the old part of Banjul – a maze of narrow streets and ramshackle houses.

Independence Dr runs northwest from July 22 Sq, becoming the main road out of Banjul. It passes the imposing structure of Arch 22 (note that only the president is allowed to drive under it – everyone else goes around!), then turns into a dual carriageway that crosses Oyster Creek after 3km, reaching the mainland.

Another 2km further west, the road splits: the right fork goes to Bakau, Fajara and the other Atlantic coast resorts; straight on leads to Serekunda, the airport and everywhere else along the southern bank of the Gambia River.

INFORMATION
Internet Access

Gamtel Internet Café (Independence Dr; per hr D30; ☽ 8am-midnight)

Quantumnet (Nelson Mandela St; per hr D30; ☽ 9am-10pm)

Medical Services

Banjul Pharmacy (☎ 4227470; Independence Dr; ☽ 9am-8.30pm) Across the road from the hospital.

Royal Victoria Teaching Hospital (☎ 4228223; Independence Dr) The RVTH has an accidents and emergencies department; for minor illnesses and malaria tests, the clinics on the Atlantic coast are better (see p98).

Money

Banks in Banjul are open from 8am to 4pm Monday to Thursday, and from 8am to 1.30pm Friday. They should change travellers cheques and have ATMs that accept Visa cards.

PHB Bank (☎ 4428144; 11 Liberation St)

Standard Chartered Bank (☎ 4222081; Ecowas Ave)

Post

Main post office (Russell St; ☽ 8am-4pm Mon-Sat) Near Albert Market. You can buy postcards, paper or envelopes from the hawkers outside.

Telephone

Gamtel office (Russell St; ☽ 8am-11.30pm) Next door to the post office.

Travel Agencies

Most of the main travel agencies have decamped to Fajara, Kotu or Kololi (see p99). Among the remaining ones, these seem to be the most efficient:

BANJUL

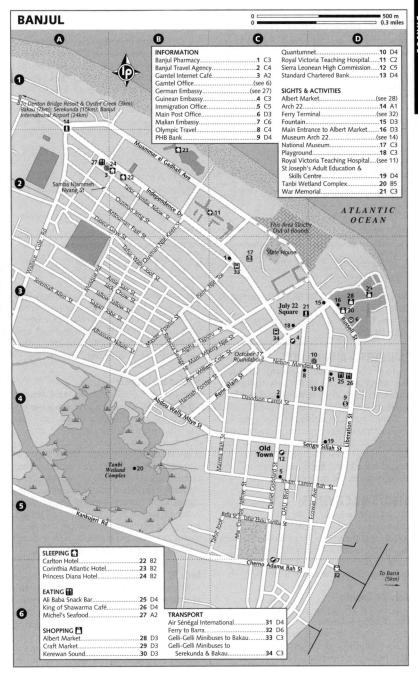

0 —————— 500 m
0 —————— 0.3 miles

INFORMATION
Banjul Pharmacy.................................**1** C3
Banjul Travel Agency..........................**2** C4
Gamtel Internet Café...........................**3** A2
Gamtel Office.................................(see 6)
German Embassy...........................(see 27)
Guinean Embassy................................**4** C3
Immigration Office..............................**5** C5
Main Post Office.................................**6** D3
Malian Embassy..................................**7** C6
Olympic Travel....................................**8** C4
PHB Bank..**9** D4
Quantumnet.....................................**10** D4
Royal Victoria Teaching Hospital.....**11** C2
Sierra Leonean High Commission....**12** C5
Standard Chartered Bank.................**13** D4

SIGHTS & ACTIVITIES
Albert Market..................................(see 28)
Arch 22...**14** A1
Ferry Terminal.................................(see 32)
Fountain...**15** D3
Main Entrance to Albert Market......**16** D3
Museum Arch 22...........................(see 14)
National Museum..............................**17** C3
Playground.......................................**18** C3
Royal Victoria Teaching Hospital....(see 11)
St Joseph's Adult Education &
  Skills Centre..................................**19** D4
Tanbi Wetland Complex...................**20** B5
War Memorial...................................**21** C3

To Denton Bridge Resort & Oyster Creek (3km);
Bakau (7km); Serekunda (15km); Banjul
International Airport (24km)

Muammar al Gadhafi Ave

Samba Njammeh
Nyang St

Tafsir Demba Ndow St
Independence Dr
Ousman Jeng St
Antouman Faal St
Dawur Cole St
Tafsir Wally Ousman Njie Keen St

Wallace Cole Rd
Mosque Rd
Annie Sarr St
Jack Chow St
Jallow Jallow St
Sagari Jobe St
Jeremiah Allen St
Alhassan Ndure St
Master Powils St
Rebecca Sharp St
Pierre Njie Tce

ATLANTIC
OCEAN

This Area Strictly
Out of Bounds

State House

July 22
Square

October 17
Roundabout
Aljoha Taputu St
Maam Mbenty Njie St
Rex William Cole St
Hannah Forster St
Rene Blain St
Abdou Wally Mbye St
Davidson Carrol St
Nelson Mandela St

Russell St

Old
Town

Serign Sillah St
Imam Lamin Bah St

Marma Bah St
Daniel Goddard St
OAU Blvd
Ecowas Ave
Liberation St

Tanbi
Wetland
Complex

Kankujeri Rd

Tafsir Toof
Balla St
Ma Cumba Tafaw St
Tafsir Ebou Samba St
Cherno Adama Bah St

To Barra
(5km)

SLEEPING 🛏
Carlton Hotel.....................................**22** B2
Corinthia Atlantic Hotel....................**23** B2
Princess Diana Hotel........................**24** B2

EATING 🍴
Ali Baba Snack Bar...........................**25** D4
King of Shawarma Café.....................**26** D4
Michel's Seafood................................**27** A2

SHOPPING 🛍
Albert Market...................................**28** D3
Craft Market......................................**29** D3
Kerewan Sound..................................**30** D3

TRANSPORT
Air Sénégal International...................**31** D4
Ferry to Barra...................................**32** D6
Gelli-Gelli Minibuses to Bakau.........**33** C3
Gelli-Gelli Minibuses to
  Serekunda & Bakau........................**34** C3

BANJUL

STREET NAME CHANGES

The city's streets, first named after the English heroes of the Battle of Waterloo, were given new designations in the late 1990s. They now carry the names of Gambia's heroes of independence. However, most people (including taxi drivers) are still more familiar with the old names, so you'll usually get a more reliable answer if you ask for directions using the old street names. We've included a list of some of the streets and their old names, but if you're still stuck, look for the addresses painted on the front of shops and businesses.

Old name	New name
Bund Rd	Kankujeri Rd
Clarkson St	Rene Blain St
Cotton St	Cherno Adama Bah St
Dobson St	Ma Cumba Jallow St
Grant St	Rev William Cole St
Hagan St	Daniel Goddard St
Hill St	Imam Lamin Bah St
Hope St	Jallow Jallow St
MacCarthy Sq	July 22 Sq
Marina Pde	Muammar al Gadhafi Ave
Orange St	Tafsir Ebou Samba St
Picton St	Davidson Carrol St
Wellington St	Liberation St

Banjul Travel Agency (☎ 4228813; bta@qanet.gm; 71 Daniel Goddard St)

Olympic Travel (☎ 4223370; olympictravels@work.gm; Nelson Mandela St)

DANGERS & ANNOYANCES

Violent crime is rare in Banjul, but pickpocketing is rife. Be particularly vigilant on the Barra ferry, at its terminal and at Albert Market.

Banjul turns its lights off after 8pm and most streets in the centre drown in darkness, making the place feel less safe than it actually is. The greatest nocturnal risk here is not armed bandits but the maze of open sewers that crisscross the streets.

SIGHTS & ACTIVITIES

Banjul feels more like a very large village than a national capital, especially if you're out birdwatching in the central Tanbi Wetlands. There are few big sights, but plenty of intimate details, from market scenes to street football, that are best taken in on a casual stroll around town.

July 22 Square

The inner-city green patch of July 22 Sq (MacCarthy Sq), a former colonial construction, was once the site of cricket matches but is now mainly used for governmental pomp and public celebrations. Look out for the **War Memorial** and the (now dried-up) **fountain** 'erected by public subscription' to commemorate the coronation of King George VI of Britain in 1937. The colourful and well-maintained **playground** will excite little visitors more than the 19th-century architecture.

National Museum

Opened in 1985, the **National Museum** (☎ 4226244, 4077461; www.ncac.gm; Independence Dr; admission D50; ☯ 9am-4pm Mon-Thu, 9am-5pm Fri-Sun) has well-presented, if slightly dusty, displays of historical and cultural artefacts, including musical instruments, agricultural tools and ethnographic items. There's an interesting archaeological section reconstructing some of the earliest periods of human habitation of the region, and a history floor that leads right up to the present with slightly yellowed though interesting photographs. You can arrange introductory talks and even art classes and craft workshops. See also the boxed text, p94.

Arch 22

With its broad columns and 35m height, **Arch 22** (Independence Dr; admission D100; ☯ 9am-11pm) is an imposing sight that stands in stark contrast to the one-storey world surrounding it. Designed by Senegalese architect Pierre Goudiaby Atepa, the enormous gateway was built as a permanent, pompous way of celebrating the bloodless military coup of 22 July 1994 (see p35).

The structure may not be to everyone's taste, but its publicly accessible balcony grants excellent views over the city and coast. There's also a good restaurant, a souvenir shop and a small **museum** (☎ 4226244) that enlightens visitors about the coup d'état and often houses temporary exhibitions.

Old Town

Head west from the ferry terminal, towards the wide Ma Cumba Jallow St (Dobson St) and beyond, and explore the old town, an unruly assembly of decrepit colonial buildings and Krio-style clapboard houses – steep-roofed structures with wrought-iron balconies and corrugated roofs (see the boxed text, p45). It's no coincidence that the houses resemble the inner-city architecture of Freetown, Sierra Leone, as many of them still belong to families who came to Banjul from Freetown, some as early as the 1830s.

Albert Market

Since its creation in the mid-19th century, this market, an area of frenzied buying, bartering and bargaining, has been Banjul's hub of activity. There are shimmering fabrics and false plaits, fresh fruits and dried fish, and tourist-tempting souvenirs at the Craft Market. You can find everything here, from loose screws to gold earrings.

Give yourself a good couple of hours to wander around Albert Market – long enough to take in the smells, sounds and sights, and get your haggling skills up to scratch. There are several drinks stalls and chop shops (basic local-style eateries) in the market to pacify shopped-out bellies.

Albert Market is never a calm spot, but if you want to avoid the busiest hours, come early in the morning or late in the afternoon.

Ferry Terminal

The terminal for the ferry to Barra, with its endless queues of lorries, the industrious hum of cargo being loaded and discharged, passengers boarding and disembarking, and the continuous chatter of patiently waiting customers, is worth experiencing. Directly opposite, the warehouses, clothes stalls and grocery wholesalers that line Liberation St resound with animated bartering that mingles with the clamour.

Royal Victoria Teaching Hospital

Gambia's main health facility, the **Royal Victoria Teaching Hospital** (☎ 4226152; www.rvth.org; Independence Dr) not only offers emergency treatment but also conducts tours of its complex of late-19th-century and modern buildings. A hospital visit might not sound like a seductive holiday idea, but the daily two-hour tours (free, donations welcome) are surprisingly interesting. They're not a show of suffering or need, but an informative introduction to the hospital's international teaching programs and research projects into malaria and hepatitis. Phone ahead to book your tour.

St Joseph's Adult Education & Skills Centre

Tucked away in an old Portuguese building, **St Joseph's Adult Education & Skills Centre** (☎ 4228836; stjskills@qanet.com; Ecowas Ave; ☒ 9am-2pm Mon-Thu, 9am-noon Fri) has provided training to disadvantaged women for the last 20 years. Visitors can take a free tour of sewing, crafts and tie-dye classes, and purchase reasonably priced items such as

---

BANJUL IN ONE DAY

Thanks to Banjul's manageable size, you can take in the town's sights in a relaxed one-day visit.

Get your energy levels up with a freshly pressed fruit juice at the **King of Shawarma Café** (p95), then head south for a visit to the inspirational, peaceful **St Joseph's Adult Education & Skills Centre** (above).

Change tempo by diving into the feverish bustle of **Albert Market** (above), then stroll past **July 22 Square** (opposite), taking in the War Memorial and fountain. Walk along Independence Dr and put in a stop at the **National Museum** (opposite) to enjoy the curious collection of historical artefacts.

Participate in a tour of the **Royal Victoria Teaching Hospital** (above), then head towards the gigantic **Arch 22** (opposite) to take in the view of the city from above.

Weave your way back through the rarely visited backstreets of Banjul's pleasant **old town** (above), and finish your day with a meal and a drink at **Michel's Seafood** (p95).

ARTS FOR THE NATION

For anyone interested in the arts, heritage and conservation, the National Museum in Banjul is an obligatory stop. Like the capital itself, the museum is a humble, slightly rickety affair, but it's still a great source of information on Gambia's history. And it's not only dusty artefacts that make a visit here worthwhile – the museum also houses the **National Centre for Arts and Culture** (NCAC; ☎ 4226244), an independent organisation devoted to the promotion of national culture. If you meet the right person here, this can be an amazing resource of information about the state of conservation projects, the opening or closing of art galleries, spots to check out and ways of getting there.

patchwork products, embroidered purses and cute children's clothes at the on-site boutique.

Tanbi Wetland Complex

Only minutes away from Banjul's built-up areas, streets are suddenly no longer lined by houses but by thick mangroves that gradually thin to a fascinating landscape of mudflats, tidal lagoons, salt plains and occasional pockets of woodland, cut through by narrow creeks. Even though human activity, construction and rice plantations have started encroaching onto the 4500-hectare site, the Tanbi Wetlands remain one of Gambia's key birdwatching spots. Caspian terns, gulls (including the grey-headed and slender-billed gulls), egrets and several species of waders are only some of its feathered inhabitants. A day out in this easily accessed wilderness is particularly rewarding in the company of a trained bird guide (see p77).

Oyster Creek

The quiet, mangrove-lined waterways of Oyster Creek, the main waterway separating Banjul island from the mainland, and its minor tributaries are brilliant for birdwatching, sport fishing and wonderfully lazy afternoons relaxing in a pirogue to the sound of the waves. Most hotels organise pirogue trips, though you can also book your tour independently at the Sportsfishing Centre (p103) at **Denton Bridge**, which crosses Oyster Creek some 3km west from Banjul city centre.

To reach Denton Bridge by public transport, take any minibus running between Banjul and Bakau or Serekunda and ask the driver to let you off at the bridge. The Sportsfishing Centre is well signposted. It's best to phone one of the companies there first and explain which activity you're interested in, though you can probably also be put in touch with a pirogue or boat owner on the spot.

SLEEPING

Not many tourists stay in Banjul city, preferring instead the beach and comforts of the Atlantic coast, and that has caused a decline in the number of places available.

Carlton Hotel (☎ 4228670; 25 Independence Dr; s/d D500/550, with air-con D800/850; ☒) Prices apparently go down here the higher up your floor. Shoestringers, do your maths: there are four storeys and rooms have already decreased by D200 on the 2nd. There's not a lot of comfort here, though some of the doors do lock properly.

Princess Diana Hotel (☎ 4228715; 30 Independence Dr; r D550) This small, dishevelled guest house has been able to maintain its modest existence since 1981. Only the name has become more glamorous, though you do get a decent bed, occasional live music in the bar, and even a kind of breakfast in the morning.

Denton Bridge Resort (☎ 7773777; s/d D800/1000; ☒) Right on the bridge at Oyster Creek, this water-sports centre, pirogue landing and excursion point also puts up sea-loving visitors in large rooms so close to the river breeze they don't need air-conditioning.

Corinthia Atlantic Hotel (☎ 4228601; www.corinthia hotels.com; Muammar al Gadhafi Ave; s/d incl breakfast D1500/2500; ☒ ☒ ☒ ☒) This plush palace sits at the entrance to Banjul like the jewel in the city's crown. Facilities include a string of good restaurants, a massage centre and a nightclub, and rooms have minibar, TV and all the equipment you expect in this class. Check out the garden, specially created by ornithologist Clive Barlow to please birds and their fans.

EATING

A dinner out in Banjul is more likely to consist of a burger and fries than three-course sumptuousness. The restaurant scene here is so calm that many eateries roll down the blinds before the evening has even started. Around Albert Market and the north end of Liberation St are several cheap chop shops and street stalls where plates of rice and sauce start at about D30. Breakfast at the ferry terminal – skewered beef on fresh bread rolls with sweet coffee – is highly recommended.

Apart from the places below, you'll find good restaurants at the Corinthia Atlantic Hotel and Denton Bridge Resort.

King of Shawarma Café (☎ 4229799; Nelson Mandela St; snacks D75-150; ☺ 9am-5pm Mon-Sat) This lovely Lebanese place has many returning guests – and for good reason. It's so friendly that the owner happily opened for us long after hours. 'There's nothing else to do in Banjul, why wouldn't I work?' he said. The meze are almost as tasty as the freshly squeezed fruit juices.

Ali Baba Snack Bar (☎ 4224055; Nelson Mandela St; dishes D100-150; ☺ 9am-5pm) More than just a kebab shop, this place is an institution with a deserved reputation for its tasty *shwarmas* (sliced, grilled meat and salad in pita bread) and falafel sandwiches.

Michel's Seafood (☎ 4223108; 29 Independence Dr; meals D150-250; ☺ 8am-11pm) Banjul's classiest restaurant offers an excellent choice of seafood and other dishes at reasonable prices. If you stay in one of the cheaper hostels, you'll appreciate its breakfast menu; if you're attempting a night out in Banjul, this is where you can have dinner.

SHOPPING

In Banjul, the best place to go shopping is Albert Market (p93). If you enter via the main entrance you'll pass stalls stacked with lustrous fabrics, hair extensions, shoes, household and electrical wares, and just about everything else you can imagine. Keep going and you'll reach the myriad colours and flavours of the fruit and vegetable section. Beyond here is the area usually called the Craft Market, with stalls selling souvenirs (see p271 for information about the sorts of items you're likely to find here).

Near the market's main entrance, you'll find **Kerewan Sound** (Russell St), Gambia's best place to buy CDs, including the latest releases from Gambian artists.

GETTING THERE & AWAY
Air

For details of international flights to/from Banjul, see p278. To confirm reservations on a flight you've already booked, it's easiest to deal directly with the airline.

Air Sénégal International (☎ 4202117; www.air -senegal-international.com; 10 Ecowas Ave)

Brussels Airlines (Map pp100-1; ☎ 4466880; www .brusselsairlines.com; Bertil Harding Hwy, Kololi)

Boat

The **Banjul–Barra ferry** (☎ 4228205; Liberation St) is a key link to the north bank and Senegal. Travelling on it is something of an assault on the senses – a mind-boggling trip through throngs of passengers, traders, pickpockets and trucks, as well as across the river. Normally, there are three boats that chug slowly back and forth between Banjul and Barra. They are supposed to run every one to two hours, officially from 7am until 9pm, but delays (and even engine failure) occur frequently. If the tide is strong, the 45-minute trip can easily stretch to an hour. Passengers pay D10, while cars cost D150 to D250.

It's best to get on as a foot passenger and catch a taxi once you're on the other side, as vehicles often have to wait for hours (and trucks for days) before getting on. Buy your ticket before going through to the waiting area and keep it until you get off; it will be checked on the other side. If you're coming from the north side by car, you need to purchase your car ticket at the weighing station near the border (just after the junction where the north-bank road to Farafenni turns off), about 3km northeast of Barra.

There are open seating areas upstairs from which you get a good view over the river. Dolphins are occasionally spotted on the passage, so keep your camera handy (but safe – this is a pickpocketing hot spot).

Gelli-Gelli & Taxi

Gelli-gelli minibuses and public taxis to Bakau (D8) and Serekunda (D10) leave from the car parks near the National Museum and July 22 Sq, respectively (they're named after their destinations). You might have to pay a bit more for luggage. Once in Bakau or Serekunda, you'll be able to jump on another taxi to take you to any other place along the coast or upcountry (see also p112).

A private hire taxi from Banjul to Fajara or Bakau will cost around D150 to D200; Kololi, Kotu and Serekunda might cost a bit more. If you don't find an empty taxi passing in the street, try the Corinthia Atlantic Hotel, where there are always a few parked outside.

For details about bush taxis to Senegal, see p284.

GETTING AROUND
To/From the Airport

Tourist taxis wait outside the airport. To Banjul, Serekunda or the Atlantic coast resorts (Bakau, Fajara, Kotu and Kololi) they'll cost around D300 to D400.

For a slightly cheaper option, walk out of the terminal until you reach the public car park, where you might find a yellow taxi that'll take you for D200 – depending on your bargaining skills.

Taxi

A short ride across Banjul city centre (known as a 'town trip') in a private taxi will cost about D25 to D50.

Atlantic Coast Resorts & Serekunda

For many tourists, the 10km stretch from Bakau to Kololi is The Gambia; for others, not at all. Lined with beaches and built up with a staggering selection of hotels and restaurants, this small zone offers everything for a relaxing beach holiday. With excellent infrastructure, wide roads and bustling neighbourhoods, it shows a chic and fashionable face that's at odds with the rest of the country – which is why some claim that the 'real Gambia' only starts where the backyards of the hotels end.

But that's not entirely true. This urbanised coastal zone is interspersed with fields, lagoons and palm groves, and the villages that have merged into this big holiday park have retained much of their original, rural character. Bakau's old town, a lively concentration of clapboard, corrugated iron and colourful market stalls, begins only a few steps away from the gleaming hotel fronts. And a short drive takes you to Serekunda, a hot and heaving market town that's bursting at the seams with traffic, people and a strictly local vibe. Even the most polished parts, such as the Senegambia Strip of Kololi, are specked with exciting small enterprises, offering sustainable alternatives to those who want to dig a little deeper into what makes this country tick.

The coast is the beating heart of Gambia's tourism industry, and it pumps energy to the surrounding areas as well. Only minutes away, small nature reserves, community projects and eco-lodges tempt you on day outings, indicating exciting new possibilities for tourism in this tiny West African nation.

HIGHLIGHTS

- Be surprised at the softness of crocodile skin when patting Charlie at the **Kachikally Crocodile Pool** (p102)
- Gibber with the monkeys at **Bijilo Forest Park** (p99)
- Track down the source of all those batik paintings in the backstreets of **Serekunda** (p112)
- Discover the next great Gambian artist in the orchid garden of the **African Living Art Centre** (p99)
- Dig your toes into the replenished sands of **Kotu beach** (p103) and watch the birds at the stream

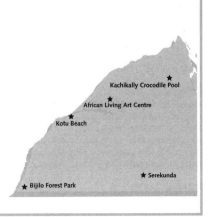

ORIENTATION

The main road from Gambia's upcountry towns leads past Banjul International Airport to Serekunda, where it divides: straight ahead is the dual carriageway leading to Banjul; to the left is Kairaba Ave, which leads to Fajara. From here, Bakau is to the northeast, while Kotu and Kololi are to the southwest.

In Bakau and Fajara the main drag is Atlantic Rd, which runs parallel to the coast, linking Kairaba Ave and Old Cape Rd. Just south of Atlantic Rd, and running parallel to it, is Garba Jahumpa Rd (formerly, and still better, known as New Town Rd). Bertil Harding Hwy (Badala Park Way) branches off Kairaba Ave at the Fajara end and leads to the hotel and beach areas of Kotu and Kololi, then on to the south coast. The busiest part of the Atlantic resort zone is Senegambia Rd in Kololi, leading from Bertil Harding Hwy (Badala Park Way) to the Senegambia Beach Hotel. Named after the hotel, it's known locally as the Senegambia Strip.

Bertil Harding Hwy (Badala Park Way) meets Kairaba Ave at the country's famous traffic lights (the only traffic lights) and links with Saitmatty Rd to the east, thus avoiding the bottleneck of Westfield Junction. The latter leads into Serekunda; from the junction the town's busy market road spreads west.

INFORMATION
Bookshops

Most supermarkets stock magazines and postcards, and informal bookstalls in Serekunda (sometimes simply spread out on the roadside) invite rummaging.

Timbooktoo (☎ 4494345; timbooktoo@qanet.gm; Garba Jahumpa Rd, Fajara; ⏰ 10am-7pm Mon-Thu, 10am-1pm & 3-7pm Fri, 10am-8pm Sat) An excellent shop with a good range of fiction, nonfiction, maps, and local and international papers. The Association of Small Scale Enterprises (ASSET) offices are upstairs.

Cultural Centres

Alliance Franco-Gambienne (☎ 4375418; alliancefg @hotmail.com; Kairaba Ave, Serekunda; ⏰ 9.30am-5pm Mon-Fri) At the southern end of Kairaba Ave. It runs language courses (in French and Wolof) as well as regular concerts, films, shows and exhibitions. The garden restaurant at the back is a calm place for a solid, cheap lunch.

Internet Access

Many of the large hotels have internet cafes, and wi-fi connections are becoming popular at restaurants and hotels (typically free for guests). Connections are usually slow. Most internet cafes charge D25 per hour.

Gamtel (www.gamtel.gm) Kololi (☎ 4377878; Senegambia, Kololi; ⏰ 9am-11pm); Serekunda (☎ 4229999; Westfield Junction, Serekunda; ⏰ 8am-11pm)

Net Bar (☎ 4498218; Atlantic Rd, Bakau; ⏰ 9am-midnight) It's possible to plug in a laptop and headsets. Small snack bar outside.

Quantumnet (☎ 4494514; Kairaba Ave, Fajara; ⏰ 8.30am-10pm) Round the corner from Timbooktoo bookshop.

Medical Services

The Accidents & Emergencies department is at the hospital in Banjul (p90).

Malak Chemist (☎ 4376087; Kairaba Ave, Serekunda; ⏰ 9am-midnight Mon-Sat, 9am-1pm Sun) Has a good reputation for stocking high-quality products from the USA and Europe.

Medical Research Council (MRC; ☎ 4495446; Fajara) If you have a potentially serious illness, head for this British-run clinic off Atlantic Rd.

Stop Steps Pharmacy (☎ 4371344; Kairaba Ave, Fajara; ⏰ 9am-10pm Mon-Sat) One of the best-stocked pharmacy chains around, with branches all along the coast.

Westfield Clinic (☎ 4398448; Westfield Junction, Serekunda)

Money

The main banks – Standard Chartered, Trust Bank and PHB – have branches in Bakau, Serekunda and Kololi.

If you need to change money after hours, ask your receptionist or local friends to put you in touch with a reliable street changer who can come to the hotel and sort you out with dalasi. (This tends to work better at smaller hotels that won't immediately insist on changing it themselves for a steep commission.)

All of the banks listed below have ATMs, though you'll often find that they're out of order and withdrawal limits can be tight. If you plan a trip upcountry, remember to change or withdraw all the money you need at the coast.

PHB Bank (☎ 4497139; Atlantic Rd, Bakau)
Standard Chartered Bank Bakau (☎ 4495046; Atlantic Rd); Serekunda (☎ 4396102; Kairaba Ave)
Trust Bank Bakau (☎ 4495486; Atlantic Rd); Kololi (☎ 4465303; Wilmon Company Bldg, Bertil Harding Hwy)

Post

The main post office is off Kairaba Ave, about halfway between Fajara and Serekunda. The

Gampost (☎ 8900587; Atlantic Rd, Bakau; ☽ 8.30am-4pm Mon-Thu, 8.30am-noon Fri & Sat) in Bakau has a telecentre and internet connection.

Telephone

The spread of mobile phones has caused many of the small telecentres to close, though you'll still find them in Serekunda and on Kairaba Ave. The easiest thing, though, is to get a local Gamtel or Africell SIM and stick it in your mobile.

Gamtel (☎ 4229999; www.gamtel.gm; Westfield Junction, Serekunda; ☽ 8am-11pm)

Tourist Information

Cultural Encounters (☎ 4497675; www.asset -gambia.com; Garba Jahumpa Rd, Fajara) The excellent information centre for ASSET is a bright, friendly place and the perfect address for finding out about sustainable tourism offers in Gambia. It's above Timbooktoo bookshop.

Tropical Tour & Souvenirs (☎ 4460536; tropical tour@gamtel.gm; Kairaba Hotel, Senegambia, Kololi) A great place for information materials, maps, books and insightful advice.

Travel Agencies

Most agents are on Kairaba Ave between Serekunda and Fajara. They tend to represent specific airlines and operators, so you might have to try a couple to get the best deal.

Good travel agencies, dealing with ticketing as well as tours, include Discovery Tours, Gambia Experience and Gambia Tours; see p287.

DANGERS & ANNOYANCES

Petty thefts and muggings are always a possibility but happen quite rarely. There are a few hot spots: be careful on the path around Fajara golf course between Fajara and Kotu and on the beaches after dark.

There's a good chance you'll be approached in the street by marijuana sellers. Note that smoking weed is illegal and punished with heavy fines, and falling into the hands of Gambian police while engaging in illegal activities is really not something you want to do.

One of the major annoyances in this area is the constant hustling of tourists by 'bumsters' (see the boxed text, p102). Single women should be careful on deserted beaches, especially after dark; several female readers have reported harassment.

SIGHTS
African Living Art Centre

A fairy-tale cross between an antique gallery, a cafe, an orchid garden and an Asian restaurant, the **African Living Art Centre** (☎ 4495131; Garba Jahumpa Rd, Fajara; ☽ 9am-8pm) is the hub of Gambia's arts scene. It's the vision of Suelle Nachif, a man with limitless imagination and skills, it seems. He cuts hair like a master, grows flowers and knows how to prepare a fabulous Asian meal. But most of all, he hosts exhibitions, brings artists together, runs workshops and does a whole lot more to infuse Gambia's contemporary scene with new life. You can arrange to meet artists here and talk to them about their work, and find out how to participate in creative exchanges. Or simply enjoy the shade of the garden setting and one of the best cocktails on the coast.

Botanic Gardens

In Bakau, at the northeastern end of Atlantic Rd, the **Botanic Gardens** (☎ 7774482; adult/child D50/free; ☽ 8am-4pm) are worth a look. They were established in 1924 and are peaceful with plenty of shade and good bird-spotting chances.

Not far away, a road turns north off Atlantic Rd and leads down to the **jetty**, where boats come and go while thousands of fish dry in the sun. Morning and late afternoon are the best times to watch this spectacle.

Bijilo Forest Park

On the coast, just a short walk from Kololi, you'll find **Bijilo Forest Park** (☎ 9996343; admission D20; ☽ 8am-6pm), a small wildlife reserve and community forest. A guided walk (4.5km, two hours) takes you along a well-maintained series of trails that pass through lush vegetation, gallery forest, low bush and grass, as you walk towards the dunes. You'll see more green vervet, red colobus and patas monkeys than you'll probably want to – feeding by visitors has turned them into cheeky little things that might come close and even steal items. Don't feed them to encourage them further. Monitor lizards are also often seen.

Birds are best watched on the coastal side. The more than 100 species that have been counted here include several types of beeeaters, grey hornbills, ospreys, Caspian terns, francolins and wood doves.

Guides can tell you more about the educational programs that are run here to combat deforestation, and the small booklet on sale

ATLANTIC COAST RESORTS & SEREKUNDA

A   **B**   **C**   **D**

ATLANTIC COAST RESORTS & SEREKUNDA

INFORMATION
Alliance Franco-Gambienne............**1** G5
Belgian Honorary Consul...................**2** H2
Cultural Encounters.........................(see 19)
Danish, Swedish & Norwegian
Consuls..**3** G3
Discovery Tours..................................**4** E3
Gambia Experience........................(see 44)
Gambia River Excursions...................**5** F3
Gampost..**6** G2
Gamtel...**7** B6
Gamtel...**8** C6
Guinea Bissau Embassy..................(see 17)
Main Post Office................................**9** G5
Malak Chemist..................................**10** G5
Mauritanian Consulate.....................**11** C6
Medical Research Council.................**12** F3
Net Bar...**13** G2
PHB Bank..**14** G2
Quantumnet......................................**15** F3
Senegalese High Commission...........**16** F4
Standard Chartered Bank..................**17** G2
Standard Chartered Bank..................**18** A5
Stop Steps Pharmacy......................(see 73)
Timbooktoo......................................**19** F3
Tropical Tour & Souvenirs...............(see 44)
Trust Bank..**20** G2
Trust Bank..**21** C6
UK High Commission........................**22** E3
US Embassy......................................**23** F4
Westfield Clinic................................**24** B6

SIGHTS & ACTIVITIES
African Living Art Centre.................**25** F3
Bijilo Forest Park Headquarters......**26** C6
Botanic Gardens...............................**27** G2
Eco Yoga Holidays..........................(see 53)
Fajara Golf Club................................**28** E4
Kachikally Crocodile Pool.................**29** H3
Sakura Arts Studio............................**30** F5

SLEEPING
African Heritage Centre....................**31** H2
African Village Hotel.........................**32** G2
Bakau Lodge.....................................**33** G2
Bakotu Hotel.....................................**34** E4
Balmoral Apartments........................**35** C6
Banana Ville......................................**36** D5
Cape Point Hotel..............................**37** H2
Coconut Residence...........................**38** C6
Fajara Guesthouse............................**39** E3
Fajara Hotel......................................**40** E3
Fountain Hotel..................................**41** E3
Holiday Beach Club Hotel.................**42** C6
Jabo Guest House.............................**43** H2
Kairaba Hotel....................................**44** C6
Kanifeng YMCA.................................**45** G4
Kombo Beach Hotel..........................**46** D4
Leybato...**47** E3
Luigi's...**48** D5
Ngala Lodge......................................**49** F3

Praia Hotel..**50** G6
Roc Heights Lodge............................**51** H2
Romana Hotel...................................**52** G2
Safari Garden....................................**53** E3
Seaview Gardens Hotel.....................**54** D4
Senegambia Beach Hotel..................**55** C6
Sunbeach Hotel & Resort..................**56** H2

EATING
Al Basha..**57** C6
Ali Baba's..**58** C6
Asie Marie Cinema............................**59** F6
Bendula Garden................................**60** H2
Bucarabu..(see 48)
Butcher's Shop.................................**61** E3
Calypso...**62** H2
Chossan..(see 99)
Clay Oven...**63** F3
Come Inn..**64** F5
Eddie's Bar & Restaurant.................**65** E3
Flavours..(see 53)
Francisco's Restaurant....................(see 41)
Gaya Art Café...................................**66** C6
Green Gate.......................................**67** H2
Green Mamba....................................**68** C6
GTS Restaurant................................**69** C6
Harry's Supermarket.........................**70** F4
Italian Connection............................**71** H2
Jojo's..**72** C6
Kairaba Supermarket........................**73** F5
Keur Bouba J & Cotton Club...........(see 92)
Kora..**74** C6
La Parisienne....................................**75** F4
Le Palais du Chocolat.......................**76** F4
Luigi's Pizza & Pasta House............(see 48)
Mandela's.......................................(see 97)
Maroun's...**77** A6
Ngala Lodge....................................(see 49)
Ocean Clipper.................................(see 37)
Pailotte...(see 1)
Paradiso Pizza..................................**78** C6
Ritz...**79** E3
Safe Way Afra King...........................**80** F5
Safeway's.......................................(see 70)
Saffie J..**81** H2
Sambou's..**82** G2
Solar Project.....................................**83** G5

Solomon's Beach Bar........................**84** C5
Soul Food...**85** F3
Sultan Sweets..................................**86** F4
Yok...(see 25)
Youth Monument Bar &
Restaurant.......................................**87** B6

DRINKING
Blue Bar..**88** F4
Chapman's..**89** G2
Churchill's.......................................(see 48)
Come Inn...(see 64)
Lana's Bar...**90** F6
Paparazzi..(see 57)
Sinatra's..**91** G2
Weezo's...**92** E3

ENTERTAINMENT
Aquarius..(see 74)
Arena Babou Fatty............................**93** F6
Destiny..**94** D4
Independence Stadium......................**95** G3
Jokor...**96** B6
Kololi Casino.....................................**97** C6
Teranga Beach Club..........................**98** C5
Waaw Nightclub................................**99** C6

SHOPPING
African Heritage Centre...................(see 31)
Bakau Market...................................**100** G2
Batik Factory...................................**101** F6
Craft Market.....................................**102** G2
Equigambia.......................................**103** D5
Salam Batik.....................................**104** F6
Tropical Tour & Souvenirs..............(see 44)

46 D4

94

54 D4

Kotu
Point

84 C5
98
48
107

Kololi
Beach

Kololi
Point

Kololi

105

103

Berting Harding Hwy

Kololi Rd

36

55 68 21
44 8
57 35
72 58 99
42 97 78
113 66 11
74

26 69

38

To Coco Ocean
Resort (1km);
Gambia Tours (1km);
Baobab Lodge (1km);
Bijilo Beach Hotel (1km);
Tanji (8km); Kartong (38km)

**Bijilo Forest
Park**

18 A5

0   200 m
0   0.1 miles

7
110
77
87
108
24
96

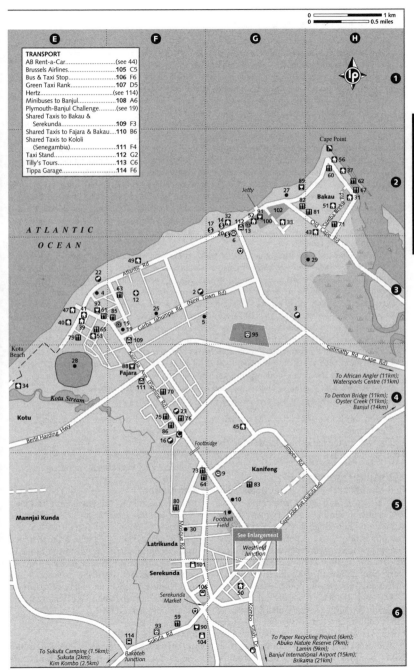

TRANSPORT
AB Rent-a-Car	(see 44)
Brussels Airlines	**105** C5
Bus & Taxi Stop	**106** F6
Green Taxi Rank	**107** D5
Hertz	(see 114)
Minibuses to Banjul	**108** A6
Plymouth-Banjul Challenge	(see 19)
Shared Taxis to Bakau &	
Serekunda	**109** F3
Shared Taxis to Fajara & Bakau	**110** B6
Shared Taxis to Kololi	
(Senegambia)	**111** F4
Taxi Stand	**112** G2
Tilly's Tours	**113** C6
Tippa Garage	**114** F6

SEX TOURISM & BUMSTERS *Katharina Lobeck Kane*

It was a short walk along the beach, barely covering 2km. The sand felt soft under bare feet, the waves were lapping against the shore, and my glass of freshly pressed fruit juice tasted delicious. And yet this was probably the most uncomfortable stroll I've ever taken. Juice sellers are unfortunately not the only guys approaching a single woman on the beaches of the Atlantic resorts. In less than an hour, I was chatted up over 20 times by young men, offering to walk with me, show me the sights, or give me the 'real Gambian experience' they thought I had come here for. On this level, male attention is no longer flattering, but deeply frustrating, to say the least.

The young men who work the beaches this way are called 'bumsters', an unflattering term for a humiliating business. Bumsters try to eke out a living by gluing themselves to tourists, offering anything from guide services and translation to sex. And, despite measures to clamp down on these persistent young men or introduce them to alternative ways of making money in the tourist industry, bumsterism is flourishing. For obvious reasons, the 'business' is kept afloat by a worryingly large sex-tourism scene that is casting a shadow on Gambia's white beaches.

In Gambia, sex tourism has a slightly different face than in countries like Thailand or the Philippines. Here, white men looking for girls constitute a much smaller group than middle-aged women, who seek out Gambian shores to look for fit, young African men. Many return regularly to meet changing partners, who depend on the ladies to earn a small income that often goes to feeding whole families.

The women involved usually argue that these 'arrangements' benefit all parties: they get their kicks; the men the cash, and perhaps even the chance to obtain a visa to Europe. But as with all forms of sex tourism, there is an obvious element of exploitation that stems from the unequal power relations involved, particularly if the practice involves under-age persons (and it often does). Certainly, no one forces youngsters to work in the industry. But, given the extreme poverty, lack of options and financial responsibilities (for a huge extended family) that young Gambians face, it's debatable how free they really are in their choices.

Besides presenting obvious health risks, including the spread of HIV/AIDS, the sex-tourism scene can also render a harmless holiday uncomfortable, as bumsters will tail you as you visit the sights. Organisations such as ASSET (see p104) have done great work in promoting a different kind of tourism, notably sustainable options. With a few pointers, it's easy to avoid the worst of the scene, while actively contributing to alternative ways of making money for Gambia's youth.

---

gives you more information about the park and its projects.

The walk to the park southwards from the Senegambia Strip only takes a few minutes.

Kachikally Crocodile Pool

In the heart of Bakau village, the **crocodile pool** (☎ 7782479; www.kachikally.com; admission D50; ☼ 9am-6pm) is one of Gambia's most popular tourist attractions. For locals, it's a sacred site. As crocodiles represent the power of fertility in Gambia, women who experience difficulties in conceiving often come here to pray and wash (any child called Kachikally tells of a successful prayer at the pool).

The pool, its adjacent nature trail and small museum, containing musical instruments and other cultural artefacts, have for years been managed by the resident Bojang family. They look after 80 fully grown and several smaller Nile crocodiles that you'll see basking on the

bank. Many of them are tame enough to be touched (your guide will point you in their direction).

A small shop nearby sells refreshments to complete a relaxed afternoon out.

Kim Kombo

Just behind Sukuta, this small family **distillery** (☎ 7229841; www.kimkombo.gm; ☼ 3-6pm Mon-Sat) makes tasty liquors from local fruit, which is grown on the plantation behind the thatched main reception. You can taste the range of flavours and buy your favourite bottle, of course – the fact that they vary according to the seasons gives you plenty of reason to come back more than once. A private taxi here should cost around D60.

Sakura Arts Studio

Just off Kairaba Ave, leading Gambian painter Njogu Touray opens the doors of his cute

ATLANTIC COAST
RESORTS & SEREKUNDA

THE KOMBOS

The four Atlantic coast resorts of Bakau, Fajara, Kotu and Kololi, along with Serekunda and other nearby suburbs of Sukuta, Kanifeng, Fajikunda and Dippa Kunda, are known collectively as the Kombos. This is because the area around Banjul is divided into several local administrative districts, called Kombo North, Kombo South, Kombo Central and Kombo St Mary.

Sakura Arts Studio (☎ 7017351; Latrikunda; ☼ 9am-6pm) to the public. Like Touray's work, the cute place is full of colour and atmosphere, granting real respite from the Serekunda bustle as well as a private view on contemporary Gambian art. Using natural media, such as shells and sand, alongside colour to paint his scenes, Touray carries the Gambian lands straight into his urban workshop. If you meet the master, don't only ask him about his fascinating career, but also about his children's workshops and work in environmental campaigns.

ACTIVITIES
Fishing
The Sportsfishing Centre at Denton Bridge is the place to organise your fishing tours.

African Angler (☎ 7721228, 7921229; www.african-angling.co.uk; Sportsfishing Centre, Denton Bridge) This brilliant little business run by Mark and Tracey specialises in light tackle, lure and anchored-bottom fishing in the creeks. They're very professional and able to accommodate experienced anglers as well as beginners.

Golf
Fajara Golf Club (☎ 4495456) is the country's main golf course (18 holes, par 69). The 'greens' are made of oil sand, so brown is in fact the dominant colour. Apart from that it's a golf course as great as any, with the added attraction of tropical scenery and plenty of birds watching you play and watch them. The club also has a pool and courts for tennis, squash and badminton, as well as a restaurant. Temporary membership is available by the day. Enquire about rates.

Swimming
Most beaches in this area are relatively safe for swimming, but currents can sometimes get strong. Care should be taken along the beach in Fajara, where there's a strong undertow. Always check conditions before plunging in.

The erosion that used to eat its way right up to the hotels has largely been reversed (see p66), so that the beaches of Kotu, Kololi and Cape Point are once again wide, sandy and beautiful. Kotu is particularly attractive, with sands and palm trees, beach bars and juice sellers on one side, and an area of lagoons a bit further north, where Kotu Stream cuts into the land (that's the bit the birdwatchers will head to).

Cape Point, at the northern tip of Bakau, has the calmest beaches. As this is a more residential area, you get less hassle.

If the Atlantic doesn't appeal, all the major hotels have swimming pools. Most places allow access to nonguests with a meal, a drink or for a fee.

Other Water Sports
Some of the large hotels – notably Kombo beach in Kotu – offer various water sports to guests. Try also the **Watersports Centre** (☎ 7773777) at Denton Bridge, which offers parasailing, windsurfing, catamaran trips and more.

COURSES
Safari Garden hotel (p106) always has something going on: African dance, drumming, batik or yoga. Phone to check the current schedule. Salam Batik (p112) offers recommended batik courses.

For total relaxation in beautiful surroundings, try Deepa Spirit's **Eco Yoga Holidays** (☎ in UK 7779 240985; www.deepaspirit.com). Both adult and children's courses are available.

ATLANTIC COAST RESORTS & SEREKUNDA FOR CHILDREN
The Atlantic coast attracts plenty of family holidaymakers, and is well equipped for young people. Most of the large resort hotels offer high chairs, cots and even babysitting services, and some of the self-contained apartments gear themselves up for family visitors. Ask hotels whether they have communicating rooms or can put an extra bed in; most of them can help. Nappies and other baby items are available at all the larger supermarkets along Kairaba Ave.

When it comes to children's entertainment you'll need to be creative, unless your offspring is the kind that's perfectly content

ATLANTIC COAST RESORTS & SEREKUNDA

INTRODUCING ASSET

One day, a group of small operators in Gambia's tourism sector had had enough. Tourism was flourishing, travellers were flocking to the coast, but instead of feeling the direct benefits of this economic growth, many private hoteliers, one-man artisan businesses and others who had hoped to make a living from tourism found it harder to compete with the big players. It only took a tiny idea to reverse that situation – unity. A handful of operators got together to form ASSET, Gambia's Association of Small Scale Enterprises in Tourism. From a simple listing, the collective developed into a vast network of small businesses, ranging from individual bird guides and organic juice pressers to crafts stalls and private guest houses. Through ASSET, they gained visibility and the possibility of putting their name on the map – all without huge marketing departments.

ASSET's efforts were honoured with the Responsible Tourism Award in 2007, but more importantly, the organisation's success has contributed to a staggering increase in community projects and responsible tourism offers. You can find out about the project and its members on a visit to its Cultural Encounters office in Fajara (p99). The ASSET advisers there can also assist you in building your very own, very unique responsible tourism itinerary.

---

with two weeks at the hotel's paddling pool and sandpit. The Kachikally Crocodile Pool (p102) is great to visit with children, and monkey spotting at Bijilo Forest Park (p99) usually goes down a storm. Njogu Touray, the artist who runs Sakura Arts Studio (p102), is brilliant at involving children in workshops.

Other kid-friendly options are just a short hop from the coast. The Tanji Village Museum (p117) has great exhibits and an area where you can watch artisans at work. Staff here really know how to explain stuff to children. Near the village museum, you can also take your kids camel riding (p117) on the beach. Pirogue tours around Oyster Creek (p94) or Kartong (p119) are brief enough to accommodate short attention spans.

Etu at Tunbung Arts Village (p118) is another artist who provides workshops for kids. Abuko Nature Reserve (p122) has more monkeys and a host of reptiles, while a trip to Makasutu Culture Forest (p123) is a full day of fun, including animal spotting, dance shows, nature trails and plenty more.

TOURS

Organised excursions in the immediate area usually take in Bijilo Forest Park and Kachikally Crocodile Pool at Bakau, or go to Banjul city for a visit to Albert Market and the museum. All of these places are easily reached by taxi, public transport or hired bicycle, but if you prefer a tour, contact the companies listed in the Transport chapter (p287) or the travel agencies listed earlier in this chapter (p99).

Boat tours through the mangroves of Oyster Creek between Banjul and the mainland or as far as Lamin Lodge (p122) are highly recommended. Gambia River Excursions (p287) has good tours from Lamin. All pirogue tours to close-by destinations depart from Denton Bridge.

SLEEPING

Gambia's Atlantic coast is dotted with hotels, ranging from plush resorts to grotty dives. The list here is not exhaustive but gives a good cross-section of options, especially for independent travellers. If you're travelling in the low season, you can usually expect rates to drop by about 50% – or find your hotel closed. For trips between June and September, always phone to check the situation.

Budget
BAKAU
Romana Hotel (☎ 4495127; aframsromanahotel@yahoo .co.uk; Atlantic Rd; r from D350) You get what you'd expect for the price: a roof over your head, swept floors, a cold shower and a ceiling fan – the clean sheets are a nice addition. Close the door and leap into one of the hammocks in the pretty garden space, and you'll probably make your peace with this place.

Jabo Guest House (☎ 4494906; 9 Old Cape Rd; d D600) Behind the intimidating compound walls hides a down-to-earth place with large and clean rooms. The biggest have good self-catering facilities and the courtyard offers chill-out space in the shade of an orange tree. You're in the heart of Bakau village here; the beach is a short walk away.

Bakau Lodge (☎ /fax 9901610; bakaulodge@yahoo .com; Bakau market; d from D600; 🖭) This small place surprises with large, two-room bungalows set around a swimming pool right in the heart of the Bakau 'hood. It's calm, considering the urban village setting, and rooms come with tea-making facilities, though there's no restaurant on site.

FAJARA & KANIFENG

Kanifeng YMCA (☎ 4392647; www.ymca.gm; Kanifeng; s/d incl breakfast D325/525; 🖳) This huge building has passable rooms and cheap meals for the budget-bound. Rooms are very, very basic (only go for the top-floor ones that come with their own bathroom), and if you carry any childhood traumas you might not think much of the school-like building. The knowledge that your stay here contributes to the impressive youth development projects run by the YMCA helps promote a sound sleep, though.

Fajara Guesthouse (☎ 4496122; fax 4494365; Fajara; s/d D600/750; 🖭 🏊) This cosy place, five minutes from the pool and restaurant at Safari Garden, exudes family vibes with its leafy courtyard and welcoming lounge. Some of the rooms are big enough to house couples with children. There's hot water – not always a given in this price range – and for an extra D250 you can get air-conditioning. Self-caterers can use the kitchen for a small extra charge.

KOLOLI

Banana Ville (☎ 9906054; njieadama@hotmail.com; Kololi; d D800; 🖭) Very tiny and very simple, this is a great budget bet. Rooms are surprisingly spacious and have good self-catering facilities. And while the furniture looks a bit wonky, the beds are comfortable enough for a good night's sleep.

SEREKUNDA

Sukuta Camping (☎ 9917786; www.campingsukuta .com; Sukuta; camping per person/car/van D100/20/28, s/d/ste D240/460/600) This exceptionally well-organised camping ground in Sukuta (southwest of Serekunda) also offers simple rooms for those who have temporarily tired of canvas. Joe and Claudia, the friendly managers, are experts on crossing the Sahara, which is why their site is something of an obligatory stop for overlanders. There are good washing and laundry facilities, the space is welcoming, and if your car is in need of a bit of TLC after a desert trip, the onsite mechanic can give professional help. A private taxi here should cost around D50.

Praia Hotel (☎ 4394887; Mame Jout St; r D500; 🖭) A few minutes' walk off Sayer Jobe Ave, right in the heart of fume-filled and garbage-strewn Serekunda, this clean, spacious hostel with its large wooden beds comes as such a surprise you may just feel like hugging Mr Ceesay, the friendly manager.

Midrange

BAKAU

African Heritage Centre (☎ 4496778; www.african heritagegambia.com; 16 Samba Breku Rd; s/d incl breakfast D900/1000, apt D1500; 🖭 🏊) Sometimes the best accommodation is found in unexpected places, such as this art-gallery-cum-restaurant near Cape Point. Out the back there are six clean, nicely furnished rooms and even an apartment for families and self-caterers. Room rates differ slightly depending on size and standard.

African Village Hotel (☎ 4495384; africanvillage hotel@yahoo.com; Atlantic Rd; s D650-1500, d D1200-2200; 🖭 🏊) Like a slightly scruffy, slightly bored little sister to the glitzy holiday clubs, this fills a gap somewhere between the bottom of the barrel and lofty palaces. The basic bungalows are a bit crammed together, but the pool is great, the location practical and extra services like bicycle hire and exchange bureau welcome.

Cape Point Hotel (☎ 4495005; Atlantic Rd; r incl breakfast D1850; 🖭 🖳 🏊) More intimate than many of the package palaces, this family-run hotel offers a good range of facilities, including free wi-fi, seating corners, satellite TV and personalised service. And though the decor reminds you a bit of a cheap furniture showroom, the balconies overlooking the pool are a nice touch.

Roc Heights Lodge (☎ 4495428; www.rocheights lodge.com; Samba Breku Rd; s/d D1600/2350; 🖭 🖳 🏊) This three-storey villa sits in a quiet garden that makes the bustle of Bakau suddenly seem very far away. Everything is held in an appealing decor of wood-and-tile simplicity. The self-catering apartments (enquire for prices) come with fully equipped kitchens, bathtub, hair dryer, TV, telephone and plenty of space – though 'penthouse' is a slightly ambitious label. The downstairs restaurant is a relaxing space, not least because of the attentive staff.

FAJARA

Leybato (☎ 4390275; www.leybato.abc.gm; Fajara beach; d incl breakfast from D800) Hidden behind a small hill off Atlantic Rd, this cosy guest house and its relaxed restaurant overlook the ocean from one of the best locations anywhere on the coast. Rooms vary in quality and price (the ones with kitchens tend to be better and D400 more expensive). They're pretty basic and slightly worn, but still, you're unlikely to find better beachfront value.

Fountain Hotel (Francisco's; ☎ /fax 4495332; franciscos hotel@yahoo.co.uk; cnr Atlantic Rd & Kairaba Ave; s/d D800/1200; P ⊠) Recently renamed, everyone still knows this family hotel as Francisco's. Its intimate character has fortunately survived the baptism: the patio is still bathed in the shade of huge trees, the restaurant still does a fabulous roast on a Sunday (D175) and staff are as friendly as ever. Rooms were undergoing renovation when we visited, and that can surely only be a good thing.

Safari Garden (☎ 4495887; www.safarigarden.com; Fajara; s/d D1100/1500; ⊠ 🖳 🖳) It's not the pretty rooms or the lovely garden that makes this place special, or even the excellent service. The real Safari Garden bonus is Geri and Maurice, a couple so dedicated to Gambia and the possibilities for eco-tourism and community action that travellers have been known to be drawn into their projects after even the briefest of stays. Ask them about Sandele Eco-Retreat in Kartong (p121), the luxurious step up from solar-powered and -heated Safari Garden.

Fajara Hotel (☎ 4495605; fax 4494575; Atlantic Rd; s/d D800/1600; ⊠ 🖳 🖳) With its long, intimidating corridors, colony of ants and bland rooms, this has all the charm of a 1960s communist camp. But the beach location and garden views are fantastic (have a drink here), and there were rumours that a group of associates was planning to invest in the place.

KOTU

Kombo Beach Hotel (☎ 4465466; www.kombobeachhotel .gm; Kotu beach; s/d from D1150/1500; ⊠ 🖳 🖳) Owned by Gambia Experience, this place mainly attracts tour groups and has a definite club feel. Rooms are a bit tired, but the location near Kotu Stream is fabulous, and the restaurant ranks among the best.

Bakotu Hotel (☎ 4465555; fax 4465959; Kotu beach; s/d D1250/1500; ⊠ 🖳) Compared with its resort neighbours, this hotel, in the strip between Fajara Golf Club and Kotu Stream, is pleasantly understated, and has comfy terrace apartments in a pleasant garden. It's particu-

larly popular with young people and, like the whole of Kotu beach, can get pretty noisy.

Seaview Gardens Hotel (☎ 4466660; www.seaview gardens-hotel.co.uk; off Bertil Harding Hwy; s/d D1500/2000; ⊠ 🖳 🖳) This tries hard to be a top-class place, and has quite a few attributes that point that way. It's pretty, tidy, friendly and bright, but doesn't really have any character. The management also has a few very well-appointed, though tiny, apartments for rent in Fajara.

KOLOLI

our pick **Luigi's** (☎ 4460280; www.luigis.gm; Palma Rima Rd; s/d incl breakfast D745/1100, apt from D2000; ⊠ 🖳 🖳) Once a pool restaurant with a couple of guest rooms, this has grown into a stunning complex with three restaurants and attractive lodgings set around the pool and hot tub. Despite this tropical growth rate, the place manages to keep its family feel and you'll soon believe that you're a personal guest of Luigi's.

Balmoral Apartments (☎ 4461079; www.balmoral -apartments.com; off Bertil Harding Hwy; apt D1200; ⊠ 🖳 ♿) Perfect for families with children, this set of spacious, self-catering apartments does most things right in providing you with a relaxed home from home in walking distance to Kololi's busy stretch of restaurants and bars. You can even organise your own barbecues here, and dig into the food under the shade of the palm trees on the patio.

Baobab Lodge (☎ 4465518; Bijilo; s/d D1200/1500; ⊠ 🖳) This family-run place has simple rooms and self-catering apartments in a garden setting, about 2km south of the Senegambia Strip. It's slightly far from the action, but not quite far enough to get away from it all. The African cookery lessons are a great addition.

Holiday Beach Club Hotel (☎ 4460418; www.holiday beachclubgambia.com; Senegambia; s/d D1500/2000; ⊠ 🖳) You're right near the Senegambia tourist mile at this resort hotel, but you'll feel miles removed once you've walked through the lush gardens to your private bungalow. The famous Bijilo monkeys leap right up to the private verandahs – great for a wildlife experience, less exciting if they start nicking your jewellery.

Bijilo Beach Hotel (☎ 4462701; www.bijilohotel .com; s/d D2000/2400; ⊠ 🖳 🖳) On the main road between Kololi and Brufut, this feels more personable than some of the resort-style places, thanks to the friendly and professional service you get. The spacious rooms are well appointed, with TV, telephone, fridge and safe box, but what really sells this hotel is its location, right on a beautiful stretch of beach and in peace-inducing distance from the busiest tourist zones.

Top End
BAKAU

Sunbeach Hotel & Resort (☎ 4497190; www.sunbeach hotel.com; Cape Point; s/d D2600/3000; 🌀 🖵 🖳) It's the location that makes this place, right at the tip of Cape Point. Staff are great and there's a reliable network of tour guides to take you around. Rooms are slightly shoddier than they should be in this price range, though, and the vibe is very much 'holiday club'.

FAJARA

our pick **Ngala Lodge** (☎ 4494045; www.ngalalodge .com; 64 Atlantic Rd; ste per person D2000; 🌀 🖵 🖳) Now here's a hotel loved, fussed over and regularly stroked by its owner. Even the simplest lodging in this red-brick palace is a large suite with its own Jacuzzi and hand-picked paintings (there's a great story about the ground-floor suite, whose ceiling was raised to make space for its chosen *œuvre d'art*). Our favourite was the Rolling Stones room, kind of a stylish shrine to one of owner Peter's passions. It's not one for families – neither laid out nor intended for children – but it's perfect for couples. The penthouse with sky-gazer dome and sea view is ideal for honeymoons. Perfect down to the frosted glasses and thoughtfully chosen book collection, the Ngala has also one of the top restaurants in Gambia.

KOLOLI

Senegambia Beach Hotel (☎ 4462717; www.senegambia hotel.com; Senegambia; s/d incl breakfast D2800/3500; 🅿 🌀 🖵 🖳) With more than 300 rooms, this is a giant on the scene. Rooms are what you would expect from such a place: standard affairs that do the job but lack character. This hotel's big winner is the stunning tropical garden surrounding the main building. It really is as brilliant as the brochure claims and attracts plenty of birds, meaning you can tick the first tail feathers off the list while still lounging at the hotel pool.

Coco Ocean Resort (☎ 4466500; www.cocoocean.com; 1 Bamboo Dr, Kombo Coastal Rd, Bijilo; ste from D5000) With its pristine white walls, sculpted domes and wide arched walkways, this aroma-drizzled wellness temple whispers relaxation, until you float back from a soul-soothing trip through

spa, *hammam* (Turkish bath), massage centre and gym to find that you've mistakenly been locked out of your luxury home. It's very possible that management has since sorted out the few service hiccups – the place was still brand new when we passed.

Kairaba Hotel (☎ 4462940; www.kairabahotel .com; Senegambia; s/d incl breakfast D4900/5700; 🅿 🌀 🖵 🖳 ♿) Knowing that this place is owned by the president might irk some, but it's very hard to dislike. Everything in this vast, labyrinthine, anything-can-be-arranged place tastes of five stars. It has more facilities than you can probably think of, including massage parlours, sports studios, a nightclub and a babysitting service. The right address for a holiday break wrapped in cotton wool.

Coconut Residence (☎ 4463377; www.coconutresidence .com; Bertil Harding Hwy; ste incl breakfast from D6500; 🌀 🖵 🖳) This is one of the few top hotels where luxury hasn't been traded for soul. All amenities and services come wrapped in a sophisticated chic, from the landscaped gardens to the lavish suites. If you're in a royal mood, go for a private villa with personal pool.

EATING

This is one of the best areas to dine in West Africa; there is no shortage of places or flavours. While many restaurants offer a standard menu, composed of a handful of dishes from all four corners of the globe plus some local flavours, there are some real gems to tickle your taste buds.

Self-caterers should head to Bakau market for fresh fruit and veg. There are plenty of supermarkets in this zone. Kairaba Ave also has several choices. **Kairaba Supermarket** (Kairaba Ave) and **Safeway's** (Kairaba Ave) are large and well stocked, while **Harry's Supermarket** (Kairaba Ave; ☽ 9am-10pm Mon-Sat) has the best hours. In Serekunda, **Maroun's** (Westfield Junction; ☽ 9am-7.30pm Mon-Sat, 10am-1.30pm Sun) is a decent choice.

Bakau

Sambou's (☎ 4495237; Old Cape Rd; dishes from D100) This small, slapdash eatery has been around for years, which is more than some of the top food temples can say. They must be doing something right, then, at this very local, no-frills place, even if it's only price or portion size.

Saffie J (☎ 9937645; Old Cape Rd; snacks D150) This is the low-key approach to restaurant management: purchase a few cheap seats, paint them with the Gambian flag, put them on the road-side and put a semblance of a fence around. Now you can charge small amounts for simple snacks with street views. Every Sunday, Lamin Sakho plays live *kora* (harp-lute) here.

Bendula Garden (☎ 4498223; www.bendulagarden .com; Kofi Annan St, Cape Point; dishes D250) This place is like an all-day happy hour where the drinks flow, the food fails to surprise, the music is live and the jokes are cheap. And though Mr Bass, the bubbly manager, insists that this spot is hassle-free, single women might disagree.

Calypso (Chez Anne & Fode; ☎ 4496292; Cape Point; dishes D250; ☉ 9am-late) This cute, round beach bar serves delicious seafood, snacks and an African dish of the day between red-brick walls and attractive paintings. Sitting right on the beach, it also grants spectacular sunset romance at the right time of day. You can order a full English breakfast (D225) here all day or, if you're the continental type, indulge in rich homemade cakes with thick cream.

Green Gate (Frank's Hungarian Restaurant; ☎ 4497362; Cape Point; dishes D100-250; ☉ 3pm-late Mon-Sat) For a cheap draught beer and solid meal in what looks like someone's living room (and probably once was), this small Hungarian restaurant is a great Bakau spot. And even if you didn't come to Africa to eat spicy Eastern European stews, they actually make a great change after days of seafood.

Other goodies in Bakau:

Italian Connection (☎ 4497462; Kofi Annan Rd; pizzas from D200) The name does not deceive – this is indeed Bakau's main pizza and pasta joint. Standard Italian fare.

Ocean Clipper (☎ 4494265; Cape Point; meals D500; ☉ 6pm-midnight) Part of the Ocean Bay Hotel & Resort complex, this lush place serves excellent Mediterranean and Asian food with a dose of exclusivity.

Fajara

La Parisienne (☎ 4372565; Kairaba Ave; cakes D30; ☉ 6.30am-midnight; ▣) French-style patisseries are very à la mode in Gambia. Excellent espresso and cappuccino, homemade ice cream, warm croissants and, well, the added incentive of free wi-fi make this a particularly worthy teatime destination.

Keur Bouba J & Cotton Club (☎ 4498249; Kairaba Ave; mains D100-200; ☉ 9am-6am) With two venues wrapped in one, this restaurant and music club only closes for three hours every night. That means morning coffee between its warm, red walls, a huge plate of rice for lunch (D75), and dinner à la carte before enjoying live jazz

and salsa. One great day and not a traffic jam suffered.

Le Palais du Chocolat (☎ 7222333; 19 Kairaba Ave; snacks D100, ☉ 7.30am-midnight; ▣) Apart from great ice creams, cakes, coffee and pastries, you can also get good *shwarma* (sliced, grilled meat and salad in pita bread) and pizzas, as well as a full English breakfast for D150 in the mornings. There's free, though slow, wi-fi.

Soul Food (☎ 4497858; Kairaba Ave; meals from D120) As the name promises, this is a place for generous portions of solid, sleep-enhancing meals. Think platters of rice dishes, mashed potato and rich sauces. The guest house upstairs has spacious but bare rooms.

our pick Butcher's Shop (☎ 4495069; www.the butchersshopgambia.com; Kairaba Ave; dishes D169-285; ☉ 8am-11pm) Driss, the Moroccan celebrity chef (and TV star), knows how to grill a pepper steak to perfection, subtly blend a sauce until the spices sing in harmony and present a freshly pressed juice cocktail like a precious gift. They do a mean Sunday brunch (D200) from 10am to 4pm, and even at this self-service occasion, Driss personally makes sure that everything runs smoothly.

Flavours (☎ 4495887; Safari Garden Hotel, Fajara; dishes D200; ☉ 8am-midnight; ▣ Ⓥ) If you've been wondering where all the great waiting staff have gone, quite a few have been hired by this fabulous little garden place, serving imaginative dishes for carnivores and vegetarians alike. Meals taste as great as they look and the atmosphere is as friendly as a hug. A dip in the pool gets thrown in free with a drink or a meal (otherwise it's D75).

Francisco's Restaurant (☎ 4495332; franciscos hotel@yahoo.co.uk; cnr Atlantic Rd & Kairaba Ave; grills D200) There are few places where mixed seafood platters and grills taste better than in the shade of the giant palm trees in Francisco's tranquil garden. The company is good, too, from the friendly owners to the loyal locals and expats.

Clay Oven (☎ 4496600; Fajara; meals D250; ☉ 7-11pm; Ⓥ) For Indian food, this place off Atlantic Rd is one of the best in the whole of West Africa. Just savour the tandoori grill or any of the original desserts. With its scrubbed white walls, leafy garden and personalised service, the surroundings are right, too. And believe us, we really tried, but Vimal wouldn't part with the slightest hint about the secret of his delicate spicing.

Ritz (☎ 9924205; Fajara; meals D250; ☽ 8am-midnight) This tiny place with the aspirational name has for six years now given the impression of teetering on the verge of closing. And yet it still serves generous portions of solid European fare in a Fajara side street. Bring a CD with your favourite music so that you don't get the endless loop of the available sounds – you'll be thanked with an extra spoonful of chips with your steak.

Yok (☎ 4495131; African Living Art Centre, Garba Jahumpa Rd; meals D300; ☽ 12.30pm-midnight; Ⓥ) No one should visit Fajara without eating at Yok, which is locally better known as the Salon. You reach this Asian restaurant via the leafy, glass-roofed alleyway behind an impressively stacked antique and arts shop. It serves excellent Singaporean, Thai and Chinese fusion cuisine against a backdrop of gently flowing waterfalls and rustling palm trees. Oh, and it has the best cocktails on the coast. You'll feel like an actor in a classic East Asian movie and be treated like a star – indulge!

Ngala Lodge (☎ 4494045; Atlantic Rd; meals D500; ☽ 11.30am-3pm & 7.30-11pm Mon-Sat; Ⓥ) When we visited, Paul the manager was bent over the CVs of a range of star-spangled European chefs. Apparently the gig to heat the stove in one of Gambia's most renowned restaurants went to a Polish celebrity cook. This has always been the top address for sumptuous and lovingly presented meals; service and sea-view setting are impeccable.

Come Inn (☎ 4391464; Kairaba Ave; mains D100-250; ☽ 10am-2am) For a hearty meal, a good draught beer and a solid dose of local gossip, there's no better place than this German-style beer garden. It's popular with overlanders and pretty much anyone else who likes big portions at decent rates.

Also try the following:

Eddie's Bar & Restaurant (Fajara; dishes D60-100; ☽ 8am-2am) It's tiny and looks unspectacular during the day, but it brims with vibrancy and locals at night. Great for Gambian food and backstreet vibes.

Sultan Sweets (☎ 4390151; sultansweets@hotmail .com; Kairaba Ave; meals D300; ▣) The varied menu ranges from full English breakfast to tasty Lebanese meze. There's a slow wi-fi connection for the information-starved.

Kololi

There are plenty of generic tourist restaurants in Kololi; following is a selection of the more interesting ones.

PALMA RIMA AREA

Solomon's Beach Bar (☎ 4460716; Palma Rima Rd; meals D100-200; ☽ 10am-midnight) At the northern end of Kololi beach, this cute round house serves excellent grilled fish in a youthful atmosphere. As light and sunny as the reggae classics on loop.

Luigi's Pizza & Pasta House (☎ 4460280; www .luigis.gm; Palma Rima Rd; dishes D75; ☽ 6pm-midnight; 🌊 ♿ Ⓥ) This is a praise song to Italy and its culinary achievements on two floors. The pasta is al dente, the pizzas are crisp and everything is cooked with the freshest ingredients. Kids get their very own menu and play area, so that parents on holiday can gaze across the sea from the terrace. There's also a breakfast parlour and tea house.

Bucarabu (☎ 7797877; Palma Rima Rd; dishes D75-200) From breakfast bar to grill party to tapas bar to cocktail lounge, there's hardly anything this place is not trying to be. The draught beer, darts and sports on a big screen lead you to suspect that the place has a loyal British following. There's live music on Friday and karaoke on Monday night.

SENEGAMBIA STRIP

GTS Restaurant (☎ 7777225; Senegambia; meals D180) This is the public face and fundraising initiative of a charity working to get Gambian youngsters into school and enable them to stay there. The relaxed restaurant has a real youth vibe, with pool tables, table tennis and occasional karaoke nights on offer. Very reasonably priced, it serves great Gambian food and seafood dishes.

Mandela's (☎ 9910986; Bijilo Park Rd; dishes from D250; Ⓥ) Meals are solid at this Gambian-Nigerian restaurant. If you love meat stew or giant steaks, you're at the right address, but vegetarians are welcome too: most dishes are available in a vegie variant (the vegetable *domodah* is particularly good).

Kora (☎ 4462727; Senegambia; dishes D275-350; ☽ 4pm-midnight; Ⓥ) This dinner favourite serves a range of very tasty meals, great cocktails and a vast selection of quality spirits in a classy ambience. If you come with friends, try the enormous mixed platter for four people (D500 per person) that gives you a taste of the best dishes on the varied menu. It also does kids' dishes (D150), a rarity in Gambia.

Ali Baba's (☎ 9905978; Senegambia; meals D300; ☽ 9.30am-2am) Everyone knows Ali Baba's, so it's as much a useful meeting point as a commendable restaurant. A fast-food joint during the day, it serves dinner with a show in its breezy garden. There are frequent live concerts (mainly reggae), and important football matches on a big screen.

Paradiso Pizza (☎ 4462177; Senegambia; pizzas D300) No one argues with Paradiso's claim of serving the best pizza in town. Amid the host of indistinguishable eateries that line the Senegambia Strip, this is a real find. Sticking with the Italian theme, the espresso here is also real.

Gaya Art Café (☎ 4464022; gayaartcafe.com; Bertil Harding Hwy; meals D350; ☪ noon-midnight Mon-Sat; ⓥ) Arty, vegie, healthy and organic, this is an unlikely addition to Senegambia's loud and boisterous food stations. The airy sculpture garden with its comfy armchairs is a great place to relax, the food absolutely fresh, the coffee made from freshly ground beans and the smoothies perfect for an energy boost after a walk around town.

Jojo's (☎ 7295711; Senegambia; dishes D370; ⓥ) Run by the former chef of the famous Ngala Lodge, Jojo's, with its earthy, minimalist ambience, sets out to rival established kitchens of the country. The saltimbocca chicken with olives and parmesan is divine, but only a build-up to the sumptuous seafood platter (order in advance). For vegetarians there's a great choice of salads, and breakfast fans will love the pancakes and coffee.

ourpick **Green Mamba** (☎ 6662622; www.greenmambagarden.com; Senegambia; Oriental wok D450; ☪ 7pm-midnight; ⓥ) A rare treat, this inspired restaurant is built around the concept of an Asian grill, meaning you get to pick the raw ingredients for your personalised stir-fry and watch them being cooked – unless you wish to relax over an original local fruit cocktail while the attentive staff bring your plate over. Spread across a large garden, tables grant a couple-enticing amount of privacy. Also check for the party and cinema nights.

Also recommended:

Al Basha (☎ 4463300; Senegambia; meals from D300; ☪ 11am-2am) Ice-cool Lebanese place with suit-'n'-tie attitude and occasional belly-dancing shows. Great meze.

Chossan (☎ 4464781; Senegambia; dishes D350) The name means 'tradition' and probably refers to the small selection of African dishes and palm wine on the menu. A busy eatery in Kololi's main tourist zone.

Serekunda

Enter the world of cheap, local eateries. You'll find them scattered across Serekunda's enormous market and taxi-station entrance, on busy side streets and near the taxi stands. Also

popular is Asie Marie Cinema, which isn't actually a cinema any more but a darkened hall with football matches on a big screen. If you're not into football, buy a cold beer and a snack, sit in the cinema's yard and turn streetwards to watch entertaining market scenes instead.

Paillote (☎ 4375418; dishes from D50; Kairaba Ave; ☪ noon-4pm) The choice at the restaurant of the Alliance Franco-Gambienne is between the African dish at a mind-boggling D50 and the European three-course meal at D120. Both are usually delicious – you'd have to try very hard to find better value anywhere.

Safe Way Afra King (dishes D50-150; ☪ 5pm-midnight) This is a popular choice among Serekunda's host of snacks, eateries and grilled-meat houses. Off the mosque road, it serves tasty *afra* (grilled meat), sandwiches, *fufu* (mashed casava) and other African dishes.

Youth Monument Bar & Restaurant (Westfield Junction; meals D100) This impressively named eatery sits right on the junction. It's a favourite with the locals, loved as much for cheap food and drinks as for the sports matches onscreen.

Solar Project (☎ 7053822; solarprojectgambia@gmx .ch; Kanifeng; snacks D50-100; ☪ 7am-midnight Mon-Sat) For ecofriendly eating options, this small solar-powered cafe and workshop is hard to beat. All of the omelettes, meatballs, cakes and dried fruit served here are cooked on the parabolic solar cookers you can observe being made in the backyard.

DRINKING

For entertainment, hotel bars compete for attention with restaurants reinventing themselves as bars at night, and a glitzy string of nightclubs near the coast. Thanks to the sizeable British and German community there are also a few pub-style places, ranging from brash to sleazy. For local-style Gambian bars and the rootsiest clubs, Serekunda is the best address.

The line between bar and nightclub is often blurred, as punters turn precious table space (or table tops) into improvised dance floors. See Entertainment (opposite) for a list of nightclubs that were actually made for dancing.

BAKAU

Chapman's (☎ 4495252; Atlantic Rd; meals D150-250; ☪ 11am-10pm Thu-Tue) In Bakau, this is labelled 'the place where everyone seems to go'. It's usually packed with a mixed crowd. Good, very generous and solid meals are washed down with pints of draught beer and good conversation.

Sinatra's (☎ 7781727; Atlantic Rd) With a different program every day (movies on Monday, live music on Friday and Saturday, grill party on Sunday afternoon) and the fixed point of cheap draught beer to guide you through it all, this is a place you're unlikely to visit only once. The vibes here shift from family fun out to smoky jazz lounge to loose club night, depending on the day and time.

FAJARA

Weezo's (☎ 4496918; Kairaba Ave) Fajara's favourite Mexican diner undergoes a fascinating transformation around sunset, when the lights are dimmed, the tables readied for spontaneous dancing, and the sumptuous tortilla dishes replaced with one of the best cocktail menus on the coast.

Come Inn (☎ 7049210; Kairaba Ave; ☺ 10am-2am) This German-style beer garden is popular with anyone knowing how to handle a few pints of draught and some solid pub humour. It's the place to compete for the biggest desert-driving stories with drink-hardy overlanders, and local Gambians, Brits and Germans.

Blue Bar (☎ 9991539; Kairaba Ave; ☺ 11am-3am) Overlooking a calm stretch of the region's main artery, this cheerful, dimly lit bar has an excellent selection of drinks to be sipped in good company on the outdoor terrace. It's a place with real atmosphere, popular with locals and expats.

KOLOLI

Paparazzi (☎ 4460600; Senegambia; ☺ 10pm-3am) This is a smart wine bar with dazzling decor and a tourist crowd. Don't stay away from your table too long or it may get pushed aside to make space for party steps to booming electronic beats.

Churchill's (☎ 4460830; Palma Rima Rd) Are clichés ever wrong? This favourite with parts of the British expat community serves fish and chips and draught beer while the Premier League on the big screen heats tempers. To round out the image, there's even a boot sale on every Sunday.

SEREKUNDA

Lana's Bar (☎ 7707684; Sukuta Rd) This reggae-coloured drinking hole will happily soak you up after a tiring, lung-clogging walk along Serekunda's main artery. Sitting here with a

cold beer, with the Serekunda bustle washing over you, is not a bad way of wasting an hour. Unless you're a single woman, when it's torture through bad chat-up lines.

ENTERTAINMENT
Live Music
The first live music you'll come across will probably be the troupes of Fula acrobats and Malinké *griots* (West African praise singers) who sometimes perform around hotel pools and outside restaurants. Though these are invariably tourist-tailored affairs, the artists are often very good, even if the hotel lobby setting may not be the ideal place to experience them. Also look out for impromptu reggae bashes, or try some of the nightclubs, which often feature live bands on weekends.

Nightclubs
Just like the coast's restaurants, the nightclubs present punters with a global mix that tries to cater to everyone – hip hop, R&B, *mbalax* (a mixture of Cuban beats and traditional, fiery *sabar* drumming), reggae and a whole lot more.

Clubs usually open their doors around 10pm, but there's no need to arrive before midnight.

KOTU & KOLOLI

Aquarius (☎ 4460247; Senegambia; ☺ 10am-3am) A smart cafe during the day, Aquarius turns into a glittering dance floor at night – a place where the dance beats are heavy and the crowds touristy. The drinks are expensive and the atmosphere is strictly party-vibe – it's no place for a quiet drink.

Teranga Beach Club (☎ 7060621; Palma Rima Rd) The future of this huge live club on the beach end of Palma Rima Rd was uncertain when we passed – the wild rumours raging were almost as exciting as the reggae and Gambian nights you'll get to experience here if it's open.

Waaw Nightclub (☎ 4460668; Senegambia) Right on the tourist strip, this is where lots of people head to when the bars have gotten too small for their desire for entertainment. It gets packed on weekends and is a bit too much of a pick-up joint to allow for innocent, relaxed fun.

Destiny (☎ 4464605; destinys@gamtel.gm; Kotu Beach) A sparkling palace on three floors, this is where parties go on late, clothes are tight, and the beat is thumping. It's the nightlife version of a holiday beach club – great for glittering parties, but the wrong address for local flavours.

SEREKUNDA

Jokor (☎ 4375690; 13 Kombo Sillah Dr) This open-air club in Serekunda, near Westfield Junction, is a raucous local affair, and makes a convincing claim to be the most entertaining club of all. It's open, and packed, every night, and there's a live band (usually *mbalax* or reggae) on Friday and Saturday.

Casinos

Kololi Casino (☎ 4460226; Senegambia, Kololi; ⏰ 4pm-1am) Near the Senegambia Beach Hotel, this casino is reckoned by most to be the best in the country. It offers roulette, poker, black-jack and jackpot machines (from 4pm), plus a bar and coffee shop. There's a restaurant attached.

Sport

FOOTBALL

The Gambia's main stadium is Independence Stadium in Bakau; this is the site for major football matches (around D30) and other sporting events, which are advertised locally on posters. Major events are impossible to miss, as seemingly the entire population of Gambia heads for the stadium, many dressed in national colours or carrying flags. The atmosphere at times like this is electric, and it's well worth going along just for that, even if you don't actually see the match.

TRADITIONAL WRESTLING

Another spectator sport popular with locals and visitors is traditional wrestling (see p51). This occasionally takes place at Independence Stadium in Bakau, but it's more interesting, and much more fun, to see the matches at **Arena Babou Fatty** (off Sukuta Rd, Serekunda), really just a dusty ground. Since the construction of a wrestling arena at the president's native Kanilai (see p133), there are fewer matches here than before. But if they happen, they're unbeatable for vibrancy. Sunday afternoons in September or October are the most popular time. The entrance fee is usually about D30 for tourists.

SHOPPING

Bakau market sells fruit and vegetables, and has an adjacent handicrafts section stuffed to the rims with carvings, traditional cloth and other souvenirs. Serekunda is the place to hunt for good-quality batiks – squeeze through its maze of backstreets to get to the small Batik Factory, where many of Gambia's ubiquitous motifs originate.

African Heritage Centre (☎ 4496778; www.african heritagegambia.com; 16 Samba Breku Rd, Bakau) Near Bakau's Cape Point tip, you'll find this beautiful boutique with a range of original sculptures, batiks, paintings and souvenirs. There's also a good restaurant and a few rooms that you can stay in down the back (see p105).

Tropical Tour & Souvenirs (☎ 4460536; Senegambia, Kololi) In Kairaba Hotel, this hassle-free place has a good range of information, books, maps, art and fashion. While there, ask about its Tropical Gardens project, an impressive little business of growing and preserving indigenous Gambian flora.

Equigambia (☎ 7798801, 7794374; www.equigambia .org; Kololi; ⏰ 10am-6pm Mon-Sat) This is the place to purchase high-quality Gambian clothing, made by selected local tailors in an excellent employment-creation and training scheme. The brightly coloured children's, men's and women's collections are sold under fair-trade conditions.

Salam Batik (☎ 9820125; salam_batik_mp_art@ yahoo.co.uk; Sukuta Rd, Serekunda) Forget about the mass-produced batik wares on display at various tourist markets. This inspiring little place sells original outfits, bags and more at very reasonable rates. You'll become the proud owner of a unique and beautiful item, while supporting local industry. Plans for batik workshops were in place when we visited. To get here, take an immediate left after Lana's Bar in Serekunda. It's on the left-hand side, after the big mango tree.

Paper Recycling Project (☎ 7707090, 7793358; gambianpaper@yahoo.co.uk; Fajikunda) A short drive out of Serekunda, this workshop, stunningly located on the edge of a *bolong* (creek), trains local residents in the art of paper making. The cards, boxes, bags and diaries on sale here are all made from recycled paper and colourful Gambian cloth. But that's almost a beautiful sideline: the real fun is in seeing this smooth project running and expanding. The owner is now planning to build a crafts village that will house other small-scale craftspeople.

GETTING THERE & AWAY

Tippa Garage (Bakoteh Junction, Serekunda) is the main transport hub for *sept-place* taxis and *gelli-gellis* (minibuses) upcountry. Destinations include Soma (D90), though for travel up-country you are better off going to Banjul

(D15 in a shared taxi, D150 in a private hire taxi), taking the ferry to Barra and getting onto taxis travelling the north-bank road from there.

For the south coast, you can get a *gelli-gelli* from Tippa Garage to Gunjur (D18), passing Brufut, Sanyang and Tujering. A private taxi to Gunjur is around D150. Vehicles for Brikama (D12) also leave from Tippa Garage.

Bush taxis (mainly *sept-places*) go from Serekunda to Kafountine and Ziguinchor in southern Senegal via the border at Séléti. See p285 for more details.

GETTING AROUND
To/From the Airport

A green tourist taxi from Banjul International Airport to Serekunda or any Atlantic coast resort costs around D400. Yellow taxis cost about D200, depending on your powers of negotiation.

Bicycle

Mountain bikes and traditional roadsters (of varying quality) can be hired from several hotels in Bakau, Kotu and Kololi, or from private outfits nearby. The Senegambia Beach Hotel in Kololi and African Village Hotel in Bakau are good addresses. Expect to pay around D40 per hour, D160 for a half-day and D200 for a full day. Bargain hunters can probably negotiate these rates down.

Car & Motorcycle

There are a few local one-man-and-his-car operations that advertise in hotels, shops and supermarkets. They can offer much better deals than the rental companies listed below; just make sure the cars are in good condition, particularly if you're travelling upcountry.
AB Rent-a-Car (☎ 9320776; abrentacar@gamtel.gm; www.ab.gm; Kairaba Hotel, Kololi)

Hertz (hertz@gamtel.gm) airport (☎ /fax 4390041); Serekunda (☎ 4473156; Tippa Garage)

Private Taxi

In the Atlantic coast resorts there are hundreds of green 'tourist taxis'. These are privately owned cars, particularly intended for tourist transport. In some of the dense tourist areas, such as the Senegambia Strip, they are the only taxis that have permission to enter.

You can pick up a tourist taxi from most of the large hotels; just ask at the reception. Sometimes drivers are waiting for clients outside. Their fares are fixed by the drivers' syndicates and are advertised on large boards outside the hotels.

Green taxis are usually more expensive than the yellow taxis that also serve as shared cabs. From Fajara to Banjul, for instance, you'll pay around D350 by tourist taxi, D150 in a yellow cab. A town trip around the coastal resorts by yellow taxi should cost around D30.

Hiring a taxi for a day to go around the Atlantic resorts and Banjul should cost around D1000 to D1500.

Shared Taxi

Shared taxis operate on several routes at the coastal resorts. The price of D6 has earned them the name 'six-six'. They connect Bakau to Westfield Junction and Serekunda, passing through Sabina Junction near the Timbooktoo bookshop in Fajara. You can also get a six-six from the traffic lights junction to the Senegambia Strip in Kololi and from there to Bakau. You simply flag a taxi down, pay your fare and get off where you want.

In Serekunda, minibuses (D8) to Banjul city leave from near Westfield Junction. If you're in any doubt, just flag down a taxi and ask where it's going. If it's not your direction, the driver will tell you where you can stop one.

Western Gambia

Where the lights of the glitzy tourist palaces fade out, the country's more intimate side reveals itself. South of the Atlantic resorts, small fishing villages line wide beaches, inviting visitors to experience local life.

Further inland, the clamorous junction town Brikama lures you to more distant destinations. Put in a stop before you jump on the next bush taxi – its dusty haze hides the homes of several renowned *griot* (West African praise singer) families. In tucked-away neighbourhoods, they can introduce you to the gentle trickle of *kora* (harp-lute) and *balafon* notes and teach you the classic songs that keep the secrets of Gambia's ancient history.

The north-bank villages of Jufureh and Albreda grant a very different view of past eras. Ever since Alex Haley's book *Roots* traced the author's ancestral lineage back to the Kinte family of Jufureh, the village has turned into a symbolic destination for those in search of answers to their past. Across the river, the crumbling walls of the ancient slaving station on James Island remain a stark reminder of the cruel trade in humans that once took place here.

Western Gambia opens itself to travellers in a way strikingly harmonious with its natural surroundings. All along the southern coast, stylish eco-lodges and wholesome community projects allow you to explore the region while keeping your footprint small. In Kartong a veritable eco-village is in the making, and further north, past a beekeeping project and organic farm, the Makasutu Wildlife Trust is working with 14 villages on the creation of a community reserve. Until it is completed, you can enjoy the same spirit at Abuko Nature Reserve, Gambia's finest and tiniest park, and on the adventure trails of Makasutu Culture Forest.

HIGHLIGHTS

- Count tail feathers at the tiny **Abuko Nature Reserve** (p122)
- Try your hand at weaving and woodcarving at **Tanji Village Museum** (p117)
- Enjoy an eco-glamorous day of hammock lounging, boat riding and yoga stretching on the beach in the tranquil river village of **Kartong** (p119)
- Imbibe the protective spirit on an eco-trail through **Makasutu Culture Forest** (p123)
- Watch the tides of time eat into the historical shores of **James Island** (p130)

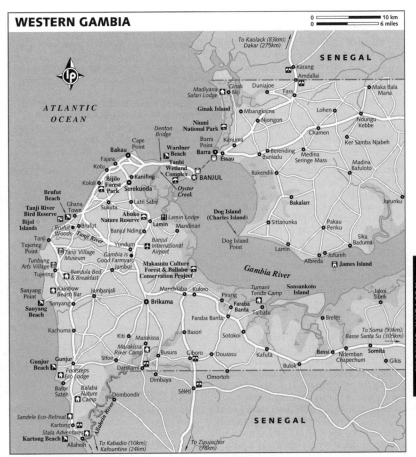

WESTERN GAMBIA

SOUTH COAST

As you leave the built-up bustle of the Kombos on the southbound Coastal Rd, gleaming hotel walls and landscaped gardens gradually give way to small fishing villages dotted with abundant greenery.

Attracted by the rural romanticism, hotels and tour operators are feverishly purchasing land and putting up structures here, and the first resorts peek out behind white strands and palm groves. The character of the holiday ventures in this area is excitingly different from the packaged entertainment that marks Kololi or Bakau. Like a tropical laboratory exploring the possibilities of re-

sponsible tourism, it sprouts solar-panelled eco-lodges and community projects in the same way that other places cultivate plasticised theme parks. From the artisan workshops at the cute Tanji Village Museum to the lush eco-palaces of Gunjur and Kartong, the responsible projects of this zone are also the most exciting ones, making sustainable travel not only effortlessly easy but also endlessly entertaining.

BRUFUT

On Brufut beach, small fishing boats still roll in and out of the sea on the tide, but this place is no longer the sleepy village that felt miles or years removed from the bustle of the coastal resorts. A lot can change in three

---

BIRDWATCHING TIPS: BRUFUT WOODS

A short but hard-to-follow track leads from Brufut town to Brufut Woods, a small forest and well-known haunt of bird lovers.

Over the years the area's woodland has permanently decreased in size due to deforestation, putting at risk one of Gambia's primary sanctuaries for species such as Verreaux's eagle owls, woodland and malachite kingfishers and various species of sunbirds.

Thanks to an enduring local initiative, the remaining area has been fenced in and equipped with a drinking pool and hide. Initially managed by the West African Bird Study Association (Wabsa), it is now looked after by the village of Brufut and is an excellent destination for birdwatchers, as long as the expansion of tourism in the region doesn't put the area at risk once more.

---

years – that's all it took for this forgotten corner to develop into a semi-urban centre with small guest houses, giant hotel complexes and rows of showy villas, luxurious enough to house even presidents, as during the OAU (Organization of African Unity) summit in 2006.

Fifteen kilometres south of Serekunda, Brufut is the next site on the Atlantic coast to which the Kombos reach out with keen, development-proffering hands. Perhaps the prettiest sign of this is **Hibiscus House** (☎ 7982929; www.hibiscushousegambia.com; r incl breakfast D2800; ⊠ 🐟), an attractive mini-hotel tucked away at the end of a bouncy dirt road in the heart of the village. The space exudes calm, perhaps because it's owned and run by a reiki specialist (who offers treatments to guests). Its centrepiece is a tall, glass-fronted lounge with a library that's so comfy you'll feel like curling up and hibernating even at 35°C. The hotel's cute pool and Jacuzzi are framed by giant plants, and as there are only a handful of rooms (each with a private terrace), you'll often have both to yourself. Should you tire of the home-cooked meals at the hotel, you can always head for **Blue Bar** (☎ 9958774; dishes around D180), a snug bar-restaurant right next door to Hibiscus House, where you can enjoy light meals and snacks in a cute garden setting.

At Brufut beach you'll find both the cheapest and most expensive food options. For some grilled fish or skewered prawns, try one of the small beach bars, or, if you're in big-spender mode, dress in your finest and book a table in one of the glamorous restaurants at the **Sheraton** (☎ 4410889; www.sheraton.com/gambia; Hwy Brufut Heights; s/d from D5000/6200; ⊠ 🖥 🐟 🏊). There are three of them, each granting fabulous sea views from behind impressive glass fronts or open-air terraces.

The mighty hoteliers designed this branch to fit beautifully into its humble surroundings. Accommodation is in tastefully designed bungalows, fully equipped with TV, hairdryer, safe, minibar, kettle and more. There's also a fabulous spa and fitness centre. Management seemed a little confused, but we might put that down to teething problems.

Don't leave Brufut without a glimpse of the arts and crafts on display at **HG Creation** (☎ 7000300; www.hgcreation.com; Brufut Gardens), opposite the Sheraton. African elegance is the theme here, covering everything from the satin *boubous* (elaborate robelike gowns) to the tiny tea sets.

To get to Brufut, take a *gelli-gelli* (minibus) from Tippa Garage in Serekunda (D15), or just jump in a cab.

TANJI RIVER BIRD RESERVE

Once you leave Brufut for Tanji, you finally ditch the urbanised areas for village life. The transition is accentuated by the 612 hectares of woodlands, tidal marshes, sand dunes, lagoons and mangrove estuary of the Tanji River that lie between the two villages. This is the area of the **Tanji River Bird Reserve** (☎ 9919219; admission D35; ☀ 8am-6pm). Called Karinti by locals, this small park was created in 1993 to protect the varied coastal and river vegetation on the mainland, as well as the nearby Bijol Islands – shifting grounds made of sand caught up and accumulated by laterite reefs.

The wide range of habitats here attracts an excellent selection of birds, including indigenous species and European migrants. More than 300 species have been recorded, and some ornithologists consider this to be Gambia's most diverse bird area. It's certainly one of the most important zones for gulls and terns, including the Caspian tern and grey-headed gull, which breed on the Bijol

WESTERN GAMBIA

Islands. Various raptor species have also been recorded. Apart from birds, Tanji, and particularly the islands, are famous for being a rare breeding area for green turtles.

The Bijol Islands form a highly sensitive animal-protection area, and any visit means a disturbance of its fragile breeding projects. Visits are normally allowed for research purposes only, though there are occasional legal tours (around D600) offered by the wildlife department outside breeding season. Other people might offer to take you there – don't take them up on it, or you'll encourage illegal and highly disruptive tours that endanger the species protected by the park. Even without a trip to the islands, a guided walk (D200 per hour) around the reserve will have you spotting plenty of birds.

If you're already at Brufut beach, a 2km walk along the road takes you to the reserve office, signposted on the right (western) side of the road, where you pay your entry fee. Otherwise, stay in the bush taxi from Serekunda and go directly to the office.

TANJI

About 3km south of the reserve office, the road crosses a small bridge to Tanji, where the smell of fresh or smoked fish introduces the community's main activity. Birdwatchers love coming to Tanji to visit the reserve, but

with its relatively calm coast, brilliant little museum (see the boxed text, below) and camel rides along the beach organised by **Pepe's Camel Safaris** (☎ 4461083), it's also great for families in search of a peaceful site with plenty of roaming space for the kids.

Opposite the riding club and only five minutes from Tanji River Bird Reserve, **Nyanya's Beach Lodge** (☎ 9808678, 4414021; s/d D400/600) puts up birdwatchers and aspiring camel drivers in bright bungalows dotted across a leafy garden that's right on the bank of a Tanji River branch. Gazing onto the water from the restaurant while sipping some baobab juice is a great way to spend an afternoon. The sea, with bathing spots and fishing activity, is also in tempting proximity, and the place offers lots of activities, from mountain biking to drumming workshops.

Those who prefer a sheltered mangrove setting to a wide beach might be better off at **Paradise Inn Lodge** (☎ 9810112; r per person incl breakfast D660). When we visited, manager Djiby Sow had just taken the place over and made an excellent start at trying to restore it to its original glory. Birdwatchers have always been the keenest clients here – the mangroves and gardens surrounding the lodge attract so many species you may not have to leave your spacious bungalow to tick vital specimens off the viewing list.

TANJI VILLAGE MUSEUM

Among the dust-covered, word-heavy dinosaurs of West Africa's museums, the **Tanji Village Museum** (☎ 9926618; tanje@dds.nl; adult/child D100/25; ⏰ 9am-5pm) stands out like a glittering disco ball. This lovingly tended place spills over with life – so much so that even easily bored kids will be reluctant to leave.

After 20 years of faithful service at the National Museum in Banjul, Tanji Village Museum founder Abdulie Bayo knew exactly what ought to be done differently to excite people about history. He came up with the brilliant idea of shaping the museum in the form of a traditional Mandinka compound and illustrating scenes of daily life through the careful selection of traditional furniture and interesting artefacts. The sneaky gaze into the interiors of typical village huts is fascinating, but it's nothing compared to the scenes of nature and life that lie outside the compound walls. A beautiful nature trail introduces Gambia's flora and fauna to you, all to the accompaniment of chirping birds that nest in the tall trees. From here, you get to the artisans' workshops, where you can see weavers and woodcarvers skilfully at work – they'll usually let you have a go if you ask. The excellent collection of traditional instruments, including examples of drum, kora, balafon and simbingo (a stringed instrument, similar to the kora), doesn't gather dust either, as resident musicians show you how they are played and pluck their strings as you enjoy a meal in the picnic area or small on-site restaurant.

If all of this entices you to find out how well you can sleep in a traditional hut, ask to book into one of the comfortable self-contained roundhouses round the back (D300 per person).

The museum lies on the coastal road, a 15-minute walk from Tanji village.

In Tanji village, **Kairoh Garden** (☎ 9903526; r per person D500) is a spacious, palm-shaded place with good-value, clean rooms. Sitting far off the beaten track, it's perfect for anyone seeking tranquillity and the minimum of company. The hotel has its own little vegetable patch, which might explain why the restaurant (meals around D200) gets such good reviews. That, or the *chef de cuisine,* who claims to excel at Asian, African and vegetarian meals, is as good as he says he is. You can also take *djembe* (a type of drum) lessons here.

Tanji lies on the coastal road; a bush taxi from Serekunda costs around D10. You can walk along the beach or through the reserve to get here.

TUJERING

About 5km south of Tanji, this tiny village is home to the nature-bound **Bendula Bed & Breakfast** (☎ 7717481; www.bendula.com; s/d D490/740) – a no-frills invitation to some remote relaxing. It has five simple, colourful huts huddled on green terrain. A long stretch of beach is in walking distance. It's the perfect place to do very little at all, but if your energy flows over you can take up drumming or dancing, watch batik makers and weavers in the village, or even produce your own herbal tea and medicine together with a local healer. Electricity is available at 12V and a pump provides water for the local-style, outdoor showers.

From the main road, a series of inconspicuous signposts takes you down a couple of dirt paths to the quirky **Tunbung Arts Village** (☎ 9982102; etundow@yahoo.com). This ragged assembly of skewed huts, wildly painted walls and random sculptures that peer out behind walls and from treetops is the creative universe of Baboucarr Etu Ndow, a renowned Gambian artist (check the Sheraton hotel in Brufut for some of his paintings). Many of the original objects scattered across this fantasy garden have been created by visitors who either stayed in one of the colour-splashed huts or took part in one of Etu's one-day workshops (enquire for rates). You can also just come and look at this piece of live art in progress, including the small museum displaying exhibits relating to local history. Visits are free; donations are welcome.

A *gelli-gelli* from Tippa Garage in Serekunda costs around D15. It'll drop you off at the turn-off to either Bendula (Batokunku mosque) or Tunbung. Both are signposted.

To get to Tunbung directly, you have to hire a taxi (around D300 return).

SANYANG
pop 6000

Whoever the founders of this fishing village were, they had not only a good sense for tracking down rich waters but also a keen eye for a stunning stretch of beach. The wide bend of the finely grained Paradise, Pelican and Osprey beaches (collectively known as Sanyang beach) were already attracting visitors to Sanyang when the neighbouring villages were still far off the tourist trail. Though it can get a little busy when the tour buses arrive, it's generally a calm stretch, perfect for wasting a few moments over fresh coconut juice, with sand between your toes. Further along, you'll find one of Gambia's ubiquitous fishing spots with colourful pirogues; behind the beach, a few palm trees invite for leisurely strolls.

Since people have often found it hard to leave after the postcard-style sunset and return to an urban rhythm, most of the original beach bars built years ago gradually converted into solid lodgings. One of the most enduring of these places is **Kobokoto** (☎ 7005511; d D300), brilliantly located on a stretch of beach that gradually shifts from soft sand to small rocks and lagoon (the bit the birds favour). You'll frequently meet Gambian and Lebanese picnic parties here – and coming here for a day trip is probably the best thing to do. Unless they've been solidly brushed, scrubbed and furnished since we visited, the rooms hardly entice you to spend the night.

On the opposite end of the sands, the **Rainbow Beach Bar** (☎ 9726806; www.rainbow.gm; d D500) does much better at combining setting, food and accommodation in one attractive package. The thatch-roof bungalows are still simple, but they're scrubbed and kept tidy. A generator provides electricity in the evenings. The best thing remains the original core – the restaurant, which serves a fantastic selection of very fresh seafood dishes, including such delicacies as grilled king prawns and lobster.

Osprey (☎ 9924010; meals D100-550; ⏰ 11am-8pm) is the first beach bar you'll hit when coming down the palm-lined laterite road that connects Sanyang beach to the main tarmac. It also serves good-quality seafood and ice-cold drinks, though its very prominent setting makes it slightly more susceptible to hustlers and bumsters.

To get to the beach, follow the coastal road towards Sanyang, then take the dirt road that branches off about 2km before Sanyang village.

GUNJUR & GUNJUR BEACH
pop 15,000

Some 10km south of Sanyang, Gunjur is one of Gambia's largest fishing centres. There's hardly a better place to absorb daily life in a fishing village than Gunjur beach (a 3km walk or D5 taxi ride from town). Boats rock on the waves and are pulled in to the shouts of the workers; nets are mended; and fish are gutted, sold and dried. There are a couple of simple beach bars that grant a view over the busy scene with the added luxury of a JulBrew in hand. Gunjur beach is less tourist-oriented than some of the neighbouring communities: scantily dressed sun seekers are better off a little bit further on, away from the nets, guts and disapproving eyes of the locals.

For great community insights, entrust some of your holiday planning to Gunjur's **Environmental Protection and Development Group** (GEPADG; ☎ 8800986; gepadg@yahoo.com). It can take you to the Bolong Fenyo Community Wildlife Reserve it manages, introduce you to its creative ways of linking the protection of Gunjur's fragile biodiversity to local job creation, and even arrange dance shows and meals. Birdwatchers will be more interested in visiting the coastal lagoon that it is helping to restore, a place that attracts over 75 species, including the white-crowned robin-chat, yellow-crowned gonolek and northern shoveler.

Sleeping & Eating

A few palm groves removed from the tourist centres, Gunjur has attracted a number of excellent small lodges built with great respect for the local environment and community.

Balaba Nature Camp (☎ 9919012; www.balaba.co.uk; Medina Salaam; huts from D550) A 5km drive from Gunjur down the coastal road will take you to this laid-back camp, set amid dense savannah woodland. Lamin, the manager, has kept things local-style with kerosene lamps and bucket showers, and at the same time maintained a small environmental footprint that's in line with his excellent efforts in environmental education and protection. Activities range from drumming, dancing and basket weaving to birdwatching excursions and boat trips.

Gunjur Project (☎ 7331818; www.thegunjurproject gambia.com; Gunjur; s/d incl breakfast D900/1500; ✇ ▣) With only six rooms, this is a humble affair, whose ambitions for working towards development far exceed its size. The UK charity that runs this place pledges to reinvest some of its profits in local development projects. In line with that ethos, it also sets up trips to the village and outings with the local fishermen.

Gecko Lodge (☎ 7778551; www.gecko-lodge.com; Gunjur; per person incl breakfast D1350) The superbly designed Gecko Lodge has cute bungalows in a leafy setting. Rooms are earthen-coloured and decorated in warm wood tones. We strongly suspect the hand of a Gambia-dedicated interior designer. There are only a handful of rooms, so you can benefit from the hammocks, beach huts and yoga classes in total peace.

our pick Footsteps Eco Lodge (☎ 7411609, 7700125; www.footstepsgambia.com; bungalows incl breakfast D2500; ✇ ▣) This eco-fabulous lodge used to be great before a bushfire ravaged it in 2007. Since it's been rebuilt, it's absolutely fantastic. From the solar panels on the roof to the vegetable garden, composting toilets and freshwater pool, you simply won't find a green fault with this place. The back garden attracts a multitude of birds, rooms are spacious, the vegetarian menu is varied and the family lodge is like a massage for tired parents.

Gunjur Beach Lodge (☎ 4486066) Gunjur's former place of pride has an uneven record of opening and closing, boasting eco-credits and being dogged by claims of bumsterism. It's worth checking what the situation is when you visit – the remote beach location alone has enough potential to attract someone with great managerial skill to turn the place around. Enquire for price details.

Getting There & Around

You can reach Gunjur by *gelli-gelli* from Tippa Garage in Serekunda or Brikama. Both cost about D18. From Gunjur village to the beach, you'll pay about D6.

KARTONG

Kartong is a calm little village that sits 10km south of Gunjur and only a short pirogue journey north of Senegal. It's one of Gambia's best-kept secrets, a picture-postcard village where gigantic palm trees sway over women with children on their backs and old men on wobbly bicycles.

THE KARTONG SPIRIT Katharina Lobeck Kane

'I never thought I'd do something quite so big in my life', says Geri Mitchell, flicking soft sand off her dress. Her tiny frame only accentuates her quiet words. Behind us, the magnificent domes of Sandele Eco-Retreat rise into the dimming skies. Another embarrassingly perfect sunset seems in the making. In Kartong, nature has a way of conspiring to make anyone who passes fall in love with it. Geri and her husband, Maurice, got caught by the village spirits a long time ago. 'Before the coastal road was built, Kartong was really far! We sometimes came here for weekends. One day we drove along the new tarmac, and suddenly realised that with this new route, it was not a question of whether tourism was going to come to Kartong, but when. So we thought, perhaps we can start this region off in a slightly different way, proposing an alternative kind of tourism.'

What Geri and Maurice didn't know then was that in the process of conceiving and creating Sandele, they'd learn how to produce compressed earth blocks, found a company to make them and send local architects to India to study the art of dome building. Sandele is today one of Gambia's most fully realised eco-lodges, and then some. Next to the domes, the learning centre of the Pathways Foundation provides a staggering array of courses, from yoga to sustainable tourism practice.

Geri unfolds a set of architectural plans, and I realise that their ambitions for altering the face of tourism in Gambia are without limits. Before us, the paper draft of a fully fledged eco-village displays their vision in thin pencil. Things have gone so well between the British couple and the local community that they've been allotted a new piece of land, where luxurious eco-lodges will be available to people who can show how their presence here will support the local community. The green homes haven't even been built yet, but demand is already high. 'They are going to go to people who can really contribute something, either sustainable business or skills', says Geri. If developing their visionary concepts has ever been a struggle, Geri and Maurice don't let it show, making it all look effortless.

Just beneath the gentle Kartong dunes, the surf hits the shore and the sun is setting so spectacularly that it soaks up all the pinks and reds from my vocabulary. 'Explain again how to get involved in the eco-village, Geri', I say. Kartong has me firmly in its grasp.

Kartong lies close to the coast, and most turn-offs leading from the main road to the holiday camps also take you to the shore. The main beach, mainly used by fishermen but suitable for bathing, is a couple of kilometres further south, past the army and customs post. Take a right at the fork, and after a pleasant 1km walk through grassy dunes you'll be rewarded with a wide, sandy strand. If you turn left instead, the road meets the Allahein River marking the border of Gambia and Senegal. There's a small harbour here, plus the Kartong Fishing Centre and several pirogues that ferry between the Gambian and Senegalese sides of the river.

As elsewhere on the coast, things are changing here. So far, the tourist ventures that have been built have merely put the sleepy village onto the map but barely interfered with the village's relaxed atmosphere and tight social structures. Such subtlety in development is rare, and much credit for this goes to Geri and Maurice, owners of Sandele Eco-Retreat and behind-the-scenes operators of **KART**

(Kartong Association for Responsible Tourism; ☎ 4495887; www.kartung.org). Check out the KART office in town to find out how to best support the association's endeavours, as well as book a tour (to watch birds or scenery) on bicycle, boat or foot.

A good time to visit this tranquil village is during the days of the rootsy **Kartong Festival** (☎ 9933193; www.kartongfestival.org), an annual dance and music event in April or May featuring a stunning array of dancing, drumming troupes and orchestras from the region.

Sights & Activities

Kartong is a great place to lean back and enjoy the slow pace of African village life, and most activities here fit right into this lazy holiday scheme. Birdwatchers don't have to go far to spot numerous species, and the area is great for walking and bicycle tours (the KART office and Boboi Beach Lodge have a few wonky bikes for hire). A pirogue tour on the Allahein River is another great way of getting birds in front of your binoculars, or just to enjoy the picturesque surroundings. For river tours try any of the lodges or KART, or if you're really up for flexing your bargaining muscles, try the local fishermen.

Tours to the local **Reptile Farm** (admission D100) consist of guided walks, complete with tape-recorded information, around some small cages with snakes and lizards. If you like your reptiles in the wild, ask your hotel or KART about tours to the sacred **crocodile pool** of Mama Bambo Folonko. You'll need guidance; it's tricky to find. The **Kartong Community Forest** is good for leisurely excursions and a great place to spot patas and red colobus monkeys. Try it just after sunrise. The light is amazing.

If personal peace and learning for life are more your thing, contact the Pathways Foundation at Sandele Eco-Retreat for a range of courses on renewal and sustainability, from alternative technologies and responsible tourism to personal development and yoga (all held in an architecturally impressive building near the beach).

The pretty **Lemon Fish Art Gallery** (☎ 9922884; www.lemonfish.gm), well signposted on the main road, is another great address. It has an excellent exhibition of contemporary paintings, sculptures and batiks by Gambian artists, and it also runs art workshops. There's a boutique where you can purchase art, jewellery and fashion at fixed prices, and you can even rent rooms here.

Sleeping

Equator Lodge (☎ 7851866; www.equatorfoundation.com; camping per tent incl breakfast D350, s/d incl breakfast D500/700) Just before reaching Kartong, a signpost takes you to one of the area's simplest accommodation options. This humble, community-owned lodge has six basic huts (four with shared toilets), friendly staff and the wholesome mission of investing profits into the local health-care centre. Solar panels and a turbine provide electricity, and the beach is only a few steps behind the dunes.

Halahin Lodge (☎ 9933193; www.halahin.com; s/d incl breakfast D600/800) Not far from Equator, Halahin Lodge is another unpretentious place with welcoming rooms in round huts, a great little restaurant and camping facilities (camping per tent D250). In line with Kartong's eco-vibes, local owner Bouba Jaiteh uses wind and solar power and promises locally grown vegetables for the sauce. Drumming and *kora* lessons can be arranged.

Lemon Fish Art Gallery (☎ 9922884; www.lemon fish.gm; r D700) You'll get so used to the great morning view from the small hill this guest house sits on that you might just forget that this isn't really your own home. It feels like a lived-in, private family house, with its colourfully decorated rooms, kitchen that's open to guests and bright verandah. Bathrooms are shared, and there are cookery, art and dance classes.

Boboi Beach Lodge (☎ 7776736; www.gambia-adventure.com; camping per person D300, d with/without bathroom D1200/800) With bungalows and hammocks set in a palm-shaded garden, an invitation to sleep under a starlit sky (mosquito net provided) and 10-step access to the beach, this place is hard to beat as far as settings go. If it just scrubbed and brushed up its rooms and shared showers, it would be a dream destination.

Stala Adventures (☎ 9915604; www.stala-adventures.com; camping per tent D245, full board per person D1500) About 5km out of Kartong and into the green, this Dutch-run fishing and bird-watching camp has five simple huts right on the river, and small boats parked outside ready to take you on a morning ride through the mangroves. With solar panelling and a waste-water-disposal system thankfully not involving the mangroves, it takes ecofriendliness seriously. Tours and courses are on offer, too.

our pick **Sandele Eco-Retreat** (☎ 4495887; www.sandele.com; half board per person r/lodge D1800/2500) There's not a single fault in the green pedigree of this luxurious eco-castle. It's entirely solar and wind powered and equipped with composting toilets. All building materials have been sourced and staff recruited from within a 20km vicinity of the hotel. Try this: lie on the huge double bed (made responsibly from dead wood) in your personal dry-brick dome and watch the morning light drift through the glass cubes in the ceiling. A great lie-in, but hard to weigh up against the option of a solitary swim under the rising sun.

Eating

All of the camps provide food and many of them use locally grown ingredients. Especially at the smaller ones, you should let them know in advance if you plan to eat so that they can heat the stove.

Morgan's Grocery (snacks & meals D50-200; ✆ lunch & dinner) About 300m west of the village along a sandy track, Morgan's stands atop a sandy hill from where it's an easy walk to the crocodile pool. The African and European meals served here are simple but good, and taste even better in the friendly company of the well-informed management.

Umpacola Bar (☎ 4419111; silwia_barke@web.de; meals around D150; ◷ lunch & dinner) On the way to the crocodile pool, Umpacola serves generous, hearty meals on a patio shaded by orange trees. The name means 'meeting place', and for making contact with locals the restaurant's central location is unbeatable. At the time of research, the management had plans for expanding into a guest house. Check how far they've progressed.

Italian Restaurant (meals around D150; ◷ 11am-midnight) Right on the river, past the fishing centre, you'll find this tiny eatery. It's no longer the real Italian restaurant that it used to be, but it still offers simple meals and coffee with views across the stream towards Senegal. You'll need a taxi or the leisure for a 3km walk to get here.

Getting There & Away

To get to Kartong from Brikama (D10) or Tippa Garage in Serekunda (D18, 30 minutes), take a *gelli-gelli* to Gunjur, where you have to change to get to Kartong (D8, 15 minutes). You can also take a private hire taxi from the Kololi resorts to Brufut Turntable (D50), and then take a bush taxi to Gunjur from there.

Note that waiting times for transport from Gunjur to Kartong can be discouragingly long. Hiring a taxi from Gunjur will cost around D220, and many of Kartong's camps offer a pick-up service. Or take a bike with you from Serekunda and cycle the remaining few picturesque kilometres between Gunjur and Kartong. Hiring a taxi all the way from Serekunda should cost around D500.

On the map, Kartong seems like the perfect launch pad for a trip to Casamance, and in theory you can easily get a pirogue at the fishing centre to take you along the picturesque Allahein River to Niafourang in Senegal. Doing this legally is the problem. You should be able to get an exit stamp at the border post in Kartong, but there's no post in Niafourang to legalise your entry there. Check with Ousmane Sané at Tilibo Horizons in Niafourang (p254) to see whether he can help.

SOUTH BANK & INLAND

There's plenty besides beach tourism in Gambia, and you don't even have to step far beyond the sand's end to find it. The following places can all be reached in day trips from the coast. The tiny village of Lamin on the main road southeast of Serekunda is worth visiting for the impressive river-set Lamin Lodge and Abuko Nature Reserve, which lies just around the corner. A few kilometres further south is dust-blown Brikama, the first 'upcountry' town on the route to the interior. And on the way to Casamance, the birdwatchers' paradise Marakissa and border town Darsilami make for peaceful stops.

LAMIN LODGE

The quirky **Lamin Lodge** (☎ 4497603; www.gambia-river.com; meals around D300; ◷ 9am-11pm) looks like a little boy's dream: it's a rugged, handmade log cabin on stilts, overlooking a mangrove creek. It's one of the most ingenious restaurant ideas around and most tour groups stop here for meals (it does great fresh oysters and lush buffets), a relaxing break or a boat excursion. **Gambia River Excursions** (☎ 4494360; www.gambia-river.com) organises plenty of imaginative boat trips on the Gambia River. At the lodge, you can hire pirogues and small motorboats by the day (from D5500) or by the hour (from D700), or you can arrange drop-offs to Denton Bridge (D1600) and Banjul (D1500). Best-loved of all is the famous Birds and Breakfast trip (D660) – think oysters and pancakes, with binoculars.

Most people get here by an organised boat tour. By road it's best to hire a taxi (D150 from Serekunda), or combine Lamin Lodge with Abuko Nature Reserve (around D400 from Serekunda, including two to three hours' waiting time). Alternatively, from Banjul or Serekunda you can take any minibus towards Brikama (D10), get off in Lamin village and then follow the dirt road for about 3km to the lodge.

ABUKO NATURE RESERVE

Despite its tiny size – 105 hectares, less than 1/8000th the size of Senegal's main national park Niokolo-Koba – **Abuko Nature Reserve** (☎ 4375888; adult/child D35/15; ◷ 8am-6pm) is possibly the mightiest of Gambia's national parks.

On the trail through the gallery forest near the field station, you pass through myriad

---

BIRDWATCHING TIPS: ABUKO NATURE RESERVE

Compact Abuko teems with birds, but the best places to spot the feathered creatures are an area of open Guinea savannah woodland, the bird extension behind the orphanage, and the main pool, where you can hope to view from photo hides collared sunbirds, green hylias, African goshawks, oriole warblers, yellowbills and leafloves. Abuko is about the only place in Gambia where you can observe green and violet turacos, white-spotted flufftails, ahanta francolins and western bluebills. The private hide near the animal orphanage is a good place to try your luck.

Early morning is the best time to observe bird activity; the gates open at 6.30am for keen spotters. You will get the opportunity to see plenty of species by following the trail through the gallery forest, then along the extension walk, with stops at the hides.

---

forms of Gambian scenery in only a few kilometres, from stretches of Guinea savannah to tall bush grasses. Such varied vegetation supports an equal diversity of wildlife. Abuko is one of the best places in Gambia for birdwatching, and the Lamin Stream that runs through part of the reserve is integral in attracting many of the more than 250 bird species regularly seen here.

Among the 52 mammal species calling Abuko home are bushbucks, duikers, porcupines, bushbabies and ground squirrels, as well as three monkey types: green or vervet monkeys, endangered western red colobus monkeys and patas monkeys.

The reserve is particularly famous for its Nile crocodiles. Unlike those found in the various sacred pools, the crocodiles of Abuko are completely wild and often enormous – you don't want to get too close, and certainly do *not* try patting them.

Crocs aren't the only reptiles here; they have the company of more than 30 other species, including an impressive array of snakes such as pythons, puff adders, green mambas and forest cobras. These can sometimes be seen sunning themselves on the paths, but usually make for the undergrowth at the slightest approach – no incidents of snake bite have been recorded by the park staff.

Assuming that the mamba you've spied does decamp into the bush, it could be sliding off underneath any one of more than 115 species of plants, many of which are labelled.

At the far end of Abuko is a small animal orphanage. Most of the animals staying here will be returned to the wild when ready, but there are also a few permanent residents, including hyenas and various monkeys.

Abuko is a great place to visit, but like all of Gambia's national parks, it's not having an easy time. It's fighting to preserve its area in its entirety, as well as its incredible biodiversity. Right at the heart of the reserve's amazing preservation work is the **Makasutu Wildlife Trust** (☎ 7782633, 4473349; m.wildlifetrust@yahoo.co.uk; http://makasutuwildlifetrust.com), an excellent biodiversity and research station, as well as an eco-tourism initiative (see p124).

Information

Even if you're not an early-rising birdwatcher, the morning hours before the midday heat are the best time to visit Abuko, although the reserve gets quieter as the sun rises.

There are several photo hides near Darwin Field Station by the crocodile pools and behind the animal orphanage (the latter is private and costs D50). You'll get the best pictures at the west-facing hides in the morning, when you've got the sun behind you.

The longest bird trail takes about two hours. If you're pressed for time, check the map at the main gate for shorter options.

A thin book about the reserve can be bought at the ticket office, and several publications on the reserve and Gambian flora and fauna are for sale at the **Darwin Field Station** (☻ 8am-4pm).

If you are visiting for research purposes or to work as a volunteer you can stay at the reserve (per person D500, less for longer stays).

Getting There & Away

A private taxi to Abuko from the Atlantic coast resorts costs about D300 to D400, including two hours of waiting time. Alternatively, you can take a minibus from Serekunda towards Brikama (D10). The reserve entrance is on the right (west) of the main road.

MAKASUTU CULTURE FOREST

Makasutu means 'sacred forest' in Mandinka, or 'cultural theme park' in the language of

---

BALLABU CONSERVATION PROJECT

This is the story of a great project that got even better. When James English and Lawrence Williams, founders of Makasutu Culture Forest, were invited to present their initiative at a sustainable tourism seminar, they didn't only return with the laurels, but also with a bagful of new ideas. Inspired by the possibilities of community conservation, they took the first steps to setting up the **Ballabu Conservation Project**, an ambitious plan to create an 85-sq-km band around the culture forest for the protection of biodiversity and elimination of poverty among the local people.

Fourteen villages are part of the protected zone, and their involvement, and the improvement of their living conditions, is at least as important a part of Ballabu as the protection of endangered animals. The support of village chiefs ensures local residents receive training to become directly involved in the conservation efforts, and will benefit from the creation of micro-projects in agriculture, tourism and other areas. A percentage of profits raised from tours along nature and heritage trails is directly invested in village development. Eventually, the communities concerned will gain full ownership over the project.

This all-singing, all-dancing queen of responsible tourism is still in its early stages and will grow gradually. Support from the UK's Eden Project has opened new possibilities. Contact Malang Jambang, Executive Director of the **Makasutu Wildlife Trust** (☎ 7782633, 4473349; m.wildlifetrust@ yahoo.co.uk; http://makasutuwildlifetrust.com) for more information.

---

tourist enterprise. Not far from Brikama, the **Makasutu Culture Forest** (☎ 9951547; www.makasutu .com; admission full/half day D750/550, night extravaganza D850; ☻ 8am-6pm Mon-Thu) occupies about 1000 hectares of land along Mandina Bolong, an area dedicated to showcasing a brushed-up, lush and certainly smiling Gambia, an oasis where everything is just a touch more perfect than in the real world beyond its gates. The setting is stunning, comprising palm groves, wetlands, mangroves and savannah plains, all inhabited by plenty of animals, including baboons, monitor lizards and hundreds of bird species.

A day in the forest includes a mangrove tour by pirogue; guided walks through a range of habitats, including a palm forest where you can watch palm sap being tapped; a visit to a crafts centre; and demonstrations of traditional dancing. The tours are well organised and run by excellent staff. This is a great day out, especially for families seeking a taste of nature away from the beaches and without the hassle of braving the roads upcountry.

James English and Lawrence Williams, the founders of this hugely successful project, don't like standing still. When we visited, they had just embarked on building the ambitious Ballabu Conservation Project (see the boxed text, above), as well as a skateboard ground.

At the far end of the forest sits **Mandina River Lodge** (☎ 9951547, 7777704; www.makasutu.com; s/d incl half board D3700/7400; ☒ ☒), one of the most extravagant places to stay in the entire country.

It's a very elegant shrug of the shoulders to anyone who still thinks that ecofriendly means cold bucket showers and worn-out batik sheets. This exclusive eco-retreat is known for its successful marriage of lavishness and respect for nature, as well as for its stunning architecture. Its four solar-powered luxury lodges float on the river, and intimate dining areas are tucked away in the mangroves. Views are breathtaking in whatever direction you turn, and the royal treatment you're given almost makes you forget about the money you paid for living the lush way.

Bookings are best made through the website. From October to April, the lodge caters principally to Gambia Experience clients (see p288); in the off season it's open to all and the prices drop by 50%.

Getting There & Away

Take a *sept-place* (seven-seater bush taxi) or *gelli-gelli* from Tippa Garage in Serekunda to Brikama, then change for one to Kembujeh village (D7), from where it's a 3km walk to the forest. A private hire taxi from Brikama costs around D150. If you phone the park beforehand, you can be picked up from Brikama at 9am and dropped off at 4.30pm by the park's bus (D100 one way).

BRIKAMA
pop 93,000

Three major junctions, crawling trucks, dust, heat and excitement – this is what Brikama is made of. Without beach access or a calm riverbank, Gambia's third-largest settlement is having a hard time competing with the nation's more spectacular locations. But don't dismiss this town too quickly. There's hardly a better place to soak up travel stories, carried here from all directions. Brikama's market is famous for its carvings but also a good place to snap up some Gambian sounds. For music, the town beats the coastal strip hands-down: it's the unlikely home of Gambia's best live club (Jokor's) and has brought forth some of the country's most renowned *kora* players (see the boxed text, below).

Information

Brikama has pretty decent facilities. There's a hospital, a post office and a Trust Bank that takes Visa and MasterCard if the ATM isn't broken (which happens frequently). At the central junction near the craft market, you can't miss the big, glass-fronted **Sonko Jileng Complex** (☎ 4483389), your address for changing money and surfing the net.

Sights

Most travellers come here to visit the famous **craft market** (⏲ 9am-6pm). You'll find it at the edge of town on the right as you come in from Banjul or Serekunda. It's a hectic corner of covered stalls crammed with souvenir-style sculptures, improvised ateliers and hordes of eager salesmen – perfect for practising your negotiating skills.

Sleeping & Eating

Brikama accommodation ranges from the barely inhabitable to the just about passable.

Roots and Culture Guesthouse (Murphy's Lodge; ☎ 9959606; r D350) This guest house lies a short drive off the Banjul Hwy. Murphy, the manager, certainly has a way of talking it up, as though he sees right through the grubby corners, dusty furniture and worn-out mattresses.

Nematulie Lodge (Chief's Compound; ☎ 9845959; nematulielodge@yahoo.com; s/d D200/400) This place is better maintained than Roots and Culture. Ask for Chief Bojang's house – that's the town's nickname for this surprisingly decent lodging. The double versions of the pink-walled bungalows are much better, and the *bantaba* (central gathering place) is best enjoyed with a JulBrew and chat with the young staff.

Alla la Daaroo Guesthouse (☎ 9912659, in UK 77267 20508; www.guesthouse.gm; Bakary Sambouya; s/d incl breakfast D350/530; ⚓) Three kilometres south of Brikama, this family house has five guest rooms and plenty of camping space in tranquil gardens. The beaten track is very far from this beautiful and solitary setting, perfect for walks around the countryside. Airport pick-up and personalised tours can be arranged, and kids are welcome.

Nice to be Nice (☎ 7281909; ytsvoorafrika@live.nl; dishes around D150; ⏲ 7am-midnight) Opposite the Trust Bank, this promisingly named place is Brikama's best and friendliest restaurant. It serves generous portions of chicken – both *yassa* (marinated and grilled) and fast-food style – as well as a couple of vegetarian dishes. There's live music every Friday and Saturday night, and always an interesting crowd.

To check if chips taste any different in another place, try the truck-stop ambience of the **Transgambia Restaurant** (Banjul Hwy; ⏲ 7pm-midnight). **Kambeng Restaurant** (Banjul Hwy) is a simple, clean, all-day address for tasty African and European

WESTERN GAMBIA

KORA COURSES

For anybody interested in African music, Brikama should be an obligatory stop on the itinerary. The dusty town is home to one of the most renowned families of *kora* (harp-lute) players in the country, a *griot* clan that reaches back several generations and has brought forth such mighty talents as Dembo Konté, his son Bakari Konté, and Malamini Jobarteh and his sons Pa and Tata Dindin Jobarteh.

Forget about the 'instant drumming courses' on the coast: this is one of Gambia's best places to learn traditional instruments – such as *kora*, *djembe*, *bolonbolong* (a three-stringed bass harp) or *balafon* – from brilliant players and teachers. You can also watch the instruments being made, and get an introduction into the *métier* (profession) of *griot*. Prices are entirely negotiable, depending on duration and whether you stay and eat in your teacher's compound. For quotes and directions call **Konté Kunda** (☎ Dembo 7776439, Jeli Bakari 9843706) or **Jobarteh Kunda** (☎ Moriba Kuyateh 9922045, 7738792; moriba143@yahoo.com). Both compounds are located in Santhiaba, Brikama.

FRESH FOOD ON THE FARM

'Gambia Is Good' shouts the world's most simplistic company slogan from big, bright posters. The logo – a bright-red, ready-to-burst tomato – completes the flashy shout for attention. It may not be the most sophisticated marketing campaign, but it's easily the most memorable one. And above all, it's one that's trying to sell you real goodies rather than a quick consumption fix.

Gambia Is Good is the link that had been missing between hard-working farmers, conscious consumers and quality-concerned restaurants. Since 2004 this socially engaged marketing company has helped more than 1000 poor (and mostly female) farmers in finding buyers for the products of their small farms, and has provided the tourist enterprises on the coast with fresh, locally grown produce. The stories of more financially secure farmers and the improved flavours of the average hotel kitchen tell of its success, while a whole shelf of awards, including the Responsible Tourism Award for poverty reduction, have provided due recognition.

The **Gambia Is Good Farmyard** (☎ Alhagie Darboe 9891560, 4494473; adult/child D100/50; ☯ 9am-6pm or by appointment) near Yundum is open to tourists and offers a whole lot more than gazing at rows of organic veg. Barely in the door, you'll already be clutching a glass of freshly pressed fruit juice. You can attend cookery classes (minimum of four people, D500 per person) and of course get to taste an organic Gambian stew in the restaurant (D250 including tour). On a tour through the farm, the farmers introduce you to local horticultural techniques, improved nursery methods, new irrigation techniques and plenty more.

If you phone the farmyard before setting out they can pick you up and crank everything into gear before you arrive – and that includes preparing fresh juice and lunch. A return trip from the coastal resorts by taxi with a bit of waiting time costs around D400. If you book a cookery class, transport is included in the fee. Negotiate a taxi for a whole day, and you can combine a trip here with a visit to Abuko Nature Reserve, Lamin Lodge and/or Sifoe-Kafo Beekeeping Association.

---

food. Sitting right next to Jokor's, it's where you want to line your stomach before a night of heavy partying.

Entertainment

Jokor's (Transgambia Hwy; admission on weekends around D100; ☯ 7pm-late) This vibrant open-air club is so fete-fabulous that it has even the glamorous folks from the coast heading to the provinces to party. International stars never miss out this multicoloured, fairy-light-adorned venue on their tours through Gambia and Senegal, and neither should you.

Getting There & Away

Brikama is easily reached by public transport as minibuses go up and down the main road between Banjul and Brikama, via Serekunda, about once every 10 minutes during the day. The fare both to and from Banjul and Serekunda is D12.

If you feel like a very rocky ride along a loosely tied chain of potholes, try a *sept-place* along the south-bank road to Soma (D90), where you can change for any other upcountry destination. There are frequent bush taxis to Gunjur (D10), where you can change for transport to Kartong.

Brikama is the junction from which to reach the Casamance region in Senegal. A bush taxi to the Senegalese border post in Séléti costs D50 (CFA1000); Séléti to Ziguinchor is CFA2500. A bush taxi from Brikama to the tiny border post in Darsilami is D10 (see the boxed text, p255).

MARAKISSA

The wide laterite road to Marakissa may be bouncy and dusty, but with its natural border of tall tropical trees, it still looks like a majestic alleyway. Stop your car at a point near the village, step out and listen: there'll be little else but the sway of branches, the chirping of countless birds and the occasional creaking of an old bicycle. You've entered the lands of blissful quiet.

Marakissa is a favourite spot for birdwatchers, who come to see white-breasted cuckoo shrikes, sunbirds, blue-breasted kingfishers, African darters and dozens of other species in the woodlands surrounding a calm river. A pirogue tour (D150) or hike around the *bolongs* (creeks) and woodlands is a good way of spotting plenty of birds, though there's a lazier option: lie back on the terrace of the friendly **Marakissa River Camp** (☎ 7779487; marakissa@

planet.nl; r per person incl breakfast D425; ⊠) and wait quietly for the chirpers to fly towards the small feeding pond downstairs. With its thatched huts snugly surrounded by forest and the waterway, Marakissa camp feels so secluded you might hatch thoughts of writing your memoirs on the balcony. In fact, the rainy season can truly leave it cut off from the rest of the country, as the large troughs in the laterite roads tend to fill up with water, making it impossible for cars to pass. If you intend to visit in the rainy months (August to October), you're better off phoning before setting out to avoid getting stuck.

SIFOE

Sifoe is a tiny community on the road from Gunjur to Darsilami and a great destination for a complete distraction from the beaches and restaurants of the coast. It's home to Gambia's most important **Beekeeping Association** (☎ 7781272; sifoe.beekeeping@yahoo.com; Sifoe-Kafo Farm). This makes it, as you'd expect, a great place to buy Gambian honey, but there's a lot more to the farm than this. Manjiki Jabang, the president of the association, gives insightful tours of the farm, including the plantation of gmelina trees behind the main building (renowned for the excellent, bright-yellow honey they give), the processing centre and the various types of hives used, including a fabulous glass model that quite literally buzzes with bee activity. He can tell you anything about African bees, from their ferocious character to the minute details of extracting honey, and even knows precise details about the introduction of particular tree species to Gambian lands. To remind you how utterly useful bees really are, you can purchase a lot more than honey. The range of products made and sold here includes candles and batiks made with Sifoe wax.

DARSILAMI

The tiny border village of Darsilami sees only the occasional tourist en route to Kafountine in Casamance. This is a shame, because it's a very pretty place, and a great birdwatching site to boot. The trip from Sifoe to Darsilami takes you along a rarely travelled but stunning stretch of tropical landscape. You'll pass imposing palm groves, wetlands and rice fields, and will frequently be tempted to stop the car and get your binoculars out to tick another rare species off your birdwatching list.

There's also a very nice place to stay, the friendly (and ecofriendly) **Timberland** (☎ 9946981; www.senegam.net; full board per person D765). It's kept in the spirit of village-style simplicity, including the experience of an outdoor shower. Rooms are equipped with the basics for a comfortable night; toilets are shared. The terrace restaurant serves excellent African and European meals, sprinkled with engaging conversations with managers Tabo and Willemina.

A *sept-place* taxi from Brikama costs D10. The drive along the road from Sifoe is more interesting, but there's no public transport. If you phone the lodge, they can pick you up for D900; hiring a taxi from the coastal resorts costs about the same. The tarmac road ends in Sifoe; from there it's 4km of picturesque laterite track to Darsilami.

TUMANI TENDA CAMP

About an hour from the coast on a *bolong* near the Gambia River, **Tumani Tenda Camp** (☎ 9903662; www.tumanitenda.co.uk; per person incl breakfast D200) is an ambitious community-tourism initiative. It's based on the very worthy concept of village ownership, with each tourist hut being managed by a family from the neighbouring Taibatu village, who use the profits to fund projects within their community. In reality, this communal ideal falls slightly flat when it comes to quality control and ongoing investment in the structure. Some of the traditional-style huts are basic but adequate, while others threaten to fold over your head. Things may have changed when you get there, and if you're prepared for a taste of the simple life, this may well be for you.

Birdwatchers venture here to try their luck spotting rare brown-necked parrots. With the help of a guide from the camp, you should also be able to observe porcupines from a hide.

Take a bush taxi from Brikama (D12) and ask to be dropped off at the turn-off to Taibatu (look for the sign). From here the camp's a 2.5km walk.

NORTH BANK

Gambia's north coast is even smaller than its south coast, stretching all of 10km from Barra at the mouth of the Gambia River to the island of Ginak, which marks the border with Senegal. Upriver from Barra are the historical sites of Albreda and James Island and the village of Jufureh, made famous by Alex Haley's book *Roots*.

BARRA

Barra's glory lies all in the past. Even the once-majestic **Fort Bullen** that tells of the town's former strategic importance is slowly being ground to dust by the hands of time. The rectangular bulwark was built by the British in 1827 to support the fort in Bathurst (now Banjul) in its prevention of illegal slave trade by controlling traffic along the mouth of the Gambia River. It was abandoned in the 1870s, then briefly rearmed during WWII before falling into disuse. At the time of research, the site was not open to visitors, as it was being used as military barracks. Contact the National Museum in Banjul (p92) to find out if things have changed and to pick up one of its informative leaflets.

Most of Barra town is dominated by the bustle near the ferry landing (see p95). While the shouting, pushing and eager trading is an urban sight to savour, keep your wits about you as many pickpockets, black-market traders and scamsters operate in the area. If you're not headed for Banjul, you can also make a getaway from here to Ginak Island. Few people spend the night here; the only tourists the basic **Barra Guesthouse** (☎ 7710271; dembisjr@ yahoo.com; Barra Point; r D500) near the ferry landing tends to see are those who have arrived too late to jump on the last boat.

The hectic taxi park near the ferry landing is a good place for picking up a *sept-place* to all eastern destinations, including Kerewan, Farafenni and Janjangbureh.

GINAK ISLAND (NIUMI NATIONAL PARK)

Niumi National Park spreads across a small corner of northwest Gambia, including the long, narrow island of Ginak (also spelt Jinack). The island is separated from the mainland by a narrow creek, and is contiguous with the Parc National du Delta du Saloum in neighbouring Senegal.

A dead-straight border dating from colonial times runs through the island, and its northern section is in Senegalese territory. There are three main villages on the island. The two in Gambia are Ginak Kajata and Ginak Niji, and the one in Senegal is Djinakh Diatako, but the locals are all Mandinka and Serer speakers and ignore the international boundary.

The island has a good range of habitats in a very small area – beach, mudflats, salt marsh, dunes, mangrove swamps, lagoons, grassland and dry woodland – and is very good for bird-watching. Waders and water birds are the main residents, but many other species can be seen, including birds of prey. Dolphins are occasionally spotted from the shore, and turtles nest on the beach. In theory, the park protects small populations of manatees, crocodiles, clawless otters, hyenas, bushbucks and duikers, plus various monkey species, but many animals have been hunted down, making the chances of spotting them slim.

Ginak is a pretty stretch of land, by all means, though claims to celestial beauty made by various tour operators are a touch exaggerated. Over the last few years, the heart of Niumi National Park has been eroded and replaced by large marijuana fields, which aren't quite as fascinating as the lush tropical forest that used to grow here. To see the remaining beautiful spots and not get lost in the illegal plantations, it's best to phone Madiyana Safari Lodge for a pick-up.

Sleeping & Eating

Madiyana Safari Lodge (☎ 4494088, 9920201; www .paradiseisland-gambia.com; per person incl breakfast D800) This lodge specialises in selling the luxury of giving up luxury. Advertising itself as a place with 'no discos, no hustlers and no electricity', it offers bird and dolphin spotting, village visits, bush trails and boat tours. Plenty to do in one day, especially as bedtime usually comes early, with nothing but the moon and a few kerosene lamps for lighting. Rooms are comfy thatched huts with brick floors, mosquito nets and open-air bucket showers – stargazing is free of charge. The food here is excellent, and the cook loves to prepare vegetarian meals on request.

Getting There & Away

It's worth phoning Madiyana Safari Lodge before arrival, so that they can organise pick-up from your front door. For D500 (one way) you'll be driven to Banjul and then taken to the lodge by boat. Another good option is joining an organised tour. The trips organised by **Hidden Gambia** (☎ in UK 01527-576239, in Gambia 7336570; www.hiddengambia.com) get good reviews.

If you insist on independence, take the ferry from Banjul to Barra, and then hire a taxi to Ginak Niji (around D400). The road to Ginak

Niji passes through Kanuma, where you turn left and follow the sandy track north to reach the lagoon opposite the village of Ginak Niji. From there you need to negotiate a canoe across the creek; once on the other side it's a 20-minute walk directly west across the island to reach the lodge.

JUFUREH & ALBREDA

pop 7000

Jufureh (also spelt Juffure or Juffereh) is a village on the Gambia River's northern bank about 25km upstream from Barra. A small Mandinka community like many others, it first changed strongly in the mid-17th century, when the development of the British trading post on James Island started to have an impact on the local economy and social make-up. After the abolishment of the slave trade and withdrawal of the British, it might have quite happily carried on existing as a tiny, unknown north-bank town, had it not been for African-American author Alex Haley and his search for historical truth and distant roots. Haley traced his ancestral origins back to Kunta Kinte and the area of Jufureh, and wrote *Roots*, a highly significant (if historically disputed) work that dared touch on the sensitive issue of the African origins of America's black communities. Its publication changed life in this remote Gambian community forever.

Jufureh and Albreda (two villages that have today almost merged into one) suddenly turned into pilgrimage sites charged with historical and emotional meaning. Tourists flocked here on 'Roots Tours', and the villagers responded to their demands, gladly exhibiting their way of life as well as the latest presumed descendants of Kunta Kinte to eager visitors. Today this area feels like a living museum. Village life is a touch too neat to feel real, and visitors in search of 'Africa' are presented with the images and stories they are thought to have come for. As soon as the tourist boats arrive, women start pounding millet at strategic points, babies are produced to be admired and filmed, the artisans in the craft market crank into gear, and one of Haley's supposed relatives – an old lady who's the sister of the deceased Binde Kinte – makes a guest appearance.

Sights & Activities

Historical tourism has become the main source of income here, as you'll notice when paying your obligatory D50 entrance fee and handling offers of taking photos of babies, photos of artisans and photos of photos in exchange for coins. This isn't entirely comfortable for most visitors. But even if the village stories do nothing but turn you into a reluctant cynic, a visit here is still worth undertaking.

The **slavery museum** (☎ 4710276, 7710276; Jufureh; admission D50; ⊙ 10am-5pm Mon-Sat), in an old trading post, has a small but impressive exhibition tracing the history of slavery on the Gambia River, including a replica slave ship of the Middle Passage. In Albreda, you also get to see a ruined 'factory' (fortified slaving station) built by French traders in the late 17th century. It's on the river's edge near the quay where the tour boats land. Nearby is a large British cannon dating from the same period.

Jufureh and Albreda are starting points for boat trips to James Island (D500). The Jufureh Albreda Youth Association (ask at the museum) offers good excursions combining tours around the villages with a trip to James Island (D600).

Sleeping & Eating

Jufureh Resthouse (☎ 5710276, 9955736; amadou .juffure@yahoo.fr; Jufureh; per person incl breakfast D400) This rootsy, slightly lethargic drumming camp works mainly with French groups but can accommodate independent travellers if there's space in the shabby bungalows.

Kunta Kinte Roots Camp (☎ 9905322; baboucarrlo@ hotmail.com; Albreda; s/d D500/1000) On the shores of Albreda, this surprisingly large hotel has decent accommodation in colourfully decorated bungalows. This is the place most tour groups stop at for lunch (African buffets are D150 per head), and if you contact them before arrival, they'll cook up an excellent three-course meal for you.

Rising Sun Restaurant (Albreda; meals D100-200; ⊙ lunch & dinner) Right on the beach, there's a good view over the river from this unpretentious place. Meals aren't particularly inspiring, and there are lot of freelance guides lurking around, but it's one of the very few food options in town.

Getting There & Away

The usual way to visit Jufureh and Albreda is by organised river tour (see p287 for operators). All the tour operators along the Atlantic coast and several hotels have the 'Roots Tour' in their catalogue. If you go independently, it's cheaper to travel here by taxi. Take the ferry from Banjul to Barra and find a shared taxi to Jufureh, which costs around D25.

Hiring a private taxi for a day trip is best done in Barra rather than Banjul, to avoid paying the steep ferry car fee. From Barra you should pay around D400 to get to Jufureh and Albreda, and up to D1000 if you ask the driver to wait and drive you back. There are only a few shared taxis per day on this route, so if you want to do the trip in a day you'll have to catch the first ferry. But if you are making the effort to come all this way, you should consider staying overnight; both Jufureh and Albreda are at their best in the evening, when the tourist groups have left.

JAMES ISLAND

Two kilometres offshore from Jufureh and Albreda, James Island is one of Gambia's most significant historical sights. It houses the remains of **Fort James** (1650s), an important British colonial trading post since 1661 and the departure point of vessels packed with ivory and gold as well as slave ships. Over subsequent decades, it was the site of numerous skirmishes. Variously held by British, French and Dutch traders, as well as a couple of privateers (pirates), it was completely destroyed at least three times (twice by the French, and once by accident when a gunpowder store exploded). Before the fort was finally abandoned in 1829, it was briefly used by the British to suppress the slave trade, which had been outlawed since 1807.

The ruins of the fort are quite extensive, though badly neglected – the only intact room is a food store, which is often called the slave dungeon for dramatic effect. The biggest threat, though, is rapid coastal erosion, which literally pulls away the ground the ruins stand on. A financial injection from the Netherlands is supposed to go towards restoration, the opening of a visitor's centre and trail, and an evaluation of the erosion. Great as this is, it's unlikely to be sufficient in stopping the river from gnawing its way into the land.

Most people take in James Island as part of a Banjul–Jufureh Roots Tour, but you can also arrange a pirogue to take you over from Albreda (D500 per pirogue). Island admission, including a visit to the museum in Jufureh, costs D100.

Central & Eastern Gambia

Gambia is made of river, with a few kilometres of savannah woodland, palm groves and crop fields on either side. You get the best view of this amazing stretch of the country on a boat tour. For most of the Gambia River's winding course, it's just you, the tranquil waters and green banks.

From Bintang Bolong to Tendaba, thick mangroves stretch out their airborne roots to oysters, providing shelter for clawless otters and nesting grounds for countless herons, ibises and other waders. Sometimes an African fish eagle will gaze proudly from a high branch, and European migrants chatter in the branches during the northern winter. The wide marshes and narrow creeks of the Baobolong wetlands are a magnificent culmination of this riverine beauty.

A little further north, the shoreline changes dramatically. Beyond the dusty junction town of Farafenni the sea ceases its saline grip on the waters, allowing lush, tropical greenery to thrive. Just after the rainy season, when the waters have swelled, this humble river takes on an almost Amazonian grandeur. Trees stand tall, their crowns shaking with the sudden leaps of baboons and colobus and vervet monkeys. As you near the River Gambia National Park, you might catch glimpses of the chimps of the Baboon Islands, and greet lazy hippos as you carry on eastwards towards the historical island town of Janjangbureh and the sprawling upcountry market of Basse Santa Su.

The ideal way of chugging to the country's far end is by a combination of road and river travel. That way, you get to immerse yourself in the culture of Gambia's more remote villages, as well as indulge in the 'behind-the-scenes' view from a privileged spot on the water.

CENTRAL & EASTERN GAMBIA

HIGHLIGHTS

- Relax to the lapping of the waves and the calls of the birds at **Bintang Bolong** (p132), where huts stand on stilts in the river
- Count herons and hoot with the owls on a river cruise around **Baobolong Wetland Reserve** (p134)
- Follow in the footsteps of histories old and new at **Janjangbureh** (Georgetown; p140)
- Wake up to the calls of chimps and outclimb the monkeys in **River Gambia National Park** (p137)
- Think peaceful thoughts to the clicking of the metal boats at Traditions in **Basse Santa Su** (p144)

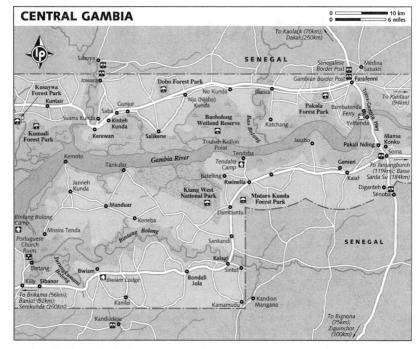

CENTRAL GAMBIA

BINTANG BOLONG

A large, meandering tributary of the Gambia River, Bintang Bolong rises in Senegal and joins the river about 50km upstream from Banjul. The banks of the tidal flow are lined with mangroves, and tucked away among the maze of shrubs near Bintang is **Bintang Bolong Lodge** (☎ 7043081, 9929362; www.bintang-bolong.com; Foni Bintang Karanai; r per person D400), an original camp that seems to grow from the mangroves surrounding it. Thirteen not very straight, not very sturdy but completely unique rooms sit on stilts right on the river – a location that equips them with the most majestic views across the water, birds and boats. A wind turbine in the village brings the energy that feeds the water pumps – which might mean occasional water shortages when the breeze fails to come in.

The lodge is a great starting point for boat trips (D800 per hour) or bus safaris (D3000 per day). There's also a crocodile pool where you can get close-up views of baby crocs, and

of course the rural life of Bintang to explore. The camp is closely tied into the local community, employing villagers and investing in schools, and community visits can easily be arranged.

Getting There & Away

Gelli-gellis (minibuses) leave daily from Brikama (D30, one hour). If you can't face the wait for the bus to fill up, you can hire a private taxi (around D2000). The driver needs to follow the main road east through the village of Somita, and at Killy turn left (north) along the dirt road to reach Bintang village and the lodge.

Otherwise, phone the lodge and arrange to be picked up. Pick-up can be arranged from Brikama (D750), Banjul or Serekunda (D1200), or Soma (D2000).

BWIAM

Until very recently, the trading town of Bwiam was a tiny Gambian village like any other, beautifully situated among plenty of tropical greenery. Today, it's a bustling rural centre, stretching in all directions. Visiting this cau-

---

TRAVELLING THE RIVER

There are two good tour operators to help you plan your trip upriver. Both can tailor excursions to your wishes. Rely on their advice and experience, though – they know which parts of the river are best, and how to avoid tedious stretches along the way. Enquire for rates.

Hidden Gambia (☎ 7336570, in England 0121 288 4100; www.hiddengambia.com) has an excellent set of excursions, including trips from Bintang to (and around) the Baobolong wetlands and longer excursions to Janjangbureh, where it operates the Bird Safari Camp, and River Gambia National Park. Tours are done in a combination of fibreglass boats and wooden, motorised pirogues.

Gambia River Excursions (Map pp100-1; ☎ 4494360; www.gambia-river.com) offers trips from Denton Bridge or Lamin Lodge, or from its eastern base, the Janjangbureh camp. Most trips are done by motorised pirogues of various sizes. Tours range from simple bird-and-breakfast excursions to trips of several days.

---

tiously developing community really is something quite special. You still get a rare insight into real village life and a vision of what could be possible here. The area surrounding Bwiam lends itself to leisurely walks, canoe rides and birdwatching excursions.

Bwiam's most impressive attribute is the surprisingly large Sulayman Junkung General Hospital, powered by one of Gambia's largest solar-energy systems. At the time of research, a large market was under construction, consisting of 40 cinderblock stalls surrounding a large, palm-lined, open-air space. By now it should be resounding with the chatter of market traders and fierce bargaining of women from the surrounding villages.

Some of Bwiam's rapid development is due to the fabulous little institution that is **Bwiam Lodge** (☎ 4489004; www.bwiamlodge.com; r D400; Ⓟ Ⓛ), a clean, bright hostel that devotes its profits to aiding children in need, thus giving a boost to the entire community. A generator provides electricity from 7pm to 7am, and staff can prepare meals on request.

Bwiam has a very active women's group, which is worth a visit for the insights you'll gain into community life, as well as for the beautiful batiks that you can watch being made and of course buy (D250 for two yards).

Sept-place taxis and *gelli-gellis* to Bwiam leave daily from Brikama (D35). A private hire taxi will be around D2500.

KANILAI

A short drive south of Bwiam, Kanilai is the birthplace of Gambia's President Yahya Jammeh. Judging by the amount of money and attention he's lavished on his native village, he must have had spent a very happy childhood here. Unlike other upcountry com-

munities, Kanilai has electricity, street lights, vast farmlands and tarmac roads. A newly built arena draws the country's wrestlers to the village, much to the detriment of the former wrestling hot spot, Serekunda. The president has also equipped the place with the **Kanilai Game Park** (☎ Kairaba Hotel 4462940; info@kairabahotel .com), unfortunately a rather disheartening affair with animals in cages. Several of the large mammals imported for the park have sadly died, some even before the opening.

The president owns a hotel here, the **Sindola Safari Lodge** (☎ 4483415; sindola@gamtel.gm; huts D1500, ste D2500; ⓧ Ⓡ), mainly intended to provide an idea of rural life, though with a thick layer of luxury, to clients of Kairaba Hotel in Kololi. The 30,000-sq-metre site offers a vast range of facilities, from tennis courts to massage parlours, lest country life should prove too rough. Birdwatching trips, walks and river fishing can be arranged, too.

Most people get here via an organised tour from Kairaba Hotel (p107). If you come here independently, phone the lodge first to check for availability. On public transport, take a bush taxi from Brikama and get off at the police checkpoint where the south-bank highway and the road to Kanilai meet. Kanilai is 6km further south.

TENDABA

On the southern bank of the Gambia River, the small village of Tendaba is 165km upstream from Banjul. The village occupies a place of honour in the upriver itineraries of many tourists, thanks to the enduring **Tendaba Camp** (☎ 6401130, 9766588; tendaba@qanet.gm; bungalows per person D280, VIP r D1000). This hotel has maintained a huge popularity since its early days as a hunting camp in the 1970s. The

---

THE STATE OF THE ROADS

Two main arteries connect the eastern and western parts of Gambia – the north-bank road, on the upper side of the river, and the south-bank road, which parallels the Gambia River in the south. While an investment in tarmac has turned the northern route into a decent, sealed road, the southern option resembled an almost artistic stretch of potholes when we last visited, so bad that most cars left the broken tarmac and drove on the side, in the dirt. Several big signs promised that this route was going to be resurfaced soon – you'll need to check the current state when you're there.

To enjoy the northern-road comforts, you can cross as a foot passenger on the Banjul ferry to Barra, and get a bush taxi to Farafenni from there. You might be able to get directly to Janjangbureh; if not, change in Farafenni. From Janjangbureh you can easily cross on the small ferry to the south, where you'll find *gelli-gellis* to Bansang and Basse Santa Su.

Gelli-gellis and *sept-place* taxis do travel along the south-bank road eastwards. If that's the kind of adventure you want, head to Tippa Garage in Serekunda to catch your taxi. For Basse and Janjangbureh, you'll probably have to change at least once. The worst stretch of road is between Brikama and Soma, and things only improve shortly before reaching Janjangbureh. From there to Basse, the road is in reasonably good condition.

Whether you're going via the northern or southern connection, allow at least 12 hours for the journey from the coast to Basse. And if you want to eschew the treacherous potholes altogether and experience the scenery at its best, combine the better bits of road with passages along the smoothest east–west connection – the Gambia River.

---

main hunting done here today is the chase for wild boar to provide the dinner buffet with its key staple.

A trip to Tendaba is a regular feature on the upriver schedules of boat and bus tours from the coast, so the village is not nearly as remote and reclusive as a look at the map would suggest. But it's still unbeatable for location. Right across the river, the mangrove-lined marshes of the Baobolong wetlands open up, and Kiang West National Park is reached easily by boat or car. Both of those places, as well as the Tendaba airfield and various spots around the spread-out village, are fantastic for birdwatching.

Book one of the VIP rooms, if they are available. No, they are not glamorous (they wouldn't need a pretentious name if they were). But they do have a bit more space, a river view and a small terrace, which is a lot more than the slightly bleak bungalows.

Getting There & Away

Many people come to Tendaba Camp as part of a tour, and most large hotels and tour operators offer two-day excursions or longer trips. A river trip is a particularly good idea (see the boxed text, p133). Prices differ widely – it's worth doing some phoning around before making your booking. Tours typically include transport, accommodation, food and a couple of side trips.

Another option is to come from the Atlantic coast resorts by green tourist taxi (about D4000 for the car, carrying up to four people). Independent travellers on public transport can take a *sept-place* along the rough road from Brikama or Serekunda to Soma. Get off at Kwinella; the camp (signposted) is 5km north along the dirt road. Camp manager Saja Touray can collect you from Kwinella. Otherwise it's a walk or trip by donkey cart.

BAOBOLONG WETLAND RESERVE

Easily explored on a boat trip from Tendaba Camp, the Baobolong Wetland Reserve is a vast area of *bolongs* (creeks), lined by thick mangroves that seem to float on the water. Fluttering egrets and herons (including the white-backed night heron) accompany your leisurely river cruise, and you might spot rarer species, such as Pel's fishing owls and mouse-brown sunbirds. Clawless otters flit out of the undergrowth and glide into the water, and the moist lands behind the mangrove curtain are home to swamp-loving sitatungas.

The mangroves in this area are some of the largest in the region, growing over 20m high in places and forming a virtual forest. This, and the biodiversity of the area, have earned Baobolong the title of a Ramsar site (wetland of international importance).

A pirogue cruise is the way to travel through Baobolong. In a couple of hours, you can chug along quite a few of the *bolongs*, ticking birds off the list as you go. To spot otters and waders, keep your eyes firmly on the undergrowth. Unless you come with an organised boat tour, you'll hire your pirogue at Tendaba Camp.

KIANG WEST NATIONAL PARK

South of the river, 145km from Banjul and to the west of Tendaba Camp, **Kiang West National Park** (admission D35) is one of the largest protected areas in Gambia, and also the wildest. Its 11,500 hectares boast a diverse animal population, though they're not easily seen.

A great place for viewing wildlife is **Toubab Kollon Point**, a river promontory in the northeast of the park where a hide grants views across a waterhole that lies 2km further west. Especially in the dry season, you stand a pretty good chance of observing various species of antelopes, baboons and red colobus monkeys. Behind Toubab Kollon Point, a laterite escarpment runs close to the riverbank, an impressive enough feature in a country as flat as Gambia – just don't come expecting the Rift Valley. From this high point, you might be able to observe baboons, warthogs and, if you've taken out a subscription to extreme luck, duikers and sitatungas on the grasslands below.

The three *bolongs* that cross the park are known to be home to dolphins, manatees and crocodiles, though they're rarely seen. And even the hyenas that live in the park are more likely to be heard than observed. As spotting wildlife isn't straightforward, a tour to Kiang West is best approached as a great excursion to a vast area of mangrove creeks and tidal flats, Guinea savannah and dry woodland – a huge range of habitats. Intrepid birdwatchers, of course, will have a great time at the park, as some 300 species have been recorded here (see the boxed text, right, for birdwatching tips).

Tendaba Camp offers 4WD tours through the park's rugged terrain, as well as pirogue trips. Visits to Baobolong Wetland Reserve can be combined with a detour to Toubab Kollon Point, and make for a great day out. The admission fee is payable at the park headquarters in Dumbuntu, though your guide will normally take care of that. Come between November and January, the best time for wildlife and bird viewing.

BIRDWATCHING TIPS: KIANG WEST NATIONAL PARK

With more than 300 recorded species, Kiang West National Park is something of a pilgrimage site for keen birdwatchers, who come here to see the large Abyssinian ground hornbill, ospreys, fish eagles, martial eagles and bateleur eagles. While raptor species are particularly common, many other varieties, including the rare brown-necked parrot and the more common white-rumped swift, are found here.

Kiang West is pretty wild terrain, and is best explored with an experienced guide from the coast, or on an excursion from Tendaba Camp. That's the way to find the most rewarding spots, without getting lost among dirt paths and mangroves.

SOMA & MANSA KONKO

Soma is a dusty sprawl of settlements, right where the road from Serekunda crosses the Trans-Gambia Hwy. It's where you change transport if you're heading upcountry by bush taxi or, crucially, fill up the tank before continuing your journey east, where service stations are rare.

Soma is a town of few graces, little more than a truckstop and the ragged businesses that have sprung up here to feed passing travellers, and refuel or repair their battered vehicles. A pirogue tour on the river makes for a nice escape, and there's a short walk you can take towards the mosque. In town, there's an internet cafe and a small health centre – but no banking facilities.

The border is only a few kilometres to the south, and the Gambian customs and immigration post is on the southern edge of town. About 10km north of Soma is Yelitenda, where you can catch the ferry across the Gambia River to Bambatenda, and then continue to Farafenni.

If you do have a day to spare here, take a day trip to Mansa Konko, originally an important local chief's capital (the name means 'king's hill'), which later became an administrative centre during the colonial era. Today it's a sleepy ghost town with a few reminders of the glory days, such as the **district commissioner's residence** and the crumbling **colonial villa**.

Sleeping & Eating

Kaira Konko (☎ 5531453; www.kairakonko.com; dm D150, r with/without bathroom D400/250) In dusty, dirty Soma,

CENTRAL & EASTERN GAMBIA

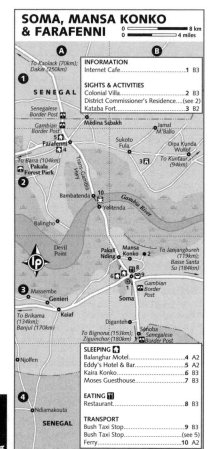

SOMA, MANSA KONKO & FARAFENNI
0 — 8 km
0 — 4 miles

INFORMATION
Internet Cafe...................................1 B3

SIGHTS & ACTIVITIES
Colonial Villa.................................2 B3
District Commissioner's Residence....(see 2)
Kataba Fort...................................3 B2

SLEEPING
Balanghar Motel.............................4 A2
Eddy's Hotel & Bar..........................5 A2
Kaira Konko...................................6 B3
Moses Guesthouse...........................7 B3

EATING
Restaurant....................................8 B3

TRANSPORT
Bush Taxi Stop................................9 B3
Bush Taxi Stop.........................(see 5)
Ferry...10 A2

this welcoming Scout centre with very decent rooms is like a friendly hug for eager Scouts and stranded tourists. Two rooms come with their own bathroom and terrace; the other five share clean toilet facilities. There's electricity (partly solar), and we'll hand the whole camp an achievement badge for its Scout-worthy hospitality, its pretty courtyard and the fruit garden out the back. The money you spend here goes partly towards the worthy Scout projects in the region, and you can also get practically involved in their activities.

Moses Guesthouse (☎ 4531462; r per person D250) Your second option is this enduring, cheap overnighter north of the main junction, with no-frills accommodation and simple food. Rooms aren't the cleanest, and the generator-

provided electricity depends on the whim of the manager or perhaps his ability to purchase fuel.

Along the central Soma roads, several street stalls serve generous portions of *benachin* (a Gambian rice dish) and omelettes soaked in oil – keep an eye open for the vinyl-covered tables on the roadside. Just north of town on the Trans-Gambia Hwy there's a small restaurant in a modern building, good for simple meals and cold drinks.

Getting There & Away
Most bush taxis from Serekunda (D90) terminate at the bush-taxi park in Soma's centre. Transport to Janjangbureh (D80) and Basse Santa Su (D90) leaves from the same park.

If you're heading north from Soma, take a local bush taxi to the Gambia River ferry at Yelitenda (D8), go across as a foot passenger (D10), and take one of the vehicles waiting on the northern bank at Bambatenda to Farafenni (D8), where you can find transport to Kaolack or Dakar. The ferry service operates between 8am and 9pm. Waits can be long, as one of the two ferries is frequently out of service, and even the functioning one might run on one engine only. Tickets are bought about 1km before you reach the ferry – anyone can indicate the office to you, and if you're on public transport, the driver normally handles this for you. Taking your own car across will cost around D100.

FARAFENNI
Soma's north-bank sister has the same junction-town ambience, though it feels a little more like an actual town than just a place to speed through. Sunday is a good day to visit, when the *lumo* (weekly market) doubles the dust and noise as traders drift in from as far as Dakar to sell their goods. There's no bank here – the nearest ATM is a longish drive away in Senegal (make sure you have all the visas you might need to cross the border).

You can also stick around for a bit and take a brief excursion to the remains of **Kataba Fort**, 10km along the eastbound dirt road. Though reduced to its dusty foundations, this 1841 Wolof construction tells a half-forgotten story of old African kingdoms.

Sleeping & Eating
Balanghar Motel (☎ 5735431; s/d D200/300) Only in the very unlikely event that Eddy's place is full,

or if you are D200 short, should you consider a night at this very shoddy motel.

Eddy's Hotel & Bar (☎ 7621197; d from D400; ⚡) The classic place to stay in Farafenni is Eddy's, which has put up stranded travellers for years (or is that decades?). Of course it's basic and a tad rundown, but it's comfortable enough, with spacious rooms and a good omelette for breakfast (D50). Room rates nearly double if you request air-conditioning. The shade of the courtyard is where you want to head for a cold beer, or just to escape the dust and heat.

Apart from Eddy's, food comes in the shape of *afra* (grilled meat) and *benachin* along the Farafenni roadsides. Look for the woman on the Kuntaur side of the main crossroads who sells excellent chicken sandwiches with fresh tomatoes and lettuce.

Getting There & Away
There are direct *gelli-gellis* from here to Serekunda (D250) via the ferry, but you don't really want to take those, seeing that you're on the side of the fabulous north-bank road. Instead, take a *gelli-gelli* to Kerewan (D90); if you're lucky there might be one all the way to Barra (D180), though you might have to change in Kerewan.

Most Dakar-bound transport goes from the Senegalese border. To get there, take a *gelli-gelli* from town (D6).

EASTERN GAMBIA

Beyond Farafenni, the Gambia River is not yet under the spell of the sea – up here, the water is fresh, not saline, and with that, vegetation and animal populations change entirely. The thick mangroves of the west thin out and make way for thick tropical forest inhabited by baboons, colobus and patas monkeys, and plenty of birds. As your boat skips past the islands of the River Gambia National Park, keep a look out for hippos bathing in the waters.

The area lends itself to a relaxed historical tour. Ancient stone circles, remnants of the region's earliest residents, are enigmatic relics of an era long gone. Further eastwards, a couple of late-Victorian warehouses tell of Janjangbureh's 19th-century role as a colonial trading station, while the spread-out market of Basse, the largest town of the region, fuels commerce across the entire eastern zone.

WASSU & KERR BATCH STONE CIRCLES
Hardly anything is known about the people who might have built the hundreds of fascinating stone circles near the riverbanks of southern Senegal and Gambia around AD 500 to AD 1000. It's assumed that they may have been farmers and hunters, who erected the mysterious rings of hewn laterite to mark the burial sites of their kings and chiefs, though this theory remains open to debate.

The **Wassu Stone Circles** are among the largest and best maintained of these sites, and there's a small, informative **museum** (admission D50) that illustrates possible theories about early human habitation of this region with images, artefacts and text. The Wassu site counts several circles, each containing between 10 and 24 laterite columns measuring 1m to 2.5m in height. Excavations have unearthed iron and bronze artefacts, spearheads, pottery shards and human bones.

The **Kerr Batch** site sits a few kilometres westwards, near Nyangabantang on the north-bank road. The small ethnographic **museum** (admission D50) raises the same questions and provides the same suggestions as the Wassu one, and assembles a number of objects that relate to life in this early period.

If you can visit only one site, go to Wassu – it's more impressive, and more easily reached.

Getting There & Away
The Wassu Stone Circles sit about 20km northwest of Janjangbureh, close to the small town of Kuntaur. Take an early ferry to the north bank from Janjangbureh and ask for the *gelli-gelli* to Kuntaur (around D25). The best day for public transport is Monday, when the Wassu *lumo* brings a better chance of taxis headed that way. Otherwise, it might be better to go on a tour with one of the Janjangbureh camps or take a private hire taxi (around D800), as transport back can be hard to come by and there's nowhere to spend the night. For Kerr Batch, you're better off hiring a taxi for a return trip (around D250), as it's a further 9km from the main drop-off point in Nyangabantang to the site.

RIVER GAMBIA NATIONAL PARK (BABOON ISLANDS)
South of Kuntaur, five islands and the surrounding waters of the Gambia River are protected as a national park. Its heart is the rather confusingly named Baboon Islands – site of

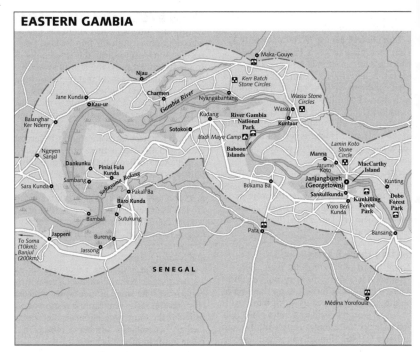

EASTERN GAMBIA

the very impressive **Chimpanzee Rehabilitation Trust** (CRA; www.chimprehab.com). Created and developed with incredible passion and dedication by the late Stella Brewer OBE, the CRA has successfully rehabilitated confiscated and pet chimpanzees from across the world back into the wild (see the boxed text, p141).

The Baboon Islands are situated in one of the most magnificent stretches of the Gambia River. Hundreds of bird species inhabit the tropical landscape, and from your pirogue you'll be able to see green vervet and colobus monkeys leaping between giant trees. In the waters, you might spot hippos and crocodiles or even a large cobra making its serpentine way between the islands. If your trip coincides with nightfall, you'll suddenly find your boat guided by the tiny lights of fireflies that rise and fade like fairy lights strung up between palm trees. You'll just make out the silhouettes of dozens of baboons roosting in the trees at the river's edge. If you're lucky you'll even spot a couple of chimps when passing the navigable channel through the national park.

Don't leave the chimp watching to chance, though. If you book a night at the CRA's Badi

Mayo Camp, you get full access to the park and can accompany the feeding boat on its tour around the chimp islands. This is the only way to see these strangely humanlike animals up close, angling for bananas and bread thrown to them. (It is not possible to enter the islands, as the chimps might violently resent your presence and, more importantly from the chimps' point of view, you might be carrying some communicable disease.)

If you spend more than just one night, you'll be able to take a tour of Sambel Kunda Village, which lies a short walk or, better yet, a ride on a horse-drawn cart from Badi Mayo through the bush. On the way Badi Mayo guides will take you to the Chasin verandah, from where you'll get a fantastic view across the river, its islands and surrounding areas. Keep an eye out for the clawless otters, bushbabies, hyenas, antelopes and multitude of bird species that inhabit this area. There are a couple of nature trails. The most impressive one leads from Samaboykongko (a high spur overlooking the river on which legend has it Gambia's last elephant met its end) to Badi Mayo.

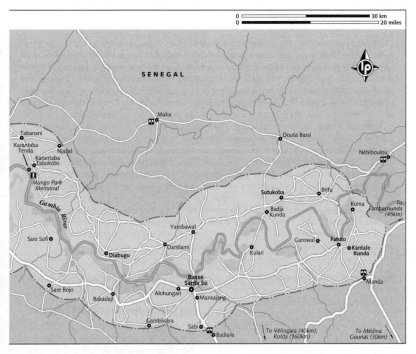

In the village, the **Gambia Horse and Donkey Trust** (www.gambiahorseanddonkey.org.uk), founded by Stella Brewer and her sister Heather Armstrong, is well worth a visit. This project looks after mistreated horses and donkeys and teaches villagers how to care better for their precious animals. Stella's philosophy was based on the premise that wildlife conservation only has a chance of working if the local community is involved and benefits directly and tangibly, and if their worries are understood (farmers, for instance, tend to be less keen on hippo protection as the giant mammals love nothing better than to eat their rice harvest). People from nearby villages not only work at Badi Mayo and the CRA, but the chimp project supports the government primary school with a sponsorship scheme, and runs a village clinic and other projects that you can visit.

Sleeping & Eating

Badi Mayo Camp (☎ 9947430; badimayo@yahoo .com; www.chimprehab.com; per person D4000) ranks among the most fantastic holiday destinations in Gambia. You get to stay in East African safari tents built on giant wooden platforms. Equipped with mosquito-netted beds, a bathroom corner, towels, bathrobes and solar lights, these aren't really tents but mobile units of luxury accommodation. From your platform, you'll see red colobus and green vervet monkeys leap from tree to tree (absolutely don't feed them!), and they'll in turn watch you while you take your outdoor shower (don't worry, they're the only ones that get to watch). At night you are surrounded by the noises of the bush – perhaps including the *'whoop whoop'* of the hyena and, if you are lucky, the plaintive sound of a manatee calling its mate.

A hot cup of coffee can be brought to your terrace in the early morning, which you'll savour to the wakening calls of the chimps on the island across from the camp.

The accommodation rate includes everything (except drinks) – pick-up from Kuntaur, all meals (cooked on site with fresh ingredients), a tour around the chimp island, and the company of David Marsden, Stella's husband and gentle spirit of this unique site. Note that you *must* book in advance. Accommodation

---

HIGHLY STRUNG HIPPOS

Giant hippopotamuses are fascinating creatures, and eastern Gambia is a zone where you get to see them perform their impressive yawns pretty reliably. Families of hippos inhabit the waters of the Gambia River eastwards of Farafenni – they love fresh water and therefore can't be found further westwards. The River Gambia National Park is a good place for reliable hippo spotting, and between there and Janjangbureh you'll find a few more sites. Local guides and boat drivers usually know where the families like to bathe. Most Janjangbureh camps, Badi Mayo Camp in the national park and the tour operators that work the river (see p133) can take you on hippo-spotting trips.

If you see a hippo, admire it from afar. These giants of the river are notoriously cantankerous creatures. Forget lions, leopards and snakes: hippos are responsible for more deaths in Africa than any other animal. Despite being vegetarian, they frequently kill animals and people with their enormous jaws and 60cm-long teeth – not to eat them, but to protect their living space. Hippos are very territorial and short-sighted, and will plough into anything they consider a threat, including, unfortunately, the occasional boat with camera-wielding tourists. The most important thing to remember is to not get between a mother and her young (very hard to do, as they usually stay close), or between the beast and the sandbank, as you'll confuse the hippo by cutting off its natural escape route. And a confused hippo is not the encounter you want to have on your holiday. Local guides are usually aware of this (and often too scared of the animals to attempt getting too close), so you don't have to worry too much.

---

is very limited, and it's not possible to just turn up.

All Badi Mayo income helps to support the CRA. If you wish to contribute further, check the website for information on how to adopt a chimp or make a donation.

Getting There & Away

The River Gambia National Park stretches over several islands. It's therefore reached by boat. Unless you are visiting Badi Mayo, access to the park is restricted to passage along the Port Authority's navigable channel. Provided that your boat has a CRA ranger on board you may move nearer to the islands. Tourists must pay the park entrance fee of D150. Phone relevant tour operators (see p287) to arrange boat trips from Kuntaur or Janjangbureh.

From the coast you can hire a taxi to Kuntaur, where Badi Mayo staff will pick you up by boat. Khadija, who takes the bookings, will put you in touch with a reliable taxi driver who can arrange to collect you from your hotel, escort you across on the Barra ferry and take you to Kuntaur. The taxi will wait two to three days and return you to the coast.

If a stay at Badi Mayo explodes your budget, you can go through the park via the navigable channel and visit Bird Island on the *Stella Brewer*, a boat run by **Faldeh** (☎ 9707770), a boatman-guide based at Kuntaur. You might still see chimps, hippos and crocodiles, and you'll spot plenty of birds, but you won't be

able to go around the park's islands, join the feeding trips or take the village tours.

JANJANGBUREH (GEORGETOWN)

Its setting on the northern edge of MacCarthy Island, 300km up the Gambia River, has earned this sleepy upcountry town the nickname Makaaty – the third label for a place that already lingers undecidedly between the colonial title Georgetown and the postindependence name Janjangbureh.

Founded by the British in 1823, Janjangbureh was a busy administrative centre and trading hub in the colonial era. Today it moves to a sluggish rhythm and falls asleep as soon as nightfall drowns most of the town in darkness. Birdsong being the local music here, it's an obligatory stop for ornithologists. Its brilliant midriver location makes Janjangbureh a great base for boat trips around the eastern region – feast your eyes on the abundant greenery that frames the river.

Information

There's little in terms of infrastructure – no banks, no hospital – though you can get online at **Gamspad** (☎ 5676159; Owen St; per hr D25; ✆ 9am-6pm).

The office of the **Forestry Department** (☎ 9908599; forest@gamtel.gm; Owen St) isn't quite as well staffed as it once was, since the German funders have withdrawn from the project. Still, it can point you reliably in the direction of the most interesting community forests of the eastern region. Ask for Ousseynou Thiam.

Dangers & Annoyances
It's hard to go for a peaceful walk here without being approached by persistent youngsters offering their services as guides. You might enjoy the company, but unless you're very directionally challenged you won't need their help. On the ferry and at the pier, young guys will often try to persuade you to stay in one particular camp or another, sometimes quite

---

COMMUNITY-BASED CONSERVATION   *Katharina Lobeck Kane*

As night falls on Badi Mayo Camp in the River Gambia National Park, the chimp calls, barking of baboons and chirping of birds finally subside, making way for the noises of the night. Suddenly the dull sound of a heavy drum mingles with the chirring of cicadas and rustling of leaves. Camp manager David Marsden explains: 'this is the sound of the hippo drum. It's beaten at night to keep the animals away from the villagers' rice fields. It's all very well protecting hippos and arguing that this is a good thing to do, but if you wake up in the morning to find your rice field totally demolished, you'll be hard to convince'. The Chimpanzee Rehabilitation Trust (CRA), which runs Badi Mayo Camp, has financed the building of hippo towers and the drum-beating watchmen. It's one of many ways in which it integrates community needs with conservation efforts.

David's wife, the late Stella Brewer (1951–2008), who famously set up the CRA, was a champion of community-based conservation. 'She always promoted a holistic approach', David says, 'knowing that nothing could be achieved if the community wasn't ready to support and defend CRA's conservation efforts'. Daughter of Eddie Brewer, the founder of the Abuko Nature Reserve and the Gambia Wildlife Conservation Department, Stella had learnt to love animals early in life and rescued her first chimp in 1968 – an act that changed her life. She soon had responsibility for a small community of chimps. As they quickly outgrew the small Abuko reserve, she moved with them to Niokolo-Koba park in Senegal (p230) in 1974, with the aim of integrating them into the wild chimp population there. In 1978 a severe drought brought the wild chimps into unremitting violent conflict with Stella's 'newcomers' and she was forced to return to Gambia with her unusual 'family'. The newly gazetted River Gambia National Park seemed a very good temporary solution for the chimps. Some 30 years later, they are still in their 'temporary' home. This makes Stella's work the longest-running project of its type in Africa. With more than 80 chimps, of whom 17 are original inhabitants, it's also one of the largest.

A trip on a horse-drawn cart to the village of Sambel Kunda behind Badi Mayo Camp illustrates David's words perfectly: Stella's name is on everyone's lips. The local nurse has nothing but praise for her, pointing to the clinic financed through her association. It's the same at the local government school, now rebuilt with solar power and a library – all thanks to the chimp project. And there's the Horse and Donkey Trust, where it's not cute chimps but the working animals of local farmers that get their dose of TLC. Their owners are taught how to prolong their animals' lives and increase their own profits by caring for them better.

This project is a real success story of how conservation can work in everyone's favour – that of the villagers, their environment and both wild and domestic animals inhabiting the surroundings. There are other examples, though stories don't exactly abound. Too often elsewhere excellent efforts have been blocked by red tape or by the project initiator's limited understanding of the surroundings they had hoped to operate in. 'The CRA's community development work is ongoing', says David, 'but it's rather more complex than it might appear from a brief glimpse from the outside'.

Individual communities have their own ways of functioning, their own beliefs, identity, knowledge and sense of 'right and wrong'. It's often tempting to fly in a solution to a problem from the outside – to an outsider it might seem so obvious what needs doing and how to do it best. Yet if it hurts local sensitivities, goes against their beliefs or is perceived to make things even harder for them, even the seemingly greatest idea is bound to fail. Badi Mayo must rank today among the most impressive efforts of gently combining wildlife conservation with community development, but it is a success that hasn't come overnight. It has been built gradually, with tremendous tenacity, for over 30 years. And perhaps its greatest strength lies there – in patience, endurance and the unfailing belief that this is a good route to take.

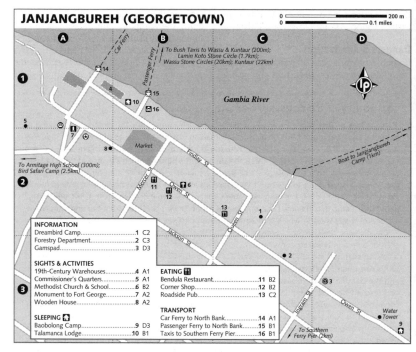

JANJANGBUREH (GEORGETOWN)

Gambia River

To Bush Taxis to Wassu & Kuntaur (200m);
Lamin Koto Stone Circle (1.7km);
Wassu Stone Circles (20km); Kuntaur (22km)

To Armitage High School (300m);
Bird Safari Camp (2.5km)

Boat to Janjangbureh
Camp (1km)

Market

Findlay St

Mercer St

Owen St

Jackson St

Queen St

Ingram St

Owen St

Water
Tower

To Southern
Ferry Pier (2km)

INFORMATION
Dreambird Camp.............................**1** C2
Forestry Department.......................**2** C3
Gamspad.......................................**3** D3

SIGHTS & ACTIVITIES
19th-Century Warehouses...............**4** A1
Commissioner's Quarters.................**5** A1
Methodist Church & School.............**6** B2
Monument to Fort George..............**7** A2
Wooden House...............................**8** A2

SLEEPING
Baobolong Camp............................**9** D3
Talamanca Lodge...........................**10** B1

EATING
Bendula Restaurant........................**11** B2
Corner Shop..................................**12** B2
Roadside Pub.................................**13** C2

TRANSPORT
Car Ferry to North Bank.................**14** A1
Passenger Ferry to North Bank........**15** B1
Taxis to Southern Ferry Pier............**16** B1

---

forcefully. If you don't want to go along with their suggestions, stay firm in your refusal.

Sights

In the centre of Janjangbureh, a few historical buildings tell of the town's colonial past. On the riverbank, the sturdy foundations of two **19th-century warehouses** continue to defy time. The old **Commissioner's Quarters** are today inhabited by the district governor, and there's a **monument to Fort George** (Owen St) outside the police station, commemorating the 1823 building of the fort by the British on demand of the local king. Further along the street, the **Methodist Church & School** (Owen St) tells of the 1824 introduction of Christianity to the region. West of town is the early-20th-century building of the **Armitage High School**, an institution once reserved for the local elite.

Janjangbureh's oldest and historically most interesting building is also its humblest. Opposite the market, a small, weather-beaten **wooden house** (Owen St) is one of the rare surviving examples of the typical housing built by freed slaves who settled here some 200 years ago.

Throughout town, prominent signposts point out the most important sights. They're particularly useful, as local kids keep setting up new sights of supposed historical significance that they'll encourage you to visit for a fee. Perhaps inspired by Jufureh's flourishing *Roots* industry (see p129), they started presenting one of the old warehouses as a 'slave prison' (the newish shackles cemented into the walls give away the scam), then added a 'slave market' and 'freedom tree' to the scene. There's no doubt that slaves were transported through Janjangbureh, yet the indicated sites don't relate to the trade – the houses were built well after slavery was abolished in British colonies in 1807. Some people are amused by this profitable rewriting of history, others insulted. Whatever your feelings, beware of the 'Visitors Book', encouraging incredibly generous donations, allegedly in memory of slavery.

Those with a penchant for ancient historical features should take a trip to **Lamin Koto Stone Circle**. It's a smaller and less impressive monument than the famous Wassu Stone Circles, but at only 1.7km away from the north bank it's closer and thus in good reach for those who can't make it to Wassu. The circle is on the right (northeast) side of the road, under a big tree.

Tours

On one- or two-day tours by boat or foot, you can explore much of the area surrounding Janjangbureh. By pirogue, you can head for River Gambia National Park (note that you need to spend a night there if you want to visit more than the main channel; see p137). A combination of boat and walking takes you to Mungo Park Memorial and Wassu Stone Circles. Dobo and Kunkilling Forest Parks (see the boxed text, below) are also within easy reach if you've got wheels. Once there, you leave the car and follow the nature trails.

The cost of pirogue tours changes quickly in line with rises or decreases in petrol prices. Expect to pay D6000 per pirogue for trips to River Gambia National Park and D2000 for a tour around MacCarthy Island. Boat hire per hour is around D1000 to D2000, depending on boat size.

Bird Safari, Jangjangbureh and Baobolong Camps all offer birdwatching tours. The ones at Bird Safari Camp are interesting, as the forest surrounding the camp attracts slightly different species.

Sleeping

Talamanca Lodge (☎ 9921100; talamancalodge@yahoo .com; Findlay St; r D200) What started as a low-key restaurant nicely located between the river and a busy street has now turned into a very basic lodge serving simple food and very cheap beer. The torn-off blade on the ceiling fan looked a little worrying, but Banna Kongira's smile and helpful attitude helped us get over that shock. You can camp here and Banna is happy to organise pirogue tours.

Jangjangbureh Camp (☎ 9816944; www.gambia -river.com; s/d D300/500) On the north bank of the Gambia River, this collection of colourful, quirky bungalows sits on a vast terrain between forest and water. Though the paint peels off the architecturally inventive huts and dust gathers in the corners, it's still a fun place to be, especially if you're in a group. A meal with a view across the river (D280) is great even if you don't stay the night. The camp belongs to Gambia River Excursions, so boat trips are easily organised. To arrange your boat to the camp, ask at Dreambird Camp (☎ /fax 5676182) in Janjangbureh.

Baobolong Camp (☎ 5676133; fax 5676120; Owen St; s/d D350/700) The bungalows of this fairly central camp are surrounded by lush riverine vegetation where the chatter of birds follows you everywhere. Rooms were in need of a clean when we passed and the number of would-be guides hanging out at the camp dipped the vibe a little. There's a generator for the torchless and a resident ornithologist for birdwatchers.

Bird Safari Camp (☎ 7336570, +44 121 288 4100; www.bsc.gm; per person incl breakfast D900; 🖳 🏊) Some 2.5km west of Janjangbureh and set

---

COMMUNITY FORESTS

One way of fighting against rampant deforestation of the central and eastern regions has been the creation of community forests. A German-funded forestry project invested great efforts in developing such forests in the surroundings of Janjangbureh. Though the main donors have pulled out of the scheme, the legacy of their work remains, and is now handled by Janjangbureh's Forestry Department. Visit its offices or, if you stay in town, ask at your hotel about trips to the forest parks. They're easily reached and make for pleasant walks through savannah woodlands and other habitats.

Dobo Forest Park is one such place. The small park stretches across 34.5 hectares of gallery forest along the north bank of the Gambia River, not far from Bansang. You'll have to be lucky to spot the park's larger inhabitants, such as crocodiles, antelopes and bushbucks, but will probably get good views of bird species, including eagles, kingfishers, bee-eaters, rollers and woodpeckers, while tracing the park's eco-trail.

Kunkilling Forest Park, on the south bank near Bansang, is a much larger affair and can either be walked or explored by donkey cart. Its 200 hectares of riparian canopy forest are jointly managed by four neighbouring villages. Four eco-trails wind through woodlands inhabited by more than 185 bird species, among them African finfoots, white-backed vultures, Adamawa turtle doves, shining-blue kingfishers and nightjars. A guided visit will also take a brief historical detour, past the tomb of the 19th-century king of Fouladou, Musa Molo.

between river and gallery forest, this place is secluded and surrounded by bird life, which is easily explored with the resident guide. Accommodation is in basic bungalows or large tents with bathroom. Solar panels function for a few hours in the evening. If they don't, try a romantic dinner on the boat landing by the light of kerosene lanterns. Hidden Gambia (see the boxed text, p133), which owns this place, can take you here and around by boat – highly recommended. If you arrive by public transport, phone to see if pick-up can be arranged from the ferry.

Eating & Drinking

Few options exist outside the camps and lodges, especially in the evenings, when life retreats behind compound walls.

Bendula Restaurant (Owen St; meals D100; 🕙 11am-9pm) A popular option is the bare hall and relaxed courtyard of this restaurant, which vibrates to a reggae beat and serves cold beers, Guinness and soft drinks. Meals can be arranged on request.

Roadside Pub (Owen St; snacks from D75; 🕙 lunch & dinner) A bit more rugged, though good for a plate of benachin and a Coke.

Corner shop (Owen St) If you find all the kitchens closed, try this small shop for corned beef, eggs or a sardine sandwich.

Getting There & Away

Ferries (D75/5 per car/passenger) reach MacCarthy Island from either the southern or northern bank of the river. The northern ferry operates from 8am to 7pm. The ferry connecting the island to the southern shore seems to run until demand dries up. Still, it's safer to get there before 7pm to avoid getting stuck. The main road between Banjul and Basse Santa Su does not go directly past the southern ferry ramp, but sept-place taxis should turn off to the ferry stop at Sankulikunda to drop off or pick up passengers if you ask them. On the island, pick-ups take people to Janjangbureh for D10, though it's always best to call your camp and arrange transport.

When leaving Janjangbureh, take a taxi to the southern ferry and cross over to the southern bank. There are occasional pick-ups or minibuses directly to Basse Santa Su (D70), though most go to Bansang (D30), where you have to change for transport to Basse. If you're heading west, go to Bansang or just to the main road. From there you can get to

Soma, cross on the ferry to Farafenni, and take the north-bank road to Barra. Remember to bring a lot of time and patience – public transport is not frequent in this part of the country and relying on bush taxis is always time-consuming and often frustrating.

BANSANG

Music lovers may know Bansang as the middle name of one of Gambia's greatest kora (harp-lute) players – Amadu Bansang Jobarteh hails from here. A pilgrimage to his birthplace will introduce you to a large town spread out between the river and the main road. It's a calm area that invites walking, particularly if you're a keen birdwatcher – spectacular red-throated bee-eaters nest in a nearby quarry. And, quite importantly, Bansang also has the largest upcountry hospital.

MUNGO PARK MEMORIAL

Historians may want to head for Karantaba Tenda, about 20km east of Janjangbureh. Near this village, on the riverbank, is the memorial pillar marking where the Scottish explorer Mungo Park set off into the interior to trace the course of the Niger River.

A bush taxi comes here most mornings from the north-bank ferry ramp opposite Janjangbureh, but if your time is limited, hiring a private taxi (around D500) may be the only certain way of getting there and back in a day. The pillar is outside the village, and local boys will guide you there for a small fee. Another option is to go by boat. You can hire one for the day from places in Janjangbureh from about D1500.

BASSE SANTA SU

Set on a beautiful waterfront, Gambia's easternmost main town is the last major ferry-crossing point on the Gambia River and an area transport hub. It's a traditional trading centre, as crammed, busy, rundown and enterprising as any West African junction town.

Information

The two main banks are **Trust Bank** (☎ 5668907) and **Standard Chartered Bank** (☎ 4668218) across the road. Neither of them has an ATM. You can change money here, but it's still best to bring enough cash with you from the coast, where you'll get better exchange rates. You can make calls and go online at the **Gamtel**

MUNGO PARK

By the end of the 18th century, scientific exploration had become another popular interest in the colonial territories. Researchers were obsessed with solving two main puzzles: the position of Timbuktu (the mysterious 'city of gold') and the route of the Niger River. Although the Niger's existence was well known, its source and mouth, and even the direction of its flow, were a mystery.

In 1795 the London-based Association for Promoting the Discovery of the Interior Parts of Africa sent a young Scotsman called Mungo Park to the Gambia River. Park followed the river upstream by boat, sailing between British trading stations. He based himself near present-day Janjangbureh, where he learnt several local languages, and then set off across the plains, with just two servants and three donkeys. He travelled northeast, crossing the Senegal River, getting captured and escaping, and eventually reached the Niger at Ségou, confirming that it flowed in a northerly direction. After more adventures and incredible hardships, he eventually managed to return to the Gambia River and to Britain, where he wrote *Travels in the Interior of Africa*.

In 1801 Park returned to the Gambia River and again set out for the Niger. This time he took a larger support crew, although most of the men were army deserters and completely unprepared for the rigours of the expedition. By the time the group reached the Niger River, many had died, and even more perished from either disease or attacks. Park and the few remaining members of his party all died under attack at the Bussa Rapids, in the east of present-day Nigeria.

office (☎ 4229999), opposite the post office. If you haven't found all the necessary immigration officials at the border, head for the immigration office in town to get your entry stamp.

Sights & Activities

Most of Basse can be explored in an afternoon stroll, which should definitely include the town's sprawling **market** and a walk along the waterfront. Every corner of every street in Basse is filled with rickety stalls, small shops and cloths that mark out street spots as improvised trading pitches. Unless cheap Chinese house wares and clothes, odd screws and car parts are the kinds of souvenirs you treasure, you won't find much to purchase here. There's some nice African cloth, though, and odd, multicoloured bicycle seats. Look out for the imaginative, hand-painted shop signs on your walk around town, dodging the bicycles and donkeys that make up the city traffic, and enjoy the feverish selling, bartering and buying. The side street past the post office has a very particular character, marked by a couple of Koranic schools where kids repeat their verses at the top of their voices, and is spread-out workshops of metal smiths.

Heading for the ferry terminal, you'll see an imposing colonial warehouse on the riverside. That's **Traditions**, a place to stay, but also a great location for a snack on its pretty riverview balcony. It overlooks a gentle bend in the river, crossed by an occasional ferry and small metal tubs driven across the water by strong wooden rudders. It's a peaceful spot, quiet enough to attract the rare Egyptian plover between June and February. This small wader might be missed when standing quietly on the riverbank, but it is instantly recognised in flight by its swept-back wings and beautiful black-and-white markings.

If you're interested in local arts and crafts, Sulayman Jallow from Traditions can organise visits to the workshops of women producing beautiful indigo, tie-dyed and mud cloth.

Both Traditions and the ferry point are good places to arrange boat rides to watch more birds (and quite possibly the occasional hippo or crocodile). Rates are negotiable and the boat owners drive a hard bargain. Expect to pay D700 an hour for a motorboat.

Sleeping & Eating

Basse doesn't exactly boast a huge amount of accommodation besides dodgy guest houses with questionable activity. The following options are recommended.

Traditions (☎ 5668760, 7335562; r D250) The very committed and utterly helpful Sulayman Jallow has divided the 1st floor of this massive colonial warehouse into several rooms, each containing a wooden bed with a good mattress and a functional fan. Electricity is provided by a generator from 7pm to 7am. The location and great views alone make this one of Basse's best accommodation options.

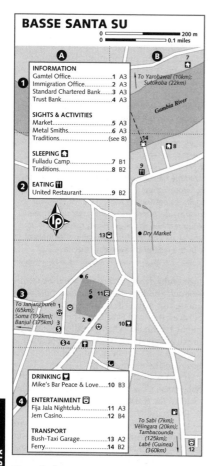

BASSE SANTA SU

0 ——— 200 m
0 ——— 0.1 miles

INFORMATION
Gamtel Office.........................1 A3
Immigration Office..................2 A3
Standard Chartered Bank.......3 A3
Trust Bank.............................4 A3

SIGHTS & ACTIVITIES
Market..................................5 A3
Metal Smiths........................6 A3
Traditions..........................(see 8)

SLEEPING
Fulladu Camp........................7 B1
Traditions.............................8 B2

EATING
United Restaurant.................9 B2

DRINKING
Mike's Bar Peace & Love......10 B3

ENTERTAINMENT
Fija Jala Nightclub................11 A3
Jem Casino..........................12 B4

TRANSPORT
Bush-Taxi Garage................13 A2
Ferry...................................14 B2

To Yarobawal (10km);
Sutokoba (22km)

Gambia River

Dry Market

To Janjangbureh
(65km);
Soma (192km);
Banjul (375km)

To Sabi (7km);
Vélingara (20km);
Tambacounda
(125km);
Labé (Guinea)
(360km)

Phone before arrival, especially if you wish to arrange (invariably simple) meals.

Fulladu Camp (☎ 9906791, 7184211; r per person D350) This vast place, on the north bank opposite Traditions, doesn't look as though it receives a lot of visitors, and yet is permanently ready for the odd person who passes by. It's a well-conceived structure with large bungalows spread across a leafy garden. To get here, you cross the river in a tiny, rusty metal tub. If you wish to eat here, make sure you phone well in advance so that fresh ingredients can be bought and prepared.

Don't expect culinary highlights in Basse. Your day here may be the occasion to appreciate a decent omelette, grilled-meat skewers sold in the street or a good plate of *benachin*

(Gambian rice dish). You can preorder food at the accommodation options listed above or try one of the tiny chop shops (basic local-style eating houses) around the taxi park. Otherwise, there's the small, reggae-coloured **United Restaurant** (ferry terminal; ☾ lunch & dinner), which blasts reggae and *mbalax* from rickety speakers and serves Gambian food.

Drinking & Entertainment

Entertainment and drinking seem very closely linked in this truck-stop trading centre. To stick with this local theme, you could head to **Mike's Bar Peace & Love** (☾ 11am-10pm), where the blackboard advertises 1L of gin for only D100 and the bizarre wall paintings inside somewhat betray the altered state of their creator. If you come here very, very regularly and consume enough to impress the managers, you might find your portrait painted on the front wall (check out the picture of the smiling guy outside). Football lovers: there's a giant satellite dish that promises football screenings, though everything obviously depends on the availability of electricity.

The **Fija Jala Nightclub** (☎ 9937121) has an inviting sign outside that proclaims it as 'the only and best nightclub in town'. That'll be the place, then, to swing a leg to distorted Gambian, Senegalese, Guinean and Jamaican rhythms. The **Jem Casino** (Jem Hotel) is a rather drunk and occasionally disorderly affair.

Getting There & Away

Bush taxis go to the ferry ramp for Janjangbureh (D70, one hour), Soma (D150, four hours) and Serekunda (D350, eight hours).

The ferry to the Gambia River's northern bank takes one car at a time, and the journey is quick. The charge for a car is D75; passengers pay D5. The small metal tubs charge D50 to take you across.

If you're heading for Senegal, you can get a very rusty *sept-place* taxi to Vélingara (D50, one hour), from where you'll be able to catch transport to Tambacounda. The border crossing is usually smooth; just make sure you get all the correct stamps (sometimes, if the border guards are on lunch break for instance, this involves visiting the immigration office in Basse). The bush taxis that travel this stretch are among the most clapped-out we've seen anywhere. Bring a cushion and plenty of patience.

CENTRAL & EASTERN GAMBIA

Senegal

ARIADNE VAN ZANDBERGEN

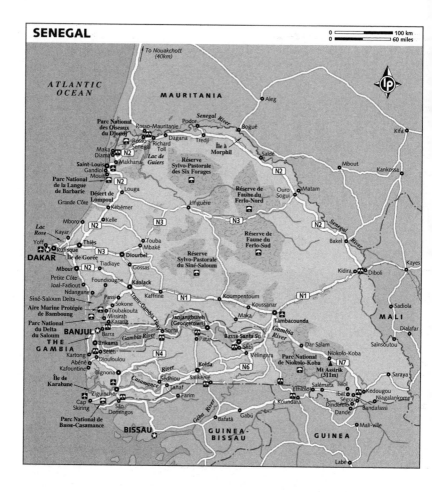

Greater Dakar & Cap Vert Peninsula

Once a tiny speck on the southern tip of Cap Vert Peninsula, Dakar has now clawed its way across almost its entire triangle, stretching, swelling and pushing against its natural boundaries. An impressive set of modern highways and ambitious interchanges has been poured onto the urban landscape to facilitate the journey from the historical Plateau past the luxurious sea-view villas of Les Almadies through to the crammed streets of Pikine – a streetwise city within the city, built on the hope and despair of Senegal's youth.

Dakar's edges are sharp and its contrasts dizzying. While development whirls on every corner and glass-fronted office blocks kiss the skies, the original fishing villages the city has swallowed in its growth – communities such as Ouakam, N'Gor and Yoff – retain their original, rural flavour, like ancient islands in a mighty, modern stream. Dakar is where horse-cart drivers chug over swish highways and gleaming 4WDs squeeze through tiny sand roads. It's where impossibly elegant ladies dig skinny heels in dusty walkways and suit-clad businessmen kneel down for prayer in the middle of the street. Made of furious drumbeats, screeching traffic, exuberant nightlife, market shouting, street hustling and boundless imagination, Dakar is like a ringing in your ear – constant sensory overload. Meet its honest hustlers, dodge the creative conmen and be awed by the gold-jingling businesswomen who walk on clouds of incense right through the fumes.

HIGHLIGHTS

- Put on your most glittering robes, hit the vibrant nightclub scene in **Dakar** (p173) and get a bout of *mbalax* fever
- Soak up the calm ambience and sense of history on **Île de Gorée** (p177)
- Indulge in a day of sea, sand and surf at the beaches of **N'Gor** (p161)
- Get in the Sunday-morning spirit at **Keur Moussa Monastery** (p182)
- Glimpse the pink shimmer of **Lac Rose** (p180) on a horse ride
- Sip coffee with artists on a private studio tour of the **Village des Arts** (p161)

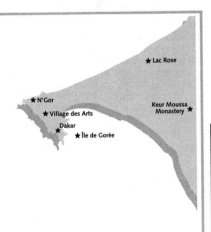

DAKAR IN...

Two Days

Start your day with croissants and coffee at the leafy **Institut Français** (p153), then dive right into city life with a stroll around the historical buildings of the centre and a visit to the **Musée Théodore Monod** (p159). Have a Senegalese lunch at **Le Djembé** (p168), then spend the afternoon strolling around the historical alleyways of **Île de Gorée** (p177). Treat yourself to dinner at **Le Cozy** (p168), then hit the club scene. Warm up with a drink at **Le Ngor** (p169), then head to the two-floor party house **Papayer Night** (p173), before rounding the night off at **Le Duplex** (p173).

Start the next day with a late breakfast at the beach on **Île de N'Gor** (p161). Enjoy the waves, then return by pirogue to the mainland and have lunch at the **Cabane des Pêcheurs** (p169). Visit the **Village des Arts** (p161), then relax and get ready for another late night of brilliant live music at **Just 4 U** (p173).

Four Days

Start your visit as for the two-day itinerary, then add a day at the **markets** (p171) and admire the view across town from the lighthouse at **Mamelles** (p160). On day four, start early and travel to **Lac Rose** (p180). Go horse riding with the guides of **Les Chevaux de Lac** (p181). Head back to Dakar for a sunset drink on the terrace of **Hôtel Sokhamon** (p166), before settling into an evening in style at **Alkimia** (p169).

DAKAR

HISTORY

Dakar started its existence as a small fishing village of the Lebou community, who have lived on the Cap Vert Peninsula for centuries. By the mid-19th century, the French port on Île de Gorée (Gorée Island) proved ineffective for the growing trade of peanuts and other products from the mainland. The French decided to relocate and in 1857 the French captain Protêt founded the town and port of Dakar on Lebou lands. By 1871 Dakar had become significant enough to be granted the special status of a self-governing commune by the French, together with Rufisque, Saint-Louis and Gorée. Following the construction of the Dakar–Saint-Louis railway in 1885, the port of Dakar became a real economic hub. Rapid urban development followed and Dakar was named the capital of French West Africa in 1902.

With Senegal's independence in 1960, it was chosen as capital of the newborn nation. It has since long outgrown its original setting on the Plateau, sprawling all the way to Rufisque via suburbs that are larger in size than the city proper.

ORIENTATION

The centre of Dakar, the historical Plateau, sits right at the tip of the peninsula, opposite Île de Gorée. Its heart is the Place de l'Indépendance, from where the busy artery Av Pompidou heads west towards the sprawling Marché Sandaga. Av Léopold Senghor leads south from here to Hôpital Principal, then connects via the wide Bd de la République to the modern Route de la Corniche-Ouest – the main route of the centre. The corniche is Dakar's proudest piece of ambitious road construction, a palm-lined wide road with bridges, roundabouts and the very controversial Soumbédioune tunnel. Traffic here usually flows smoothly, past Mamelles, all the way to Les Almadies and N'Gor, where it turns into Route de N'Gor and leads eastwards to Yoff.

A second main artery out of the Plateau is Av Blaise Diagne, which passes through the old Senegalese quartier of Médina, before slicing as Av Cheikh Anta Diop through fashionable Point E, with its bars and restaurants, Mermoz and the old Lebou village Ouakam.

At writing, the journey out of Dakar to the surrounding regions was still a tough trip through slow traffic jams from the Patte d'Oie interchange, past Pikine and Thiaroye, through to Rufisque. This is bound to change soon – from Av du Président Lamine Guèye to Patte d'Oie you can already see the first completed stretch of the modern, six-lane autoroute out of the city. It'll eventually take you all the way to Diamniadio – in time to connect with the new airport that is planned near there (see the boxed text, opposite).

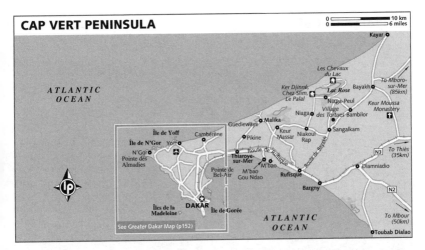

CAP VERT PENINSULA

To get into town from Léopold Sédar Senghor International Airport, you can either travel along the Route de N'Gor and the corniche, or take the Route de Yoff, which connects, via an interchange, with the VDN, which runs straight to Point E.

Maps
The best city map is the one produced by **Editions Laure Kane** (www.editionslaurekane.com, in French; maps CFA4000), which features the latest road layouts, shows the names of all quartiers, streets, hotels, restaurants, embassies and more. You can find it in all major bookshops in Senegal.

Some hotels and mobile phone outlets stock copies of a free, but less detailed Dakar map, as well as the cute but outdated *Dakar Bird View* map.

INFORMATION
The exhaustive site www.au-senegal.com gives you an answer to almost any question about Senegal. Most parts of this French site are available in software-translated English.

BUILDING A NEW CITY

In a massive urban makeover, the Senegalese government has poured extraordinary amounts of money into the construction of roads, interchanges and bridges in the capital city. Street lights crowd the sidewalks, and new luxury hotels, residential homes and sparkling office blocks are being raised…right on the erosion-threatened littoral of the corniche.

The words West African Dubai have been mentioned and, though that is a very steep exaggeration, the works have turned Dakar into one of West Africa's most modern, well-connected cities. Ever since these so-called 'grand works of President Wade' started, there has been controversy about their extent and focus, and many query this outpouring of money over Dakar, pointing quite persuasively at the often disastrous state of the roads in the countryside (including major economic arteries). There may be some truth in the suggestion that all that feverish infrastructure creation is the president's way of achieving immortality.

What it means for you is that things may change quickly. Traffic in town now flows reasonably quickly. Getting out of Dakar, however, can be a nightmare trip through suffocating congestion. Once the construction of the impressive new autoroute has been completed, it should be a swift ride, though by then the planned construction of the brand new airport is likely to cause another set of difficulties.

To keep track of the progress of works, ask around or check www.investinsenegal.com for the latest on the new autoroute, plans for the railway and all other structural projects handled by the government. The site www.anoci.com contains information on hotel and house construction.

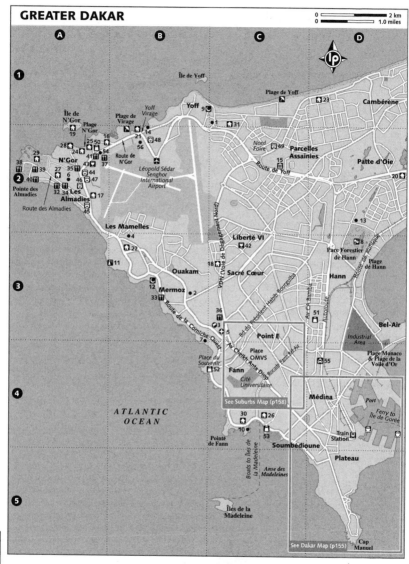

GREATER DAKAR

The excellent pocket-sized glossy *221* (CFA100) contains a printed version of the site's cultural calendar, as well as interesting write-ups on music, arts and sports around the country. It's available at newsagents, shops, restaurants and hotels.

Waaw is a free pocket-sized mag full of advertising and useful lists of restaurants, travel agencies and embassies (for some embassies, see p265).

Bookshops

All of the following bookshops have a good range of books, magazines and maps, though there's little in English. The secondhand street stalls around the Marché Sandaga don't offer much choice, but you might find the occasional dog-eared curiosity among last season's women's magazines and outdated school books.

PLATEAU
Librairie 4 Vents (Map p156; ☎ 33 821 8083; 55 Rue Félix Faure; 🕑 9am-1pm & 3-7pm Mon-Sat)
Librairie Clairafrique (Map p156; ☎ 33 822 2169; Rue de Thiong; 🕑 8.30am-6.30pm Mon-Sat)

POINT E & MERMOZ
Librairie 4 Vents (Map p152; ☎ 33 869 1037; Av Cheikh Anta Diop, Mermoz; 🕑 9am-1pm & 3-7pm Mon-Sat)
Librairie Clairafrique (Map p158; ☎ 33 864 4429; Université Cheikh Anta Diop, Av Cheikh Anta Diop; 🕑 8.30am-6.30pm Mon-Sat)

Cultural Centres
PLATEAU
Institut Français Léopold Sédar Senghor (Map p156; ☎ 33 823 0320; www.institutfr-dakar.org; 89 Rue Joseph Gomis) This spacious arts centre occupies a whole city block and is one of the main hubs of cultural activity in Dakar. It has an open-air stage, a good cafe, and exhibition and cinema rooms, and also houses a couple of artists' workshops and shops in its vast garden. Information on events is found online and in a printed guide available at the centre.

POINT E
British Council (Map p158; ☎ 33 869 2700; www .britishcouncil.org/senegal; Rue AAB-68, Amitié Zone A-B) This small centre has a pretty garden cafe and a library with a small selection of English-language books, magazines and DVDs. Has a good internet cafe.
Goethe-Institut (Map p158; ☎ 33 869 8880; www .goethe.de/ins/sn/dak; Rue de Diourbel) Near the Piscine Olympique, the German cultural centre frequently hosts exhibitions and has a cinema. On the top floor of the brand new building, you'll find Café Vounda Bar, great for simple meals, overlooking Dakar from the 5th-floor terrace.

YOFF
Centre Culturel Vivre et Apprendre (Map p152; ☎ 33 820 5484; culturevivreetapprendre@gmail.com; Av Seydina Limmamou Laye) New in 2009, this initiative of the Global Ecovillage Network offers dance, percussion and Wolof courses, exhibitions and exchanges in Yoff village.

Emergency
Dakar's main emergency department is at Hôpital Principal. If you've had a very serious accident, get yourself flown out to Europe.
SAMU (☎ 33 628 1213; 🕑 24hr) Emergency ambulances.
SOS Médecin (Map p152; ☎ 33 889 1515; Baie de Soumbédioune, cnr Rue 62 & Rue 64; 🕑 24hr) Can visit you at home and arrange transport to hospital.
Suma Urgences (Map p158; ☎ 33 824 2418; Av Cheikh Anta Diop; 🕑 24hr) Emergency transport and home visits.

Internet Access

Almost every hotel and many restaurants in Dakar offer free wi-fi access. With the rapid advance of wireless, the number of internet cafes has declined. The following offer a speedy service:

Business Centre (Map p158; Bd du Sud; ⏲ 8am-10pm) Opposite the Restaurant Jardin Thaïlandais.

Cyber-Business Centre (Map p156; ☎ 33 823 3223; Av Léopold Senghor; ⏲ 8am-midnight)

Espacetel Plus (Map p156; ☎ 33 822 9062; Bd de la République; ⏲ 8am-midnight)

Medical Services

Compared to other West African cities, Dakar has a fairly good medical network.

Clinique de la Madeleine (Map p155; ☎ 33 821 9470; 18 Av des Jambaars) Well-equipped private clinic with general services and a maternity department.

Clinique du Cap (Map p155; ☎ 33 889 0202; Av Pasteur) Private clinic with intensive-care unit.

Clinique Pasteur (Map p156; ☎ 33 839 9200; 50 Rue Carnot) A privately run clinic that is a good address for malaria blood tests.

Hôpital Principal (Map p155; ☎ 33 839 5050; Av Léopold Senghor) Though Dakar's main hospital compares well to other public health-care facilities in the country and region, it's still understaffed and underequipped.

Bio-24 (Map p156; ☎ 33 889 5151; 13 Rue St Michel) The best place for malaria tests and other blood screenings. Open 24 hours a day.

There's a pharmacy on almost every street corner. In addition to the 24-hour pharmacy and the late-night option listed below, there's a rotational 24-hour standby system; you'll find details of the current all-hour place outside every pharmacy door. Otherwise, most open from 8am to 8pm Monday to Saturday.

Pharmacie Guigon (Map p156; ☎ 33 823 0333; 1 Av du Président Lamine Guèye; ⏲ 8am-11pm Mon-Sat) Dakar's best-stocked pharmacy.

Pharmacie Mandela (Map p156; ☎ 33 821 2172; Av Nelson Mandela; ⏲ 24h) Near the Hôpital Principal.

Money

The main banks are CBAO, BICIS and SGBS. They all have central branches near Place de l'Indépendance and others all over Dakar – there are plenty more than those listed below. All have security-guarded ATMs and change money. See p259 for business hours and p268 for more details on managing money in Senegal.

PLATEAU

BICIS (Map p156; ☎ 33 839 0390; www.bicis.sn; Place de l'Indépendance)

CBAO (Map p156; ☎ 33 849 9300; www.cbao.sn; Immeuble SDIH 2, Place de l'Indépendance)

SGBS (Map p156; ☎ 33 842 5039; Av Léopold Senghor; www.sgbs.sn)

POINT E

CBAO (Map p158; ☎ 33 849 9318; Rue de Kaolack)

SGBS (Map p158; ☎ 33 839 55 00; Bd de l'Est)

Photography

Photo Ciné (Map p156; ☎ 33 821 7758; Place de l'Indépendance) Best for passport photographs and digital prints.

Post

DHL (Map p158; ☎ 33 823 1394; Rue F; ⏲ 8am-6.30pm Mon-Fri, 8am-noon Sat) The Senegal agent for all express mail.

Main post office (Map p156; ☎ 33 839 3400; Bd el Haji Djily Mbaye; ⏲ 7am-7pm Mon-Fri, 8am-5pm Sat) Near Marché Kermel.

Post office (Map p156; ☎ 33 839 3400; Av Pompidou) Smaller, with a *télécentre* (privately owned telephone bureau) and a Western Union service.

Telephone

Before the rise of mobile phones, there used to be a couple of public telecentres in every street. You still find a few, especially around Av Hassan II (formerly Avenue Albert Sarraut) and in the side streets off Av Pompidou. It's best, however, to buy a local SIM card.

Tourist Information

There is no official tourist information office in Dakar. Private travel agencies (see p291 and below) can help with enquiries but will invariably try to sell you something.

Travel Agencies

The following agencies can help with finding good flight deals and booking tickets. For companies specialising in tours around the country, see p291). Most airlines have offices in central Dakar (see p279), where you can reconfirm your ticket.

Dakar Voyages (Map p156; ☎ 33 823 3704; www.dakarvoyages.com; 29 Rue Assane Ndoye) Tends to have the best deals on charter flights.

Nouvelles Frontières (Map p152; ☎ 33 859 4447; www.nfsenegal.com; Lot 1 Mamelles Aviation;

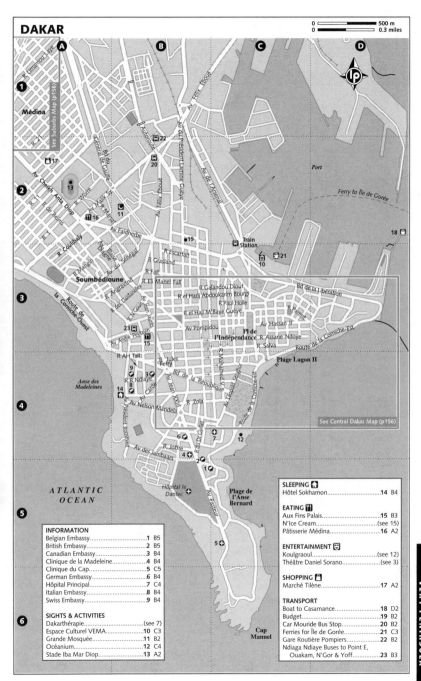

DAKAR

| 0 | 500 m |
| 0 | 0.3 miles |

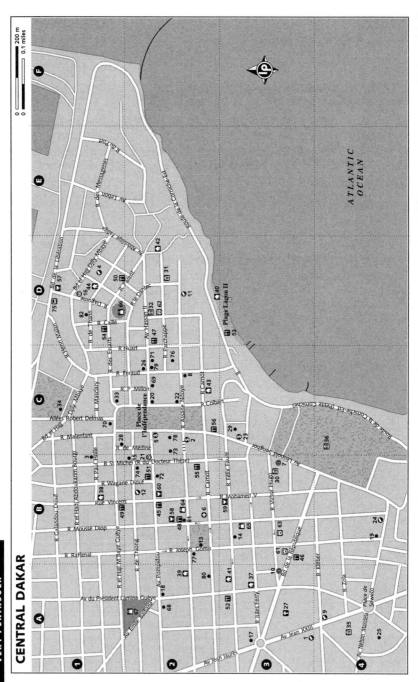

CENTRAL DAKAR

ATLANTIC
OCEAN

🕑 8.30am-6pm Mon-Fri, 9am-12.30pm Sat) This large French tour operator can book seats on charter and regular flights.

Senegal Tours (Map p156; ☎ 33 839 9900; 5 Place de l'Indépendance) Large tour operator that deals with ticketing as well as tours.

Universities

Dakar's sprawling **Université Cheikh Anta Diop** (Map p158) occupies most of the Fann suburb, south of Point E. It's like a vibrant city within itself, with plenty of little eateries, internet cafes and copy shops catering to students. Watch out for occasional student riots, usually caused by the late payment of scholarships or demands for better facilities.

DANGERS & ANNOYANCES

Compared to other capitals of the world, Dakar is a fairly safe place, where violent crime and guns are rare. However, as rising prices have worsened conditions for many Senegalese and frustrations are felt more widely, street crime has also increased.

Muggings at knife point have become more common, as well as thefts by youngsters on scooters or rollerblades or in passing cars. Nights are obviously more dangerous and it's always advisable to get transport directly from the venue of your choice back to your hotel, rather than walking in the dark.

Areas to be particularly careful in at night include the Petite Corniche (behind the *palais présidentiel*), the Route de la Corniche-Ouest, the industrial area near Hann and all beaches.

During the day, pickpocketing is a risk, especially in the crammed streets around Av Pompidou and Marché Sandaga, as well as beaches and *gares routières* (bush taxi stops). Avoid carrying large bags and be on your guard. Less worrying, but potentially very annoying, are the street traders, hustlers, scamsters and womanisers that stick to you like shadows on a walk around the inner city. For ideas on how to shake them off, see p261. The 'Remember me?' scam is particularly popular here (see Scams, p263).

GREATER DAKAR & CAP VERT PENINSULA

lonelyplanet.com

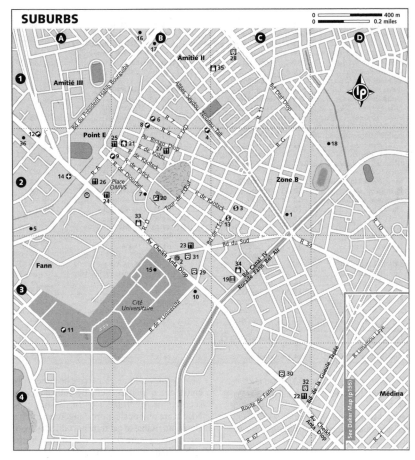

SUBURBS

Some vigilance and common sense should help you get around unharmed – inner-city Dakar can be a pain to walk around, but Lagos it ain't, and none of the areas mentioned are no-go zones.

SIGHTS

Dakar is hardly a city for a leisurely stroll – randomly parked cars, over-eager telephone-top-up-card touts and a nauseating network of open sewers ensure that your gaze never lingers for too long on the magnificent historical buildings, colourful market scenes or urban sculptures that dot the city. Then again, Dakar's organised chaos is part of this city's unique charm and infuses the historical town with an intense sense of the now.

PLATEAU

The vastness that is Dakar's central Place de l'Indépendance is the beating heart of the city. Circular home to countless cars and crooks, its boulevards describe a wide loop around artfully neglected greens that house a blow-up cinema and dried-up fountains. Between 1960s concrete blocks and building sites where supermodern structures are being grown, you find some majestic old houses, including the **gouvernance** (governor's office; Map p156) and the **chambre de commerce** (Chamber of Commerce; Map p156). A few steps to the north of the Place de l'Indépendance is the stately **Hôtel de Ville** (town hall; Map p156; Bd el Hajj Djily Mbaye), from where a short walk takes you to the elegant facade

INFORMATION			SIGHTS & ACTIVITIES			Le Balajo................................**26** A2		
British Council.............................**1** C2			ACI Baobab................................**16** B1			Sabura.....................................**27** B2		
Business Centre.........................**2** B3			Africa Park................................**17** B1					
CBAO...**3** C2			Centre Culturel Blaise			ENTERTAINMENT 🖲		
Côte d'Ivoire Embassy.................**4** B2			Senghor....................**18** D2			Chez Anthiou............................**28** C1		
DHL...**5** A2			Galerie Kemboury.....................**19** C3			Just 4 U...................................**29** B3		
Ghanaian Embassy.....................**6** B1			Piscine Olympique...................**20** B2			Le Madison..............................**30** C4		
Goethe-Institut..........................**7** B2						Pen'Art...................................**31** B3		
Guinea-Bissau Embassy..............**8** B1			SLEEPING 🛏			Sun Set Sahel...........................**32** C4		
Guinean Embassy.......................**9** B2			Auberge Marie-Lucienne..........**21** B2					
Librairie Clairafrique..................**10** B3						SHOPPING 🛍		
Malian Embassy........................**11** A3			EATING 🍴			Espace Agora...........................**33** B2		
Moroccan Embassy....................**12** A2			Centre Commercial			Fil & Pampilles.........................**34** C3		
SGBS..**13** C2			Sahm....................**22** C4			Sigil.......................................**35** C1		
Suma Urgences.........................**14** A2			Jardin Thaïlandais.....................**23** B3					
Université Cheikh Anta			La Provençale...........................**24** A2			TRANSPORT		
Diop.....................**15** B3			Lalibela...................................**25** B2			Coseloc...................................**36** A2		

of Dakar's famous **train station** (Map p155; Bd de la Libération).

The nearby **Marché Kermel** (Map p156; see p171) is a pretty building and busy trading site, restored in 1997 to its original 1860s beauty (the original was destroyed in a fire).

Heading southwest, the awe-inspiring **palais présidentiel** (Map p156; Av Léopold Senghor) is surrounded by sumptuous gardens and guards in colonial-style uniforms. It was originally built in 1907 for the governor of the time, General Roume, who lent his title to the street outside (since renamed Av Léopold Senghor). The **assemblée nationale** (national parliament; Map p156; Place de Soweto), with its modern glass facade, is easy to reach from here, as is Dakar's central **cathedral** (Map p156; Bd de la République), a large 1920s building.

Museums & Art Galleries

A testament to former President Senghor's interest in promoting African art and culture, Dakar's **Musée Théodore Monod** (Musée IFAN; Map p156; ☎ 33 823 9268; Place de Soweto; adult/child CFA2200/200; 🕙 9am-6pm Tue-Sun) is a major centre of West African cultural studies. Though exhibits are gathering dust, displays of masks, traditional dress, musical instruments and other artefacts from across West Africa are imaginative and interesting. Behind the main museum, a newly renovated gallery often houses excellent exhibitions of contemporary art.

If that's more your scene, you'll enjoy a stroll through the many small art galleries and ateliers hidden in the city's side streets. The leafy garden of the **Institut Français Léopold Sédar Senghor** (p153) is a hub of creativity. The scrap-metal bird sculptures by Mamadou Tall Dhiedhiou and charmingly chaotic workshop of the famous *sous-verre* (reverse glass paint-

ing) artist Moussa Sakho alone are worth a visit. The brilliant little **Galerie Le Manège** (Map p156; ☎ 33 821 0822; 3 Rue Parchappe; 🕙 9am-5pm Tue-Sat), in a beautifully restored 19th-century building, is also part of the French cultural complex. The space of the **Galerie Nationale** (Map p156; ☎ 33 821 2511; Av Hassan II; admission free; 🕙 9am-6pm) is a bit drab, but its frequently changing exhibitions of photography and paintings are usually very good. Across the road, **Atiss** (Map p156; ☎ 33 823 1877; 12 Av Hassan II) exhibits artfully woven items by Aïssa Dione.

Galerie Arte (Map p156; ☎ 33 821 9556; www.arte.sn; 5 Rue Victor Hugo) displays its original selection of sculptures, paintings, jewellery and furniture like a shop and, while items are indeed for sale, there's no pressure to buy. At the **Galerie Antenna** (Map p156; ☎ 33 822 1751; 9 Rue Félix Faure; 🕙 9.30am-1pm & 4-7.30pm Mon-Sat) nearby, the commitment to African arts and antiques spills over even into the decoration of the gallery's impressive facade.

The **Espace Culturel VEMA** (Map p155; ☎ 33 821 7026; Embarcadère de Gorée; 🕙 8am-6pm) is a ray of hope in the dreary industrial lands near the Île de Gorée ferry stop. Its spiced-up warehouse frequently houses exhibitions and events, but you need to phone first to see if anything's on. At **Dakarthérapie** (Map p155; ☎ 33 839 5072, 33 839 5066; Hôpital Principal; 🕙 9am-1pm & 3-6pm Mon-Fri), you get a very unique insight into the forgotten corners of Senegalese society as well as a display of artwork. This completely innovative and support-worthy project showcases work by psychiatric patients, created during artist-led workshops organised by the association Nit Nit Garabam.

Beaches

Central Dakar isn't really the place to go swimming and **Plage de l'Anse Bernard** (Map

GREATER DAKAR & CAP VERT PENINSULA

p155), the classic spot of coast for the residents of the area, is quite plagued by rubbish. Clients at Hôtel Lagon II (Map p156) get access to its private metre of beach.

MÉDINA TO MAMELLES

Each of the suburbs that surround the town centre has its very own character and is worth visiting just to explore the many faces of the city. Closest to the Plateau is the Médina, a bustling popular quartier with tiny tailor's shops, a busy **market** (see p171) and streets brimming with life. It was built as a township for the local populace by the French during colonial days and is the birthplace of Senegalese superstar Youssou N'Dour. Besides being a very real neighbourhood, where creative ideas and new trends grow between crammed, makeshift homes, it's also home to Dakar's **Grande Mosquée** (Map p155; Av Malik Sy). Built in 1964, it is impressive for its sheer size and landmark minaret.

Following the corniche northwards, you pass the large **Place du Souvenir** (Map p152). It was built in 2007 as a site of commemoration for the victims of the *Joola* ferry disaster (see p37), and is a wide and windy spot that houses occasional arts exhibitions and has a view across the Atlantic. Further along the corniche, you'll see the tall **Mosquée de la Divinité** (Map p152; Route de la Corniche-Ouest) perched on a calm stretch of shore. The **Mamelles**, Dakar's only two hills, are further north, off the Route de la Corniche-Ouest. Mamelles means 'breasts', and you don't need a great amount of imagination to guess why the pair of sloping mounds have been given that name. On one of them sits the pretty 1864 **Mamelles lighthouse** (Map p152). The leisurely 25-minute walk up there is rewarded with a great view across town. The second one is being adorned (or spoilt?) by a gigantic monument to 'African Renaissance'. Rumour has it that it's been designed by North Koreans. We haven't been able to confirm this – but it's certainly got all the charm of a socialist statue. Eastwards from here, the neighbourhood **Ouakam** (Map p152) has retained the close-knit character of the Lebou village it used to be.

Museums & Art Galleries

Among Dakar's suburbs, the best address for art galleries is the affluent residential quartier Point E. This is where you find the fabulous little oasis that is **Espace Agora** (Map p158; ☎ 33

864 1448; Rue D, Point E). In its tree-shaded patio, you can look at (and purchase) carefully selected Moroccan and Senegalese sculptures and paintings. If you're lucky, you'll catch one of the special exhibitions that are frequently on show. A short walk from here, **Galerie Kemboury** (Map p158; ☎ 33 825 4843; Bd Canal IV; ◷ 3.30-7pm Mon, 9.30am-1pm & 3.30-7pm Tue-Sat) has a reputation for tracking down new works by some of Senegal's most promising artists.

Beaches

The beaches along the Route de la Corniche-Ouest are popular with local joggers and fitness fanatics, but were unsuitable for swimming even before the coast was built up with grand hotels and office blocks. The tiny spot of beach next to the Mosquée de la Divinité (Map p152) is a popular surfing spot and grants great views over the Mamelles cliff.

LES ALMADIES, N'GOR & YOFF

Framed by beaches and brushed by strong winds, these three northwestern neighbourhoods each have their own unique character. Les Almadies is Dakar's *quartier chic,* a plush neighbourhood where the polished villas of Senegal's richest look out onto private beaches. It's one of the fastest-developing zones of the capital. Almost every month a new bar, restaurant or glitzy club seems to open its doors here, drawing punters away from the inner city. To dive into the street vibes behind the luxurious facades, head along the coastal branch of the Route des Almadies towards the westernmost point of the African continent, the **Pointe des Almadies** (Map p152), beautifully understated with its street-side food stalls, small cafes and secret surfer spots.

The small Lebou village of N'Gor is rarely visited by tourists as their attention is entirely taken up by the area's wide beach and the small island across from it (see Beaches, p161).

In Yoff, the situation is exactly the reverse. The beaches close to the Lebou community are industrial sands – launching pads for pirogues and garbage dumps for fish guts. Yoff is Dakar's most independent zone, where the Lebou village ties and traditions continue to dominate life and even local governance; the community is self-administering, with no government officials, no police force and, apparently, no crime. The Lebou of Yoff are nearly all members of

---

SAND MINING

The huge posters that line the walls of the Dakar-based dive centre and environmental agency Océanium (see below) are as shocking as they are eerily beautiful. One shows a bird's-eye view of the small fishing village Malika. The tracks of multiple trucks have left tattoolike imprints along the coast and long rows of sand-filled lorries leave the shore, lined up like beads on an endless necklace. Every day 7000 sq km of sand, equivalent to 400 truckloads, is mined here illegally. The effects are devastating: where a wide, sandy shore used to border the small community, the sea advances today right up to the first habitations. Trees have lost their grounding and the pontoon bridge of an abandoned holiday camp sits deserted in the ocean. 'Everyone cries that our coasts are being eaten up, but no one puts a stop to the illegal mining', says Jean Goepp, tireless project coordinator at the Océanium. The busy construction of multistorey buildings, roads and public infrastructure demands tons of cement, yet the sand that goes into its making doesn't always come from certified sources. 'People are in such a rush to build that they buy sand of unverified origin and then they don't even take the time to treat it properly', explains Jean, 'a lot of the sand used is actually not ideal for construction as it contains too much sea salt'.

---

the Layen, one of the brotherhoods that dominate life in Senegal (see p46). The founder of the brotherhood, Saidi Limamou Laye, is believed to be a reincarnation of the Prophet Muhammad. His large **Layen Mausoleum** (Map p152), an impressive 1950 construction with gleaming white walls and a green onion-shaped dome, is an important pilgrimage site for members of the brotherhood. The Muslim faith of Yoff's residents strongly colours life in this community. Smoking is not allowed here, there are no bars and you have to wear long clothing while walking through the village streets.

Museums & Art Galleries

Without a stop at Dakar's famous **Village des Arts** (Map p152; ☎ 33 835 7160; www.vdesarts.com; Route de Yoff), an arts tour around Dakar is simply not complete. More than 30 photographers, painters and sculptors create, shape and display their works in this large garden space. An on-site gallery shows a selection of their work and the nearby restaurant is the place to have a drink and chat to the artists.

In the heart of Les Almadies, take a look at the **Céramiques Almadies** (Map p152; ☎ 77 533 0134, 33 820 0338; Route des Almadies, 2nd turn-off left), where Mauro Petroni, a real 'Dakar original' and annual organiser of the Off-Biennale, displays his beautiful ceramics and frequently the works of other artists, too. The **Centre Culturel Vivre et Apprendre** (Map p152; ☎ 33 820 5484; culture vivreetapprendre@gmail.com; Av Seydina Limmamou Laye) in Yoff hosts occasional arts exhibitions and runs workshops.

Beaches

The sheltered **Plage N'Gor** (Map p152) is the main escape spot for flirtatious youth and *dakarois* families armed with picnic baskets. The CFA500 access fee you pay is intended to go towards maintaining the cleanliness of this busy stretch of sand. A short boat ride (CFA500 return) across the bay takes you to **Île de N'Gor** (Map p152), a tiny island with a couple of other beaches. As on Plage N'Gor, you can hire parasols and mats here for a small fee.

Winds and currents get stronger as you head towards Yoff, where the **Plage de Virage** (Map p152) is popular with surfers and bodyboarders, though swimming is also possible. Past the bustle and litter of Yoff's fishing beach (great for taking in the sights of pirogues rolling in on the surf), the sands of **Plage de Yoff** (Map p152) stretch out temptingly into the distance. The windy shore is great for mind-clearing walks; strong currents make it unsuitable for bathing.

ACTIVITIES
Diving

Good scuba-diving (*plongée sous-marine*) sites include the rocky reefs and islets around the Pointe des Almadies and the islands of Gorée, N'Gor and La Madeleine. By far the best address for diving excursions is the **Océanium** (Map p155; ☎ 33 822 2441; www.oceanium. org; Route de la Corniche-Est; ☺ Mon-Sat), which offers half-day dives, as well as longer excursions, and has introductory courses. The Océanium also houses a very active and effective

GREATER DAKAR & CAP VERT PENINSULA

ACCRO ROLLER

You see them all across town: young guys with rollerblades, performing heart-stopping moves right there, in the thick Dakar traffic. Reckless? Absolutely. But also a sign of the exciting urban culture that makes this city on the Atlantic tick.

The spread of the roller-skating craze can be blamed on one individual – Babacar Ndiaye, a man who was seemingly born with wheels on his feet. 'I fell in love with skating, that's all. I couldn't stop', he laughs from behind oversized sunglasses. Since skating alone isn't much fun, he taught others, managed to get grants to purchase skates, protectors and helmets, and eventually founded the **Association Accro Roller** (☎ 77 649 5180; www.accro-roller.com) with a few associates. Today the group has hundreds of members and they do a lot more than just take risks in traffic jams. Trained in teaching others, they run classes for dozens of kids, offering the youngsters a healthy activity and fun in a group setting. Marketing companies have been attracted by the Accro Rollers, and now hire them to distribute leaflets; fashion designers and artists have used them as models and dancers. The money made goes back into supporting the group and helping its members advance other small-scale businesses they may be running. 'That's the beauty of our group', says Babacar, 'we unite every skill you could imagine. That's how we can support one another, build projects, go further'.

The Accro Rollers can also arrange roller-skating holidays in and around Dakar. Contact them to find out more.

---

environmental protection agency, so its courses come with eco-awareness and as much extra environmental input as you like. Divers can stay at the Océanium for more-than-reasonable rates; don't forget to ask about its eco-tourism projects (see p161).

Fishing

At Plage de N'Gor, **Atlantic Evasion** (Map p152; ☎ 33 820 7675; www.atlantic-evasion.com; Plage de N'Gor) offers both deep-sea fishing and angling excursions. The restaurant **Lagon I** (Map p156; ☎ 33 889 2525; Route de la Corniche-Est) arranges deep-sea fishing trips and boasts several world-record catches.

Swimming & Sports

From December to January, temperatures drop significantly in Dakar. The 17°C reached at night often feels even colder as the harmattan winds blow in; not everyone is brave enough to swim then.

Apart from the beaches around Dakar, there are several excellent pools. If swimming is sport rather than relaxation to you, the 50m-long pool at the **Piscine Olympique** (Map p158; ☎ 33 869 0606; Tour de l'Œuf, Point E) is your address. It's part of a huge fitness complex, housing other (smaller) pools, a gym, basketball courts and football grounds, plus restaurants and even rooms to spend the night.

Don't confuse it with the **Club Olympique** (Map p152; ☎ 33 864 5655; www.olympique-club.com; Route de la Corniche-Ouest), a state-of-the-art fitness centre with a large pool (heated in the colder months, admission adults/children CFA5000/4000), a tennis centre, playground and squash hall.

Most hotels open their pools to nonguests for a fee. Pullman Teranga (admission CFA8000) and Le Méridien President (CFA10,000) both have good, though expensive, pools.

Surfing

A swimmer's disappointment is a surfer's dream – the wave-beaten beaches around Dakar aren't always suitable for bathing, but make excellent surfer haunts. The main addresses for surfing:

Pantcho Surf Trip (Map p152; ☎ 77 534 6232; Plage de N'Gor; 7-day course CFA145,000) Senegal's double surf champion offers a package that's just as interesting. Courses available for adults and children. Accommodation in N'Gor hotels can be arranged for those booking a surfing holiday. Internationally qualified trainer.

Tribal Surf Shop (Map p152; ☎ 33 820 5400; www .tribalsurfshop.net; Yoff Virage) You can rent boards here or get yours fixed. It has a surfing school that does classes for adults and children (two-hour courses cost CFA25,000), as well as longer-term holidays. Trainers are qualified to international standard. Also offers skateboarding, kayaking and bodyboarding and can arrange accommodation in villas around Yoff.

Wrestling

Dakar's main arena for traditional wrestling is the **Stade Iba Mar Diop** (Map p155). Fights of big-name wrestlers are national sports events, held in **Stade Léopold Sédar Senghor** (Map p152), Dakar's main stadium in Yoff. Senegal's entire population awaits the results of the traditional star match held on 1 January.

Most matches are commentated only on the radio and will be talked about incessantly by the locals. Saturday and/or Sunday are the usual days for the fights, starting around 4.30pm or 5pm.

COURSES
Language

Recommended language courses are run at the following centres:

ACI Baobab (Map p158; ☎ 33 825 3637; Villa 509, Allées Seydou Nourou Tall) Small, friendly Wolof teaching centre set up by former Peace Corps volunteers.

Centre Culturel Vivre et Apprendre (Map p152; ☎ 33 820 5484; culturevivreetapprendre@gmail.com; Av Seydina Limmamou Laye) Runs Wolof, French, English and Spanish courses.

Pôle Linguistique de l'Institut Français (Map p156; ☎ 33 823 8483; 3 Rue Parchappe; ☽ Oct-May) Runs Wolof and French classes.

Dance

For dance courses or to watch rehearsals, try Yoff's Centre Culturel Vivre et Apprendre (see Language, above) or the **Centre Culturel Blaise Senghor** (Map p158; 33 824 6600; Bd Dial Diop), whose bleak facade doesn't do justice to the creative bustle going on inside.

DAKAR FOR CHILDREN

As a big, brash city, Dakar probably doesn't feature highly on a parent's list of must-sees. But the locals' overwhelmingly friendly attitude towards children, the surrounding beaches and a few child-focused activities make it surprisingly family friendly – as long as you avoid the inner city.

Dakar's affluent citizens love taking their kids out to **Magic Land** (Map p152; ☎ 33 842 7307; Route de la Corniche-Ouest; adult & child over 2/child under 2 CFA2500/free; ☽ 5-10pm Tue & Thu, 4-10pm Wed & Fri, 2-10pm Sat & Sun), a trendy theme park fully equipped with merry-go-rounds, Ferris wheels and other attractions. For something smaller, try **Sun Park** (Map p156; Jardin de la Cathédrale; adult/child CFA500/300; ☽ 4-10pm), a cute little playground in the cathedral gardens, or the **Africa Park** (Map p158; Av Bourguiba; admission free, per ride CFA500; ☽ 11am-8pm Fri-Sun).

If your children are older than five, the glass-painting workshops by Moussa Sakho

in the Institut Français (p153) are worth checking out.

Other than that, a ferry trip to Île de Gorée (Map p179) and a pirogue tour to the beaches of N'Gor (p161) or, if they're old enough to cope with a slightly rougher journey, to the Îles de la Madeleine (p179) make for good family escapes from hectic Dakar.

An absolute must-do with kids is a day trip to Bandia Reserve and Accrobaobab (see p186) – the guaranteed sight of giraffes, rhinos and monkeys, followed by a safe climbing adventure in the branches of a baobab make for a one-day minivacation.

With kids, you're better off staying in a hotel around Yoff or N'Gor rather than in town, for the sake of sanity, space and proximity to the beaches of Plage Virage and N'Gor (the waters at N'Gor are calmer). The Club Olympique (see opposite) has a good children's pool, a small playground and sports activities for little ones.

The green, picnic-perfect area of the Parc Forestier de Hann (Map p152) is worth a visit, particularly for its **Poney Club** (Map p152; ☎ 33 832 0652; www.poneyclubdakar.com), offering horse riding for kids from four years of age onwards (it's advisable to bring your own helmet). Hann Zoo (Map p152) in the same area is supposed to be a kids' attraction, but the sight of caged, neglected animals is more likely to make them cry.

It's next to impossible to push a pram around anywhere in Dakar. You'll lose the battle against parked cars and sand. Nappies, baby food and other baby products are readily available in all big supermarkets. See also p260.

TOURS

All of Senegal's tour agencies offer day trips around the city and the peninsula. A one-day tour costs around CFA15,000. See p291 for details of agencies.

FESTIVALS & EVENTS

Dakar's cultural calendar is packed and, outside the wettest months (July and August), you're almost certain to stumble across a festival, awards ceremony or concert series of some sort.

Dak'Art Biennale (☎ 33 823 0918; www.dakart.org) This biennial festival of painting and sculpture drowns the town in colour for the whole of May, with exhibitions all across Dakar.

PIKINE STREET VIBES

Past Dakar's dignified old Plateau and beyond the ostentatiousness of Les Almadies, the city is surrounded by the tough belt of sprawling, ever-expanding *banlieues* (suburbs). Pikine, Guediewaye and Thiaroye – those are the rough boroughs where youngsters get swept up when they move to the city and from where many emigrate on perilous journeys across the ocean, hoping for a better life in Europe. They're hard and poor, made of ramshackle housing and improvised streets that can barely contain the sheer numbers of people living there. Few people believe in the youth of the *banlieues* and many are scared of them, as despair, unemployment and frustration lead many to violence and crime.

Matador, a leading hip hop star of the 1990s, grew up here and knew that there was more to the *banlieue* generation than the aggression and destruction everyone associates them with. While his rap lyrics harshly depict the circumstances of life here, his actions work towards changing them. 'In 2006, just after the rainy season, inadequate sewerage systems left our *banlieue* flooded, and nothing was done for weeks. People who had nothing lost their homes, died of illness and weren't supported for a long time. That's when I decided to do something. We organised our first solidarity concerts for the victims of the floodings.' The events were hugely successful. Fuelled by people's evident hunger for cultural activities and their desire to help lift their community up, he created Africulturban, a vibrant organisation that organises festivals and workshops, and, above all, provides a place of activity and hope to youngsters with too much time and few perspectives. 'I'm a rapper. I know hip hop. And I know what hip hop can do.'

Based at Pikine's huge cultural centre, Africulturban promotes creative skills, from music to radio and event management. 'We build projects where no one thought there could be any. We educate, provide an outlet and amplify the voices of our young people who decry the disastrous conditions in the *banlieues*', says Matador.

Festivals and concerts happen here regularly, but the big annual focus is the mighty Festival 2H, a celebration of street culture, grown from the street. There's no better place to experience the sheer force of Dakar's urban youth culture than this. It knocks you over. Contact **Africulturban** (☎ 33 853 2422, 76 583 5175; thieba88@hotmail.com; www.myspace.com/festa2hfestival; Complexe Culturel de Pikine) if you plan to visit – they will be your guardian angels, making sure that you get hit by the vibrancy of the event, not by random street robbers. Far off the regular tourist trail, this is where Dakar's urban heart beats.

Kaay Fecc (☎ 33 824 5154; www.kaayfecc.com) One of Africa's best dance festivals, Kaay Fecc, held in early June, features contemporary and traditional choreography from all across Africa and beyond.

Festival International du Film de Quartier (☎ 33 821 0771; www.festivaldufilmdequartier.com) Film lovers shouldn't miss this annual December showcase of Senegal's best contemporary film work. For the duration of the festival many cultural centres, restaurants and other spaces mount screens to show films.

Festival Banlieue Rythme (www.banlieuerythme.org) Annual music festival with concerts across Dakar, but a focus on the *banlieue* Guediewaye.

SLEEPING

Dakar has a wide range of accommodation, from dodgy dosshouses to palatial hotels. This is a city that overcharges for most things – reasonably priced rooms can be hard to come by.

Budget

Dakar doesn't cater well for backpackers on a budget. Some of the cheapest hostels are of dubious cleanliness and clients. If you're on a shoestring budget and on a tour around the country, try to save money in rural regions and save up for something a little nicer when in the capital.

PLATEAU

Chez Nizar (Map p156; ☎ 77 319 1224; 25 Av Pompidou; r CFA15,000) Just above the famous fast-food joint Ali Baba's, this hostel stretches an amazing 100 basic rooms into the Dakar skies. It's got all the charm of social housing, and it's just as cheap as that.

MÉDINA TO MAMELLES

Espace Thialy (Map p152; ☎ 33 855 0260; espace.thialy@orange.sn; Impôts et Domaines, Patte d'Oie; s/d incl breakfast

CFA14,000/18,000; 💻) Since it's far from the tourist bustle, this pretty guest house, with a leafy garden and a quiet terrace, can afford to charge very little for its homely, well-maintained rooms. It's not that close to the centre or the beach but is well placed if you're planning to head for the regions outside Dakar.

Hôtel du Phare (Map p152; ☎ 33 860 3000; info@ lesmamelles.com; Les Mamelles; s with/without bathroom CFA22,000/15,000, d with/without bathroom CFA28,000/20,000; ❄ 💻) Tucked away in a side street off Route de la Corniche-Ouest, this family-friendly guest house has a handful of rooms with simple charm and a homely atmosphere. The leafy patio provides quality relaxing space.

LES ALMADIES, N'GOR & YOFF

Via Via (Map p152; ☎ 33 820 5475; viavia@orange.sn; Route des Cimetières; s/d incl breakfast CFA10,000/16,000) What it lacks in style, it makes up with friendliness. This backpacker option isn't the prettiest but has a nice patio restaurant and supports a street children's project with its profits. There are *djembe* (drum) courses on offer, too.

Keur Diame (Map p152; ☎ 33 855 8908; Parcelles Assainies; www.keurdiame-senegal.com; s/d incl breakfast CFA13,000/21,300) Right in the strictly local neighbourhood Parcelles Assainies, you get the immersion in Senegalese life on one side and the vastness that is Yoff beach a few steps in the opposite direction. Rooms here come with mosquito nets and fans, there's a roof terrace to sunbathe on and manager Ruth is fantastically friendly.

Hôtel Cap Ouest (Map p152; ☎ 33 820 2469; capouest @arc.sn; Yoff Virage; s/d from CFA19,500/23,000) This family hotel next to Plage Virage is the only address in Dakar where you get to dangle your feet in the ocean and lounge in a hammock on the shore for less than the rate of a downtown dosshouse. The newly decorated 1st-floor

rooms with sea views cost CFA4000 more, an investment absolutely worth making.

Midrange

All hotels in this price range have rooms with private bathrooms. Most offer free wi-fi and accept credit cards.

PLATEAU

Hôtel Saint-Louis Sun (Map p156; ☎ 33 822 2570; fax 33 822 4651; Rue Félix Faure; s/d CFA23,500/29,500; ❄ 💻) Although one of the few hotels to maintain reasonable prices, it hasn't exactly invested in its rooms. Its greatest attribute is the central courtyard with huge palm trees, which turns the space into a calm oasis amidst the crowds and fumes of central Dakar. There's free wi-fi.

Hôtel Ganalé (Map p156; ☎ 33 889 4444; hganale@ orange.sn; 38 Rue Assane Ndoye; s/d CFA34,000/42,000; ❄ 💻) Rooms are more welcoming than the sinister-looking lobby, though the slapdash design is carried over. Your air-conditioning might hum a little, the table wobble or the wi-fi stutter, but on the whole it's still the low-key, relaxed corner travellers have come to appreciate.

Hôtel Farid (Map p156; ☎ 33 821 6127; www.hotelfarid .com; 51 Rue Vincens; s/d from CFA36,100/41,200; ❄ 💻) The tiny reception and elevator turn out to be a narrow gateway you squeeze through to reach three floors of spacious, clean and well-maintained rooms. It's by no means luxurious, but a valid, safe and comfortable option that's fair value for the city centre. The Lebanese restaurant on the ground floor is fabulous.

Hôtel Al Afifa (Map p156; ☎ 33 889 9090; gmbafifa@ telecomplus.sn; 46 Rue Jules Ferry; s/d CFA39,000/42,000; ❄ 💻 📶) With dark wood panelling and black leather couches, it appears that the owner's idea of stylish decor is based on a 1950s men's club. But apparently that will soon be back in vogue. And if it isn't by the time you

---

GETTING UNDER DAKAR'S SKIN

A brilliant way of getting to know this city, its changeable moods and early morning faces is by staying with a local family, partaking in their lives for a few days and finding out what their Dakar looks like. There are now a couple of excellent organisations that can put you in touch with recommended families and help you out should things go wrong. **Senegal Chez L'Habitant** (☎ 77 517 2666; papeaidara@hotmail.com, www.senegalchezlhabitant.com) maintains a regularly updated register of families across the country who would like to open their houses. Océanium (p161) has built an excellent database of private stays on Île de N'Gor. Both organisations have checked the places they recommend and can find you the home that fits your profile, from the most basic to a more luxurious stay.

come here, focus on the garden and pool – they really are pretty. Ask for room 103 – it's the only one with a terrace.

Hôtel Sokhamon (Map p155; ☎ 33 889 7100; www.hotelsokhamon.com; cnr Av Président Roosevelt & Av Nelson Mandela; s/d CFA48,000/53,000, with sea view CFA63,000/68,000; P 🏊 🖳) Like a slightly confused film set, this boutique hotel reminds you of Mali, the Middle East, then the Caribbean and has a medieval-style wine cellar – and that's only the walk to the bar. All the furnishings of this hand-sculpted place have been designed, sourced and made locally. The terrace is Dakar's best spot for sipping sundowners.

Résidence Les Arcades (Map p156; ☎ 33 849 1500; www.arcades.sn; 8 Av Djily Mbaye; apt from CFA56,000; 🏊 🖳) Right in the centre of town, these discreetly decorated apartments with satellite TV and balcony provide a touch of homeliness many hotels can't match. Ideal for longer stays and self-caterers, they come with an equipped kitchen. There's no restaurant, but room cleaning is included in the rate.

MÉDINA TO MAMELLES

Auberge Marie-Lucienne (Map p158; ☎ 33 864 3756; Rue A, Point E; s/d CFA30,000/36,000; 🏊 🖳) A bit slow and grumpy, this large guest house doesn't really try to charm its guests, and yet it's usually full. Rooms are much prettier than the dark corridors have you expect, however, and the unfussiness turns out to be quite pleasant. Proximity to the university and music clubs means that you often bump into interesting guests – from visiting lecturers to jazz bands on tour.

Auberge Good Rade (Map p152; ☎ 33 860 6030; goodrade@orange.sn) This is by far not as humble as the word *auberge* (hostel) suggests. With spacious rooms, welcoming staff and minimalist, modern decor, this rivals many of the more expensive hotels.

Le Djoloff (Map p152; ☎ 33 889 3630; www.hoteldjoloff.com; s/d CFA50,000/60,000; Fann Hock; 🏊 🖳) This very pretty place in a quiet neighbourhood of Dakar near the corniche has rooms designed to make you feel like Malian royalty. The space is a little dark, but the stunning roof terrace with views across the corniche, sun deck, patio and smiling staff make up for that entirely.

LES ALMADIES, N'GOR & YOFF

Keur Yaadikoone (Map p152; ☎ 77 638 5526; www.yaadikoone.com; Île de N'Gor; r CFA20,000) Alassane, your open-armed host, placed every tiny piece of colourful mosaic on the floors and walls of the cute houses and apartments he rents out. The wooden furniture, paintings and decorative batiks are hand-picked and, if the small beach outside weren't so tempting, you'd find it hard to leave your cute holiday home at all.

La Brazzérade (Map p152; ☎ 33 820 0683; www.labrazzerade.com; Plage de N'Gor; d/ste CFA20,000/35,000; 🏊 🖳) Mainly known for its fabulous grill, this place also has a hotel floor, perched above the restaurant like a half-forgotten afterthought. The more expensive rooms have a small balcony and views over Île de N'Gor – an investment you should make.

Chez Carla (Map p152; ☎ 33 820 1586; Île de N'Gor; d incl breakfast CFA25,000) The classic choice on Île de N'Gor has been given an impressive makeover. A wooden pontoon reaches right from the sunny rooms and excellent restaurant to the sea – perfect for setting off on your boat trip or sipping sundowners as night falls.

Maison Abaka (Map p152; ☎ 33 820 6486; www.maison-abaka.com; r from CFA30,000; 🏊 🖳 🖳) Pool conversations here usually deal with waves and where to catch them – this family-style place is a favourite with surfers. Apparently water sports and interior design are more closely linked than expected – rooms are airy and lovingly decorated. A great place for an active holiday in beautiful surroundings.

La Madrague (Map p152; ☎ 33 820 0223; madrague-resa@orange.sn; Plage de N'Gor; r from CFA39,000; 🖳) This place is like one long bikini party where everyone gets to sleep over. With gaudy pink walls, a pool-centric set-up and, of course, the prime location on a private stretch of N'Gor beach, it tempts you to take nothing too seriously for a few days.

Le Lodge des Almadies (Map p152; ☎ 33 869 0345; hotellelodge@orange.sn; Route des Almadies; r CFA40,000) Its restaurant ranks among Dakar's finest, and that's in the competitive field of refined French cuisine. However, accommodation can be variable. The rooms in the main house are cute, with luxurious, mosaic-decorated bathrooms. Next door, they've forgotten to breathe in a bit of soul.

Ambre (Map p152; ☎ 33 820 6338; www.ambre.sn; Route des Almadies; r from CFA42,000; 🏊 🖳 🖳) Green, adorned with art and beautifully designed, this small guest house is as friendly as a smile. Each of the six rooms has its own subtle colour scheme, and the harmonious decor continues all the way through the downstairs lounge, garden and restaurant. A unique gem close to the city's best hotels and bars.

Airport Hôtel (Map p152; ☎ 33 869 7878; Route de N'Gor; s/d CFA45,000/56,000; ✴ ⬛ ⬛) Here's a hotel that does most things right, without even trying very hard. No outlandish concepts here, no overblown identity. Just good-quality, practical and welcoming accommodation with satellite TV, fridge and minibar, large windows with views across an inviting pool and the swish of palm trees to lull you to sleep.

Top End

In 2009 the mighty hotel moguls Sheraton, Radisson and Kempinski, alongside a couple of other gold-endowed investors, were set to complete six brand-new hotel complexes, all rumoured to be swanky five-star palaces. They're all perched close to the waters left of the Route de la Corniche-Ouest.

PLATEAU

Résidence Madame! (Map p152; ☎ 33 869 5964; www.residencemadamel.com; Les Almadies; r CFA56,000-106,000; ✴ ⬛ ⬛) Located in the north of Dakar, it calls itself a guest house but secretly aspires to become an intimate wellness haven – the *hammam* (Turkish bath), massage parlour, terrace solarium and gym give it away. From the pool in the centre, the view is 360 degrees of white stone and wholesomeness.

Novotel (Map p156; ☎ 33 849 6161; h0529@accor.com, www.accorhotels.com; Av Abdoulaye Fadiga; r CFA100,000; ✴ ⬛ ⬛) This hotel spent so much energy styling the airy lobby that none was left for the rooms. They were (finally) being redecorated when we passed – if the same goes for the service, this might become a great place.

Hôtel Lagon II (Map p156; ☎ 33 889 2525; www.hotel-lagon-senegal.com; Route de la Corniche-Est; s/d CFA106,000/110,000; ✴ ⬛) Careful. Behind the ginger-coloured cabin door lie the 1960s, when orange was all the rage and round-edged formica tables every woman's dream. Lying back on the impressive 2m-by-2m bed, thoughts of the sexual revolution proved a distraction from the fantastic views over Île de Gorée. The pontoon-perched restaurant is highly recommended for its fish dishes.

Pullman Teranga (Sofitel; Map p156; ☎ 33 889 2200; h0563@accor.com, www.accorhotels.com; 10 Rue Colbert; r from CFA113,500; Ⓟ ✴ ⬛ ⬛) Comfortable, practical and as smooth as a boardroom table, Dakar's most central hotel is squarely aimed at business travellers and gets eight out of 10 on

the postseminar evaluation sheet for its conference rooms, wi-fi, business centre, dimly lit bars and hair salon. The breakfast buffet is fantastic (and pricey at CFA12,000).

MÉDINA TO MAMELLES

Terrou-Bi (Map p152; ☎ 33 839 9039; www.terroubi.com; Route de la Corniche-Ouest; r from CFA159,000; Ⓟ ✴ ⬛ ⬛) Brand new in 2009, this business hotel with sea views has classy, comfortable rooms in minimalist red and white tones. It's part of a complex that houses one of Dakar's top restaurants and casinos, with a massage centre under construction. While the space is fantastic, it falls flat when it comes to service – in line with most of Dakar's top-end places.

LES ALMADIES, N'GOR & YOFF

Méridien President (Map p152; ☎ 33 869 6969; www.starwoodhotels.com; Pointe des Almadies; r from CFA166,000; Ⓟ ✴ ⬛ ⬛) The drive through the abundant garden, the discreet politeness of the valets and the opulent lobby all make you all feel like a very privileged person, until you float right off your plush carpet and into an almost ordinary bedroom. The theme is 'junior executive in provincial estate agency', rather than 'royalty on sojourn', and even the higher-bracket rooms are only set apart by their (admittedly very attractive) views.

EATING

Dakar's restaurant scene is definitely one of the capital's highlights. There are about 100 eateries in the town centre alone, and that's before you've even headed for the suburbs, where chic new restaurants open all the time.

French cuisine, a hangover from the colonial past, is a particular highlight, but there's more to Dakar than *entrecôte* (rib steak) and *crème brûlée* (cream dessert covered in caramelised sugar). The styles of kitchens stretch from the Cape Verde islands over Vietnam, Thailand, Lebanon, Italy and India to Mexico.

Restaurants are usually open all day, though they'll only serve food from midday to 2pm and 7pm to midnight or later. (Many only close when the last guest has staggered out.) Note that most of Dakar's restaurants are closed on Sunday.

African

Almost every restaurant in Dakar has a Senegalese *yassa poulet* (grilled chicken marinated in a thick onion and lemon sauce) or *thiéboudienne* (Senegal's national dish; rice cooked in a thick sauce of fish and vegetables) on the menu. Some places particularly renowned for knowing how to spice a sauce are listed here. Thanks to large communities from other African countries, you'll also find a range of restaurants offering flavours from across the continent.

PLATEAU

Keur N'Deye (Map p156; ☎ 33 821 4973; 68 Rue Vincens; dishes from CFA2000; **V**) Highly recommended, this place offers well-prepared Senegalese specialities and a reasonable range of vegetarian dishes including large bowls of salad. At most times, the tinkling of the *kora* (harp-lute) accompanies the eager clattering of cutlery.

Chez Loutcha (Map p156; ☎ 33 821 0302; 101 Rue Moussé Diop; dishes CFA2500-4000; ☽ noon-3pm & 7-11pm Mon-Sat) A restaurant like a bus stop, this always overflowing place serves huge portions of Cape Verdean and Senegalese cuisine. Even the strong smell of bleach cleaner near the entrance and the deafening noise at lunchtime don't seem to deter punters – perhaps they even add to the workman's vibe that makes this enduring eatery what it is.

Le Djembé (Map p156; ☎ 33 821 0666; 56 Rue St Michel; dishes CFA3000-5000; ☽ 11am-5pm Mon-Sat) Behind Place de l'Indépendance, this humble eatery is the whispered insider tip for anyone in search of a filling platter of *thiéboudienne* in a peaceful oasis right in the heart of town.

MÉDINA TO MAMELLES

Sabura (Map p158; ☎ 33 864 1295; 18b Av Birago Diop, Point E; mains CFA4000-6000; ☽ 8am-1am) This Guinea-Bissau restaurant serves the best Cape Verdean, Portuguese and Creole cuisine in town. If you want a royally prepared *catchoupa* – Cape Verde's porky answer to paella – this is your place. The number of loud, lusophone party people here is a safe indicator of authentic Portuguese food.

Lalibela (Map p158; ☎ 77 510 1569; Rue A, Point E; dishes around CFA6000; ☽ 11am-2am; **V**) When you've tired of *thiéboudienne*, head for this cute Ethiopian restaurant. You'll sense the hosts' nostalgia for their Abyssinian homeland in every detail of the colourful decor, the rich Ethiopian coffee and the perfectly soured *injera* (bread). It's open late and there's occasional live music.

International
PLATEAU

La Galette (Map p156; ☎ 33 823 1516; 16 Av Pompidou; ☽ tea house 7am-11.30pm, restaurant noon-2.30pm & 7.30-11pm Sun-Fri, 7.30-11pm Saturday; **V**) Mornings and afternoons, people queue at the excellent patisserie downstairs for croissants and bread. Walk right past them to the tea house on the 1st floor for the best espresso in Dakar or to the adjacent restaurant, where creative French cuisine is served with skill and smiles.

Restaurant Farid (Map p156; ☎ 33 823 6123; 51 Rue Vincens; dishes CFA3500-6000; ☽ 6am-midnight; 🖳 **V**) Squeezed between grey inner-city walls, this little oasis serves the best Lebanese meze in town. It also does a fantastic Asian-style stuffed lamb and renders even a simple plate of grilled prawns outstanding by adding just the right touch of garlic and oil.

Le Bideew (Map p156; ☎ 33 823 1909; 89 Rue Joseph Gomis; dishes around CFA5000; ☽ 9am-11pm; **V**) In the cool shade of the Institut Français' mighty *fromager* (kapok tree), this colourful arts cafe is perfect for a break from the city. Little touches, like the drizzle of honey on the chicken and avocado salad or the fresh herbs sprinkled over the *brochettes de lotte* (fish skewers), make all the difference. Even the burgers taste slightly healthier here than they should.

Lagon I (Map p156; ☎ 33 821 5322; Route de la Corniche-Est; mains around CFA8000; ☽ 7am-midnight) This is very deservedly known as one of Dakar's best seafood places. Though it rather overstresses the point a little by pursuing the nautical theme relentlessly, from the cruise-ship decor and cabin-style toilets to the pontoon and uniformed waiters. If you are with company, get a scrumptious seafood platter to share.

our pick **Le Cozy** (Map p156; ☎ 33 823 0606; www .lecozy.com; Rue des Essarts; dishes around CFA10,000; ☽ noon-3pm & 7pm-midnight; **V**) The heavy wooden doors don't look like gates to a secret world, they really do sweep you off the market streets behind Marché Kermel into a temple of refined cuisine. Small, imaginative touches render even the simplest meal divine here – the creamy risottos and Japanese dishes are particularly recommended. Presentation and service are as perfect as the classy restaurant and bar spaces. And in the evening, the space transforms into a smart lounge bar, serving delicious cocktails.

La Fourchette (Map p156; ☎ 33 821 8887; 4 Rue Parent; meals CFA10,000-15,000; ☽ noon-2.30pm & 7.30-11pm Mon-Sat; **V**) The humble exterior betrays nothing of the polished parlour that hides within. Impeccable sushi and dishes from around the world prepared by two of Dakar's most renowned chefs attract expats and the trendiest Senegalese folks.

Le Fuji (Map p156; ☎ 33 821 6000; mains CFA17,000; 🕐 noon-3pm & 7pm-1am Mon-Sat) Very new and very glamorous, this is one of the top sushi houses in West Africa. The fish is so fresh your tongue might be startled and the surroundings are pretty enough to while the evening away. It's an investment, as prices are sky high, but justified.

MÉDINA TO MAMELLES

Fiesta (Map p152; ☎ 77 587 3483; VDN; dishes CFA4000; 🕐 10am-2am) It has a thatched roof and is cooled by busy ceiling fans, yet it exudes subtle class. We first discovered it when expats from across Europe gathered in front of the big screen to watch World Cup matches, swigging pints of draft beer and savouring pizzas. Usually, though, it's a quiet place for a relaxed meal served by attentive staff.

La Terrasse du Terrou-Bi (Map p152; ☎ 33 839 9039; Route de la Corniche-Ouest; meals CFA5000-8000; 🛒) Right on the sea, this chic garden restaurant serves highly recommended French cuisine. It's a favourite with Dakar's moneyed classes and is the perfect place to sip cocktails near the pool before blowing the holiday budget in the adjacent casino.

Jardin Thaïlandais (Map p158; ☎ 33 825 5833; 10 Bd du Sud; meals around CFA8000; 🕐 10am-4pm & 6pm-1am Mon-Sat) There's no better Thai, perhaps no better Asian food, in the whole of Senegal than that served at this understated place in Point E. Prices are a bit steep, but every bite is worth it.

LES ALMADIES, N'GOR & YOFF

La Crêpe Bretonne (Map p152; ☎ 76 699 4231; Pointe des Almadies; crêpes from CFA1500) This is where Dakar's youth comes out to play on Sunday afternoon, eating crêpes, drinking cola and falling in and out of love. It's a low-key, local-style place, made up of a few plastic tables placed on the sand. On a packed day, it's unbeatable for *ambiance*.

Chez Fatou Kim (Map p152; ☎ 33 820 9208; dishes CFA3000-6000; Route des Almadies; 🕐 9am-11pm) Many a Dakar family has whiled away a Sunday afternoon at this log cabin overlooking the Atlantic, partly because the setting is so lovely, with the waves crashing against smooth black rocks, partly because the service is so slow. It does generous portions of chicken-and-chips

and other such kids' favourites, and a great selection of seafood.

our pick **Le Ngor** (Map p152; ☎ 77 504 3006; Route des Almadies; dishes CFA4000; 🕐 Tue-Sat) From the roadside, it looks like a humble beach hut. Come closer, and a quirky, seashell-adorned maze of a building invites you in for grilled fish and cocktails with views over the Atlantic. Since it doesn't advertise, every punter here feels like this is his or her personal discovery. Most people who've stepped in here by chance became regulars from the first bite of ginger prawns. And why wouldn't you? The restaurant, with its wall-painted Dakar scenes, is a breezy place for a Sunday lunch of lobster and fresh juice, and the mosaic-styled tapas bar is where you kiss a perfect day goodbye with a sundowner.

Art et Afrique (Map p152; ☎ 77 783 6686; Route des Almadies; dishes CFA5000) The three-floor climb through an infinite collection of African masks and sculptures is almost as enjoyable as the international cuisine you enjoy up on the straw-roofed terrace. The Mamelles lighthouse provides an almost cinematic background.

Sao Brasil (Map p152; ☎ 33 820 0941; Station Shell, Route de N'Gor; pizzas CFA5000; 🕐 noon-4pm & 6.30pm-midnight; 🛒) Very confusingly named, this is one of Dakar's best Italian addresses. Properly baked in a stone oven, the huge pizzas come with a thin base and there's many choices of toppings. The house cocktails (CFA4000) are equally impressive and can be consumed in peace while the kids get busy on the small playground.

Le Récif des Almadies (Map p152; ☎ 33 820 1160; Pointe des Almadies; dishes CFA5000-7000; 🕐 noon-midnight Thu-Tue) This seafood restaurant sits in a prime location right on the Pointe des Almadies, with views across the Atlantic. The menu is as big as a book, packed with seafood dishes (all depending on the season) and a good selection of Asian (especially Vietnamese) food.

Alkimia (Map p152; ☎ 33 820 6868; Route des Almadies; tapas CFA6000; 🕐 noon-2.30 & 7.30-11pm Tue-Sun) You might want to practise that nonchalant, carelessly affluent walk before testing it walking onto the select pebbles of this chic garden space. The size and quality of the tapas and sushi (prepared by a Japanese chef) almost justify the steep rates. Dress smart so as not to get caught out among the white shirts and expensive heels.

Cabane des Pêcheurs (Map p152; ☎ 33 820 7675; meals CFA6000-9000; 🕐 11am-3pm & 7-11pm) Dakar's best fish restaurant serves you treats like amberjack and dolphinfish that you'll find hardly anywhere else in the city. Everything is absolutely fresh (it also runs a busy fishing centre) and served with style, and there's lovely decor and sea views to boot. Also has a couple of excellent rooms to rent.

Le Dionevar (Map p152; ☎ 33 820 0911; Pointe des Almadies; meals around CFA8000; ☺ 10.30am-2.30pm & 7.30-10.30pm) This may well be the place with the most solid reputation in Dakar for serving top-quality seafood at competitive prices. You get to choose from 23 different, equally good fish dishes, and that's only once you've managed to pick one of 33 delicious starters. Views from Africa's westernmost tip thrown in.

Le Mogador (Map p152; ☎ 33 820 0402; Route des Almadies; dishes CFA10,000) You wonder how this ubertrendy restaurant keeps all the covers, walls and seats so white, when everything else around is covered in dust. Walking into the Japanese garden and yin-and-yang restaurant is like a trip into an interior design magazine. The place is styled like a model, and serves delicious, light meals and cocktails.

Quick Eats

All across Dakar you'll see women stirring pots of *mafé* (rice covered with a thick, smooth groundnut sauce with fried meat and vegetables), grilling fish in the street and in makeshift *tanganas* (cafes) and selling steaming glasses of *café touba* (spicy coffee) with a slice of bread and butter.

A favourite snack is the *shwarma* (CFA1000), sold in small restaurants. Av Pompidou in the town centre has lots of them, a few more are listed below. They're open all day, until about 2am.

PLATEAU

Ali Baba Snack Bar (Map p156; ☎ 33 822 5297; Av Pompidou) Dakar's classic fast-food joint has always looked rough and smelt of hot oil. That hasn't deterred anyone yet from picking up their lunchtime kebab or *shwarma* here.

Caesar's (Map p156; ☎ 33 823 8400; 27 Bd de la République) Sometimes only fried chicken wings, burgers and fries will do, and for those moments Caesar's is your place. Come here regularly and you'll gain precious insights into the complexities of teenage love.

MÉDINA TO MAMELLES

Le Balajo (Map p158; ☎ 33 864 1113; Av Cheikh Anta Diop; ☺ 7.30am-3pm & 7-11pm) This tiny eatery with

the huge, colourful sign outside serves great Senegalese cuisine and snacks from around the world. Every office worker in the vicinity orders lunch here, but if you eat on site, you can often enjoy live concerts by rising folk star Biba.

La Provençale (Map p158; ☎ 33 825 1425; km 2.5 Av Cheikh Anta Diop) There's a narrow alleyway that takes you from the patisserie on the road through to a cute courtyard with tiled floors, shade and a tranquil atmosphere. Croissants, sandwiches and *shwarmas* are served quickly and there's live jazz every weekend.

LES ALMADIES, N'GOR & YOFF

Katia's (Map p152; ☎ 33 820 8082; 6 Route de N'Gor; pizzas CFA4000) A strong contender for the top pizza place in town, this is equally great for takeaway or sipping Flag beer while watching hustlers and tourists, dressed-down locals and blinging babes drift in to quench that late-night hunger.

Cafes & Patisseries

In Dakar a patisserie is not somewhere to buy your bread but a place to take your date if you really want to make an impression. Patisseries are springing up all over the place, most of them air-conditioned to freezing point and scrubbed till they shine.

PLATEAU

La Royaltine (Map p156; ☎ 33 821 9994; Av du Président Lamine Guèye) You know that a millefeuille is perfect when the pastry is buttery but light and the vanilla cream rich without being too sweet – this is where you get to taste one. At this top address for sweet indulgence, cakes, pralines and other delicacies are fussed over like precious pearls. And when the uniformed guard opens the glass doors for you, you know that you've just invested in something very special.

Aux Fins Palais (Map p155; ☎ 33 823 4445; 97 Av Peytavin; ☺ 6.45am-8.30pm) Sticks of white French bread are found on every corner in Dakar. This, however, is one of the very rare places to buy wholemeal bread in enough varieties to make even a German bakery proud. With excellent coffees, pancakes and original creations such as thyme-sprinkled puff pastries, it's a great place for breakfast.

N'Ice Cream (Map p155; ☎ 33 823 3545; 97 Av Peytavin; per scoop CFA1000; ☺ 11am-10.30pm Mon-Fri, 10am-11pm Sat & 11am-9pm Sun) This is where you find Dakar's widest selection of ice creams, including fla-

---

MARKET HOPPING

Dakar's markets are among the city's most fantastic features. Just take plenty of energy, some money (best hidden in your pockets, where it's harder to steal) and brush up your bartering skills.

If you want to plunge in head first, start at **Marché Sandaga** (Map p156; Av Pompidou), Dakar's largest, busiest and most central market. Officially, it lies at the intersection of Av du Président Lamine Guèye and Av Émile Badiane, though in reality its makeshift stalls claim most of the pavements in this part of town. There's little you won't find here and eager traders will try to satisfy even the most extraordinary requests. Hi-fi systems, folds of fabric, clothes and pirated videos are sold at stalls and hang off the shoulders of walking merchants. In Av Émile Badiane you'll find some of Dakar's best ranges of CDs.

Next stop: Marché Kermel (Map p156). This covered market behind Av Hassan II is worth a visit for its beautiful building alone, a 1997 reconstruction of the original 1860s construction. Push past the tourist stalls and you arrive at the local stalls, where women sell fish, fruit and veg.

Then it's time to head out of the city centre and into the heart of the Médina (a taxi there will cost around CFA1500). Created in colonial days as a 'township' for African residents, this is still a popular and slightly deprived quartier, though one that buzzes with sights, sounds and smells. The bustling **Marché Tilène** (Map p155; Av Blaise Diagne) mainly sells fruit, vegetables and daily household objects. The quartier itself has plenty of tiny tailor's shops, perfect to get your clothing of choice made at a fraction of the retail price.

The market at the Village Artisanal Soumbédioune (Map p152), on the Route de la Corniche-Ouest, is one of the most popular places to buy woodcarvings, metalwork, ivory and batiks. It's squarely aimed at tourists, so prepare for some serious bargaining. Soumbédioune is also home to a busy fish market. Come in the late afternoon to catch sight of colourful pirogues rolling in to unload stacks of fish, prawns and crabs. You can buy the fish directly from the local women, who sort, prepare and sell it right behind the boats.

Saving the best for last, head to **Marché des HLM** (Map p152; Av CA Bamba) to pick up some African fabrics. Hundreds of rolls of wax-dyed *bazin* (dyed fabrics beaten to a shine with wooden clubs), vibrant prints, embroidered cloth, lace and silk lend colour to the ramshackle stalls and dusty streets of this popular quartier. You can have your new ensemble sewn right here. And ladies, don't miss out on the street stalls selling the ingredients for the fabled Senegalese seduction techniques. Here is where you pick up your incense, the earthenware to burn it in, homemade perfumes and jingling waist beads.

---

vours made with local fruit – we loved the *corosol* (soursop) cream. Everything is made under rigorous hygienic conditions – a rarity among ice-cream parlours in Senegal.

Time's Café (Map p156; ☎ 33 821 2168; Av Léopold Senghor; snacks CFA4000; ⊗ 7am-11pm; **V**) The name is not a chance pick – New York was without a doubt the inspiration for this colourful breakfast parlour. It does the best latte in town – though you pay a staggering CFA2000 per cup – and has a tasty range of salads, snacks and light meals on the menu.

MÉDINA TO MAMELLES

Pâtisserie Médina (Map p155; ☎ 33 823 1713; Av Faidherbe; ⊗ 24hr) Dakar's 'terminus'. Every night out ends here at 5am, with coffee, croissants and cream doughnuts. With some luck, you'll even see some of Senegal's biggest music and football stars huddled around cups of hot chocolate. Far more hilarious and 'real' than the nightclub you've probably just left.

Self-Catering

Corner shops stacked sky high are scattered all across Dakar, selling basics like milk, oil, onions, the ubiquitous stock cubes and tinned sardines. Fresh fruit and vegetables are sold from roadside stalls across town. For a wider selection, Marché Kermel or Marché Tilène (see above) are great, and a trip to the Soumbédioune market is an experience – you can buy cheap sole, barracuda and white grouper *(thiof)* fresh off the boat.

Senegal imports most of its food, including staples. Dakar's supermarkets are well stocked with French brands of groceries, including good wine selections and household

GREATER DAKAR & CAP VERT PENINSULA

and sanitary items – often sold for up to twice the price they go for in Europe. The ones with the widest selection belong to the Casino chain. Try **Casino Centre** (Map p156; 31 Av Hassan II) near the Place de l'Indépendance, the giant **Centre Commercial Sahm** (Map p158; Bd de la Gueule Tapée) near Point E or the large, commercial **Dakar City** (Map p152; Route de N'Gor), which has a big supermarket and several shops.

DRINKING

Dakar by night can be almost as busy as Dakar by day. The glitziest, most pretentious and utterly good-looking party parlours are in Les Almadies.

PLATEAU

Ozio (Map p156; ☎ 33 823 8787; 21 Rue Victor Hugo) This ubertrendy bar-cum-club is a favourite with Dakar's glittering classes. Decor and attitude are ice-cool, as is the air-conditioning. Heavy electronic beats reduce conversation to gestures.

Le Viking (Map p156; ☎ 77 244 8056; 21 Av Pompidou) While slick new R&B clubs with chilled Champagne and skinny crowds open daily, this old-style pub is a beer-scented, slightly musty place, where shirts are still allowed to crumple and draught pints are poured into glasses that are certainly not frosted. It's friendly and slightly tipsy, and women will feel safer if they've come with a few friends.

Le Mex (Map p156; ☎ 33 823 6717; 91 Rue Moussé Diop; ⏰ noon-2am) This colourful place transforms from a Mexican restaurant into a lively bar once the sun has set. It's popular with the French military and their obligatory female following.

Le Seven (Map p156; ☎ 33 842 6911; 25 Rue Mohamed V) This is the glittering queen of Dakar's bars. Think Champagne bubbles, tiny tank tops, the latest hits. So *branché* (cool; literally 'plugged in') that you risk electrocution, this is where the in-crowd parties.

Casino du Port (Map p156; ☎ 33 849 0649; Bd de la Libération) One of several casinos in this money-burning capital, the Casino du Port doubles as a stylish bar and good restaurant, with live jazz on weekends. A good place to start the night.

New Africa (Map p152; ☎ 33 827 5371; newafrica@ orange.sn; ⏰ 7pm-2am Mon-Sat) Possibly Dakar's most relaxed bar (the meals are great too), this fills the gap between the chic 'in bars' and the dodgy drinking holes. Come here on Friday

nights, when the courtyard explodes with couples dancing superbly to contemporary Latin beats. Unmissable.

LES ALMADIES, N'GOR & YOFF

Le Patio (Map p152; ☎ 33 820 5823; Route de N'Gor) Past the broad-shouldered bouncers and across the red carpet, this large outdoor place looks like a private garden party. The cocktails here are divine, and it's only a short stumble to the next club.

Tolosa Caliente (El Toro; Map p152; ☎ 77 435 6516; tapas from CFA1500; ⏰ noon-midnight Mon-Sat) If you miss the *ambiance* in bars before the general smoking ban (or the smell of your clothes the next day), you'll love this tiny, smoky tapas bar. It's a hoot, full of pre-party folk lining their stomachs with very reasonable snacks before the long night ahead.

Magnetic Terrasse (Map p152; ☎ 33 820 0754; Route des Almadies; ⏰ 8pm-2am) Far from the style dogma of Les Almadies, this is a great down-to-earth bar for enjoying a game of snooker, a couple of beers and, well, a cigarette – it can get smoky in here. A rare pocket of untrendy fun on the party mile.

ENTERTAINMENT

New nightclubs seem to open here on a weekly basis, and several live music venues allow you to see some of Senegal's biggest artists play to their excited home crowds. The cultural calendar in the publication *221* and online at www.ausenegal.com has the best listings.

For a fun night out, don't even get your kit on before midnight. Leaving the house around 1am is impeccable timing; returning home before 4am, a sign of weakness. Now go party!

Live Music

Dakar's live music scene is booming, and the boundaries between restaurants, bars and nightclubs are often fluid. Below you'll find a few favourite venues, but it's worth checking out some of the eating, drinking and dancing venues as well – many pack bands in corners on occasions. In restaurants and bars admission is often free, while clubs charge between CFA3000 and CFA10,000.

Pen'Art (Map p158; ☎ 33 864 5131; Bd du Sud, Point E) Around the corner from Just 4 U, this is a cosy jazz club with good bands in a relaxed atmosphere. Come here when a reggae outfit like Timshell is playing and the place turns into a sweaty, swaying cave of excitement.

Yengoulene (Map p152; ☎ 33 820 7626; Nord Foire) During the day, this colourful cultural complex looks like a hangover-troubled party animal. It comes alive on most Saturday nights, when the distorted sound system is cranked up and Senegal's *mbalax* stars drive their audience to daring dance moves under the disco ball. Check cultural listings – it's not open every weekend.

Just 4 U (Map p158; ☎ 33 824 3250; just4u@orange.sn; Av Cheikh Anta Diop; ☽ 11am-3am) The stage of this outdoor restaurant looks barely large enough to hold a small jazz combo, and yet it has been graced by all of Senegal's finest stars and a glittering procession of international greats. There's a concert on every day and, on weekends, this is where you usually get to catch the big names, including Orchestra Baobab, Omar Pene and occasionally even Youssou N'Dour himself.

Papayer Night (Map p152; ☎ 77 513 1841; Route de Yoff) Some of Dakar's best parties happen here, at this nightclub with live music. Upstairs you can warm up to the whispering guitars and moaning voices of folk stars like Pape & Cheikh or Yoro, before you head downstairs for *mbalax* fever, spread by the big masters, such as Mbaye Ndiaye Faye or Thione Seck.

Blue Note (Map p152; ☎ 33 820 4551; Route de N'Gor) Between the white walls and the pizza tables, this relaxed jazz club features acoustic shows from blues to folk, often by international artists.

Chez Anthiou (Map p158; ☎ 77 634 0290; Rue 10, Amitié II) A visit here is like an invitation to the house party of a greying salsa lover. Couples contemplate their marriages while sweeping elegantly across a dance floor that trembles to the classic sounds of Pape Fall and his band. An intimate place that manages to be classy and raunchy at the same time.

Sun Set Sahel (Map p158; ☎ 33 821 2118; Centre Commercial Sahm, Bd de la Gueule Tapée) The Sahel has been here forever, a veritable slice of Dakar's musical history. As streetwise as the Médina neighbourhood surrounding it, it's still a great place for a Senegalese party, with dizzying *mbalax* vibes and occasional live music by Thione Seck.

Nightclubs

PLATEAU

Koulgraoul (Map p155; ☎ 77 532 2648; Route de la Corniche-Est; admission CFA3000) Every first Saturday of the month, Dakar's most dressed-down party happens in the sea-bordering backyard of the Océanium. This may be the only event that reliably attracts everyone, from hustling Rasta boys to glammed-up Lebanese ladies and most of the expat community.

Café de Rome (Map p156; ☎ 33 849 0200; 32 Bd de la République) Everyone congregates in this cushy basement club, from shady businessmen to the ambassadors of various nations. You could put on a suit, pose in a leather armchair and suck on cigar, and no one would even flinch at the glamour cliché.

MÉDINA TO MAMELLES

Le Madison (Map p158; ☎ 77 738 7308; km 1 Av Cheikh Anta Diop) Once all the lights are plugged in, this place glitters like a department store at Christmas. From Monday to Wednesday, you can practise your *mbalax* moves at the Senegalese nights; on weekends, there's often live music.

LES ALMADIES, N'GOR & YOFF

K Club (Map p152; ☎ 33 820 6467; Route des Almadies; ☽ noon-3am) Hip hop star Akon has invested here and footballer El Hajj Diouf is regularly booked in for Champagne nights. With a shimmering pool in the middle and VIP sections that you purchase with a CFA100,000 bottle, it's the stuff R&B clips are made of. The crowd is very young and slightly too serious about having fun.

Le Duplex (Map p152; ☎ 77 354 2954; Route de N'Gor) Behind the glass and white walls lies a hip interior and a booth only accessed by Dakar's most renowned DJs and their international guests. Dress smart, look cool and practise the lines 'Normally I only drink Cristal' and 'My cousin lives right next door to Diddy. Apparently he's a really nice guy.'

Le Nirvana (Map p152; ☎ 77 366 8814; Route de N'Gor) This is the grown-up version of the kids' clubs across the road. Still supersmart and polished, it has several intimate seating areas for those that can buy privacy with precious liquor bottles and booming beats through to the early morning hours.

Le Castel (Map p152; ☎ 33 860 6030; VDN, Sacré Cœur 3 Extension) Dakar's glitziest clubs, with their booming hip hop and posing stance, have a way of making anyone over 18 feel old. That's why we love Le Castel, where you're allowed to be an adult, listen to your favourite old-school tracks and swig Champagne not to be cool but because you can pay for it yourself.

DAKAR STYLE

Dakar emanates chic. At any time of day, the city's sandy pavements are dotted with a dazzling range of colours, fabrics designed to reflect the sunlight in shimmering sparks, and myriad imaginative versions of the classic *boubou* (elaborate robelike outfit worn by men and women). Your holiday wardrobe will have a hard time competing. Time to check out some of the city's many stylists who propose designer wear, often at very affordable rates. The choices are almost endless. You can go for classic African fabrics, like woven cloth and *bazin,* worked into modern cuts, or get clad in fashionable street wear that does the African look with style. Here's a list of some of our favourite designers and their brands:

Colle Ardo Sow (☎ 33 821 2529) She was one of the first to rework humble hand-woven cloth, fashioning fabulously elegant kaftans and robes from the handworked strips. Fabulous evening wear with an African touch.

Fitt (Map p152; ☎ 77 562 0890; Route de N'Gor, near Station Shell) Stylish jackets, shirts and trousers with original, flattering cuts and minimalist designs are the staples of Ndiaga Diaw's quality collection.

Kira (☎ 77 698 7279; kiralingerie@yahoo.fr) Kira's sensual lingerie is inspired by the sexy waist beads and *petits pagnes* (small, see-through wraparound cloths) of the Senegalese seduction repertoire. Not for the shy.

Sigil (Map p158; ☎ 77 501 97 54; sigil.com@free.fr; Villa 134, Amitié II, Mermoz) Denim has never looked better than in Cheikha's Senegalese street wear. His accessories, like bags, hats and scarfs, all adorned with the unmistakable logo, brush up any outfit.

Also try the following:

Casino du Cap Vert (Map p152; Route de N'Gor; ☎ 33 820 0974) One of Dakar's oldest and busiest nightspots. Gleaming 4WDs still pull up here at 3am to start the party.

Senat (Map p152; ☎ 33 869 6969; Le Méridien Président) Another magnet for Dakar's flashy young crowd. To spot famous footballers, singers and the like, head here.

Theatre & Cinema

In the absence of a regular cinema, the national **Théâtre Daniel Sorano** (Map p155; ☎ 33 822 1715; Bd de la République) has screenings (as well as plays and dance shows).

At the relaxed bar **Kadjinol Station** (Map p156; ☎ 33 842 8662; www.kadjinol-edu.com; off Av Hassan II), you can watch DVD versions of world cinema and Hollywood blockbusters in an arty setting.

SHOPPING

CENTRAL DAKAR

Dakar isn't really the place for a relaxed shopping stroll. You'll be too busy clutching your purse, shaking off hustlers and dodging parked cars to appreciate a relaxed promenade around the inner city. Still, there are a few places worth venturing into town for, most of them in the side streets between Av Pompidou and Bd de la République.

The 'Moroccan mile' on Rue Mohamed V, between Av Pompidou and Rue Assane Ndoye, has a line of small shops with masks, carvings and Maghreb craftswork. Try one of the Moroccan shoemakers to get your favourite designer footwear copied. Check also the galleries mentioned under Sights, p158.

Maam Samba (Map p156; ☎ 33 973 3040; www .ong-ndem.org; Institut Français, 89 Rue Joseph Gomis) The beautiful clothes, bed throws and hammocks on sale here are all made from stunningly coloured, organic cottons. The fabrics are woven, dyed and sewn by the Mouride community of the village Ndem, where the project has had huge successes in combating rural exodus by providing local infrastructure and employment.

Cajou (Map p156; Rue Assane Ndoye) This tiny shop is a fabulous address for children's clothes and cute toys, all handmade with love. You can even get a traditional *boubou* for your daughter's dollies.

Cocktail du Sénégal (Map p156; ☎ 33 823 5315; 108 Rue Moussé Diop) One of Dakar's most original souvenir shops, this spacious shop has a wide selection of clothes, original gifts, souvenirs and jewellery.

Naaj (Map p156; ☎ 33 825 7546; 66 Rue St Michel) The glass tableware on sale here is both original and beautiful, inspired by Senegal's tradition of *sous-verre* (reverse glass painting).

MÉDINA TO MAMELLES

At writing, the large shopping and entertainment complex **Sea Plaza** (Route de la Corniche-Ouest) was about to open. It's a large mall with shops, bars, restaurants and clubs, and includes outlets of some of Senegal's most famous fashion designers.

Fil & Pampilles (Map p158; ☎ 33 824 0931; Bd Canal IV) This small shop sells unique, contemporary craftwork, ranging from gaudily painted furniture and woven handbags to silver jewellery and classy *sous-verre* art.

Espace Agora (Map p158; ☎ 33 864 1448; Rue D) This airy patio displays beautiful Moroccan artwork, home wares and select products by local artisans.

Soumbédioune Souvenirs (Map p152; Route de la Corniche-Ouest) Opposite Soumbédioune market, this large shop and the small stalls near it sell lots of funky souvenirs, including bags, toys, CD stands, lamps and various other objects made from recycled cans.

LES ALMADIES, N'GOR & YOFF

Suska (Map p152; ☎ 33 865 2158; Route de N'Gor) The colourful woven bags, pillowcases and decorative items are all handmade, and are a cut above some of the stuff you'll find at the market.

GETTING THERE & AWAY
Air

The Léopold Sédar Senghor International Airport is in Yoff. For details of flights between Dakar and international or regional destinations, see p278. There were no regular internal flights at the time of research.

The following airline offices in Dakar can answer flight enquiries, confirm flights and make reservations:

Afriqiyah Airways (Map p156; ☎ 33 849 4930; 67 Av Peytavin)
Air Europa (Map p152; ☎ 33 822 0299; Route de N'Gor)
Air France (Map p156; ☎ 33 829 7777; 47 Av Hassan II)
Air Ivoire (Map p156; ☎ 33 889 0280; 12 Allées Robert Delmas)
Air Sénégal International (Map p156; ☎ 33 865 2242; Av Hassan II) Had grounded all flights at time of research.
Alitalia (Map p156; ☎ 33 849 9900; 5 Av Pompidou)
Brussels Airlines (Map p156; ☎ 33 823 0460; Immeuble la Rotonde, Rue Docteur Thèze)
Delta Airlines (Map p156; ☎ 33 849 6955; Senegal Travel Services, Fayçal Bldg, 19 Rue Parchappe)
Ethiopian Airlines (Map p156; ☎ 33 823 5552; Immeuble la Rotonde, Rue Docteur Thèze)
Iberia (Map p156; ☎ 33 889 0050; 2 Place de l'Indépendance)
Kenya Airways (Map p156; ☎ 33 823 0070; Av Hassan II)
Royal Air Maroc (Map p156; ☎ 33 849 4748; 1 Place de l'Indépendance)
South African Airways (Map p152; ☎ 33 869 4000; Villa 5, Route de Yoff)

TACV Cabo Verde Airlines (Map p156; ☎ 33 821 3968; 105 Rue Moussé Diop)
TAP Air Portugal (Map p156; ☎ 33 821 5460; Rue Assane Ndoye)
Virgin Nigeria (Map p156; ☎ 33 889 9010; 22 Rue de Thann)

Boat

The ferry *Aline Sitoé Diatta* travels between Dakar and Ziguinchor twice weekly in each direction. For more details, see p236.

Ndiaga Ndiaye & Sept-Place Taxis

Ndiaga Ndiayes (white Mercedes buses, used as public transport in Senegal) and *sept-place* taxis for long-distance destinations leave from Gare Routière Pompiers (Map p155), at the junction of the autoroute and Av Malick Sy (3km north of Place de l'Indépendance), and from Gare Routière Colobane (Map p152).

Journey durations are impossible to quote with certainty, as they depend on tyre punctures, the number of people and the time it takes to get out of Dakar.

Taxis and minibuses only leave when they're full, and most people travel early. To get a quick start, be at the station well before 9am. (The only way to avoid Dakar's gridlock is to get out of town before 7am).

Sept-place taxis are slightly more expensive but infinitely better than Ndiaga Ndiayes. They are safer, fill up quicker and arrive faster as there are fewer people to drop off on the way. You have to pay extra for luggage (around CFA500 to CFA1000).

Keep your ear to the ground for the latest roadworks, as itineraries, congested areas and the road layout on the whole change pretty fast. They'll tell you about changing itineraries and let you guess where the traffic jams are worst when you're planning to set out. The road layout of this city changes incredibly fast.

Car & Motorcycle

There are dozens of car rental agencies. For a full list, see www.ausenegal.com/Location-de-voitures.html. Agencies include the following.
Avis (Map p152; ☎ 33 849 7757; www.cfaogroup.com) Also at the airport.
Budget (Map p155; ☎ 33 889 7676; Av du Président Lamine Guèye) Also has agents at the airport.
Coseloc (Map p158; ☎ 33 869 2525; www.coseloc.sn; km 5.5 Av Cheikh Anta Diop) Tends to give good deals.
Dakar Location (Map p156; ☎ 33 823 8610; 7 Rue de Thiong)

GREATER DAKAR & CAP VERT PENINSULA

Hertz (Map p156; ☎ 33 822 2016; www.hertz.sn; 64 Rue Joseph Gomis) Has branches at the airport and on the Plateau.
Senecartours (Map p156; ☎ 33 889 7777; www .senecartours.sn; 64 Rue Carnot) One of Senegal's biggest operators; also has branches in Les Almadies.

Car Mouride

This long-distance bus service is financed by the Sufi brotherhood of the Mourides (hence the name). Most buses are clean and safe, and the service is fairly reliable. Still, they are generally much slower than bush taxis and are not particularly comfortable.

Book your seat ahead of time (a couple of days' notice is usually enough) at the office of the **Gare Routière Pompiers** (Map p155; ☎ 33 821 8585), off Av du Président Lamine Guèye. It's always safer to go there in person rather than phone. Most buses leave in the middle of the night (check exact departure times at the office) and, thanks to the booking system, they don't take too long to fill up.

Buses leave from a petrol station that doubles as a bus stop at the intersection of Av Malik Sy and Av Félix Éboué, near the Gare Routière Pompiers. Incoming transport sometimes terminates at Gare Routière Kolobane, about 2km north of Gare Routière Pompiers.

Train

Only one of Senegal's train lines survives – the train that goes from Dakar to Bamako (Mali) via several towns, including Thiès, Diourbel and Tambacounda. The service is completely unreliable and derailments are frequent. If you're keen on the adventure (which it certainly is), check the latest state of the service at Dakar's train station. If you really want to get somewhere, take a bush taxi. For details of the train to Bamako, see p281.

GETTING AROUND
To/From the Airport

On arrival, you'll find taxis parked to the right of the exit, though you have to cut a way through the throngs of overeager guys trying to push you to a taxi, change money, beg or pick your pocket. A journey into the town centre is supposed to cost CFA4000, though you might have to pay more. Yoff and N'Gor are closer and should cost around CFA2000.

If you want to save a couple of hundred CFA francs, walk out of the airport onto the main road and flag down a taxi there.

Bus

Dakar's DDD (Dakar Dem Dikk) bus service is surprisingly good. The large, blue DDD buses run pretty regularly along most major routes. They have fixed stops (some clearly visible, with small waiting cubicles, others simply marked by a tiny DDD sign stuck in the ground) and theoretically go every 10 minutes, depending on how tight the gridlock is. Short distances cost CFA150, longer ones range from CFA175 to CFA250, with prices conforming to a system of zones. Pay for your ticket at the conductor's booth on the bus (make sure you have change). The main bus garage in town is on Bd de la Libération.

Buses are particularly useful in off-peak hours; they get extremely full in the morning and afternoon rush hours. For Les Almadies, Yoff and N'Gor they can be useful as taxis get pricey on those longer distances.

You can view the full network, complete with maps and prices, at www.demdikk.com.

Some useful circuits:

No 1 Parcelles Assainies–Place Leclerc From the heart of town via the suburbs all the way up the peninsula.
No 7 Ouakam–Palais de Justice Travels the length of Av Cheikh Anta Diop into the centre of town.
No 8 Aéroport (Yoff)–Palais de Justice The direct bus route from the airport to the centre of town.
No 11 Keur Massar–Palais 1 Takes you from Keur Massar right through to the centre of town.
No 16 Malika–Palais A direct connection between the village Malika and the town centre.

Car Rapide

These colourfully decorated, blue-and-yellow minibuses are Dakar icons and, while travelling in these pretty (though battered) vehicles is certainly an experience, the routes they follow are hard to understand if you don't know the city well. Destinations aren't marked, and the assistants perched dangerously on the back shout directions so fast that untrained ears won't understand a thing.

Car rapide drivers have a reputation for driving dangerously, and stop frequently and randomly. When you want to get off, just tap a coin on the roof or window. Journeys cost between CFA50 and CFA150.

Ndiaga Ndiaye

This is another one for Dakar insiders. These privately owned, white 30-seater minibuses, adorned with colourful decorations (most

---

TAXI SISTER

Among the mass of clapped-out taxis plying Dakar's roads, the bright-yellow Chinese Cherys stand out like flowers in a field. Not only because the tiny model is unusual or because they're in a well-polished condition, but because they are the only public vehicles in town driven by women. Under a government scheme designed to get women working, a handful of female drivers were given cars to start their own one-woman taxi business. They now gradually pay them off, carrying clients through the city's hectic streets, defying all the male prejudice raining down on them. For women passengers, this is an obvious way of travelling safely, and without the constant marriage offers male taxi drivers tend to weave into conversations. Taxi Sisters are parked outside Novotel in the centre of town, and you can order them on ☎ 88 408 4084.

---

with *Alhamdoulilai,* meaning 'Thanks be to God', across the front), roughly follow the same routes as the DDD buses. Fares are between CFA100 and CFA150, depending on the length of your trip. Destinations and routes are not marked, so you'll have to ask or listen for the call from the apprentice.

Senbus

These are Indian-made Tata buses, assembled in Senegal. They were supposed to replace the battered *cars rapides* one day but have only really managed to provide an additional service. Though they also get packed, they are much more comfortable and user friendly, with clearly marked destinations and fairly fixed stops. They don't do many routes, though. Rates are the same as for *cars rapides.*

Taxi

Yellow-and-black taxis, from ancient Peugeots that barely hold together to modern Iranian Samands (assembled in Senegal), fill the Dakar streets. It's the most expensive, but also the easiest way of getting around the city.

Prices are entirely up for negotiation, and Dakar taxi drivers will often propose outrageous rates if they think you don't know the city well. Try to get cues about approximate rates from locals. For a short ride across the Plateau, you'll pay CFA500 to CFA700. Place de l'Indépendance to Gare Routière Pompiers is around CFA1000, and Dakar Centre to Point E is around CFA1500. For Yoff and N'Gor you'll easily pay CFA3000 to CFA4000. Drivers tend to charge more at night.

Hiring a taxi for day trips around Dakar should cost around CFA35,000.

CAP VERT PENINSULA

Just off the shores of Dakar, two small islands provide a welcome escape from the city and its wiles. Île de Gorée, with its meditative mood and tragic past, stands as an eerily beautiful symbol of the horrors of the slave trade, and has become something of a pilgrimage site for many in search of distant roots. Arts lovers flock here too – some of Senegal's greatest painters have set up workshops here, among the bougainvilleas, historical houses and rocky shores. The tiny Îles de la Madeleine are a very different place – specks of volcanic land, home to cormorants and turtles, and the occasional pirogue traveller drawn here by a clear, natural pool that nature has carved into the stone.

Any journey into the country's interior passes through the peninsula's northeastern bottleneck. Before Dakar really fades out into open savannah lands, it first puts on the street culture really thickly in the huge *banlieues* (suburbs) Pikine, Guediewaye and Thiaroye. These sprawling conurbations are where many hopeful rural emigrants en route to the city's fame and fortune get stranded. Many of Senegal's famous wrestlers, rappers and other streetwise, self-made heroes have grown up among their flooded, broken streets. Further eastwards, fishing villages and a tranquil monastery announce the city's end – you have now officially escaped Dakar's grip.

ÎLE DE GORÉE

It's only a 30-minute ferry ride from Dakar's hectic port to Île de Gorée – 23 hectares of almost complete stillness. Where Dakar is all traffic noise, car fumes and beeping horns, Gorée's calm is only disturbed by breaking waves, rustling leaves and voices.

REGARDS SUR COURTS

Gorée is at her most beautiful during the annual festival **Regards sur Courts** (☎ 33 842 1622; www.goree-regards-sur-cours.org). For one May weekend, the island's historical houses open their doors to the public, granting rare glimpses into leafy patios framed by ancient stone walls. Not only that – most courtyards are adorned with spontaneous art exhibitions, from the most informal community project to the precious works of sculptors and painters, many of whom have their workshops on the island.

There are no tar roads and no cars on this island, just narrow alleyways filled with trailing bougainvilleas and colonial brick structures whose wrought-iron balconies suggest Mediterranean love stories.

But Gorée's calm is not so much romantic as meditative. Ancient buildings, particularly La Maison des Esclaves, bear witness to the island's role in the Atlantic slave trade. Most visitors are drawn to Gorée by its history; for many it's a painful, symbolic journey in search of ancient roots. Cultural initiatives, such as the December **Gorée Diaspora Festival** (☎ 33 823 9177; www.goreediasporafestival.org; Mairie de Gorée), explore the connections between Africa and America in music, film and debates.

Information

Any tourist entering Gorée must pay a tourist tax of CFA500. You pay this at the tourist information booth near the ferry landing. You can also hire tourist guides here, though you're unlikely to really need one.

Gorée has a post office and an internet cafe, **Espace Multimedia** (per hr CFA500; ⏲ 10am-1pm & 3-10pm), both near the ferry jetty.

Sights

There's plenty to see on the island to fill a day, but don't come on a Monday, as all the museums and historical buildings will be closed.

The island's most famous house is the 1776 Dutch building **La Maison des Esclaves** (admission CFA500; ⏲ 10.30am-noon & 2.30-6pm Tue-Sun), a powerful symbol of the horrors of slavery, with its famous arched staircase opening onto the ocean (see the boxed text, p180).

The base of the **Castel**, at the southern tip of the island, was erected by the Dutch in the

17th century, well before the slave house was built. Over the centuries other fortifications were added, including massive WWII guns, which sank a British warship in the harbour. Walking up to the top of the Castel, you pass the homes of the Baye Fall disciples who live here (see the boxed text, p46); from the top you get great views across the island.

On the other end of the island, the ancient French Fort d'Estrées (1850) houses the **IFAN Historical Museum** (☎ 33 822 2003; Fort d'Estrées; admission CFA500; ⏲ 10am-1pm & 2.30-6pm Tue-Sat), which has old Gorée maps, pictures and artefacts under low, white arcs. A walk up its stairs affords views across to Dakar.

Gorée's two sacred buildings are also worth seeing. The 1830 **Saint Charles Borromée Church** is an imposing building that's usually open to visitors, while the **mosque** (near the Castel), built in 1892, is one of the oldest stone mosques in Senegal.

The permanent exhibition at the **Musée de la Femme** (Rue du Port; admission CFA500; ⏲ 10am-5pm Tue-Sun), dedicated to the role of Senegalese women throughout history, is interesting, while the displays of the **Musée de la Mer** (☎ 33 821 5066; admission CFA500) aren't quite as scintillating as the 18th-century French West India Company building they are housed in. Both the old **Navy Hospital** and the **Hôtel de Ville**, just north of the hospital, are beautiful buildings, and the **Ancienne Résidence du Gouverneur** remains impressive, even though it's almost in ruins now – walk through to the back yard, a tranquil spot with a view.

Near the jetty, drop in to the **Gorée Institute** (☎ 33 849 4849; www.goreeinstitute.org; Rue du Jardin) to find out about its fantastic work in culture, human rights and community development. It often hosts exhibitions in the Gorée houses it has lovingly restored.

A walk around the Castel takes you to a great viewing spot, as well as to the workshops of two famous artists who have set up shop here: Gabriel Kemzo, one of Senegal's great sculptors, and the painter Cheikhou Keita.

Sleeping

Many Gorée residents keep a spare room for unexpected (and paying) visitors. One of the prettiest private options is **Chez Valerie** (ASAO; ☎ 33 821 8195; 7 Rue Saint Joseph; csaodakar@orange.sn; r from CFA15,000), a private, old Goréen house, whose four rooms are lovingly decorated with the colourful works of Gorée artists and surround a shady patio. Gorée's classic address

ÎLE DE GORÉE

0 — 200 m
0 — 0.1 miles

INFORMATION
Espace Multimedia...............................1 B4
Hôtel de Ville...2 A4
Navy Hospital..3 A4

SIGHTS & ACTIVITIES
Ancienne Résidence du Gouverneur...........4 A4
Atelier Cheikhou Keita...........................5 B5
Atelier Gabriel Kemzo.............................6 B5
Gorée Institute......................................7 B4
IFAN Historical Museum...........................8 A3
La Maison des Esclaves............................9 B4
Mosque..10 A4
Musée de la Femme...............................11 B4
Musée de la Mer....................................12 A3
Saint Charles Borromée Church...............13 B4

SLEEPING
Auberge Keur Beer................................14 B4
Chez Valerie...15 A3
Hostellerie du Chevalier de Boufflers........16 A3

To Dakar (4km)

Tacoma Shipwreck

Ferry Jetty

Bars & Restaurants

Tourist Market

Public Gardens

Steps

Castel

is the **Hostellerie du Chevalier de Boufflers** (☎ 33 822 5364; www.boufflers.com; r from CFA18,000), which has a terrace restaurant with harbour views and tastefully decorated rooms in a building behind. The top-floor ones are much better, but CFA5000 more expensive. **Auberge Keur Beer** (☎/fax 33 821 3801; keurbeergie@yahoo.fr; Rue du Port; s/d CFA20,000/25,000) has simple rooms (some,

cheaper than those listed above, have shared bathrooms). The helpful management can also arrange accommodation in private homes should the *auberge* be full.

Eating
The restaurant at the Hostellerie du Chevalier de Boufflers is Gorée's most famous, as well as most expensive address. For more options, head for the beach opposite the ferry jetty, where small eateries fight for space. From Chez Tonton to the Kooly Tengala to Ann Sabran, they offer similar, standard menus at similar prices (around CFA3000). At the Castel, your choice is between the local *gargotte* (basic eatery) Chez Madame Siga or Le Castelo, superbly located on top of the Castel.

Shopping
Just behind the row of bars and restaurants facing the ferry jetty is a little tourist market crammed full of crafts and batiks, and the ascent to the Castel is lined with street stalls, selling cheap paintings, more tie-dye and souvenirs.

Getting There & Away
A **ferry** (☎ 33 849 7961, 24hr info line 77 628 1111; www .dakar-goree.com) runs every one to two hours from the *embarcadère* in Dakar, just north of Place de l'Indépendance, to Île de Gorée. The trip across takes 20 minutes and costs CFA5000 return for foreigners. For the ferry timetable, phone the info line or check the website.

ÎLES DE LA MADELEINE
From Dakar's shores, the **Îles de la Madeleine** (admission CFA1000, guide CFA5000, pirogue CFA4000) look like a couple of bare, hostile rocks. The beauty of their volcanic formations reveals itself only as the waves carry your pirogue into the natural harbour of Sarpan, the main island.

The site was declared a national park in 1985 to protect the rare bird species that inhabit it (see p181), and its unusual vegetation of dwarf baobabs.

If small trees and big birds don't make your heart beat faster, you can come here for some snorkelling, diving or swimming in the clear rock pool.

Remember to bring all the food and water you'll need. These are uninhabited, natural islands with nothing but peace.

GREATER DAKAR & CAP VERT PENINSULA

LA MAISON DES ESCLAVES

Île de Gorée was an important trading station during the 18th and 19th centuries, and many merchants built houses in which they would live or work in the upper storey and store their human cargo on the lower floor.

La Maison des Esclaves (The Slave House) is one of the last remaining 18th-century buildings of this type on Gorée. It was built in 1786 and renovated in 1990 with French assistance. With its famous doorway opening directly from the storeroom onto the sea, this building has enormous spiritual significance for some visitors, particularly African Americans whose ancestors were brought from Africa as slaves.

Walking around the dimly lit dungeons, you can begin to imagine the suffering of the people held here. The curator, Joseph Ndiaye, provides a commentary full of gruesome details that is less sober historical fact than emotive illustration. And that really describes La Maison des Esclaves as a whole – its historical significance in the slave trade may not have been huge, but the island's symbolic role is immense.

There's no doubt that Gorée was a slave-trading station, though of the 20 million slaves that were taken from Africa, only around 300 per year may have gone through Gorée and, even then, the famous doorway would not have been used – ships could not get near the dangerous rocks and the town had a jetty a short distance away.

But the number of slaves transported from here isn't what matters in the debate around Gorée. The island, and particularly La Maison des Esclaves, stands as a terrible reminder of the immense suffering inflicted on African people as a result of the Atlantic slave trade.

Getting There & Away

Pirogues to Îles de la Madeleine go from the **National Park Office** (☎ 77 113 2108, 76 633 7664) on the Route de la Corniche-Ouest, south of Hôtel Terrou-Bi and Magic Land. It's obligatory, as well as useful, to take a guide with you (CFA5000) to show you around the islands. There's a minimum group size of four people per boat. If you are a lone traveller, contact the office and see if you can join another group.

The **Océanium** (Map p155; ☎ 33 822 2441; www .oceanium.org; Route de la Corniche-Est) runs diving trips to the islands.

VILLAGE DES TORTUES

On the Route de Bayakh, just north of the village of Sangalkam, is the fascinating **Village des Tortues** (Turtle Village; ☎ 77 658 9984; adult/child CFA3000/2000; ⌚ 9am-5.30pm). This 'village' is a sanctuary for more than 400 injured and neglected turtles. There are several species of land and sea turtles, but the main attractions are the giant African spurred tortoises *(Geochelone sulcata)*. This is the largest continental tortoise on earth, and the neatly kept reserve has got scores of them, ranging from newly hatched ones to a 92kg giant.

The wide turtle enclosures are spread across a large botanical garden, full of local medicinal plants, and the turtle tours conducted by passionate staff are packed with information on tortoises and trees.

There's also a small boutique where you can purchase locally made craftwork, and a pretty cafe to sip a *bissap* (hibiscus drink) with your packed picnic. People interested in volunteering should call the village, as it regularly hires volunteer workers.

To get here, take DDD bus 15 or a Ndiaga Ndiaye to Rufisque and then another Ndiaga Ndiaye heading for Kayar; ask to be let off at the village (you'll see the huge sign on your left). Alternatively, a taxi from Rufisque will cost about CFA3000, or CFA14,000 from Dakar.

LAC ROSE

Also known as Lac Retba, this shallow lagoon surrounded by dunes is a popular day-trip destination for *dakarois* and tourists alike, all coming to enjoy the calm and catch the lake's magic trick – the subtle pink shimmer that sometimes colours its waves. The spectacle is caused by the water's high salt content: 10 times that of your regular ocean. It's a beautiful sight but can only be enjoyed when the light is right. Your best chance is in dry season, when the sun is high. But even if nature refuses to put on her show, a day out here is still enjoyable. You can swim in the lake, buoyed by the salt, or check out the small-

---

BIRDWATCHING TIPS: ÎLES DE LA MADELEINE

The 45-hectare park of the Îles de la Madeleine is home to an exclusive selection of birds. The rare red-billed tropical bird, with its narrow, swept-back wings, and long tail streamers in the breeding season, is the islands' emblem. The islands are small and on a short walk you might also see breeding colonies of common cormorants, northern gannets, bridled terns and ospreys as well as dozens of black kites that circle across the city and the island.

---

scale salt-collecting industry on its shores (see below). Better still, venture out on horseback with the excellent hosts at Chevaux du Lac (see Sleeping & Eating).

Sleeping & Eating

Up until the demise of the Dakar rally, Lac Rose is where the Sahara drivers would arrive and celebrate their victories or drown their woes. The annual event, combined with the beauty of the lake, has spawned a small tourist industry that unfortunately also brought hustlers, souvenir sellers and the odd con man to the shores of the lake. For a peaceful stay, pick one of the hotels away from the small holiday village near the artisans' village. All places can arrange camel rides, beach buggy tours and excursions to the surrounding villages and beyond. Apart from the hotels, you can also stay in one of the many residences near the lake. Find out more from Dakar travel agencies or www.ausenegal.com.

Ker Djinné (☎ 77 634 0468; r with/without air-con CFA19,000/14,000; ☒ ☎) Opposite the artisans' village, this is a relaxed place, with accom-modation in well-maintained round huts and a recommended restaurant where a *griot* (West African praise singer) usually strums his *kora*.

our pick **Chevaux du Lac** (☎ 77 630 0241, 77 633 5201; www.leschevauxdulac.com; half-/full board CFA14,000/19,000) Tucked away on the north-ern side of the lake, this friendly *campement* and horse farm is wonderfully secluded. The cute bungalows are simple but impeccable, and the surrounding garden provides the right shade for your hammock. Vincent and Stephanie, the friendly hosts, arrange excur-sions on horseback for beginners, includ-ing children, and advanced riders (1½ hours costs CFA10,000; three hours, CFA20,000) – a brilliant way of exploring the lake and its surroundings.

Chez Salim (☎ 33 836 2466; www.chez-salim.com; d CFA20,000; ☒ ☒ ☎) Among the cluster of places near the artisans' village, this is a more upmarket option with reasonable rates. It has spacious, comfortable bungalows set in a vast garden. The bivouac excursions are highly recommended.

Le Palal (☎ 33 836 2651; www.lac-rose-palal.com; s/d CFA33,000/48,000; ☒ ☎) This is group tour cen-tral, an all-round holiday factory that mass-produces fun. Not one for quiet contemplation of the lake's natural spectacle, then, but great if you like your holidays club style.

Getting There & Away

It's best to get here by hire taxi from Dakar (return trip with some waiting time costs around CFA20,000). Otherwise, take public transport to Keur Massar (bus 11, Ndiaga Ndiayes and *cars rapides* all go here from Dakar) and hire a taxi from there (around CFA5000). You can also join an organised excursion (see p154).

SALT COLLECTING AT LAC ROSE

On the southern side of Lac Rose is a village called Niaga-Peul, from where local people go out to collect salt from the lake. The lake is shallow, so they wade up to their waists and use digging tools to scrape the salt off the lake bed and load it into flat-bottomed pirogues. When the canoe is full and the water only millimetres below the rim, it is punted back to the shore and the salt carried onto the bank in buckets. Each salt collector builds his own pile of salt – marked by his initials – and members of his family are involved, too; the women do most of the carrying work. The good-quality salt is put straight into 25kg sacks and sold to middlemen from Dakar who come each morning with trucks and pick-ups. The poorer-quality salt gets loaded in bulk and is taken elsewhere for processing. The workers get paid less than CFA400 for each 25kg sack, and even less for the low-grade salt.

If you're driving from Dakar, take the main road towards Rufisque and, about 6km beyond Thiaroye-sur-Mer, turn left on the tar road, which takes you to Keur Massar. About 3km beyond the village, in Niakoul Rap, turn left for Niaga-Peul and Lac Rose. Alternatively, go to Bambilor, shortly behind the Village des Tortues, and take the road directly to the southern end of Lac Rose.

RUFISQUE

Rufisque was one of the first and most important French settlements during colonial days, but unlike Saint-Louis or Gorée it hasn't managed to preserve many of its old buildings or its cosmopolitan character. Today, it mainly acts as the gateway from Dakar to the regions, clogged by traffic jams and hazy with pollution. You could stop for a bit, check out the architectural remains that tell of the town's former glory, or take a horse-and-cart ride. Otherwise, do as the locals do – pass through.

If you want to spend the night, the cosy **Oustal de l'Agenais** (☎ 33 836 1648; Route de Rufisque; r CFA15,000; 🖳) is a good option with clean, comfortable rooms, a cosy restaurant and friendly management.

Getting There & Away

Rufisque is on the main road out of Dakar and, until the new autoroute is completed, every vehicle going out of town squeezes through here, including DDD bus 15, frequent Ndiaga Ndiayes and *cars rapides*. Due to the building of the autoroute, the roads here are notoriously congested. To avoid getting stuck, leave Dakar early in the morning, best around 7am.

KEUR MOUSSA MONASTERY

About 12km southeast of Lac Rose and 50km from Dakar on the road to Kayar, Keur Moussa Monastery is a great place to spend a reflective Sunday morning. The building itself is pretty unremarkable, apart from altar paintings that evoke the ancient Coptic Christian art of Ethiopia. But the real reason to visit is

the 10am mass, famous for its unique music – a stunning mixture of *kora* playing and Gregorian chants in Wolof.

You can buy CDs of this beautiful sound after the service (CFA10,000), and even have a *kora* made to learn on yourself. Most locals come here to purchase the monks' famously delicious goat's cheese.

Getting There & Away

Take bus 15 to Rufisque and change for a minibus to Bayakh or Kayar (CFA150). Tell the driver where you're headed and you'll be dropped off at a junction, from where it's a 1.5km walk to the monastery. It's signposted and all the drivers know it. Getting a lift back to Dakar shouldn't be difficult, as many people will be going that way after the mass.

If you are driving, take the Route de Rufisque from Dakar, turn left at Rufisque in the direction of Kayar, drive for 21km to Bayakh and then turn right (south) and continue for 5km to the monastery.

KAYAR

The pretty Lebou village of Kayar marks the point where the coast swings from the east towards the north – the beginning of Senegal's Grande Côte. It's one of the largest fishing centres in Senegal and, on its wide beach, you can watch the whole cycle of a fisherman's day unfold, from the rolling out to sea in the morning, to gutting and selling the glistening catch right on the beach.

The northern beaches aren't particularly recommended for swimming as the current here is very strong. But the coastline is an impressive sight and a great place to relax. Pirogue trips, as well as walks to the sand dunes behind the village, fill a day nicely, and watching pirogue makers at work is fascinating. Kayar isn't far from Lac Rose and the two destinations can easily be combined into a weekend excursion.

You can sometimes get direct transport from Dakar; otherwise, jump off at Rufisque and change for a Kayar taxi or minibus.

Petite Côte & Siné-Saloum Delta

Where Dakar relaxes its urban grip, tall baobabs line the road towards Mbour, forming a majestic gateway to Senegal's favourite seaside escape. The sandy shore line of the Petite Côte is where city folk unpack their picnic baskets on weekends, joining the hundreds of other travellers on a break from the bustle. The sunny beaches and gentle currents are hard to resist and, since the '80s, a veritable tourist industry has grown here, between the palm trees and tiny fishing villages.

The pulsating heart of the zone is Saly-Portudal, a thriving holiday centre that lives on sunshine and surf. Things are more understated and the beaches emptier just to the north and south, where local communities retain much of their original character, small nature reserves have inviting strolls, and fishermen unload their glistening catches on the shores.

Past the twin villages Joal and Fadiout, where seashells crunch under your feet and the gods live in harmony, the Saloum River cuts into the coast, opening up a vast maze of mangroves and marshes. Léopold Sédar Senghor, Senegal's first president, grew up here and it's said that the beauty of the place and its people inspired much of his renowned poetry. This region has an undeniable magic, best explored with plenty of time. In Palmarin lone baobabs stretch out from endless salt plains like solitary thoughts. Further south, narrow creeks and slim sand banks are perfect for pirogue tours, presenting you with rich bird life as your boat cruises through the narrow waterways.

HIGHLIGHTS

- Indulge in lazy beach life at **Saly-Niakhniakhal** (p188), the quieter part of Senegal's sea-resort zone
- Watch dozens of colourful fishing pirogues roll in with their glistening catches at **Mbour** (p190)
- Walk the wooden bridge from **Joal** to **Fadiout** (p192) and listen to the crunching seashells under your toes
- Take a donkey cart to the edge of the world – or so it seems – from the mangrove fringes of **Bamboung** (p198)
- Fly over the wetlands, shimmering waters and salt patches of the **Siné-Saloum Delta** (p193)

PETITE CÔTE

This is where Senegal greets the Atlantic with kilometres of sandy coast. Safe swimming beaches attract large numbers of tourists, causing the flashy holiday village of Saly-Portudal to spill over its boundaries. If you like your holiday more low key and your beach body slightly less exposed, the villages Toubab Dialao, Popenguine and La Somone in the north, as well as Mbodiène and Nianing in the south have beaches that still swing to the local rhythm.

TOUBAB DIALAO & NDAYANE

pop about 4000

Once a tiny fishing village, Toubab Dialao has gradually turned into a second home for affluent *dakarois*. Their villas in various stages of completion stretch over the gently sloping hills and small cliffs that frame the original village and its coastline.

Despite all the developments, Toubab Dialao has retained its tranquil atmosphere. It's a great spot for swimming, hiking or a tour around the hills and plains on horseback. The excellent guides at **Les Cavaliers de la Savane** (☎ 77 569 0365) take beginners and advanced riders on tailor-made excursions (two hours costs CFA12,500). Phone them and they'll take you right into the village hinterland, from where their tours start (food is provided there, and they were working on accommodation when we passed).

Toubab Dialao is mainly famous for being the home of the internationally renowned dance school **Jant Bi** (L'École des Sables; ☎ 33 836 2388; www.jantbi.org), run by dancer and choreographer Germaine Acogny. Situated a short drive along a dirt track out of town, it frequently hosts international dance courses. Even if it's deserted, a walk up to the school is worth undertaking. The main arena is a great spot for watching sunsets, rendered embarrassingly perfect by the pink wings of flamingos. If the school isn't fully booked, you can stay in its huts; phone to enquire.

Sleeping & Eating

There are three small hotels in the heart of Toubab Dialao, which form a seashell-adorned village within the village. The trend was started by a Frenchman, Gérard, who owns the highly rated Sobo-Bade, the hub of much of the activity in the village.

Sobo-Bade (☎ /fax 33 836 0356; www.espacesobobade.com; dm per person CFA4000, r from CFA12,000) With its quirky rooms, colourful mosaics, tiny towers and low roofs, this enduring haunt looks like the original home of the hobbits. A chapel-shaped performance space and medieval-style theatre complete the set. There are batik, pottery and dance courses on offer, and bicycles (two hours costs CFA5000) and horses (two hours costs CFA10,000) can be hired.

La Mimosa (☎ /fax 33 836 0015; lamimosa@gmail.com; s/d CFA10,000/12,000; 🐷 🖳) Opposite the Source, this place has a lovely garden with sculptures, flowers and even a couple of sofas. The bright upstairs rooms are much better than their darkish counterparts downstairs. Bubbly Astou serves great food here (from CFA1500 to CFA3000) and the massage centre gets good reviews.

La Source Ndiambalane (☎ 33 836 1703; ndiambalan@orange.sn; d/tr CFA12,000/15,000) This place continues the shell-art theme to such perfection that it looks almost like an extension of Sobo-Bade, next door. Rooms here are smaller and lack the original character of the famous neighbour, but the airy sea-view terraces are great for sitting, gazing and enjoying a good meal.

Centre Mampuya (☎ 77 569 3773; www.mampuya.org; s/d incl breakfast CFA18,000/28,000) You need determination to get here; we spent an hour in the burning heat pushing a Yamaha bike over sand mounds. But there's a sweet reward on arrival: the naturally cool rooms come with stunning views across the baobab-specked lands and the bar serves cool drinks. The centre's main attraction is the large tropical garden, where the village community is involved in cultivating and preserving rare and medical plants. Don't do what we did – phone the centre and arrange pick-up from Toubab Dialao.

La Pierre de Lisse (☎ 33 957 7148; www.itineraire lisse.net; r per person from CFA33,500; 🐷 🖳 🖳 🛁) What started with a couple of huts in Baba Mbengue's backyard has grown into a luxurious holiday oasis in the middle of nowhere. Baba's trademark stone-wall bungalows come with shiny bathrooms, comfy double beds and wardrobes large enough to hide someone. The vast garden space, huge pool and choice of excursions make it a family favourite.

Also recommended:

À la Bonne Auberge (Chez Pierino; ☎ 33 836 0888; s/d CFA12,500/15,000; 🐷) Has three simple rooms with optional air-conditioning (CFA5000) and serves good Senegalese food (order in advance).

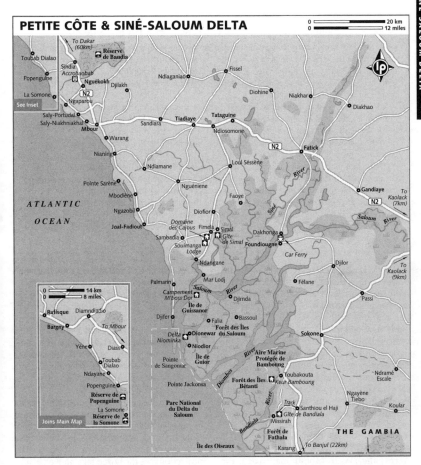

PETITE CÔTE & SINÉ-SALOUM DELTA

Chez Paolo (☎ 77 658 7594; pizzas from CFA4000; ☒ 11am-10pm) Great views from a bare concrete terrace. Pizzas are tasty and opening hours flexible.

Getting There & Away

To get here from Dakar, take any transport headed for Mbour and get off at Diamniadio junction. Minibuses run from here to Toubab Dialao (CFA300). Or go to Rufisque, take a taxi to Yène (near Toubab Dialao) and change there for a taxi to Toubab Dialao. A hire taxi from Dakar should cost around CFA20,000.

RÉSERVE DE BANDIA

This private **wildlife reserve** (☎ 33 958 2024; adult/child CFA10,000/5000; guide CFA3500; ☒ 8am-6pm) sits 65km from Dakar on the road to Mbour,

about 5km east of Sindia. It's well managed and crowded with wildlife, including species indigenous to Senegal, as well as rhinos, giraffes, buffaloes, ostriches and other mammals that have either never inhabited West Africa or have long been extinct here. In that sense it's more of a zoo, but an amazingly beautiful one with not a cage in sight. And because of its compact size, animal sightings are almost guaranteed.

For those more interested in human tradition than beasts, the Serer burial mounds and giant baobab, once used to bury *griots* (West African praise singers), may be an enticement to visit.

Walking around the reserve isn't allowed. You can normally enter with your own car or

---

WOMEN IN ENVIRONMENT: RÉSERVE DE POPENGUINE & TOUBAB DIALAO

While the fishermen of the villages along the Petite Côte struggle to preserve their traditional way of life in the face of dwindling stocks, the women have often been quick to adapt, building on their existing cooperatives to seek out new projects. In Popenguine, a collective of energetic ladies took on the task of looking after the local community reserve, setting an impressive precedent in the region.

To care for the 1000 hectares of protected savannah woodland that make up the Réserve de Popenguine, they set up the small Campement Keur Cupaam, whose revenue is partly invested in the minipark, partly used to support other small enterprises run by the women. You can see both the successful preservation efforts and the local development projects on tours they arrange. Guided birdwatching can also be arranged.

Their small but significant success inspired the female community of neighbouring Toubab Dialao to set up their own project. They obtained an environmental grant to start working on the sustainable management of local resources, and have so far started on reforestation and the protection of Toubab Dialao's lagoon. Seeing that the project also includes training in irrigation, planting, accounting and other skills, the women look set to surprise their men with more projects to come. To find out more or arrange a visit, contact the **groupement des femmes** (☎ 77 564 0180). For Popenguine, see below.

---

hire a 4WD at the entry (CFA40,000). Note, however, that during and shortly after the rainy season access is restricted to 4WDs only and you may have to leave your private vehicle and rent one of the park's 4WDs. Hiring a guide is obligatory.

Even if you don't take a tour around the park, a visit to Bandia's **restaurant** (☎ 33 958 2024; dishes from CFA6000) is highly recommended. It overlooks a pond where you can usually spot buffaloes, crocodiles and plenty of birds. Even if they're too cute too resist, don't feed the monkeys or you risk losing your entire, pricey meal to their greedy paws.

ACCROBAOBAB

Across the Dakar–Mbour main road, the treetop adventure park **Accrobaobab** (☎ 77 637 1428; www.accro-baobab.com; adult/child CFA17,500/12,500) turns adults into kids and kids into passionate climbers. Along an adventure course constructed to European safety norms, you can climb, glide and clamber through the crowns of baobab trees, bounce on a mighty trampoline and do the Tarzan liana leap. The main track is suitable for children from 10 years old; kids from four years old get their own miniature version. Hard to pack more family fun into one day.

POPENGUINE
pop around 1700

This calm village has an ambience all of its own. Perhaps that's due to a mix of ethnici-

ties and religions rarely found in such a small community, or maybe because it's a famous Pentecostal pilgrimage site, ever since an apparition of the Black Madonna was seen here in 1986 (check www.sanctuaire-popenguine .sn for details on the annual event). The central **Église Notre Dame de Délivrance** was completed in 1988 and features contemporary altar paintings, stained-glass windows and a statue of the Black Madonna. Sunday service is held in both French and Serer.

Popenguine lies on the edge of a small **nature reserve** (see the boxed text, opposite), which is home to plenty of bird life and has generated tentative projects in responsible tourism and community involvement in environmental protection (see the boxed text, above).

Sleeping & Eating

Popenguine's most original accommodation options are at the end of the laterite road that leads right through the village.

Campement Keur Cupaam (☎ 33 956 4951; rnpo-penguine@gmail.com; dm/d CFA6000/12,000) Run by a boisterous women's cooperative, this is the starting point for tours around the Réserve de Popenguine. There's a knowledgeable ornithologist on site and the women prepare tasty, home-cooked meals. Staying here is certainly good for the soul – after all, your cash supports a community-based project for environmental protection – but if the rooms were a bit better maintained, doing good would be a whole lot more enticing.

Keur de Sable (☎ 33 957 7164; s/d CFA7500/12,000; houses CFA25,000-60,000) Don't bother with the small rooms with shared bathrooms – the thing to do here is rent a house with quick access to the beach. Phone first to check availability and allow staff to prepare your lodging. The restaurant offers excellent three-course meals (CFA8000), homemade cocktails and musical entertainment on request.

Restaurants are small here and menus limited. **L'Écho-Côtier** (☎ 77 637 8772; meals CFA5000) is a decent beach restaurant located behind Keur de Sable. Further along, **Chez Ginette** (☎ 77 957 7110; ☺ Wed-Mon) is the place to sip a beer as waves lap at your feet, while the manager at **Chez Fatou** (dishes around CFA4000), in the village centre, swears that she prepares real Italian cuisine, and the whole village comes in just to try it.

Getting There & Away

From Dakar, head for Mbour and get off at Sindia, from where infrequent bush taxis run to Popenguine for CFA350.

LA SOMONE & NGAPAROU
pop around 13,000

Some 80km from Dakar, La Somone and Ngaparou form a gentle medium between the mass tourism of Saly-Portudal and the village intimacy of Toubab Dialao. The hotel-lined main road takes you through to the lagoon, great for birdwatching and pirogue tours, though slightly plagued by self-styled tour guides.

The recommended tour operator **Africa Dream** (☎ 33 957 0328; www.baladesafricaines.com; Ngaparou) has its base in a Ngaparou backstreet, though its tours can start anywhere.

Ngaparou's **Africa Lodge** (☎ 33 958 5330; www.africa lodge-senegal.com; Ngaparou; r per person incl breakfast from CFA16,000; P ⚛ ⬜ ⚛ ♿) is a fabulous, family-friendly guest house, designed with plenty of love and taste. Each room is given its very own character, complete with atmospheric lighting and hand-picked fabrics. The studios upstairs are spacious and lead out onto a private terrace. Pick-up from Dakar can be arranged.

Under the easygoing management of party-joker, coffee-importer and dressed-down businessman Formica, **Le Tamarin** (Chez Formica; ☎ 77 570 9674; www.letamarin-somone.com; r incl breakfast CFA17,000; ⚛ ⚛) has turned into the welcoming soul of La Somone. Accommodation comes in the form of simple rooms and miniapartments, and the busy restaurant is a place for news, gossip and good food. Every Saturday there are grill parties with live music at the pool.

For similar prices, the mask-adorned *campement* **Le Bassari** (☎ 77 567 3917; d/tr/q CFA17,000/25,000/34,000; ⬜) offers direct access to the beach, though the *ambiance* and the rooms aren't quite as vibrant.

The **Africa King** (☎ 33 958 5343; africaking@arc.sn; r/villas CFA20,000/75,000; ⚛ ⬜ ⚛) is a smallish set-up with rooms and large villas set in a small garden. It's much quieter and friendlier than the Africa Queen across the road, whose pool and stretch of beach you can access with a reservation at the King.

Le Phénix (☎ 33 957 7517; www.lephenix.net; villas CFA40,000; ⚛) rents villas with two bedrooms and a living room at reasonable rates and, though they're not exactly in sparkling condition, the space and beach location they offer make them a valid option, particularly for families.

BIRDWATCHING TIPS: POPENGUINE & LA SOMONE

Réserve de Popenguine was declared a protected zone in 1986, after the blue rock-thrush was spotted here. Since then, efforts to rehabilitate flora and fauna have shown impressive results and species have multiplied. Campement Keur Cupaam (opposite) works with ornithological guides from the National Parks Authority who can point out the rock-thrush as well as other species, including guinea fowls, cormorants, purple swamphen, glossy starlings and different types of heron. Tours cost CFA2500 per person.

In La Somone, the main birdwatching spot is the Réserve de la Somone, a community-managed reserve that covers a stunning lagoon bordered by mangroves. It was classified a reserve in 2002 following demand from the village. You can book a guided tour at Keur Cupaam or at the park headquarters at the edge of the reserve. A tour combining boat rides and walks is the best way of exploring the reserves. Over 100 species have been recorded here, with flamingos, pelicans, herons and terns being the most prominent.

For food and drinks try **Café Creole** (☎ 33 958 5191; dishes CFA2500-3000), at the junction of the roads to Ngaparou and La Somone, mentioned here despite the wish for no more publicity from the already overworked manager. At the much calmer **Le Vivier** (☎ 77 656 6581; dishes around CFA4000; 🍴), meals are served under thatch roofs between the pool and the beach.

Right on the lagoon, the **Lookea Club Baobab** (oliver.singer@decameronpty.com; www.decameron.com; 🍴 📶 🍴) has snatched up a prime location, but deals almost exclusively with tour groups. Have a meal on its terrace restaurant if you can't stay in one of the stylish bungalows – the setting is worth it.

To get to La Somone or Ngaparou, take a Mbour-bound taxi, then get off at Nguékokh, where taxis leave for La Somone and Ngaparou (CFA350).

SALY
pop around 20,000
Loved by many, despised by some, Saly sits like a hedonistic queen among the villages of the coast. This is Senegal's buzzing centre of beach tourism, home to a multitude of hotels, sandy shores and packed nightclubs. But things haven't always been this way. Until the 1980s, only a few hundred residents went about their agricultural and fishing business here. Just steps away from the tourist bustle, you can still catch small glimpses of the area's former character. Walk along the beach towards Mbour and you'll pass the community of Saly-Niakhniakhal, where intimate hotels and local-style bars allow you to enjoy the luxuries of beach life without the hassle.

Saly-Portudal
Depending on your personal taste, this is either Saly's 'burnt zone', as locals like to put it, or the fun part of town. It's certainly where you'll be headed to withdraw cash from either **BICIS** (☎ 33 957 3331) or **SGBS** (☎ 33 957 37 03) near King Karaoke. There are several internet cafes.

SIGHTS & ACTIVITIES
Everything's about beach life here, but for a sight other than bronzing bodies, check out the giant metal sculptures on the route to La Somone and **Musée d'Art Khomdon** (behind Centre Commercial) with its gigantic, brightly coloured animal shapes.

Fishing & Water Sports
Most fishing clubs offer similar deals at similar rates. The Lamantin Beach Hotel has a highly rated water sports and fishing centre, and the club at Espadon is recommended.

Aqua Passion Plongée (☎ 33 958 5049; www .aquapassion-plongee.com) Offers scuba diving (CFA55,000 per day) for beginners, advanced and children.

Blue Marlin Fishing (☎ 77 442 2025; Plage Centre Commercial) Fishing club and booking point for Dakar–Gorée–Saly boat tours.

Marlin Club (☎ 33 957 2477; marlinclub@arc.sn) Popular fishing club in the heart of Saly's tourist zone. You can taste the fresh catch in the restaurant downstairs.

Senegal Loisirs (☎ 77 638 7626; contact@senegal -loisirs.com, www.senegal-loisirs.com; Plage Saly-Sud) Next to Habana Café, this good address for water sports hires out jet skis (CFA16,000 per 15 minutes), beach buggies, catamarans (CFA16,000 per hour), sailing boats (CFA10,000 per hour) and banana boats.

Beach-Buggy Tours
Love them or hate them, the showy, big-wheeled beach buggies are a staple of the Petite Côte tourist scene. **Sénégal Raids Quads** (☎ 33 957 3710; seneraidquad@orange.sn; opposite Résidences du Port) offers tailor-made tours, aimed at discovering the country rather than breaking speed limits.

Boat Tours
The Liaison Maritime Dakar–Gorée offers Dakar–Gorée–Saly **boat trips** (☎ in Dakar 33 849 7960, in Saly 77 442 2025; one-way/return CFA15,000/20,000). Tickets can be bought at Embarcadère Gorée (see p179) or at the Blue Marlin Club in Saly (see Fishing & Water Sports, above).

Golf
The **Golf de Saly** (☎ 33 957 2488; www.golfsaly.com) golf course is located at the end of town towards La Somone.

SLEEPING
This is a tiny selection of the dozens of hotels Saly offers, not even counting the fenced-in residences that rival local hotels.

La Médina (☎ 33 957 4993; www.ausenegal.com/la -medina-hotel-saly-senegal.html; s/d 15,000/20,000; Saly Village; 🍴 📶 🍴) This Mediterranean-style place has simple rooms on three balcony-adorned floors surrounding a leafy patio. An unexpected oasis of peace in the heart of Saly.

Les Flamboyants (☎ 33 957 0770; www.hotelsenegal flamboyant.com; s/d from CFA24,600/25,000; 🍴 🍴) With its understated decor, offhand service and simple rooms, this is a good backpackers' choice, until you switch focus to the large pool, pretty garden, massage centre and *hammam* (Turkish baths) and you feel as though you've received an upgrade to first class.

Savana Saly (☎ 33 939 5800; www.savana.sn; s/d CFA45,000/55,000; P 🍴 💻 🐾 👯) What the rooms and family apartments lack in style, the hotel makes up for with its vast garden space, enormous pool and forthcoming service. There are plenty of activities on offer and children are not just accepted but utterly welcomed.

Espadon (☎ 33 939 7099; www.espadon-hotel.com; s/d incl breakfast CFA67,000/107,000; 🍴 💻 🐾) For once a place that doesn't just boast four stars but actually deserves them. The double-storey bungalows are bright and classy and have a private, sunny terrace, the restaurant is one of the best in the country, and there's a good wellness centre for relaxation.

Lamantin Beach Hotel (☎ 33 957 0777; www .lelamantin.com; s/d incl breakfast from CFA85,000/130,000; 🍴 💻 🐾) This glitzy establishment calls itself paradise on earth and, if your idea of heaven involves being pampered in a spa or relaxing in a *hammam* or on a private beach, then you'll probably agree with them. Other Saly hotels draw equal in the set-up of the rooms, but few match the quality of service and food here.

EATING & DRINKING

Don't underestimate Saly's hotels: the Lamantin Beach Hotel and Espadon (see above) offer cuisine to outshine (and out-price) most of Saly's restaurants. Self-caterers can find all they need at **Supermarché Plein Sud** (☎ 33 957 3347).

Le Tam Tam (☎ 33 957 8813; Saly main street; ice creams CFA2000) For an afternoon coffee and a trip through the endless possibilities of flavouring homemade ice cream, this arty, green-walled cafe is unbeatable.

Habana Café (☎ 33 957 1730; Plage de Saly-Sud; dishes around CFA5000; 😊 11am-1am Mon-Sat) The skilled chef here shapes dishes from fresh ingredients and friendly waiters serve them to you on the beach-view terrace. That's why Saly locals keep coming back. Afternoon coffee and ice cream here can easily stretch to sundowners.

La Riviéra (☎ 33 957 0724; Place du Carousel; meals from CFA5000; 😊 10am-11pm) A large swimming pool is the centrepiece of this vast restaurant

and around it gather tourists and tourist-chasing youngsters over concerts, cheese fondue and the bikini parades of aspiring Miss Salys. During the day, the games and merry-go-round make it a popular family choice.

Le Sapoti (☎ 77 575 4076; Centre Commercial; meals from CFA5000; 😊 Wed-Mon) This large and friendly place gets busy on Sunday night, when tango and waltz, mussels and white wine turn back time for punters. If you don't remember when Clark Gable died, the Sunday crowd isn't yours, but the food is good here on any day.

Le Soleil (☎ 77 541 2526; opposite Marché Artisanal; dishes CFA5000; 😊 9am-4am) One day the 1st-floor terrace of this boisterous restaurant-cum–live venue will break and bury the stiff attitude of the downstairs piano bar under it. It's so packed with tables that even the aspiring-model waitresses are barely able to squeeze through. Great for party vibes, although the food is unspectacular.

Les Tables du Marlin (☎ 33 957 2477; marlinclub @arc.sn; near Centre Commercial; dishes CFA6000; 😊 10am-7pm) Cute, with wooden floors, this lunchtime venue looks like a living room that opens onto the beach. The seafood platter, heaving under half a lobster, prawn skewers and a selection of grilled fish (CFA16,000) is best washed down with a freshly pressed fruit juice.

Le Patio du Mary Sol (☎ 33 957 0777; 😊 4.30-10pm) Not only the restaurant's pretty decor but also the excellent cuisine has survived several changes of management. The poolside attracts leisurely crowds in the afternoon; the French kitchen draws smart couples for dinner and drinks.

ENTERTAINMENT

Saly turns into a raucous, heaving, noisy beast in the evening. Most night venues are notorious pick-up joints where no one is apparently supposed to leave or be left alone. The thumping bass at **Rolls Club** (☎ 77 631 1578; Centre Commercial) lures in everyone at some point of the night. **King Karaoke & L'Étage** (☎ 33 957 5966; opposite Sonatel), near the roundabout, is a weekend magnet made of snooker, pizza and a crowd jumping to the top-10 favourites.

SHOPPING

The **Marché Artisanal** (main street) is a good place to pick up wooden sculptures, recycled toys and colourful handbags. Across the road, the **Maison d'Afrique** (☎ 33 957 1233; Route de Golf; 😊 9.30am-1pm & 4-7.30pm Mon-Sat) has more unusual items of better quality. For a colourful woven hammock or throw, try the fair-trade boutique **Maam Samba** (☎ 76 590 1527; Saly entry; ⏰ 9am-7pm) near the Sénélec. The most original place by far is the **metal sculptor's workshop** (☎ 77 341 1322) on the route from Saly to La Somone, which is easily recognisable by the giant, rusty baobab sculpture outside. He also does items that fit into a suitcase.

GETTING THERE & AWAY
Saly-Portudal's hotels are 3km off the main road, about 5km north of Mbour. There is no public transport and taxis charge CFA1500 from the main road to the hotels and other facilities at the beachfront.

Saly-Niakhniakhal
Between Saly-Portudal and Mbour, this suburb affords you a much calmer and a touch more integrated holiday. It begins just behind Habana Café and stretches south from there.

SLEEPING
our pick **Ferme de Saly & Les Amazones** (☎ 77 638 4790; farmsaly@yahoo.fr; www.farmsaly.com; half board Ferme/Amazones CFA16,500/30,200) Jean-Paul, a man like a bear, received travellers on his organic farm and horse stable when Saly was still a tiny fishing village of 300 souls. The original backpackers' haunts are still there (and still good), but if you've long pushed your rucksack into a dusty corner, book a room at the beachside farm's jewel, the Résidence les Amazones. It has airy apartments with sea views and possibly Saly's most amazing pool. And with all of this, you get Jean-Paul's stories of the old days, and homemade cuisine.

Auberge Khady (☎ /fax 33 957 2518; auberge_khady@hotmail.com; s/d incl breakfast CFA16,700/25,100; 🖭) The best part of this cute, mosaic-decorated hotel is the airy terrace restaurant, where Friday night is often animated, with live music and dance. Rooms are simple and entirely adequate for the price you pay.

L'Éden du Pescadou (☎ 33 957 5158; www.edendupescadou.com; s/d from CFA18,000/20,000; 🖭🖭) In the kitchen, the chef successfully experiments with the marriage of European and African flavours (dishes around CFA4000). Rooms are bright and spotless. Fishing and tailor-made excursions can be arranged.

Au Petit Jura (☎ 33 957 3767; www.aupetitjura.ch; d CFA23,000; 🅿🖭🖭🖭) This pretty, Swiss-

owned retreat has huts so spotless you can't help but be reminded of the best clichés about Switzerland. It's a hard choice between the central swimming pool and the quiet beach only steps away from your bed.

Auberge Treizeguy (☎ 33 957 0509; www.autreizeguy.com; r incl breakfast CFA26,000; 🖭🖭) This is as far from a hotel as you can get. The lovely couple that runs this intimate place rents out a handful of rooms in the main house. They've got kids and welcome other parents with children. The beach is right outside the front door.

EATING
All of the hotels listed do food; the restaurants at L'Éden du Pescadou and Ferme de Saly are particularly recommended.

Chez Poulo (☎ 77 659 6331; dishes around CFA1000; ⏰ 11am-midnight) No one seems to be able to remember a time before Chez Poulo. This is where you get the best Senegalese food in the area, as well as tasty local juices and rustic European meals.

Escale Jappo (☎ 33 957 2222; ⏰ 7am-11pm) Jappo is a local NGO that helps young people get an education and find employment. Its restaurants are one way of doing that – the young staff are all locals who have been trained under the scheme. With its wood and brick decor, leafy patio and frequent live music, this is one of Saly-Niakhniakhal's best places for a simple meal, snack or relaxed drink.

MBOUR
pop around 150,000
Five kilometres south of Saly, Mbour is the region's most important fishing centre. Cut a path through the main streets thronged with people, traders and horse-drawn carts and head for the main beach. Hundreds of pirogues are launched into the sea from here daily. As they come in, their catch is immediately brought up, gutted and dispatched at the spectacular, if slightly nauseating, 200m-long fish market.

The *gare routière* is near the Dakar end of town, behind a wide gate. Mbour has banks with ATMs, several internet cafes, a post office and a hospital, all along the alley at the heart of town.

Sleeping
Most places offer free wi-fi.
Ndaali (☎ 33 957 4724; www.ndaali.com; zone résidentielle; r CFA15,000; 🖭🖭) Every cent Aziz Samb

earned while working in France's hotel kitchens has gone into the bricks from which he patiently grew one of Mbour's most welcoming small *campements*. Bungalows are attractive and sleep up to four on two floors, and Aziz personally makes sure that your stay is as perfect as the delicious meals he serves.

Hôtel Club Safari (☎ 33 957 1991; www.hotelclub safari.com; s/d incl breakfast CFA16,000/22,000; ✷ ☐ ⛴) This intimate, seashell-adorned hotel has comfy rooms set around a pool and boasts a range of facilities (including a massage centre) and activities that put larger hotels to shame.

Le Paradou (☎ 33 957 4008; www.paradou-senegal .com; s/d incl breakfast CFA21,000/25,000; ✷ ☐ ⛴) This family enterprise near Mbaïla Hôtel extends a very warm welcome, with impeccable rooms, lovely hosts and a homely atmosphere.

Keur Marakiss (☎ 33 954 7454; www.marakiss.com; Mbour Serere-Souf; s/d incl breakfast CFA22,750/26,000 ✷ ☐ ⛴) If you have enough friends, you can rent out this homely thatched-roof cottage entirely. Rooms are attractive – with whitewashed walls and wooden beams – and there's an equipped country kitchen and day trips to see really interesting community projects.

New Blue Africa (☎ 33 957 0993; Route de Niakhniakhal; s/d CFA23,000/28,000) Rooms here are of a standard breed, but the location of this small hotel is unbeatable – it sits right behind a gentle dune on the finest stretch of beach in the area. Young manager Fode is not only a fabulous host but also mixes a mean house cocktail.

Mbaïla Hôtel (☎ 33 957 4300; www.mbailahotel. com; Route de Saly-Niakhniakhal; s/d CFA26,000/35,600; ✷ ☐) This beachside place has a lovely garden adorned with wooden sculptures and crunchy seashell grounds. The all-day breakfast, with a bottomless cup of coffee and local jam, is another convincing reason to stay here.

Tama Lodge (☎ /fax 33 957 0040; www.tamalodge .com; s/d from CFA33,000/46,000) Right on the Plage des Cocotiers, Tama Lodge is more a piece of art than a hotel. The sublime mud bungalows look like the homes of West African kings and are surrounded by amazing wooden sculptures. Try the excellent cuisine during a candlelit dinner on the beach.

Eating & Drinking

The kitchens of Tama Lodge and Ndaali are also recommended.

Chez Paolo (☎ 33 957 1310; dishes from CFA2500; ⛤ 11am-11pm) Anyone in town can show you the way to this favourite local eatery, right on the main road. It may look unpretentious, but the Senegalese food here is divine– the large number of locals is proof of its popularity.

Le Kassoumaye (☎ 33 957 3524; dishes CFA4000; ⛤ 9am-11pm Thu-Tue) This garden restaurant serves generous plates of standard European fare and an impressive range of desserts. The beach location is an added attraction.

Les Jardins Plage (☎ 77 527 8963; Route Saly-Niakhniakhal–Mbour) At the time of research, two enterprising youngsters showed great promise in turning this beachfront venue between Mbaïla Hôtel and New Blue Africa into the area's foremost place for live music. Check it out to see whether they've succeeded.

Getting There & Away

There's frequent public transport between Mbour and Dakar (minibus CFA1000, *sept-place* taxis CFA1300). Mbour–Joal transport is a little less regular (minibus CFA500, *sept-place* taxis CFA600). Hiring a taxi from Mbour to Warang is a time-saving option (CFA1000). Hire taxis cost around CFA15,000 from Dakar to Mbour or Warang, CFA20,000 all the way to Joal.

WARANG
pop around 5000

The almost aristocratic building of **Liqueur de Warang** (☎ 77 524 5416; gambanar@yahoo.com; ⛤ 11am-1pm & 3-7pm) is the first place you come across on entering town. Stop for a break and a very persuasive tasting session of the local fruit liqueurs (CFA8000 per litre) this family enterprise makes.

If you now need a place to stay that doesn't involve driving, you have a choice of two. There are the white, Mediterranean-style bungalows of **Les Manguiers de Warang** (☎ 33 957 5174; www.lesmanguiersdewarang.com; s/d CFA14,500/15,600; ✷ ☐ ⛴), with a rooftop you can sleep on (mosquito net provided). Between batik courses and trips to the massage centre, time passes quickly here.

Warang Hôtel (☎ 33 957 2010; lewarang@orange.sn; s/d incl breakfast CFA20,000/30,000; ✷ ⛴) is slightly more geared towards tour groups and associations. Accommodation is provided in simple, slightly dark huts. It gets an extra star for direct access to the sea and attentive management.

NIANING
pop around 2000

Nianing is quieter and more local in character than Saly, though the wide beach continues its flawless sway down to here.

The small town has its own tour operator, **Afrika Touki Voyages** (☎ 33 957 1420; www.afrikatouki .com), particularly recommended for women who seek the safety net and company of other females on their travels (see p291). Nadine Diop, who runs it, also owns Nianing's classic stay **Le Ben'Tenier** (☎ 33 957 1420; www.lebentenier.org; s/d incl breakfast CFA15,000/23,200; ✖ ☐ ☎). With its spacious bungalows and well-kept gardens, this is not only a welcoming place, it also invests a percentage of its profits into the improvement of local education.

Across the road in the heart of the village, the tiny **Le Girafon** (☎ 33 957 5266; gabykader@hotmail.com; s/d with/without air-con CFA15,000/10,000) had just been taken over by two young locals when we visited. A handful of bungalows and the hammock-dotted garden had already been done up in style. **Nianing Oasis** (☎ 33 957 4256; www.nianing-oasis .com; s/d incl breakfast CFA12,800/21,000; ✖ ☎) is a large, bright place slightly devoid of character.

The most delicious meals are served in the stylish surroundings of **Le Coco Diop** (☎ 77 570 9404; meals around CFA4000; ⌚ 11.30am-3pm & 6.30pm-midnight Tue-Sun; Ⓥ). It does a great range of salads and can do lobster on special order. The liqueur ice creams are divine; staff, utterly welcoming. On the main road, the **Palme d'Or** (☎ 77 321 2615; dishes around CFA3000; ⌚ noon-2pm & 6pm-midnight Wed-Mon) serves simple meals quickly and gets lively in the evenings.

Le Domaine de Nianing (☎ 33 957 1085; www .domainedenianing.com; s/d around CFA50,000/80,000) is a huge resort hotel with a seemingly endless supply of rooms and plenty of activities to choose from.

Getting There & Away

Nianing is on the main road between Mbour and Joal and all public transport stops here. Bush taxis from Mbour to Nianing cost CFA250; hiring a car shouldn't be more than CFA1000. Mbour–Joal, a seat in a public taxi is CFA800 and car hire around CFA8000.

MBODIÈNE
pop around 3000

Halfway between Nianing and Joal, Mbodiène sits right next to a beautiful lagoon, perfect for birdwatching and bathing. The place to

stay is the popular **Plein Soleil** (☎ /fax 33 957 8823; pleinsoleilmbo@orange.fr; d incl breakfast CFA25,200; ✖ ☐ ☎ ⚕), where families are welcome, the beach is within walking distance and oysters can be plucked fresh from the nearby lagoon. Phone first to check availability.

If you prefer your hotel vast and beach activities in plentiful provision, rent a bungalow at the resort-style **Laguna Beach** (☎ 33 957 8802; www.lagunabeach.sn; half board per person CFA34,500/52,000; ✖ ☐ ☎ ⚕).

JOAL-FADIOUT
pop around 38,000

Follow the winding coastal road from Dakar 110km southwards and you'll reach the twin villages Joal and Fadiout. Joal, the place where former president Léopold Sédar Senghor grew up, is on the mainland. Its sister, Fadiout, sits on a century-old island composed entirely of shells, reached via a long wooden bridge from Joal. Everything is shells here – they are embedded in houses and streets, as well as the shared Muslim and Christian cemetery, reached by another bridge crossing.

The citizens of Joal and Fadiout are proud of their religious tolerance: Christians and Muslims live in harmony, and Fadiout's impressive church and shrines to the Virgin Mary rub shoulders with the mosque. Fadiout's maze of narrow alleyways is great for relaxed walks – it gets more tranquil the further you move away from the artisans' market on the main street.

The beauty of Joal is unfortunately hard to detect under all the garbage and plastic bags in the street. It's a great starting point for pirogue excursions; trips to the cemetery, an oyster cultivation centre, and a set of stilt-balanced granaries, modelled on ancient, fire-eaten originals, are all recommended.

To arrange your pirogue tour, head for the Fadiout bridge, where you'll find the small office of the pirogue owners' association. Like a taxi park, they'll tell you which boat goes first and have a price list – no need to negotiate tariffs.

Sleeping & Eating

The tiny *auberge* (hostel) **Le Thiouraye** (☎ 77 515 6064; s/d incl breakfast CFA10,000/12,000; ✖) on the riverside is a great budget option. Rooms are basic, but good value, and the terrace restaurant sits right on the water. The menu (composed by one of Senegal's top chefs) is fantastically varied: try the pork in coconut sauce or the house-style prawn salad. The **Hôtel de la Plage** (☎ 33 957 6677; www.hoteldelaplagejoal .com; Diamaguène; d/tr incl breakfast CFA25,000/28,000; ⓟ ☻) is a fine, no-frills affair with bright, large rooms.

If your budget stretches just an inch further, try **Keur Seynabou** (☎ 33 957 6744; www.keurseynabou. com; r CFA35,000; ☒ ▢ ☻), whose three first-floor rooms are magazine perfect. Every detail has been taken care of, from the atmospheric lighting to the hand-stitched bed covers, homemade lamps and lush garden.

Getting There & Away

A minibus to/from Mbour is CFA700. If you're heading on down the coast, it costs CFA1300 from Joal to Palmarin. A *sept-place* taxi goes directly to Dakar most mornings (without changing at Mbour) for CFA2000.

SINÉ-SALOUM DELTA

The red dust and sudden potholes of the laterite route from Joal to Palmarin have been known to elicit outbursts of verbal violence from even the calmest souls. But just as you start doubting your travelling plans, an area of otherworldly beauty opens up before you. Endless salt and sand plains stretch into the distance, and singular baobabs rise from the glistening lands like watchful giants. This is the gateway to the Siné-Saloum Delta, a 180,000-hectare zone of shimmering flats, small palm groves, mangrove creeks and lagoons where the Saloum River spills artfully into the Atlantic.

PALMARIN
pop around 5000

Some 25km south of Joal, Palmarin sits where the beaches of the Petite Côte merge with the myriad landscapes of the Siné-Saloum Delta. Encompassing four small villages, Palmarin is a breathtaking spot with tall palm groves, salty plains and patches of gleaming water.

Sleeping & Eating

Signposts along the main road indicate the locations of Palmarin's handful of unique *campements*. The area is best explored by pirogue or *charrette* (horse-drawn cart) – all the *campements* organise reasonably priced tours.

Djidjack (☎ 33 949 9619; www.djidjack.com; d/q CFA25,000/35,000, camping CFA2500) The centrepiece of this welcoming *campement* is a massive *case à impluvium* (traditional house) that contains a good restaurant, a varied library and the slightly eccentric company of the Swiss hosts. Accommodation is in large bungalows set in a lovingly maintained garden.

Yokam (☎ 77 567 0113; www.au-senegal.com/pages /yokam; Palmarin Facao; per person incl breakfast CFA8000) Palmarin's cheapest room option has a few lightweight straw huts close to the beach. The place is well maintained and manager François receives you with a five-star smile.

Lodge de Diakhamor (☎ 33 957 1256; www.lesenegal .info; s/d half board CFA23,000/41,000) With its red, mud-walled bungalows, this place looks like a cross between a medieval fort and a Fula village. It's apparently modelled on ancient local architecture and feels like the adventure attraction at an inspired theme park. Pirogue excursions, and horse-riding, bicycle and fishing trips are included in the room rate.

ourpick Lodge des Collines de Niassam (☎ 77 639 0639; www.niassam.com; half board per person CFA52,000; ☒ ☻) Senegal's most original hotel has swish log cabins wedged between the mighty branches of baobabs or seemingly suspended over the shallow waters of the delta. The views are breathtaking and the home-mixed fruity rums tempting.

Royal Lodge (☎ 33 957 6000; www.le-royal-lodge.com; Palmarin; ste incl breakfast CFA103,000-226,000) Palmarin's regal choice has carefully crafted apartments with DVD, satellite TV and private hot tub. The hotel's biggest asset is the lagoon pool, which seems to stretch to the horizon.

Getting There & Away

Palmarin is most easily reached from Mbour via Joal-Fadiout and Sambadia (where you may have to change). The fare from Joal to Sambadia is CFA500 in a Ndiaga Ndiaye, and from Sambadia to Palmarin it's CFA400.

AROUND PALMARIN
M'boss Dor

Campement M'boss Dor (☎ Nov-Jun 77 541 9683, Jul-Oct +33 5 58 77 91 89; www.mboss-dor.com; full board per person CFA53,800) Manager Frédéric is a curious character, skilled ultralight-aircraft pilot and man of quick decision. On a long-distance trip over the Siné-Saloum, he spotted a tiny, uninhabited island and decided that that is where he'd retire, then he informed his wife. Today, the

LE CUISINIER NOMADE

Maybe it's the seclusion of the place and its magical landscapes or maybe there really *is* something in the water – no community in Senegal seems to attract enterprising oddballs and conceptualisers of unusual holiday ideas as reliably as Palmarin. Professional kitesurfer and top-ranking chef Thomas Morin is certainly one of them. Fascinated by the solitary sandbanks surrounding the village, the self-styled nomad chef had the fantastically strange idea of offering luxury picnics among the mangroves and beaches. On exclusive outings, he lures you into a parallel world that feels very glamorous, classy and a bit like the pecs of a young Robert Redford. A gramophone plays old records on the sand, crystal glasses and silver cutlery sparkle under a Mauritanian tent, and plates heave under lobster, prawns and other delicacies, personally prepared by the master chef himself. It's not just a little indulgent and is perfect for a – rather out of the ordinary – Sunday.

Contact **Rêve de Nomade** (☎ 77 727 5717; www.revedenomade.com; luxury lobster lunch per person CFA72,000, enquire for weekend rates) to book.

charming couple have built a tiny neighbourhood of four classy log cabins, in which they receive guests in search of solitude in comfort. The huts are so lovingly decorated that even the bucket shower feels somewhat glamorous. The amazing views across the island are only topped by the bird's-eye perspective you gain from the ultralight-aircraft flights (20 minutes costs CFA25,000). The island is rich in bird life and is also home to jackals, hyenas, servals, and patas monkeys. Suitable for kids from six years onwards.

You need to book in advance. Your hosts can arrange transport from Dakar (from CFA40,000 to CFA50,000) or pick-up from the mosque at Palmarin Ngallou.

Djifer
pop around 2000

Ten kilometres south of Palmarin, the fishing village of Djifer is a litter-strewn calamity and not even the sight of colourful pirogues on the waves and a few swaying palm trees distract sufficiently from the pollution, fish guts and plastic bags at your feet. It is, however, a major jumping-off point for pirogue trips into the Siné-Saloum Delta. You can charter boats for Dionewar (around CFA30,000), Ndangane, Mar Lodj, Îles des Bétanti and other places in the delta. These trips take you along the waterways through the mangroves and are highly recommended for the scenery and bird life you get to see.

Unless you arrive by pirogue here from Ndangane or Foundiougne, you'll either have to spend most of a day waiting for public transport from Palmarin (CFA500) or simply hire a taxi from there (around CFA2000).

Dionewar & Surroundings

Dionewar is on one of the larger islands in the delta, a great base for pirogue excursions through narrow *bolongs* (creeks). A couple of days are enough to take in several of the small islets nearby, including the deserted **Pointe de Sangomar**, great for picnics in solitude. More interesting are the tranquil islands **Guior** and **Guissanor** across the river mouth. The villages **Dionewar** and **Falia**, the oldest settlements on Guior, nestle right in the web of *bolongs*, labyrinthine paths that are best explored aboard a small pirogue.

The plush **Delta Niominka** (☎ 33 948 9935; www.deltaniominka.com; s/d incl breakfast CFA45,000/60,000; 🞬 🞭) offers all of those trips and plenty more. Nestling among the lush greenery of Dionewar, it has stylish accommodation in two-storey bungalows that hide under massive thatch roofs. Run by the very capable management of the Lamantin Beach Hotel in Saly, it offers the same personalised service you get there, though in a more intimate setting.

If you stay at the hotel, pick-up and drop-off can be arranged (one-way costs CFA6000). There's also a crammed public pirogue that leaves Djifer around 3pm every day and returns from Dionewar the morning of the following day (CFA1000 per person).

PARC NATIONAL DU DELTA DU SALOUM

Covering over 76,000 hectares of mangrove-lined creeks, sandy islands, large sea areas and woodland, the **Parc National du Delta du Saloum** (admission CFA2000) is Senegal's second-largest national park. The park's main attraction is the fantastically varied landscape and the hundreds of bird species it attracts. In the gallery forest and savannah woodlands of the Forêt de Fathala in the south, you might also spot wild boars and patas monkeys. You need a bit of luck to view the park's common duikers, bushbucks and red colobus monkeys – they're becoming very rare as human settlements, deforestation and hunting impact on the park despite its protected status.

The northern creeks and wetlands of the park can be explored on pirogue tours from Palmarin, Dionewar or Djifer. The Fôret de Fathala and the southern islands are best reached from Missirah (see p199).

NDANGANE & MAR LODJ
pop around 2500

Next to the small fishing village of Ndangane (pronounced ndan-gan) on the northern side of the Siné-Saloum Delta, a thriving tourist zone has developed along a stretch of coast-bound tarmac. You'll find some good hotels here, as well as internet cafes and souvenir shops, though no bank. It's also haunted by would-be guides and persistent traders. Mar Lodj, the island opposite, is much calmer, and great for swimming and island walks or horse-cart tours. If you're spiritually inclined, try Mar Lodj's Sunday Mass *(messe au tam-tam)*, a Catholic service with local music (Mar Lodj church, 10am Sunday).

Both places are starting points for fishing, birdwatching and pirogue tours through the *bolongs* of the delta and the nearby Île des Oiseaux (Bird Island). In Ndangane the im-pressively organised GIE des Piroguiers (see Getting There & Away, p196) is the place to book and pay for your trips; on Mar Lodj you simply ask your *campement*.

Sleeping & Eating
NDANGANE

Most of the accommodation and eating op-tions are located in close proximity to the ferry jetty.

Le Barracuda (Chez Mbacke; ☎ 33 949 9815; r per person CFA6000) This cheap and very cheerful family-run place has simple, brick-floored rooms promisingly labelled 'Luck' and 'Happiness'. The furniture is a bit rickety; you're better off sitting on the restaurant terrace with its panoramic river views.

Les Anacardiers (☎ 33 949 9804; www.lesanacardiers.net; r per person CFA11,000; ☒ ☐) The nicest rooms in this small hostel are the ones with the tiled floors in the straw-covered huts. Add CFA1000

to the regular room rate for air-conditioning and another CFA2000 for hot water.

Le Cormoran (☎ /fax 33 949 9316; www.lecormoran.net; r per person CFA12,000; ☒ ☒) Rooms are simple in this popular *campement*, but the garden and small pool in the back provide welcome refuge from Ndangane's Rasta hustlers. Check out the ambitiously named souvenir shop, Le Louvre, across the road.

Auberge Bouffe (☎ 33 949 9313; www.aubergebouffe.com; s/d incl breakfast CFA16,000/24,000; ☒) Run by a Swiss-Italian couple who never wanted to grow up, this airy hostel sparkles with bright reds, blues and yellows. Rooms are cute and well maintained and come with hot water. The restaurant serves delicious Italian food made from superfresh ingredients.

Les Cordons Bleus (☎ 33 949 9312; cordons-bleus@orange.sn; www.lescordonsbleus.com; s/d/tr CFA34,000/46,000/58,000; ☒ ☒ ☐ ☒) It's named after the world's leading hospitality school and would probably pass with flying colours. Each room is given a personal touch and the restaurant looks out on a mangrove-framed spot of the river. Unless you're too busy with day trips or minigolf, give the massage centre a try.

Le Pélican du Saloum (☎ 33 949 9320; resapelican@senegal-hotels.com; half board CFA40,000/60,000; ☒ ☐ ☒) This typical resort hotel has activi-ties ranging from minigolf to tennis, and a ter-race for sunset amazement. Kids have of plenty space to run around in the tropical garden.

In addition to the hotels, a handful of small restaurants provide welcome variety. **Le Tamarko** (☎ 77 574 9413; dishes from CFA3000; ☒ 11am-10pm) opposite the jetty has a standard menu but is a lovely place to watch the coming and going of the pirogues. **La Maroise** (☎ 33 949 9320; dishes from CFA3000) serves excellent cof-fee and European food in a welcoming set-ting. For Senegalese food and local gossip, **Le Picbœuf** (☎ 77 638 7601; dishes CFA1500) remains unbeaten.

MAR LODJ

The island has no mains power, though most places have either solar panels or generators. Make your booking before setting off so that you benefit from hotel pick-up.

Le Limboko (☎ 77 429 9908; www.limboko.com; s/d incl breakfast CFA10,000/12,000) This slowly evolv-ing *campement* has a couple of pretty rooms with walls covered in crushed seashells. Thomas, the owner, has plenty of great ideas, including a women's initiative dealing with juice, jam and honey making, oyster picking and fabric dyeing. Check out whether it's off the ground yet.

Le Marsetal (☎ 77 637 2531; half/full board CFA16,000/21,000; 🏊) In the north of the island, this is the *campement* closest to Ndangane (only a CFA2500 pirogue ride away). Kurt, the Austrian owner, is the soul of this place and remains unfazed even if all the large family bungalows are taken up with kids discovering their freedom. Food is clean and healthy (and occasionally Austrian), and the set-up relaxing, with cute bungalows and plenty of hammock-lounging space. Bring your own mosquito net.

Essamaye (☎ 77 555 3667; www.senegalia.com; Marfafako; full board per person CFA17,500) At Xavier's homely place you're greeted like a long-lost member of the family and get to sleep under the roof of a huge, Casamance-style *case à impluvium* decorated with artefacts from southern Senegal. Rooms are simple with shared bathrooms; the restaurant serves home-cooked Senegalese meals and grants fabulous views over the mangroves. Phone Xavier to arrange free transport from Ndangane and maybe even a tour around the country – he's a fabulous guide.

Le Bazouk (☎ 77 633 4894; www.bazoukdusaloum .com; half board per person CFA18,000; 🏊) This family-friendly place has spacious bungalows scattered over a vast, sand-covered garden where bougainvilleas lend shade and palm trees carry hammocks. Kids have plenty to do testing the board-game tables, play areas and clean beach, leaving mum to check out the Toureg jewellery on sale near the restaurant. Electricity is provided by solar panels and the organic garden provides vegetables for the tasty meals. At noon and 5pm every day, there's a free transfer from Ndangane.

La Nouvelle Vague (☎ 77 566 2648; khadynv@gmail .com; r CFA20,000) The long dining tables set out in the garden space indicate quite correctly that this place is a popular lunch address (a three-course meal costs CFA5000). The brightly tiled rooms with their wound Rhun-palm ceilings are comfortable and any problems are swiftly dealt with by Khady, the engaging manager. Transfer from Ndangane is included if you reserve in advance.

Kooniguy (☎ 77 647 3741; kooniguy@gmail.com; half board per person CFA27,500; 🍴🖥) Mar Lodj's most upmarket place is a 10-minute horse-cart ride

from the main beach (direct Ndangane transfer costs CFA20,000). It's beautifully designed, with a good restaurant, though we found the atmosphere rather chilly.

Getting There & Away

Take any *sept-place* between Mbour and Kaolack (CFA1000) and get off at Ndiosomone, from where bush taxis shuttle back and forth to Ndangane. A direct *sept-place* from Dakar to Ndangane costs CFA1800.

To reach Mar Lodj from Ndangane, head for the jetty. On the left-hand side, you'll find the small office of the **GIE des Piroguiers** (☎ 77 213 7497, 77 226 6168), the boat owners' association. It has a list of fixed prices (for both trips to Mar Lodj and excursions in the area) and will point you to the next available boat. If you stick to that, you'll have no hassles and no need to bargain.

FIMELA, DJILOR & SIMAL
pop around 1500

The villages of Fimela, Djilor and Simal lie just north of Ndangane, past the tourist trail, in lush natural settings overlooking the Saloum River. Djilor is the birthplace of the first Senegalese president, Léopold Sédar Senghor, which is why the friendly, riverside *campement* **Domaine des Cajous** (☎ 77 615 7365; tesoufaye@yahoo.fr; Djilor; s/d from CFA15,000/30,000; 🖥) offers the curious attraction of theatre pieces about his life, performed by women from the village.

In Simal the rootsy **Gîte de Simal** (☎ 77 957 1256; www.lesenegal.info; Simal; s/d half board CFA21,000/37,000) is attractively located at a riverside spot in the shade of kapok trees. You stay in traditional-style thatched huts and get to experience the pleasure of an open-air shower. All activities, including *charrette* (horse-drawn cart) tours, and pirogue and angling trips, are included in the rate.

The stunning **Souimanga Lodge** (☎ 77 638 7601; www.souimanga-lodge.com; Fimela; s/d CFA80,000/120,000; 🖥🖳🖴) in Fimela is honeymoon perfect with luxury log cabins, wide glass front windows and a breathtaking setting between tropical gardens and green mangroves. We highly recommend dinner on the wooden terrace at dusk, when the place gets drenched in a magical pink light and resounds with the chatter of herons.

There are fairly frequent *sept-places* from Ndangane to Fimela (CFA400), from where you can hire a taxi to either Gîte de Simal or Souimanga Lodge for about CFA2000 to CFA3000. Bush taxis from Fimela to Ndiosomone cost CFA600.

FOUNDIOUGNE
pop around 5000

Once a French colonial outpost, today's Foundiougne is a slow-moving corner that revolves around the rhythm of the local fishing community. If you visit in September, you'll often get the chance to see Serer wrestling matches, watched by entire villages in the dim light of kerosene lanterns. Once a year, usually in June or July, the Foundiougne festival breathes life into the town with cultural performances and pirogue regattas.

This area has notoriously bad drinking water – stick to bottles.

Sleeping & Eating
Many *campements* have come and gone here. Anne-Marie has seen them all and has always maintained a full house, whatever the competition. Her small riverside hotel, **Le Baobab sur Mer** (Chez Anne-Marie; ☎ 33 948 1262; s/d incl breakfast CFA10,000/17,000), is Foundiougne's sparkling soul – a place for generous meals on the terrace, lively drink-ups, sparkling company and simple accommodation.

In town the small Senegalese eatery **Bingo-Bingo** (☎ 77 565 4400; dishes CFA1500) serves a mean *thiéboudienne* (rice with fish), while the Italian restaurant **La Cloche** (☎ 77 544 4242; meals CFA4000) near the jetty convinces with a clean kitchen and great river views.

Getting There & Away
Foundiougne is reached by ferry (CFA100/1500 per person/car). It leaves the departure jetty at Dakhonga at 8.30am, 10.30am, 12.30pm, 3.30pm and 6.30pm. From Foundiougne departure times are 7.30am, 9.30am, 11.30am, 3pm and 5pm. There's no ferry on Wednesday afternoon.

From Dakar a direct daily bus leaves Patte d'Oie for Dakhonga (CFA3000) at around 1pm – possibly much later. You can also jump on a *sept-place* to Fatick (CFA2500) at Pompier station (they're more frequent than the buses). In Fatick, you change for a bush taxi to Dakhonga. Coming from the south, you reach Foundiougne from Passi, on the pothole-studded tarmac road between Kaolack and Sokone.

SOKONE
On the way from Kaolack to Toubakouta, Sokone barely sees any tourists, which makes it a great place for anyone wanting to catch a glimpse of village life in Senegal. That's what the small *campement* **Fadidi Niombato** (☎ 77 215 6860; www.niombato.com; s/d CFA15,000/20,000) is there for. Run in association with the village, it organises small-scale encounters with families from the community and offers meals made from fresh, locally grown ingredients. You can simply enjoy daily life here (homestays can be organised), or go on excursions to the nearby *bolongs* of the Parc National du Delta du Saloum or the Forêt de Fathala. Ask one of the camp staff to take you to try some fresh or grilled oysters – they're delicious.

BIRDWATCHING TIPS: BIRDWATCHING IN THE SOUTH OF THE SINÉ-SALOUM DELTA

Toubakouta offers enough bird life to have keen spotters stay here for days and return every year. It's mostly an area for sea birds and waders, though the nearby forest areas house some other species, including hornbills and sunbirds.

A good place to start a birdwatching tour is Diorom Boumag, an ancient seashell mound where giant baobabs have taken root, a 20-minute pirogue ride from Toubakouta. In their branches nestle numerous Senegalese parrots and rose-ringed parakeets. It's best to visit this place by pirogue in the late afternoon and move further along the river to arrive around dusk at the Reposoir des Oiseaux, where you can watch swarms of pelicans, cormorants, egrets and plenty of other species prepare noisily for the night.

Île de Bamboung is much less visited and is a perfect place for independent travellers to observe birds in a peaceful environment.

A trip to Île des Oiseaux takes up an entire, thoroughly worthwhile day. Near Îles des Bétanti south of Toubakouta, this small islet houses impressive colonies of Caspian terns, royal terns, herons, grey-headed gulls, slender-billed gulls and flamingos. With a bit of luck, you might even spot a sacred ibis.

For a quick meal, the **Restaurant Cailcedrat** on the main road is a good option.

Gambia-bound *sept-place* taxis from Dakar (CFA7500) and Kaolack pass through town.

TOUBAKOUTA & BAMBOUNG
pop around 9500

Nestled among mazes of mangroves and tropical forest, Toubakouta is a beautiful spot and a great base for excursions to the nearby Forêt de Fathala and the impressive eco-project the Marine Protected Area of Bamboung (see the boxed text, below). Teeming with birds, the area is an ornithologist's dream, and watching flamingos, fish eagles, herons and egrets prepare to roost on the shore at nightfall is fascinating, even if you're not a keen birdwatcher.

Toubakouta has a couple of *télécentres*, a post office, and online access via internet cafes (CFA500 per hour) or wi-fi at Hôtel Keur Saloum. There's no bank.

Sleeping & Eating
Keur Youssou (☎ 33 948 7728; s/d CFA6250/12,500; ✖) For a budget place, this is impressively well run. The Rhun-palm scented and nicely furnished rooms are a bargain and the atmosphere is friendly and relaxed. Youssou can arrange car hire, excursions and fishing trips.

Chez L'Épicier (☎ 77 652 0960; assenghor@hotmail .com; d CFA12,000; ✖ ▢) The small restaurant is a popular meeting place and the adjacent grocery store is fairly well stocked. Rooms at the back are large, but slightly dark and dusty.

Les Coquillages du Niombatto (☎ 77 645 3036; layeloum@hotmail.com; d incl breakfast CFA12,500) It's the friendly management that has people coming back to this Toubakouta classic. The rooms in the red round huts could do with a lick of paint and sweeping of the corners.

Keur Thierry (Brasserie de Toubakouta; ☎ 77 439 8605; d incl breakfast CFA12,500; ✖) The gleaming, open kitchen in the middle of the patio even prepares oddities like traditional French beef bourguignon – best washed down with the cold Belgian beer on offer. Rooms are simple and clean, but you have to bring your own mosquito net. Add CFA2500 for air-conditioning.

ourpick Keur Bamboung (☎ 33 842 4052, 77 510 8013; www.oceanium.org; half/full board CFA17,000/22,000)

MARINE PROTECTED AREA OF BAMBOUNG

The Marine Protected Area of Bamboung (Aire Marine Protégée du Bamboung) near Toubakouta today ranks among the most effective such zones worldwide. Its evolution has been complex, but the initial concept was a simple one: the protected area is primarily managed by the 14 villages located on its periphery and the local communities are also the primary beneficiaries of the project.

The villages finance 24-hour guards and motorised pirogues that patrol the *bolongs* (small creeks), preventing attempts at illegal fishing. The guards are relatively well paid (for local conditions). The money comes from the *eco-campement* Keur Bamboung (see above), created for exactly that purpose on the southern edge of the area. With solar power, a water-filtering system and small vegetable gardens, the humble camp tries to remain as respectfully integrated into its surroundings as possible. Set in a strikingly beautiful area of tidal mangrove lands and woodlands, it's not only good for the soul but a great site to stay at as well. It's a fantastic base for walks or pirogue tours through thick mangrove forests, birdwatching excursions or early morning trips to see wild boars at their drinking pools. At night, the cackle of hyenas accompanies the dreams of visitors; during the day it's the monkeys that have a laugh at the 'intruders'.

The results of this project have been overwhelming: annual tests have shown that some fish species have started recovering here from a point of near extinction. Their proliferation has given such a boost to the ecosystem that the area has become home to rare animals, such as the manatee, and attracts increasing numbers of birds, including Goliath herons, pink-backed pelicans, flamingos and pied kingfishers.

A much needed silver lining in the overwhelming task of helping the marine areas of Senegal recover from overfishing, the project has since inspired similar initiatives elsewhere in the country. The eco-camps of Haer (Marine Protected Area Petit Kassa) and Pointe St George (manatee sanctuary) are still in their early stages, but you can already take fascinating birdwatching and pirogue tours of the area (see p244) – with guaranteed sightings of the rare manatee.

STRAW-HUT CUISINE

'*Boum*' means 'party' in French and it seems an unlikely nickname for the humble old man who stands outside his tiny restaurant, stroking the hand-painted letters that invite visitors into **Chez Boum** (☎ 77 719 0389; Toubakouta village), a rickety straw hut barely big enough to hold four tables. What looks like any other rice bar magically transforms into a star-studded restaurant once you've tasted Boum's saffron-flavoured curry and chicken in balsamic vinegar. 'It can be hard to find the right ingredients', he says, 'but you have to try. A meal can be simple, but it still has to be cooked properly'. His kitchen creativity comes as a delicious surprise in such humble surroundings, and only starts making sense when Boum reveals that he used to work in some of Senegal's finest kitchens, before scraping together the money to set up his own little business. 'I worked in restaurants my whole life. It was time to do something for myself', he smiles, while we savour the best chocolate mousse Senegal has offered so far. 'This is small, but it's mine. And that's the way I prefer it.'

Campements rarely come more remote than this village-run eco-lodge, composed of a handful of terrace-adorned huts on the edge of a mangrove-lined island. Rooms are all equipped with a water tank, solar-powered lights, mosquito netting and the occasional bat flapping its wings underneath the straw roof. Camp profits go towards paying the all-important patrols of the marine reserve. Contact Keur Bamboung before arrival and they'll arrange your pirogue pick-up from Toubakouta and 2km donkey-cart ride to the camp. Transport and all activities (mangrove walks, pirogue trips, canoeing, birdwatching) are included in the price.

Hôtel Keur Saloum (☎ 33 948 7715; www.keursaloum .com; s/d incl breakfast CFA34,200/55,000; P ⊠ ⬛ ⬛ ⬛) The classiest place in town occupies the prime spot facing the river and mangroves. You get the best views from the spacious restaurant terrace and the private balconies in the suites (CFA50,000 per person). The double bungalows in the back of the large garden are great for families with young children.

Domaine les Palétuviers & L'Île des Palétuviers (☎ 33 948 7776; paletuv@orange.sn; s/d half board CFA47,000/63,000; P ⊠ ⬛ ⬛ ⬛) This expansive hotel offers a range of activities and likes to think of itself as a plush holiday haven – but the rooms and atmosphere disappoint. The thing to do is ask at reception for a trip to its *campement*, L'Île des Palétuviers, on the Îles des Bétanti, west of Toubakouta. It's in a lovely spot and has the touch of exclusivity the Domaine lacks.

Getting There & Away

Toubakouta is close to the Gambian border at Karang, 70km south of Kaolack. It's on the main route from Dakar to Banjul, hence it is well served by *sept-place* taxis (CFA7500 from Dakar).

MISSIRAH

Right next to the Fôret de Fathala (see p194), Missirah is a tranquil village, defined by the huge kapok tree in its centre. It's a great starting point for excursions into the forest, best done under the excellent guidance of the couple that runs Missirah's vast **Gîte de Bandiala** (☎ 33 948 7735; www.gite-bandiala.com; half/full board per person CFA16,300/22,600). This reclusive *campement* is completely in step with its natural setting. You're surrounded by greenery and there's a waterhole that attracts monkeys and wild boars – which is especially great if you're staying with children too small for extended hiking tours. You can also take pirogue or fishing trips to the nearby creeks and lagoons (minimum four people) from the *gîte*.

Getting There & Away

From Toubakouta bush taxis take you to Missirah for CFA500, but they're very rare (fewer than one daily) and will still drop you off on the main road, from where it's a 2km hike to the *campement*. There's always someone in town willing to hire their car or motorbike (around CFA6000) for a direct trip. A private taxi from Kaolack costs around CFA40,000.

West-Central Senegal

The route from Dakar to Touba may not exactly be the road to paradise, but it's a journey straight to Senegal's religious and economic core. Past the old railway city of Thiès, an understated urban centre, lie the triplet towns of Diourbel, Mbaké and Touba – the heartland of Senegal's Mouride brotherhood. Apart from the giant mosque of Touba, these towns offer little in conventional sightseeing and seem unspectacular – draped in dust and made of randomly sprawling streets. But don't let this deceive you: their combined spiritual strength and monetary power sweeps the entire country like a powerful wave, influencing every aspect of Senegalese society from culture to politics. Travel here during the Grand Magal, the annual Mouride pilgrimage, and you'll feel the full force of religious devotion, as a staggering two million people descend onto Touba to unite in prayer.

Although central Senegal is home to the country's largest cities outside Dakar, it also spans its most deserted region. The wide Ferlo plains are barely known to anyone but the Fula cattle herders who lead their herds across the parched soils. And in the far west, the strong coastal winds have swept up a veritable desert near Lompoul, where you can feel like Bedouin royalty for a day, seated under a Mauritanian tent or on the swaying back of a dromedary.

HIGHLIGHTS

- See the fruits of religious devotion and raw capitalism working hand in hand in **Touba** (p204), the centre of the Mouride Muslim brotherhood
- Join the most relaxed party at the Palais des Arts in **Thiès** (opposite), the best live stage outside Dakar
- Learn to milk a cow in the nomads' land around **Koba** (p204)
- Sip sweet tea between the windswept dunes of **Lompoul** (p203)

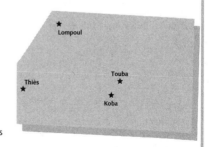

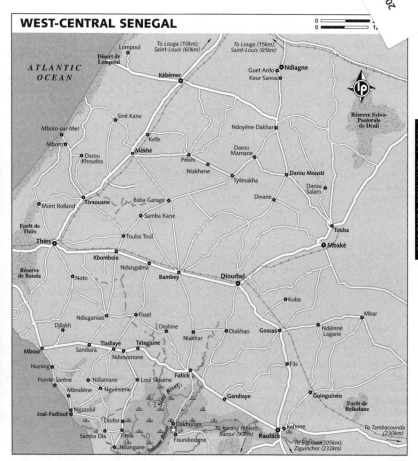

WEST-CENTRAL SENEGAL

THIÈS
pop 500,000

When the French colonial administration laid out their planning for West Africa's railways, they fixed the crossing point of the two major lines (Dakar–Niger and Dakar–Saint-Louis) at Thiès, inadvertently creating a vibrant new urban centre. It's still called the 'railway city' today, though it's devoted less to celebrating the famous tracks than the man who tried to stop their completion – the legendary Lat Dior, who famously troubled the French colonial administration in their expansionist plans (see p29).

Unlike those hectic, dirt-plagued towns where major roads converge, Thiès, the railway junction, is a quiet urban centre. It is neither as rough as Kaolack nor as dusty as Tambacounda, and yet it's more modern than Ziguinchor. In close proximity to Dakar, its tree-lined roads make a great escape from the hectic peninsula.

Orientation & Information

The main artery of town is Av Léopold Senghor, where there are a string of good eateries. It leads north to the train station and another small cluster of restaurants and bars. Recently all the attention seems focussed on the suburbs surrounding the centre – the southwestern corner near the *gare routière* is evolving particularly fast. Thiès is wi-fi central – almost every hotel and restaurant offers the service.

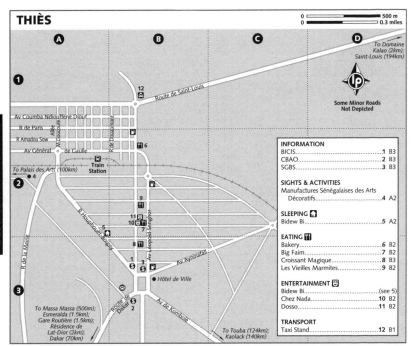

All these banks have withdrawal facilities and standard opening hours:

BICIS (☎ 33 951 8339; Place de France)
CBAO (☎ 33 952 0505; Rue Nationale 2)
SGBS (☎ 33 951 8225; Av Léopold Sédar Senghor)

Sleeping

Apart from Domaine Kalao, all places listed have free wi-fi.

Domaine Kalao (☎ 77 277 8893; Route de Saint-Louis; r CFA12,500) Just out of Thiès, where the bush waves the town goodbye, you'll find this little gem. Greenery hugs its handful of rooms and the kitchen, with its inspired selection of African and European meals, is the envy of Thiès' leading restaurants.

Massa Massa (☎ 33 952 1244; www.massamassa.com; Cité Malick Sy; r with/without air-con CFA26,000/16,000; ⊠ ⌨) New hostels seem to open their doors in Thiès every day, but so far no one has been able to push this pretty guest house off its prime spot. Things are simple, but small touches, like comfortable mattresses and a brilliant restaurant, give it the edge most others lack.

Bidew Bi (☎ 33 952 2717; bidewbi@orange.sn; Av Houphouët-Boigny; s/d CFA25,000/30,000; ⊠ ⌨) Part

of a huge entertainment complex, this is the right address for those out to party. A nightclub, bar and restaurants are part of 'home', yet sleep in the attractive, warmly lit rooms doesn't get too disturbed.

Résidence Lat Dior (☎ 33 952 0777; www.hotel-residencelatdior.com; s/d CFA27,600/35,200; P ⊠ ⌨ ⌨) For a place with a pool and fitness centre, seek out this pink-painted business hotel. It's got a whole book of services; the only thing missing on the list is atmosphere.

Eating

There are several good restaurants in town – again, usually equipped with a free wi-fi connection.

Les Vieilles Marmites (☎ 33 951 4440; dishes around CFA3000; ⊗ 11am-2pm & 6pm-midnight) This is the kind of Senegalese place where mealtime begins when the Maggi sauce and chilli pot are put on the vinyl-covered table. If you don't mind waiting a little for your meal (in good company), this is a brilliant little corner for rice and sauce.

Croissant Magique (☎ 33 951 1878; Av Lamine Guèye; dishes around CFA2000; ⌨) Quiet and centrally located, this friendly Lebanese place is Thiès' top address for excellent pizzas, fast food and the whole gamut of snacks. Chat with the manager or any of the regulars – they'll make you fall in love with this town.

Big Faim (☎ 33 952 0622; Escale; meals CFA1000-5000; ❤ 6am-2am; 🖵) Even if hunger strikes at the most unlikely hours, Big Faim throws you a lifebuoy in the form of chicken and chips, pizza and pasta or coffee and croissants.

Esmeralda (☎ 33 951 0248; Cité Malick Sy; 🖵) Just read the prominent flags at the door: Senegalese, Italian and French food are all on the menu of this classy restaurant near the *gare routière*. Meals are good here and, from the lovers' corridor to the VIP parlour, there's a space for every client.

There's a good bakery for breakfast stuff off Av Général de Gaulle on the route towards the main taxi stand. There are also a number of small shops around town for groceries and other items.

Entertainment

Since Senegalese *mbalax* star Ma Sané, who hails from Thiès, invested her cash in the creation of the magnificent **Palais des Arts** (☎ 33 951 7010; Sounoumakane; ❤ 6pm-3am) the town has had a stage and exhibition space to rival Dakar's best. There's always something happening – try to catch Ma Sane with her band Waflash here on her home turf.

For something more intimate, settle into the low chairs of **Chez Nada** (☎ 33 951 0700; Rue Sans Soleil; ❤ 9pm-2am), a small club with good acoustic shows every Friday and Saturday.

Dosso (☎ 33 951 2640; Rue Sans Soleil; ❤ Tue-Sun; 🗬), the 'grandfather' of Thiès nightlife, and

the glitzy **Bidew Bi** (☎ 33 952 2717; ❤ 7pm-4am) have the best dance floors in town.

Getting There & Away
BUSH TAXI
Sept-place taxis and Ndiaga Ndiayes leave from the *gare routière*, 1.5km from the centre on the southern outskirts. There are frequent *sept-place* taxis to Dakar (CFA1500, one hour, 70km), Kaolack (CFA2300, two hours, 140km) and Saint-Louis (CFA3000, four hours, 196km).

TRAIN
The train station and ticket office are on Av Général de Gaulle. The Bamako (Mali) trains pass through Thiès whenever they happen to arrive here – ask at the station what their astrologers predict in terms of derailments and delays. Thiès–Tambacounda is around CFA10,000 and Thiès–Bamako CFA30,000.

Tickets are hard to get in Thiès because most people travel from Dakar and few get off here, so the train is often full. For more details, see p281.

Getting Around
Any taxi trip around town should cost CFA500. There's a taxi stand in the north of town.

DÉSERT DE LOMPOUL
Near the Grande Côte, where you expect wide beaches rather than dry desert sands, nature has decided to play a little trick. From the coast far into the country's interior, huge dunes stretch as far as you can see, suggesting camel rides and solitary contemplation.

TAPESTRIES OF THIÈS

The crafts centre of the **Manufactures Sénégalaises des Arts Décoratifs** (☎ /fax 33 951 1131; admission CFA1000; ❤ exhibition room 8am-12.30pm & 3-6.30pm Mon-Fri, 8am-12.30pm Sat & Sun), off Rue de la Mairie, was one of many artistic endeavours inspired by President Senghor during the 1960s. Today the factory is run as a cooperative, with designs for the brightly coloured cotton tapestries chosen from paintings submitted by Senegalese artists.

All of the weaving is done on manual looms and two weavers complete about 1 sq metre per month. Only eight tapestries are made of each design. Most find their way around the world as gifts from the government to foreign dignitaries; there's a huge tapestry hanging in Atlanta airport and another in Buckingham Palace. Others are for sale, but, at CFA500,000 per square metre, most of us will be content to admire them in the exhibition room.

The centre is currently experiencing financial troubles and is not always open to visitors. If you find the doors locked, knock anyway; there's usually someone there to take you around the exhibition space.

The two *campements* that have opened here offer all of that and more. Both have accommodation in huge Mauritanian tents, as well as campfires and camel tours through the dunes. **Le Gîte de Lompoul** (☎ 33 957 1256; www .lesenegal.info; s/d half board CFA21,000/37,000) has a simple but attractive set-up. The **Lodge de Lompoul** (☎ 33 869 7900; www.africatravel-group.com; s/d half board CFA50,000/70,000), in contrast, makes you feel like the chief of the Bedouins (or the lead actor in *Out of Africa* – views differ), with tents raised on wooden platforms, artfully scattered earthen and metal wares, and stylish outdoor washing corners. The managing team was preparing the first desert festival when we passed – it's supposed to turn into an annual extravaganza of Sahel music. Keep your ear to the whispering dunes to find out the latest (see also p266).

To get here, contact the relevant travel agency – TPA for the Le Gîte de Lompoul, ATG or Sahel Découverte for the Lodge de Lompoul (see p291 for their contact details).

KOBA

The dry, sparse Ferlo plains, home to Fula nomads and their herds, are about as far off the beaten track – off any track, really – as you can get. At **Campement de Koba** (☎ 33 957 1256; www.lesenegal.info; s/d CFA21,000/37,000) you get to stay nomad style in small, thatched huts, where simple beds are protected by mosquito nets. On the way here, you'll see slow-moving herds of cattle grazing on small herbs, their brown hides almost merging with the dry surroundings. Nightfall under the dim glow of kerosene lamps is fascinating – the huge, starlit skies even more so.

To get here, contact the tour operator TPA (see p292) and join one of its excursions.

DIOURBEL
pop 110,000

The steaming-hot, sand-blown town of Diourbel (jur-bell) is of enormous significance to the Mourides as it was home to Cheikh Amadou Bamba (opposite), the founder of the Mouride Sufi brotherhood, from 1912 until his death in 1927. The colonial government held him here under house arrest and forbade him from entering the holy city of Touba, 48km to the northeast.

The Bamba family still lives in the town, in a palatial compound that is said to have walls 313m long (313 is the number of proph-

ets in the Koran and a mystical number for Muslims). Nearby is the town's main mosque, a 1919 building that's smaller but more aesthetically pleasing than the vast structure at Touba. To arrange a visit, ask for the caretaker and (if you're dressed appropriately) he may take you around. Remember to take your shoes off at the gate. There's a small hostel, but most people tend to stay in Mbaké (see opposite) or come on a day trip from Kaolack, Thiès or Dakar.

Getting There & Away

Frequent *sept-place* taxis go to Dakar (CFA2000, three hours, 146km), Thiès (CFA900, 80 minutes, 76km) and Touba (CFA700, one hour, 50km), and you can get a *car mouride* daily to Thiès, Dakar and Kaolack.

TOUBA & MBAKÉ
pop 500,000

Dubbed the Holy City, Touba is the sacred focus of the Mouride Sufi brotherhood (see p46), the place where their spiritual leader, Cheikh Amadou Bamba, lived and worked. A dazzling network of commercial links and large-scale control over the nation's groundnut (peanut) plantations – not to mention reverential offerings from followers – make the Mouride community Senegal's major economic force, meaning that humility and devotion sit here right on the rawest edge of capitalism. The town is home to the country's biggest mosque, whose minaret dominates the whole area, and the biggest (and blackest) market, a mind-boggling sprawl of official business and even more undercover activity.

The construction of the mosque started in 1936 under Bamba's son, who became caliph (brotherhood leader) upon his father's death. It houses an impressive Koranic library containing the complete works of Cheikh Amadou Bamba and many of his students. Take a close look at the building and you'll notice the architectural signs of various phases of construction, ranging from vast concrete columns to detailed plaster decorations. Since its foundation, the structure has been constantly enlarged, improved and refined, and this process still continues.

And it's not only the mosque that is swelling in size. The whole of Touba is under permanent construction, with new houses, streets and entire neighbourhoods extending the city's sprawl in ever-larger circles. If you

---

BAMBA – A SENEGALESE ICON

Cheikh Amadou Bamba, who founded the Mouride brotherhood in 1887, is without doubt Senegal's most iconic religious figure. His veiled portrait looks down earnestly on the population from thousands of paintings spread across walls, shop signs, cars, stickers and even T-shirts. Born in 1850, he was a relative of the powerful Wolof leader Lat Dior and a member of the wealthy Mbacke clan but initially renounced his noble heritage and chose a path of religious devotion. His preachings attracted an increasingly large following, the most famous disciple being the eccentric Cheikh Ibra Fall, leader of the Baye Fall, an offshoot of the Mouridiya (the local name for the Mouride brotherhood). Both branches emphasise the importance of physical labour as a path to spiritual salvation. This initially fitted in neatly with the French administration's attempts to improve its territory's economic output, but Bamba's anticolonial stance and the colonialists' fear of his growing Islamic power base led them to exile the charismatic leader in 1895. Bamba returned to Senegal in 1907 and, despite his continued anticolonial rhetoric, entered into hushed negotiations with the French.

Long after his death, the influence of Bamba and his teachings keeps growing; the ever-increasing masses of people descending on Touba for the Grand Magal are proof of the immense popularity the Mouridiya enjoys.

---

consider that the entire town literally belongs to the descendants of Cheikh Amadou Bamba, you'll begin to get an inkling of the brotherhood's immense wealth.

If you really want to see the combined forces of faith and fortune at work, join the two million religious followers on the **Grand Magal**, a pilgrimage that takes place 48 days after the Islamic New Year (for details see the boxed text, p47). It celebrates Bamba's return from exile in 1907 after having been banished for 20 years by the French authorities. With the rapidly increasing popularity of Mouridism, the pilgrimage has turned into the biggest event in Senegal. Dakar mysteriously empties on the day, as buses, *sept-place* taxis and Ndiaga Ndiayes all converge on Touba. You'll probably have to squeeze into a car a couple of days beforehand if you try to make the pilgrimage by public transport. This is a mind-boggling event and is certainly unforgettable, but you need to be very comfortable being surrounded by huge, enthused crowds for days.

There are no places to stay in Touba, but during the Magal people open their homes to strangers (though the competition for their mattresses is tough). Most people visit Touba on day trips from Dakar, Kaolack or Thiès. Close to Touba, Mbaké, another town in the 'Mouride circle', has the small *campement* **Le Baol** (☎ 33 976 5505; s/d CFA13,800/15,800; ⚙). It's quite spartan, but adequate, and staff here are great at explaining the deeper aspects of Mouridism to you, as well as taking you to Touba, Diourbel and beyond.

Getting There & Away

To reach Touba from Dakar (2½ hours, 165km) costs CFA3500 in a *sept-place* taxi or CFA1700 by Ndiaga Ndiaye. If you're going to the Mbaké *campement* first, take a *sept-place* taxi and let the driver know (and insist), otherwise he'll take a short cut to Touba and you'll be left stranded. By *car mouride* (bus service financed by the Mouridiya) from Dakar, it's CFA1600.

For the pilgrimage, you're better off making private arrangements. Though there'll be plenty of buses, they will all be full to breaking point. And don't count on transport to take you back to Dakar before the pilgrimage is over – all of Senegal's public transport (with the exception of the odd taxi) is owned and run by the Mouride community – they won't leave their biggest annual event to take you home.

KAOLACK
pop 420,000

'Kaolack isn't a town to live the good life', mumbled a punter at Anouar's outdoor eatery into his glass of Flag beer. That's probably right, if a bit cruel. Senegal's biggest junction town is made of dust, sweaty lines of traffic and a huge garbage problem that piles up on its outer edges. To add to Kaolack's troubles, its water is almost undrinkable due to a dangerously high fluoride content.

But this town with few blessings is also one of Senegal's biggest cities and, as such, has a fascinating urban vibe. At Kaolack's famous covered **market** (one of the biggest in

---

NDEM – STITCHING THE COMMUNITY TOGETHER

The winds that sweep the arid lands around Bambey are hot and unforgiving. Every gust brings the desert a little closer and whispers persuasive words of departure into the ears of the villages' youngsters. Many – too many – accept defeat, leaving their communities to seek a better life in Dakar, that brightly lit beacon on the horizon.

Babacar Mbow, however, did the opposite. This great mystic and guide of the Baye Fall community was living in the 'Eden' so many young people here dream of – France – when he had a spiritual calling. 'I knew that it was time to go home', he says, adjusting his giant turban of dreadlocks. 'God told me to return and so I did, thinking that I would set up a centre of religious learning.' But God's plans were different. When he arrived in his home village, Ndem, there were hardly any people left to pass on his teachings to. He found the community deserted. 'I realised that I needed to do something else – give people a reason to stay.' With ingenuity and perseverance, he and his wife set up Maam Samba – a clothing label with a difference. Reviving techniques of manual weaving and dyeing in the community, they hired villagers to produce brightly coloured clothes, stunning hammocks, bedspreads and a whole range of other items. The beautiful products quickly became sought after and the business started growing. Today Maam Samba employs over 300 people – the number of villagers benefiting from its revenues is far greater still. A school and a health centre have been built and a biofuel project uses the waste from groundnut plantations to heat the brand new bakery, saving the few remaining trees in the vicinity.

In the Bambey region, Ndem is suddenly that radiant light, attracting people rather than seeing them leave. And Babacar, divine predictions being what they are, has become the revered spiritual guide he was destined to be. A hush goes through the crowds when he passes, people avert their eyes as though struck by his radiance and they fall to their knees in respect. It's hard to think of a better example of passing on Baye Fall's teachings of hard work and complete dedication.

You can see and purchase Maam Samba items at outlets in Dakar (see p174), Saly (p190) and Saint-Louis (p218). To arrange visits to the village, you first need to contact **Maam Samba** (☎ 33 973 3040; www.ong-ndem.org).

Africa), you can observe the daily congregation of traders from across the country. Also in the centre, the colourful building of the **Alliance Franco-Sénégalaise** (☎ 33 941 1061; www .kaolack.af-senegal.org; Rue Galliène) hosts excellent concerts and exhibitions by local artists. The Moroccan-style **Grande Mosquée** of the Baye Niass points to another Kaolack advantage – it's a great spot for exploring Senegal's spiritual corner, the central region, from where the nation's brotherhoods spread their faith.

Information

Banks with ATMs include **CBAO** (Rue de la Gare) and **SGBS** (Rue de la Gare). There are several points to go online; the **internet cafe** (Rue Cheikh Tidiane Cherif; per hr CFA150) has a fairly speedy service. There's a **hospital** (☎ 33 941 1029; Av Valdiodio Ndiaye) and several pharmacies.

Sleeping

Kaolack has a number of good lodgings – a definite enticement to stay and glance beyond the town's troubled exterior. All offer free wi-fi.

Djolof Inn (☎ 33 941 9360; Fass; r with/without air-con CFA15,000/11,000; 🔀 🖵) Near the *gare routière* for Dakar, this is a very decent cheapie with clean rooms, a great community of random travellers and a downstairs restaurant that does a tasty omelette for breakfast.

Arc en Ciel (☎ 33 941 1212; Av Valdiodio Ndiaye; s/d CFA18,000/21,000; 🔀 🖵) The patio of this pretty guest house is a real oasis in the city – framed by Moroccan-style walls and specked with greenery. Rooms are impeccable and come with satellite TV and hot water, and you get to use the pool and tennis courts of Le Relais.

Hôtel de Paris (☎ 33 941 1019; Rue de France; s/d CFA24,200/30,700; 🔀 🖵 🐾) This stately turn-of-the-century building is the grandfather of Kaolack's hotels and exudes a classic charm, with wooden furniture, coffee tables and soft lighting. Stay here for a sense of what Kaolack might have felt like a few decades ago.

Le Relais (☎ 33 941 1000; Plage de Kundam; s/d CFA25,000/30,000; 🔀 🖵 🐾) A pool, quality restaurant and even that Kaolack rarity of a great location make this the star among

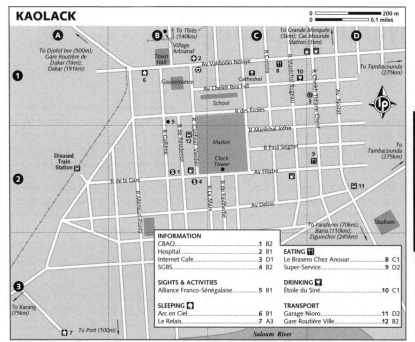

KAOLACK

INFORMATION
CBAO.............................1 B2
Hospital...........................2 B1
Internet Cafe....................3 D1
SGBS..............................4 B2

SIGHTS & ACTIVITIES
Alliance Franco-Sénégalaise.......5 B1

SLEEPING
Arc en Ciel.......................6 B1
Le Relais.........................7 A3

EATING
Le Brasero Chez Anouar...........8 C1
Super-Service....................9 D2

DRINKING
Étoile du Siné...................10 C1

TRANSPORT
Garage Nioro....................11 D2
Gare Routière Ville.............12 B2

WEST-CENTRAL SENEGAL

the local lodgings. It's got all the amenities of a modern business hotel, but a lot more atmosphere.

Eating & Drinking
All listed hotels have good restaurants – the variety and quality reflects the standing of each place. All across town (and especially near the market), you'll find small, local eateries – one will always have your favourite sauce to go with the rice.

Everyone's favourite stopover, though, is the enduring **Le Brasero Chez Anouar** (☎ 33 941 1608; Av Valdiodio Ndiaye; meals about CFA3000; 🕐 7am-11pm) It's laid-back, serves a different *plat du jour* every day and is the kind of place to head to for advice on anything from car repairs to party spots.

The busiest bar in town is the indefatigable **Étoile du Siné** (Av Cheikh Ibra Fall), where cold beers, cheap gin and the company of the whole town (or so it seems) get you through the night.

For self-caterers, there's a **Super-Service** and a few corner shops, a good bakery and, of course, the main market.

Getting There & Away
Sept-place taxis to all northwestern destinations, including Dakar (CFA3000, three hours), leave from Gare Routière de Dakar, on the northwestern side of town. East- and southbound vehicles, eg to Karang on the Gambian border (CFA2500, two hours) and Tambacounda (CFA6000), go from **Garage Nioro** (Sud).

Getting Around
Shared taxis cost CFA600; they also connect to the northern and southern *gares routières* (CFA150). Gare Routière Ville is where they're based.

Otherwise you can hop on the back of a *taxi-mobylette* (scooter taxi; CFA300) or take a horse-drawn *calèche* (cart; CFA750).

Northern Senegal

Northern Senegal's defining feature is the tranquil Senegal River, which marks the border between Senegal and Mauritania before spilling into the Atlantic near the historical island of Saint-Louis. Watered by its flow, the riverine zone is an area in which the Senegalese government places high agricultural hopes. But only a short distance away the soil cracks with dryness and hot desert winds brush harshly through the tops of thin acacia trees.

Many historical movements have swept through this region, each leaving its mark on the local cultures, religion and traditions. Homeland of the Tukulor people, the north was influenced by early Arab traders who brought their wares and religion from the north. The 16th-century Tukulor kingdom (Fouta Toro) was later integrated into El Hajj Omar Tall's vast Islamic empire, which spanned large parts of West Africa. His forces clashed with the French, who set up their first settlement, the historic town of Saint-Louis, here and dotted the shores of the river with majestic forts.

An immediate sense of history pervades this region, just as the grains of sand carried in from the northern Sahara do. From the peaceful old centre of Saint-Louis to the Sudanese-style Omarian mosques on the remote Île à Morphil, you'll often feel as though you're walking in a different time, breathing ancestral air. But perhaps that's only the blistering heat playing tricks on your brain, or the strong, syrupy tea you may have enjoyed with the residents of an earthen-coloured Tukulor village.

The best spot to soak up the region's extraordinary spirit is Podor. Sit on the quay next to the beautifully restored colonial warehouses, the classic fort at your back, the tranquil flow of the river in front, and feel the magic envelop you. The old men near the shore will happily share stories of their past with you.

NORTHERN SENEGAL

HIGHLIGHTS

- Walk to a jazz beat through the colonial old town of **Saint-Louis** (p210)
- Duck under clouds of pelicans at the mighty **Parc National des Oiseaux du Djoudj** (p221)
- Trail historical battles along the **Île à Morphil** (p225), gazing at ancient French forts and stunning Sudanese-style mosques
- Whisper to the river in **Podor** (p224), nudging it to pass on its secrets

Parc National des Oiseaux du Djoudj ★

★ ★ Île à Morphil
Podor

★ Saint-Louis

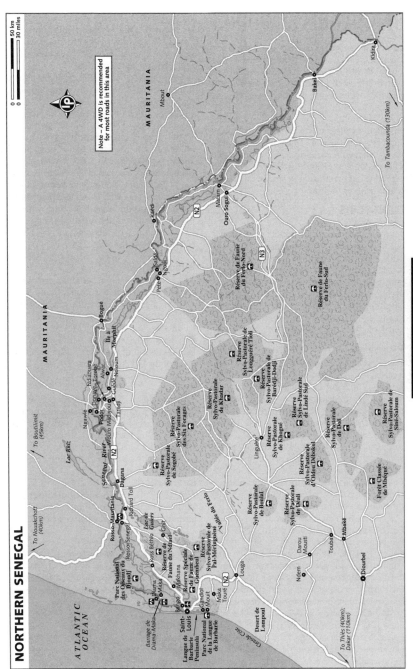

SAINT-LOUIS & AROUND

Sheltered from the ocean by the long sandbank, the Langue de Barbarie, Saint-Louis is one of West Africa's most fascinating towns. The first French settlement in Africa, it expanded beyond its original island setting long ago and tells stories of centuries past with its colonial warehouses and bustling fishing centres. Better still, the town makes a great jumping-off point for trips to the Parc National de la Langue de Barbarie, Parc National des Oiseaux du Djoudj and the Réserve Spéciale de Faune de Guembeul – all within easy reach from the river mouth.

SAINT-LOUIS
pop 155,000

Like a monument to colonial aspirations, Saint-Louis impresses its sense of the past with every step you take along its narrow streets. The madness of European expansionism in Africa, the beauty of its 19th-century architecture and the unique culture born from the difficult encounters between different civilisations – Saint-Louis' historical buildings speak of all of that and more.

History

Founded in 1659 by Louis Caullier on the easily accessible, seemingly inundation-proof Île de N'Dar, Saint-Louis was the first French settlement in Africa. A busy centre for the trade of goods and slaves, it had developed into a large and wealthy town by the 1790s, marked by the cosmopolitan culture of a large *métis* (mixed-race) community (see also p27), which defines Saint-Louis' cultural make-up to this day. The *signares* – women of mixed race who married wealthy European merchants temporarily based in the city – are the most famous example of this.

By 1885, with an established train connection to the growing urban centre of Dakar, Saint-Louis had achieved its bustling height. It already looked a lot like it does today, with its symmetrical road system and the town's characteristic Portuguese and French buildings, with their shady patios, wrought-iron balconies and large gates, made of massive pieces of wood.

With the creation of Afrique Occidentale Française (French West Africa) in 1895, Saint-Louis became the capital of the French colonial empire, spanning today's Senegal, Sudan, Guinea and Côte d'Ivoire. When Dakar became the capital in 1902, Saint-Louis' prestige faded. It remained capital of Senegal and Mauritania until 1958, when all Senegalese administration was moved to Dakar (Nouakchott became the Mauritanian capital in 1960).

Over the years Saint-Louis expanded beyond the confines of the island, covering part of the mainland (Sor) and the Langue de Barbarie Peninsula, where most of the Senegalese inhabitants lived. Though the old town centre wasn't actively preserved, it wasn't hugely modified either, and it was labelled a Unesco World Heritage Site in 2000. Advancing neglect, however, threatened this exclusive status a few years later. The private restoration of some houses, as well as an excellent initiative to support impoverished homeowners to preserve the historical structures, promises not only to maintain the heritage label but also to restore a new shine to the town.

Orientation

The city of Saint-Louis straddles part of the Langue de Barbarie Peninsula, Île de N'Dar and the mainland. From the mainland you reach the island via the 500m-long Pont Faidherbe; Pont Mustapha Malick Gaye links the island to the peninsula, where the thriving fishing community of Guet N'Dar inhabits the areas of the old African quarter.

MAPS

The map *Saint-Louis et la Région du Fleuve Sénégal* (CFA3000), a cross between a cartoon and an aerial photograph, is available at the Syndicat d'Initiative. It's quite outdated but is still useful for the layout of the roads – it shows the city's houses in amazing detail.

Information

The website www.saintlouisdusenegal .com contains links to all major hotels and restaurants and a good events calendar.

CULTURAL CENTRES

Institut Jean Mermoz (Map p211; ☎ 33 938 2626; www.ccfsl.net; Av Jean Mermoz; ☉ 8.30am-12.30pm & 3-6.30pm Tue-Fri, 8.30am-4pm Sat) It has a library and cafe, publishes a regular guide to events in Saint-Louis, and hosts films, concerts and art exhibitions.

EMERGENCY

Saint-Louis Hospital (Map p211; ☎ 33 938 2400; Bd Abdoulaye Mar Diop) Has an accident and emergency department.

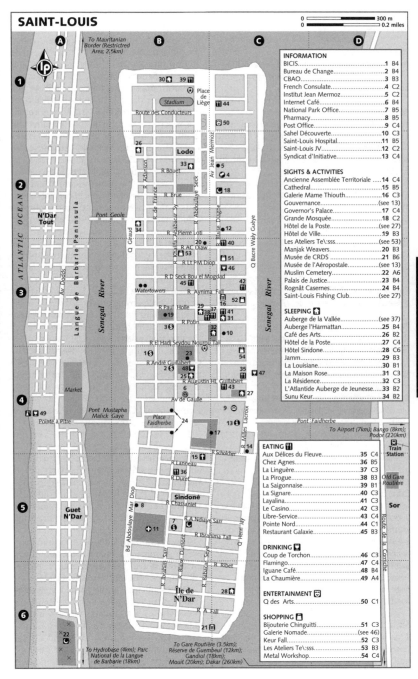

SAINT-LOUIS

INFORMATION	
BICIS	1 B4
Bureau de Change	2 B4
CBAO	3 B3
French Consulate	4 C2
Institut Jean Mermoz	5 C2
Internet Café	6 B4
National Park Office	7 B5
Pharmacy	8 B5
Post Office	9 C4
Sahel Découverte	10 C3
Saint-Louis Hospital	11 B5
Saint-Louis JV	12 C2
Syndicat d'Initiative	13 C4

SIGHTS & ACTIVITIES	
Ancienne Assemblée Territoriale	14 C4
Cathedral	15 B5
Galerie Mame Thiouth	16 C3
Gouvernance	(see 13)
Governor's Palace	17 C4
Grande Mosquée	18 C2
Hôtel de la Poste	(see 27)
Hôtel de Ville	19 B3
Les Ateliers Te\:sss	(see 53)
Manjak Weavers	20 B3
Musée de CRDS	21 B6
Musée de l'Aéropostale	(see 13)
Muslim Cemetery	22 A6
Palais de Justice	23 B4
Rognât Casernes	24 B4
Saint-Louis Fishing Club	(see 27)

SLEEPING	
Auberge de la Vallée	(see 37)
Auberge l'Harmattan	25 B4
Café des Arts	26 B2
Hôtel de la Poste	27 C4
Hôtel Sindone	28 C6
Jamm	29 B3
La Louisiane	30 B1
La Maison Rose	31 C3
La Résidence	32 C3
L'Atlantide Auberge de Jeunesse	33 B2
Sunu Keur	34 B2

EATING	
Aux Délices du Fleuve	35 C4
Chez Agnes	36 B5
La Linguère	37 C3
La Pirogue	38 B3
La Saigonnaise	39 B1
La Signare	40 C3
Layalina	41 C3
Le Casino	42 C3
Libre-Service	43 C4
Pointe Nord	44 C1
Restaurant Galaxie	45 B3

DRINKING	
Coup de Torchon	46 C3
Flamingo	47 C3
Iguane Café	48 B4
La Chaumière	49 A4

ENTERTAINMENT	
Q des Arts	50 C1

SHOPPING	
Bijouterie Chinguitti	51 C3
Galerie Nomade	(see 46)
Keur Fall	52 C3
Les Ateliers Te\:sss	53 B3
Metal Workshop	54 C4

NORTHERN SENEGAL

Pharmacy (Map p211; Bd Abdoulaye Mar Diop) Stays open late; next to the hospital.

INTERNET ACCESS

Internet Cafe (Map p211; Av de Gaulle; per hr CFA500; 8am-11pm) Decent terminals and several phone booths.

MONEY

Both BICIS and CBAO change money and have ATMs that should accept Visa and MasterCard. Reception desks at the larger hotels will also change cash, though they might accept euros only.

BICIS (Map p211; ☎ 33 961 1053; Rue de France; 7.45am-12.15pm & 1.40-3.45pm Mon-Thu, 7.45am-1pm & 2.40-3.45pm Fri)

Bureau de Change (Map p211; ☎ 33 961 8585; Rue Khalifa Ababacar Sy; 7.30am-1pm & 2.30-7.30pm)

CBAO (Map p211; ☎ 33 938 2552; Rue Khalifa Ababacar Sy; 8.15am-5.15pm Mon-Fri)

POST

Post office (Map p211; Av de Gaulle) In the art-deco-style building opposite the Hôtel de la Poste.

TOURIST INFORMATION

National park office (Map p211; ☎ 33 961 8621; bipramp@yahoo.fr; Maison du Combattant, Rue Ibrahima Tall; 8am-1pm & 3-6pm) Dusty, disorganised office that has plenty of information on national parks though seems strangely reluctant to share it.

Syndicat d'Initiative (Map p211; ☎ 33 961 2455; sltourisme@orange.sn; Gouvernance; 9am-noon & 2.30-5pm) This tourist office opposite Pont Faidherbe is a haven of information and publishes an excellent range of booklets, brochures and maps. Multilingual staff can organise activities around town and tours around the entire region.

TRAVEL AGENCIES

Sahel Découverte (Map p211; ☎ 33 961 4263; residenc@orange.sn, www.saheldecouverte.com; Rue Blaise Diagne) This is the mogul of Saint-Louis' travel agencies, with roots in the region as deep as a baobab's. It knows every tree and stone in northern Senegal and offers a range of insightful tours in and around Saint-Louis (see p214).

Saint-Louis JV (Map p211; ☎ 33 961 5152; sljv @orange.sn; Rue Blaise Diagne) The place to purchase, change or confirm tickets. Offers tours on special request. Agents speak French, English and Spanish.

Sights

The metal arches of the low-lying **Pont Faidherbe** (Map p211), are the city's most significant landmark, and you'll cross its clicking

and hole-riddled steel planks when driving into town. Built in 1897, the 507m-long bridge is a masterpiece of 19th-century engineering, particularly noteworthy for its rotating middle section that allowed boats to steam up and down the Senegal River.

Right opposite the bridge, you'll see the **Gouvernance** (Map p211), built on the ruins of an 18th-century colonial fort. A tour around the back rooms of the Syndicat d'Initiative still grants a glimpse of the ancient walls. That's where you'll find the **Musée de l'Aéropostale** (Map p211; ☎ 33 961 2455; admission CFA1000; 9am-1pm & 3-5.30pm), which has displays about the colonial airmail service that played an important historical role in the development of Saint-Louis. This is the place to read up on the life and achievements of famous 20th-century pilot Jean Mermoz, who spent plenty of nights in the **Hôtel de la Poste** (Map p211; ☎ 33 961 1118; www .hotel-poste.com; Av de Gaulle), diagonally opposite the Gouvernance, when delivering airmail from France.

Place Faidherbe (Map p211), with its statue of the French governor who led the colonial expansion eastwards and initiated many ambitious infrastructural projects, is in front of the **governor's palace** (Map p211). It's flanked north and south by the 1837 **Rognât Casernes** (Map p211), as well as by other essentially intact 19th-century houses. This central space is where Saint-Louis splits into its southern part (Sindoné) and northern part (Lodo); the former the old Christian town, the latter the original home to the Muslim population.

In the south next to the governor's palace, you'll find the 1828 **cathedral** (Map p211), with a neoclassical facade. The Maghreb-style building of the **Grande Mosquée** (Map p211; Av Jean Mermoz) in the north was constructed in 1847 on order of the colonial administration to appease the growing Muslim population. The oddity of an attached clock tower betrays the designers' religious affiliation.

The island has plenty of other historical buildings, some in a semiruinous state, others lovingly restored. The walking tour, opposite, takes you past the most beautiful places.

At the southern tip of the island, the **Musée de CRDS** (☎ 33 961 1050; Quai Henri Jay; adult/child CFA500/250; 9am-noon & 3-6pm) contains faded photos of famous Saint-Louis personalities, an informative history section (in French) and several exhibits relating to northern Senegal. The top-floor gallery sometimes houses exhibitions of contemporary art. **Galerie Mame Thiouth** (p211; ☎ 33 961 3611; Rue Blaise Diagne; ☺ 8am-7pm) displays works by local artists and artisans under the arched ceilings of a restored house. **Les Ateliers Tësss** (p217) are a treasure trove of silk threads and woven patterns. Watch the **Manjak weavers** (Map p211) at work, check out samples of their ancient weaving methods, view contemporary prints on display and purchase some craft work if your budget allows.

What mainland Saint-Louis lacks in classic architecture, it compensates for with buzz and vibrancy. Every morning some 200 pirogues are spectacularly launched into the sea from the shores of **Guet N'Dar** (Map p211). And when the first pirogues ride in on the surf, the neighbourhood's roads turn into spontaneous fish markets. Fresh catches are gutted on the sand, dripping parcels loaded onto trucks and the rest dried and smoked by local women.

At the southern end of Guet N'Dar is the **Muslim cemetery** (Map p211), where each fisherman's grave is covered with a fishing net, and the **Hydrobase** (Map p219), from where Jean Mermoz took off on his numerous flights.

Activities

ADVENTURE SPORTS

Saint-Louis Quad (Map p219; ☎ 77 710 8303; www.saint louisquad.com; Bango) organises beach-buggy tours around the dusty, isolated paths of the region. Pick-up from anywhere around Saint-Louis can be arranged.

SWIMMING

On the island of Saint-Louis (Île de N'Dar), the restaurant and live-music venue Flamingo (p217) has a pool next to the bar. The courage to jump into this publicly displayed party boat is rewarded with a great view across the river. Beach-bound travellers should head straight for the Hydrobase on Langue de Barbarie, where you have a choice between bathing in the sea, the river or the pool.

Festivals & Events

The **Saint-Louis International Jazz Festival** (p60), held annually in early May, is an event of international renown that regularly attracts jazz greats from around the world. The main event usually happens at the Quai des Arts (see p217) or on an open-air stage in Place Faidherbe, and there are fringe events all over town.

In October you might witness the **Regatta of Guet N'Dar**, a hugely entertaining pirogue race,

which passes through the river arm between Saint-Louis and Guet N'Dar. The entire population of Guet N'Dar participates – women sing to encourage the pirogues to go faster, salesmen shout to encourage buyers and young fishermen paddle in unison to try to win the race. Ask the Syndicat d'Initiative for dates.

Les Fanals, historic processions with decorated lanterns as big as carnival floats, are a tradition unique to Saint-Louis. They were initiated by the *signares* and have their roots in their lantern-lit marches to midnight Mass. Today Les Fanals, held around Christmas and sometimes during the jazz festival, act to evoke Saint-Louisian history and reaffirm the town's unique identity.

Walking Tour

The chequered pattern of the island's streets is easily covered in a day's walk. Take your time to gaze into some of the patios, adorned with pink bougainvilleas and leafy trees, and count the number of 19th-century buildings that have been restored to a new shine. The old town is Saint-Louis' most famous feature, but the city spills far beyond the island. Your tour around town is really only complete if it's taken you through the bustling streets of Guet N'Dar, where the tide determines the rhythm of the local fishing community.

Saint-Louis' preferred postcard image, the elegant iron construction of **Pont Faidherbe** (**1**; opposite), is the best starting point for a trip around town. Opposite you'll see the majestic building of the **Gouvernance** (**2**; opposite) and, diagonally opposite Pont Faidherbe, the **Hôtel de la Poste** (**3**; p216), whose cosy cafe nods nostalgically to the days of the Aéropostale, the colonial airmail service and its hero Jean Mermoz.

Pass the hotel and turn into Rue Blaise Diagne, where tiny art shops, galleries and restaurants breathe new life into ancient buildings. Around the corner, the mighty warehouses **Maurel** and **Prom (4)** are among the town's most famous facades. Some of the most impressive restoration efforts can be seen in Saint-Louis' hotels. **La Résidence (5**; p216) is owned by one of the town's old *métis* families, whose history speaks out from the carefully assembled collection of memorabilia in the restaurant. Around the corner, **Jamm (6**; p216), with its tall ceilings, is one of the most striking works of restoration.

Along Quai Bacre Waly Guèye a proud line of warehouses such as **Keur Fall (7**; p218)

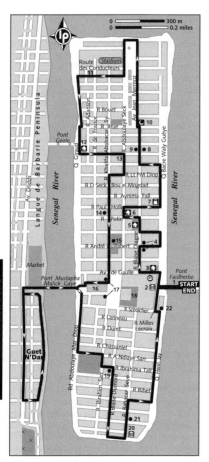

WALK FACTS

Start Pont Faidherbe
Finish Pont Faidherbe
Distance 7km to 9km
Duration One day

looks out onto the river. Enjoy the river stretch for a couple of blocks before heading back inwards to glance at the facade of **Saint-Louis JV (8**; p212). Across the road another **colonial house (9)** was being saved from crumbling to dust when we visited, under a community-benefit restoration scheme (you can find out more about this at the offices of Sahel Découverte).

Continuing northwards the **Grande Mosquée** (**10**; p212) announces the old Muslim quarters and a short walk along the neem-tree-lined Av Jean Mermoz takes you to the island's north-ern point, where you can just about glimpse Île Bop Thior – the island where many of the Saint-Louisian bricks were made.

Past the football stadium, a right turn takes you through a scattering of **army quarters (11**). Walk through to Quai Giraud and take in the sight of pirogues on the opposite shore. The charming guest house **Sunu Keur (12**; p216), completely rebuilt according to the plans of the old, ruined house it replaced, is a good place for a drink or a bite to eat. Take in the woven cloths at **Ateliers Tèsss (13**; p217), before setting off for a promenade along the animated Rue Khalifa Ababacar Sy. Check out the facades of the old **Hôtel de Ville (14)** and the **Palais de Justice (15)**. Then weave your way to **Place Faidherbe (16**; p212), where **Rognât Casernes (17**; p212) and the **Governor's Palace (18**; p212) replace the vibrancy of the local people with military pomp.

The 1856 Pont Mustapha Malick Gaye takes you from the island onto the Langue de Barbarie Peninsula. The scent of history is left behind as you plunge head first into the colourful vitality of the Guet N'Dar. Children play in the sandy streets and dozens of pirogues roll in on the shores.

Crossing the bridge to return to the island, turn south for a tour around the ancient Christian quarter. Opposite the hospital, the **Ancienne Maison des Sœurs de Saint-Joseph-de-Cluny (19)** is waiting for the moment it will be restored.

Walk south down Rue Blaise Dumont, then east around the southern tip of the island and turn left (north) up Rue Babacar Seye. You'll pass the **Musée de CRDS (20**; p212) and the **Lycée Ameth Fall (21)**. Built in 1840 on the site of the old Christian cemetery, the *lycée* has housed a hospital and a college. Today the laughter of school children rings from its leafy courtyard. Walking back towards Pont Faidherbe, don't miss the impressive work done on the **Ancienne Assemblée Territoriale (22)**.

Tours

An organised tour is a great way of explor-ing the northern region. The leading tour operator is Sahel Découverte (p212), which has dozens of exciting trips in its catalogue. Its proudest offering is a cruise aboard the historic ship *Bou El Mogdad* (six-day cruise

---

THE BOU EL MOGDAD – SENEGAL'S CLASSIC CRUISE SHIP

From the 1950s to the 1980s, this pretty little liner used to chug back and forth on the Senegal River, connecting villages and facilitating trade. A whole generation grew up to the rhythm of its tours and disappointment was harsh when the '*Bou El*' left the northern waters during the construction of the Maka Diama dam. Jean-Jacques Bancal, head of Sahel Découverte, never quite stopped missing the sight of it on the river and decided to bring the vessel back home. In November 2005 the boat returned to the river in all its former glory and, for the first time in decades, the classic Pont Faidherbe was creaked open, while onlookers watched with bated breath and sweaty palms, fearing for Saint-Louis' symbolic iron construction.

A trip on this classic ship feels like an adventure straight out of an Agatha Christie novel. The planks creak, the bars are wood panelled, the furniture exudes old-time elegance and the clinking of the ice cubes in your rum glass makes you feel like a spy on a mission. But if any of the guests mysteriously disappear, rest assured – they've probably just hopped off at one of the stops. You can join the journey from Saint-Louis, Podor or any of the other stops along the river. The whole trip lasts a week, but it's possible to join the boat for a day or two if your budget doesn't stretch to cover the full treat.

See www.saheldecouverte.com and www.compagniedufleuve.com for details on the cruise.

CFA325,000, per day CFA73,000) upriver from Saint-Louis to Podor, which affords a stunning 'behind the scenes' view of the river region. See also the boxed text, above.

The Syndicat d'Initiative (p212) also has a range of excellent tours. Its two-day trips tracing the river valley from Saint-Louis over Podor to Bakel take you far off the beaten track (two days including accommodation costs CFA110,000).

Syndicat d'Initiative offers a tour of Saint-Louis (around CFA6000), a trip to Parc National des Oiseaux du Djoudj (around CFA20,000), excursions to Mauritania (around CFA40,000) and more. Prices are per person and include transport and admission fees. There's a minimum of four people per group; independent travellers may be able to join a larger excursion.

FISHING & BOAT TOURS

Several hotels and *campements* offer fishing tours. The following clubs enjoy a good reputation:

Ranch de Bango (Map p219; ☎ 33 961 1981; www .ranchdebango.com) Deep-sea fishing from June to December; angling (sea and river) all year.

Saint-Louis Fishing Club (Map p211; ☎ 33 961 1118; www.hotel-poste.com) Deep-sea fishing from May to October; angling all year round.

Sleeping

Saint-Louis offers accommodation for all budgets, of all types and in many different surroundings. You can stay on the island in

walking distance to all the bars and restaurants and the town's historic architecture or try the beach-lined places on the Langue de Barbarie Peninsula (see page p220).

BUDGET

Café des Arts (Map p211; ☎ 33 961 6078; Quai Giraud; s/d CFA5000/10,000) This quite unglamorous hostel has plenty of beds squeezed between colourful walls. The top-level terrace up the wonky concrete staircase is a nice, though slightly rough, touch (beware of the metal rods angling for a 3rd-floor construction). Not bad if you're on a peanut budget.

Auberge de la Vallée (Map p211; ☎ 33 961 4722; Rue Blaise Diagne; r per person CFA5000) There's really nothing special about this centrally placed cheapie. Staff seem vaguely uninterested in you and their jobs and the 1st-floor rooms are basic with little more than beds and mosquito nets – but that's all fair for the price you pay.

L'Atlantide Auberge de Jeunesse (Map p211; ☎ 33 961 2409; pisdiallo@yahoo.fr; Rue Bouet; s/d CFA5750/11,500) Behind the scrubbed white walls and blue shutters hides a typical youth hostel: cheap, mosquito netted, ventilated, clean, slightly rough around the edges and full of travellers with stories to tell. If Papis, the friendly host, is around, don't miss the chance to drink *ataaya* with him.

La Louisiane (Map p211; ☎ 33 961 4221; www.auberge lalouisiane.com; Pointe Nord; r from CFA14,500; 🐱 🖵) It's hard to tell whether it's the enviable river-view location, the great food or the engaging company of the owner, Marcel, that has travellers

NORTHERN SENEGAL

return regularly to this small hotel. The outdoor veranda is a great addition, shielding you from the chilly river wind while you dig into a fantastic meal with views over the waves.

MIDRANGE

Auberge l'Harmattan (Map p211; ☎ 33 961 8253; mimi-saintlouis@hotmail.com; Rue Abdoulaye Seck; d/tr CFA15,000/20,000; ⬛) With huge rooms packed with trinkets, paintings of topless beauties and odd bits of old furniture, this looks like the illegal sublet of a naughty grandmother. The glamour piece is the glass-paned top floor, packed with heirlooms and a double bedroom directly behind the private bar.

Sunu Keur (Map p211; ☎ 33 961 8800; www.sunu-keur.com; Quai Giraud; s/d from CFA18,000/23,000; ⬛ ⬛) Whatever it was that bit the owners and made them leave France and restore a derelict Saint-Louisian house to its former glory, you should be grateful that they caught that bug. This is a calm, comfortable guest house with excellent food, a homely atmosphere and magnificent views across town from the terrace.

Hôtel Sindoné (Map p211; ☎ 33 961 4245; www.hotelsindone.com; Quai Henri Jay; s/d from CFA30,000/36,000; ⬛) This narrow historical building houses a surprising number of rooms, all decked out in discreet shades and classy fabrics. The hotel is most famous, however, for its riverside restaurant – and for good reason – but doesn't a delicious three-course meal just make the perfect prelude to a romantic night between elegant sheets?

La Résidence (Map p211; ☎ 33 961 1260; www.hoteldelaresidence.com; Rue Blaise Diagne; s/d/ste CFA30,000/36,000/40,000; ⬛ ⬛ ♿) This is one of Saint-Louis' most ancient hotels and the Bancals, the old Saint-Louisian family who own it, have done a great job of evoking history. Every item and picture in the patio-style restaurant has a meaningful link to Saint-Louis' colourful past. Invest in a suite: they've got a lot more space and are quieter. The restaurant is one of the town's very best and there's even a baby-sitting service.

Hôtel de la Poste (Map p211; ☎ 33 961 1118; www.hotel-poste.com; Av de Gaulle; s/d CFA30,000/36,000; ⬛ ⬛) Dating from the 1850s, this historic Saint-Louis hotel was the point of call for the pilots of the colonial airmail service. The famous pilot Jean Mermoz used to stay in room 219. It has recently been renovated and the 2nd floor, with its bare-brick arches, tiled floors, white walls and a gaze onto the hotel's

centrepiece – the leafy patio – has turned out particularly nicely.

ourpick Jamm (Chez Yves Lamour; Map p211; ☎ 77 443 4765; http://jamm-saintlouis.com; Rue Paul Holle; s/d incl breakfast CFA50,000/55,000; ⬛ ⬛) This magical guest house is a strong contender for the most beautifully restored building in Saint-Louis. The tiled and brick-walled rooms have ceilings high enough to impress even regular churchgoers and every tiny decorative detail has been restored with such care that you suspect the owner, Yves Lamour, to be something of a renovation maniac. We're glad to report, however, that he's perfectly nice – and provides great company on the tours he offers around the region.

TOP END

La Maison Rose (Map p211; ☎ 33 938 2222; www.lamaisonrose.net; Rue Blaise Diagne; s/d/ste from CFA53,000/65,000/91,500) Discreetly glamorous like an old-school Hollywood diva, this beautifully restored Saint-Louisian villa has stylish suites personalised with antique furniture and contemporary paintings. The *hammam* (Turkish bath), massage centre and sauna are irresistible.

Eating

Many of Saint-Louis' hotels double as restaurants – the kitchens of Hôtel Sindoné, La Louisiane and La Résidence are rated among the best places to eat in town. They fall into the midrange bracket for price, though they'd certainly deserve a 'top end' for the quality of their meals.

Self-caterers will save money and have more fun shopping in the market just north of Pont Mustapha Malick Gaye in Guet N'Dar. For European goods and French wine, head for the **Libre-Service** (Map p211; Rue Blaise Diagne).

BUDGET

Chez Agnes (Complexe Aldiana; Map p211; ☎ 33 961 4044; Rue Duret; meals around CFA2500) In this pretty, tree-lined patio-restaurant, lovely Agnes serves portions of Senegalese rice and sauce so generous that the word generosity itself ought to be redefined. It's the perfect lunch break on your walk around historical Saint-Louis.

Pointe Nord (Map p211; ☎ 33 961 8716; Av Jean Mermoz; dishes around CFA3000; ⊗ 11am-4pm & 7pm-midnight Mon-Sat) Nowhere else in Saint-Louis but in this laughter-filled greasy spoon do you get half a juicy chicken of such quality for CFA3000 or grilled fish served Ivory Coast style with *athieke* (cassava couscous) and *aloko* (fried plantains).

La Pirogue (Map p211; ☎ 77 376 8104; Rue Potin; meals around CFA3000) This eatery is so small it barely has enough space for its four tables, which heave under the generous portions. Besides freshly grilled fish, there's also a small selection of vegie dishes on the menu.

For a solid local meal on a vinyl-clad table, try the following:

La Linguère (Map p211; ☎ 33 961 3949; Rue Blaise Diagne; meals around CFA2000)

Restaurant Galaxie (Map p211; ☎ 33 961 2468; Rue Abdoulaye Seck; meals CFA2000-4000)

MIDRANGE & TOP END

Aux Délices du Fleuve (Map p211; ☎ 33 961 4251; Quai Bacre Waly Guèye; pastries around CFA500; ☻ 7.30am-1pm & 3pm-midnight) For a relaxed continental breakfast or some afternoon espresso-and-cake indulgence, this patisserie near the river has long been the best address. And if you stay on after your coffee, you may as well enjoy your prenightclub aperitif here, too.

Layalina (Map p211; ☎ 33 961 8102; Rue Blaise Diagne; meals around CFA4000) In the morning hot croissants, cakes and pastries entice you to a lush breakfast in this Moroccan-style restaurant; later in the day, you can stop here for rich kebabs and other fast food, before relaxing into the cushions of the dimly lit tea house for a luxurious dinner.

Le Casino (La Terrasse; Map p211; ☎ 33 961 5398; Quai Bacre Waly Guèye; mains around CFA5000; ☻ Wed-Mon 7pm-midnight) Yes, this is a place to lose money in poker games, but you're better off investing your cash in a meal. It serves the best pizzas in town and also offers gems such as goat's cheese salad with local honey and homemade bread, and artichokes baked in Roquefort.

La Signare (Map p211; ☎ 33 961 1932; www.lasignare .com; Rue Blaise Diagne; mains CFA5000) The management may have changed, but not the list of refined starters (try the hot goat's cheese salad or the squid in garlic butter) and the excellent selection of main courses that made this diner one of Saint-Louis' most popular addresses.

La Saigonnaise (Map p211; ☎ 33 961 6481; Place de Liège; mains CFA6000; ☻ noon-midnight) This restaurant, at the northern end of Rue Abdoulaye Seck, complements its great location on the river with very tasty Vietnamese fare (the owner and the chef are both from Vietnam). The setting is lovely, with a glass verandah that adds to the atmosphere as well as sheltering from the wind.

Drinking & Entertainment

In addition to the following, try Le Papayer on Hydrobase (p220), one of the best nightclubs around.

Coup de Torchon (Map p211; ☎ 77 518 5408; Rue Blaise Diagne; ☻ 11am-3pm & 7pm-1am) It's hard not to make new friends in this cosy bar-restaurant. The bar staff are too friendly and the space too small to push past the fun. Not only do pre-party drinks go down well here, but you also eat well and sometimes get to enjoy live music.

La Chaumière (Map p211; ☎ 77 495 6086; Pointe à Pitre; admission from CFA2000; ☻ from 10pm) Two bars, a VIP space and a dance floor complete with mirror walls, air-con and an old-school disco ball: such are the ingredients that have gone into the making of Saint-Louis' hottest club. Every Wednesday and Friday, you can get down Senegalese style; on Saturday and Sunday, the place is heaving to global beats.

Flamingo (Map p211; ☎ 33 961 1118; htlposte@orange .sn; Quai Bacre Waly Guèye; ☻ 11am-2am) The biggest parties in Saint-Louis happen here, without fail. Every weekend, a live band, often of international stature, plays precariously close to the swimming pool, while the crowd parties before the magnificent backdrop of Pont Faidherbe. For live music, this is the most reliable address.

Quai des Arts (Map p211; ☎ 33 961 5656; Av Jean Mermoz) Saint-Louis' biggest live venue really comes to life during the annual jazz festival (see p60). It's a great place for concerts all around the year, though, and, bizarrely, also houses a gym for those who prefer weight lifting to shaking it.

Iguane Café (Map p211; ☎ 77 633 4956; Rue Abdoulaye Seck) Dressed in fluffy red, this is where the margaritas spill over and the mood improves as people drink to long health and a hilarious night out on the town – and all under Che Guevara's watchful gaze.

Shopping

Les Ateliers Tèsss (Map p211; ☎ 33 961 6860; atelier _tesss@yahoo.fr; Rue Khalifa Ababacar Sy) Passionate designer Maï Diop collects and recreates the beautiful patterns of Manjak weaving. Round the corner you can watch the craftsmen working on the gigantic, patterned cotton rugs – seeing the work involved in making

NORTHERN SENEGAL

the quality fabrics explains the steep prices charged for them.

Bijouterie Chinguitti (Map p211; ☎ 33 961 5059; Rue Blaise Diagne) We've passed this small jewellery shop at impossible hours and the friendly Mauritanian owners were always standing in the door ready to receive customers. This is a great place for silver jewellery (worked before your very eyes).

Keur Fall (Map p211; ☎ 33 961 6238; keurfall@yahoo .fr; Quai Bacre Waly Guèye; ☺ 9am-1pm & 3-7.30pm Mon-Sat) On the nicely brushed-up ground floor of a historical building, Keur Fall sells a colourful range of clothes, shoes and toys – all made by the residents of the community project in the village of Ndem and sold under fair-trade conditions.

Metal Workshop (Map p211; ☎ 77 611 9852; Quai Bacre Waly Guèye) Thiam's workshop smells of grease and swings to the beat of his hammers. This is where he creates unique metal sculptures, including weighty crocodiles made from bicycle chains.

Galerie Nomade (Map p211; ☎ 33 961 9956; www.chez ismael.com; Rue Blaise Diagne) This Saint-Louis–based gallery sells precious beadwork from West Africa's nomad cultures (see also p221).

Getting There & Away
AIR
Saint-Louis has its own airport, 7km out of town, but ever since Air Sénégal stopped its services here from Paris and Dakar, it has been dormant, though there are occasional rumours of charter companies taking over the Paris–Saint-Louis route.

TAXI
The *gare routière* (Map p219) sits on the mainland 4.5km from town, south of the Pont Faidherbe. A private hire taxi from here to the city centre on the island costs CFA500. The fare to or from Dakar is CFA4500 by *sept-place* taxi.

The Saint-Louis–Richard Toll trip by *sept-place* taxi costs CFA2000.

Getting Around
Taxi prices in Saint-Louis are fixed (CFA500 at the time of writing), so there's no need to negotiate for trips around the city. Prices to destinations in the surrounding areas depend on your negotiating skills. You can either hire private taxis at the *gare routière* or stop any driver in town and start bargaining.

AROUND SAINT-LOUIS
Réserve Spéciale de Faune de Guembeul
South of Saint-Louis on the way to Gandiol, the **Réserve Spéciale de Faune de Guembeul** (Map p219; ☎ 33 832 2309, 77 556 3712; admission CFA1000, guide CFA3000; ☺ 7am-6pm) stretches over 720 hectares of saline lagoon, mangrove wetlands and savannah woodland. The area was gazetted in 1983 and is listed as a Ramsar (the international wetland conservation convention) site – a wetland of international importance.

Near the entrance of the reserve there's a small museum that gives a great overview of the flora and fauna of the reserve, its research and protection projects and its history (all displays are in French, with lots of illustrations).

The area is essentially inhabited by wild boars and patas monkeys, as well as less common species such as desert hedgehogs, lesser gerbils, porcupines and African spurred tortoises. An important centre for the protection of endangered animals and reintroduction of species now extinct in Senegal, it's home to a group of dama gazelles and scimitar oryx.

On a morning walk, you are likely to spot a few of the more common animals and, even if you don't, the stroll through the Guembeul flora is enjoyable.

The reserve is also an excellent birdwatching spot. Apart from flamingos and grey and white pelicans, you might spot little egrets, black-tailed godwits and various types of plover, such as the common ringed and grey plovers.

Gandiol & Mouit
pop around 5000
During the wet months, shallow seawater lagoons sparkle on either side of the 18km road from Saint-Louis to Gandiol. From November onwards the waters recede, leaving behind shimmering salt flats (*tann*). Gandiol and its neighbour Mouit lie on the edge of the mainland, facing the palm-tree-specked sandbank that is the Langue de Barbarie. People come here and fall in love with the place, hence the rapid buying up of the lands surrounding the fishing villages.

When you've reached the Gandiol lighthouse, you've almost arrived at the village. This is a spot to remember: pirogues cross from here to the two *campements* on the southern end of the Langue de Barbarie and it is also the starting point for organised boat tours of the national park (see p212).

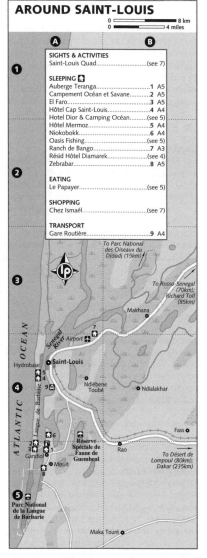

AROUND SAINT-LOUIS

0 |========| 8 km
0 |========| 4 miles

SIGHTS & ACTIVITIES
Saint-Louis Quad............................(see 7)

SLEEPING 🛏
Auberge Teranga...............................1 A5
Campement Océan et Savane...........2 A5
El Faro...3 A5
Hôtel Cap Saint-Louis.......................4 A4
Hotel Dior & Camping Océan.........(see 5)
Hôtel Mermoz...................................5 A4
Niokobokk..6 A4
Oasis Fishing.................................(see 5)
Ranch de Bango................................7 A3
Résid Hôtel Diamarek....................(see 4)
Zebrabar..8 A5

EATING
Le Papayer.....................................(see 5)

SHOPPING
Chez Ismaël....................................(see 7)

TRANSPORT
Gare Routière....................................9 A4

agers, put up the first hut. You can live here simply (as in the cut-off cabin of an old truck) or in spacious, two-floor bungalows, which are as beautiful as they are practical (with Swiss mattresses and double glazing). There's a miniplayground and plenty to explore for younger children. Older kids (and that includes adults) can set out on kayak and canoe tours and birdwatching excursions.

Auberge Teranga (Map p219; ☎ 33 962 5853; www .gandiole-teranga.com; Gandiol; r CFA17,000; 🐾) Once you find yourself in the loving care of the Saint-Louisian family that runs this place, you may just forget that you're not at home here, right between the stunning lagoon and the colourful *car rapide*–turned-bar that serves delicious coconut punch. Every Sunday afternoon you can indulge in massages here – just in case all that relaxing in the flower garden and the home-cooked food have exhausted you too much.

Niokobokk (Chez Isabelle & Didier; Map p219; ☎ 33 962 0562; niokobokk@gmail.com; Gandiol-Mbotou; r from CFA26,000; 🐾 💻 🐾) From across the lagoon, this red, double-storey building looks like an atrocity, but once inside it turns out to be quite a stunning house with magnificent views and pretty rooms. You eat well here, too, and are made to feel utterly welcome by the multilingual owners.

GETTING THERE & AWAY
Hiring a taxi from Saint-Louis to Mouit or Gandiol should cost you around CFA5000. All of the hotel owners can arrange pick-up if you call them from Saint-Louis. If you're driving to Gandiol, turn off the tar road where it swings a sharp right (west) just before Mouit.

La Langue de Barbarie
West of Saint-Louis island (Île de N'Dar), this long, sandy peninsula sits on the waters like the glamorous front yard of the old town. The southern tip is protected as a national park; the area further north houses villages and the hotel cluster of the Hydrobase.

Once a continuous stretch of land, the area is today split in two, ever since an opening was drilled right into the middle of the bank in 2003. A misguided attempt to shelter Saint-Louis from flooding, this was the beginning of a gradual environmental disaster. The force of the sea has pushed the small embouchure open with dramatic speed and force, turning it into a continuously growing breach of several

Around Gandiol there is a handful of places to stay, each a unique set-up.

Zebrabar (Map p219; ☎ 77 638 1862, 33 962 0019; www.zebrabar.net; Mouit; camping per person CFA2500, s CFA4000-20,000, d CFA7000-25,000) This vast *campement* in a secluded spot has been a favourite with overlanders and families ever since Ursula and Martin, the charming Swiss man-

NORTHERN SENEGAL

hundred metres in only five years. Worse, the new course of water also causes the natural gap between the tip of the bank and the mainland near Mouit to close with the drift sand, changing the face of the Langue de Barbarie completely, and with it the Unesco-protected habitat of hundreds of birds.

In terms of natural developments, this is all happening at an incredible speed – though it's still a process of many years for us mere mortals. You'll still find the national park in its full beauty and the *campements* will be here for a long while before ultimately being washed away. And yet if you walk up towards the widening gash after Hydrobase, you can't help ponder both force of nature and foolishness of man.

PARC NATIONAL DE LA LANGUE DE BARBARIE

Some 25km south of Saint-Louis, the **Parc National de la Langue de Barbarie** (Map p219; admission CFA2000; ⏰ 7am-7pm) includes the far southern tip of the Langue de Barbarie Peninsula, the estuary of the Senegal River and a section of the mainland on the other side. The park covers a total area of 2000 hectares and is home to numerous sea birds and waders – notably flamingos, pelicans, cormorants, herons, egrets and ducks. From November to April, bird numbers swell due to the arrival of migrants from Europe.

You can walk along the sandy peninsula, but to explore the whole park and do some birdwatching you'll need to take a pirogue (CFA9000 for one or two people, each extra person CFA2500), which can cruise slowly past the mudflats, inlets and islands where birds feed, roost and nest.

If you come here independently, first go to the park office at Mouit to pay your entrance fee. Pirogues can be hired at Gandiol lighthouse.

Sleeping & Eating

In a paradisiacal spot on the southern half of the Langue de Barbarie, about 20km from Saint-Louis and across the river from Gandiol, you'll find two *campements*.

El Faro (Map p219; ☎ 33 961 1118; r per person CFA15,000) This place had just come under new management at the time of research. Even in its closed state, it had us fall under its charms with its beautiful setting and pretty yellow bungalows with African decor. Contact the Hôtel de la Poste (p212) for the latest information.

Campement Océan et Savane (Map p219; ☎ 77 637 4790; www.oceanetsavane.com; tents per person CFA10,000; bungalows from CFA30,000) At this relaxed *campement,* you can stay in low-roofed Mauritanian tents or choose the comfort of a log cabin right on the river, featuring the attraction of a river-view bath-tub. There's electricity, warm water, and a fabulous restaurant under a huge Mauritanian tent. You can relax in tucked-away corners or try fishing, windsurfing, kayaking and birdwatching.

Getting There & Away

For El Faro, you make reservations and travel arrangements through the Hôtel de la Poste (p216) in Saint-Louis; for Campement Océan et Savane, via La Résidence (p216). Otherwise get a taxi to the Gandiol lighthouse (around CFA3000), then either get on the free pirogue at noon, 4pm and 5pm, or phone Jules (☎ 77 656 4633) to book his boat outside those hours for CFA2500.

HYDROBASE
Sleeping & Eating

Saint-Louis has many faces: some dashing, some rugged. To see the city in all its guises, take a taxi ride from the old town to Hydrobase. You'll leave an island built on nostalgia, then cross the busy fishing village N'Dar, where your taxi will hardly be able to push through carts stacked with fresh catch, cooling vans, eager traders and fish-smoking stalls, before arriving at the secluded sandy beaches of the Hydrobase. This is a great place for anything beach related, as well as walks and pirogue tours along the Langue de Barbarie. It's hard to choose between the hotels here – most of them are fantastically friendly.

Hotel Dior & Camping Océan (Map p219; ☎ 33 961 3118; www.hotel-dior.com; camping CFA3500, s CFA24,100-32,000, d CFA31,200-40,000) Once you're tucked into your sleeping bag under a huge Mauritanian tent and you hear the wind whistling across the dunes, you might forget you're right on the ocean and not in the heart of the desert. If you're an overlander who's just crossed the Sahara, that may be the last thing you want. In that case book a classy bungalow with hot water, wi-fi and minibar, looking out onto a village-style courtyard.

Oasis Fishing (Map p219; ☎ 33 961 4232; oasisnico@arc.sn; s/d CFA15,000/21,000; 🖳 🖳) This simple and welcoming place has small, unpretentious huts decked out in busy African prints that often get booked up with overlanders. If shared toilets are an edge too rough, book one of the bungalows (they house up to three people).

Hôtel Mermoz (Map p219; ☎ 33 961 3668; www .hotelmermoz.com; s/d/tr from CFA15,500/20,950/26,500; P ⊠ ⌨ ⌥ ⌖) The bungalows of this vast hotel are fine – but the real bonus here is the accessories. Huts are spread out across a vast, beautiful garden, there's lots to do (including jet skiing and horse riding), and it boasts the indulgence of a beauty parlour and massage centre. And all of that without feeling like a soulless resort hotel.

Résid Hôtel Diamarek (Map p219; ☎ 33 961 5781; www.hoteldiamarek.com; d from CFA25,000; ⌧ ⌨ ⌥ ⌖) The friendly French couple who own and run this cute hotel have poured a decade of love into its walls. You sense it in every corner, from the well-stocked library (with wi-fi) to the hand-stitched blankets. The double bungalows are family friendly, the pool is large enough for proper exercise and their souvenir shop features such a unique selection of gifts it deserves a special mention.

Hôtel Cap Saint-Louis (Map p219; ☎ 33 961 3939; www.hotelcapsaintlouis.com; s/d CFA28,000/35,000; P ⌧ ⌨ ⌥ ⌖) This family-run place has it all: a fantastic sea-view restaurant, vast sand beaches and one of the best swimming pools around. It's also child friendly all the way down to the kids' menu. Groups or families can rent beautifully private five-bed bungalows.

Le Papayer (Map p219; ☎ 77 566 8382; Carrefour de l'Hydrobase; ⌚ 10am-5am) If you want a change from your hotel food or you're after a great night out, try Le Papayer. Food is fine here, though the menu is pretty uninspired, but the dance floor is one of the best in the Saint-Louis area.

Getting There & Away
A taxi from Saint-Louis to Hydrobase costs CFA1500.

Bango
pop around 2000
Bango is a tiny village north of Saint-Louis, mainly known to travellers for being home to the popular **Ranch de Bango** (Map p219; ☎ 33 961 1981; www.ranchdebango.com; s/d CFA35,00/45,000; ⌧ ⌥), where locally produced sculptures sprout amidst lush greenery and activities include horse riding, fishing and tennis.

Accommodation ranges from comfortably simple to vast and elegant, and bars and restaurants cater to every taste. Check out its enticing trip through the river region.

Once in Bango put in a stop at **Chez Ismaël** (☎ 77 639 0974; www.chezismael.com), near the football field, where honorary nomad Ismaël collects, displays and sells historical beads in the inviting Mauritanian tea tent he put up at the back of his castlelike home. These beads are real treasures and, if they're out of your price range, you're welcome to just look and enjoy, or perhaps purchase something cheaper, like a pretty desert tent.

A hire taxi takes you here in less than half an hour (around CFA7000). Alternatively, phone to see if pick-up from Saint-Louis can be arranged.

Parc National des Oiseaux du Djoudj
On a great bend in the Senegal River, this 160-sq-km **park** (☎ 33 968 8708; admission CFA2000, pirogue CFA3500, car CFA5000; ⌚ 7am-dusk) is 60km north of Saint-Louis. It protects a stretch of the main river with its numerous channels, creeks, lakes, ponds, marshes, reed beds and mud flats, as well as surrounding areas of woodland savannah. This, along with the fact that it's one of the first places with permanent water south of the Sahara, means that migratory birds love it here, making it the third most important bird sanctuary worldwide (see p222). It is protected as a Unesco World Heritage Site, and the wetlands have been listed as a Ramsar site.

Even if you're not a keen ornithologist, it's hard to escape the impact of seeing vast colonies of pelicans and flamingos in such stunning surroundings. Experienced birdwatchers will recognise many of the European species, assembling here in impressive numbers. Around three million birds pass through the park annually, and more than 350 separate species have been recorded.

There are also a few mammals and reptiles in the park, most notably populations of wild boars, mongooses, serpents and crocodiles, as well as jackals, hyenas, monkeys and gazelles.

Trips around the park are usually done by pirogue. It's officially open from 1 November to 30 April, though you might well get access outside that period if you knock on the entrance doors or speak to the Station Biologique. The best time for birdwatching is from December to January.

NORTHERN SENEGAL

BIRDWATCHING TIPS: TOURING THE PARC NATIONAL DES OISEAUX DU DJOUDJ

The Parc National des Oiseaux du Djoudj is a protected and internationally renowned bird sanctuary. Birdwatchers flock to the protected area to observe spur-winged geese, purple herons, egrets, spoonbills, jacanas, cormorants, harriers and a multitude of European migrants that settle here from November to April. The park is most famous for its impressive flocks of pelicans and flamingos and all tours offered by agencies, hotels and guides focus on these birds.

Tours usually leave Saint-Louis at 7am to reach the park by 8.30am. They start with a two-hour boat ride through the creeks, the highlight of which is a view of the enormous pelican colony. After lunch you drive to see flamingo flocks on the lake's edge.

You'll be able to spot other species, no doubt, but if it's the rarer varieties you're after, a tourist trip might not be satisfying. Keen birdwatchers are better off coming with their own guide or explaining their interest to the park director or the team at the Station Biologique (below). They should be able to put you in touch with a trained ornithological guide and will have up-to-date research findings about the park.

SLEEPING

Hôtel du Djoudj (☎ 33 963 8702; www.hotel-djoudj .com; r CFA27,000; ☷ Nov-May; ☲) This grand place sits near the park headquarters and main entrance. Rooms are comfortable and staff could hardly be more helpful. The swimming pool is open to nonguests who eat at the hotel. You can arrange boat rides around the park (adults/children over two CFA3500/2500) and hire bicycles (half-/full day CFA3000/6000).

Station Biologique (☎ Ibrahima Camara 77 524 0105, Ibrahima Diop 77 656 7038; full board per person CFA16,000) Situated at the park headquarters and main entrance, this low-key camp with clean rooms and good vibes is mainly intended for research groups and students, though tourists can be accommodated if spaces are available. Camping is allowed.

GETTING THERE & AWAY

There's no public transport from Saint-Louis to Djoudj, so you have to negotiate a hire taxi (around CFA25,000) or join an organised tour, which might work out cheaper. If you're driving, take the paved highway towards Rosso for about 25km. Near Ross-Béthio you'll see a sign pointing to the park, from where it's another 25km along a dirt road. You can also book a night on the *Bou El Mogdad* (see p215), which puts in a stop here.

SENEGAL RIVER ROUTE

The arid north, where desert winds sweep over the tranquil flow of the Senegal River, is a zone where history comes alive. From Saint-Louis, the urban heart of the French expansion, the route along the river valley is lined with monuments of the French conquest, such as the forts and colonial warehouses of Dagana, Podor, Matam and Bakel. On the Île à Morphil, ancient, Sudanese-style mosques tell of the resistance to colonial occupation and the Islamic expansionism of religious leader El Hajj Omar Tall and his forces. At its height El Hajj Omar Tall's Islamic empire reached across large parts of West Africa, from Timbuktu (Mali) to northern Senegal, where he met with French opposition. Today the 18th-century Omarian mud mosques still seem to oppose the French forts in a silent, architectural battle.

On the cultural trail through the small towns that developed around the forts and their trading centres, you'll also pass small, sand-blown Tukulor villages, where smooth *banco* (mudbrick) huts seem to rise naturally from the soil. Made from dried mud and sand, they blend in as completely with their surroundings as do the dust-covered acacia trees and shrubs. In this otherworldly scene, the dazzling blues of the Tukulor gowns (*boubous*) and the women's shimmering gold earrings, worn even for simple trips to the river, provide a striking contrast.

MAKHANA

Some 18km from Saint-Louis, an easily missed turn-off and a brief drive through the bush takes you quite unexpectedly to a 19th-century pumping station, placed next to a tiny Tukulor village on the river arm Kassak. Although left to rust, the ambitious 1882 construction is an impressive feat of engineering that contains two of Africa's oldest steam engines. Its huge metal wheels furnished the entire region with fresh water until 1952. Since then it hasn't been used, but it remains a remarkable site.

To visit it, you pay a small fee to the adjacent village. In exchange you'll be shown around the plant (and if you want, the village too) on a short, informative tour. You can just turn up, as there's always someone there. If you want to eat in the village though or get the community to organise a concert or dance, you need to set up your visit. Contact Sahel Découverte (p212) to find out how to do that.

A hire taxi from Saint-Louis to Makhana should cost around CFA10,000.

ROSSO-SENEGAL

pop around 10,000

The fly-blown frontier town of Rosso-Senegal is around 100km northeast of Saint-Louis on the Senegal River, where a ferry crosses to Rosso-Mauritania. This is the main connection between the two countries, and the only reason that you'd want to visit Rosso. If you get stuck, there's a small, rather grim hostel.

The journey from Rosso-Senegal to Dakar costs CFA5500 by *sept-place* taxi; to Saint-Louis the fare is CFA2000. A Ndiaga Ndiaye to Richard Toll costs CFA800. For information on crossing the border, see p283.

RICHARD TOLL

pop around 80,000

Before the arrival of the polluting and job-providing sugar company CSS, Richard Toll

was a tiny agricultural community. Today it is inhabited by 80,000 people of the most diverse ethnic mix, has two banks (with ATMs), a garbage-strewn market, three small hotels and a fantastic little dairy (see p80), whose products you must try when there (the best place to purchase its yoghurt and fresh milk is the bakery in the centre of town).

If it weren't clogged with litter or blurred by the sugary clouds of the factory, Richard Toll would be an exciting urban centre, with busy main streets that smell of fresh mint and resound with the happy jingling of colourful horse-drawn carts *(calèches)*. Jump on one to visit the **Folie de Baron Roger** – a crumbling ruin of a once overly ostentatious French castle, built as a statement of glamour by the colonial governor Baron Jacques-François Roger in the 1820s. The red-coloured ruin is surrounded by overgrown plants – the remnants of an experimental garden, in which Jean Michel Claude Richard tested the adaptability of various European plants and, incidentally, lent the town its name.

With its pink walls, greasy tables and boisterous atmosphere, the **Auberge de la Cité** (☎ 33 963 3361; r incl breakfast CFA12,000) is a typical truck drivers' stop. The restaurant, a converted nightclub, serves huge portions of Senegalese food (CFA1000) and sways drunkenly in the evenings. Behind the *auberge* on the river, the **Hôtel la Taouey** (☎ 77 531 4010; r incl breakfast CFA19,000; P ⊠) has large rooms where odd bits of frayed furniture stand around like lost

NORTHERN SENEGAL

OMAR LY – HISTORY THROUGH THE LENS

Right in the heart of Podor's small market, between sheep, tea-brewing kids and corner stores, Omar Ly rolls up the blinds of his tiny photo studio, Thioffy – and opens a small window on Podor's past. All across the front of the studio, yellowing B&W photographs document both moments of daily life and proud studio stances through 30 years of local history. There's a lanky disco chick with a huge Afro, her tiny baby on a chair. A veiled Mauritanian lady proudly clutches her ghetto blaster. And two *griots* (West African praise singers) in huge '70s sunglasses strike a regal pose before a painted baobab.

Omar Ly smiles knowingly and walks over to a large wooden box – his first homemade camera. He built the simple machine to gain an edge over competitors and, once he scraped together enough to buy a portable camera, he assumed the role of Podor's roaming reporter, documenting every minor or major event on B&W film. 'First I walked, then I was able to hire a bicycle, eventually even a motorbike. So things advanced', he says with a grin. Then he hands me a series of small prints from a pile so tall it threatens to tumble. One shows a young woman in fine dress and make-up, challenging the camera with that serious expression the Senegalese like to assume when facing the lens. 'She came in the other day. I showed her the picture and she almost started crying. She had completely forgotten about this. But I haven't. I don't forget a face.' And thanks to his astounding life's work, Podor's people won't be forgotten either.

kids. The restaurant turns into a nightclub every last Saturday of the month.

The clean and bright **Gîte d'Étape** (☎ /fax 33 963 3240; s/d CFA29,400/32,800; 🕮 🖳) on the river is the town's best hotel by far. Its wooden pontoon is perfect for sundowners or an overpriced meal.

Cheaper food options include the two smaller guest houses and a handful of greasy spoons along the main road.

PODOR
pop 15,000

Apart from prayer hours, when the call of muezzins near and far ring across town, Podor is so quiet that every bleating of a goat is an event on the aural landscape. Built in the 1860s, Podor was once the centre of the ancient kingdom of Tekrur on the trade route of Arabs from the north and the Tukulor of Fouta Toro. Today when the flickering heat brushes over Podor's ochre *banco* huts and dust-covered trees, history still seems strangely alive in this camouflaged town.

If you arrive by boat, you get the best glimpse of Podor, famous for its quay with a row of partly restored colonial warehouses (see the boxed text, below). The town's most notable sight is the renovated fort. Built in 1744, it has seen various periods of decay and rebuilding. Its current structure was erected in 1854 by Louis Faidherbe to secure the commerce of French companies along the river. Upstairs you can visit a few 'historical showrooms', while downstairs a good display explains Podor's past (in French) and a brilliant photo exhibition shows photographs by Podor's oldest local photographer, Omar Ly (see the boxed text, p223).

Podor is the gateway for excursions to the historic sites of the Île à Morphil (see opposite) and Wouro Madiyou, home to the unique, mosaic-ornamented brick mausoleum of Cheikh Ahmadou Madiyou (a celebrated contemporary of El Hajj Omar Tall). Only a short drive from Podor, the abandoned site of Donaye village tells a sad story of flooding in an eerily beautiful setting. The small travel association Daande Maayo, based at the Maison Guillaume Foy on the quay, can arrange excellent tours around the region.

Festivals & Events

The Festival des Blues du Fleuve (see p265) is the brainchild of famous singer Baaba Maal and is a fascinating way of listening to the myriad musical cultures of the river region and beyond.

Sleeping & Eating

When we visited, a pretty hotel was being constructed opposite the fort. Check whether it's open when you visit.

Keur Ninon (Gîte d'Étape; ☎ 33 965 1642; s/d incl breakfast CFA6600/13,200) Rooms in this guest house opposite the *gare routière* are only for those who don't fear dust, neglect and the odd cockroach, but you can eat excellent Senegalese meals here (CFA1000, order in advance) and party Podor-style on Saturday.

Catholic Mission (Quai; r CFA7000; 🖳) The mission has a couple of dusty rooms for stranded tourists. Bring a few beers or a good bottle of red wine and the talkative Père Mohiss will bless you with his kindness.

Centre de Formation (☎ 33 965 1222; Quartier Thioffy, Podor; d/tr CFA10,000/15,000; 🕮) This vocational college has a few clean, well-maintained rooms to let. You'll be looked after by hospitality students and can purchase the works of the tie-dye and pottery classes held on site. Ask in town and follow the signposts to get here.

Maison Guillaume Foy (☎ 33 965 1682; Quai; r incl breakfast CFA15,000) Right next to the mission, this is the first quay building to have been magnificently restored. You could watch the

---

PODOR RIVE GAUCHE

Only a few years ago, Podor used to be far off the beaten track, a small northern town only of interest to intrepid travellers and fans of dry Sahel landscapes. Today the place is climbing out of its forgotten corner – and doing so with style. The restoration of the old fort was a first crucial step and the efforts of the association **Podor Rive Gauche** (☎ 33 965 1682; www.podor-rivegauche .com, in French; Maison Guillaume Foy) are building interest in the town in the most beautiful way. The most visible aspect of its work is the renovated waterfront on Podor's historical quay. Other projects include cultural exchanges, the promotion of local creative talent and the publication of historical and artistic materials. Visit the association at the Maison Guillaume Foy to find out more.

ÎLE À MORPHIL

Between the main Senegal River and a major channel that runs parallel to it for over 100km, Île à Morphil is a long, thin island with Podor at its western end. It's a fascinating area with rugged terrain and washed-out dirt tracks, which wind through its dry lands, passing by the beautiful *banco* villages typical of the zone. You can stop at any of them and will be welcome, especially if you pay a quick visit to the *chef de village* (village chief), who can also show you around his fief. Guédé, the ancient capital of Fouta Toro, is found here, with its refined Omarian mosque. The oldest of these Sudanese-style buildings is further east in Alwar, the birthplace of El Hajj Omar Tall. It's amazing to think that the historic leader used to pray in this 18th-century building.

You reach this rarely visited zone about 2km after the Podor bridge. A signpost indicates the turn-off and distances to its string of traditional villages. If you have time (and your own wheels), you can go as far as Saldé at its eastern end, home to some of the Fouta Toro's greatest families. From here, a ferry crosses over to Ngoui on the mainland, from where you can reach Pete on the main road.

---

river forever from your window or the terrace, unless the library and courtyard downstairs or the excellent company of the staff prove too distracting. Book in advance – at the time of writing there were only three rooms.

Getting There & Away

Sept-place taxis travel fairly regularly between Podor and Saint-Louis (CFA4500, four hours, 262km), sometimes continuing all the way to Dakar (CFA9000). Coming from Saint-Louis, you will have to get off at Taredji (CFA4500) and jump on a minibus to Podor from there (CFA500). If you're heading east, a *sept-place* taxi to Ouro Sogui (CFA6000, five hours, 222km) is best. Hiring a taxi from Saint-Louis to Podor costs around CFA50,000.

MATAM & OURO SOGUI
pop 21,000

Lying 230km southeast of Podor, Matam was once a proud administrative centre but over the years has lost in status to its neighbour Ouro Sogui, which is now a trading and transport hub for the Vallée du Ferlo. Apart from the remains of Matam's old warehouses and the beautiful river, there isn't much to see here, though the tranquil village is worth taking in and intrepid travellers can explore the hinterland.

Ouro Sogui is the kind of place you need to fill the tank, get cash from the ATM (if

it's working) and maybe spend a night. The town's two hotels face one another. **Oasis du Fouta** (☎ 33 966 1294; s/d incl breakfast CFA15,000/17,000; ☒) has decent rooms around a small courtyard and a lively bar. **Hôtel Sôgui** (☎ 33 966 1536; s/d CFA18,500/23,000; ☒) is the larger hotel, with similar rooms but less atmosphere.

Battered *sept-place* taxis run to Dakar (CFA10,500, 10 hours, 690km) and Bakel (CFA2000, two hours, 148km).

BAKEL

A backdrop of gentle hills and the fascinating, crumpled earth mounds of the Falémé tributary lend Bakel a unique charm. The **fort**, built in 1854 under Faidherbe, is nowadays the seat of the *gouvernance* (governor's office) but can usually still be visited. There's not much left of the **Pavilion René Caillé**, once temporary home to the famous French voyager, and it's inhabited by a local family. Still, climb onto the hill and enjoy the view onto Bakel town.

To spend the night, head towards Kidira and stay at Étoile de Boundou (see p234).

If you come from Kidira on a vehicle bound for Ouro Sogui, you might be dropped off at the junction 5km south of Bakel, from where local bush taxis shuttle into town. Normally there's a once-daily connection to Tambacounda (CFA4000, four hours, 184km) via Kidira (CFA1700, one hour, 60km).

Eastern Senegal

For years Senegal's best-kept secret, the mountainous Bassari lands, with their steep waterfalls and green hillsides, used to be reached only be those determined enough to brave over 400km of broken tarmac. Now that work on Senegal's main artery is visibly advancing, the country's remotest parts have become more attractive than ever. Yet should the trip still be a trying quest when you visit, the rewards of your efforts will be as sweet as finely perfumed Kédougou honey.

Named after the largest ethnic group in the area, Bassari country is the only mountainous region of Senegal and fabulous for extended hikes. On a walk over craggy mountain paths, past steep waterfalls and through thick forests, the distinctive landscape will impress itself on you, as will the unique cultural make-up of this region. The Bassari and Bédik people who live here continue to follow their traditional ways of life. Their tiny villages, beautiful hamlets of stone and mud huts, are often arranged around an enormous, shade-giving kapok tree. Fetishes tied to its trunk tell of the animist faith most people adhere to.

Before reaching Bassari country, the Tambacounda–Kédougou road passes through Niokolo-Koba, Senegal's largest national park. On an early-morning journey you just might see a lion lazing at the roadside or slow the car to allow huge troupes of baboons to cross. Better still is a leisurely boat tour along the bends of the Gambia River – a sure chance to see hippos and crocodiles basking on the banks.

HIGHLIGHTS

- Watch warthogs chill in termite mounds and dream of lions at **Parc National de Niokolo-Koba** (p230), Senegal's largest protected reserve
- Cool off under the deep drop of the waterfall at **Dindefelo** (p233)
- Go for solitary hikes around the hills of **Bassari country** (p231) and visit tiny, half-hidden Bédik villages

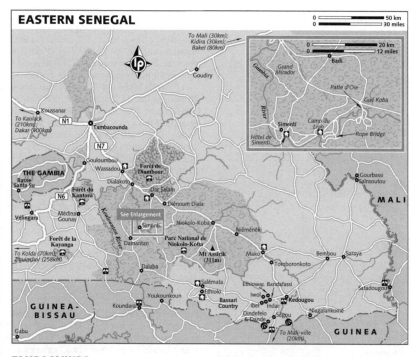

TAMBACOUNDA

pop 300,000

Tamba, as the locals affectionately call it, is a rough lover, made of dust, sand and sizzling temperatures. This is Senegal's eastern junction town, and artfully loaded trucks line every street, sweating in the heat before heading off to their next destination. Tamba is a tough gateway to the stunning Bassari lands, but it reveals its charming soul on an early-evening stroll. That's when the traffic fumes subside, the dust settles, and the roadsides turn into improvised cinemas, as people carry their TV sets into the street to watch the latest series together.

Information

INTERNET ACCESS

The Oasis Oriental Club and Relais hotels have wi-fi access. Ask if you can get online with purchase of a meal or drink.

Cyber Misat (☎ 33 981 5444; Av Léopold Senghor; per hr CFA250; ☯ 8am-9pm) One of several central internet cafes.

MEDICAL SERVICES

Hôpital Régional (☎ 33 981 1218) The regional hospital, but still not a place you want to be treated in.

Pharmacie Orientale (☎ 33 981 2519) Next to Hôtel Niji.

Pharmacie Thiaala (☎ 33 981 1323; Av Léopold Senghor)

MONEY

The ATMs at both banks are slightly unreliable. You can also change money at both banks.

CBAO (☎ 33 939 8900; Bd Demba Diop)

SGBS (☎ 33 981 1530; Av Léopold Senghor) ATM not accessible outside bank opening hours.

TOURIST INFORMATION & TRAVEL AGENCIES

Agence de Voyage (☎ 33 981 0084; Quartier Abattoir) Can sort out tours and car hire.

National park office (☎ 33 981 1097; ☯ 7.30am-5pm) Can help with enquiries about the park and point you in the direction of drivers hiring 4WDs.

Syndicat d'Initiative (☎ 33 981 1250; nijihotel@orange.sn; Hôtel Niji) General tourist information is provided by the desk next to the hotel's reception.

Sleeping

Everyone, and that obviously includes hotels, runs tours to the Parc National de Niokolo-

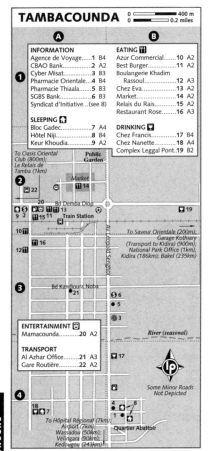

TAMBACOUNDA

0 ——— 400 m
0 ——— 0.2 miles

Ⓐ   **Ⓑ**

INFORMATION
Agence de Voyage......1 B4
CBAO Bank..............2 A2
Cyber Misat.............3 B3
Pharmacie Orientale....4 B4
Pharmacie Thiaala......5 B3
SGBS Bank..............6 B3
Syndicat d'Initiative...(see 8)

SLEEPING
Bloc Gadec.............7 A4
Hôtel Niji.............8 B4
Keur Khoudia..........9 A2

EATING
Azur Commercial.......10 A2
Best Burger............11 A2
Boulangerie Khadim
   Rassoul...........12 A3
Chez Eva..............13 A2
Market................14 A2
Relais du Rais........15 A2
Restaurant Rose.......16 A3

DRINKING
Chez Francis..........17 B4
Chez Nanette..........18 A4
Complex Leggal Pont..19 B2

ENTERTAINMENT
Mamacounda..........20 A2

TRANSPORT
Al Azhar Office........21 A3
Gare Routière..........22 A2

To Oasis Oriental
Club (800m);
Le Relais de
Tamba (1km)

Public
Garden

Market

Bd Demba Diop

Train Station

To Saveur Orientale (200m);
Garage Kothiary
(Transport to Kidira) (900m);
National Park Office (1km);
Kidira (186km); Bakel (235km)

Bd Kandioura Noba

River (seasonal)

Some Minor Roads
Not Depicted

To Hôpital Régional (7km);
Airport (7km);
Wassadou (50km);
Vélingara (90km);
Kédougou (243km)

Quartier Abattoir

EASTERN SENEGAL

Koba (see p230), but arrangements can be strangely haphazard. Prepare for hard negotiation of car-hire rates.

Bloc Gadec (☎ 77 531 8931; dm/r CFA3000/8000) The clean rooms have little more than a roof, a double bed with a fresh sheet, a mosquito net and a fan, but a little tidiness can even make the simplest place feel welcoming. Bathrooms are shared (one for three rooms).

Keur Khoudia (☎ /fax 33 981 1102; Bd Demba Diop; s/d CFA16,000/22,000; ☒) Deteriorating rooms and rising prices have greatly diminished the charm of this budget hotel. Hôtel de Simenti in Niokolo-Koba park belongs to the same owners, but car hire is still to be fiercely negotiated.

Hôtel Niji (☎ 33 981 1250; www.hotelniji.com, in French; s/d CFA18,500/22,000; P ☒ 🖵 🕰) Ever

expanding, this hotel has rooms for every pocket, ranging from simple, garden-set bungalows (Niji Annexe) to lush but soulless quarters near the pool. Add CFA7000 for hot water, air-conditioning and breakfast. A good address for information about the region.

Le Relais de Tamba (☎ 33 981 1000; www.horizons-bleus-senegal.com; Rte National; s/d/tr incl breakfast CFA25,000/30,000/37,000; P ☒ 🖵 🕰) The Relais hotel chain has a reputation for classy simplicity, and this place has all the niceties of the Kaolack and Kédougou (Bédik) branches. At 1km from the hothouse that is Tamba, this quiet, pool-centred retreat lets you breathe again.

Oasis Oriental Club (☎ 33 981 1824; www.oasis oriental.com, in French; Rte de Kaolack; s/d incl breakfast CFA27,500/34,500; P ☒ 🖵 🕰) After swallowing 12 hours worth of dust en route to Tamba, a lazy afternoon at the pool of this upmarket hotel is a massage for the soul, particularly if you're looked after by such a friendly staff team.

Eating

Tambacounda isn't exactly blessed with great culinary choices, but there are a number of decent *gargottes* (small, simple, local-style eating houses) and other cheap eateries in the centre of town.

Restaurant Rose (☎ 77 554 6542; dishes from CFA1000; ☺ noon-2.30pm & 6-11pm) 'I love pink and cooking' is how lovely Ada introduced her rickety roadside restaurant. Hence the solid Senegalese meals and decent steak served between rose-tinted walls and fake flower arrangements. There's no alcohol on the menu, though you may be allowed to bring your own.

Relais du Rais (☎ 77 552 7096; dishes from CFA2000; ☺ noon-2.30pm & 6-11pm) This well-known local eatery is good for solid plates of rice and sauce. The European dishes on offer don't get more adventurous than chicken and chips.

Saveur Orientale (☎ 77 322 5619; Garage Kothiary; meals CFA2500; ☺ 11am-1am) By Tamba standards, this neon-lit place with its small front yard qualifies as close to classy. A cut above the grub-grabber eateries on Bd Demba Diop, it serves pizzas, snacks and mainly meat dishes.

The local market is where you buy your fruit and veg. **Azur Commercial** (☺ 9am-1am), opposite Relais du Rais, is a good place to stock up on groceries, especially because it's open late. Next door, the **Boulangerie Khadim Rassoul** is where you get your bread and croissants in the morning.

Also recommended:

Best Burger (☎ 33 981 3203; Bd Demba Diop; ⏰ 9am-2am) Popular local hang-out serving impressively sized burgers.

Chez Eva (Bd Demba Diop) One of several reasonable *gargottes* on Bd Demba Diop.

Drinking & Entertainment

Entertainment in Tamba comes mainly in the form of dubious drinking holes complete with cheap beer, hookers, fly-encircled neon lights and a thriving male population.

Mamacounda (Bd Demba Diop; ⏰ Thu-Sun) This dance floor, drowned in feet and strobe lights, is where Tamba's youth spends Saturday night. Don't let Tamba's general scruffiness fool you – you'll look out of place here if not dressed to the nines. Things get going around 1am, and there's live music on weekends.

Chez Francis (☎ 77 643 1231; Av Léopold Senghor; snacks CFA2000; ⏰ 11am-2am) This small snack bar serves *shwarmas* (sliced, grilled meat and salad in pita bread) and other culinary simplicities in a courtyard permanently animated by a noisy TV set. The beers here are cheap and cold.

Chez Nanette (meals CFA1500; ⏰ 8am-midnight) This is one of Tamba's more spacious bars and gets lively most nights of the week. As Senegalese women don't tend to drink or smoke, the audience is mainly male or very lightly dressed female, but there's less hassle than at other places.

Complex Leggal Pont (☎ 33 981 1756; Bd Demba Diop; ⏰ 11pm-4am) If the state of some people during our visit is anything to go by, expect alcohol-fuelled nights. It looks gloomy but is still something of a Tamba institution, though not one for unaccompanied women.

Getting There & Away

AIR

Tambacounda has an airport and used to be served for a couple of months each year by Air Sénégal International. Check whether another company has taken over the trip by the time you travel.

BUS & BUSH TAXI

From the *gare routière* (station) Garage Kouthiary, on the eastern side of town, *sept-place* taxis go to the Malian border at Kidira (CFA5000, three hours). For all other desti-

nations, go to the *gare routière* north of Bd Demba Diop.

Vélingara is well served by minibuses (CFA1500, two hours) and *sept-place* taxis (CFA2000), as it's a popular place to cross into Gambia. To Dakar by *sept-place* is CFA9000 (12 hours), Kédougou CFA6000 (four hours), Kolda CFA6000 (four hours) and Ziguinchor CFA9000 (10 hours).

The *car mouride* bus leaves daily at 4.30am for Dakar (CFA6000, eight hours). Contact the **Al Azhar office** (☎ 33 937 8125; Bd Kandioura Noba) for confirmation and departure point (uncertain at the time of writing due to roadworks). The Malian and Nigerian long-distance buses that travel from Dakar to Bamako, Niamey and Cotonou also take on passengers in Tamba. Ask at your hotel or the petrol station near Mamacounda where they normally pick up passengers.

TRAIN

The train between Dakar and Bamako (Mali) should pass through Tambacounda twice a week but usually goes much less frequently (see p281). The ticket office opens a few hours before the train arrives, but tickets can be bought in advance. First-class sleepers are CFA33,000 to Kayes and CFA52,000 to Bamako. First-class seats are about CFA15,000 cheaper.

Getting Around

All taxi trips around town cost CFA400 – no need to bargain.

WASSADOU & MAKO

Off the route from Tamba to Kédougou, often in superb riverbank locations, you'll find a scattering of small *campements* (hostels) that provide an attractive alternative to the hotels in Tamba for visits to the national park.

Campement de Wassadou (☎ 33 982 3602; wassadou@niokolo.com; s/d CFA17,000/24,200), 50km southeast of Tamba, tempts with well-equipped, thatched huts and fabulous views across the Gambia River. Its bivouac, campfire and hippo-viewing boat trips are possibly better than a 4WD tour through Niokolo-Koba. A favourite with overlanders and families.

Mako lies another 150km further southeast, at the entry to Bassari country. This small village has a handful of *campements*. Some cater for hunters; the ones listed below boast an ecofriendly approach.

Keur Annick (☎ 77 405 1941; half board per person CFA12,500) overlooks the tranquil flow of the Gambia River from its vast terrain. Its solar-powered bungalows provide simple but adequate accommodation, and there are excellent tours on offer. Paul, the former pharmacist who runs this place, pledges to invest a percentage of all earnings in the close-by village.

A short walk along the river (this area lends itself to tranquil walks), near a fabulous hippo spot, **Eco-Campement Badian** (☎ 77 653 2741; asociacion @campamentos-solidarios.org; half board per person CFA12,000) is a simple Spanish-run camp built in harmony with the cultural values and architectural styles of the region. A touch rootsier than Keur Annick, it's also run in conjunction with the neighbouring village and offers community exchanges and tours.

Don't pass Mako without purchasing some of the tasty honey sold by an NGO on the side of the road to Tamba. There's no sign; watch out for the board indicating 'Poste de Mako' and ask where to turn.

PARC NATIONAL DE NIOKOLO-KOBA

The World Heritage Site of Niokolo-Koba, a vast biosphere reserve spanning about 9000 sq km, is Senegal's major national park. The landscape is relatively flat, with savannah woodland, plains, marshes and a few hills – the highest being Mt Assirik (311m) in the southeast.

The Gambia River and its two tributaries, the Niokolo-Koba and the Koulountou, cross the vast wilderness and are crucial sources of water for the 80 mammal species and 350 bird species that inhabit the park. On a tour through its vast woodlands, you may however be forgiven for thinking that there's little else but wild boars, a few antelopes and baboons. Sadly, many species have been hunted down and the few remaining lions are very rarely spotted. You can have a great day out here – just don't expect anything like the wildlife parks in East or Southern Africa.

The most stunning spots in the park are the banks of the Gambia River, from where you often see hippos, and Nile, slender-snouted and dwarf crocodiles. Other commonly viewed animals include waterbucks, bushbucks, kobs, duikers, roan antelopes, giant derby elands, hartebeests, baboons, monkeys (green and patas) and warthogs. Chimpanzee troops inhabit parts of the eastern area, though

they're as rarely seen as the few leopards that still exist here.

The best part for animal spotting is Simenti, with its hide overlooking a waterhole where animals regularly come to drink, and a lovely river bend that's great for crocodile sightings. A boat tour on the Gambia River (CFA6500) is very highly recommended – much more exciting than hours of driving around the park's dry woods.

Your guide will be able to point out other drinking holes, as well as the picture-perfect rope bridge left here by a Hollywood team years ago.

Information

Dar Salam, on the road between Tambacounda and Kédougou, is the main park entrance for tourists. The small information booth at the entrance gate is where you hire your obligatory guide. At Simenti, there's another park office, a visitors centre and the large Hôtel de Simenti, where you can find out about boat tours. In Tamba, try the **national park office** (☎ 33 981 1097; 7.30am-5pm).

WHEN TO GO

Parc National de Niokolo-Koba is officially open from 15 December to 30 April – the park centres and hotels are closed for the rest of the year – though you can visit at any time. The best viewing season for wildlife is from January to March, when the vegetation has withered and animals congregate at waterholes. The park gates are open from 7am to 6pm daily. Early morning is best for animal sightings.

FEES & GUIDES

The entrance fee (adult/child under 10 CFA2000/free, vehicle CFA5000) gives you access for 24 hours. It's obligatory to hire a guide (CFA8000 per day), even if you've got one already. Most guides are good at pointing out mammals and plants, but unfortunately less impressive at spotting birds. Many speak English and/or Spanish.

TRANSPORT & TOURS

You enter the park at Dar Salam, and by car only. Walking is allowed near accommodation sites or in the company of a guide. During and just after the rainy season, a 4WD is obligatory, and it's highly recommended even in the dry season. Clapped-out *sept-place* taxis break down easily on the uneven paths, lie too low for good animal sightings and aren't even much cheaper.

All the main tour operators arrange trips from Dakar to Niokolo-Koba (see p291). **Agence de Voyage** (☎ 33 981 0084), opposite Hôtel Niji in Tamba, offers tours, as does any good hotel in Tamba, Mako or Wassadou. One-day tours from Tamba cost around CFA100,000 to CFA120,000, including car hire, fuel, driver, guides and admission fees.

Since you need to take a guide at Dar Salam, you might as well just hire a car and arrange your own trip. Your hotel reception, the national park office or Agence de Voyage can organise a 4WD. Rates should not exceed CFA80,000 to CFA100,000 per day, including petrol and driver.

In the park, you can arrange tours from Simenti (CFA6500 per person, minimum group size four people), as well as highly recommended trips by motorised pirogue along the river (CFA6500 per person, minimum group size four people).

Sleeping & Eating

Dar Salam Campement (☎ 33 984 4275; Dar Salam; camping per tent CFA5000, s/d/tr CFA5000/8000/9500) At the park entrance, this *campement* has clean bungalows and a simple restaurant that's perfect for a cold beer after your park tour. You can hire bicycles (CFA2000 per day) and check out the Biodiversity Centre.

Camp du Lion (☎ national park office 33 981 2454; camping per tent CFA4000, s/d CFA8000/12,000) This tiny *campement* about 10km east of Simenti has thatched huts so flimsy you fear they might get blown into the Gambia River. There's a viewing point within walking distance that's great for spotting hippos and crocs on the riverbank.

Hôtel de Simenti (☎ 33 982 3650; Simenti; s/d CFA15,000/25,000; P ⊠ ⊠) Overlooking a majestic, crocodile-frequented bend of the river, this hotel sits in a prime location. Shame that most rooms are housed in a concrete block that evokes memories of bad schooling. The bungalows round the back are much nicer. Even if you don't sleep here, come to enjoy a drink and the view, or a picnic at the hide opposite the animal-frequented waterhole.

Getting There & Away

Most people get here on a tour or by hired 4WD (see opposite). Rates hardly drop travelling the hard, bush-taxi way. If you jump in a *sept-place* taxi from Tambacounda to Dar Salam (CFA6000), you'll either have to hire a 4WD there (CFA70,000 or more) or phone Hôtel de Simenti to pick you up and drop you off (CFA30,000 one way, CFA6500 for a tour around the park).

BASSARI COUNTRY

Bassari country, characterised by the unique and reclusive culture of its inhabitants, is the only mountainous region of Senegal and a fabulous area for hiking through green hillsides and tiny, traditional villages. If you drive in from Tamba, you'll rejoice at the first soothing sight of a distant hill. You will also see mud-covered men riding towards you on bicycles. They are returning from one of the many gold mines of this area, carrying buckets of washed-out soil that they'll rinse again and again to draw out even the finest gold powder. Rich in gold and iron, Bassari country is ironically also the poorest region in Senegal. This paradox led to uprisings in December 2008, when administrative buildings and cars were burnt in protest of poverty and low local employment in the face of rising exploitation of the mines. It seems that many changes lie ahead for this remote part of Senegal.

Kédougou
pop 75,000

Kédougou is the largest town in the southeast of Senegal, though it remains very rural in character, with its large traditional huts, tall trees and red laterite roads. The tranquil market in the centre of town is famous for its indigo fabrics, and is the place to buy your groceries.

There's no bank here; the nearest one is in Tambacounda. **Netekoto Cyber** (☎ 33 985 1512; Daande Maayo; per hr CFA300) has internet access on sluggish computers and a laptop point, and Le Bédik and Relais hotels have wi-fi.

Kédougou has an impressively large regional **health centre** (Rte de Tamba). The nearby **Pharmacie Kénéya** (☎ 33 985 1525; Rte de Tamba) is fairly well stocked.

SLEEPING

Most places in Kédougou can arrange tours to Bassari country or to Parc National de Niokolo-Koba.

Le Nieriko (☎ 33 985 1459; Togoro; r CFA8000; ⊠) Managed with a smile but also the minimum

---

GUIDED TOURS

The company of a clued-up guide is invaluable for exploring the myriad mountain paths of Bassari country. The best place to find a reliable and knowledgeable guide is the hotel **Le Bédik** (☎ 33 985 1000) in Kédougou. Two recommended guides there are **Alpha Diallo** (☎ 77 652 6450; dialloa95@ yahoo.fr, http://alphaguia.blogspot.com, in French) and **Doba Diallo** (☎ 77 360 6401; dobadiallo@yahoo.fr, http://dobadiallo.mi-website.es, in Spanish). They come from the area, know the best routes through the hills and have a good relationship with the villagers, which will make you, the visiting stranger, much more welcome. It remains up to you, though, to show the proper respect and perhaps present kola nuts, money and small gifts to the *chefs de village* (village chiefs).

Guides can arrange anything from leisurely day trips to strenuous hikes of up to eight days through the forests, mountains and tiny Bédik, Bassari and Fula villages, with the possibility of sleeping either in the homes of locals or in *campements* (hostels).

If you're after more far-flung destinations, take them up on their offer to cross over the border to Guinea. You'll need a valid visa before setting out and a 4WD (hire can be arranged for around CFA100,000 per day, including petrol and driver). The rocky trip via Fongolimbi (220km from Kédougou) is spectacular, passing through almost mountainous terrain and thick forest.

Alpha and Doba both charge CFA10,000 per day for accompanying you on 4WD tours, and CFA15,000 per day for hikes.

---

of energy expenditure, this small *campement* at the edge of the Togoro dirt road has slightly dark and dusty rooms. You need at least bicycle wheels to get to this rootsy place; otherwise it's a longish walk in the hot sun.

La Giraffe (☎ 77 107 4196; Togoro; r CFA10,000) This forlorn little *campement* behind Togoro quartier looks like a tiny village out in the bushlands. If you're in a small group, you can have a fantastic, camping-style time in this little hamlet between bush and river, with views across the woodlands. Call before you get here, or you might find it deserted.

Le Soninke (☎ 33 985 1107; Daande Maayo; s/d incl breakfast CFA16,000/24,000; ⚡ 🏊) Among Kédougou's *campements*, this is one of the cleaner options, with a view across the Gambia River to boot. The spacious rooms are pretty bare and lack practical features like wardrobes, but boast a riverside balcony and hot water.

our pick **Le Bédik** (☎ 33 985 1000; s/d incl breakfast CFA25,000/30,000; ⚡ 🏊 🖥 🏊) If you invest in comfortable, relaxation-inducing accommodation anywhere, do it here. On your arrival after a 15-hour car journey from Dakar, or your return from a three-day hike through the Bassari mountains, you'll be grateful for the hot shower, cold beer, inviting pool, stunning river view and friendly welcome. Big bonus: Kédougou's most serious guides tend to work with this hotel.

Other options:

Chez Diao (☎ 33 985 1124; Kédougou centre; d CFA6600; 🏊) Very basic, with shared toilets that would

not feature in a commercial for cleaning products. Rates double for air-con.

Relais de Kédougou (☎ 33 985 1062; lerelais@orange .sn; s/d from CFA17,000/21,000; ⚡ 🏊 🖥 🏊) A hunter's favourite, opposite Le Bédik. The restaurant has fantastic river views. Cheaper rooms with shared bathrooms are available.

EATING & DRINKING

Le Bédik and the Relais have the best kitchens. The Nieriko chef also rustles up a solid meal, though you have to order in advance. Otherwise it's down to the cheap eateries near the market for large platters of rice and sauce (around CFA1500). For dinner, drinks and dancing, try the **Black & White** (🕗 8pm-2am) in the town centre, the biggest party spot of this backwater town.

A place to seek out for a tasty dairy dessert is **Mussolia** (☎ 77 355 6500; mussolia@yahoo.fr), a tiny shop near the *gendarmerie* (police station) on the road to Tamba, where Ndeye Coumba sells divine frozen yoghurt (CFA150 to CFA300).

GETTING THERE & AWAY

There's plenty of traffic between Tamba and Kédougou (*sept-place* taxi CFA6000, Ndiaga Ndiaye CFA4500, four hours). At the time of writing, work had been started on the road connecting Saraya in Senegal (about 60km northeast of Kédougou) to Kita in Mali. Scheduled to be finished in 2010, this will open a brilliant new route to connect the two countries.

Friday is the best day to find a public pickup or 4WD to Labé in Guinea (CFA20,000, two days) – the ride along the treacherous dirt roads is extremely rough.

GETTING AROUND

For car hire try your hotel, or Doba and Alpha, the guides at Le Bédik. You'll pay around CFA55,000 per day for a 4WD (fuel not included). You can also hire cars for specific journeys. Ethiolo by 4WD costs around CFA70,000 and Dindefelo CFA60,000, both including petrol. The Bédik guides can arrange motorbike hire at CFA15,000 a day (not including fuel) and organise a relatively sturdy mountain bike for CFA5000.

Around Kédougou

Kédougou is a pretty town, but mainly it's the starting point for visits to the hills of Bassari country. The best way to explore Kédougou's stunning surroundings is a combination of driving (a 4WD) and hiking – best done in the company of a good guide (see opposite).

KÉDOUGOU–SALÉMATA ROUTE

The washed-out westbound road from Kédougou towards Salémata is lined with small roadside villages, typically inhabited by Fula and Bassari people. In the background, hillsides rise on either side. Climbing the narrow mountain paths to the top, you reach the hamlets of the Bédik, seminomadic people who adhere strongly to traditional lifestyles and are keen to preserve their relative isolation.

One of the nearest villages is **Bandafassi**, 15km from Kédougou and the capital of the Kédougou district. The inhabitants are mainly Fula and Bassari, and the village is renowned for its basket makers. In Indar, a part of Bandafassi, is the wonderfully welcoming *campement* **Chez Léontine** (☎ 77 554 9915; d CFA7500), with solar-powered lights and delicious meals prepared by the charming owner. It's a great base for hikes up the hill to the Bédik village of **Ethiowar**, from where you get fabulous views over the surrounding savannah.

Ibel, a Fula village, lies another 7km up the road from Bandafassi. Visits here are usually combined with a steep hike up to **Iwol**, a postcard-perfect village stretched out between a giant *fromager* (kapok tree) and a sacred baobab. Plenty of legends are associated with this place, and the local teacher will share them with you for a donation (CFA1000). The

local women make beautiful pottery – tiny Bassari statuettes and small incense burners (CFA300 per piece).

While Ibel and Iwol have by now become fixed points on most tourist circuits, **Salémata**, 83km west of Kédougou, is still rarely visited. This is a regional hub, with a health centre, small boutiques and the friendly *campement* **Chez Gilbert** (☎ 77 107 4584; r CFA6000). In April and May, the entire region surrounding Salémata is plunged into weeklong festivities during the annual Bassari initiation ceremonies. Observers are accepted, but keep a respectful distance, so as not to turn a local celebration into a tourist event. Gilbert can invite Bassari dancers to perform some of their spectacular masked and costumed dances outside this season.

The 15km trip to **Ethiolo** leads mainly through thick forest and bush grass, and there's a good chance of spotting chimpanzees in the trees (some of the few wild chimps left in Senegal). Ethiolo's brilliant *campement* **Chez Balingo** (☎ 33 835 1570; r CFA7000) has accommodation in traditional Bassari stone huts, and is run by the enthusiastic and knowledgeable Balingo. Like a character who's leapt right out of a book of legends, he can feed you morsels of local lore while taking you on exciting tours of Ethiolo's surroundings.

Getting There & Away

Public transport along this route is sporadic, and the road is rough. A 4WD is recommended.

A reliable daily vehicle is the Nenefecha minibus, which takes patients and visitors to Nenefecha hospital (about halfway between Kédougou and Salémata) and also transports visitors to the villages on the way. The bus leaves Kédougou Monday to Friday at 9am and 3pm, returning from Nenefecha at 1pm and 7pm, and costs around CFA2500. The best day to visit Salémata is Tuesday, when the *lumo* (weekly market) brings the village to life, and with it a better chance of public transport (minibus from Kédougou CFA2500, four hours).

DINDEFELO & DANDE

One of the most popular destinations from Kédougou is Dindefelo, famous for its impressive 100m **waterfall** with a deep, green pool suitable for bathing. It's a 2km hike through lush forest from Dindefelo village to the cascade. The starting point is the **Campement Villageois** (☎ 77 354 8911; r per person CFA2500), where you pay your CFA1000 waterfall admission. Accommodation is much better at the adjacent **Dogon du Fouta** (☎ 33 985 2187, 77 552 3831; moktardiallo @hotmail.com; per person from CFA2500). You can stay in rootsy stone (the cheapest) or bamboo huts, or for an extra CFA4500 book yourself into a thatched hut on stilts that seems to have emerged from an old explorer's tale.

If you have time and strong legs, take a hike up to **Dande**, a village on the plateau above Dindefelo. From here you can walk to the source of the waterfall. Don't go here without a guide, as the deep drop is hidden by some innocent-looking shrubs! Nearby there's an impressive cave – gigantic and smoothly hollowed out as if human made or shaped by water. Watch out for the beehives in the bushes. Throw in a trip to the nearby potters' village, and night might fall too early for a return. Try the *campement* **Chez Doba** (☎ 77 360 6401; http://aubergechezdoba.blogspot.com, in French; per person CFA2500), where a handful of traditional Fula huts put up dedicated hikers.

As Dindefelo has become part of the regular tourist trail, the waterfall of **Ségou** is now the new Dindefelo for the tour-group-allergic hiker. From Ségou village on the Bandafassi–Dindefelo road, it's a 7km hike through stunning woodlands and rarely visited hills to the beautiful falls. You can bathe in the basin and

there's a small **campement** (r per person CFA3000) that also serves meals (CFA2500).

If you're relying on public transport, go to Dindefelo and Ségou on Sunday, the day of the *lumo*. The minibus costs CFA1000 from Kédougou and takes at least two hours. Again, the road is so bad that a hired 4WD or motorbike is a better option.

Goudiry & Kidira

Kidira is the place to cross into Mali. To get your passport stamped quickly, book a taxi (CFA2000) to take you to both immigration posts and your Mali-bound bus. The border closes at 6pm. If you fear that you'll arrive after hours, you can stop in Goudiry (65km before Kidira), where the **Savane Safari Club** (☎ 33 983 7165; www.savanesafari.com; s CFA12,500, d with air-con CFA26,000; ⊠ ⊴) has welcoming accommodation in clean bungalows, is blessed with a pool and has a great restaurant. From January to March it mainly attracts hunters. Another option is to head for Kidira, then turn into the Kidira–Bakel road and stay at **Étoile de Boundou** (☎ 33 983 1248; r with/without air-con CFA18,600/15,000; ⊠), just outside Kidira on the road to Bakel. It has spotless rooms and a staff team that will soon have you excited about the region.

If you're not immediately crossing the border, take a day trip to Bakel from here.

Casamance

Every September when the tropical downpours have subsided to the occasional bolt of lightning in the distance, the king of Oussouye is honoured with a week of spectacular wrestling matches and dances. In his brilliant red robes, sceptre clutched, he cuts a stately figure. As a baldachin provides shade, he observes hundreds of youngsters from across the Casamance compete with skill, speed and the spiritual support of their protective charms. Dust whirls up and the urging cheers from the crowds rise to a deafening noise. Oussouye's monarch is an animist leader, political chief and skilled fetishist, an adviser and sovereign revered across the entire region. As you witness the devotion displayed and the spectacle unfold, you know that you're far – very far – from Dakar, with its highways, skyscrapers and Wolof society.

Not only the unique Diola culture but even the lands conspire to impress on you the region's distinctive qualities. For once your eyes feast on abundant greenery, pushed to magnificent heights by fertile soils and the waters of the Casamance River. Small islands all along its course invite for a spell of soul searching in complete isolation. Bird calls ring from the thick mangroves that line the river and, in the far west, the land greets the sea with wide, powdery beaches.

People travel to the Casamance and never leave – discrete, lush and welcoming, the region is quick to cast its spell on you. But the Casamance's distinctiveness has also had serious consequences. For decades the region has been troubled by simmering separatist sentiments that have at times flared up in civil war. Though conflicts have largely been quelled, Senegal's most fertile zone remains slightly unstable and, while it's perfectly possible to spend the holiday of your life here, you're advised to listen to the local people and heed their advice before setting off on those tempting tours through remote villages and palm-shaded islands.

HIGHLIGHTS

- Swim by day and party by night at **Cap Skiring** (p246), home to the best beaches in Senegal
- Cycle over sandy paths and kayak through the creeks at **Oussouye** (p249)
- Learn the art of cooking *thiéboudienne* (rice and fish), then treat yourself to a dolphin tour at **Cachouane** (p249)
- Follow the seductive call of the wattle-eye all the way to the manatee sanctuary at **Pointe St George** (p244)
- Sip sundowners between the roots of a giant kapok tree on historical **Île de Karabane** (p245)

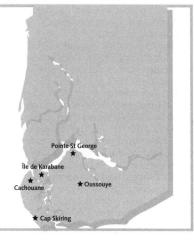

TO GO OR NOT TO GO

Separatist conflicts officially ended in 2004, yet occasional clashes continue to occur, though they are more commonly caused by street robbers with access to arms than motivated by any real secessionist sentiment.

The vast majority of tourists visit the Casamance without experiencing any problems, but some caution is still advisable. The biggest concern is the sporadic occurrence of road ambushes, mainly along the Ziguinchor–Bignona artery. They are most likely to happen at night or in the early hours of the morning – if you stick to daytime travel, you're very unlikely to get caught up in anything. The route from Ziguinchor to Cap Skiring was considered completely safe at the time of research and all major roads are manned by military, stationed in order to dissuade the robbers.

Check your embassy for travel advice before setting out and, if you're already in Casamance, ask your hotel about the latest situation and the safety of a particular destination. Casamance residents, especially those working in the tourist industry, are always the ones who are best informed and are a reliable source of advice.

HISTORY

The Diola people of Casamance have a long history of resisting the rule of outsiders. It's a sentiment that underlined their outright rejection of slavery, their refusal to accept France's colonial administration and enduring secessionist wars.

In the 19th and early 20th centuries, the French colonial authorities controlled their colonies through local chiefs and frequently installed leaders from other ethnic groups to administer Diola territories. This increased the resentment that colonisation itself had provoked and Diola resistance against foreign interference remained strong into the 1930s.

The last Diola rebellion against the French was led in 1943 by a traditional priestess from Kabrousse called Aline Sitoé Diatta. Forced into exile in Timbuktu (Mali) by the French after the uprising was quelled, she died far from home and is today revered as the greatest heroine of the Casamance.

The conflicts that have plagued the region for the last 20 years originated from a proindependence demonstration held in Ziguinchor in 1982, after which the leaders of the Mouvement des Forces Démocratiques de la Casamance (MFDC) were arrested and jailed. As the government clamped down on separatist sentiments with increasing severity, the north–south divide only increased and the secessionist movement gained in strength.

Throughout the '90s periods of civil war alternated with fragile ceasefire agreements, causing destruction and a rising death toll among civilians. When the disappearance of four French tourists in 1995 was blamed on the MFDC, their leader, Father Diamacoune

Senghor, accused the army of trying to turn international opinion against the rebels. Peace talks continued but, following the government's refusal to consider independence for Casamance, a group of hardliners broke away from the MFDC and resumed fighting.

Against a background of ongoing clashes, causing the death of over 500 people in the late 1990s, Father Diamacoune urged his supporters to continue to pursue reconciliation with the government. Several peace deals were made and broken, until the final one in 2004 suddenly promised success. Violence still erupts occasionally, though these acts can rarely be attributed to the concerted action of separatists, but rather to street robbers and bandits who profit from a politically charged situation and the availability of firearms in the region since the years of conflict.

INFORMATION

The web portals www.casamance.net and www.voyagerencasamance.com contain a wealth of information, from political news to events calendars and hotel bookings.

GETTING THERE & AWAY
Air

There are airports at Ziguinchor and Cap Skiring. Until its bankruptcy in 2009, Air Sénégal International used to have regular flights. Check whether another carrier has resumed them.

Boat

Cheaper than planes and far more comfortable than *sept-place* taxis, boats are a great way of travelling between Dakar and Ziguinchor.

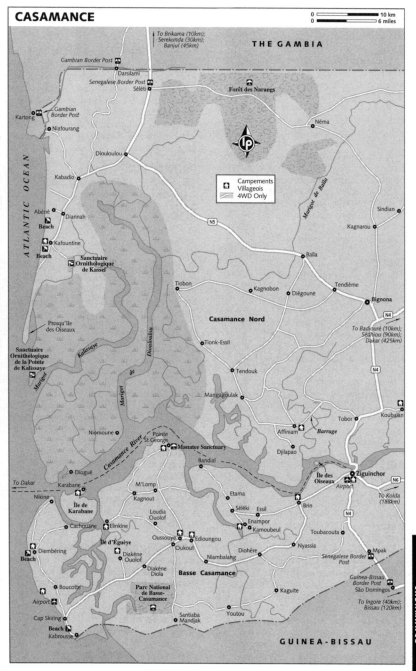

CASAMANCE

| 0 | 10 km |
| 0 | 6 miles |

THE GAMBIA

To Brikama (10km);
Serekunda (30km);
Banjul (45km)

Gambian Border Post
Darsilami
Senegalese Border Post
Séléti

Forêt des Narangs

Gambian Border Post
Kartong
Niafourang

Diouloulou

Kabadio

ATLANTIC OCEAN

Abéné
Beach
Diannah

Kafountine
Beach

Sanctuaire
Ornithologique
de Kassel

N5

Néma

Sindian

Kagnarou

Baïla

Tiobon
Kagnobon
Diégoune

Tendième

Bignona

N4

To Badioure (10km);
Sédhiou (90km);
Dakar (425km)

N4

Casamance Nord

Presqu'île
des Oiseaux

Sanctuaire
Ornithologique
de la Pointe
de Kalissaye

Kalissaye

Marigot

Dioulouku

Marigot

de

Tionk-Essil

Tendouk

Mangagoulak

Niomoune

Pointe
St George
Manatee Sanctuary

Casamance River

Affiniam
Barrage

Tobor

Koubalan

Djilapao

Île des
Oiseaux
Ziguinchor

N6

To Dakar

Diogué

Karabane
Nikine

Île de
Karabane

Cachouane
Elinkine

Île d'Égueye

Diembéring
Beach

Boucotte

Airport
Cap Skiring
Beach
Kabrousse

M'Lomp

Kagnout

Loudia
Ouolof

Oussouye
Oukout

Diakène
Ouolof

Diakène
Diola

**Parc National
de Basse-
Casamance**

Santiaba
Mandjak

Bandial

Etama

Séléki
Essil
Enampor
Kamoubeul

Ediongou
Niambalang

Diohère

Brin

N4

Toubacouta

Nyassia

Airport

To Kolda
(188km)

Senegalese Border
Post

Mpak

Guinea-Bissau
Border Post
São Domingos

To Ingore (40km);
Bissau (120km)

Kaguite

Youtou

Basse Casamance

GUINEA-BISSAU

Campements
Villageois
4WD Only

CASAMANCE

The overnight trip takes 16 hours and you arrive in the Casamance just in time for brilliant views as you start moving up the Casamance River.

The German-built 500-passenger boat *Aline Sitoé Diatta* that travels the route has a variety of price classes, ranging from seats (CFA15,500) to two-bed cabins (per person CFA30,500). It leaves Dakar every Tuesday and Friday at 8pm (check-in is open from 2.30pm to 5.30pm) and returns from Ziguinchor every Thursday and Sunday at 2pm (check-in is from 11.30am to 1pm). You have to book your place on the overnight trip in advance and in person – seats frequently fill up. Contact the **Cosama ticket office** (☎ in Ziguinchor 33 991 7200, in Dakar 33 821 2900; cosama@orange .sn) for more information. Its Dakar offices are located next to the Gorée ferry pier; in Ziguinchor they're at the port.

Sept-Place

There are plenty of *sept-place* taxis daily between Dakar and Ziguinchor (CFA9000, eight to 12 hours, 450km). The ambitiously named Trans-Gambia Hwy was being given a new layer of tarmac at the time of research; until it's newly paved, you'll spend a large part of your journey on dirt paths between Kaolack and Farafenni. The journey is also broken by two Senegal–Gambia border crossings (usually smooth, though you may be asked for random payments) and a ferry crossing that can take anything from 15 minutes to four hours, depending on the current state of the boat and whether one or two ferries are in circulation.

GETTING AROUND

Casamance can be toured by car, public transport, pirogue or bicycle or on foot. In Ziguinchor and Cap Skiring you can hire cars (around CFA40,000 per day; ask your hotel). For *sept-place* services, see individual destinations.

Most places on the river or one of its branches (including Cap Skiring, Ziguinchor, Affiniam, Niomoune and Île de Karabane) can be reached by scheduled or hire pirogues. In Ziguinchor regular boats leave from the pirogue point Ancien Bac, near Hôtel Kadiandoumagne; private pirogue hire is also arranged from there. For specialised hiking, biking and kayak tours, contact **Casamance VTT** (☎ 33 993 1004; casavtt@yahoo.fr) in Oussouye.

ZIGUINCHOR

pop 230,000

Depending on your state of mind, Ziguinchor can either be a slowly swinging, charming town or a gradually crumbling provincial capital. True, the roads are increasingly dented by potholes and most buildings haven't seen a lick of paint in years. But huge mango trees, old colonial houses and a decidedly friendly vibe provide real atmosphere worth exploring for a couple of days.

ORIENTATION

The old Ziguinchor centre is compact and easily covered on foot. Major roads radiate from the traffic circle Rond-Point Jean-Paul II, including busy Rue Javelier, which leads past Marché Escale to Rue du Commerce on the river. This is where you find the ferry terminal.

Heading eastwards from Rond-Point Jean-Paul II, Av Carvalho takes you to the *gare routière*, from where Route 54 leads south to Guinea-Bissau and north to Banjul and Dakar.

INFORMATION

The sites www.voyagerencasamance.com and www.casamance.net have exhaustive lists of hotels, restaurants and events.

Bookshops

The bookshop at the northern end of Rue Javelier has a good selection of titles about Senegal and Casamance (mostly in French).

Cultural Centres

Alliance Franco-Sénégalaise (☎ 33 991 2823; Av Lycée Guignabo; ☉ 9.15am-noon & 3-7.15pm Mon-Sat) This giant *case à impluvium* (see the boxed text, p240), decorated with South African Ndebele and Casamance patterns, has exhibition spaces, a large concert hall and a welcoming restaurant and bar. There's a visiting fee of CFA1000.

Internet Access

Most hotels have free wi-fi and there's an internet cafe at the Alliance Franco-Sénégalaise.
Sud-Informatique (☎ 33 991 1573; www.sudinfo.sn; Rue Javelier; per hr CFA1000; ☉ 9am-midnight)

Medical Services

If you're in need of urgent treatment, Véronique Chiche at Le Flamboyant hotel can recommend reliable doctors in town.

CASAMANCE

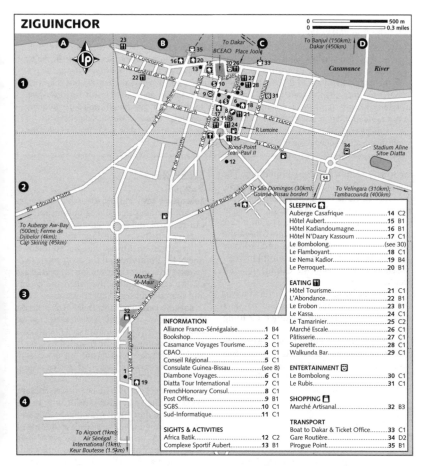

ZIGUINCHOR

| 0 | 500 m |
| 0 | 0.3 miles |

INFORMATION
Alliance Franco-Sénégalaise.................1 B4
Bookshop...2 C1
Casamance Voyages Tourisme.............3 C1
CBAO..4 C1
Conseil Régional...............................5 C1
Consulate Guinea-Bissau...............(see 8)
Diambone Voyages............................6 C1
Diatta Tour International.....................7 C1
FrenchHonorary Consul......................8 C1
Post Office.......................................9 B1
SGBS...10 C1
Sud-Informatique............................11 C1

SIGHTS & ACTIVITIES
Africa Batik....................................12 C2
Complexe Sportif Aubert..................13 B1

SLEEPING
Auberge Casafrique.........................14 C2
Hôtel Aubert...................................15 B1
Hôtel Kadiandoumagne.....................16 B1
Hôtel N'Daary Kassoum.....................17 C1
Le Bombolong...........................(see 30)
Le Flamboyant................................18 C1
Le Nema Kadior..............................19 B4
Le Perroquet..................................20 B1

EATING
Hôtel Tourisme...............................21 C1
L'Abondance..................................22 B1
Le Erobon......................................23 B1
Le Kassa..24 C1
Le Tamarinier.................................25 C2
Marché Escale................................26 C1
Pâtisserie......................................27 C1
Superette.......................................28 C1
Walkunda Bar.................................29 C1

ENTERTAINMENT
Le Bombolong................................30 C1
Le Rubis..31 C1

SHOPPING
Marché Artisanal.............................32 B3

TRANSPORT
Boat to Dakar & Ticket Office...........33 C1
Gare Routière.................................34 D2
Pirogue Point.................................35 B1

Hospital (☎ 33 991 1154) Has an accident and emergency department but is not well equipped.

Money

The following banks change money and have ATMs that take Visa and MasterCard.

CBAO (☎ 33 991 1362; Rue Javelier)
SGBS (☎ 33 991 1251; Rue de la Poste)

Post

Post office (Rue du Général de Gaulle) A beautiful old building.

Tourist Information

Plans for a tourist information centre with a focus on community tourism were well advanced when we passed. Check whether it

has opened at the **Conseil Régional** (Rue Javelier) as intended.

Travel Agencies

Casamance Voyages Tourisme (☎ 33 991 4362; cvtzig@orange.sn; Rue Javelier) Good for purchasing plane and boat tickets, arranging tours and car hire.
Diambone Voyages (☎ 77 641 5132; www.diambone voyages.com; Rue de France) Great for anything from flight bookings to arranging full-blown Casamance holidays.
Diatta Tour International (☎ 33 991 2781; aessibye@ yahoo.fr; Rue du Général de Gaulle) Arranges tours and hotel reservations. Also has a branch in Cap Skiring.

SIGHTS

A relaxed walk through the mango-tree-lined streets of central Ziguinchor takes you past

CASAMANCE

CASES À IMPLUVIUM

Huge and round, with gently sloping thatched roofs, the *cases à impluvium* are impressive structures. They're unique to Casamance and beautifully adapted to the region. Senegal is drenched by annual tropical downpours and the *case à impluvium* is built to collect rainwater. Its roof slopes in the middle, channelling drops into a basin, thus not only keeping the hut dry but collecting water for drier times as well. Several Casamance *campements* are housed in *cases à impluvium*. When you wake up in your room, open the door to the round corridor and you'll get to enjoy the wonderful diffused light the roof construction produces as an accidental side effect.

A great example is the *campement villageois* in Enampor (p243), while the fanciest of all is the Alliance Franco-Sénégalaise (p238) in Ziguinchor.

---

the town's colourful colonial buildings. The central **post office** on Rue du Général de Gaulle, the office of **Diatta Tour International** next door and the old **Conseil Régional** on the corner of Rue Javelier are all impressive. The huge *case à impluvium* of the **Alliance Franco-Sénégalaise** (p238), with its mosaic floors and Ndebele patterns, is one of the most beautiful in West Africa and regularly hosts exhibitions and events.

On **Rue du Commerce** in the north, you can see dozens of pirogue makers and painters at work, as well as watch women cleaning mussels.

Heading 5km west out of town, the **Ferme de Djibelor** (☎ 33 991 1701; admission CFA2000; ⏰ 9am-6pm) has a large, tropical fruit and flower garden, though it's more famous for the oddity of the crocodile farm at the back.

ACTIVITIES
Pirogue Excursions
From Ziguinchor you can easily arrange pirogue excursions, from short trips to Affiniam (see p250) to extended tours to the remote manatee sanctuary at Pointe St George (p244) and Niomoune (p245). Enquire at the pirogue point Ancien Bac in Ziguinchor for scheduled boats and hire (see also p238), or ask your hotel or a travel agency (see p239).

Sports
For fitness facilities and a pool, try **Complexe Sportif Aubert** (☎ 33 938 8020; Rue Diallo; per month CFA10,000, pool admission CFA1000).

FESTIVALS & EVENTS
The Alliance Franco-Sénégalaise (p238) hosts regular events. The cultural calendars on www.voyagerencasamance.com and www.au-senegal.com are regularly updated.

SLEEPING
Budget
Auberge Aw-Bay (☎ 33 936 8096; Kolobane; per person CFA3600) For the price of a camping spot, you can get a real roof over your head in this clean *auberge* with its sky-blue doors and hammock-adorned garden. Owner Adama Goudiaby is one of the brains behind the *campements villageois* and knows that even the simplest place can be rendered attractive when the rooms and shared toilets are kept spotless.

Auberge Casafrique (☎ 33 991 4122; Santhiaba; s/d with air-con CFA17,000/19,000, without air-con CFA11,000/13,000; ❄) Rooms are well maintained and set in bungalows surrounded by a leafy garden. There are several chill-out spaces and, for a cover charge of CFA3000, you can camp here.

Le Perroquet (☎ 33 991 2329; perroquet@orange.sn; Rue du Commerce; s/d CFA11,000/13,000) Come in the right season and you'll hear this backpacker favourite long before you see it as dozens of yellow-billed storks attract you with their noisy chatter. For 1st-floor rooms with a balcony you pay an extra CFA1000 – a small investment for stunning river views.

Also in town:

Hôtel N'Daary Kassoum (☎ 33 991 1472; ndaary@hotmail.com; Rue de France; s/d CFA12,000/15,000; ❄) It's adorned with great masks and statues, though rooms lack light and lustre.

Le Bombolong (☎ 33 938 8001; Rue du Commerce; r CFA10,000) Expect all sorts of noise at night in this hotel famous for its nightclub.

Midrange & Top End
Ferme de Djibelor (☎ 33 991 1701; s/d CFA15,000/22,000) With their kitchen corner, fold-down beds and timber walls, the three log cabins on the crocodile farm are strangely reminiscent of ski chalets, until the lush gardens remind you where you are.

CASAMANCE

Le Flamboyant (☎ 33 991 2223; www.casamance.info; Rue de France; s/d without air-con CFA16,000/18,000, with air-con CFA20,000/22,000; 🍴 💻 🖥) Satellite TV, quality mattresses, free wi-fi and spot lighting aren't steady companions in this price range, but this lovingly designed place has made an attractive habit of underselling its great accommodation and service. Manager Veronique Chiche is not only an excellent host but also the honorary French consul in Ziguinchor.

Le Nema Kadior (☎ 33 991 1052; nemakadior@orange .sn; Av Lycée Guignabo; s/d incl breakfast CFA20,000/26,000; 🍴 💻 🖥) The fact that half of its straw-covered bungalows are closed certainly indicates decline, but the fading is done with style. Having crossed the unkempt gardens, the well-maintained state of the rooms comes as something of a surprise. There's a tennis court and a pool that outsiders can use for a cover charge of CFA2000.

Hôtel Aubert (☎ 33 938 8020; hotelaubert@orange .sn; Rue Fargues; d/tr CFA22,000/25,000; 🍴 💻 🖥) Ziguinchor's oldest hotel is not quite the queen of town it used to be, though it's still a valid option. The central setting and sports centre across the road are a bonus.

Hôtel Kadiandoumagne (☎ 33 938 8000; www .hotel-kadiandoumagne.com; Rue du Commerce; s/d from CFA25,000/30,000; 🍴 💻 🖥 ♿ 🏊) The tongue-twisting Kadiandoumagne (kaj-an-dou-man) has picked the prime spot on the Casamance River. The garden and views are fabulous, and almost worth the cost of the slightly unspectacular rooms (they do have satellite TV, minibar and free wi-fi).

EATING

There are lots of small eateries, though they're hardly magnificent.

Le Erobon (☎ 33 991 2788; Rue du Commerce; meals CFA2000; 🕐 10am-1am) A few years ago, a few youngsters started selling grilled fish on the edge of the river, then put them on plates with a bit of garnish and today they've apparently sold enough to build a rough roof and buy tables. Every Wednesday night, a local musician entertains beer drinkers with guitar tunes.

Le Tamarinier (☎ 33 992 0022; Av Carvalho; meals around CFA2000-4000) Manager Marie-Agnès runs this lively, local-style bar-cum-restaurant with the cunning and strength of a judoka (which she is, black belt) and the smile of a flight attendant. The grilled prawns here taste even better with the live music on weekends.

Le Kassa (☎ 33 991 1311; Rond-Point Jean-Paul II; mains around CFA2500-4000; 🕐 8am-2am) It's proven itself for years, this patio-pretty place on the Ziguinchor roundabout. It's spacious and relaxed and, best of all, the good kitchen stays open late. The live shows on weekends are often great.

Walkunda Bar (☎ 33 991 1845; Rond-Point Jean-Paul II; mains CFA3000-5000; 🕐 9am-1am) A popular haunt for affluent locals and localised expats, the Walkunda often gets referred to as Zig's classy place. Don't dress up too smart, though, as the *ambiance* is still healthily relaxed. The garden tables are the best.

Hôtel Tourisme (☎ 33 991 2223; Rue de France; mains CFA4000; 🕐 noon-2.30pm & 7-10pm) Across the road from Le Flamboyant and managed by the same couple, this is a great place to wind down over a plate of seafood or the usually excellent Senegalese *plats du jour*.

Ferme de Djibelor (☎ 33 991 6855; dishes around CFA5000) If the thought of crocodile meat on a skewer is too much, you can pick from a good range of standard meats (and even a vegetarian option). The surrounding garden is as attractive as the menu is unusual.

L'Abondance (Rue du Général de Gaulle; 🕐 5pm-3am) This small *dibiterie* (grilled-meat place) is where you round off a night out on the town with pork skewers, grilled lamb and cold beers.

Self-caterers can get the fresh stuff at **Marché Escale** (Rue Javelier), right in the heart of town. There's also a small **superette** (Rue Lemoine), as well as a good **pâtisserie** (Rue Javelier).

DRINKING & ENTERTAINMENT

If you like small, circumspect drinking holes, then you'll enjoy Ziguinchor – keep an eye open for pink neon lights drifting through half-open doors – those are your places. Follow your drink-up with a dance at **Le Bombolong** (☎ 33 938 8001; Rue du Commerce; admission CFA1500-3000), Zig's enduring nightclub. The paint at the nightclub might be peeling a little, but it still has plenty of fun in it. More upmarket, **Le Rubis** (Rue de Santhiaba; admission CFA1000-2000) is owned by football star François Bocandé and sparkles like a gold medal.

Wrestling

Most wrestling matches take place on Sunday afternoons in the arena, east of Av Lycée Guignabo.

DYEING PICASSO

For decades Mamadou Cherif Diallo has produced some of Ziguinchor's most original batiks and taught his skills to passing travellers. Between mouldy walls, puddles of waste water and basins of colourful dye, he tells us his incredible story, while a monkey on a chain nods in bored agreement. 'I came to Senegal in 1973, but not as a batik maker', he says. 'I had studied boat engineering but couldn't find work in Guinea, my home country. Someone told me that they needed a lot of engineers in Senegal and so I decided to come here. But when I arrived, I realised that I'd been tricked. There was no work for me! I didn't have any money to go back, so I had to think of something else. And that's when I taught myself how to make batiks.' Inside his house a small gallery is covered from ceiling to floor with a dazzling array of colours and motifs. 'I think of something to print, then cut the stamps from wood and mix the colours. For more difficult designs, I call in a local artist who will draw the sketch on the cloth. Hold this!' He passes us the end of a massive piece of cloth and unfolds the fabric. A second later a brightly coloured batik version of Picasso's *Guernica* spans an entire wall. Painted in wax and soaked in brilliant blues and reds, the famous motif has been drawn with amazing precision. Mamadou smirks at our obvious bewilderment. 'I try to come up with new ideas all the time. This is one I made to order for a client. It was a lot of work! I can print anything you want, even your portrait. You just have to bring your picture along.'

To book a batik course, buy prints or just visit Mamadou's workshop, contact him at **Africa Batik** (☎ 77 653 4936; Ziguinchor).

SHOPPING

Marché Artisanal is great for a street stroll and picking up a couple of those ubiquitous wooden sculptures. **Marché St Maur** is more local in character.

Massoumé (☎ 77 573 3388; behind Marché Escale; ⏰ 9am-7pm Mon-Sat, 10am-1pm Sun) Marie Carton, who set up this lovely little shop, spends her time searching Casamance villages for the region's most original artisans and artists. It's a great place for rare finds, unique items and the products of tiny community associations.

Keur Boutesse (☎ 33 991 6620; jofettweis@gmail .com; Grand Dakar) The minimalist prints on hand-woven fabrics produced by Joëlle Fettweis, who studied local printing techniques for three decades, are perfect for throws and curtains. Call her before you visit and she'll pick you up at the nearby hospital.

GETTING THERE & AWAY
Boat
See p236 for details about the boat service between Dakar and Ziguinchor and p238 for information on pirogues around the region.

Bush Taxi
The large *gare routière* is 1km east of the centre. If you want to get all the way to Dakar (CFA9000, eight to 10 hours), get there around 6am or 7am; see also p238. Other *sept-place* destinations include Bissau (CFA6000, three to five hours), Cap Skiring (CFA1500, two hours), Kafountine (CFA3500), Kolda (CFA4500) and Tambacounda (CFA9000).

GETTING AROUND
Car
The set-up for hiring cars in Ziguinchor is quite informal. Most hotels can help, as can travel agencies (see p239).

Taxi
The official rate for a taxi around town or to the *gare routière* is CFA500. For a longer ride, you might have to pay a bit more. The main taxi rank is at Rond-Point Jean-Paul II.

BASSE CASAMANCE

However long you stay, you'll never feel that you've fully discovered this region. A relaxed pirogue tour around tiny bird islands, the manatee sanctuary at Pointe St George and historical Île de Karabane can keep you excited for longer than you can stretch your vacation. The road from Ziguinchor parallels the river and takes you through culturally and architecturally amazing Diola villages and thick forests to the wide, white beaches of Cap Skiring. Whether you like your holiday club style, sipping coconut juice in a hammock, or prefer to explore local culture in one of the

CASAMANCE

region's community *campements,* you'll be well served here.

ENAMPOR & SÉLÉKI

The 19km track along the deserted dirt road from Brin to Enampor teaches you the meaning of heading into the middle of nowhere. You know you've arrived when you see the straw roof of the huge, beautiful *case à impluvium* that houses the **Campement Villageois** (☎ 77 563 3801, per person CFA4000), where photographs and artefacts gently introduce you to the sacred aspects of Diola culture. It's a tough choice between this and the very attractive round house of the Spanish **Eco-Campement Séléki** (☎ 77 653 2741; www.campamentos-solidarios .org) close by, also run for the benefit of the local community. Both run tours to sacred sites, including forests used for initiation ceremonies (you won't be allowed to enter those) and seats associated with the region's animist king.

There's an unreliable Ndiaga Ndiaye from Ziguinchor to Enampor (CFA600). Hiring a private taxi will set you back CFA8000 to CFA10,000 and a hire pirogue from Ziguinchor CFA20,000.

OUSSOUYE

Roughly halfway between Ziguinchor and Cap Skiring, Oussouye (oo-soo-yeh) is the main town in the Basse Casamance area and seat of the region's Diola king. Shaded by mighty kapok and palm trees, it swings to its own relaxed rhythm, which speeds up briefly during wrestling season in September and October, when large matches attract the best fighters from across the region.

You can see the whole town in a day, including a variety of community projects, such as **Kalaamisoo** (☺ on request), a weaving workshop for disabled people, and the **Association des Femmes Évangéliques**, where your purchase of delicious jams and juices supports a female employment project.

Oussouye is a fantastic base to explore the interior of Basse Casamance, including M'Lomp, Ediougou and Elinkine. Ask your hotel about excursions or, even better, arrange hiking, biking and kayak tours through the local Casamance VTT (see the boxed text, p244).

There's no bank, but there's a small health centre and a post office.

Sleeping

Auberge du Routard (☎ 33 993 1025; r per person CFA3000) In the centre of this small *case à impluvium* the ladies of the hut can be found making batiks – an art they will teach you for a small fee. Rooms are basic but clean; bathrooms are shared.

Aljowe (Chez François; ☎ 77 517 0267; s/apt per person CFA4000/7000) This huge, red-brick *case à impluvium* really is as welcoming as it looks. For a private bathroom, you need to rent one of the cute apartments, which also give you extra legroom.

Campement Villageois d'Oussouye (☎ 33 993 0015; http://campement.oussouye.org; s/d CFA4500/6000) This

---

CAMPEMENTS VILLAGEOIS

In the 1970s, long before responsible travel became the buzzword it is today, two inspired thinkers – Adama Goudiaby and Christian Saglio – came up with the idea of fuelling village development by encouraging community tourism. They initiated the *campements villageois,* traditional-style lodgings that allowed travellers to explore life the rural way and were built, owned and run by the local community. The project was hugely successful for the first decade. Then, with the looming Casamance conflict and declining tourist numbers, the camps started running into problems. Many closed, others were destroyed, and even those that lasted were troubled by problems of maintenance and management – partly caused by the communal management that made them special.

Today an injection of finance and training is breathing new life into the pretty lodgings. The *campements* of Affiniam, Enampor, Koubalan and Oussouye have all been restored in their traditional architectural styles. But that's almost secondary – the real legacy of Goudiaby and Saglio's model is the responsible thinking it has sparked across the region. Villages, local residents and private hoteliers are all experimenting with ways of marrying local benefits with private management. From Cachouane to Koubalan, you can today go village hopping across the Casamance region, warmed by the thought that your money is helping the community you have just visited.

TWO WHEELS, TWO LEGS & ONE BOAT

Flat lands, tropical landscapes and gigantic, shade-providing trees make the Basse Casamance an attractive destination for mountain-bike tours, best combined with kayak trips through the *bolongs* (creeks). The place to arrange all of this and more is **Casamance VTT** (Chez Benjamin; ☎ /fax 33 993 1004; www.casamancevtt.com; Oussouye). This inspiring little company offers guided bike and kayak tours through the region's most beautiful parts (a half-/full day costs CFA6500/13,500). A guided tour combining cycling and kayaking costs CFA15,000 per day and takes you all the way to the river island Éguèye (see p246). Child seats and kids' bikes are available but should be booked in advance.

Benjamin, the Spanish- and English-speaking brains behind the company, also handles the organisation of the (in theory) annual Casamance Semi-Marathon, which usually takes place at the beginning of December. Check beforehand whether it's being organised in your year of travel.

Casamance VTT has its offices on the way to Campement Emanaye. Any local can show you the way.

---

impressive *case à étages* (two-storey mud building), beautifully restored in the region's typical mud architecture, has small rooms with shared bathrooms and good Senegalese food. Rooms can get hot in the summer months.

Campement Emanaye (☎ 77 573 6334; emanaye@ yahoo.fr; s/d CFA4500/7000) Maxim is the soul of this *campement*. You've just seen him make beds, then he's at the bar to pour you a beer and organise tours (plenty on offer here). Rooms are basic, but from the 1st floor you get fantastic views across the rice fields. Add CFA2000 for a fan.

Eating & Drinking
In the shade of a huge kapok tree, **Le Kassa** (☎ 77 563 7186; Route Nationale; dishes around CFA2000) serves tasty Senegalese meals, best enjoyed with fresh *bissap* (hibiscus drink) from the women's project next door. **Le Passager** (☎ 77 512 0243; meals around CFA2000), next to the *gare routière*, is busier and slightly drunk in the evenings when the band is playing.

If you want to test the village discos, **Chez Papis** promises 'multidimensional dance nights' and tries hard to rival **Elusaye** in popularity. If you're over 16, you'll feel old in both places.

Getting There & Away
All bush taxis between Ziguinchor and Cap Skiring pass through Oussouye. Most continue to the Cap and rates to Oussouye are usually CFA1000, though you might have to pay the whole fare to the Cap (CFA1500).

EDIOUNGOU
A short bike ride or pleasant walk from Oussouye, Edioungou is famous for its pottery. You can watch the local women create

their pretty wares, and purchase them. The 1st-floor terrace of **Campement Les Bolongs** (☎ 33 993 1001; s/d CFA7000/10,000) is an obligatory stop: it affords fantastic views over rice fields and a particularly beautiful spot of mangrove. Even if you don't stay the night here, you should drop by for a meal (CFA4000 to CFA6000).

M'LOMP
On the bouncy track between Oussouye and Elinkine, you pass through the village of M'Lomp, the best place to admire the local *cases à étages*, unique to this part of West Africa. The huge kapok tree that towers above the first *case à étages* is over 400 years old and sacred. Nearby, the **Small Museum of Diola Culture** (☎ 77 563 3833; admission by donation) is a cute but random display of Diola artefacts. Ask for Yannick Manga, who set it up; he's a good source of information and a reliable guide.

Decent food in a welcoming setting can be found at **Les Six Palmiers** (meals CFA1000-1500).

Oussouye–M'Lomp is CFA300 by Ndiaga Ndiaye and CFA500 by *sept-place*.

POINTE ST GEORGE & PETIT KASSA
Couched between bright-green rice fields, the magnificent belt of the Forêt de Kanoufa and the Casamance River, the rarely visited Pointe St George boasts perhaps the most stunning surroundings in the whole region. In 2008 the environmental agency Océanium established a Marine Protected Area here to revive dwindling fish stocks and protect the rare manatees, which are seen here more reliably than anywhere else in Senegal or Gambia (just make sure you're here at low tide).

Pierre, the friendly village chief, can put you up in the first completed rooms of the *campement villageois* on the river. Your stay helps pay the guards that man the observation tower in the river, making sure no illegal fishing takes place. Further inland, the tall viewing platform of the Forêt de Kanoufa grants magnificent views over the lands and the many birds inhabiting this varied scenery (see also the boxed text, p72).

A short boat ride from here, the Petit Kassa is another protected area, with a slightly different but equally enticing landscape. Stays are possible here, too, otherwise it's a day trip from Pointe St George.

The best way of getting here is by pirogue. Contact **Océanium** (☎ 33 822 2441; www.oceanium .org) to arrange your trip – either a mere return from Cap Skiring or Elinkine, or a hop over several islands in the vicinity.

NIOMOUNE

On the north bank of the Casamance River, between a tiny Diola village, mangrove creeks and the river, and accessible only via a long, picturesque pirogue journey, Niomoune is about as far off any classic land or river trail as you can get. At **Campement Alouga** (☎ 77 576 0977; www.alouga.com; half board per person CFA8500), you stay village style (and that includes open-air showers), taste scrumptious oysters in lemon sauce and other fresh, delicious meals and explore the village in the endearing company of lodge-owner Hyacinthe.

There's a public pirogue from Ziguinchor every day (except Tuesday and Saturday) that returns daily (except Monday and Thursday; CFA1300, four hours). Chartering a boat from Elinkine is CFA35,000 (one hour).

ELINKINE

The beaches of this busy village are dotted with colourful pirogues, either taking the local fishermen out to sea or residents of this multiethnic, multinational community and the odd tourist across the river to Île de Karabane and other destinations.

After years of closure, the **Campement Villageois d'Elinkine** (☎ 77 376 9659; campement elinkine@free.fr; r per person CFA8000) had just reopened its doors when we visited and looked enticing with its straw-covered beach huts under coconut palms, six pretty rooms with private bathrooms, and a river-facing restaurant. It's managed privately today but operates in the spirit of a true village camp, meaning profits flow back into the community.

Accommodation is more basic at the **Campement Le Fromager** (☎ 77 525 6401; s/d CFA3000/6000) near the jetty. Manager Mamadou Ndiaye is something of an institution here and is more than happy to share his vast regional knowledge with visitors.

Ndiaga Ndiayes from Ziguinchor to Elinkine are CFA1400, CFA700 from Oussouye. A hire taxi from Oussouye costs around CFA10,000. There are regular pirogues from here to Île de Karabane (CFA1500) and hire boats can take you to Cachouane, Niomoune and any other place on the river.

ÎLE DE KARABANE

This tranquil island near the mouth of the Casamance River was the first French trading station in the region (1836–1900). The remains of this historical legacy include the crumbling walls of a Breton-style church and school, the *gouvernance* (governor's office) and mission that houses the island's main hotel, and the Catholic cemetery with graves of French settlers and sailors. Large and centrally located, this is a great base for pirogue trips, including a spell of fishing, oyster plucking, birdwatching or dolphin spotting. Or just kick back on the beach, sipping palm wine or cocktails at **Africando** (☎ 77 533 3842), the cutest bar in Casamance, wedged between the roots of the big kapok tree between Campement Le Barracuda and Hôtel Carabane.

Sleeping & Eating

Mobile coverage isn't great here. Always leave a message if you don't get an answer on any of the numbers given – you will be called back. All places mentioned can arrange pick-up from Elinkine (around CFA15,000) and organise excursions.

Badji Kunda (☎ 77 556 2856; s/d CFA4000/6000) Artfully scattered with small statues and colourful wall paintings, the hotel is the extension of sculptor Malang Badji's busy workshop. It's great for atmosphere – rooms are adequate. You can try your hand at local glass painting or pottery for the cost of materials.

Chez Helena (☎ 77 654 1772, 77 642 3476; s/d CFA4500/7000) If the rooms were as pretty as the bright restaurant terrace, this would be a fantastic place to stay. They're not, but boisterous manager Marie-Hélène Mendy will make you forget the curious assembly of furniture by wrapping you up in sparkling conversation.

Campement Le Barracuda (☎ 77 659 6001; half/full board CFA7300/9800) Many travellers, aspiring anglers or daytime tourists wouldn't consider going anywhere else. Not because the accommodation is anything special, but because Amath, the manager, is a gentle spirit and generous host whom you trust to sort out any minor request or problem. The hotel operates Karabane's popular fishing centre.

Hôtel Carabane (☎ 77 569 0284; hotelcarabane@ yahoo.fr; half/full board CFA16,500/25,000) This delightful hotel is set in a lush and shady tropical garden. You'll have the honour of staying in what used to be the colonial *gouvernance* and enjoying your drink in the former Catholic mission.

Getting There & Away

Île de Karabane is best reached by pirogue from Elinkine. A regular boat *(navette)* leaves Elinkine daily at around 2.30pm and 5pm, reaching Île de Karabane half an hour later, before continuing to the village of Diogué on the north bank. It returns at 10am the next day. The fare for each stretch is CFA1500. Chartering a pirogue costs around CFA15,000 to CFA20,000 each way – just ask at the harbour or arrange pick-up with your hotel.

ÎLE D'ÉGUÈYE

About 17km from Oussouye, the Casamance River hugs this pretty islet with two slim arms. If you want to hide from the world for a day, book a room at the welcoming **Campement de l'Île d'Éguèye** (☎ 77 544 8080; r with full board CFA11,000). It works closely with Casamance VTT (see the boxed text, p244) in Oussouye, which has a kayak point here and organises guided tours. It can also get you here by bicycle from Oussouye and pirogue from Diakène Ouolof (between Oussouye and Cap Skiring).

CAP SKIRING & KABROUSSE

Cap Skiring's beaches are rumoured to be among the finest in West Africa. They're certainly Senegal's best and, considering their awesome beauty, the tourism industry here is enticingly low-key. Even in high season, you get a few hundred metres of white sand to yourself and all along the beachfront you find intimate guest houses and *campements*.

Orientation

The village of Cap Skiring is 1km north of the junction between Ziguinchor and the coastal

roads, past the main road with shops and restaurants.

There are some places to stay in the centre itself, but most hotels and *campements* sit on the beach south of Cap Skiring village, 5km along the coastal road towards Kabrousse.

Information

Casa Loisirs (☎ 33 993 5393; clpassion@orange.sn; village centre) Your place for hiring kayaks, beach buggies and cars. Ask for Tonton: he knows everyone.
CBAO (☎ 33 938 8111; Place du Marché; ☷ 9am-1pm & 2.45-4.15pm Mon-Fri, 9am-12.30pm Sat) The ATM should take Visa and MasterCard.
Diatta Tour International (☎ 33 991 2781; aessibye@yahoo.fr; opposite Auberge le Palmier) Check for excursions, especially to Diembéring and the tropical garden near Boucotte. It also owns Oudja Hôtel in Boucotte.
Health centre (☎ 77 643 3414) Very basic.
Net's Cap (☎ 77 245 5380; net-s-cap@orange.sn; per hr CFA300; ☷ 9am-10pm) Fast and well-equipped internet cafe.
Pharmacie du Cap (☎ 33 993 5122) In the centre of the village.

Activities

Most of the midrange and top-end hotels offer access to the beach and seaside activities. At Hôtel Katakalousse (see opposite), kayaking, quad hire, fishing and other options are open to nonguests. The fishing trips of the Villa des Pêcheurs (see opposite) enjoy a particularly good reputation.

The **Club Med** (☎ 33 993 5135) is normally a members-only place, though the Cap's club is rumoured to allow 'outsiders' in for meals and use of the golf course (with sea views).

For pirogue excursions to Île de Karabane (around CFA50,000), Île des Oiseaux (CFA25,000 to CFA30,000) and other destinations, as well as angling trips (half-/full day CFA15,000/35,000) head for the Pont Katakalousse, opposite the hotel of the same name (3km south of Cap Skiring on the main road). **Jean Baptiste** (☎ 77 555 2415) and **Philippe Gomis** (☎ 77 631 4836) are only two of several reliable and experienced *piroguiers*.

Sleeping

You'll find accommodation for all budgets in Cap Skiring, most of it close to the beach. Unless otherwise stated, the hotels listed below are all situated along the beach that parallels the road from Cap Skiring to Kabrousse.

BUDGET

Auberge Le Palmier (☎ 33 993 5109; Cap Skiring village; d with bathroom from CFA10,000; 🍴) Opposite Club Med, this is a clean, small family hotel. Rooms are well maintained with comfortable mattresses, though slightly dark. If you like pastis, you can usually join the owner for a few glasses on the terrace. Room rates go up by CFA2000 if you want hot water and by another CFA3000 for air-con.

Le Paradise (☎ 33 993 5303; r CFA14,000; 🍴) Among the handful of rootsy *campements* that line the beach, this is the best pick. You get direct beach access from the lush gardens. The king of this cheap castle can stay in the one air-conditioned chamber with sea views; budget-bound travellers can get a cheap bed with a shared bathroom for CFA6000.

Noopalou Coussene (Chez Bruno Diatta; ☎ /fax 33 993 5130; www.casamance-peche.org; r incl breakfast CFA15,000) This self-declared fishing paradise doesn't look quite as pristine as the publicity suggests and, after a visit to the unkempt restaurant space (great views, though!), the cleanliness of the rooms came as a surprise.

MIDRANGE

Kaloa les Palétuviers (☎ 33 993 5210; www.hotel-kaloa .com; Cap Skiring village; s/d incl breakfast CFA15,000/26,000; 🍴 🛁) This is one of few Senegalese-owned and Senegalese-managed places at the Cap and it offers the amenities of a well-organised hotel at fantastic rates. It doesn't have beach access but sits on a stretch of mangroves that you can explore on kayak and pirogue tours.

Villa des Pêcheurs (☎ 33 993 5253; www.villa despecheurs.com; s/d incl breakfast CFA19,000/23,500; 🍴) Rooms with their wooden decor are comfortable and the tropical garden is huge. The kitchen (including the in-house bakery) is so great that they've started organising cookery courses. Widely renowned for its excellent-value fishing trips, it also appeals to anyone without any interest in casting nets.

Hôtel Katakalousse (☎ 33 993 5282; www.katakalousse .com; Pont de Katakalousse; r CFA25,000) Cap Skiring's main address for water sports and excursions caters primarily to sports fishermen. Outside main catch season, you can talk about things other than catch sizes, and enjoy the hot tub and well-appointed bungalows. Cap Skiring's main pirogue point is right across the road from here.

Les Hibiscus & La Palmeraie (☎ 33 993 5136; hibiscus@orange.sn; Kabrousse; s/d incl breakfast from CFA29,200/42,800; 🍴 🛁 🏊) Two hotels in one, this vast place lets you choose between comfortable bungalows in a lush tropical garden (Les Hibiscus) and spacious villas where you're completely independent (La Palmeraie; enquire for rates). Resort style, it lacks the soul of the smaller places.

La Mer (☎ 33 993 5280; Kabrousse beach; d from CFA30,000) Right on the beach, this little bar has four small studios (or is that large rooms?) with walls made of crushed seashells and a private, hammock-adorned terrace. DVD player and sound system are provided.

Mansa Lodge (☎ 33 993 5147; www.capsafari.com; s/d CFA30,000/44,000; 🍴 🏊) The couple that runs this cosy family guest house effortlessly makes you feel at home. They've lived in the Casamance for 30 years and are both trained and experienced hoteliers – hence the eye for detail, lovely decor, personal care and profound knowledge of the region.

Fromager Lodge (☎ 33 993 5421; www.fromagerlodge .com; Kabrousse village; s/d incl breakfast CFA35,000/56,000; 🍴 🏊) The design here is as colourful as the homemade punch is potent. Its double bungalows are lovingly decorated with fabrics and wood. The bar winds itself around a kapok tree and the restaurant near the pool serves real Italian cuisine (dishes cost CFA5000).

Les Bougainvilliers (www.bougains.info; studios per week CFA150,000; 🍴 🛁) Run by the same managers as Le Paradise, long-term travellers can rent large studios here.

TOP END

La Maison Bleue (☎ 33 993 5161; www.lamaisonbleue .org; r per person CFA43,000/66,000) As styled as a supermodel strutting down the catwalk, this airy place oozes sophisticated chic. Rooms have individual colour schemes, and a designer's skilled hand lends the cosy lounge and garden restaurant a special touch. Its most exciting offerings, though, are the weekend trips to Guinea-Bissau's archipelago, the Bissagos Islands.

La Paillote (☎ 33 993 5151; www.paillote.sn; s/d incl breakfast CFA71,000/84,000; 🍴 🛁 🏊 👶) This is the charming grandmother of Cap Skiring's hotels. It's been here the longest and spoils visitors the best. It's a luxurious stay with access to a supreme variety of activities and services – including tailoring, golf, tennis, beauty treatments and, crucially, babysitting – alongside the obligatory pirogue excursions and water sports.

CASAMANCE

Résidences Les Alizés (☎ 33 993 5288; www.les-alizes-hotel.com; d per week CFA280,000, villas per week CFA1.6 million; 🔀 🖵 🐾 🍴) It ticks all the luxury boxes in the hotel handbook. There's the set of pools, hot tubs and bubble baths, the solarium, relaxation parlour, sports centre and all-round service. And it may be the only time you'll be asked to choose between a whisky cellar and a surfboard. Accommodation is in gigantic, stylish villas that sleep six people on three floors – not ideal for intimacy seekers.

Eating

There are plenty of good restaurants here, most sit along the main road in the village. Three hotel restaurants are also worth exploring: the Fromager Lodge has an excellent Italian kitchen, La Maison Bleue does great Asian food and the Villa des Pêcheurs is still the best for seafood dishes.

In the village, try the following:

Chez Les Copains (☎ 77 548 1593; Allée du Palétuvier; dishes around CFA2000) Tucked away behind Kaloa Les Palétuviers, this local-style eatery with vinyl-covered tables built to carry heavy bowls is one of the best places to enjoy a large plate of Senegalese *thiéboudienne*.

Le Kassala (☎ 33 653 0382; Cap Skiring village; roast meat per kg CFA5000; 🕐 8pm-4am) This lively *dibiterie* is what the Senegalese call a *terminus*: the almost obligatory 3am food stop for rumpled clubbers before heading home. It's also a fine and friendly place to hang out in the evenings, savour some delicious roast meat and catch up on local gossip.

Bar de la Mer (☎ 33 993 5280; Kabrousse beach; d from CFA30,000) In French places this close to the beach are described as 'feet in the water'. It's a beach bar that does a great seafood platter. In the evenings it often turns into a party parlour. The house cocktails may be to blame.

Le Djembé (Chez Nadine & Patrick; ☎ 77 533 7692) This colourful place continues the musical theme way beyond the name – you can enjoy live jazz here on Friday while relishing mouth-watering French and Italian dishes. It serves a refined cuisine, often made from local ingredients. A good place for family meals.

Drinking & Entertainment

Party picks at the Cap range from the rootsy to the glamorous. The noisy, hilarious and utterly lively **Bakine** (☎ 33 641 5124; Croisement du Cap; 🕐 10pm-3am) is the place to enjoy, or join in with some live drumming, wild dancing and arty talk with the Cap's most random folks. In Cap Skiring village, **Kassoumaye** (admission CFA500-1000; 🕐 10pm-4am) has the most local vibes – think *mbalax* leaps in front of big mirrors and a dusty glitter ball to complete the look. **Kaloa Les Palétuviers** (☎ 33 993 5210; admission around CFA2000) serves up a reliably good mixture of Senegalese and international grooves. The classiest clubs are **Case Bambou** (☎ 33 993 5178; moise_dasylva@yahoo.fr; admission CFA2000), a brilliant restaurant during the day and glitzy dance floor after 11pm, and the waxed-and-shined **Savane Café** (admission CFA3000; 🕐 9pm-3am).

Getting There & Away

AIR

Air CM (www.aircm.com) is one of several charters to **Cap Skiring Airport** (☎ 33 993 5194).

BUSH TAXI

Sept-place taxis (CFA1500) and minibuses (CFA1000) run regularly throughout the day between Ziguinchor and Cap Skiring.

Getting Around

A taxi from the main *campement* area to Cap Skiring village is around CFA1000, as is the trip from the Cap to Katakalousse.

Check your hotel for bike hire. For car hire, try Casa Loisirs (see p246) or the noticeboards at the hotels.

BOUCOTTE

The beach at Cap Skiring will seem unremarkable compared to the seemingly endless stretch of white sand at Boucotte beach, 7km to the north.

In the village the small **Boucotte Museum** is worth a quick look (ask any local to take you there). It has a small exhibition of Diola artefacts along the roots of some giant kapok trees.

Just north of Boucotte you can walk through a lush **tropical garden** (☎ Diatta Tour 33 992 0648) with fruit trees, medicinal herbs, tropical greenery and magnificent views across the rice fields from a small hill. Phone Diatta Tour before setting out to get directions and find out whether the restaurant there has been completed.

Located right behind the beach, **Oudja Hôtel** (☎ 33 992 0648; diattatour@yahoo.fr; s/d incl breakfast CFA11,000/14,000) has simple, ventilated rooms in a vast garden. Accommodation is basic, but adequate for the price charged.

A short walk further along the beach, **Hôtel Maya** (☎ 77 575 6177; www.hotel-maya.com; s/d incl breakfast CFA23,000/36,000; 🌐 📶 ♿ 👶) is more upmarket, with 20 spacious rooms overlooking the sea and pool (much nicer than watching the TV that's also offered). Communicating family rooms and the babysitting service allow stressed parents to keep their kids close while catching up on couple time.

Both hotels offer a free pick-up service. Hiring a taxi from Cap Skiring to Boucotte should cost around CFA2000 to CFA3000; a seat in one of the regular but rare (once or twice a day) bush taxis costs CFA500 – but careful, you'll be dropped off on the main road, from where it's still a long trek down a sand track to your hotel. Alternatively, you can walk the 7km along the beach.

DIEMBÉRING

Diembéring is so pretty that a chart-topping ballad has been devoted to it. The crowns of several giant kapok trees watch over it and their roots dominate the small village square and paths to the sand beach. Now that a handful of *campements* offer adventurous travellers a bed for the night, it's no longer as reclusive as it used to be.

Right on the village square, **Campement Asseb** (☎ 77 541 3472; sembesene@yahoo.fr; per person incl breakfast CFA5500) is run by a Diembéring native, who has turned this once-neglected space around with an investment in paint and simple repairs. For local *ambiance*, this is the best address.

Just outside the village on the route from the Cap, the tiny five-room affair that is the **Auberge Les Rizières** (☎ 77 721 3281; www.casamance -les-rizieres.com; per person CFA10,000) seems mainly geared towards *djembe*, dance and batik lovers. It has basic accommodation, a bubbly manager and camping space. You can hire bicycles here and ride along the wide beach.

On the main square, **Le P'tit Maxim** is mainly a place for a drink in the company of tropical greenery, and there's a small Spanish-run *campement*-cum-bar on the beach.

Diembéring is great for excursions to Cachouane and Île de Karabane, as well as for beach lounging and a taste of village life. For the latter, ask about the crafts workshops run by the local women's collective.

The route from Cap Skiring to Diembéring is a bouncy, dusty dirt track – unless the

promise of paving has really been kept. A seat on a minibus or *sept-place* costs CFA800. You're best off phoning your *campement* for pick-up options, or hiring a taxi (around CFA7000) or a 4WD.

CACHOUANE

Just north of Diembéring and across a river branch from Île de Karabane, this tiny Diola village tempts with white sands, palm trees, mangrove-lined creeks and dolphins close by. Since it's not exactly easy to access, it remains a peaceful place, where only the highly recommended **Campement Sounka** (☎ 77 645 3707; half board per person CFA8500) has put down roots. Things are kept simple and tidy in this large *case à impluvium* (bathrooms shared) and meals (vegie options possible) are often served African style, on a large plate where everyone digs in. Papis, who runs this relaxed place, can take you on pirogue excursions and dolphin-spotting tours to the islands of the Casamance River.

You can walk here from Diembéring – a spectacular hike through tropical landscape – or phone the *campement* to arrange a pirogue from Elinkine (CFA8000).

CASAMANCE NORD

The route northwards from Ziguinchor is best explored with plenty of time available, as several *campements villageois* will tempt you to leave the main road and venture along sandy tracks to tiny settlements.

KOUBALAN & DIOUBOUR

Koubalan is a small village, 22km northeast of Ziguinchor. Its **campement villageois** (☎ 77 527 7130) was just being restored when we passed – and is set to look excellent. In the neighbouring village, the *banco* (mudbrick) building of the **Gîte de Dioubour** (☎ 33 957 1256; infotpa@orange.sn; enquire for rates) is privately managed, engaged in training local staff and dedicated to putting a percentage of profits back into the community (see also p291). It's slightly more upmarket, but still a typical village setting.

Both Koubalan and Dioubour are great sites for excursions to the nearby Forêt des Kalounayes, pirogue trips through the mangroves (check out the promising reforestation being done here) and birdwatching tours.

REFORESTATION IN ACTION *Katharina Lobeck Kane*

Our pick-up truck flies over the Casamance street. Today is the last weekend of the mangrove reforestation project run by Océanium (p161), the final leg of a huge program that has already exceeded its goal of five million plants by over a million. And we're running late. Partly because our car broke down, partly because the very energetic project manager, Elise Kabo, keeps shouting out to halt from the back of the pick-up. We stopped so that she could talk to a local fisherman who had carelessly knocked over recently replanted mangroves. We stopped for a lecture in community work. 'Stop the car!', her voice rings out again, followed by a knock on the car window. 'Look at that, just look at those people selling our forests!' She jumps off the truck and struts over to a couple of women crouched behind a tower of charcoal bundles. She talks to them for a while, then returns to us, shaking her head. 'They'll kill our forests. Their forests... But you have to understand them. It brings in more money than anything else. That's hard to argue with.' All along the road, bunches of charcoal are lined up. 'The other day, I came across this guy burning teak to coal', exclaims Elise, 'Precious teak! You could smell it for miles.' Ahead of the clearing of land for agriculture and building, the burning of charcoal is one of the main reasons for which the lush forests of Senegal and Gambia are being cut down. Efforts are being made to replace the old-fashioned heating material with solar ovens or gas, but habits are hard to shift.

As we approach the Casamance town of Tobor, however, we finally catch a glimpse of the successes of Océanium's tireless efforts. To the left and right, young mangrove plants peek out of the shallow water – it's the association's most successful reforestation site. A few villages further along, we see how such success is shaped. A group of elders walks up to the scheduled community gathering, each carrying his own stool under his arm. Ali El Haidar, director of Océanium, asks them to speak to the youngsters, tell them how they remember the Casamance of their youth. And they do. They tell of abundance of fish and oysters as the mangroves covered every shoreline. And while there's certainly some 'back in the day' sentiment, it's hard to deny the obvious: the construction of roads and cutting of the oxygen circulation has led to the death of vast mangrove swamps and caused a decline of fish and other animals. The youngsters of the village listen and shortly after clamber onto the Océanium truck, singing loudly. A few minutes later, they all wade knee deep in river water, placing young mangrove spores into the mud. And perhaps they'll soon start shouting at careless anglers too: 'don't step on the work I did this summer!'

Getting There & Away

You can reach both villages by hire taxi from Ziguinchor (CFA7000, 45 minutes). They lie along the dirt road on the turn-off from Tobor. You can also get here by hire pirogue from Ziguinchor (around CFA35,000, two hours).

AFFINIAM

A few kilometres north of the river, Affiniam is located between forest and river, and is easily reached from Ziguinchor by boat. The **campement villageois** (☎ 77 567 0044; per person CFA4000) is in a large *case à impluvium* (see the boxed text, p240) on the edge of the village, shaded by giant kapok trees and close to the pirogue point. The guides there can take you to the low-key artisans' centre, where you can normally watch batiks being made and buy local jam. Affiniam is also great for pirogue trips to bird habitats and the *case à étages* in Djilapao.

Getting There & Away

The *campement* can pick you up by pirogue from Ziguinchor (around CFA25,000), or you can take the public boat leaving Ziguinchor daily except Thursday and Sunday (CFA600, two hours). Hiring a taxi from Ziguinchor costs CFA15,000 (one hour, 30km).

BIGNONA

Bignona is a crossroads town, a place where trucks are lined up on the sides of the roads while their drivers grab a quick plate of rice in one of the many tiny eateries. Spend a day or so here to have a look at the old colonial buildings (including the old Hôtel le Palmier) or venture into the lands behind the town for birdwatching or a tour around local villages (ask your hotel for a guide).

The best place in Bignona to stay is the cosy **Auberge Kayanior** (☎ 33 994 3014; kayanior@yahoo.fr; Quartier Château d'Eau; s/d CFA10,000/12,000; 🖳), with clean, pretty rooms in a family house, free wi-fi and a garden to relax in. If Rosalie, the manager, isn't available to share her passion for the region with you, she'll find someone who is.

In Badiouré, 11km from Bignona on the road towards Séléti, **Relais Fleuri** (☎ 33 994 3002; fax 33 994 3219; s/d CFA15,000/22,000; ⊠ ⊋) caters mainly to hunters. As long as you avoid the main hunting season (January to April), you can enjoy the pool and peaceful surroundings without talk about prey and rifles.

There are frequent *sept-places* from Ziguinchor to Bignona (CFA800).

KAFOUNTINE

Numerous illegal marijuana plantations near the town have spawned the kind of holiday centre where the tie-dye sporting *babas cool* (hippies) swing their dreadlocks to the all-pervading *djembe* beat. Kafountine is reasonably well equipped, with a *télécentre*, a slowish internet cafe, a health centre and a post office, but no bank. Most hotels and *campements* are scattered along a wide, sandy beach that reaches from the wetlands in the north past the fishing village in the south.

Sights & Activities

The typical Kafountine tourist does very little, very slowly. A day fills nicely with relaxing swims, some hammock lounging and a spell of *djembe* drumming in the evening. But don't get sucked into Kafountinian apathy before taking a birdwatching tour to Kassel (see p254). The trips organised by Esperanto Lodge are particularly recommended.

The **fishing village** is great to visit at high tide, when boats are launched into the sea. Nearby you can watch pirogue makers carve and paint the colourful boats. A completely different attraction is the **Village d'Outouka** (see the boxed text, p253), a world of stunning creation near Campement Sitokoto. On the main road through the village, put in a stop at **Chez Gilbert**, where you can purchase tasty local honey, bottled, filtered and labelled to good hygienic standards.

Sleeping

Unless otherwise stated, places are situated along the beach.

Campement Sitokoto (☎ 33 994 8512; per person incl breakfast CFA4500) Kafountine's *campement villageois*, located between river and sea, has basic rooms with shared bathrooms. It has seen better days but is very cheap and pledges to give back to the community.

Le Bolonga (☎ 33 994 8515; per person incl breakfast CFA7500) This quality place really is as warm and welcoming as the bar-reception in the wide brick building at the entrance suggests. The red-brick design is carried through to the pretty rooms, but the absence of fans might mean sweaty summer nights.

Le Paradise (☎ 77 327 2123; awa@club-internet.fr; r per person CFA9000) In one swift clearing of the smoke, this former Rasta haunt near Le Flamant Rose has now been turned into an arty *campement* with hand-sculpted chairs, a whiff of red wine hanging over the restaurant and world music drifting from the speakers. The restaurant serves a good selection of salads.

Le Kelediang (☎ 77 542 5385; www.senegam.net; full board CFA10,000) Sitting in a 3-hectare forest, this nature-bound *campement* is designed to be rootsy – as basic as a bucket shower and outdoor pit toilet. Everything is very clean and well kept. The restaurant serves delicious three-course meals (local ingredients, what else?) on a large terrace behind the sea.

Le Mampato (Chez Kiné Basse; ☎ 77 575 1684; btwn village & beach; s/d CFA12,000/15,000) Kiné Basse is something of a local institution, renowned for her love of parties – making you wonder how she keeps this pretty little place together so well. Her very good restaurant has gradually grown into a small hostel with four bright and tiled rooms. In Kiné's backyard, you can have a look at the squashed car the author of this book had an accident in and wonder why people would risk their lives to write travel guides. I do, regularly.

our pick **Esperanto Lodge** (Chez Eric; ☎ 33 936 9519; www.esperantolodge.com; per person incl breakfast CFA13,500; ⊠ ⊡) This relaxed place on the river is a real gem. Bungalows (some family sized) are large and designed with taste, but it's the landscaped garden with its palm trees and bamboo bridges and the enviable location between river and sea (and the bird life this attracts) that hold the greatest appeal. Then again it might be the restaurant, which wakes you with pancakes and fresh orange juice and puts you to sleep with local-juice cocktails.

Mama Maria (☎ 33 994 8541; www.hotelmamamaria .com; s/d incl breakfast CFA14,400/23,000) It looks like a country mansion, this Spanish-owned lodge, except that it sits just behind the beach. The heart of this impressive wood construction is the living room, where DVDs and books (mostly in

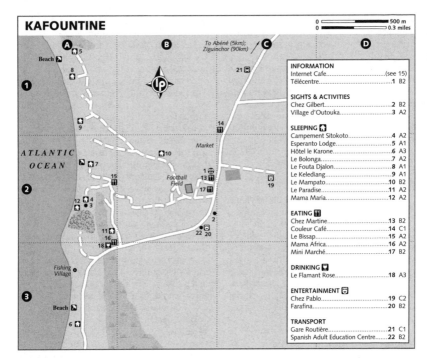

Spanish) fill the walls to the ceiling. The simple, colourful rooms will definitely feel homely after your first breakfast of omelette, coffee, prawns and fresh fruit on the sunny terrace.

Le Fouta Djalon (☎ 77 503 9922; lefoutadjalon@ yahoo.fr; r CFA15,000; ☒) The slope of a large dune shades the lodge's red-brick huts from the sea winds and gently whispers 'beach' until you succumb and climb up it, then down and into the sea. This is one of the most reliably managed and maintained places in Kafountine, with an unusually clean beach, thanks to daily litter picking.

Hôtel Le Karone (☎ 33 994 8525; www.lekarone.net; s/d CFA16,500/27,000; ☒ ☒) This very nice place with the only pool in Kafountine and a welcoming garden setting had just been put up for sale when we passed. Could it have been improved further or has it been turned into a car park? It's worth trying to find out, as it's a great place to stay.

Eating & Drinking

The kitchens at Esperanto Lodge, Le Fouta Djalon, Le Mampato and Hôtel Le Karone are also worth visiting.

Mama Africa (dishes CFA1500) Ask anyone where to eat and you'll be shown the way to Mama Africa. This is all about generous portions and welcoming smiles and, since everyone eats here, it's also where you'll find out anything you need to know.

Couleur Café (☎ 33 994 8555; couleur.cafeym@yahoo.fr; dishes CFA4000) The menu offers excellent grilled fish, good prawn dishes and homemade desserts. The setting is cute as well – inside there's a collection of random furniture and artefacts; outside, the view over Kafountine's lazy main street.

Le Bissap (☎ 33 994 8512; dishes CFA3000-4000; ☺ 8am-midnight) A cute eatery that advertises a unique *cuisine de métissage* (fusion cuisine). The food is tasty and you can check your emails and buy your groceries here, too.

Le Flamant Rose (☎ 77 541 2504) The name is *'rose'* (pink), the walls pink and the *ambiance* veers towards the redly lit. A very popular bar in town, it's one to visit before and after a trip to the local nightclubs.

Self-caterers can stock up in the centre of the village. The **Mini Marché** (☺ 9am-11pm) sells a good variety of foodstuffs and is a popular hang-out for local youth. A few metres along, the minimarket **Chez Martine** has a good selection of wine, foodstuffs and toiletries.

Entertainment

This is a town full of party-ready inhabitants. The nightclubs are usually packed with dreadlocked youngsters, fuelled with smoke and liquor. The **Farafina** (admission CFA1500-2000) is the most upmarket place of the lot. The local-style **Chez Pablo** (admission CFA500-1000) plays mainly Guinean and Senegalese music. Most nights you'll hear drumming coming from one direction or another. Follow the sound and you'll find yourself at an impromptu street party, where you can show off your Senegalese dance moves and tie-dyed trousers.

Getting There & Away

From Ziguinchor *sept-place* taxis run directly to Kafountine (CFA2200). You can also get bush taxis from Serekunda or Brikama in Gambia (around CFA1500). Traffic sometimes goes via the back roads and the sleepy Darsilami border, rather than the main crossing at Séléti, causing difficulties for your entry stamp (see the boxed text, p255).

Getting Around

To get from the hotel-lined beachfront to the village centre, it's a long walk, a bike ride through the sand or a taxi trip (around CFA1000; you need to order it with the hotel). You can hire clapped-out bicycles pretty much everywhere; a good place is the **Spanish Adult Education Centre** on the main road.

ABÉNÉ

Abéné (6km north of Kafountine) only really comes to life over Christmas and New Year's, when the **Abéné Festivalo** (www.alnaniking.co.uk/senegal /festival) attracts *djembe* drummers from around the world. Anyone is welcome – whether budding percussionist or professional. This event is all about community spirit, rather than big names.

Sleeping

La Belle Danielle (☎ 77 936 9542; r per person CFA3500) If the rooms were as great as the helpful and well-connected manager, Mamadou Konta, this would be a star-studded place. Things are very basic – a mattress, a roof and shared toilets – but also dirt cheap.

Maison Sunjata (☎ /fax 33 994 8610; info@senegambia .de; s/d CFA10,000/16,000) Staying here is like a visit to grandma's. There's a nicely tended garden, the spacious guest rooms are brushed to shine and you'll get fussed over a fair bit. The communicating rooms with shared bathrooms are great for families. Meals need to be specially ordered.

Le Kossey (☎ 77 223 8052; r per person CFA6000) The vast tropical garden is luxuriously large for the 10 round huts it contains. Rooms are clean and nicely understated and the whole place is only a few metres away from the beach. Candles and petrol lamps provide light. It's rumoured to have the best party on New Year's Eve.

Le Casamar (☎ 77 565 8939; per person CFA10,000) The garden is vast, the bungalows spacious and the beach around the corner – all of which spells great holiday haven. The thatch-covered

---

VILLAGE D'OUTOUKA

'If a child loves drawing and you step in his way, you'll disturb his life forever', explains Joachim while spreading out dozens of brightly painted canvasses on large tables. Behind us children's paintings in various stages of completion dot the entire wall of Outouka's central building. Inside giant sculptures made from household waste and colourful cloth lurk lazily in corners, next to giant carnival masks that wait patiently for their annual day out. Every day dozens of kids come running to Joachim's village and spend their free hours drawing, painting and modelling. When the storm of daily creativity passes, Joachim carefully traces the figures in each work with a thin black line, giving them the typical 'Outouka' look. 'I've seen children deal with issues here that they haven't been able to express elsewhere,' he says. 'Many of these kids have seen violence, sometimes war.' But this is a place of laughter and creative overflow.

Village d'Outouka (Chez Joachim; ☎ 77 633 9418; www.associationadiama.com), next to Campement Sitokoto, is open every day; just drop by. Paintings can be purchased – the profits are used to keep the village going, buy new paints and brushes, and organise exhibitions.

restaurant is not only pretty but also serves good food (order in advance).

Le Kalissai (☎ 33 994 8600; www.kalissai.com; s/d CFA28,000/32,000; 🛏 🖳) Past a winding dirt track through lush greens, you reach this polished place, where large bungalows are surrounded by lawns that are greener and more precisely cut than your average golf course. Right on the beach, with plenty of activities on offer, this is Abéné's classiest choice.

Eating

Chez Vero (☎ 77 617 1714; meals around CFA3000; 🕙 10am-10pm) is the much-loved auntie of Abéné's restaurant scene. The consistently good food is served on a terrace, under the watchful eyes of gaudy Madonnas and *griots* (West African praise singers) painted on the wall. **Bistro Café** (☎ 77 229 2649) is another good option with decent pizzas (CFA2000 to CFA3000), a well-stocked boutique selling batiks and clothes, bicycle hire and the occasional drumming soirée.

Getting There & Away

All public transport to and from Kafountine stops at the Diannah turn-off to Abéné. The village is 2km off the main road and the beach is a further 2km; you can walk or get a taxi (CFA1000). A private taxi from Kafountine is CFA3000.

NIAFOURANG

Here, where the *djembe* drumming makes way for the chatter of hundreds of birds, you find the utterly friendly **Tilibo Horizons** (☎ 77 501 3879; r with half board CFA11,000), wedged between the river and the sea. Ousmane Sané, the humble manager who runs the simple place like a *campement villageois*, can indicate walking

routes, arrange meals cooked to your taste and pirogue excursions along the mangroves. Highly recommended are the excursions with the eco-operator Casamance Horizons (p291), which take you far east to rarely visited stretches near Sédhiou.

For a sundowner in more stylish surroundings, cross the creek via the wooden planks to the **Domaine de Kabadio** (☎ 77 605 7009) and wait for the sun to set.

Phone Tilibo Horizons to pick you up from Ziguinchor or Bandikaki, where the *sept-place* from Ziguinchor to Kafountine can drop you off.

HAUTE CASAMANCE

SÉDHIOU

Some 100km east of Ziguinchor, river-lined Sédhiou is the largest town in this part of Casamance, a tranquil place that sleepwalks through an existence rarely disturbed by visitors. From 1900 to 1909, this was the main trading post of the French colonial administration. The old Fort Pinet-Laprade and a weather-beaten assembly of other old buildings still bear witness to this faded glory. The river is at its widest point east of the delta and lush forests and rice fields surrounding the historical town are fantastic for solitary walks.

Surrounded by majestic palm trees, the upmarket hunter's hotel **La Palmeraie** (☎ 33 995 1102; philippe.bertrand@apicus.net; s/d CFA20,000/28,000; 🛏 🖳) is Sédhiou's main address. It's located on a proud spot on the river but lacks the intimacy of the rustic **Auberge Le Faradala** (☎ 77 566 4846) on the edge of the village. This is where you get to sip tea with the locals, enjoy a gen-

---

BIRDWATCHING TIPS: BIRDWATCHING SITES AROUND KAFOUNTINE

An easy boat ride from Kafountine are two major bird areas of Senegal: the Sanctuaire Ornithologique de la Pointe de Kalissaye, a group of sandy islands (usually hidden by the waters), at the mouth of the Marigot Kalissaye; and the Sanctuaire Ornithologique de Kassel, some 5km southeast of Kafountine. The first is a great spot for observing waders and gulls, including Caspian terns with their massive wingspan, royal terns and pelicans. The island of Kassel has some of the tallest mangroves in the surroundings, home to herons, egrets and cormorants. If you've already settled too comfortably into the Kafountine beat, you can also do your birdwatching right in town. One of the best spots is the Esperanto Lodge, where you can look for birds in the *bolongs* (creeks) while imbibing a sunset drink. Esperanto Lodge and several other hotels organise trips to the famous birdwatching sites further afield, including the Presqu'île des Oiseaux, a narrow spit of land between the ocean and a creek, noted for its huge population of Caspian terns.

DARSILAMI BORDER

Bush taxis from Brikama to Kafountine sometimes go via the remote Darsilami border. The *sept-place* taxi will stop at Darsilami so you can be stamped out of Gambia. However, there's no border post in Senegal. If you arrive in Abéné or Kafountine without a stamp, you must arrange to get it as soon as possible. Ask your *campement* for help – they know the procedures – or head for the Séléti border, where you can get your entry made official. Don't travel around without it – even if you don't get problems on your tour, you definitely will when you try to leave the country.

---

erous plate of *thiéboudienne* in their company and even witness village school being held under the palm tree.

A short diversion off the smooth tarmac road from Kolda to Carrefour Diaroumé takes you to Sédhiou (bush taxi CFA3500); the turn-off is signposted.

KOLDA & DIAOUBÉ

Kolda's glory lies in its past, when it was the capital of a 19th-century Fula kingdom. The legacy of this grand past is a large Fula population, whose culture and language predominate. The town itself is unspectacular, though there are some pretty spots near the river,

where islands attract birds and monkeys. On a Wednesday, a day trip to the famous market of **Diaoubé** (38km from Kolda on the route to Vélingara) is a must. Once a week the population of this tiny town doubles, as traders from as far as Mali come here to peddle sacks of peanuts and rice, bars of soap and folds of cloth. As it's market day, you'll find plenty of public transport headed there (CFA1000).

To spend a night in Kolda, try **Le Firdou** (☎ 33 996 1780; www.lefirdou.com; s/d CFA16,000/19,000; P 🖳 🕽), pleasantly located a short walk from the centre. It's a pretty little oasis in a dusty town, with attractive bungalows in a palm-shaded garden. Another option is the impressively sized **Hôtel Hobbe** (☎ 33 996 1170; www.hobbe-kolda.com; s/d incl breakfast CFA20,000/25,000; 🞰 🖳 🕽), where black-crowned cranes stalk around the swimming pool and hunters take pictures with prey at their feet.

Outside the two hotels, food is limited to the vinyl-covered tables that pose as eateries. For a local-style party, try **Moya Nightclub** or the **Badaala**; both get packed with local youth on weekends.

Kolda is well served by public transport. There are regular bush taxis to Ziguinchor (CFA4500, six hours, 493km), Vélingara (CFA2500, 3½ hours, 290km) and Tambacounda (CFA4000, six hours, 443km). All bush taxis leave from the *gare routière* about 2km outside of town on the road to Sédhiou.

Directory

CONTENTS

BOOK YOUR STAY ONLINE

For more accommodation reviews and recommendations by Lonely Planet authors, check out the online booking service at www.lonelyplanet.com/hotels. You'll find the true, insider low-down on the best places to stay. Reviews are independent and thorough. Best of all, you can book online.

ACCOMMODATION

In both Gambia and Senegal, there's a huge discrepancy between tourist facilities available in the coastal areas and cities, and those inland. This is most strongly felt in Gambia, where a highly built-up and developed resort zone at the Atlantic coast contrasts with limited choices upcountry. At the luxury end, options are particularly thin outside the tourist centres. Backpackers, by contrast, will find that their budget stretches further inland, where most accommodation offers are not only simpler but also cheaper.

Senegal being larger, you'll find built-up areas with a good range of choices across the country, and some regions, such as the Siné-Saloum area, have developed a small scene of luxurious hotels in remote zones. In the Casamance, small holiday camps open increasingly in tucked-away corners. They are often run with village involvement, and tend to be simple but well maintained and set in brilliant locations.

Generally, the cost of accommodation is higher here than in East or Southern Africa, and noticeably more than in most parts of Asia. Rates vary enormously within the countries, though. Dakar is particularly expensive – you can easily pay more than a European rate here for a hotel that's not even that great. The cheapest area is the Casamance, where simple rooms in village *campements* (hostels) start at CFA4000.

Top-end hotels have well-appointed rooms with private bathrooms and hot showers, 24-hour electricity and air-conditioning. They are normally equipped with satellite TV, wi-fi, telephone, minibar and safe, and many have gyms or massage centres. Rates frequently include breakfast. Apart from a handful of notable exceptions, service can be pretty lousy, even in the most expensive places.

Rooms in the midrange section have a private bathroom and hot water. They will have fans and most probably even air-con, though you might have to pay extra for it (in places where electricity depends on generator power, this can push up prices quite a bit). You'll find a few cute family-run places, guest houses and original holiday camps in this bracket.

Budget places can occasionally be real bargains, with good, clean, midrange-type rooms for much better rates. Sometimes, however, they can be pretty basic dives of doubtful cleanliness. Cheapies won't normally have hot water or internet connections. If

---

PRACTICALITIES

■ The following English-language magazines cover the region and are mostly published monthly. *Focus on Africa* (BBC) has well-researched news stories, accessible reports and a concise rundown of recent political events. You'll find it in bookshops in Gambia and Senegal. *New African* (IC Publications) has a reputation for accurate and balanced reporting, with a mix of politics, finance and economic analysis. It has features on social and cultural affairs, sport, art, health and recreation. There are many more periodicals produced in French. The most widely available are *Jeune Afrique* and *L'Intelligent,* popular monthly magazines covering regional and world events. You'll find those magazines in the better bookstores of Gambia and Senegal, as well as some street stalls.

■ The electricity supply in both Gambia and Senegal is 220V. Plugs in Senegal usually have two round pins, like those in France and the rest of continental Europe. This plug type is also used in Gambia, but you'll also find plugs with three square pins, as used in Britain.

■ The metric system is used in both Gambia and Senegal. To convert between metric and imperial units, refer to the conversion chart on the inside front cover of this book.

---

bathrooms are shared, we've indicated that in the review.

See the inside front cover for price ranges of budget, midrange and top-end accommodation in Gambia and Senegal.

Many places, especially those in the top-end and midrange brackets, have high- and low-season rates. This book quotes high-season rates throughout, applicable from October to April. During low season (May to September) you can often get rooms about 25% to 50% cheaper. Especially in Gambia and Cap Skiring (Senegal), where tourist numbers vary most strongly from one season to the next, some hotels might close completely for low season. Call first if that's when you intend to travel. Many hotels raise rates above high-season tariffs over Christmas and New Year.

For comprehensive listings of hotels, check the following sites:

Access Gambia (www.accessgambia.com) Lists most hotels in Gambia, outlining facilities and contact details, and has links to their pages.

Au Senegal (www.au-senegal.com, in French) Has an almost exhaustive listing of Senegal hotels, and booking facilities for many.

Tourist Tax

In Senegal, a tourist tax is payable per night and per person. At the time of research, this was fixed at CFA600. Throughout the book, accommodation rates are quoted exclusive of this tax.

Types of Accommodation

In Gambia, the title 'lodge' is popular, supposed to imply a higher degree of comfort

(which is sometimes true). In Senegal, you'll hear the names *auberge* (hostel) and *gîte* (inn). A *maison d'hôte* is a guest house, usually a small, family-like place. A *maison de charme* is similar to a *maison d'hôte,* often with welcoming decor. An *hôtel de passe* is always at the low end of basic, generally implying the availability of rooms by the hour.

CAMPEMENTS & CAMPS

Campements are the most common accommodation in Senegal. The name implies not a camping site, but a hotel or lodge with accommodation in bungalows or traditional-style round huts. They exist in all price ranges, from very basic to all-singing, all-dancing luxury versions, though the majority sit in the midrange bracket. The Gambian equivalent is called a camp.

CAMPING

There are not many camping grounds in Gambia and Senegal, and those that do exist cater mainly for overlanders with their own vehicles. However, some hotels and *campements* allow camping for a small fee. Always check first, and don't just pitch a tent in a village without asking – you might run into problems with the local community.

ECO-LODGES

The term 'eco-lodge' is supposed to refer to a place that actively tries to reduce the environmental impact of hotel activity on its setting. Gambia has some excellent examples, powered by solar and wind energy, with dry toilets, and built with local materials from sustainable

DIRECTORY

LAUNDRY

Throughout Gambia and Senegal, finding someone to wash your clothes is fairly simple. The top-end and midrange hotels charge per item. At cheaper hotels, a staff member will do the job (by hand!), or find you somebody else who can. If you do hand your washing over, never include your underwear. No one washes anyone else's briefs and handing your dirty drawers to the laundry lady will cause her embarrassment.

---

sources. An eco-lodge should also train and employ staff from the local community, and respect and remain integrated with local customs and culture. If you wish to travel responsibly, it's worth checking the pedigree of your chosen eco-lodge carefully – the title is sometimes used liberally for places that don't actually qualify. We've indicated particularly outstanding examples in the GreenDex (p319).

HOTELS

Hotels come in all shapes and sizes, from cheap *hotels de passe* to glittering five-star palaces. You'll find star systems in use in both Gambia and Senegal, but they don't exactly correspond to the European and American equivalents – the respective Ministries of Tourism apply their own rules for awarding stars. Don't rely on the stars; check what facilities really are on offer.

Note that breakfast is not always included in the room rate and can be a substantial extra cost in top-end hotels. Only the most expensive places tend to offer a full breakfast buffet. In budget hotels, breakfast is more commonly a mug of Nescafé served with French bread and butter.

Some hotels charge by the room, though most places have single and double rates. The rate for two people sharing is always cheaper than that of two singles added up.

RESORTS

You can spend your entire holiday at resort hotels without venturing out. They are usually large complexes with several restaurants, bars, a nightclub, possibly a hair salon, a massage parlour, a souvenir shop and bike- or car-hire facilities. They also tend to have a wide range of activities on offer. In Senegal, most resort hotels are clustered around Saly, with a few

places in Cap Skiring and Dakar. In Gambia, you'll find them all along the Atlantic coast.

ACTIVITIES

Most tourist activities on the coast of Senegal and Gambia tend to be related to the sea, beach tourism being an important slice of the holiday industry. Upcountry it's all about the scenery and wildlife, with birdwatching, tours around the national parks and hiking among favourite pursuits.

Birdwatching

Senegal and Gambia are among West Africa's best birdwatching destinations. In Gambia, tourists interested in birdwatching benefit from a well-organised network of trained guides, tours and camps. Senegal has equally interesting birdwatching sites, but no comparable set-up. While some national parks have ornithological guides, birdwatchers will mainly have to organise their own excursions. See p70 for details on birdwatching sites, species that can be seen, and contact details for birdwatching associations.

Boat Trips

Boat trips are a great way of exploring regions of Senegal and Gambia. Gambia is almost more river than land, and going upcountry by boat is infinitely more rewarding than braving the roads. You can go from the coast all the way to Basse Santa Su in the east, but smaller excursions in the coastal area are also possible. In Senegal, the myriad mangrove-lined waterways of the Siné-Saloum and Casamance are best explored by boat.

Most trips are done by small, brightly painted wooden boats (pirogues), usually equipped with a motor. Motorised pirogues require a lot of petrol to run, the cost of which is carried by the person who hires the boat. This can make pirogue trips expensive. As the amount of petrol needed is the same for one person or a group of 10, you're better off if you're travelling with a group.

On the Senegal River, you also have the opportunity to travel by cruise ship, the *Bou El Mogdad,* an old, dignified boat, which has real historical importance in Senegal. See p215 for more information.

Cycling

Senegal and Gambia are good for the off-road, dirt-track variant of cycling. If you can bear the heat it can be a great way of exploring the countryside. The best-organised cycling company in Senegal is **Casamance VTT** (☎ /fax 33 993 1004; www.casamancevtt.com) in Oussouye, Casamance.

Hiking

The most interesting region for hiking is southeastern Senegal, the only area in Senegal and Gambia where you'll find mountains (see Bassari country, p231). Walks lead along small, steep paths, through tiny villages and occasionally through thick forest. It's best to go with a guide (see the boxed text, p232), not so much to avoid getting lost, but mainly to find the best spots and ensure a welcoming reception in the villages.

Swimming

In the tourist areas of Senegal and Gambia most major hotels have pools that nonguests are able to use for a fee or a small consumption at the hotel restaurant or bar. If you like your swim with less chlorine and more saline, you've got a long stretch of coast from where to jump in. Most areas along the Gambian coast are suitable for swimming. In Senegal, the best beaches are found on the stretch from Cap Skiring to Diembéring and along the Petite Côte. Dakar has a few beaches, but they're not on the same scale. Along the strands of the Grande Côte, currents are too strong for bathing, and still remain fairly strong around Saint-Louis.

Water Sports & Fishing

In Senegal, the places for diving, fishing and water sports are Dakar (p161) and Saly (p188), while the best surfing spots are found around Dakar (p162). In Gambia, the Atlantic coast resorts (p103) are your best bet. Also check the Sleeping sections in the relevant chapters – large resort hotels usually have water-sports equipment for hire, or make it available at no cost to guests.

The most popular activities include kayaking, waterskiing, parasailing and bodyboarding. If you're a skilled kitesurfer, head for Palmarin, where Thomas Morin offers renowned kitesurfing holidays (see the boxed text, p289).

Deep-sea sport fishing can be arranged in Dakar and Saly in Senegal, and in the hotel resorts of the Atlantic coast in Gambia. More relaxed outings in creeks, rivers and mangroves are possible all along the Petite Côte, Cap Skiring and the Siné-Saloum region in Senegal, and on the Gambian coast. Depending on the season, ocean catches include barracuda, tuna, sailfish, blue marlin, swordfish, sea bass and wahoo. See regional chapters for more details, and check www .au-senegal.com (in French).

BUSINESS HOURS

The further you're away from the city, the more flexible opening times seem to get. Note that Friday afternoon is never a good time to try to find people in their offices – for Muslims, this is the holy day of the week, and many take a longer break for the afternoon prayers, or simply go home. Unless otherwise indicated, listings throughout the book conform to the business hours listed below.

The Gambia

Government offices and businesses are open from 8am to 3pm or 4pm Monday to Thursday, and 8am to 12.30pm on Friday.

Banks open from 8am to 4pm Monday to Thursday, 8am to 1pm and 2.30pm to 4pm on Friday, and 9am to 1pm on Saturday.

Shops often close for lunch, opening from 8.30am to 12.30pm or 1pm and 2.30pm to 5.30pm Monday to Thursday, and 8am to 12.30pm on Friday and Saturday.

Restaurants may be open all day, but usually only serve lunch from 11am to 3pm and dinner from 6pm to 11pm. Most restaurants in the cities stay open until the last guest leaves, though in smaller towns many close around 10pm, or whenever the food runs out.

Bars usually open around 8pm, tend to get going from 11pm onwards, and close around 3am or 4am.

Senegal

Businesses and government offices are open from 8am to 1pm and 2pm to 5pm Monday to Friday.

Banks seem to be strangely keen on very complex opening hours. In Dakar, they are usually open from 7.45am to noon and 1.30pm to 4.45pm Monday to Thursday, and from 7.45am to 12.30pm and 2.45pm to 4pm on Friday. Some key branches open from 8.45am to 12.30pm on Saturday morning.

Shops are usually open from 9am to 1pm and 2.30pm to 7pm Monday to Saturday, and 9am to 12.30pm on Sunday. Some shops are open all day. Supermarkets open all day from 8am to 8pm and are closed on Sunday.

The larger restaurants in the urban centres may serve food all day, but it's more common for places to offer lunch (noon to 3pm) and dinner (7pm to 11pm). Most restaurants in Dakar are closed on Sunday. Many places that serve food in the day turn into bars at night, and can stay open (disguised with a new ambience) until 3am or 4am. For a night out in Dakar, don't even think of leaving the house before midnight; most places only get going around 1am.

CHILDREN

With an average of five children per mother, you may guess that Senegal and Gambia are places where children are very welcome. No one will be surprised to see travelling families and people will generally be happy to accommodate children.

However, you need to bring a certain amount of courage and sense of adventure. If you're an easily worried parent, you might not want to brave some journeys upcountry, and even if you are happy to take certain, sensible risks, you should come prepared, having done some reading on the country, and investigated facilities and the state of roads.

Practicalities

Travel with older children, from about the age of five, is fairly straightforward. Most hotels and *campements* offer the option of adding an extra bed to a room, usually at a very reasonable rate, and many have family rooms, with a double bed and a single, either in the same room or in a second room. Ask whether your hotel has communicating rooms; these are often the best solution for travelling families.

Children under two don't pay; in some places this extends to children of five if they share a room with their parents. Most hotels offer 50% discounts for under-12-year-olds.

Child-minding facilities are only available in a few hotels, most of them in the upper midrange or top-end bracket, and there's little in the way of professional babysitting agencies. Other extra provisions for kids, such as high chairs, hire cots and nappy-changing facilities, are generally only found in top-end places. Small midrange hotels and guest houses are usually very accommodating, trying to find solutions even if they don't have all the gear available.

All of the major supermarkets in urban areas, and even some smaller boutiques, stock throw-away nappies, though they're more expensive than in Europe. In smaller places less frequented by tourists or expats, you might not find them so readily; muslin cloths and plastic wraps are the locally used variant. If you're still feeding formula, take as much as you need with you; formula on sale here is not always of the best quality, even if the packaging looks the same as your usual brand. Breastfeeders, by contrast, have it much easier. Many local kids are breastfed to the age of one and beyond, and breastfeeding in public isn't frowned upon. There are no baby-changing facilities, so a changing mat will be absolutely useful.

Safety while travelling is a problem. Most bush taxis don't have seatbelts, let alone child seats. However, if you hire the whole taxi for the trip, or a day (usually by paying for all the seats), you can mount your own child seat, if you've brought it. That's absolutely recommended – the dangers of road travel in the two countries are very real, and it's a good idea to avoid unnecessary risks, particularly if travelling to remote areas where hospital facilities are limited.

Leave your pram behind! Trying to push a buggy around sandy footpaths, performing a slalom around ambulant traders and parked cars, is frustrating to say the least. A baby rucksack is much, much more useful – or you can just learn to strap your little one on your back, local style.

On public transport you'll have to pay for your child if they have their own seat. If they are young enough to sit on your lap, they travel for free.

If you travel with children, a well-stocked first-aid kit is absolutely essential, as is malaria medication, sunscreen, a sun hat and an impregnated mosquito net.

Throughout the book, particularly child-friendly features have been highlighted in individual reviews with the 🧒 icon. Lonely Planet's *Travel with Children* provides more detailed advice, as well as ideas for games on those long, bouncy bus rides.

Sights & Activities

While Senegal and Gambia offer little in the way of child-dedicated facilities, such as playgrounds or theme parks, there are plenty of activities that will excite children – you just need a little bit of imagination.

Of the urban centres, Dakar is the one with the biggest kids' scene, complete with a theme park, workshops and regular children's events (see p163), as well as a quick escape to the Village des Tortues (p180) and Accrobaobab (p186).

In Gambia, many of the resort hotels along the coast cater well for children, with shallow kids' pools, board games and the occasional slide and swing. The country has the great advantage that most things are in close proximity to the coastal centre, including Makasutu Culture Forest (p123) and Abuko Nature Reserve (p122).

Saint-Louis in Senegal (p210) is a calm city with fairly safe streets, where pelican- and flamingo-watching tours around the Langue de Barbarie (p219) and the Parc National des Oiseaux du Djoudj (p221) are not far away.

Some of the national parks can be pretty boring for little ones, as animals aren't always easily spotted. Senegal's Réserve de Bandia (p185) is a notable exception, with almost guaranteed sightings of buffaloes, monkeys, rhinos and crocodiles.

Pirogue tours are usually a hit, as are trips on a horse or donkey cart. The latter are possible in many places, but particularly in Senegal's Siné-Saloum region, Rufisque and the Casamance.

CLIMATE CHARTS

In Gambia, the coolest period is from December to mid-February, with an average daytime maximum of around 24°C (75°F). In October and November, and from mid-February to April, the average daytime maximum rises to 26°C (79°F), rising further through May and June to sit around 30°C (86°F) from July to September. Senegal has a wider range. In Dakar the average daytime maximum is around 24°C (75°F) from January to March, and between 25°C and 27°C (77°F and 81°F) in April, May and December. From June to October it rises to around 30°C (86°F). In southern Senegal, temperature patterns are similar to those in Gambia. Temperatures along the coast are generally lower than these averages, and feel even colder due to strong winds, while inland they are higher. The northern and eastern parts of Senegal, bordering Mauritania and Mali, generally have the highest temperatures.

Rainfall is another significant factor. The wet season is shorter (with lower total rain-

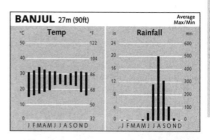

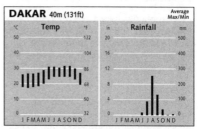

fall) in the north. The rainy period also gets shorter, and the amount of rainfall decreases, as you go inland. For example, in the far north of Senegal, the average annual rainfall is just 300mm, while in the far south it can top 1500mm. Dakar, about halfway down the country on the coast, gets around 600mm annually, while inland Tambacounda, at approximately the same latitude, normally gets half of this or less.

CUSTOMS REGULATIONS
The Gambia

There are no restrictions on the import of local or foreign currencies, or on the export of foreign currency, but you cannot export more than D100 – not that you'd want to. The usual limits apply to alcohol (1L of spirits, 1L of wine) and tobacco (200 cigarettes).

Senegal

There are no limits on the import of foreign currency; CFA200,000 is the maximum amount of local currency foreigners may export. Duty must be paid on some electronic items, such as computers and DVD players.

DANGERS & ANNOYANCES

On a world scale Gambia and Senegal are fairly safe places to visit, though crime in Senegal's capital, Dakar, was increasing at a worrying rate at the time of research. Outside Dakar violent crime is almost unheard of.

REALITY CHECK

Lest you get too paranoid, remember this. Considering the wealth of most tourists and the unimaginable poverty of most locals, the incidence of robbery or theft in most of Gambia and Senegal is incredibly low. Even a shoestring traveller's daily budget of about US$40 a day is what some Gambians make in a month. When you sit in a bus station sipping a soft drink that costs half a US dollar, look around you. You'll see an old man selling fans carefully woven from palm leaves for about half this price, or a teenager trying to earn that amount by offering to clean your shoes. It reminds you with a jolt that the vast majority of local people are decent and hardworking, and want from you only respect and the chance to make an honest living.

Street robberies happen in the Casamance and in Dakar. Take extra caution in these places and avoid moving around at night. See Precautions, opposite, for more safety tips.

For specific threats to women, see p277.

Begging

In most of Africa there is no government welfare for the unemployed, sick, disabled, homeless or old. If there's no family to help, stricken people may be forced to beg.

Especially in Dakar, groups of beggars squat near traffic lights or junctions, and will walk up to your car once it's come to a stop. Particularly hard to digest is the sight of many young boys begging in Dakar's streets with empty tomato cans. They are the so-called *talibe,* who may have been sent by their religious teacher into the streets (see p48).

It's up to you to decide when to give and how much. Many locals give spare coins or food – after all, charity is an integral part of Muslim culture.

Bribery

Bribery is a pretty widespread vice that you'll probably encounter at some point if you travel around the region. Police and military have gained notoriety for trying to extract bribes from people, which is partly due to the fact that they're very poorly paid. The most likely case is that you'll be stopped by a uniformed official who'll try to find fault with your papers or behaviour, then imply that the 'problem' can be solved with a small 'gift'. As long as you're not breaking the law in any way and have your papers in order, there's absolutely no reason why you should pay a fine. The trouble is that this is a game of time and a gradual wearing down of the opposite side. The person stopping you may not be in a hurry to get anywhere, while you might not necessarily be so keen on a lengthy

discussion over rights and obligations. And that's when most people grudgingly cede and pay.

Whatever happens, try to stay patient and polite if faced with tedious border procedures or police checks. Anger or rudeness can quickly keep you there all day. And remember that there are many officials who aren't corrupt. Don't freely offer to bribe your way out of a tricky situation; always wait for the official to announce that there's a fee of some sort involved in dealing with your apparent infraction of the law. Trying to bribe a noncorrupt official can get you into real trouble. See also p42.

Civil Unrest

This mainly concerns the Casamance region in Senegal. Though officially at peace with Dakar since 2004, the area isn't entirely safe, largely due to common robbers profiting from the precarious political situation. Occasionally street robbers will block a road and demand your belongings. If you're faced with this situation, give them your stuff, and they'll probably leave you alone. See p236 for more information on how to travel safely here.

In the university towns of Dakar and Saint-Louis, student riots over late payments of bursaries and learning conditions take place occasionally. They're usually confined to university areas, and quite easily avoided.

Mugging

The danger of robbery is much more prevalent in cities and larger towns than in rural or wilderness areas. The riskiest place is Dakar, where pickpockets and street hustlers roam the inner city (see p157 for more details). In the resorts near Banjul attacks are less frequent but not unknown; tourists have on occasion been pushed to the ground and had bags or cameras stolen, but they haven't been knifed or otherwise seriously injured (see p99). Gun crime is virtually unheard of.

Police Checks

Particularly in Gambia, police checks happen frequently. Normally, the driver will have to show his or her licence and insurance papers, though you may sometimes be asked to show your papers too. In Senegal, checks happen mainly in Dakar (by traffic police) and in Casamance (by the military). In Dakar, you'll be waved aside; in the Casamance, as in Gambia, you're more likely to be stopped at a fixed checkpoint. These points can be hard to detect if you don't know the area. Keep an eye out for them if you're driving; you'll get into trouble if you drive past.

Senegalese cars tend to get checked in Gambia frequently, and vice versa. That's why it's much easier to hire a car in each country, rather than trying to take it across the border.

Precautions

Taking some simple precautions will hopefully ensure your journey to Senegal or Gambia is trouble-free. Remember that many thousands of travellers enjoy trips without any problems whatsoever, usually because they were careful. Most of the precautions that we have suggested below are particularly relevant to cities.

- Don't make yourself a target. Carry around as little as possible; leave your day pack, camera, credit card and MP3 player in your hotel room – provided you feel safe about the place. In Senegal, even your passport can usually be left behind, though it's a good idea to make a copy of it and keep that with you. An exception is the Casamance, where you'll encounter police checkpoints. In Gambia, you need to keep your passport and vaccination certificate with you at all times.
- Don't display your money and other symbols of wealth. Use a separate wallet for day-to-day purchases, and keep the bulk of your cash out of sight, hidden in a pouch under loose-fitting clothing.
- Walk purposefully and confidently, even (or especially) if you're lost. If scamsters spot that you don't know the area, they'll be quick to try one of their latest con jobs on you. If you need to find a route, you're better off asking someone than consulting a map. That's what everyone does,

so it won't make you a target – maps are only used by tourists, and by pulling it out, you're 'outing' yourself.
- Don't walk in the backstreets, or even on some of the main streets, at night. Take a taxi. A dollar or two for the fare might save you a lot of trouble.
- Take someone you trust with you if you intend to travel to a risky area of town. It's usually not too difficult to find someone who wouldn't mind earning a few dollars for the task of guiding you safely around the streets – ask at your hotel reception.
- Avoid crowded events, such as football matches and stadium concerts, as they can lead to violence and crowd control is always very poor. Particularly if the political situation is charged when you visit, such events can be the trigger to vent lots of frustrations, and you don't want to get caught in it. During the research for this book, occasional street marches with violent consequences occurred, fuelled by very real grievances over the steeply rising cost of living and power cuts. Be extra cautious during times like these and keep your ear to the ground.

Scams

The hustlers of Dakar and Banjul, and some other places frequented by tourists, have perfected a dazzling array of scams and con tricks. Some are imaginative and amusing; others are serious and cause for concern. Their aim is always to get some (or all) of your money.

REMEMBER ME?

A popular trick in the tourist areas involves a local lad approaching you in the street with the words 'Hello, it's me, from the hotel, don't you recognise me?' You're not sure. You don't really remember him, but you don't want to seem rude, so you stop for a chat. Can he walk with you for a while? Sure. Nice day. A few more pleasantries. Then comes the crunch: how about a visit to his brother's souvenir shop? Or do you need a taxi? A tour? By this time you're hooked, and you probably end up buying or arranging something.

A variation involves the con artist pretending to be a hotel employee or 'son of the owner' out to get supplies for the bar or restaurant. There's been a mix-up in the shop, or he's just out of petrol and needs to get the food stock back. Can you lend him some money? You can take it off the hotel bill later. And there's more. Once you've passed him some bank notes (or even if you haven't) and he's gone, a couple of guys approach you, introducing themselves as tourist guards (with ID cards and all), out to protect visitors to their country from the low-down con artists, such as the one you've just fallen for. They explain his trick and accompany you for a while, and, grateful for their help and understanding, you make a small donation to their fund.

The best way of avoiding this trap is, well, to remember the people you have met. And shut your ears to anyone just whistling at you or calling you 'my friend' *('mon frère')* in the inner city. If they don't know your name, you probably have never been introduced. Tell people confidently you're not staying in any hotel, you've spent years living here, and throw in a couple of Wolof words; that'll probably put them off.

STREET SELLERS
A youth approaches you in the street with some random items for sale. Even though you make it clear you don't want them he follows you for a bit – checking you out. Then his buddy approaches you from the other side, distracting you with more wares. You get irritated and distracted, and while you focus on him, whoosh, the other guy goes straight for the wallet in your pocket.

The solution? Walk purposefully, don't be distracted, and keep your eyes open for odd behaviour. And don't carry your wallet in your back pocket.

VISITORS BOOK
In both Gambia and Senegal, the 'visitors book' has become one of the most popular and definitely the most effective means of extracting cash from tourists. There are several variations, but the following scenario is a classic of the genre.

You're in the market, carrying your camera, when a man approaches telling you he has a newborn child. Could you please, if it's no problem at all, come to his compound and take a photo of him and the child. It's not far away, it won't take long, and it would mean the world to him and his sick wife. When you get to the compound you meet his sick 'wife' but the baby is nowhere to be seen. Dad explains that his child is also unwell and has

---

COPIES

Photocopies of all your important documents, plus airline tickets and credit cards, will help speed up replacement if they are lost or stolen. Keep these records and a list of travellers cheque numbers separate from other valuables, and also leave copies with someone at home so they can be faxed to you in an emergency.

---

been taken back to the hospital, but seeing as you're here would you like a Coke? It's free! 'It is our duty to be hospitable', he says. 'We have lots of tourists here, and we never take money for a drink.' When you get up to leave, the 'visitors book' appears, listing the names of dozens of other Western tourists who've allegedly donated money to the family to help pay for rice – D500 being the average 'donation'. When it gets to this stage, you'll either be rude or pay.

Watch out for these situations from the start. As a general rule, most honest people will not just approach random strangers in the street and invite them to their homes. You're allowed to be suspicious if anyone does.

Security
To keep your money and other valuables (such as passport and air ticket) safe from pickpockets, the best place is out of sight under a shirt or skirt or inside your trousers. Some travellers use a pouch or money belt that goes around their neck or waist, while others go for invisible pockets and other devices.

EMBASSIES & CONSULATES
The Gambia
The following list includes embassies of some 'home' countries and of neighbouring countries for which you might have to get a visa. It's always best to go at the beginning of the morning session, as lunch hours can be very flexible.

Some embassies and consulates are in Banjul, and others are scattered along the Atlantic coast. For details of embassies in Gambia not listed here, check in the phone book or ask when there.

Germany (Map p91; ☎ 4227783; 29 Independence Dr, Banjul; ⊗ 8am-1pm, closed Tue)

Guinea (Map p91; ☎ 4226862; top fl, 78A Daniel Goddard St, Banjul; ⊗ 9am-4pm Mon-Thu, 9am-1.30pm & 2.30-4pm Fri)

Guinea-Bissau (Map pp100-1; ☎ 4226862; Atlantic Rd, Bakau; ◷ 9am-2pm Mon-Fri, to 1pm Sat)
Mali (Map p91; Cherno Amada Bah St, Banjul; ◷ 9am-1pm)
Mauritania (Map pp100-1; ☎ 4491153; off Bertil Harding Hwy, Kololi; ◷ 8am-4pm Mon-Fri)
Senegal (Map pp100-1; ☎ 4373752; off Kairaba Ave, Fajara; ◷ 8am-2pm & 2.30-5pm Mon-Thu, to 4pm Fri)
Sierra Leone (Map p91; ☎ 4228206; 67 Daniel Goddard St, Banjul; ◷ 8.30am-4.30pm Mon-Thu, to 1.30pm Fri)
UK (Map pp100-1; ☎ 4495133/4; http://ukingambia.fco.gov.uk; 48 Atlantic Rd, Fajara; ◷ 8am-1pm Mon-Thu, to 12.30pm Fri)
USA (Map pp100-1; ☎ 4392856, 4392856; http://banjul.usembassy.gov; 92 Kairaba Ave, Fajara; ◷ 8.30am-12.30pm)

Several European countries have honorary consuls in Gambia, including **Belgium** (Map pp100-1; ☎ 4497619; belconbanjul@yahoo.com; Bakau), and **Denmark, Sweden and Norway** (Map pp100-1; above Tina's Grill, Saitmatty Rd, Bakau). French diplomatic affairs are dealt with by the French embassy in Dakar, Senegal.

Senegal

For visa requests to neighbouring countries you usually need to provide two passport photos and a photocopy of your passport. Fees vary widely, from CFA15,000 to CFA50,000. Visits to your own embassy in Senegal are usually by appointment.

Many embassies are in or near central Dakar, but there is a steady movement of the diplomatic corps towards the Point E and Mermoz areas. If you need one that's not listed here, or if the information given has changed, phone directory enquiries from Senegal (☎ 1212), or check www.au-senegal.com (in French; click on 'Senegal Pratique', then 'Ambassades').

Most embassies open from 8am to noon. The following are located in Dakar unless otherwise indicated.
Belgium (Map p155; ☎ 33 889 4390; www.diplomatie.be; Av des Jambaars, Plateau)
Canada (Map p155; ☎ 33 889 4700; Immeuble Sorano, 3rd fl, 45-47 Bd de la République, Plateau)
Cape Verde (Map p156; ☎ 33 821 3936; 3 Bd el Haji Djily Mbaye, Plateau)
Côte d'Ivoire (Map p158; ☎ 33 869 0270; www.ambaci-dakar.org; Allées Seydou Nourou, Point E)
France (Map p156; ☎ 33 839 5100; www.ambafrance-sn.org; 1 Rue Assane Ndoye, Plateau) There's also a

consular service at Saint-Louis (Map p211; www.arc.sn/consulatstlouis) and an honorary consul in Ziguinchor (Map p239; Rue de France).
Gambia (Map p156; ☎ 33 821 7230; 11 Rue de Thiong, Plateau)
Germany (Map p155; ☎ 33 889 4884; www.dakar.diplo.de; 20 Av Pasteur, Plateau)
Ghana (Map p158; ☎ 33 869 4053; Rue 6, Point E)
Guinea (Map p158; ☎ 33 824 8606; Rue de Diourbel, Point E)
Guinea-Bissau Dakar (Map p158; ☎ 33 824 5922; Rue 6, Point E; ◷ 8am-12.30pm Mon-Fri); Ziguinchor (Map p239; ☎ 33 991 1046; Rue de France; ◷ 8am-2pm Mon-Fri)
Italy (Map p155; ☎ 33 889 2636; www.ambdakar.esteri.it/Ambasciata_Dakar; Rue Alpha Hachamiyou Tall, Plateau)
Mali (Map p152; ☎ 33 824 6252; 23 Route de la Corniche-Ouest, Fann; ◷ 9am-1pm Mon-Fri)
Mauritania (Map p152; ☎ 33 823 5344; Fann; ◷ 8am-2pm Mon-Fri)
Morocco (Map p158; ☎ 33 824 3836; Av Cheikh Anta Diop, Mermoz)
Netherlands (Map p156; ☎ 33 849 0360; 37 Rue Kléber, Plateau)
Spain (Map p156; ☎ 33 821 3081; 18-20 Av Nelson Mandela, Plateau)
Switzerland (Map p155; ☎ 33 823 0590; Rue René Ndiaye)
UK (Map p155; ☎ 33 823 7392; 20 Rue du Dr Guillet) One block north of Hôpital Le Dantec.
USA (Map p156; ☎ 33 823 4296; Av Jean XXIII)

FESTIVALS & EVENTS

There's always a festival on somewhere in the region: some so small and informal that you'll hardly hear about them; others huge, international events. You'll find a selection of key festivals below. In Senegal, check www.au-senegal.com (in French) for a calendar of cultural events. In Gambia, www.onegambia.com has free online music and clips, as well as information on upcoming events.
Abéné Festivalo (☎ 33 994 8615; www.alnaniking.co.uk) Informal event, mainly featuring *djembe* players and percussion troupes of varying standards. Happens every New Year in Abéné, Senegal.
Dak'Art Biennale (☎ 33 823 0918; www.dakart.org) One of Africa's largest contemporary arts events, held biennially in Dakar, Senegal, usually in May. Next editions 2010 and 2012.
Gorée Diaspora Festival (☎ 33 823 9177; www.goree diasporafestival.org; Mairie de Gorée) Music from Africa and the Americas on Île de Gorée, Senegal, every December.
Les Blues du Fleuve (☎ 33 868 2126; www.festivalles bluesdufleuve.com) Held in the northern Senegalese river

town of Podor, this festival brings together a wide range of artists from across West Africa. Initiated by famous Senegalese singer Baaba Maal.

Festival International du Film de Quartier (☎ 33 821 0771; www.mediacentredakar.com) Every December, this Dakar film festival showcases local productions with a strong focus on fringe projects.

International Roots Festival (☎ 4226244; www .rootsgambia.gm) Biennial festival held in April or May showcasing traditional and contemporary acts from Gambia and the African diaspora; also hosts seminars and debates. The main focus is Jufureh, but events happen all over the country. Next editions 2010 and 2012.

Kaay Fecc (☎ 33 824 5154; www.kaayfecc.com) One of Africa's best contemporary dance festivals. Held annually in Dakar, in late May or early June.

Kartong Festival (☎ 9933193; www.kartongfestival .org) Village festival in southern Gambia that features an amazing array of traditional and contemporary groups from Gambia and Senegal. It usually happens in March or April.

Regards sur Courts (☎ 33 842 1622; www.goree -regards-sur-cours.org) Annual community arts festival held in May, where Gorée's old houses open their doors to the public.

Sahel Festival (☎ 33 869 7900; www.africatravel -group.com) Set to become an exciting festival of Sahel music, it promises to showcase the best talents from the region in the magical surroundings of Senegal's Lompoul dunes. First edition in November 2009.

Saint-Louis International Jazz Festival (☎ 33 961 2455; www.saintlouisjazz.com) Renowned international jazz festival held in the beautiful old town of Saint-Louis, Senegal, annually in late May.

FOOD

The availability and quality of restaurants differ enormously between the urban and rural areas of the region. Dakar and the Atlantic resort zone in Gambia have a fantastic selection of restaurants serving anything from cheap, local rice dishes to sophisticated three-course cuisine. In smaller towns, your options may be limited to hotels or tiny roadside eateries (called *gargottes* in Senegal, chop shops in Gambia). Most restaurants only serve food during meal hours (around midday to 3pm and 6pm to 11pm), and in small villages it's often best to order in advance – many kitchens there can't afford to prepare food on the off-chance of a visitor and will only crank into gear when they know you're coming. A good thing to do is pass by the restaurant in the morning, order your meal for 1pm or 2pm, go on an excursion and come back in time for food.

Prices for meals vary enormously. Local rice dishes with fish or a meat sauce are always the cheapest. They go for around CFA1500 or D30 in the chop shops. A classy restaurant will charge around CFA6000 to CFA8000 or D250 to D350 for a dish. The higher rate doesn't always mean better food, and some of the best meals can be found in the most inconspicuous corners. Check our restaurant reviews for a selection of recommended places to eat.

Alcoholic drinks (apart from beer) in Senegalese restaurants are expensive – expect European rates or more. You might pay around CFA3500 for a glass of red wine, CFA5000 for a gin and tonic. Self-caterers can get by cheaply if they live on local veg, fruit and rice. As soon as the menu gets more varied, you'll need a generous budget, both in Senegal and Gambia. European imports, including things like cheese, coffee and cornflakes, can cost up to three times more than in Europe. Fresh fruit and veg, and fish from the market are all cheap.

See also the Food & Drink chapter (p79).

GAY & LESBIAN TRAVELLERS

Homosexuality is illegal in both Senegal and Gambia, under the Offences Against Morality Act. In Senegal it's punishable with fines or imprisonment of up to five years; in Gambia, up to 14 years. In the case of intercourse with under-21-year-olds, the maximum sentence is always applied. Despite this legal situation, homosexuals in Senegal were quite easily able to make contact, meet and flirt in the bars and nightclubs of Dakar and Saly. Even though large parts of the population harbour strong antigay resentments, people would generally 'look away' rather than become aggressive.

This quiet, though grudging, acceptance of homosexuality by Senegalese society was shaken up in early 2008, when a lifestyle magazine published an article about a 'gay wedding ceremony' of two Senegalese men in the tourist centre of Saly. If keeping silent about the taboo topic had enabled people to remain disengaged and quietly tolerant of homosexuality, the feature had broken that 'false peace'. The article provoked violent reactions from all corners of society, causing one of the men featured to flee the country and even gain refugee status in the USA due to the persecution he suffered. The justice system has also clamped down more severely than ever before, condemning a group of nine men to eight years in prison in December 2008, the harshest sentence ever pronounced against homosexuals in Senegal (the five-year maximum penalty was exceeded, as the men's group was described as a criminal organisation. Following an appeal and significant international support, the men were freed in April 2009).

Gay and lesbian groups report a general rise of homophobia in Senegal, and the public pronouncements of Gambia's president, Yahya Jammeh, don't inspire much hope for broader acceptance either. Religious leaders from both the Christian and Islamic communities in Senegal and Gambia have publicly condemned homosexuality, and fuelled homophobia by claiming to fight 'a moral combat'.

Against this rather gloomy background, it's still possible to make contact with gays and lesbians. Beaches, bars and nightclubs are popular meeting places, and Dakar, Saly and the Atlantic resort zone in Gambia have the largest scenes. Note that open displays of affection are frowned upon even among heterosexual couples – you don't see couples kissing or holding hands in the street. Gay and lesbian couples need to be even more discreet in the public arena.

For more information, see the following websites:

Behind the Mask (www.mask.org.za) This South Africa–based organisation has dedicated pages for individual African countries, containing legal and social information that's regularly updated.

ILGA (www.ilga.org) The site of the International Lesbian, Gay, Bisexual, Trans and Intersex Association features regular updates on the situation of homosexuals worldwide.

HOLIDAYS

Between the Christian, Muslim and national holidays, there's barely a month that goes by without a public celebration. For important holidays, the countries sometimes choose to take more than one day off.

The Muslim holidays, such as Korité, Tabaski, Tamkharit and Eid al-Moulid, are determined by the lunar calendar, and occur on different dates each year (for dates and details, see the boxed text, p47). The exact dates of these holidays are only announced just before they occur, as they depend on sightings of the moon.

Governmental departments shut on public holidays, as do many businesses and shops, though there'll always be a place open where you can get your bread and coffee. Public trans-port will be less frequent, and taxis usually increase their prices.

The Gambia
Holidays include the following:
New Year's Day 1 January
Independence Day 18 February
Good Friday March/April
Easter Monday March/April
Workers' Day 1 May
Anniversary of the Second Republic 22 July
Christmas 25 December

Senegal
Holidays include the following:
New Year's Day 1 January
Independence Day 4 April
Easter Monday March/April
Whit Sunday/Pentecost Seventh Sunday after Easter
Whit Monday Day after Whit Sunday
Ascension Fortieth day after Easter
Workers Day 1 May
Assumption 15 August
Christmas Day 25 December

Other annual festivals include the Grand Magal pilgrimage, held in Touba 48 days after the Islamic New Year to celebrate the return from exile of the founder of the Mouride Islamic brotherhood.

INSURANCE

An insurance policy covering you for medical expenses and an emergency flight home is essential. You're travelling in countries where risks of illness or traffic accidents are elevated, and hospitals in Senegal and Gambia are neither cheap nor good – it's important to know that you can get airlifted out should you have a serious problem.

Most travel insurance also covers your baggage in case of loss, and cancellation. That's a useful thing to have, as some of the airlines travelling to Senegal have a terrible record of losing or delaying luggage.

If your travel agent, insurance broker or credit-card company can't help you with a good policy, try a student travel service. It's preferable to get a policy from an insurance company that will directly pay any costs you incur, rather than reimburse you after you pay your bills.

Worldwide cover for travellers from over 44 countries is available online at www.lonelyplanet.com/travel_services.

DIRECTORY

INTERNET ACCESS

In Senegal, internet access is cheap and easy in all but the most remote areas. Service tends to be slower and more difficult in Gambia. Wi-fi is becoming increasingly popular in both countries and is well advanced in Dakar. Other regions in Senegal and Gambia are catching up fast. It's therefore useful to bring a small laptop or mobile phone that gains you access instantly. The internet symbol (🖳) used in reviews refers to places equipped with either wi-fi access or a business centre.

The Gambia

There are many internet cafes in Banjul and on the Atlantic coast, and even upcountry towns usually have a place to go online. Gamtel and Quantumnet (www.qanet.gm) have several internet cafes, and there are plenty of others. All charge about D30 an hour as a base rate. Service can be slow, though the main cafes have microphones, headphones and webcams. Frequent power cuts can ruin any well-planned day. Check if the cafe has a back-up generator, or at the very least a surge protector, before logging on.

Senegal

Senegal is one of the leading countries in Africa for web services, and you'll have no problem logging on. In Dakar, most hotels and many restaurants have wi-fi access, and the service is usually free of charge. Major towns in the regions are catching up fast. The spread of wi-fi means, though, that there aren't quite so many internet cafes (called cybercafes) anymore. We have indicated a few – note that service can be slow. Even small communities usually have somewhere to connect to the net, but prices upcountry are often higher than the CFA300 per hour you tend to pay in Dakar.

LEGAL MATTERS

While marijuana is widely available in both Gambia and Senegal, its use is illegal in both countries. If you're caught in possession you could face up to two years in an African jail – a less-than-attractive proposition. However, unless you're caught by an unusually straight cop, or are carrying a particularly large quantity of the drug, it's more likely you'll be 'persuaded' to buy your way out of trouble, which usually results in a very one-sided bargaining session.

Homosexuality is illegal in both countries – see p266 for more information.

MAPS

Most maps of Senegal also show Gambia, but the level of detail on the smaller country is generally poor. The Freytag & Berndt (scale 1:500,000) and Reise Know-How (1:550,000) maps are relatively good. The two-country map (1:350,000) and Gambia plan (1:350,000) by International Travel Maps tend to be more widely available.

Macmillan's *Traveller's Map of Gambia* (1:400,000, latest edition 2004) is clear and easy to read, with most roads, tourist sights and places of interest marked, though it can be hard to find.

For Senegal, the locally produced *Carte du Senegal* (1:912,000) is comparatively cheap and good, and includes a basic street map of Dakar. You won't find it outside Senegal though. More widely available is the *Senegal Carte Routière* (1:1,000,000) produced by the Institut Géographique National (IGN).

In Senegal, the **DTGC** (Direction des Travaux Géographiques et Cartographiques; www.dtgc.au-senegal .com) produces very detailed regional maps that are on sale in Dakar bookstores, while the **ADM** (Agence de Developpement Municipal; www.adm .sn) has started publishing a series of maps of towns and individual neighbourhoods, containing more detail than you're ever likely to need.

If your journey through Gambia and Senegal is part of wider travels in West Africa, the Michelin map *Africa – North & West* (1:4,000,000) is an essential purchase. It's the classic map, regularly updated and with a good level of detail.

MONEY
The Gambia

Gambia's unit of currency is the dalasi (da-la-see), abbreviated to D or d. Throughout this book, we have put it before the amount, eg D200. The dalasi is not fixed and varies enormously. At the time of writing it was steadily decreasing in value. Unconfirmed rumours blame this on the influx of drug money from Guinea-Bissau. Whatever the cause, it's creating all sorts of problems for local entrepreneurs. For you, it means bearing the changes in mind when looking at prices quoted throughout this book – they may have changed by the time you visit.

The dalasi is divided into 100 butut, and there are coins for five, 10, 25 and 50 butut, although apart from the 50 these are rarely seen. Notes in circulation are D5, D10, D25, D50 and D100.

Gambia's main banks are Standard Chartered, Trust Bank and PHB, which have branches in Banjul, Serekunda, Brikama and the Atlantic coast resorts. Further east, only Basse Santa Su has branches of Standard Chartered and Trust Bank, but they don't have ATMs.

Senegal

The currency of Senegal is the West African CFA franc, called the 'franc CFA' in French (pronounced franc seh-eff-ahh). CFA stands for Communauté Financière Africaine, and is also the official currency of Benin, Burkina Faso, Côte d'Ivoire, Guinea-Bissau, Mali, Niger and Togo.

The value of the CFA is tied to the euro at a fixed rate of €1 to CFA655.957. There are coins for CFA5, CFA10, CFA50, CFA100 and CFA250, and notes for CFA500, CFA1000, CFA5000 and CFA10,000.

The main banks are BICIS, SGBS (both affiliated to French groups) and CBAO (affiliated to the Moroccan Attijari bank). Most major towns have one or more branches with ATMs.

ATMs

There are ATMs at several banks (notably Standard Chartered) and a couple of petrol stations in Banjul and around the Atlantic coast. Senegal is amazingly well served, with ATMs in all major and some minor towns, and all across Dakar. Still, even in Senegal it's not wise to rely on their presence if you travel upcountry, as a broken or empty machine can leave you stranded.

In theory ATMs accept credit and debit cards from banks with reciprocal agreements. Visa and MasterCard are most widely accepted, and Visa tends to work more reliably in both countries.

In Senegal, your typical withdrawal limit is CFA300,000, though some bank branches only allow up to CFA150,000. In Gambia, limits can be tight, with some banks only allowing withdrawals of up to D2000.

Black Market

The huge black market that used to dominate money changing in Gambia has shrunk in size. The main points for changing on the street are the borders with Senegal (where you can barely step out of your taxi for women pushing crumpled bank notes in your face) and the Barra ferry jetty. Naturally, those are also the places you're most likely to get cheated when changing. If you arrive from Senegal without dalasi, you don't necessarily need to change at the border, as CFA notes are accepted by taxi drivers and many shopkeepers. It's usually a better idea to hold off changing large amounts until you've arrived at your hotel (receptionists usually know reliable money changers), rather than pulling out your bills in a shady restaurant at a busy border crossing.

In Senegal, the airport is a popular place for changing underhand. Since the CFA is pegged to the euro, you don't usually get a better rate if changing on the black market.

Credit Cards

The use of credit cards is mainly limited to midrange and top-end hotels and restaurants, car-rental outfits, purchasing air tickets and some tours. Visa is the most widely accepted. You won't usually be able to use them in supermarkets and only in very few shops (such as Senegal's large bookshops).

Certainly don't rely on plastic when travelling upcountry, not even for use in ATMs. Some banks in the interior of Senegal and Gambia can give cash advances on credit cards, though readers have reported this being too much hassle to try.

Your card company will tell you which banks in Gambia and Senegal will accept your card. You'll also need to ask your bank or card company about charges, and arrange a way to pay card bills if you're travelling for more than a month or so. Debit cards can be used to draw cash and because there's no bill to pay off they are good for longer journeys.

International Transfers

Unless you've got a bank account with a major bank in France, it's highly unlikely that your bank will accept international wire transfers. And even if it does, chances are it'll take longer than your holiday and cost you almost as much.

Faster and a lot simpler than banks is Western Union money transfer, where all you need to do is phone someone with money, get them to send their cash and tell you the password, and you can pick up the cash at a branch the next day. This doesn't come cheap either, but if you're really stuck for cash in a small village in the sticks of Gambia or Senegal, this might sometimes be your only option. Western Union offices are springing up quicker than potholes in Gambia's tarmac, and even small towns often have a branch.

Money Changers

In Senegal and Gambia, major international currencies such as euros, US dollars and British pounds can be changed in banks in the capital cities, major towns and tourist areas. All the major bank branches change money, as do exchange bureaus, which are mostly present in the tourist zones. The airports in both countries have exchange bureaus that open late. Should you find them closed, you can always change enough for your taxi fare to the hotel with one of the guys lurking around the airport (you can't miss them – they're on your back as soon as you step out). In urban areas, you can usually change money at hotel reception desks, although rates are often lousy or commissions high.

Try to do all your changing in the cities before heading upcountry. In remoter areas, you'll usually have to rely on informal money changers. Rates at hotels and with informal changers get worse the further you're away from the capital.

Tipping

In restaurants (apart from cheap, local ones), it's typical to give a tip of up to 10% of the total amount. Sometimes this is already included in the bill. Nobody will expect you to tip in a small roadside eatery (though you can, of course). You don't usually give tips to taxi drivers (that's why you negotiated your rate so hard beforehand). At supermarket checkouts, guys will pack your bags and carry them to the car – they'll expect a tip, though you may also refuse the service in the first place.

Travellers Cheques

In Gambia, you can change Amex travellers cheques in pounds sterling or euros at most branches of Standard Chartered and Trust Bank, although smaller banks upcountry are highly unlikely to accept them. In Senegal, only the central CBAO branch in Dakar accepted travellers cheques at the time of writing. Commissions can be high.

PHOTOGRAPHY & VIDEO

You don't need a permit to take pictures or film videos for noncommercial use, but there are limitations to what you can do. People don't like being randomly snapped by strangers in either country. Shooting in markets is particularly difficult – traders may harshly ask you to stop. If you're filming or photographing public events, stick to the events on stage if possible; punters don't want to get caught on camera.

Absolutely don't point your camera at things like military installations, airports, ferries, harbours and government buildings. This is particularly pertinent in Gambia, where you might get your camera confiscated or be taken to the police station. Always ask before taking pictures of places of worship or a natural feature with traditional religious significance.

Photographing & Filming People

Taking pictures of strangers is a sensitive issue, and you will find that people are hardly excited about becoming part of your postcard collection. This is particularly true of the 'daily life' situations you'll probably be tempted to document on your travels. The street, beach or market scene that's so wonderfully typical and colourful to you contains people going about their daily business, perhaps in situations of poverty or hard work they feel embarrassed about.

In Senegal and Gambia, people usually take pictures of ceremonies or parties when they've dressed their best. They'll pose for the photographer, rather than him taking random shots. You might find that limiting, but as a matter of respect you should always ask permission before taking pictures. If you get no for an answer, accept it.

The best way of getting varied pictures, including daily-life shots, is by making Gambian and Senegalese friends. Once people know you, they'll be happy for you to get out your camera – just make sure you mail the shots to them later.

Technical Tips
CAMERA CARE

Heat and humidity can take a toll on your camera, but the biggest danger is the all-pervading dust that accompanies almost every trip out of town. Especially during harmattan season (December to March) and on long bush-taxi rides, particles of dust get blown everywhere, challenging even the best sensor cleaner. Find a camera bag that closes well and put extra lenses and other accessories in a zip-lock bag when you're not using them.

EXPOSURE

When photographing animals or people, take light readings from the subject and not the brilliant African background, or your shots will turn out underexposed. Senegalese skies can look frustratingly bland and grey in photographs (especially during harmattan season). Try using bracketing to get the best out of your shot.

TIMING

The best times to take photographs on sunny days are the first two hours after sunrise and the last two before sunset. This takes advantage of the colour-enhancing rays cast by a low sun. A polarising filter can help to cut out glare, which is especially useful during hazy periods before the rainy season. The midday sun is often too harsh for good photographs.

For further tips, check out Lonely Planet's *Travel Photography*.

EQUIPMENT & PRINTING

Dakar is the best place to purchase CF, SD and other storage cards, as well as other accessories. Look for IT shops; they stock the stuff. The city also has a couple of places where you can print your photographs on good paper. That can be quite expensive, though it's a good solution if you want to give someone a copy of a picture you took. Gambia isn't quite as well equipped, though you'll find cards, accessories and possibilities for printing around the main streets of the Atlantic coast resorts.

POST

Postal services can be unpredictable and unreliable in both countries. While simple letters tend to arrive without difficulties, thick envelopes and small parcels often get lost in transit. Post is much quicker and more reliable from the main centres.

In both countries the postal services are relatively cheap. Postcards, envelopes and packaging materials can be purchased at bookshops and stationery stores.

Sending Mail

Letters sent from Dakar or Banjul take about a week or two to reach most parts of Europe,

and at least 15 days to reach North America or Australasia. If speed is more important than money, you're better off using a DHL service – especially in Senegal.

Receiving Mail

If you need to receive mail, you're probably living in Senegal or Gambia, or staying for a longer period of time. If you are here working, you might be able to use your office address for any letters you need to receive. Otherwise you can open a postbox at the main post office for a small monthly fee. Apart from courier services, mail does not get delivered to private homes.

It can take a week or much longer for mail to arrive from Europe, North America or Australasia. If the letter contains any larger items, such as CDs, it may well get stuck in customs, and you'll have to pay a small fee to retrieve it. If you've been waiting for mail for long periods of time, ask at the post office; they'll know if customs kept it.

SHOPPING

Small commerce is something of a national sport in Senegal and Gambia. Makeshift stalls get erected overnight on busy spots, at bus stops or on any other unclaimed patch. And as if that weren't enough, ambulant traders walk all major streets, peddling anything from framed paintings to Christmas trees and top-up cards.

For souvenirs, try the artisan markets (*marchés artisanals* in Senegal) that you'll find in all major towns. On small stalls and cloths spread out on the floor, you'll find the 'classic souvenirs' of the region on display: small wooden masks (the same designs endlessly repeated), wide patchwork trousers, batik T-shirts and cheap glass paintings. In Senegal, Dakar, Saint-Louis and Saly have the largest markets. In Gambia, try Bakau and Banjul. For genuine traditional art, seek out the galleries of Dakar and Fajara; for contemporary works, head straight for the artist workshops in Serekunda, Fajara, Tujering, Dakar, Gorée or Saint-Louis. See individual sections for more details.

Senegal and Gambia are great places to snap up some African fabrics, ranging from Lagos wax prints to glitter-adorned *laze*. If it's Malian-style *bazin* (bright, starched, dyed cotton cloth) you're after, go with someone who knows their stuff – fabrics vary enormously in quality and price. A 6m stretch of *bazin riche*

FUNKY SOUVENIRS

So you're the type of traveller who steers clear of 'tourist tat' but still wants to bring home something special? Try the following:

■ a lampshade or CD shelf made from old cans, sold at Dakar's Soumbédioune Souvenirs (p175)

■ an Afro-funky outfit from Ndiaga Diaw's urban label Fitt (p174) in N'Gor, Senegal

■ a colourful outfit that supports a village, from Equigambia (p112) in Kololi, Gambia, or Maam Samba (p174) in Dakar, Senegal

■ a *sous-verre* (glass painting) in a chunky metal frame, sold by Moussa Sakho at his workshop at the Institut Français Léopold Sédar Senghor (p159) in Dakar

■ a jar of delicately scented *churay* (a mixture of seeds and fragrant wood) to burn – it'll do wonders for your love life

■ a perfect copy of your favourite sandals, made to fit at the Moroccan workshops in Dakar's Rue Mohammed V

■ a batik copy of Picasso's *Guernica,* or any other masterpiece you fancy, made by Africa Batik in Ziguinchor, Senegal (see the boxed text, p242)

■ a scrap-material bird made by Mamadou Dhiedhiou Tall (or one of his apprentices), on sale at the Institut Français Léopold Sédar Senghor (p159) in Dakar

■ a diary, handmade from recycled paper at the Paper Recycling Project (p112) near Serekunda, Gambia

---

can be more than US$200; cheaper versions go for US$40.

For jewellery, try the ambulant traders who roam the beaches peddling cheap bead necklaces. Saint-Louis is particularly good for Mauritanian and Touareg silver craft, and jewellery shops in Dakar sell high-quality gold (again, go with someone who knows about quality and prices).

There are plenty of street stalls selling Gambian and Senegalese music. CDs go for around US$10. Try to buy originals where possible – piracy is a major problem for artists.

If you like incense, ask at the markets for *churay* and you'll be shown to small jars of brown roots and seeds soaked in perfume. Put in an incense burner, it not only makes for a nice scent but is also considered a potent aphrodisiac. That's why it's usually sold next to tables laden with sexy waist beads (to be worn under skirts) and mood-enhancing perfumes.

Bargaining

As soon as you flag down your first taxi in Dakar, you'll be introduced to the art of bargaining, an aspect of daily life in this part of the world.

Bargaining accompanies almost every purchase, with the exception of supermarkets, some fixed-price boutiques and pharmacies. With very few exceptions, such as the shared cabs on the Atlantic coast and the fixed-rate deals of Tambacounda and Saint-Louis, taxis need to be (fiercely) negotiated. Bus and bush-taxi prices are fixed, though you'll have to negotiate your luggage fee (see the boxed text, p288).

It takes a while to get used to bargaining. Especially if you have no idea of what the going rates are, you won't feel on solid ground and may think you're constantly being ripped off. That may happen – but the much-propagated myth that tourists are constantly being charged double or triple the general price isn't entirely true. Some traders might push their luck if they think you don't know your stuff, or you're more affluent than the average local (which you probably are), but the fact is that Senegalese and Gambians have to haggle the same way you do.

The first rule of successful bargaining is to relax and treat the whole procedure as an entertaining aspect of travel, rather than getting too serious about it. You show interest in an item; the vendor names a price. You pretend to faint with shock and make your first offer. Now the vendor's jaw drops. He'll probably feign indignation, indicating a clear no. You plead abject poverty, insisting on your first rate for a bit, and he'll come down. Then you go up a little. This carries on until you've found a mutually agreeable price. And that's the crux – mutually agreeable. You hear travellers all the time moaning about how they were 'overcharged' by souvenir sellers. When things have no fixed price, nobody gets overcharged. If you've paid a certain price, you did it because that's what you felt it was worth when you bought it, right?

Confidence in bargaining comes from knowing the going rate. You'll find this out easily if you know locals, and you'll get a feel for it once you've spent some time in the countries. We've roughly indicated prices for transport, food and other items throughout the book to give you some guidance. If sellers won't come down to a price you feel is fair (or that you can afford), it either means that they really aren't making any profit, or that if you don't pay their prices, they know somebody else will.

SMOKING

Public smoking bans have so far not reached Gambia or Senegal, and there were no immediate plans when this book went to press.

You'll very rarely see a Senegalese or Gambian woman sucking on a filter. Among young men, though, smoking is very common, and you'll see them purchase individual cigarettes from street stalls. If your taxi driver pulls out his cigarettes and you'd rather not inhale the fumes, politely ask him not to smoke while you're in the car. You'll normally get a nod and either an apology or a vexed look, as well as a smoke-free ride.

As many restaurants and bars are outdoor venues, they don't really get too smoky, even if all the cool clubsters light up. Where smokiness is an issue, we have tried to mention it in reviews. Note that smoking is forbidden in the village of Yoff (near Dakar), which is governed by the Islamic principles of the Layen community.

SOLO TRAVELLERS

It's perfectly possible to explore Senegal and Gambia on your own, though you probably won't end up spending much time alone as people will start talking to you, take you out for drinks and chat to you in the bush taxi. There's none of the embarrassed staring at the ceiling here that frustrates Westerners

---

PLAYING THE MARKET

The markets in Gambia and Senegal are large, vibrant, colourful and always fascinating, and well worth a visit even if you don't want to buy anything. There are markets with ramshackle stalls, where women sell carefully arranged fruits and vegetables, and those made of lines of boutiques crammed with cheaply imported electrical items, clothes and shoes, endless rolls of gaudy fabrics and pretty much anything else anyone might want. Most larger towns also have craft markets, where carved masks, statues and other items are sold mainly to tourists.

The biggest markets are in large towns such as Banjul, Serekunda, Dakar and Kaolack, but those in smaller places are also well worth a visit.

In rural areas, many villages hold a weekly market called a *lumo*. It always takes place on a particular day of the week, and it's possible to explore an entire region by travelling from the *lumo* of one village to the next. This is a great option, not only because you'll see the villages from their liveliest side, but also because in remote areas the day of the *lumo* is often the only one on which you'll find relatively frequent bush taxis.

Lumos are often major events. They're once-weekly possibilities to meet people from the surrounding villages, and therefore social events as well as opportunities to buy and sell. Especially in small communities, they'll attract street musicians, women displaying their finest gold jewellery, and whole communities out to enjoy themselves.

Market strolls are great, though dealing with overeager traders requires a particular cool and self-control. The Senegalese are famous for their skill of selling anything to anyone, so you need to be equally clever if you don't want to return home with bags full of unwanted stuff. Walking around town (especially the inner city of Dakar), you'll often be approached by walking traders, decorated with their wares like Christmas trees. A confident *'bakhna'* (meaning 'it's OK') or *'après'* (literally 'later', intended to mean 'I'm pretending to come back later but never will') should shake them off. If that doesn't work, keep looking straight past them, and keep walking on.

on their daily schlep to work – people talk to one another.

Travelling solo is by far the most expensive way of travelling. Many hotels charge the same rate for single and double rooms. On boat trips, you'll be paying for the entire boat, when it can actually hold a dozen others, and some tours require a minimum of four people. Then again, if you're reasonably communicative, you'll find it easy to link up with other travellers interested in sharing a boat or doing a tour together.

Women travelling alone will have to put up with a lot of unasked-for attention from men; see Women Travellers (p276) for details.

TELEPHONE & FAX

While few Gambian and Senegalese households have private landlines, the mobile-phone business is booming. Mobiles are a top status symbol here – you'll be surprised at the number of cutting-edge camera-internet-whatnot phones you'll see. Lots of people have at least two numbers, giving them relatively affordable access to two networks. The best way to stay connected is to take an unlocked mobile phone (or get it unlocked by a crafty mobile salesman – they're everywhere) and insert a local SIM card. That way, you avoid high international bills on your regular number. SIM cards can be bought anywhere in the street or at dedicated outlets. You simply insert the SIM and purchase credit via top-up cards sold by hundreds of youngsters on the street.

If for some reason you can't insert a local SIM, you can always make calls from telecentres, which also offer fax services. There's usually one in every town, though the rapid advancement of mobile phones is gradually pushing them out of business.

International connections are usually good. Calls to other African countries can be tough, depending on the place you're calling.

The Gambia

Gambian mobile providers are Gamcel, the former national provider, and Africell. Both give good coverage in most parts of the country. SIM cards cost D200 to D300. Costs are around D2 per minute for calls to the same network, and around D3.50 for calls between different networks or to landlines. Calls to Senegal are around D8, to the USA and Europe D22, and to other countries D24. Reductions

apply after 9pm. Fixed lines are provided by Gamtel, which also runs telecentres (some with internet access), though several of these have closed in recent years.

Senegal

The national telephone provider Sonatel is owned by Orange, which is also the most popular mobile provider. Orange mobile numbers start with 77; landline numbers are preceded by 33. If you're travelling widely in francophone West Africa, Orange numbers are useful as they work, and receive calls free of charge, in Guinea-Conakry, Guinea-Bissau, Mali, Côte d'Ivoire and possibly a few other countries by the time you read this (though you can only purchase top-up credit in the country where you purchased the SIM). The other two providers are Tigo (starting with 76) and Expresso (prefixed by 70). All three have similar rates, charging around CFA90 per minute for local calls (Tigo rates are slightly higher if you call other networks) and around CFA180 per minute for international calls. SIM cards cost around CFA2500.

Coverage is excellent. Apart from the odd stretch of remote bush, you'll get reception almost anywhere in the country.

Phone Codes

To phone Senegal or Gambia from another country, you need to dial your country's international access code (for example, ☎ 00 or ☎ 010), then the country code: ☎ 220 for Gambia, ☎ 221 for Senegal. There are no area codes in Gambia or Senegal; the first figures of a phone number allow you to identify which region a call comes from, or whether it's a landline or mobile.

To phone overseas from either Gambia or Senegal, first dial the international access code (☎ 00 for both Gambia and Senegal), then the number with international dialling code.

In Gambia the number for directory assistance is ☎ 151; in Senegal it's ☎ 1212.

TIME

Gambia and Senegal are at GMT/UTC, which for most European visitors means there is no or very little time difference. Neither country has daylight-saving time. When it's noon in Gambia or Senegal, it's 7am in New York, noon in London, 1pm in Paris and 10pm in Sydney.

TOILETS

There are two main types of toilet in Africa: the Western style, with a bowl and seat; and the African one – a hole in the floor, over which you squat. Standards for both vary tremendously, ranging from the pristine to the unusable. The lack of running water in rural areas often makes Western-style loos hygienic disasters. Suddenly the noncontact squat toilet doesn't look like such a bad option any more (as long as you roll up your trouser legs).

Public toilets are virtually nonexistent. In urban areas, you're never far from a restaurant that'll allow you to use the loo (you might have to buy a drink). If you're on a long bush-taxi trip through the country, things aren't quite so easy. Not even the buses have toilets, and there are no comfy service stations on the way. Near borders or ferries you'll usually find a few squalid toilets, and sometimes locals will allow you to use their loo. Some petrol stations have filthy toilets in the back – don't be shy to ask. Drivers will put in (strangely rare) toilet stops, usually near an empty field – easy for men, tough for women. Always carry some toilet paper with you on long trips, and perhaps some disinfectant hand wash – and keep your hands off the water bottle!

A couple of clued-up eco-lodges in Gambia have installed compost toilets – a great, nonsmelling, biodegradable solution. You'll be shown how to use these.

TOURIST INFORMATION

There isn't much in the way of tourist information on the ground. Apart from the organisations and websites listed below, hotels and travel agencies are good sources of information.

The Gambia

The national tourist office in Gambia is the **Gambia Tourism Authority** (☎ 4462491; www.visitthegambia.gm). It has a fairly informative website but doesn't operate any public-access offices on the ground. **Cultural Encounters** (Map pp100-1; ☎ 4497675; www.asset-gambia.com; Garba Jahumpa Rd, Fajara), the welcoming office of the Association of Small Scale Enterprises in Tourism (ASSET), is a great source of information about travelling responsibly. It can indicate exciting local projects, from restaurants and hotels to shops and tour operators.

In Kartong, the local organisation **KART** (Kartong Association for Responsible Tourism; ☎ 4495887; www.kartung.org) tries to improve eco-tourism options in southern Gambia. It's small, but worth checking out for information about the Kartong Festival (see p266) and local excursions.

For information online, ranging from sights to hotel listings and much more, try **Access Gambia** (www.accessgambia.com).

Senegal

Senegal's Syndicats d'Initiatives are supposed to provide information and activities in each of the country's regions. Some are very good, others hardly more than a phone on a desk somewhere.

The main branch is in Saint-Louis, a busy office and excellent resource for tourists. The Tambacounda branch produces a local map and can give good information. Joal and Sokone are mainly one-person operations.

Syndicats d'Initiatives include the following:

Gorée (☎ 33 823 9177; methiourseye@hotmail.com; Mairie de Gorée)

Saint-Louis (☎ 33 961 2455; sltourisme@orange.sn; Gouvernance)

Siné-Saloum (☎ 33 948 3140; www.au-sinesaloum .com, in French; Limboko, Mar Lodj)

Tambacounda (☎ 33 981 1250; nijihotel@orange.sn; Hôtel Niji)

Ziguinchor (☎ 33 938 8000; www.lacasamance.info, in French)

An excellent online source for travelling to Senegal is **Au Senegal** (www.au-senegal.com, in French).

TRAVELLERS WITH DISABILITIES

Neither Senegal nor Gambia are easily accessible to travellers with disabilities. Hotels that make provisions, such as wheelchair access, are few and far between. The sandy and obstacle-ridden pavements can be hard to negotiate for the visually or mobility impaired. However, if you stick to the large, established (and unfortunately expensive) hotels you can expect help, a general awareness, and things such as accessible toilets and wheelchair access. If you plan to travel upcountry, you're best off travelling with a tour company, and explaining to them your particular requirements beforehand.

VISAS

Depending on your nationality, you could need to buy a visa and have it stamped in your passport in order to enter one or both countries.

Some information is given below, but it's best to phone your nearest Senegalese or Gambian embassy before travel. Don't forget to ask how long it takes to issue the visa, and whether you need to enter the country within a certain period. Websites such as www.lonelyplanet.com, or the governmental webpages of each country, can also be useful.

Multiple-entry visas can be handy if you're flying into Senegal and then visiting Gambia before returning to Senegal for your homeward flight (or vice versa).

Visas at Borders & Airports

It is not possible to get visas to Senegal at the airport. In Gambia, last-minute travellers without a visa might be allowed in but will have to get a visa within 48 hours from the **immigration office** (Map p91; ☎ 4228611; OAU Blvd, Banjul; ⏱ 8am-4pm). This is usually more hassle than it's worth, as entry and speed of entry depend entirely on the whims of the immigration officials you encounter.

Purchasing a visa at the land borders between Senegal and Gambia is sometimes possible but too unpredictable to be recommended. You may get across the border without problems, but you may also be sent back.

Note that even travellers who don't need a visa are sometimes asked to pay CFA1000 for a tourist stamp when crossing from Senegal to Gambia. If you pay, you still won't get a stamp but will avoid a tedious conversation about rights and duties with a Gambian border official.

The Gambia

Visas are not needed by nationals of Commonwealth countries, Germany, Italy, Luxembourg, the Netherlands, Economic Community of West African States (Ecowas) and Scandinavian countries for stays of up to 90 days. For those needing one, visas are normally valid for one month and cost around US$50; you'll need to provide two photos. Always double-check visa requirements with your nearest Gambian consulate, and ask it what its processing times are (the standard period is three working days).

Last-minute travellers are sometimes allowed to enter and obtain a proper visa by submitting their passport to the immigration office and making a demand. However, it's obviously much safer to arrive with all your papers in order. The immigration office in Banjul (left) handles requests for extensions (D250).

Senegal

Visas are not needed by citizens of the EU, Ecowas, Canada, South Africa, Japan, Israel, the USA and several other (mainly African) countries. Australians, New Zealanders and Norwegians do need a visa. Tourist visas for one to three months cost about US$15 to US$20.

VISA EXTENSIONS

Most people wishing to stay beyond the initial three-month period that you are granted when entering simply take a quick trip to Gambia, and on returning earn another three months. Otherwise you can submit a request to the **Ministère de l'Intérieur** (Map p156; Av Jean Jaurès, Dakar) who will explain the (tedious) procedure to you.

VISAS FOR ONWARD TRAVEL

For Mali and Mauritania you can get visas at the border. For Guinea-Bissau, you should arrange your visa beforehand, at the consulate in either Dakar or Ziguinchor (see p265). For Gambia, it's also better to get a visa beforehand, as the availability at the border largely depends on the whims of the officials you encounter.

WOMEN TRAVELLERS

While it's not exactly dangerous to travel on your own as a woman in Gambia and Senegal, you do need to know how to live with a grinding background noise of constant male attention. Unwarranted and usually unwanted interest is a pretty steady companion of lone female travellers. There are several reasons for this. In this part of the world, it's unusual for women to travel alone, particularly if you leave your husband in another country or, God forbid, don't even have one. Western women are perceived as 'easy prey', partly because their generally greater sexual independence can sometimes be misinterpreted, and partly because of sex tourism. A third reason is a general flirtatiousness that colours conversations between young people. Guys approach women pretty directly, and see how far they can go. It's up to you to set the boundaries.

Dress Code

The way you dress can make a difference to how you are regarded, to a certain extent.

SAI-SAIS

A *sai-sai* is a womaniser, a smooth operator, a charming hustler, a con man or a dodgy mixture of all of these. These guys are usually young, often good-looking men, who approach women (sometimes bluntly, sometimes with astonishing verbal skills) in towns, nightclubs, bars and particularly on beaches. While some of them are fairly harmless (just don't get your heart broken), others can pull some pretty sly jobs, involving sexual advances, tricking you out of money or downright stealing. Use the same yardsticks you would at home before getting involved with men. Would you give your phone number to someone you just met? Would you accept a dinner invitation from a stranger? If not, then don't do it here.

Senegal is a Muslim country, and though few women are veiled, most wear long trousers or skirts in the street. Length is important: trousers and tops can be supertight and sparkling, with 'sexy bitch' spelt out in scarlet sequins, but a miniskirt will cause much staring, unless worn with leggings underneath.

Staggeringly sexy is the dress code for most nightclubs. Anything goes here, from stripper heels to microskirts and as much make-up as you can manage without weighing your head down.

Things are a little different when you travel through rural areas or visit someone's house (especially for the first time). That's when more modesty is recommended: go for understated elegance, with long trousers or skirt, and a blouse or T-shirt.

Married women and females from 30 years upwards tend to dress more modestly, usually preferring a smart city look to downright sexiness.

Sexual Harassment

Reports of serious sexual harassment, rape or violent threats suffered by women travelling to Senegal or Gambia are very rare. What you will experience are comments, kissing noises, chat-ups and possibly proposals by random strangers when walking on your own, especially on city streets and beaches. While this isn't dangerous, it's usually annoying, and you do need to know how to deal with such situations. The best way of shaking off hangers-on is to shrug off their advances, state your lack of interest firmly and stride on. Watch how the local women handle things – then practise that ice-cold stare and use it liberally. Avoid getting involved in conversation, but keep it cool – chilly politeness is more effective than anger.

Inventing a husband is a pretty good strategy, and can help ward off suitors. On the same note, it's always better to refer to serious partners as husbands – the fact that you might have a boyfriend usually doesn't deter (and will possibly awaken some sort of male competitive instinct – the last thing you want).

If you follow some common-sense ground rules – don't stroll along deserted beaches or dark city roads alone, don't hitchhike – you're unlikely to get into serious trouble.

Tampons

Tampons are only available at supermarkets and pharmacies in large towns such as Dakar and Banjul. They're quite expensive, too, so you might want to take a sufficient supply with you. In Senegal, a tampon is usually called a *tampon hygiénique*. By simply asking for a *tampon* you'll be requesting a stamp, as in a passport stamp, which just won't suffice.

Transport

CONTENTS

GETTING THERE & AWAY

ENTERING THE GAMBIA & SENEGAL
Passports

A full passport is essential for entering both Gambia and Senegal, or an ID card if you're a citizen of an Ecowas (Economic Community of West African States) country. Check the expiry date before you set out; it should be at least six months after your return. Passport controls between Senegal and Gambia can be tedious. Francophone citizens tend to find entry into Gambia a hassle; anglophones may encounter some red-tape tedium at the Senegalese immigration post. As long as your papers are in complete order, meaning you've got a passport with a valid visa (if you need one) and your vaccination certificate (see p293), you should encounter no serious difficulties.

AIR

West Africa isn't particularly cheap to reach from other parts of the world, and the best connections still follow the old colonial ties. For cheap flights to Senegal, you're best off checking websites and travel agents in France. For those to Gambia, the UK is a better address. Charter flights are popular for both countries; contact details of the major operators are given below.

Airports & Airlines
THE GAMBIA

The Gambia's main airport is **Banjul International Airport** (BJL; ☎ 4473117; www.gambia.gm/gcaa) at Yundum, about 20km from Banjul city centre, and about 15km from the Atlantic coast resorts. It's an impressive building, designed by Senegalese architect Pierre Goudiaby Atepa, but small with few facilities. There is no airport bus – see p96 for transport options.

Most travellers from Europe arrive on the competitively priced charter flights of the **Gambia Experience** (☎ in UK 0845 330 2060; www.gambia .co.uk). At writing, airlines with scheduled flights included the two carriers below, though the future of Air Sénégal International was extremely uncertain (see the Senegal section, opposite).
Brussels Airlines (airline code SN; ☎ in Kololi 4466880; www.brusselsairlines.com; hub Brussels Airport, Brussels)
Air Sénégal International (airline code V7; ☎ in Banjul 4202117; www.air-senegal-international.com, in French; hub Aéroport International Léopold Sédar Senghor, Dakar)

THINGS CHANGE

The information in this chapter is particularly vulnerable to change: prices for international travel are volatile, routes are introduced and cancelled, schedules change, special deals come and go, and rules and visa requirements are amended. Petrol prices in particular have become more unpredictable than they used to be. This has its impact on airfares as well as on local transport in country.

To arrange international trips, it's worth spending some time doing careful research, seeking out special offers and comparing rates. For in-country travel, talk to the locals to find out if any major price shifts have occurred recently. If you plan to do a fair bit of bush taxi travelling, you can rest assured that *sept-place* drivers will rarely try to overcharge you on the price of a seat. Private taxi rides have to be negotiated anyway, and thus depend as much on your bargaining skills as on the going oil rate.

The details given in this chapter should be regarded as pointers and are not a substitute for your own careful, up-to-date research.

TRANSPORT

CLIMATE CHANGE & TRAVEL

Climate change is a serious threat to the ecosystems that humans rely upon, and air travel is the fastest-growing contributor to the problem. Lonely Planet regards travel, overall, as a global benefit, but believes we all have a responsibility to limit our personal impact on global warming.

Flying & Climate Change

Pretty much every form of motor travel generates CO_2 (the main cause of human-induced climate change) but planes are far and away the worst offenders, not just because of the sheer distances they allow us to travel, but because they release greenhouse gases high into the atmosphere. The statistics are frightening: two people taking a return flight between Europe and the US will contribute as much to climate change as an average household's gas and electricity consumption over a whole year.

Carbon Offset Schemes

Climatecare.org and other websites use 'carbon calculators' that allow jet-setters to offset the greenhouse gases they are responsible for with contributions to energy-saving projects and other climate-friendly initiatives in the developing world – including projects in India, Honduras, Kazakhstan and Uganda.

Lonely Planet, together with Rough Guides and other concerned partners in the travel industry, supports the carbon offset scheme run by climatecare.org. Lonely Planet offsets all of its staff and author travel.

For more information check out our website: lonelyplanet.com.

SENEGAL

Until the new mega-airport 40km from Dakar is built, the **Léopold Sédar Senghor International Airport** (Aéroport International Léopold Sédar Senghor; DKR; ☎ 33 869 5050, 24hr information line 77 628 1010; www.aeroportdakar.com) in Yoff is Senegal's main international airport. It's pretty well organised (most shady characters are now confined to the adjacent taxi park) and has ATMs, exchange facilities, car-hire companies and offices of major airlines and tour operators.

The tiny airport of **Cap Skiring** (☎ 33 993 5194) also has international connections to France.

When this book went to press, the national carrier **Air Sénégal International** (airline code V7; ☎ in Dakar 81 804 0404, in France 08 20 20 21 23; www.air-senegalinternational.com, in French) had just filed for bankruptcy, following the pull-out of Royal Air Maroc. By the time you travel, another carrier may have taken over its excellent West African connections. Check before setting out.

Other main airlines:

Afriqiyah Airways (airline code 8U; ☎ in Dakar 33 849 4930; www.afriqiyah.be; hub Tripoli International Airport, Libya)

Air Algérie (airline code AH; ☎ in Dakar 33 823 5548; www.airalgerie.dz; hub Houarie Boumedienne Airport, Algiers)

Air Europa (airline code UX; ☎ in Dakar 33 822 0299; www.air-europa.com; hub Madrid Airport, Madrid)

Air France (airline code AF; ☎ in Dakar 33 839 7777; www.airfrance.fr; hub Airport Charles de Gaulle, Paris)

Air Ivoire (airline code VU; ☎ in Dakar 33 889 0280; www.airivoire.com; hub Abidjan Airport, Abidjan)

Brussels Airlines (airline code SN; ☎ in Dakar 33 823 0460; www.brusselsairlines.com; hub Brussels Airport, Brussels)

Delta Airlines (airline code DL; ☎ in Dakar 33 849 6955; www.delta.com; hub Hartsfield-Jackson International Airport, Atlanta)

Ethiopian Airlines (airline code ET; ☎ in Dakar 33 823 5552; www.flyethiopian.com; hub Bole International Airport, Addis Ababa)

Iberia Airlines (airline code IB; ☎ in Dakar 33 889 0050; www.iberia.com; hub Madrid Barajas Airport, Madrid)

Kenya Airways (airline code KQ; ☎ in Dakar 33 823 0070; www.kenya-airways.com; hub Jomo Kenyatta International Airport, Nairobi)

Royal Air Maroc (airline code AT; ☎ in Dakar 33 849 4748; www.royalairmaroc.com; hub Mohammed V International Airport, Casablanca)

South African Airways (airline code SA; ☎ in Dakar 33 869 4000; www.flysaa.com; hub Johannesburg International Airport, Johannesburg)

TACV Cabo Verde Airlines (airline code VR; ☎ in Dakar 33 821 3968; www.flytacv.com; hub Praia Airport, Praia)

TAP Air Portugal (airline code TP; ☎ in Dakar 33 821 5460; www.tap.pt; hub Lisboa Portela Airport, Lisbon)
Virgin Nigeria (airline code VK; ☎ in Dakar 33 889 9010; www.virginnigeria.com; hub Lagos International Airport, Lagos)

Tickets

Regular flights to both Senegal and Gambia tend to be comparatively expensive, and rising petrol prices keep pushing ticket rates up. Particularly in Dakar, airport tax is also steep, as it includes an amount for the construction of the new hub. However, most airlines run frequent promotional deals and there are charter options too – you need to invest some time in online research.

Especially in larger towns, it's worth seeking out the help of a travel agent who knows about special deals, has strategies for avoiding layovers and can offer advice on everything from which airline has the best vegetarian food to the best travel insurance to bundle with your ticket. Several airlines offer 'youth' or 'student' tickets, with discounts for people under 26 (sometimes 23) or in full-time education. If you're eligible, ask the travel agent if any student fares are available – they might 'forget' to tell you. Regulations vary, but you'll need to prove your age or student status.

Africa

There are plenty of connections to other West African capitals, though not all airlines are in an equally good state. Delays, cancellations and reroutings are common, and prices are often forbiddingly high, even for short distances.

Many East and Southern African destinations can be difficult to reach and may involve multiple changes, long waiting times and high costs. Dakar is well connected to Kenya and Ethiopia, but most long-haul destinations within Africa are more commonly, and cheaply, reached via Europe.

SENEGAL

Dakar is one of Africa's travel hubs, though all of Air Sénégal's flights (to Benin, Burkina Faso, Cape Verde, Côte d'Ivoire, Gambia, Guinea, Guinea-Bissau, Mali, Mauritania, Morocco and Niger) had been suspended at writing as the company had filed for bankruptcy. Check for the latest when you travel. Kenya Airways and Ethiopian Airlines stop in Mali. TACV Cabo Verde Airlines flies three times a week

to Praia, from where you can even connect to Recife (Brazil). Côte d'Ivoire and Ghana are best reached by Air Ivoire. For Nigeria, the most reliable connection is provided by Virgin Nigeria, with twice-weekly connections.

For northern Africa, Afriqiyah Airways connects Senegal to Libya (and further to Europe), Royal Air Maroc is the main carrier to Morocco, and Air Algérie flies to Algeria.

Dakar also has a direct daily connection to South Africa with South African Airways and Delta Airlines, and a direct link to Ethiopia via Ethiopian Airlines.

Asia

The best connections between Asia and Senegal tend to go via Dubai, then with Ethiopian Airlines or Kenya Airways via Addis Ababa or Nairobi, respectively, to Dakar. For Gambia, you have to travel via Europe or Senegal.

Australia & New Zealand

Reaching Senegal or Gambia from Australia and New Zealand involves several changes. You can fly via South Africa, then go to Senegal with one of the direct flights with South African Airways or Delta Airlines. Another option is flying via Europe.

Continental Europe

THE GAMBIA

The only airline serving Gambia from Europe is Brussels Airlines. Most visitors come on charter flights with the Gambia Experience (p288). Flights depart from Gatwick, Manchester and Bristol, and connect to other European cities.

SENEGAL

Senegal has good direct connections to European countries, including Belgium (Brussels Airlines), Portugal (TAP Air Portugal), Spain (Iberia Airlines) and, of course, France (Air France). All of these airlines operate at least three times a week, and most have daily flights to Europe. TAP Air Portugal, Iberia, and Royal Air Maroc (via Casablanca) tend to have the cheapest deals.

There are plenty of charter flights to Senegal with French and Belgian package-tour companies that are usually cheaper than the scheduled flights. In Senegal, the best agency for charter flights is Nouvelles Frontières (p154) in Dakar.

USA & Canada

No flights are scheduled from the USA to The Gambia, but Senegal has direct flights from New York and Atlanta with South African Airways and Delta Airlines. All other flights from North America go on European airlines via Europe, and it may be cheaper to fly to London or Paris and buy a discounted ticket onwards from there.

Citizens of Canada will probably find the best deals travelling via Europe, especially London or Paris (and especially from Montreal).

Discount travel agents in the USA and Canada are known as consolidators. San Francisco is the ticket consolidator capital of America, although some good deals can be found in Los Angeles, New York and other big cities.

LAND & RIVER
Car & Motorcycle

Driving your own car or motorbike to Senegal or Gambia is getting ever easier, as far as road conditions are concerned, though also riskier – there were terrorist attacks on overland travellers in Mauritania in 2007. See p16 for manuals covering the many issues to be dealt with in planning such an undertaking.

It's important to know that it's illegal to import vehicles older than five years to Senegal. If your car is older and you are just trying to cross Senegal to reach Gambia, you'll have to deal with some border formalities and will be accompanied by a border official all the way to Gambia.

If you want to travel around Senegal and Gambia using your own car or motorcycle but don't fancy the Sahara crossing, another option is to ship your vehicle. The usual way of doing this is to load your car or motorcycle on board at a port in Europe and take it off again at either Dakar or Banjul. Getting a vehicle out of a port is almost always a nightmare, requiring visits to several different offices where stamps must be obtained and mysterious fees paid at every turn. Consider using an official handling agent or an unofficial 'fixer' to take you through this process.

In Gambia, **Sukuta Camping** (www.campingsukuta .com) has all sorts of overland information. In Senegal, try **Zebrabar** (www.zebrabar.net).

Train

The only functioning passenger train in the region is the one linking Dakar with Bamako (Mali), with several stops on the way. In theory, a train links the two capitals once a week on a 35-hour journey. In practice, this almost never occurs. The train is frequently out of action, sometimes only transports freight and, due to frequent derailments and other unexpected occurrences, tends to take much longer (some travellers have reportedly spent up to a week to reach their destination). The train is part of the Senegalese government's ambitious program of infrastructure improvements and plans are in place for standardising the width of tracks and improving service. While this gives hope for the distant future, it might also mean that things will get even worse while the works are going on. Phone the **train station** (☎ 33 849 4646) in Dakar for the latest information, or check the train travellers cult site **Seat 61** (www.seat61 .com/Senegal.htm), which provides regular updates on the journey.

If it's adventure you're after, do the journey by all means. You'll have plenty to tell your friends about: breakdowns, unexplained stops, nonworking lights, dust, heat, traders squeezing through packed carriages and blind passengers clinging onto the outside of the rusty coaches. If you just want to get from Dakar to Bamako, take a plane.

The train normally leaves from the main train station in Dakar, though since 2008 the Hann train station has sometimes been used as the departure point. The main stops on the way to Bamako are Thiès and Tambacounda.

Tickets are available at all the stations the train passes, during office hours. You're always at an advantage buying your ticket in, and travelling from, Dakar – the train is often full on leaving the capital. Dakar to Bamako costs CFA52,000 for a 1st-class sleeper, CFA34,250 for 1st class and CFA25,000 for 2nd class.

Seats are numbered, but that usually means little: people squeeze into any place they can get and there's little point in insisting on your rights. It's advisable to bring your own clean camping mat and bedding as well as water. You can buy cheap food and snacks on the way, or rather, you'll hardly be able to escape the pushy offers of the ambulant traders at the stops. You'll probably find mineral water, though.

At each border post you'll have a short hike to the immigration office. Foreigners sometimes have their passport taken by an immigration inspector on the train, but you

TRANSPORT

OVERLAND THROUGH THE WESTERN SAHARA

Safety

There are three main routes across the Sahara leading to West Africa: the Route de Hoggar (through Algeria and Niger); the Route de Tanezrouft (through Algeria and Mali); and the Atlantic Route through the western Sahara (through Morocco and Mauritania). The Algerian routes have not been safe for years, plagued by rebel insurgencies, army clashes and smugglers, and the situation is certainly not improving (and perhaps getting worse). Nearly all travellers come to Senegal via the Atlantic Route.

Paved all the way from Morocco to Dakar, the Atlantic Route has perhaps become too boring for adventure driving. For people less prone to risk-taking, it's made the fabled desert drive possible – you don't even need a 4WD. Still, caution is advised on this route as well. Following the murder of French tourists in 2007, the famous Dakar rally was moved from here to South America, as the area was considered unsafe. Overland drivers do arrive in Senegal along this route all the time, and things seemed calm at the time of writing. Check the latest travel advice, though, before setting out, balance it against reports from other travellers and use your own good judgment.

The Route

The Atlantic Route leads essentially from Tangier via Tan-Tan and Dakhla to Nouâdhibou, Nouakchott and finally Dakar, crossing Morocco, Mauritania and the western Sahara to arrive in Senegal. Dakhla is a major centre for refuelling, with cheap hotels and a decent camping ground. It's also the place to find other drivers you can team up with.

From Nouâdhibou, you can go south down the coast to Nouakchott, through the Banc d'Arguin National Park, or you can go east on the iron-ore train to Choûm and then take the route via Atar and Akjout to Nouakchott.

If you have your own vehicle, don't bother with the hustler-ridden Mauritania–Senegal border crossing at Rosso. Take the dirt track via the Maka Diama dam (bouncy, but decent to drive on outside the rainy months), where border formalities are swiftly completed.

Paperwork

It's important to note that the *carnet de passage* overlanders used to purchase in Europe to drive their car legally into Senegal is no longer accepted. You need to purchase a *passavant* (normally CFA2500) at the Senegalese border, which legalises your stay for 10 days, and can be easily renewed twice (for 15 days each time) at customs posts in Dakar, Saint-Louis, Tambacounda, Kaolack, Matam, Diourbel and Ziguinchor.

Note that it's illegal to import cars older than five years into Senegal. If you take part in the Plymouth–Banjul banger race (see the boxed text, p284), you'll probably be escorted through Senegal to the Gambian border. Don't attempt to do anything but cross to Gambia – people have gotten into trouble that way.

Resources

Pretty much anyone who's completed this Sahara rite of driving passage ends up publishing a travel report online. Type in the words 'Sahara' and 'overland', and start communicating with your virtual desert buddies. A solid internet resource is Chris Scott's enduring site www.sahara-overland.com. Try also www.the153club.org.

---

still have to collect it yourself by getting off at the border post. Nobody tells you this, so if your passport is taken, ask where and when you have to go to get it back.

This train is a popular working ground for pickpockets. Keep all valuables with you and be sure to carry a torch. Good luck!

Guinea

Nearly all traffic between Senegal and Guinea goes via Labé, a large town in northwestern Guinea, to Diaoubé, a busy market town near Kolda in the Casamance. From there, you can catch connections to other places in Senegal. There are also regular cars via Koundara and

Mali-Diembering in Guinea to Kédougou in Senegal. The Diaoubé route has the better roads, and the trip should take around 24 hours (CFA20,000). The Kédougou–Labé route is so bad that even public transport is by 4WD (CFA20,000, two days). From Kédougou, your best chance for public transport to Guinea is on a Friday. Diaoubé is best served on Wednesday, when traders and buyers head there for the weekly *lumo* (market).

Guinea-Bissau

Bush taxis run several times daily between Ziguinchor and Bissau (CFA6000, 147km) via São Domingos (at the border) and Ingore. The road is in good condition and border crossings usually swift. At the time of research, the toll bridge across the wide Cacheu River on the Guinea-Bissau side was nearing completion (July 2009 was the intended opening date). Once that's usable, the Ziguinchor–Bissau connection will be temptingly easy, and should take no longer than two to three hours (depending on the border). As long as the ferry remains in operation, you can spend anything from four to seven hours on the road.

Mali

At the time of writing, the Dakar–Tambacounda road was still the worst nightmare of all truck and taxi drivers – a string of potholes from Kaolack onwards so bad that vehicles drive beside the road for most of the time. Roadworks started near Tambacounda in 2008. That meant long, dusty diversions through the bush, but once works are completed (supposedly in early 2010), the journey should become easier than ever. Once you're in Tambacounda, things get much easier. The road to the border crossing in Kidira (three hours, 184km) is good, and from there it's good tarmac all the way to Bamako in Mali.

Dakar–Tambacounda costs CFA9000 by *sept-place* and Tambacounda–Kidira CFA5000. In Kidira, you can hire a taxi to take you quickly from one immigration post to the next (around CFA2000) and drop you off in Diboli on the Malian side, at the stopping point of the long-distance buses most people take from here to Kayes and Bamako (CFA13,000). You can even take the long-distance bus all the way from Dakar to Bamako (CFA22,000, two days), but that's a hell of a trip.

At the time of research roadworks had also started along the track from Saraya in Senegal to Kita in Mali. Once they're completed (expected in 2010), this will be an attractive option for entering Mali from the Bassari lands, much quicker than the long tour via Kidira.

Mauritania

The main border point is at Rosso, a town full of garbage, pickpockets and pushy salesmen. The border is marked by the flow of the Senegal River, which you cross on a ferry (CFA2000/3000 per passenger/car) that runs four times daily. The immigration post on the Mauritanian side is only open from 8am to noon and 3pm to 6pm, meaning you might have to wait until lunch is over to get your crucial stamp. From the Mauritanian immigration post it's 500m to the *gare routière* (bus and bush-taxi station), from where bush taxis go to Nouakchott. Keep some CFA1000 and CFA2000 notes handy – you might be asked to pay some curious exit and entry taxes at the border and will almost certainly be obliged to place your bags on a wheelbarrow and have them pushed a small distance by overeager youngsters. Visas can be obtained at the border. If the ferry isn't working or you arrive at an odd time, you can also cross by pirogue (canoe) for around CFA1000.

A much easier way of getting from Mauritania to Senegal is the crossing at the Maka Diama dam, 97km southwest of Rosso and just north of Saint-Louis. There's no public transport here, so it's only an option if you've got your own wheels. The route is a dirt track and can be washed out during and just after the rainy season. The rest of the year it's a bouncy but doable drive. The border crossing here is usually swift – no hassle, no hustlers – but you might be asked to pay a CFA6000 exit and entrance fee on either side, as well as around CFA5000 for the bridge toll. These fees might vary, or not be demanded at all.

SEA

The days of working for your passage on commercial boats have long gone, although a few lucky travellers do manage to hitch rides on private yachts sailing from Spain, Morocco or the Canary Islands to Senegal, Gambia and beyond.

Another nautical option available is taking a cabin on a freighter. Several cargo ships run from European ports, such as London-Tilbury,

Bordeaux, Hamburg and Rotterdam, to various West African ports (including Dakar), with comfortable officer-style cabins available to the public. A typical voyage from Europe to Dakar takes about eight days, and costs vary according to the quality of the ship. It's not a way of saving money, but an option for anyone wanting to travel long distances and avoid planes. For more information see *Travel by Cargo Ship*, a handy book written by Hugo Verlomme, or contact a specialist agent.

Freighter World Cruises (☎ 1-626 449 3106, 1-800 531 7774; www.freighterworld.com; 180 South Lake Ave, No 340, Pasadena, CA 91101-2655, USA) Publishers of *Freighter Space Advisory*.

Maris Freighter Cruises (☎ 1-203 222 1500, 1-800 996 2747; www.freighter-cruises.com; 1320 State Rte 9, Champlain, NY 12919, USA)

Strand Voyages (☎ 020-7010 9290; www.strandtravel .co.uk; 357 Strand, London WC2R 0HS, UK)

GETTING AROUND

TRAVELLING BETWEEN THE GAMBIA & SENEGAL
Air

There were no regular flights between the Gambia and Senegal at the time of research.

Boat

At the time of writing, there were no scheduled boat services between Senegal and Gambia. Large pirogues take passengers from Djifer in the Siné-Saloum area to Banjul, but these boats are unsafe and overcrowded, and the ride is rough, as it involves leaving the shelter of the delta for the open sea.

Kartong in Gambia sits a short pirogue ride across the Gambia River from Niafourang in Senegal, and you can easily hire a pirogue from Kartong to take you there. While the trip is easy, smooth, beautiful and cheap, border formalities are not. You can get an exit stamp at Kartong, but there are no border posts in Niafourang. To get your immigration stamp on the Senegalese side, you have to head straightaway to Kafountine, where the officials there are likely to query your right to be in the country without a stamp taken at the border.

Bush Taxi
TO/FROM DAKAR

Sept-place taxis run frequently between Dakar and Banjul. Ferry crossings and tedi-

---

PLYMOUTH–BANJUL CHALLENGE

Now that the massive beast that was the Dakar rally has moved to South America, its quirky sister, the Plymouth–Banjul banger race, is aspiring to take the prime spot. This is a race of a different kind, though. Participants leave from the UK in clapped-out vehicles (though still good enough to make it through two weeks of Sahara driving), and on arrival in Gambia the cars are auctioned for charity. The event takes place annually in December. Contact the **Plymouth–Dakar Challenge** (Map pp100-1; ☎ 4497675; www.plymouth-dakar.co.uk; above the Timbooktoo bookshop, Garba Jahumpa Rd, Fajara) for more information.

---

ous, sometimes unpredictable, immigration procedures can stretch the 305km journey to eight hours or more.

The main route from Gambia to Senegal takes you via the Barra ferry (p95) to Amdallai and Karang at the border, then to Kaolack and Dakar. On the Barra side of the Gambia River there's plenty of transport to Amdallai (CFA1000 per person or around CFA5000 to hire a taxi), where you complete border formalities. From the Gambian immigration post, you walk across to the Senegalese post; from there it's best to hire a taxi (around CFA700) for the short stretch to the *gare routière*, from where *sept-place* taxis to Kaolack and Dakar leave. The road to Dakar is tarred most of the way, the stretch from Sokone to Kaolack being the only really tricky bit. If starting out from Dakar, make sure you get on an early taxi to be certain that the border hasn't closed or the ferry stopped operating (11pm).

A second important border crossing is the one at Farafenni (p136). You get there via the Trans-Gambia Hwy from Dakar (under construction when we visited, causing dusty diversions through the bush). From Farafenni, you can take taxis along the north-bank road eastwards to Janjangbureh (Georgetown) or westwards to Kerewan and Barra. To get to Soma and join the south-bank road, cross via the ferry at Farafenni (CFA300/D10); you can take a taxi from Soma westwards to Bwiam, Bintang, Brikama and Banjul. It's far more advisable to stick with the north-bank road, as the south-bank road east of Brikama still counted among West Africa's worst stretches of broken tarmac when we visited.

Most Senegal-bound drivers take both dalasi and CFA. There's no bank in Barra or Karang, so you should change dalasi into CFA in Banjul. This will be much calmer than at the border, where money changers will push themselves in your way to get your currency.

If you're coming from Dakar and think you might miss the last ferry across to Banjul (it leaves at 11pm), you're far better off staying in Toubacouta and getting the ferry from Barra to Banjul the next morning.

TO/FROM TAMBACOUNDA

From Basse Santa Su bush taxis go through Sabi to Vélingara (CFA1500/D50, 45 minutes, 27km). *Sept-place* taxis in Basse are not only rare, they're also in a terrible state – prepare for long waiting times and an uncomfortable ride.

On the upside, this is one of the few borders where you don't have to change vehicles. Your transport arrives in Vélingara at a small garage on the western side of town. Vehicles for Tambacounda go from another garage on the northern side of Vélingara and *calèches* (horse-drawn taxis) shuttle between the two for CFA250 per person. From Vélingara to Tambacounda is CFA2000 by *sept-place* taxi, CFA1500 by minibus.

TO/FROM ZIGUINCHOR & KAFOUNTINE

To get to Ziguinchor, take a bush taxi from Serekunda's Tippa Garage to the Gambian border at Giboro (D60). From there it's about 3km to the Senegalese border post at Séléti, where a bush taxi to Ziguinchor costs CFA2500. *Sept-places* also link Brikama and Giboro (D40). It's tarmac from Serekunda to Brikama, then pretty decent laterite track to the border. Note that this border sometimes closes around 8pm, though you can sometimes get your stamp at the house of the immigration official.

If you're heading for Kafountine, you can get a taxi from Giboro to Diouloulou (D60), then change for Kafountine. It's also possible to go from Brikama to Kafountine via the tiny border town of Darsilami. This route isn't frequently used by public transport but is perfectly doable (see p255).

For details about the crossing from Kartong to Senegal by pirogue, see opposite.

Car & Motorcycle

Taking a rental car across a border in this region is usually forbidden. You can take a personal car from one country to the other, provided you have purchased Ecowas insurance (you can usually get this at the border). Driving through Gambia with a Senegalese number plate and vice versa is often not much fun: you tend to get stopped at every checkpoint. Make sure your papers are in perfect order – and even then you may get asked to pay random fines for unheard-of infractions of the law.

THE GAMBIA
Air

There are no internal flights in Gambia.

Bicycle

Cycling is a cheap, convenient, healthy and environmentally sound way to travel, and gives you a deeper insight into Senegal and Gambia, as you often stay in small towns and villages and interact with the local people.

If you've never cycled in Africa before, this region is a good place to start. The landscape is flat and in Gambia distances between interesting points are relatively short.

A mountain bike or fat-tyred urban hybrid is most suitable, as even in cities there are occasional dirt tracks and potholes in the tarmac. Note that drivers in this part of the world are not used to seeing cyclists on the street. Especially in the city, where traffic follows the law of survival of the fittest, riding a bike can be very dangerous. A helmet is essential and it's worth considering getting a small helmet-mounted rear-view mirror.

The best time to bike is the relatively cool period from mid-November to the end of February. Even then, you'll need to carry lots of water and smother yourself with sunscreen. If you get hot or tired, or simply want to cut out the boring bits, bikes can easily be carried on buses and bush taxis for a small luggage fee. If you're camping near settlements in rural areas, ask the village headman each night where you can pitch – randomly put-up tents can create confusion and even provoke hostility from villagers.

It's important to carry sufficient spares, and have a good working knowledge of bike repair and maintenance – punctures will be frequent.

Anyone considering doing some serious cycling in Senegal and Gambia should

TRANSPORT

contact their national cycling association. The following associations also have useful information.

Cyclists' Touring Club (☎ 0844 736 8450; www.ctc .org.uk) Based in Britain, it provides members with route details and information for many parts of the world.

International Bicycle Fund (☎ /fax 206 767 0848; www.ibike.org/bikeafrica) A US-based, socially conscious organisation that arranges tours, provides information and has an excellent website with information on cycling in Africa, a huge range of links and a list of cyclist-friendly airlines.

Boat

Seeing that Gambia consists mainly of a waterway, with a few kilometres of land on each shore, it's surprising how little the river is used as a means of transport. There are no scheduled passenger boats, which is a shame, as a picturesque river journey is a great way of seeing the country.

A handful of private tour operators organise trips upriver (see opposite). They are absolutely worth checking out, and even spending some money on – the river is only rarely seen from the side of the road, and the leisurely boat trip takes you through mangroves and further north past islands and tropical vegetation, with a chance of spotting monkeys, chimpanzees and hundreds of birds.

Travelling by boat tends to be slightly more expensive than trips by car as the fuel consumption is higher. But note that quoted prices are usually per boat. As soon as you travel in a small group (some tour operators demand a minimum of four people), the price goes down. If you are on your own, check with the company if it's possible to join a group.

If you want to stay close to the Atlantic coast, you can take part in pirogue day trips around the mangroves between Banjul and Lamin, and through the Tanbi wetlands. The best place to book boats to do that is Denton Bridge (p94). In the south, you can take pirogue trips along the Allahein River. Near Tendaba Camp, the Baobolong wetlands are best explored by pirogue.

Along the river there are several ferry crossings connecting the north and south banks. The main ones are the Barra ferry (see p95) between Barra and Banjul, and the ferry connecting Farafenni and Soma (see p136).

Bus

When we visited, the once-deceased national bus service had just been revived via the purchase of several good express buses that ply Gambia's major routes. The green vehicles (still shiny in 2008) connect the major coastal centres of Serekunda, Bakau, Sukuta, Banjul and Brufut from 7am to 7pm daily. A good place to get them is Brufut Turntable or Tippa Garage in Serekunda. Short distances (eg Banjul to Serekunda) cost D5. Beware, though: much like your average bush taxi, these buses tend to move when they're full, which means that you'll sometimes spend more time waiting than travelling. The same buses travel longer distances, such as to Kerewan, Janjangbureh and Basse from Barra. Note that even bush taxis can spend 10 hours on the 360km to Basse – think twice before jumping on a bus.

Car & Motorcycle

There are two main routes through Gambia: the tarmac road on the northern bank of the river, and the string of potholes posing as asphalt along the southern bank. Plans are in place to adorn the south-bank road with a layer of asphalt too, but until that has happened, don't take it if you can avoid it. From the coast to Brikama it's still fine, and then again in the east from Janjangbureh to Basse. All other stretches are anything from bearable to barely existent. The main roads near the coast are all good, though you only need to look for something slightly off the beaten track and you'll be driving on dirt.

Gambia's resort areas are best for hiring cars or motorbikes (see p113), but before doing this read the boxed text, opposite. Most hire agencies are small operators, Hertz being the only big name represented. To drive yourself, you need to have an international driving licence and be at least 23 years of age.

It's common to hire a car with a driver, and you can also negotiate daily rates with *sept-place* or private taxi drivers.

Despite the British heritage, people in Gambia drive on the right, in line with Senegal and most other countries in West Africa.

For minor repair works, there are improvised garages all along major roads, and every village has someone who can weld your oil tank back together. Careful, though: some of those mechanics aren't that familiar with vehicles other than the standard Peugeots they deal with, and might do more damage than good in trying to get your car back on the road.

TRANSPORT

WARNING

Unless you're very familiar with the state of the streets in Senegal and Gambia, driving around the two countries is not something that should be taken lightly.

Road conditions inland are often terrible. What looks like a promising stretch of racing tarmac on the map may in reality turn out to be a string of large potholes, vaguely connected by tired asphalt. If you don't want to bust a tyre here, you'll have to perform that careful slalom around the cracks and obstacles you'll see the local taxi drivers perform – and sometimes even leave the route entirely to drive beside it. A straight dirt road can be easier to drive on than perforated asphalt, but you also have to get used to it. Keep the speed down, and watch out on bends, as it's easy to slide off the road.

Other dangers involve cars and animals moving unexpectedly into your path. Cows in particular never give way to a car. If you see a herd approach, take your foot off the gas and keep moving along slowly, careful not to touch the animals. Don't come to a full stop, as they might feel tempted to do the same. Take particular care if driving through Senegal's national park Niokolo-Koba, especially in the early-morning hours. Many wild animals sleep on the tarmac at night, and you really don't want to risk hitting a lion.

If you want to hire a car, it's worth considering getting one with a driver (many agencies only rent with drivers for long-distance travel), as he'll be familiar with the territory, and any mechanical problems that arise will be his responsibility, rather than yours. Neither country has automobile associations to assist you in case of an accident.

Local Transport
TOWN TAXIS
Town taxis operate in the Atlantic coast resorts. They are painted yellow with green stripes and can be hired privately. Operated as shared taxis, they are often called 'six-six', as you pay D6 for the ride. Six-six routes include the stretches between Bakau and Westfield Junction, and Bakau and Serekunda. Both pass Sabina Junction in Fajara. You can also get a six-six from the Senegambia Strip to the so-called traffic light junction. If you don't want to share or wish to travel a different route, you can book a yellow tourist taxi for a town trip, which will cost around D30.

TOURIST TAXIS
Green tourist taxis are specifically for tourists and can go anywhere in the country, though they mainly operate in the tourist resorts and along the coastal road. Tourist taxis can be found at ranks near large hotels. A list of rates is on display outside most hotels and at the airport. They are considerably more expensive than town taxis, though tariffs are negotiable within reason.

Sept-Place Taxis & Gelli-Gellis
Gambia has borrowed the French term *sept-place* to refer to the seven-seater Peugeots that link all major towns in the country. *Gelli-gellis* are minibuses, a bit cheaper but endlessly more tedious than *sept-place* taxis. They're usually rusty metal hulks that defy all laws of physicality by holding together and even moving with boxes, bags and sheep strapped to the roof.

They both ply the south-bank road, despite its dismal state, going from Serekunda's Tippa Garage to Brikama and Soma (for Janjangbureh and Basse, you have to change at one of those places). For a north-bank trip, they leave from Barra to Kerewan, Farafenni and Janjangbureh before heading south for the trip from Janjangbureh to Basse.

Other public transport routes include the coastal road to Kartong and the good dirt track from Brikama to the Séléti border.

Prices for both *sept-place* taxis and *gelli-gellis* are fixed (though change fairly often in line with fluctuations in the cost of petrol). You'll almost always be quoted the correct price; the bit to bargain over is the additional luggage fee (see the boxed text, p288). They move only when they're full and fill up quickest early in the morning (around 7am).

Tours
Taking an organised tour can be a good way of exploring the country if you want to avoid the hassles of travelling on public transport. On the Atlantic coast, you'll find several private tour operators. Independent travellers can often join a group for an excursion. For specialised vacations, see the boxed text, p289.

> **LUGGAGE FEES**
>
> Whenever you travel by bush taxi, there is always an extra fee for luggage, which varies according to the size of the baggage and the distance you travel. Drivers have introduced this charge as a desperate measure because fares are generally fixed by the government and are often too low to include a profit for the driver. The baggage charge may sometimes be the only money he takes home.
>
> Unless the charge is beyond all reason, there's no reason to debate the fee. For most journeys, you're likely to pay around CFA500/D25 to CFA1000/D50 per item, roughly 10% to 20% of your fare. Anything above CFA2000/D100 per bag is likely to be an overcharge, unless you're transporting something outsized.

Discovery Tours (Map pp100-1; ☎ 4495551; www .discoverytours.gm; 10 Atlantic Rd, Fajara) Has a good selection of country tours and can put personalised tours together. Has multilingual staff.

Gambia Experience (Map pp100-1; ☎ 4461104; www.gambia.co.uk; Kairaba Hotel, Kololi) Gambia's biggest tour operator offers everything from charter flights to all-inclusive holidays and in-country tours. Good Senegal-Gambia combined tours via second branch Senegal Experience.

Gambia River Excursions (Map pp100-1; ☎ 4494360; www.gambia-river.com) This long-standing company with offices in Fajara and at Lamin Lodge does trips from Denton Bridge or Banjul all the way up to Janjangbureh. Most trips are done by motorised pirogues of various sizes. Tours range from simple bird-and-breakfast excursions to tailor-made trips of several days.

Gambia Tours (Map pp100-1; ☎ 4462601/2; www .gambiatours.gm) Efficient, family-run enterprise offering tours around the country since 1983. Also deals with car rental, airport transfers etc. Multilingual staff.

Hidden Gambia (☎ in UK 01527-576239, in Gambia 7336570; www.hiddengambia.com) This company has an excellent set of excursions, including trips from Bintang to (and around) the Baobolong wetlands, and longer excursions to Janjangbureh and the River Gambia National Park. Tours are done in a combination of fibreglass boats and wooden, motorised pirogues.

Tilly's Tours (Map pp100-1; ☎ 9800215; www .tillystours.com; Senegambia Strip, Kololi) Small company aiming to offer responsible tourism products where possible. Recommended birdwatching and inland trips. Profits go partly to UK-based charities working in Gambia.

SENEGAL
Air
With Air Sénégal International's bankruptcy, all internal flights had ceased at the time of writing. If the company does get rescued (and there was still hope at writing), you should be able to use the carrier for trips from Dakar to Cap Skiring (from October to May), and to Ziguinchor and Tambacounda (January to March).

Bicycle
See p285 for information on travelling by bicycle in this region.

Boat
The most important boat service in Senegal is the 500-seater passenger ship *Aline Sitoé Diatta*, which connects Dakar twice weekly to Ziguinchor in the Casamance, providing an easy and good-value way of reaching Senegal's south. See the Casamance chapter (p236) for more details.

If it's a trip up the Senegal River you're after, you can travel on the *Bou El Mogdad* (p215), a stunning old boat with a long historical connection to the region. This is not a public transport alternative to road travel but a small 1950s cruise ship that chugs leisurely from Saint-Louis to Podor over several days. The *Africa Queen* is a similar boat that usually operates in Guinea-Bissau's Bissagos Islands, but comes to Saly and the Siné-Saloum region in the rainy season.

Various towns and islands in Senegal can be reached by regular ferry services, including Île de Gorée (see p179) and Foundiougne (see p197). Regular pirogues connect Dakar and Île de N'Gor (see p161), Dakar and Îles de la Madeleine (see p180), Ndangane and Mar Lodj (see p196), and various places in the Siné-Saloum region. Note that only the regular, ferry-type pirogues are equipped with life vests; self-hired boats don't necessarily come with the requisite features.

Africa Queen (☎ 33 957 7435; Saly) Contact Saly's Espadon hotel to see if the boat is in Senegal during your stay (it usually is from around May to October).

Aline Sitoé Diatta (☎ in Ziguinchor 33 991 7200, in Dakar 33 821 2900) Departs from Dakar every Tuesday and

HOLIDAYS WITH A DIFFERENCE

If you're the kind of person who feels uncomfortable as part of a tour group that ticks off the sights and buys the T-shirts, and wish to put a completely different edge on your holiday, you should check out some of the small, informal tours on offer. There are plenty of organisations, community associations and inspired individuals around that propose holidays with a difference. The following list gives you some pointers.

- **Skate through the city** Dakar's largest association of inline skaters can organise urban explorations for dedicated or amateur skaters. You get to discover the city on wheels, including the most vibrant, young and difficult urban boroughs. Contact **Association Accro Roller** (☎ 77 649 5180; www.accroroller.tk, in French).

- **Breathe deeply on the beach** From November to May, gentle Deepa runs the most relaxing holidays of all, offering yoga courses for beginners and advanced at Gambia's eco-fantastic Sandele Eco-Retreat (Kartong) and Safari Garden (Fajara). You get to dive into the beauty of the country while inhaling deeply, and a percentage of the profits is invested in sustainable tourism projects. Contact **Eco Yoga Holidays** (☎ in UK 7779 240985; www.deepaspirit.com).

- **Picture it** On a photography holiday suitable for beginners and professionals, you don't only get to see Gambia's most beautiful corners, you also learn how to capture those special moments the professional way. Contact **Focus Gambia** (☎ in UK 01258-453504; www.focus-gambia.com).

- **Ride the waves** Thomas Morin is not only a star-studded French chef, he also organises spectacular kitesurfing holidays in the stunning surroundings of Palmarin, Senegal. Contact **Kite Aventure** (☎ 77 727 5717, in France 04 83 14 92 57; www.kiteaventure.com).

- **Go local** This inspired little organisation can arrange your stay with carefully selected local families. Part of the profits go to the host communities that you'll get to dive into deeply. Contact **Sénégal Chez l'Habitant** (☎ 77 517 2666; papeaidara@hotmail.com; www.senegalchez lhabitant.com, in French).

- **Be eco-fabulous** Discover remote Marine Protected Areas in Senegal's Siné-Saloum and Casamance regions, watch rare manatees and bird species, stay in village camps and know that your spending in stunning surroundings directly supports the protection efforts. Homestays on N'Gor are also on the menu. Contact **Océanium** (☎ 33 822 2441; www.oceanium.org, in French).

- **Become a wildlife volunteer** If you're serious about community-based conversation and biodiversity research, find out how you can support the work of Gambia's wildlife trust and its eco-tourism agenda. Contact **Makasutu Wildlife Trust** (☎ 7782633; m.wildlifetrust@yahoo.co.uk, http://makasutuwildlifetrust.com).

Friday around 8pm; returns from Ziguinchor every Thursday and Sunday around 2pm.

Bou El Mogdad (☎ 33 961 4263; www.sahel decouverte.com) One- to four-day trips can be booked through Sahel Découverte in Saint-Louis.

Gorée Ferry (☎ 33 849 7961, 24hr info line 77 628 1111; www.dakar-goree.com) Provides several daily boat connections between Dakar and Île de Gorée (see p179), and organises recommended minicruises between Gorée and Îles de la Madeleine, as well as Gorée and Saly.

Bus

Senegal's long-distance buses are operated by the Touba-based Mouride brotherhood, hence the name *cars mourides*. *Cars mourides* go from Dakar to most major towns in the country. They leave from the Shell station at Av Malick Sy near *gare routière* Sapeurs-Pompiers (usually just referred to as Pompiers), usually in the middle of the night. You have to book your seat in advance. There's no central phone number, so the best thing is to go to the Shell station (every taxi driver knows it), ask for the person responsible for the *cars mourides*, and let them know the direction you're going. They should, in theory, book you on the bus.

Even though many *cars mourides* are in good condition, travelling by bus can be very tedious and is always time-consuming. Departure times are quite flexible and sharing a vehicle with tens of others and their usually substantial luggage always means enduring many stops for people to get off on the way, waiting for them to untie their bags from the roof, and watching smaller cars pass you by. Punctured tyres take longer to repair, too.

If you feel really adventurous, ask at Pompiers for the Ghanaian, Malian and Nigerian buses that link Dakar to Bamako, Nouakchott and even far-flung places like Cotonou.

Bush Taxi

Bush taxi (*taxi-brousse* in French) is the term for all public transport smaller than a big bus. They leave once they are full; this might take half an hour, or several days if you're out in the sticks.

The best time for catching bush taxis is usually between 6am and 9am. In remote locations, your best chances for transport are the market days, when people will be heading to the market town (or village) in the early morning and returning in the evening.

Tickets are sold by seat, so if you want extra legroom or want to speed up the process, you can purchase two seats or more. This is also the best way to calculate taxi hire. If you want to hire the whole vehicle, take the cost of a ticket, multiply it by the number of seats in the vehicle and add a sum for the usual luggage fee to get the amount you should be paying.

Though public transport prices are fixed, they frequently increase (and even drop) in line with fluctuating petrol prices. Drivers will almost always quote the correct fee.

Sept-place taxi destinations from Dakar include Saint-Louis (CFA4500, five to six hours), Ziguinchor (CFA9000, nine to 10 hours) and Tambacounda (CFA9000, 10 to 12 hours). Minibuses are typically about 20% to 25% cheaper than *sept-place* taxis, and Ndiaga Ndiayes about 30% to 35% cheaper.

MINIBUS

With a capacity of about 20 people, these are smaller versions of the Ndiaga Ndiaye (most of them are Nissan Urvans). They are sometimes referred to as '*petits cars*'. Minibuses mainly operate on rural roads, and cost a few francs more than Ndiaga Ndiayes.

NDIAGA NDIAYE

Also called '*grands cars*', these Mercedes minibuses, named after the first entrepreneur who introduced them to Senegal, are usually the cheapest and slowest form of transport. The ubiquitous 32-seaters are recognisable by their white colour and the word *Alhamdoulilahi* (Thanks to God) painted across their fronts.

Ndiaga Ndiayes tend to stop frequently to drop off or collect passengers, which is why they can take almost twice as long for a short journey as a *sept-place* taxi. Or is it because of frequent punctures, engine failure or the occasional accident? It all sounds grim, but in the more remote regions they might be your only choice of transport, and with the right attitude, the journey can even be hilarious.

PICK-UP

Leaving the city and heading for the rather remote regions, you'll occasionally encounter covered pick-up trucks on the street (called '*bâchés*' in Senegal). These battered vehicles, crammed with people, chickens, sacks of rice and live goats, are sometimes the only type of bush taxi you'll find out in the sticks.

SEPT-PLACE TAXI

Sept-place taxis (also sometimes referred to as 'brakes' or '*cinq-cent-quatre*') are Peugeot 504s, and are considered the top end of public transport, though you might disagree. Most are in a pretty rough state, occasionally reduced by the rough roads to little more than chassis, body and engine. With three rows of seats, Peugeot taxis are built to take the driver plus seven passengers (hence the name '*sept-place*') – that's not counting the goats, mattresses and occasional motorbike on the roof. If you come first, you're supposed to get the front seat; late arrivals have to squeeze in the back (but don't have to sit around and wait for the car to fill up).

Car & Motorcycle

Some general points about driving your own vehicle to and around the region are covered on p281.

DRIVING LICENCE

You need an international driving licence to drive or hire a car in Senegal. Most hire companies request a minimum age of 23.

HIRE

Car hire is generally expensive. By the time you've added up the cost of the car, the distance travelled, plus insurance and tax, you can easily end up paying over US$1000 per week. You will need a credit card to pay the large deposit.

Hiring 4WDs is even more expensive and hire rates often shoot up if you want to go up-country, where bad road conditions increase the risk of accidents. Some hire companies can provide a chauffeur at very little extra cost – sometimes it's cheaper because you pay less for insurance.

Most car-rental companies are based in Dakar; for details see p175. There are large international names (Hertz, Avis, Budget etc), and also smaller independent operators.

If you're not worried about air-conditioning and are flexible on comfort, you can also rent a *sept-place*. Negotiate a daily rate (let the driver know where you want to go, as a day around Dakar doesn't go for the same rate as out-ings over washed-out dirt roads), fill the tank (make sure you've made clear who pays for petrol) and head off. To calculate how much you should be paying, multiply the number of seats by the usual fare.

Local Transport
CALÈCHE & CHARRETTE
You have herewith left the world of the motorised vehicle. Horse-drawn *charrettes* and their 'upmarket' counterparts, *calèches*, are used as means of public transport in places such as Rufisque, Richard Toll and Dagana. A *charrette* is little more than a simple board attached to a wheel and strapped behind a horse, and it's more typically used to transport bags of sand and bricks. A *calèche* actually has seats and a sunroof, and can be a fun means of getting around town (especially if you've got kids), provided that you're not pressed for time.

CAR RAPIDE
This colourfully decorated, blue-and-yellow Dakar minibus is one of Senegal's symbols; you'll see it on postcards and as souvenirs. While it really is cute to look at, it's not a great way to get around unless random stops, dare-devil overtaking manoeuvres and crammed seats are your thing. *Cars rapides* only really operate in Dakar and pretty much cover any journey you can imagine, though not always as directly or quickly as you might hope. You'll pay CFA75 for a short hop, CFA150 for slightly further, and never more than CFA200.

MOBYLETTE
The only place *mobylettes* (mopeds) are used as regular means of public transport is in Kaolack. You pay for the passenger seat, hang on, and be patient while the driver gets you from A to B, at the speed of either a slow motorbike or a battered bicycle, depending on his and your combined bodyweight.

SENBUS
These white, Indian-built minibuses were introduced in Dakar as a modern alternative to the *cars rapides*. They have predetermined stops and tend to carry fewer people, though as with *cars rapides* their destinations aren't always easily recognised.

TAXI
Yellow taxis, from very battered Peugeots to brand-new Iranian and Indian vehicles, are found in all major cities. In Dakar, you need to negotiate quite fiercely. If you know the approximate rate to your destination, hit the driver with it right away, or you'll be drawn into a several-minute negotiation. In Ziguinchor and Saint-Louis, rates for small hops are fixed at CFA500. You just wave them down on the roadside and jump in. Dakar also has a great service of female-driven taxis – see the boxed text, p177, for more information.

Tours
Most places of interest in Senegal can be reached by either public transport or car, but if you're short on time you could get around the country on an organised tour.

A small selection of tour operators is included below. See also individual chapters for more options. For activities and tours with a twist, see the boxed text, p289.

Africa Connection Tours (Map p155; ☎ 33 849 5200; www.actours-senegal.com; 32 Rue Mass Diokhané) Multilingual agency (English, Spanish, French and more) that specialises in themed cultural tours and excursions to rural areas.

Africa Dream (☎ 33 957 0328; www.africadream.org; Ngaparou) This tiny, French-run agency proposes personalised circuits to even the most unlikely corner. Very friendly and able to cater to tiny groups.

ATG (Map p152; ☎ 33 869 7900; www.africatravel -group.com; Rte du Méridien Président, Dakar) A big player with a vast range of quality excursions to all regions, a number of lodges and excellent partners across the country. Particularly good for Spanish, Portuguese and French clients. Also organises festivals and plenty more.

Casamance Horizons (☎ 77 709 3241; www .casamance-horizons.com, in French) Tiny, rootsy and lovely, this is a great local initiative wholly devoted to responsible tourism. A large part of your money goes directly to the communities you visit, channelled via the village associations. Tours are based in the Casamance and usually include a stop at the cute *campement* Tilibo Horizons at Niafourang.

Gambia Experience (☎ in UK 0845 330 2060; www .gambia.co.uk) Gambia's biggest tour operator has the monopoly on flights from the UK and organises a huge variety of stays.

Mboup Voyages (Map p156; ☎ 33 821 8163; www .mboupvoyages.com, in French; 2 Place de l'Indépendance, Dakar) One of the most enduring agencies, with good Dakar tours.

Origin Africa (Map p158; ☎ 33 860 1578; www .origin-africa.sn, in French; Cité Africa, Ouakam) This small tour operator has a good selection of tours around even remote regions.

Sahel Découverte (Map p211; ☎ 33 961 4263; www .saheldecouverte.com, in French & Spanish; Saint-Louis) Brilliant for tours around northern Senegal. Also caters to Spanish and English speakers.

Senegal Experience (☎ in UK 0845 330 2080; www .senegal.co.uk) The Senegal branch of Gambia Experience specialises in tours to Siné-Saloum for travellers from the UK.

Senegal Tours (Map p156; ☎ 33 839 9900; fax 33 823 2644; 5 Place de l'Indépendance, Dakar) Large, reliable operator.

our pick **TPA** (☎ 33 957 1256; tpa@orange.sn; www .lesenegal.info, in French) A tour operator with a difference, TPA is the leading agency for rural tourism, offering unique tours to lesser-travelled routes, typically with its original tourist trucks. Its *campements* are built in local architectural styles and run in the spirit of community *campements* – a percentage of earnings is locally invested, and staff are locally recruited and trained.

Touki Voyages (☎ 33 957 1420; www.afrikatouki.com, in French) Has excellent tours, and invests a percentage of profits in local education development projects. Particularly great are the women's tours, aimed at making travel for individual female tourists more comfortable.

Health

CONTENTS

Travel health depends on your predeparture preparations, your daily health care while travelling and how you handle any medical problem that does develop. While the potential dangers can seem quite frightening, in reality few travellers experience anything more than an upset stomach.

BEFORE YOU GO

If you wear glasses, take a spare pair and your prescription. If you require a particular medication, take an adequate supply, as it may not be available locally. Take the part of the packaging showing the generic name rather than the brand, which will make getting replacements easier, but be sure to remove or black out the price you paid at home or you could encounter a sudden dose of hyperinflation. It's a good idea to have a legible prescription or letter from your doctor showing that you legally use the medication.

RECOMMENDED VACCINATIONS

Plan ahead for getting your vaccinations, as some require more than one injection, and certain vaccinations should not be given together. Note that some vaccinations should not be given during pregnancy or to people with allergies – discuss with your doctor.

It is recommended that you seek medical advice at least six weeks before travel. Be aware that there is often a greater risk of disease for children and during pregnancy.

Discuss your particular requirements with your doctor, but vaccinations you should consider for a trip to Gambia or Senegal are listed in the boxed text, p294 (for more details about the diseases themselves, see the individual disease entries later in this chapter). Carry proof of your vaccinations on an international health certificate. In both Senegal and Gambia, you will need a yellow-fever vaccination certificate if you're coming from a yellow-fever-infected area.

INTERNET RESOURCES

There is a wealth of travel-health advice on the internet. For further information, the Lonely Planet website (www.lonelyplanet .com) is a good place to start. The World Health Organization publishes a superb book called *International Travel and Health,* which is revised annually and is available online at no cost at www.who.int/ith. Other websites of general interest are MD Travel Health at www.mdtravelhealth.com, which provides complete travel-health recommendations for every country, updated daily, also at no cost; the Centers for Disease Control and Prevention at www.cdc.gov; and Fit for Travel at www.fitfortravel.scot.nhs.uk, which has up-to-date information about outbreaks and is very user-friendly.

It's also a good idea to consult your own government's travel-health website, if one is available, before departure. The following is a selection of government travel-health websites:

Australia (www.dfat.gov.au/travel)
Canada (www.hc-sc.gc.ca)
UK (www.doh.gov.uk/traveladvice)
USA (www.cdc.gov/travel)

FURTHER READING

Lonely Planet's *Africa: Healthy Travel* is a handy pocket size and is packed with useful information on pretrip planning, emergency first aid, immunisation and disease information, and what to do if you get sick on the road.

For those planning on being away for a while or working abroad (eg as a Peace Corps worker), *Where There Is No Doctor* by David

REQUIRED & RECOMMENDED VACCINATIONS

It is essential to have a vaccination certificate to show you've been jabbed for yellow fever.

Diphtheria & tetanus Vaccinations for these two diseases are usually combined and are recommended for everyone. After an initial course of three injections (usually given in childhood), boosters are necessary every 10 years.

Hepatitis A Vaccines for hepatitis A (eg Avaxim, Havrix 1440 or VAQTA) provide long-term immunity (possibly more than 10 years) after an initial injection and a booster at six to 12 months. Alternatively, an injection of gamma globulin can provide short-term protection against hepatitis A – two to six months, depending on the dose given. It is not a vaccine but a ready-made antibody collected from blood donations. It is reasonably effective and, unlike the vaccine, it is protective immediately, but because it is a blood product there are concerns about its long-term safety. A hepatitis A vaccine is also available in a combined form, Twinrix, with a hepatitis B vaccine. Three injections over a six-month period are required; the first two provide substantial protection against hepatitis A.

Hepatitis B Travellers who should consider vaccination against hepatitis B include those visiting countries where there are high levels of hepatitis B infection, where blood transfusions may not be adequately screened or where sexual contact or needle sharing is a possibility. Vaccination involves three injections, with a booster at 12 months. More rapid courses are available if necessary.

Meningococcal meningitis Vaccination is recommended, especially for visits during the dry season from November to June. A single injection gives good protection against the major epidemic forms of the disease for three years. Protection may be less effective in children under two years.

Polio This is still prevalent in Gambia and Senegal, so everyone should keep up to date with this vaccination, which is normally given in childhood. A booster every 10 years maintains immunity.

Rabies Vaccination should be considered by those who will spend a month or longer in a country where rabies is common, especially if they are cycling, handling animals, caving or travelling to remote areas, and for children (who may not report a bite). Pretravel rabies vaccination involves having three injections over 21 to 28 days. If someone who has been vaccinated is bitten or scratched by an animal, they will require two booster injections of vaccine; those not vaccinated require more.

Tuberculosis The risk of TB to travellers is usually very low, except for those living with or closely associated with local people. Vaccination against TB (BCG) is recommended for children and young adults living in these areas for three months or more.

Typhoid Vaccination against typhoid may be required if you are travelling for more than a couple of weeks. It is available either as an injection or as capsules to be taken orally.

Yellow fever A yellow-fever vaccine is now the only vaccine that is a legal requirement for entry into Gambia and Senegal, usually only enforced when coming from an infected area. At the time of research, yellow fever was still affecting small numbers in Senegal. For immunisation you may have to go to a special yellow-fever vaccination centre.

Werner is a very detailed guide, ideal for self-diagnosing almost anything.

IN TRANSIT

JET LAG & MOTION SICKNESS

Eating lightly both before and during a trip will reduce the chances of motion sickness. If you are prone to motion sickness, try to find a place that minimises movement – near the wing on aircraft, close to midship on boats, and near the centre on buses. Fresh air usually helps; reading and cigarette smoke don't.

Commercial motion-sickness preparations, which can cause drowsiness, have to be taken before the trip commences. Ginger (available in capsule form) and peppermint (including mint-flavoured sweets) are natural preventatives.

IN THE GAMBIA & SENEGAL

AVAILABILITY & COST OF HEALTH CARE

The Gambia's main government-run hospital is in Banjul, but there is a better selection of private clinics and doctors in the area around the Atlantic coast resorts. If you're upcountry, there are hospitals in Bansang, Brikama, Bwiam and Janjangbureh.

In Senegal you'll find the country's main hospitals, as well as many private clinics and doctors, in Dakar. Around the country, most large towns have hospitals, doctors and clinics; if you need to find any of these, ask at an upmarket hotel.

INFECTIOUS DISEASES

Self-diagnosis and treatment can be risky, so you should always attempt to seek medical help. Your embassy or consulate usually has a list of doctors in the area that speak your language, and good hotels should be able to recommend a local doctor or clinic. Although we do give drug dosages in this section, they are for emergency use only. Correct diagnosis is vital. In this section we have used the generic names for medications – check with a pharmacist for brands available locally.

Note that antibiotics are ideally administered only under medical supervision. Take only the recommended dose at the prescribed intervals and use the whole course, even if the illness seems to be cured earlier. Stop immediately if there are any serious reactions and don't use the antibiotic at all if you are unsure that you have the correct one.

Some people are allergic to commonly prescribed antibiotics such as penicillin; carry this information (eg on a bracelet) when travelling.

Cholera

This is the worst of the watery diarrhoeas and medical help should be sought.

Cholera is usually transmitted via contaminated human excrement. This might sound like a rather unlikely source of infection – but beware, as an infected person preparing meals without having washed their hands properly might transmit the disease. Infection is unlikely outside known problem areas, but if you really want to be safe, prepare your own food and choose restaurants with excellent standards of cleanliness.

Note that, in Senegal, cholera outbreaks are frequently reported after the annual mass pilgrimage.

Fluid replacement is the most vital treatment – the risk of dehydration is severe as you may lose up to 20L a day. If there is a delay in getting to hospital, then begin taking tetracycline. The adult dose is 250mg four times daily. It is not recommended for children under nine years or for pregnant women. Tetracycline may help shorten the illness, but adequate fluids are required to save lives.

Dengue

This viral disease is transmitted by mosquitoes and is fast becoming one of the top public-health problems in the tropical world. The disease has been reported in small numbers in both Gambia and Senegal. The *Aedes aegypti* mosquito, which transmits the dengue virus, is most active during the day (unlike the malaria-carrying mosquito), and is found mainly in urban areas in and around human dwellings. Symptoms of dengue fever include a sudden onset of high fever, headache, joint and muscle pains (hence its old name, breakbone fever) and nausea and vomiting. A rash of small red spots sometimes appears three to four days after the onset of fever. In the early phase of illness, dengue may be mistaken for other infectious diseases including malaria and influenza. Minor bleeding such as nosebleeds may occur in the course of the illness, but this does not necessarily mean that you have progressed to the potentially fatal dengue haemorrhagic fever (DHF). This is a severe illness, characterised by heavy bleeding, which is thought to be a result of secondary infection due to a different strain (there are four major strains) and usually affects residents of the country rather than travellers. Recovery even from simple dengue fever may be prolonged, with tiredness lasting for several weeks.

There is no vaccine and no specific treatment for dengue. Aspirin should be avoided, as it increases the risk of haemorrhaging. The best prevention is to avoid mosquito bites – see p297.

Filariasis

This mosquito-transmitted parasitic infection is found in many parts of Africa, including Gambia and Senegal. Possible symptoms include fever; pain and swelling of the lymph glands; inflammation of lymph drainage areas; swelling of a limb or the scrotum; skin rashes; and blindness. Treatment can eliminate the parasites from the body, but some of the damage caused may not be reversible. Prompt medical advice should be obtained if the infection is suspected.

Fungal Infections

These occur more commonly in hot weather and are found on the scalp, between the toes (athlete's foot) or fingers, in the groin and on the body (ringworm). You get ringworm (a fungal infection, not a worm) from infected

HEALTH

MEDICAL KIT CHECKLIST

The following is a list of items you should consider including in your medical kit – consult your pharmacist for brands available in your country.

- antibiotics – consider including these if you're travelling well off the beaten track; see your doctor as they must be prescribed, and carry the prescription with you
- antifungal cream or powder – for fungal skin infections and thrush
- antihistamine – for allergies, eg hay fever; to ease the itch from insect bites or stings; and to prevent motion sickness
- antiseptic (such as povidone iodine) – for cuts and grazes
- aspirin or paracetamol (acetaminophen in the USA) – for pain or fever
- bandages, Band-Aids (plasters) and other wound dressings
- basic set of children's medication – if you're travelling with children
- calamine lotion, sting-relief spray or aloe vera – to ease irritation from sunburn and insect bites or stings
- cold and flu tablets, throat lozenges and nasal decongestant
- insect repellent, sunscreen, lip balm and eye drops
- loperamide or diphenoxylate – known as 'blockers' for diarrhoea
- multivitamins – consider for long trips, when dietary vitamin intake may be inadequate
- prochlorperazine or metaclopramide – for nausea and vomiting
- rehydration mixture – to prevent dehydration, which may occur, for example, during bouts of diarrhoea; particularly important when travelling with children
- scissors, tweezers and a thermometer – note that mercury thermometers are prohibited by airlines
- sterile kit – in case you need injections in a country with medical hygiene problems; discuss with your doctor
- water-purification tablets or iodine

animals or other people. Moisture encourages these infections.

To prevent fungal infections, wear loose, comfortable clothes, avoid artificial fibres, wash frequently and dry yourself carefully. If you do get an infection, wash the infected area at least daily with a disinfectant or medicated soap and water, and rinse and dry well. Apply an antifungal cream or powder such as tolnaftate. Try to expose the infected area to air or sunlight as much as possible. Wash all towels and underwear in hot water, change them often and let them dry in the sun.

Hepatitis

This is a general term for inflammation of the liver, a common disease worldwide. Several different viruses cause hepatitis, and differ in the way they are transmitted. Similar symptoms in all forms include fever, chills, headache, fatigue, feelings of weakness, and aches and pains, followed by loss of appetite, nausea, vomiting, abdominal pain, dark urine, light-coloured faeces, jaundiced (yellow) skin and yellowing of the whites of the eyes. People who have had hepatitis should avoid alcohol for some time afterwards; the liver needs time to recover.

Hepatitis A is transmitted by contaminated food and drinking water. You should seek medical advice, but there is not much you can do apart from resting, drinking lots of fluids, eating lightly and avoiding fatty foods. Hepatitis E is transmitted in the same way as hepatitis A; it can be particularly serious in pregnant women.

There are almost 300 million chronic carriers of hepatitis B in the world. It is spread through contact with infected blood, blood products or body fluids – for example, through sexual contact, unsterilised needles and blood transfusions – or through contact with blood via small breaks in the skin. Other risk situations include shaving, tattooing or body piercing with contaminated equipment. The symptoms of hepatitis B may be more severe than those of type A and the disease can lead to long-term problems such as chronic liver damage, liver cancer or a long-term carrier state. Hepatitis C and D are spread in the same way as hepatitis B and can also lead to long-term complications.

There are vaccines against hepatitis A and B, but there are currently no vaccines against the other types of hepatitis.

HIV & AIDS

Infection with the human immunodeficiency virus (HIV) may lead to acquired immune deficiency syndrome (AIDS), which is a fatal disease. With an HIV prevalence rate of 0.8%, according to a 2003 estimate, Senegal has one of the lowest HIV/AIDS rates in Africa, and the prevalence in Gambia is also relatively low. Still, that's no reason for taking risks. Any exposure to blood, blood products or body fluids may put the individual at risk. The disease is often transmitted through sexual contact or dirty needles – vaccinations, acupuncture, tattooing and body piercing are all potentially as dangerous as intravenous drug use. HIV/AIDS can also be spread through infected blood transfusions; some developing countries cannot afford to screen blood used for transfusions. If you do need an injection, ask to see the syringe unwrapped in front of you, or take a needle and syringe pack with you.

There are two types of HIV, and both are fairly common in West Africa. Unfortunately, many HIV tests do not test for both variations. What this means is that unprotected sex with someone who has tested negative for the virus might not be as safe as it sounds. Fear of HIV infection should, however, never discourage treatment for serious conditions.

Leishmaniasis

This is a group of parasitic diseases transmitted by sandflies, which are found in many parts of the Middle East, Africa, India, Central and South America and the Mediterranean. Cutaneous leishmaniasis affects the skin tissue, causing ulceration and disfigurement; visceral leishmaniasis affects the internal organs. Seek medical advice, as laboratory testing is required for diagnosis and correct treatment. Avoiding sandfly bites is the best

precaution. Bites are usually painless and itchy and are yet another reason to cover up and apply repellent.

Malaria

This serious and potentially fatal disease is spread by mosquito bites. Nowhere in Gambia and Senegal is completely free of malaria, so it's extremely important to avoid mosquito bites and to take tablets to ensure a good degree of protection.

Symptoms range from fever, chills and sweating, headache, diarrhoea and abdominal pains to a vague feeling of ill health. Seek medical help immediately if malaria is suspected. Without treatment the disease can rapidly become more serious and can be fatal.

Antimalarial drugs do not prevent you from being infected, but kill the malaria parasites during an early stage in their development and significantly reduce your risk of becoming very ill or dying. Expert advice on medication should be sought as there are many factors to consider, including the area to be visited, the risk of exposure to malaria-carrying mosquitoes, the side effects of medication, your medical history and whether you are a child or an adult, or pregnant. Travellers to isolated areas in high-risk countries may like to carry a treatment dose of medication for use if symptoms occur.

If medical care is not available, malaria tablets can be used for treatment. You need to use a different malaria tablet from the one you were taking when you contracted malaria. The standard treatment dose of mefloquine (Larium) is two 250mg tablets and a further two six hours later. For Fansidar, it's a single dose of three tablets. If you were previously taking mefloquine and cannot obtain Fansidar, then other alternatives are Malarone (atovaquone-proguanil; four tablets once daily for three days), halofantrine (three doses of two 250mg tablets every six hours) or quinine sulphate (600mg every six hours). There is a greater risk of side effects with these dosages than in normal use if used with mefloquine, so medical advice is preferable. Also be aware that halofantrine is no longer recommended by the WHO as emergency standby treatment because of side effects, and should only be used if no other drugs are available.

Travellers are advised to prevent mosquito bites at all times. The main messages:

HEALTH

- Wear light-coloured clothing.
- Wear long trousers and long-sleeved shirts.
- Use mosquito repellents containing the compound DEET on exposed areas (prolonged overuse of DEET may be harmful, especially to children, but using it is preferable to being bitten by disease-transmitting mosquitoes).
- Avoid perfume and aftershave.
- Use a mosquito net impregnated with mosquito repellent (permethrin) – it may be worth taking your own.
- Impregnate your clothes with permethrin; this effectively deters mosquitoes and other insects.

In Gambia you absolutely need to take precautions against malaria.

Malaria is a killer and exists year-round throughout Senegal. It is essential that you take appropriate precautions, especially if you're heading out of Dakar.

Meningococcal Meningitis

This is a serious disease that attacks the brain and can be fatal. There are recurring epidemics in various parts of the world, including the interior regions of Gambia and Senegal.

A fever, severe headache, sensitivity to light and neck stiffness that prevents forward bending of the head are the first symptoms. There may also be purple patches on the skin. Death can occur within a few hours, so urgent medical treatment is required.

Treatment consists of large doses of penicillin given intravenously, or chloramphenicol injections.

Rabies

This fatal viral infection is found in many countries. Many animals can be infected (such as dogs, cats, bats and monkeys) and their saliva is infectious. Any bite, scratch or even lick from an animal should be cleaned immediately and thoroughly. Scrub with soap and running water, then apply alcohol or iodine solution. Seek medical help promptly to receive a course of injections to prevent the onset of symptoms and death.

Schistosomiasis

Also known as bilharzia, this disease is common in Gambia and Senegal. It is transmitted by minute worms that infect certain varieties of freshwater snails found in rivers, streams, lakes and particularly behind dams. The worms multiply and are eventually discharged into the water.

The worm enters through the skin and attaches itself to your intestines or bladder. The first symptom may be a general feeling of being unwell, or a tingling and sometimes a light rash around the area where it entered. Weeks later a high fever may develop. Once the disease is established, abdominal pain and blood in the urine are other signs. The infection often causes no symptoms until the disease is well established (several months to years after exposure) and damage to internal organs irreversible.

Avoiding swimming or bathing in fresh water where schistosomiasis is present is the main method of preventing the disease. Even deep water can be infected. If you do get wet, dry off quickly and dry your clothes as well.

A blood test is the best way to diagnose the disease, but the test will not show positive for some weeks after exposure.

Sexually Transmitted Diseases (STDs)

HIV/AIDS and hepatitis B can be transmitted through sexual contact – see the relevant sections earlier for more details. Other STDs include gonorrhoea, herpes and syphilis. Sores, blisters or rashes around the genitals and discharges or pain when urinating are common symptoms. With STDs such as the wart virus or chlamydia (both common in Gambia and Senegal), symptoms may be less marked or not observed at all, especially in women. Chlamydia infection can cause infertility in men and women before any symptoms have been noticed. Syphilis symptoms eventually disappear completely, but the disease continues and can cause severe problems in later years. While abstaining from sexual contact is the only 100% effective prevention, using condoms is also effective. Gonorrhoea and syphilis are treated with antibiotics. The different STDs each require specific antibiotics.

Sleeping Sickness

In parts of tropical Africa tsetse flies can carry trypanosomiasis, or sleeping sickness; however, it is seldom seen in Gambia and Senegal. The tsetse fly is about twice the size of a housefly and recognisable by the scissor-like way it folds its wings when at rest. Only a small proportion of tsetse flies carry the disease, but it is a serious disease. No protection is available except avoiding tsetse fly bites. The flies are attracted to large moving objects such as safari buses, to perfume and aftershave and particularly to the colours purple and dark blue (avoid dark blue hire cars). Swelling at the site of the bite, five or more days later, is the first sign of infection; this is followed within two to three weeks by fever.

Tetanus

This disease is caused by a germ that lives in soil and in the faeces of horses and other animals. It enters the body via breaks in the skin. The first symptom may be discomfort in swallowing, or stiffening of the jaw and neck; this is followed by painful convulsions of the jaw and whole body. The disease can be fatal. It can be prevented by vaccination.

Tuberculosis (TB)

This bacterial infection is usually transmitted from person to person by coughing but may be transmitted through consumption of unpasteurised milk. Milk that has been boiled is safe to drink, and the souring of milk to make yoghurt or cheese also kills the bacilli. TB is quite a problem in parts of Gambia, though travellers are usually not at great risk as close household contact with the infected person is usually required before the disease is passed on.

Typhoid

This is a dangerous gut infection caused by contaminated water and food. While it's seldom seen in Gambia and Senegal, if you suspect you have typhoid seek medical help immediately.

In its early stages sufferers may feel they have a bad cold or flu on the way, with headache, body aches and a fever that rises a little each day until it is around 40°C (104°F) or more. The victim's pulse is often slow relative to the degree of fever present – unlike a normal fever where the pulse increases. There may also be abdominal pain, vomiting, diarrhoea or constipation.

In the second week the high fever and slow pulse continue and a few pink spots may appear on the body; trembling, delirium, weakness, weight loss and dehydration may occur. Complications such as pneumonia, perforated bowel or meningitis may occur.

Typhus

This disease is spread by ticks, mites or lice. It begins with fever, chills, headache and muscle pains, followed a few days later by a body rash. There is often a large painful sore at the site of the bite and nearby lymph nodes are swollen and painful. Typhus can be treated under medical supervision. Seek local advice on areas where ticks pose a danger and always check your skin carefully for ticks after walking in areas that may harbour them, such as tropical forests. An insect repellent can help, and walkers in tick-infested areas should consider having their boots and trousers impregnated with benzyl benzoate and dibutylphthalate.

Yellow Fever

This viral disease is endemic in many African and South American countries and is transmitted by mosquitoes. The initial symptoms are fever, headache, abdominal pain and vomiting. Seek medical care urgently and drink lots of fluids.

TRAVELLER'S DIARRHOEA

Simple things such as a change of water, food or climate can all cause a mild bout of diarrhoea, and many people experience a few rushed toilet trips soon after arriving in Africa. If there are no other symptoms, then don't worry, as this is just your body dealing with the change – it doesn't mean you've got dysentery!

Dehydration is the main danger with any diarrhoea, particularly in children or the elderly as dehydration can occur quite quickly. In all circumstances fluid replacement is the most important thing to remember. Weak black tea with a little sugar, soda water, or flat soft drinks diluted 50% with clean water are all good. With severe diarrhoea, a rehydrating solution is preferable to replace minerals and salts lost. Commercially available oral rehydration salts (ORS) are very useful; add them to boiled or bottled water. In an emergency you can make up a solution of six teaspoons of sugar and half a teaspoon of salt to a litre of boiled or bottled water. You need to drink at least the same volume of fluid that you are losing in bowel movements and vomiting. Urine is the best guide to the adequacy of replacement – if you have small amounts of concentrated urine, you need to drink more. Keep drinking small amounts often. Stick to a bland, fat-free diet as you recover.

HEALTH

Gut-paralysing drugs such as loperamide (Imodium) or diphenoxylate (Lomotil) can be used to bring relief from the symptoms, although they do not actually cure the problem. Only use these drugs if you do not have access to toilets, eg if you must travel. Note that these drugs are not recommended for children under 12 years.

In certain situations antibiotics may be required: diarrhoea with blood or mucus (dysentery), any diarrhoea with fever, profuse watery diarrhoea, persistent diarrhoea not improving after 48 hours and severe diarrhoea. These suggest a more serious cause of diarrhoea and, in these situations, gut-paralysing drugs should be avoided. A stool test may be necessary to diagnose what bug is causing your diarrhoea, so you should seek medical help urgently.

Where this is not possible, the recommended drugs for bacterial diarrhoea (the most likely cause of severe diarrhoea in travellers) are norfloxacin 400mg twice daily for three days or ciprofloxacin 500mg twice daily for five days. These are not recommended for children or pregnant women. The drug of choice for children would be co-trimoxazole with dosage dependent on weight. A five-day course is given. Ampicillin or amoxycillin may be given in pregnancy, but medical care is necessary.

Two other causes of persistent diarrhoea in travellers are giardiasis and amoebic dysentery. You should seek medical advice if you think you have either, but where this is not possible tinidazole (Fasigyn) or metronidazole (Flagyl) are the recommended drugs. Treatment is a 2g single dose of tinidazole or 250mg of metronidazole three times daily for five to 10 days.

Amoebic Dysentery

Caused by the protozoan *Entamoeba histolytica,* amoebic dysentery is characterised by a gradual onset of low-grade diarrhoea, often with blood and mucus. Cramping abdominal pain and vomiting are less likely than in other types of diarrhoea, and fever may not be present. It will persist until treated and can recur and cause other health problems.

Giardiasis

A common parasite, *Giardia lamblia,* causes giardiasis. Symptoms include stomach cramps, nausea, a bloated stomach, watery, foul-smelling diarrhoea and frequent gas. Giardiasis can appear several weeks after you have been exposed to the parasite. The symptoms may disappear for a few days, then return; this can go on for several weeks.

ENVIRONMENTAL HAZARDS
Food

There is an old colonial adage that says: 'If you can cook it, boil it or peel it, you can eat it…otherwise forget it'. Vegetables and fruit should be washed with purified water or peeled where possible. Beware of ice cream sold on the streets of Banjul or Dakar or anywhere it might have been melted and refrozen. Seafood is generally some of the safest food available in Senegal and Gambia, but shellfish such as mussels, oysters and clams should be treated with caution, while undercooked meat, particularly in the form of mince, should be avoided. If a place looks clean and well run and the vendor also looks clean and healthy, then the food is probably safe. In general, places that are packed with travellers or locals will be fine, while empty restaurants are questionable. The food in busy restaurants is cooked and eaten quite quickly with little standing around, and is probably not reheated.

Heat Exhaustion

Dehydration and salt deficiency can cause heat exhaustion. Take time to acclimatise to high temperatures, drink sufficient liquids and do not do anything too physically demanding.

Salt deficiency is characterised by fatigue, lethargy, headaches, giddiness and muscle cramps; salt tablets may help, but adding extra salt to your food is better.

Anhidrotic heat exhaustion is a rare form of heat exhaustion that is caused by an inability to sweat. It tends to affect people who have been in a hot climate for some time, rather than newcomers. It can progress to heatstroke. Treatment involves removal to a cooler climate.

Heatstroke

This serious, occasionally fatal, condition can occur if the body's heat-regulating mechanism breaks down and the temperature rises to dangerous levels. Long, continuous exposure to high temperatures and insufficient fluids can leave you vulnerable.

The symptoms are feeling unwell, not sweating very much (or at all) and a high body temperature (39°C to 41°C or 102°F to 106°F). Where sweating has ceased, the skin becomes flushed and red. Severe, throbbing headaches and lack of coordination will also occur, and the sufferer may be confused or aggressive. Eventually the victim will become delirious or convulse. Hospitalisation is essential, but in the interim get victims out of the sun, remove their clothing, cover them with a wet sheet or towel, then fan continually. Give fluids if they are conscious.

Insect Bites & Stings

Filariasis, leishmaniasis, sleeping sickness, typhus and yellow fever are all insect-borne diseases, but they do not pose a great risk to travellers.

Bed bugs are a particular problem in the budget-accommodation places of Gambia and Senegal. These evil little bastards live in various places but are found particularly in dirty mattresses and bedding, and are evidenced by spots of blood on bedclothes or on the wall. Bedbugs leave itchy bites in neat rows, often along a line where your body touched the mattress. They won't kill you, but bites often itch for days, making sleep difficult. Calamine lotion or a sting-relief spray may help, but your best bet is to just find another hotel.

Parasites

You should always check all over your body if you have been walking through a potentially tick-infested area as ticks can cause skin infections and other, more serious diseases. If you find a tick attached, press down around its head with tweezers, grab the head and gently pull upwards. Avoid pulling the rear of the body as this may squeeze the tick's gut contents through the attached mouth parts into the skin, increasing the risk of infection and disease. Smearing chemicals on the tick will not make it let go and is not recommended.

Water

The number one rule is be careful of the water and especially of ice. If you don't know for certain that the water is safe, assume the worst. Having said that, we travelled throughout Senegal and Gambia and in most towns the tap water was OK to drink. However, people respond differently, and water that's fine for some might spark a marathon session on the throne for others – you'll soon know where you stand (or sit).

Bottled water and soft drinks are generally fine and are widely available, although in some places bottles may be refilled with tap water – check the seals. Take care with fruit juice, particularly if water may have been added. Tea or coffee should also be OK, since the water should have been boiled.

The simplest way to purify water is to boil it thoroughly. Alternatively, you could buy a water filter for a long trip. There are two main kinds of filter. Total filters take out all parasites, bacteria and viruses and make water safe to drink. They are often expensive, but they can be more cost effective than buying lots of bottled water. Simple filters (which can even be a nylon mesh bag) take out dirt and larger foreign bodies from the water so that chemical solutions work much more effectively; if water is dirty, chemical solutions may not work at all. It's very important when buying a filter to read the specifications, so that you know exactly what it removes from the water and what it doesn't. Simple filtering will not remove all dangerous organisms, so if you cannot boil water it should be treated chemically. Chlorine tablets will kill many pathogens, but not some parasites such as giardia and amoebic cysts. Iodine is more effective in purifying water and is available in tablet form. Follow the directions carefully and remember that too much iodine can be harmful.

WOMEN'S HEALTH
Gynaecological Problems

Antibiotic use, synthetic underwear, sweating and contraceptive pills can lead to fungal vaginal infections, especially when travelling in hot climates. Fungal infections are characterised by a rash, itch and discharge and are usually treated with Nystatin, miconazole or clotrimazole pessaries or vaginal cream. Maintaining good personal hygiene and wearing loose-fitting clothes and cotton underwear may help prevent these infections.

Sexually transmitted diseases are a major cause of gynaecological problems. Symptoms include a smelly discharge, painful intercourse and sometimes a burning sensation when urinating. Medical attention should be sought and sexual partners must also be treated. For more details see p298. Besides abstinence, the best thing is to practise safe sex.

Both in Gambia and Senegal, tampons and the tiny, discreet and comfortable types of hygienic pads are only available in the super-markets and service stations of the larger towns – and they tend to be comparatively expensive. Upcountry, it'll all be less-than-sexy towels. Best bring a good supply of pads and tampons with you.

Pregnancy

It is not advisable to travel to some places while pregnant as some vaccinations against serious diseases (eg yellow fever) are not advisable during pregnancy. In addition, some diseases are much more serious for the mother during pregnancy (eg malaria) and may increase the risk of a stillborn child.

Most miscarriages occur during the first three months of pregnancy. Miscarriage is not uncommon and occasionally leads to severe bleeding. The last three months of pregnancy should be spent within reasonable distance of good medical care. A baby born as early as 24 weeks stands a chance of survival, but only in a good modern hospital. Pregnant women should avoid medication, although vaccinations and malarial prophylactics should be taken where needed.

Language

EUROPEAN LANGUAGES

The sheer number of indigenous tongues spoken in Gambia and Senegal means that a single official language is very useful for administrative purposes. The languages of the former colonial powers – French in Senegal; English in Gambia – have come to serve this purpose, and also act as lingua francas.

FRENCH

Note that the French of France differs from the French of West Africa: for starters, the French of West Africa is pronounced with an accent that makes it easier to understand for English speakers. Conversely, the French you speak with *un accent terrible* is more likely to be understood in *les marchés de Dakar* than on *les boulevards de Paris*.

Though we've generally only included the polite form of address – *vous* (you) – with the following phrases, the informal form – *tu* (you) – is used much more commonly in West Africa than in France; you'll hear less *s'il vous plaît* (please) and more *s'il te plaît* (please; considered impolite in France unless spoken between good friends). If in doubt (eg when dealing with border officials or any older people), it's always safer to use the polite form.

If you fancy getting stuck into your *français* to a greater extent than is possible with what we include here, Lonely Planet's compact *French* phrasebook offers a handy, pocket-sized guide to the language that will cover all your travel needs and more.

Alongside French, Wolof (p308) acts as a lingua franca in much of Senegal. So try out some Wolof phrases if you find that your French is falling on deaf ears.

Pronunciation

Most letters in the French alphabet are pronounced more or less the same as their English counterparts. Here are a few that may cause confusion:

c	before **e** and **i**, as the 's' in 'sit'; before **a**, **o** and **u** it's pronounced as English 'k'. When it has a cedilla (**ç**), it's always pronounced as the 's' in 'sit'
j	**zh** in the pronunciation guides; as the 's' in 'leisure'
n, m	where a syllable ends in a single **n** or **m**, these letters are not pronounced, but the preceding vowel is given a nasal pronunciation
r	pronounced from the back of the throat while constricting the muscles to restrict the flow of air

The pronunciation guides included with each French phrase should help you in getting your message across. Syllables in French words are equally stressed.

Accommodation

I'm looking for a ...	Je cherche ...	zher shersh ...
camping ground	un camping	un kom·peeng
guesthouse	une pension (de famille)	ewn pon·syon (der fa·mee·yer)
hotel	un hôtel	un o·tel
youth hostel	une auberge de jeunesse	ewn o·berzh der zher·nes

Where is a cheap hotel?
Où est-ce qu'on peut trouver un hôtel pas cher?	oo es·kon per troo·vay un o·tel pa shair

What is the address?
Quelle est l'adresse?	kel e la·dres

Could you write the address, please?
Est-ce que vous pourriez écrire l'adresse, s'il vous plaît?	e·sker voo poo·ryay ay·kreer la·dres seel voo play

Do you have any rooms available?
Est-ce que vous avez des chambres libres?	e·sker voo·za·vay day shom·brer lee·brer

SIGNS

Entrée	Entrance
Fermé	Closed
Interdit	Prohibited
Ouvert	Open
Renseignements	Information
Sortie	Exit
Toilettes/WC	Toilets
Femmes	Women
Hommes	Men

I'd like (a) ...	*Je voudrais ...*	zher voo·dray ...
double-bed	*une chambre*	ewn shom·brer
room	*avec un grand*	a·vek un gron
	lit	lee
room with	*une chambre*	ewn shom·brer
two beds	*avec des lits*	a·vek day lee
	jumeaux	zhew·mo
single room	*une chambre*	ewn shom·brer
	à un lit	a un lee

How much is	*Quel est le*	kel e ler
it ...?	*prix ...?*	pree ...
per night	*par nuit*	par nwee
per person	*par personne*	par per·son

May I see it?
Est-ce que je peux voir   es·ker zher per vwa
la chambre?   la shom·brer
Where is the bathroom?
Où est la salle de bains?   oo e la sal der bun
Where is the toilet?
Où sont les toilettes?   oo son lay twa·let

air-conditioning	*climatisation*	klee·ma·tee·za·syon
bed	*lit*	lee
blanket	*couverture*	koo·vair·tewr
hot water	*eau chaude*	o shod
key	*clef/clé*	klef/klay
sheet	*drap*	drap
shower	*douche*	doosh
toilet	*les toilettes*	lay twa·let

Conversation & Essentials

In common with many other predominantly Muslim groups, the Wolof and Mandinka use the traditional Arabic greeting: *salaam aleikum* (peace be with you); the response is: *aleikum asalaam* (and peace be with you).

Hello.	*Bonjour.*	bon·zhoor
Goodbye.	*Au revoir.*	o·rer·vwa
Yes.	*Oui.*	wee
No.	*Non.*	no

Please.	*S'il vous plaît.* (pol)	seel voo play
	S'il te plaît. (inf)	seel ter play
Thank you.	*Merci.*	mair·see
You're welcome.	*Je vous en*	zher voo·zon
	prie. (pol)	pree
	De rien. (inf)	der ree·en
Excuse me.	*Excusez-moi.*	ek·skew·zay·mwa
Sorry. (forgive me)	*Pardon.*	par·don

(Have a) good evening.
Bonne soirée.   bon swa·ray
What's your name?
Comment vous   ko·mon voo
appelez-vous? (pol)   za·pay·lay voo
Comment tu   ko·mon tew
t'appelles? (inf)   ta·pel
My name is ...
Je m'appelle ...   zher ma·pel ...
Where are you from?
De quel pays   der kel pay·ee
êtes-vous? (pol)   et·voo
De quel pays es-tu? (inf)   der kel pay·ee e·tew
I'm from ...
Je viens de ...   zher vyen der ...
I like ...
J'aime ...   zhem ...
I don't like ...
Je n'aime pas ...   zher nem pa ...

Directions

Where is ...?
Où est ...?   oo e ...
Go straight ahead.
Continuez tout droit.   kon·teen·way too drwa
Turn left.
Tournez à gauche.   toor·nay a gosh
Turn right.
Tournez à droite.   toor·nay a drwat
How many kilometres is ...?
À combien de kilomètres   a kom·byun der kee·lo·me·trer
est ...?   e ...

Health

I'm ...	*Je suis ...*	zher swee ...
asthmatic	*asthmatique*	as·ma·teek
diabetic	*diabétique*	dee·a·bay·teek
epileptic	*épileptique*	ay·pee·lep·teek
ill	*malade*	ma·lad
I'm allergic	*Je suis*	zher swee
to ...	*allergique ...*	za·lair·zheek ...
antibiotics	*aux antibiotiques*	o zon·tee·byo·teek
nuts	*aux noix*	o nwa
peanuts	*aux cacahuètes*	o ka·ka·wet
penicillin	*à la pénicilline*	a la pay·nee·see·leen

LANGUAGE

antiseptic	*l'antiseptique*	lon·tee·sep·teek
aspirin	*l'aspirine*	las·pee·reen
condoms	*des préservatifs*	day pray·zair·va·teef
contraceptive	*le contraceptif*	ler kon·tra·sep·teef
diarrhoea	*la diarrhée*	la dya·ray
medicine	*le médicament*	ler may·dee·ka·mon
nausea	*la nausée*	la no·zay
sunblock cream	*la crème solaire*	la krem so·lair
tampons	*des tampons*	day tom·pon
	hygiéniques	ee·zhe·neek

Language Difficulties

Do you speak English?
Parlez-vous anglais?   par·lay·voo zong·lay
Does anyone here speak English?
Y a-t-il quelqu'un qui   ya·teel kel·kung kee
parle anglais?   par long·glay
I don't understand.
Je ne comprends pas.   zher ner kom·pron pa
Could you write it down, please?
Est-ce que vous pourriez   es·ker voo poo·ryay
l'écrire, s'il vous plaît?   lay·kreer seel voo play
Can you show me (on the map)?
Pouvez-vous m'indiquer   poo·vay·voo mun·dee·kay
(sur la carte)?   (sewr la kart)

Numbers

0	*zero*	zay·ro
1	*un*	un
2	*deux*	der
3	*trois*	trwa
4	*quatre*	ka·trer
5	*cinq*	sungk
6	*six*	sees
7	*sept*	set
8	*huit*	weet
9	*neuf*	nerf
10	*dix*	dees
11	*onze*	onz
12	*douze*	dooz
13	*treize*	trez
14	*quatorze*	ka·torz
15	*quinze*	kunz
16	*seize*	sez
17	*dix-sept*	dee·set
18	*dix-huit*	dee·zweet
19	*dix-neuf*	deez·nerf
20	*vingt*	vung
21	*vingt et un*	vung tay un
22	*vingt-deux*	vung·der
30	*trente*	tront
40	*quarante*	ka·ront
50	*cinquante*	sung·kont
60	*soixante*	swa·sont
70	*soixante-dix*	swa·son·dees

Emergencies

Help!
Au secours!   o skoor
There's been an accident!
Il y a eu un accident!   eel ya ew un ak·see·don
I'm lost.
Je me suis égaré(e). (m/f)   zhe me swee zay·ga·ray
Leave me alone!
Fichez-moi la paix!   fee·shay·mwa la pay

Call …!	*Appelez …!*	a·play …
a doctor	*un médecin*	un mayd·sun
the police	*la police*	la po·lees

80	*quatre-vingts*	ka·trer·vung
90	*quatre-vingt-dix*	ka·trer·vung·dees
100	*cent*	son
1000	*mille*	meel

Question Words

Who?	*Qui?*	kee
What?	*Quoi?*	kwa
What is it?	*Qu'est-ce que*	kes·ker
	c'est?	say
When?	*Quand?*	kon
Where?	*Où?*	oo
Which?	*Quel?/Quelle?*	kel
Why?	*Pourquoi?*	poor·kwa
How?	*Comment?*	ko·mon

Shopping & Services

I'd like to buy …
Je voudrais acheter …   zher voo·dray ash·tay …
How much is it?
C'est combien?   say kom·byun
I don't like it.
Cela ne me plaît pas.   ser·la ner mer play pa
May I look at it?
Est-ce que je peux le voir?   es·ker zher per ler vwar
I'm just looking.
Je regarde.   zher rer·gard
It's cheap.
Ce n'est pas cher.   ser nay pa shair
It's too expensive.
C'est trop cher.   say tro shair
I'll take it.
Je le prends.   zher ler pron

Can I pay by …?	*Est-ce que je peux*	es·ker zher per
	payer avec …?	pay·yay a·vek …
credit card	*ma carte de*	ma kart der
	crédit	kray·dee
travellers	*des chèques*	day shek
cheques	*de voyage*	der vwa·yazh

LANGUAGE

less	*moins*	mwa
more	*plus*	plew
smaller	*plus petit*	plew per·tee
bigger	*plus grand*	plew gron

I'm looking for ...	*Je cherche ...*	zhe shersh ...
a bank	*une banque*	ewn bonk
the ... embassy	*l'ambassade de ...*	lam·ba·sad der ...
the hospital	*l'hôpital*	lo·pee·tal
the market	*le marché*	ler mar·shay
the police	*la police*	la po·lees
the post office	*le bureau de poste*	ler bew·ro der post
a public phone	*une cabine téléphonique*	ewn ka·been tay·lay·fo·neek
a public toilet	*les toilettes*	lay twa·let
the telephone centre	*la centrale téléphonique*	la san·tral tay·lay·fo·neek
the tourist office	*l'office de tourisme*	lo·fees der too·rees·mer

Time & Dates

What time is it?
Quelle heure est-il?　　kel er e til
It's (eight) o'clock.
Il est (huit) heures.　　il e (weet) er
It's half past (seven).
Il est (sept) heures et demie.　　il e (set) er e day·mee

in the morning	*du matin*	dew ma·tun
in the afternoon	*de l'après-midi*	der la·pray·mee·dee
in the evening	*du soir*	dew swar
yesterday	*hier*	yair
today	*aujourd'hui*	o·zhoor·dwee
tomorrow	*demain*	der·mun

Monday	*lundi*	lun·dee
Tuesday	*mardi*	mar·dee
Wednesday	*mercredi*	mair·krer·dee
Thursday	*jeudi*	zher·dee
Friday	*vendredi*	von·drer·dee
Saturday	*samedi*	sam·dee
Sunday	*dimanche*	dee·monsh

January	*janvier*	zhon·vyay
February	*février*	fayv·ryay
March	*mars*	mars
April	*avril*	a·vreel
May	*mai*	may
June	*juin*	zhwun
July	*juillet*	zhwee·yay
August	*août*	oot

September	*septembre*	sep·tom·brer
October	*octobre*	ok·to·brer
November	*novembre*	no·vom·brer
December	*décembre*	day·som·brer

Transport

What time does ... leave/arrive?　　*À quelle heure part/arrive ...?*　　a kel er par/a·reev ...

the boat	*le bateau*	ler ba·to
the bus	*le bus*	ler bews
the train	*le train*	ler trun

I'd like a ticket to ...
Je voudrais un billet à ...　　zher voo·dray un bee·yay a ...
I want to go to ...
Je voudrais aller à ...　　zher voo·dray a·lay a ...
Which bus goes to ...?
Quel autobus/car part pour ...?　　kel o·to·boos/ka par poor ...
Does this bus go to ...?
Ce car là va-t-il à ...?　　ser ka·la va·til a ...
Please tell me when we arrive in ...
Dîtes-moi quand on arrive à ... s'il vous plaît.　　deet·mwa kon·don a·reev a ... seel voo play
Stop here, please.
Arrêtez ici, s'il vous plaît.　　a·ray·tay ee·see seel voo play

the first	*le premier* (m)	ler prer·myay
	la première (f)	la prer·myair
the last	*le dernier* (m)	ler dair·nyay
	la dernière (f)	la dair·nyair
ticket	*billet*	bee·yay
ticket office	*le guichet*	ler gee·shay
timetable	*l'horaire*	lo·rair
train station	*la gare*	la gar

daily	*chaque jour*	shak zhoor
early	*tôt*	to
late	*tard*	tar
on time	*à l'heure*	a ler

I'd like to hire a ...	*Je voudrais louer ...*	zher voo·dray loo·way ...
4WD	*un quatre-quatre*	un kat·kat
bicycle	*un vélo*	un vay·lo
car	*une voiture*	ewn vwa·tewr
motorbike	*une moto*	ewn mo·to

diesel	*diesel*	dyay·zel
petrol/gas	*essence*	ay·sons

Is this the road to ...?
C'est la route pour ...?　　say la root poor ...
Where's a service station?
Où est-ce qu'il y a une station-service?　　oo es·keel ee a ewn sta·syon·ser·vees

Please fill it up.
Le plein, s'il vous plaît.   ler plun seel voo play
I need a mechanic.
J'ai besoin d'un   zhay ber·zwun dun
mécanicien.   may·ka·nee·syun

AFRICAN LANGUAGES

The diverse tribes and ethnic groups of Gambia and Senegal are spread across the national boundaries, and each has its own language or dialect. According to the Summer Institute of Linguistics *Ethnologue*, there are up to 50 distinct languages spoken in the region, at least 15 of which have over 15,000 speakers. Some of the native tongues spoken as a first language by a significant proportion of people are listed here (although many people speak at least two indigenous languages). Note that the phrases reflect pronunciation and not correct spelling.

DIOLA

The Diola people inhabit the Casamance region of Senegal, and also southwestern Gambia, where their name is spelt Jola. Their language is Diola or Jola – not to be confused with the Dioula or Dyola, spoken in Burkina Faso and Côte d'Ivoire. Diola society is segmented and very flexible, so several dialects have developed which may not be mutually intelligible between groups even though the area inhabited by the Diola is relatively small.

Hello./Welcome.   *kahsoumaikep*
Greetings. (reply)   *kahsoumaikep*
Goodbye.   *oukahtorrah*

FULA

The Fula people are found across West Africa, from northern Senegal to as far east as Sudan and as far south as Ghana and Nigeria. The Fula are known as Peul in Senegal, and are also called Fulani and Fulbe. There are two main languages in the Fula group:

- Fulfulde/Pulaar, spoken mainly in northern and southern Senegal; includes Tukulor and Fulakunda dialects
- Futa Fula (aka Futa Djalon), one of the main indigenous languages of Guinea, also spoken in eastern Senegal

These far-flung languages have numerous regional dialects and variants that aren't always mutually intelligible between different groups.

The following phrases in Fula should be understood through most parts of Senegal. Note that **ng** is pronounced as one sound (like the 'ng' in 'sing'); practise isolating this sound and using it at the beginning of a word. The letter **ñ** represents the 'ni' sound in 'onion'.

Hello.   *no ngoolu daa* (sg)
   no ngoolu dong (pl)
Goodbye.   *ñalleen e jamm* (lit. 'Have a
      good day.')
   mbaaleen e jamm (lit. 'Have a
      good night.')
Please.   *njaafodaa*
Thank you.   *a jaaraamah* (sg)
   on jaaraama (pl)
You're welcome.   *enen ndendidum*
Sorry/Pardon.   *yaafo* or *achanam hakke*
Yes.   *eey*
No.   *alaa*
How are you?   *no mbaddaa?*
I'm fine.   *mbe de sellee*

Can you help me, please?
   ada waawi wallude mi, njaafodaa?
Do you speak English/French?
   ada faama engale/faranse?
I speak only English.
   ko engale tan kaala mi
I speak a little French.
   mi nani faranse seeda
I don't understand.
   mi faamaani

What's your name?   *no mbiyeteedaa?*
My name is ...   *ko ... mbiyetee mi*
Where are you from?   *to njeyedaa?*
I'm from ...   *ko ... njeyaa mi*
Where is ...?   *hoto woni?*
Is it far?   *no woddi?*
straight ahead   *ko yeesu*
left   *nano bang-ge*
right   *nano ñaamo*
How much is this?   *dum no foti jarata?*
That's too much.   *e ne tiidi no feewu*
Leave me alone!   *accam!/*
   oppam mi deeja!

1   *go-o*
2   *didi*
3   *tati*

4	*nayi*
5	*joyi*
6	*jeego*
7	*jeedidi*
8	*jeetati*
9	*jeenayi*
10	*sappo*
11	*sappoygoo*
12	*sappoydidi*
20	*noogaas*
30	*chappantati*
100	*temedere*
1000	*wujenere*

MALINKÉ

Malinké is spoken in Senegal's east. With speakers numbering over 250,000, it is recognised as one of the country's six national languages. While it is similar in some respects to Mandinka, the two are classed as separate languages.

Good morning.	*neesoma*
Good evening.	*neewoola*
How are you?	*tanaste?*
Thank you.	*neekay*
Goodbye.	*mbarawa*

MANDINKA

Mandinka, a national language of Senegal, is the language of the Mandinka people found largely in central and northern Gambia, and in parts of southern Senegal. The people and their language are also called Mandingo and they're closely related to other Manding-speaking groups such as the Bambara of Mali, where they originate.

In this guide, **ng** should be pronounced as in 'sing' and **ñ** represents the 'ni' sound in 'onion'.

Hello.	*i/al be ñaading* (sg/pl)
Goodbye.	*fo tuma doo*
Please.	*dukare*
Thank you.	*i/al ning bara* (sg/pl)
You're welcome.	*mbee le dentaala/*
	wo teng fengti (lit. 'It's nothing.')
Sorry./Pardon.	*hakko tuñe*
Yes.	*haa*
No.	*hani*
How are you?	*i/al be kayrato?* (sg/pl)
I'm fine.	*tana tenna* (lit. 'I am out of trouble.')
	kayra dorong (lit. 'Peace only.')
What's your name?	*i too dung?*

My name is ...	*ntoo mu ... leti*
Where are you from?	*i/al bota munto?* (sg/pl)
I'm from ...	*mbota ...*

Can you help me, please?	
i/al seng maakoy noo, dukare? (sg/pl)	
Do you speak English/French?	
ye angkale/faranse kango moyle?	
I speak only English.	
nga angkale kango damma le moy	
I speak a little French.	
nga faranse kango domonding le moy	
I don't understand.	
mmaa kalamuta/	
mmaa fahaam	

Where is ...?	*... be munto?*
Is it far?	*faa jamfata?*
Go straight ahead.	*sila tiling jan kilingo*
left	*maraa*
right	*bulu baa*
How much is this?	*ñing mu jelu leti?*
That's too much.	*a daa koleyaata baake*
Leave me alone!	*mbula!*

1	*kiling*
2	*fula*
3	*saba*
4	*naani*
5	*luulu*
6	*wooro*
7	*woorowula*
8	*sey*
9	*kononto*
10	*tang*
11	*tang ning kiling*
12	*tang ning fula*
20	*muwaa*
30	*tang saba*
100	*keme*
1000	*wili kiling*

WOLOF

Wolof (spelt *ouolof* in French) is the language of the Wolof people, who are found in Senegal, particularly in the central area north and east of Dakar, along the coast, and in the western regions of Gambia. The Wolof spoken in Gambia is slightly different to the Wolof spoken in Senegal; the Gambian Wolof people living on the north bank of the Gambia River speak the Senegalese variety. Wolof is used as a common language in many parts of Senegal and

LANGUAGE

Gambia, often instead of either French or English, and some smaller groups complain about the increasing 'Wolofisation' of their culture.

In this guide, **ng** should be pronounced as in 'sing' and **ñ** represents the 'ni' sound in 'onion'.

For more Wolof phrases, check out Lonely Planet's *Africa* phrasebook or buy and download the Wolof chapter online at www.lonelyplanet.com/shop.

Hello.	*na nga def* (sg)
	na ngeen def (pl)
Good morning.	*jaam nga fanane*
Good afternoon.	*jaam nga yendoo*
Goodnight.	*fanaanal jaam*
Goodbye.	*ba beneen*
Please.	*su la nexee*
Thank you.	*jai-rruh-jef*
You're welcome.	*agsil/agsileen ak jaam* (sg/pl)
Sorry./Pardon.	*baal ma*
Yes.	*wau*
No.	*deh-det*
How are you?	*jaam nga am?* (lit. 'Have you peace?')
I'm fine.	*jaam rek*
And you?	*yow nag?*
What's your (first) name?	*naka-nga sant?*
My name is ...	*maa ngi tudd ...*
Where do you live?	*fan nga dahk?*
Where are you from?	*fan nga joghe?* (sg)
	fan ngeen joghe? (pl)
I'm from ...	*maa ngi joghe ...*
Do you speak English/French?	*deg nga angale/faranse?*
I speak only English.	*angale rekk laa degg*
I speak a little French.	*degg naa tuuti faranse*

I don't speak Wolof/French.	*mahn deggumah wolof/ faranse*
I don't undestand.	*degguma*
I'd like ...	*dama bahggoon ...*
Where is ...?	*fahn la ...?*
Is it far?	*soreh na?*
straight ahead	*cha kanam*
left	*chammooñ*
right	*ndeyjoor*
Get in!	*dugghal waay!*
How much is this?	*lii ñaata?*
It's too much.	*seer na torob*
Leave me alone!	*may ma jaam!*

Monday	*altine*
Tuesday	*talaata*
Wednesday	*allarba*
Thursday	*alkhyama*
Friday	*ajuma*
Saturday	*gaawu*
Sunday	*dibeer*

0	*tus*
1	*benn*
2	*ñaar*
3	*ñett*
4	*ñeent*
5	*juroom*
6	*juroombenn*
7	*juroomñaar*
8	*juroomñett*
9	*juroomñeent*
10	*fuk*
11	*fukakbenn*
12	*fukakñaar*
20	*ñaarfuk*
30	*fanweer*
100	*teemeer*
1000	*junneh*

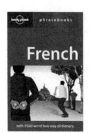

Also available from Lonely Planet:
French and *Africa* phrasebooks

LANGUAGE

Glossary

Items marked G or S are used only in Gambia or Senegal respectively.

auberge – hostel or small hotel

balafon – wooden xylophone typically played by *griots*
bazin – dyed fabrics that are beaten to a shine with wooden clubs
bolong (G) – literally 'river' in Mandinka; when used in an English context, it means creek or small river
boubou – common name for the elaborate robelike outfit worn by men and women (also called *grand boubou*)
bumsters (G) – 'beach boys' who loiter around the coastal resort zones of Gambia and make a living by offering their services, including sex, to female tourists

cadeau (S) – gift, tip, bribe or handout
calèche – horse-drawn cart used to carry goods and people, particularly in the rural regions of Senegal
campement (S) – could be loosely translated as 'hostel', 'inn' or 'lodge', or even 'motel'; it is not a camping ground
campement villageois (S) – rural, village-managed lodgings typical of the Casamance
car mouride – long-distance bus service financed by the Sufi brotherhood of the Mourides
car rapide (S) – usually decrepit, yellow-blue minibus, a popular form of public transport in Dakar
case (S) – hut
case à étages (S) – two-storey mud house
case à impluvium (S) – large round traditional house, with a roof constructed to collect rainwater in a central tank or bowl
confrérie – brotherhood

dibiterie – grilled-meat stall
djembe – (also spelled *jembe*) short, goat-hide-covered drum

Ecowas – Economic Community of West African States

factory – fortified slaving station
fanals – large lanterns of the *signare* women; the processions during which the lanterns are carried through the streets
fromager (S) – kapok tree, also known as silk-cotton tree

garage (G) – bus and bush-taxi station
gare routière (S) – bus and bush-taxi station; also called *autogare* and *gare voiture*
gargotte (S) – basic eating house or stall

gelli-gelli – type of minibus
gendarmerie (S) – police station/post
gîte (S) – used interchangeably with *auberge* and *campement*
gouvernance (S) – governor's office
grigri – charm or amulet worn to ward off evil (pronounced gree-gree); also written as *grisgris* or *grisgri*
griot – traditional musician and praise singer who also acts as historian for a village, family or leading personality
groupement de femmes – women's cooperative

harmattan – light winds from the north that carry tiny particles of sand from the desert, causing skies to become hazy from December to March
hôtel de ville (S) – town hall

IMF – International Monetary Fund

kora – 21-string harp-lute
Koran – Islamic holy book (also spelled Qur'an)

lumo – weekly market, always on a fixed day for every village

mairie (S) – town hall; mayor's office
marabout – Muslim spiritual guide
marigot (S) – creek
mbalax – traditional *sabar* drumming and a mix of other influences; the heart and soul of Senegalese music
MFDC – Mouvement des Forces Démocratiques de la Casamance
mobylette – moped

Ndiaga Ndiaye (S) – white Mercedes bus, used as public transport

pagne (S) – length of cloth worn around the waist as a skirt
paillote (S) – shelter with thatched roof and walls; usually on the beach or around an open-air bar-restaurant
palétuviers (S) – mangroves
pirogue – traditional wooden canoe, either a small dugout or a long, narrow seagoing fishing boat

quartier – neighbourhood

Ramsar – an international convention concerned with the conservation of wetland habitats and associated wildlife

sabar – tall, thin, hourglass drum

sai-sai – Wolof term for a womaniser; used for youngsters who smooth-talk women

sept-place – usually a Peugeot 505, with seven seats

signares (S) – women of mixed race who married wealthy European merchants during colonial times, particularly in Saint-Louis and Gorée

six-six (G) – popular term for shared taxis travelling fixed routes around the Atlantic coastal resorts

sous-verre (S) – reverse-glass painting; technique in which images are drawn onto the back of a glass surface, particularly in Saint-Louis

syndicat d'initiative (S) – tourist office

tama – small tension drum of variable pitch

tampon (S) – stamp (eg in passport)

tampon hygiénique (S) – tampon (also called *tampon périodique*)

taxi-brousse (S) – bush taxi

telecentre (G) or **télécentre** (S) – privately owned telephone bureau

thiéboudienne (S) – rice with sauce (national dish)

tontin – informal community banking system

toubab – white person

village artisanal (S) – craft market

Behind the Scenes

THIS BOOK

This and the previous edition of *The Gambia & Senegal* were written and researched by Katharina Lobeck Kane. The 1st edition was written by David Else and the 2nd by Andrew Burke. This guidebook was commissioned in Lonely Planet's Melbourne office and produced by the following:

Commissioning Editors Stefanie Di Trocchio, Shawn Low
Coordinating Editor Robyn Loughnane
Coordinating Cartographer Ildiko Bogdanovits
Coordinating Layout Designers Nicholas Colicchia, Jacqui Saunders
Managing Editor Bruce Evans
Managing Cartographer Shahara Ahmed
Managing Layout Designer Sally Darmody
Assisting Editors Stephanie Pearson, Sarah Bailey
Assisting Cartographers Khanh Luu, Ross Butler, Valentina Kremenchutskaya
Cover Designer Katy Murenu
Project Manager Craig Kilburn

Thanks to Lucy Birchley, Andras Bogdanovits, Melanie Dankel, Rachel Imeson, Indra Kilfoyle, Darren O'Connell, Raphael Richards, Branislava Vladisavljevic

THANKS
KATHARINA LOBECK KANE

Thanks first of all to an amazing team of editors and cartographers for their support during impossibly hectic times.

Jules and Ishema, sorry for travelling on my own so much that I'm now too tired for family holidays. Coming home after the long absences has been fabulous. Cherif Bodian, once you've got your new bike, let's do the Casamance!

For sharing your passion for your home or adopted countries and pointing out favourite corners, thanks go to PJ, Haidar, Elise, Marcel, Geri and Maurice, Ursula, Tomm, Lamine, Jean-Jacques and Muriel, Ines, Alpha and Doba, Mark and Jayne, James, Peter and Malang, Deepa, Jess Tyrell, Clara and Jean Pierrot, Mwana, Julien, Hassoum, Fatime, Romuald, Laure, Jean-Paul and Henryk Stuelpner (thanks for the books, backpack and B52s!). Apologies to anyone I've forgotten – hundreds of thoughts from dozens of minds go into the making of such a guide.

OUR READERS

Many thanks to the travellers who used the last edition and wrote to us with helpful hints, useful advice and interesting anecdotes:

Hilda Cabral, Anne-Grete Camara, Ben Clayden, Sara Hollerich, Lucy Hunt, David Montagnier, Daniela Smits

ACKNOWLEDGMENTS

Many thanks to the following for the use of their content:

Globe on title page ©Mountain High Maps 1993 Digital Wisdom, Inc.

THE LONELY PLANET STORY

Fresh from an epic journey across Europe, Asia and Australia in 1972, Tony and Maureen Wheeler sat at their kitchen table stapling together notes. The first Lonely Planet guidebook, *Across Asia on the Cheap,* was born.

Travellers snapped up the guides. Inspired by their success, the Wheelers began publishing books to Southeast Asia, India and beyond. Demand was prodigious, and the Wheelers expanded the business rapidly to keep up. Over the years, Lonely Planet extended its coverage to every country and into the virtual world via lonelyplanet.com and the Thorn Tree message board.

As Lonely Planet became a globally loved brand, Tony and Maureen received several offers for the company. But it wasn't until 2007 that they found a partner whom they trusted to remain true to the company's principles of travelling widely, treading lightly and giving sustainably. In October of that year, BBC Worldwide acquired a 75% share in the company, pledging to uphold Lonely Planet's commitment to independent travel, trustworthy advice and editorial independence.

Today, Lonely Planet has offices in Melbourne, London and Oakland, with over 500 staff members and 300 authors. Tony and Maureen are still actively involved with Lonely Planet. They're travelling more often than ever, and they're devoting their spare time to charitable projects. And the company is still driven by the philosophy of *Across Asia on the Cheap*: 'All you've got to do is decide to go and the hardest part is over. So go!'

SEND US YOUR FEEDBACK

We love to hear from travellers – your comments keep us on our toes and help make our books better. Our well-travelled team reads every word on what you loved or loathed about this book. Although we cannot reply individually to postal submissions, we always guarantee that your feedback goes straight to the appropriate authors, in time for the next edition. Each person who sends us information is thanked in the next edition – and the most useful submissions are rewarded with a free book.

To send us your updates – and find out about Lonely Planet events, newsletters and travel news – visit our award-winning website: **lonelyplanet.com/contact**.

Note: we may edit, reproduce and incorporate your comments in Lonely Planet products such as guidebooks, websites and digital products, so let us know if you don't want your comments reproduced or your name acknowledged. For a copy of our privacy policy visit lonelyplanet.com/privacy.

Index

INDEX

INDEX

GreenDex

The following associations, hotels, restaurants, shops and tour operators have been selected by Lonely Planet authors because they demonstrate a commitment to sustainability. We've selected restaurants for their support of local producers – so they might serve only seasonal, locally sourced produce on their menus. We've also highlighted the local producers themselves. In addition, we've covered accommodation that we deem to be environmentally friendly, for example for their commitment to recycling or energy conservation. Attractions are listed because they're involved in conservation or environmental education. For more tips about travelling sustainably in Gambia and Senegal, see the boxed text in the Environment chapter (p68). We want to keep developing our sustainable-travel content. If you think we've omitted someone who should be listed here, email us (see www.lonelyplanet.com/contact for email addresses). For more information about sustainable tourism and Lonely Planet, see www.lonelyplanet.com/responsibletravel.

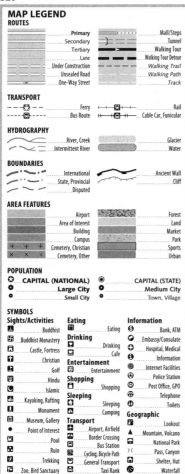

MAP LEGEND

ROUTES

Primary
Secondary
Tertiary
Lane
Under Construction
Unsealed Road
One-Way Street

Mall/Steps
Tunnel
Walking Tour
Walking Tour Detour
Walking Trail
Walking Path
Track

TRANSPORT

Ferry
Bus Route

Rail
Cable Car, Funicular

HYDROGRAPHY

River, Creek
Intermittent River

Glacier
Water

BOUNDARIES

International
State, Provincial
Disputed

Ancient Wall
Cliff

AREA FEATURES

Airport
Area of Interest
Building
Campus
Cemetery, Christian
Cemetery, Other

Forest
Land
Market
Park
Sports
Urban

POPULATION

CAPITAL (NATIONAL)
Large City
Small City

CAPITAL (STATE)
Medium City
Town, Village

SYMBOLS

Sights/Activities
Buddhist
Buddhist Monastery
Castle, Fortress
Christian
Golf
Hindu
Islamic
Kayaking, Rafting
Monument
Museum, Gallery
Point of Interest
Pool
Ruin
Trekking
Zoo, Bird Sanctuary

Eating
Eating
Drinking
Drinking
Cafe
Entertainment
Entertainment
Shopping
Shopping
Sleeping
Sleeping
Camping
Transport
Airport, Airfield
Border Crossing
Bus Station
Cycling, Bicycle Path
General Transport
Taxi Rank

Information
Bank, ATM
Embassy/Consulate
Hospital, Medical
Information
Internet Facilities
Police Station
Post Office, GPO
Telephone
Toilets
Geographic
Lookout
Mountain, Volcano
National Park
Pass, Canyon
Shelter, Hut
Waterfall

LONELY PLANET OFFICES

Australia
Head Office
Locked Bag 1, Footscray, Victoria 3011
☎ 03 8379 8000, fax 03 8379 8111
talk2us@lonelyplanet.com.au

USA
150 Linden St, Oakland, CA 94607
☎ 510 250 6400, toll free 800 275 8555,
fax 510 893 8572
info@lonelyplanet.com

UK
2nd fl, 186 City Rd,
London EC1V 2NT
☎ 020 7106 2100, fax 020 7106 2101
go@lonelyplanet.co.uk

Published by Lonely Planet Publications Pty Ltd
ABN 36 005 607 983

© Lonely Planet Publications Pty Ltd 2009

© photographers as indicated 2009

Cover photograph: Baobab against red sky at dusk, Senegal, Sylvain Grandadam/Age Fotostock. Many of the images in this guide are available for licensing from Lonely Planet Images: www.lonelyplanetimages.com.

Mixed Sources
Product group from well-managed forests and other controlled sources
www.fsc.org   Cert no. SGS-COC-005002
© 1996 Forest Stewardship Council

Although the authors and Lonely Planet have taken all reasonable care in preparing this book, we make no warranty about the accuracy or completeness of its content and, to the maximum extent permitted, disclaim all liability arising from its use.